# OPIUM *and* EMPIRE

## The Lives and Careers of William Jardine and James Matheson

RICHARD J. GRACE

McGill-Queen's University Press
Montreal & Kingston · London · Chicago

*For Sadie and Bud – my mother who taught me to love history and my father who taught me how to tell a story well.*

© McGill-Queen's University Press 2014

ISBN 978-0-7735-4452-9 (cloth)
ISBN 978-0-7735-4726-1 (paper)
ISBN 978-0-7735-9681-8 (ePDF)
ISBN 978-0-7735-9682-5 (ePUB)

Legal deposit fourth quarter 2014
Bibliothèque nationale du Québec

First paperback edition 2016
Printed in Canada on acid-free paper that is 100% ancient forest free
(100% post-consumer recycled), processed chlorine free

McGill-Queen's University Press acknowledges the support of the Canada
Council for the Arts for our publishing program. We also acknowledge the
financial support of the Government of Canada through the Canada Book
Fund for our publishing activities.

---

**Library and Archives Canada Cataloguing in Publication**

Grace, Richard J., 1940–, author
    Opium and empire: the lives and careers of William Jardine
    and James Matheson / Richard J. Grace.

    Includes bibliographical references and index.
    Issued in print and electronic formats.
    ISBN 978-0-7735-4452-9 (bound). – ISBN 978-0-7735-4726-1 (paper)
    ISBN 978-0-7735-9681-8 (ePDF). – ISBN 978-0-7735-9682-5 (ePUB)

    1. Jardine, William, 1784–1843. 2. Matheson, James, 1796–1878.
    3. Jardine, Matheson & Co. – History. 4. Great Britain – Commerce –
    China – History – 19th century. 5. China – Commerce – Great Britain –
    History – 19th century. 6. China – History – Opium War, 1840–1842.
    7. Businesspeople – Great Britain – Biography. I. Title.

    HF486.J372G73 2014        382.0941'05109034        C2014-903880-1
                                                       C2014-903881-X

---

This book was typeset by Interscript in 10.5/13.5 Baskerville.

# CONTENTS

# FOREWORD

My aim is to tell the story of two lives that were interwoven by their partnership in commerce and by their influence on British government in
the early Victorian period. Along the way, I intend to demonstrate that
these two men, William Jardine and James Matheson, serve as test cases
corroborating the Cain-Hopkins thesis of "gentlemanly capitalism" in
the growth of the Victorian empire.

Others have told the story of the expansion of the empire in South
Asia and East Asia more deliberately than I intend to do in this book,
which is more concerned with the two lives in the foreground than with
the fullness of the imperial narrative that surrounds them. To give the
reader some depth of context for their lives and activities, it has been
necessary to provide detailed information about the settings and circumstances in which they operated (such as British trade with India and
East Asia, the Canton System, the origins of the first Opium War, and
the conditions of life in the Hebrides). All that is essential background
for a reader new to this arena of history, but it is not my central purpose.
Nor have I been principally concerned with retelling the history of
Jardine, Matheson and Company, whose lifespan extends to this day
and goes far beyond the temporal boundaries of the combined biogra-
phies. The history of that firm has been done ably by other writers in
several instances.

What I propose to offer the reader is a microcosm of the imperial
experience, the account of a collaboration of two entrepreneurs in
British trade in East Asia in the 1820s and 1830s, and their lives preceding and following the commercial and political drama at Canton in
which they played such prominent roles. It is a study of empire writ
small – informal empire, in which these agents of history are not

Hegelian world-historical figures, though their impact on the events of their time was extraordinary. Rather, my book is history on a human scale which tells of the personalities, trials, challenges, mistakes, disappointments, and achievements of two Scots whose epic journey took them from post-Jacobite "North Britain" to the coast of China and eventually returned them to a much-changed Britain, decades after they had risked their futures on the tenuous commerce of the Celestial Empire.

Jardine and Matheson have often been recognized as giant figures on the scene at Macao and Canton and Hong Kong; but until this volume no one has offered a full-length biography of either man, let alone both of them. In numerous instances they have been caricatured by writers who mention them briefly, depicting them as one-dimensional villains whose opium commerce was "ruthless" and whose imperial drive was "war-mongering." Such cardboard figures fail to represent with any adequacy the complex, multifaceted personal and business histories of Jardine and Matheson. This study attempts to explore the depth of each man, his complicated and sometimes inconsistent internal workings, and his successes and failures. It seeks to represent the two men as human beings, fallible like the rest of us, more influential than most of us, and, like all of us, ultimately accountable to our contemporaries, to history, and to God.

Since this study is essentially biography, rather than business history, the method of exposition employed here is primarily narrative. However, the narrative slows down in chapters seven and eight to allow the reader to examine at close range the partners' business practices, their ideas of free trade, their political behaviour in relation to the Chinese and British governments, and their standards of business ethics.

The Scotland in which they were born was a land that was exporting many of its energetic young men because of its political subordination after the Union of 1707 and because of its enforced cultural change after the last Jacobite rising. Born in the late eighteenth century, they emerged from Scottish schools in the early nineteenth century determined to pursue careers in the East Indian trade. They returned home wealthy men, owing in large part to their involvement with the traffic in opium between sources in India and markets on the coast of China. The trade was illegal in China, but Jardine and Matheson were very talented at inventing ways to skirt the prohibition. During their commercial years, opium was not an internationally regulated substance, and it was readily available legally from many sources in Britain. But opium hardly tells the full story of their lies.

I have endeavored diligently to present these men as three-dimensional figures whose private lives were to some degree buried with them in Scotland at Lochmaben and Lairg. Much of the challenge confronting me has been to exhume those private lives and to reveal more about them than would be possible in a strategically distanced thesis about the informal empire built upon trade in East Asia. Jardine and Matheson left us volumes of personal correspondence about their commerce, but they also left us a trail of clues as to their inner selves, their letters speaking to us indirectly but clearly. My research into their story has involved detective work that was often frustrating, as in the case of the estate records for Lewis, Matheson's island in the Hebrides, which were consumed by fire at the Stornoway town hall in 1918. Piecing together the threads of their private lives – from site visits, local histories, regional newspapers, genealogies, gravesites, and stray references in unlikely sources, with good luck and bad luck mixed in – has been the most daunting dimension of this project.

When the threads are woven together, they constitute a remarkably colourful story which challenges the reader to assess the impact of these two figures on their times, just as it has challenged me. Taken together, their two lives tell us a great deal about the type of tough-minded men who expanded the global markets of Victorian Britain and played major roles in changing the course of modern history in East Asia.

For the sake of consistency, I have generally retained the spellings that Jardine and Matheson's correspondence employed, rather than substituting more modern usage. Hence, for example, Canton does not become Guangzhou, nor is Peking replaced by Beijing.

The people who helped this book see the light of day are legion. The administration of Providence College, Rhode Island, granted me sabbatical leaves which enabled me to conduct the research and to do the writing of this book. I am deeply indebted to my colleagues at Providence, whose encouragement and criticism improved the manuscript immeasurably. In that regard I am especially grateful to Mario DiNunzio, Brian Barbour, Hugh Lena, and Peter Johnson. Tony Hopkins and Tom Devine offered me their sound critical advice on sections of the text and I am grateful for their kindness and encouragement. I am also indebted to Matheson and Company for granting me permission to examine the

Jardine Matheson Archive at Cambridge University Library, and to their honorary archivist, the late Alan Reid, who was very kind and helpful during the early stage of my research.

I thank the Syndics of Cambridge University Library for allowing me access to the resources of the Manuscript Room. I also received invaluable assistance from Godfrey Waller, the library's superintendent of manuscripts, and from Margaret Pamplin, whose extensive knowledge of the Jardine Matheson Archive provided me with important direction and well-rooted insights in the initial stage of this project. I must also thank the masters and fellows of St Edmund's College, Cambridge, for granting me a visiting fellowship on two occasions and for extending to me the hospitality and friendship of that community. Sir Richard Laws, Paul Luzio, Father Michael Robson, OFM Conv, and Bruce Elsmore were particularly kind and generous.

There are many people in Scotland – too numerous to mention by name – who welcomed me into their homes at Inverness, Lairg, Stornoway, and Lochmaben and offered valuable advice. I must also acknowledge all the kind librarians at Stornoway, Dumfries, Inverness, and Edinburgh for their knowledgeable assistance.

Kyla Madden, senior editor at McGill-Queen's University Press, has been the guardian angel of this project. I am so very grateful to her for her interest in the manuscript, for her encouragement through the various stages of revision, and for her regularly sound and patient counsel in bringing this project to fruition. I need also to acknowledge the painstaking assistance of Curtis Fahey as copy editor. His keen eye for clarifications of the text and improvements to elements of style and citation have made this a much better book.

Most of all, I am everlastingly grateful to my family for their love, support, and endurance during the long years of research and writing which produced this book. William Jardine and James Matheson became virtual lodgers at our home, and I have to confess that I dragged the family to remote locations in Scotland where the children must have wondered what on earth Dad was up to. Marianne crossed the Minch with me to serve as amanuensis on a research expedition to Lewis; Ben became sufficiently fond of his grandmother's homeland to return in later years to study at Glasgow; and Elizabeth as a wee child learned that historical research could mean feeding apples to a horse at Jardine's childhood home. My wife, Madeleine, has been a saint. She has sustained me with good advice about the narrative, abundant patience when I was hanging out with Jardine and Matheson, and unwavering encouragement that the whole endeavour was worthwhile. Without them, dear reader, you would not be reading this book.

Richard J. Grace
July 2014

## A NOTE FOR THE PAPERBACK EDITION

Thomas Weeding was an early business associate of William Jardine and later became the principal London banker handling Jardine's long-distance financial business from China. When *Opium and Empire* was first published, John Goold, a reader in Tasmania, Australia, contacted me regarding Weeding and the ship *Sarah*, which was jointly owned by Weeding, Jardine, and a Bombay merchant named Framjee Cowasjee. Goold, who is a relative of Weeding at a distance of many generations, has done extensive research into Weeding, his connections with Jardine, and their joint venture with the *Sarah*. On the strength of his recommendations I am offering the following corrections and clarifications for the paperback edition of this book.

Page 35: Thomas Weeding was never a member of the East India Company staff at Canton. His first acquaintance with Jardine may have occurred in 1802 while the vessels on which they served were being prepared to sail from England with an E I C fleet bound for India and China. It was customary for officers of a fleet's ships to meet before sailing and such gatherings probably extended to surgeons and mates.

Page 71: The *Bombay Calendar* lists William Jardine's arrival at Bombay on 13 April 1819, aboard the *Partridge* (rather than the *Bombay Merchant*, which arrived later in the year). The surety required by the E I C for Jardine's "free merchant's indentures," permitting Weeding to send Jardine to India as his agent (£2,000), was posted by Weeding and his father-in-law, James McCallum.

Pages 72, 79: There were actually three vessels named *Sarah* sailing to and from Bombay during the years Jardine first became engaged in the Eastern trade as a private merchant at Bombay. Information provided by Mr Goold establishes the fact that the *Sarah* owned by Weeding,

Jardine, and Cowasjee was not engaged in the country trade (private trade between India and China not conducted under EIC auspices) and that this vessel sailed between London and Bombay for its first seven voyages (1819–27). Accordingly, Jardine could not have been serving as supercargo aboard the ship between Bombay and Canton, nor was he travelling back and forth between London and Bombay.

Page 370n75: When Jardine sold his share in the *Sarah* in 1827, Weeding became the majority shareholder and Cowasjee retained his one-third interest in the vessel, which continued sailing from London to Eastern ports until 1843.

RJG
October 2015

William Jardine, by George Chinnery. (© National Portrait Gallery, London.
Asset reference number: D36485)

Sir Nicholas James Sutherland Matheson, by James Lonsdale. (© National Portrait Gallery, London. Asset reference number: D38310)

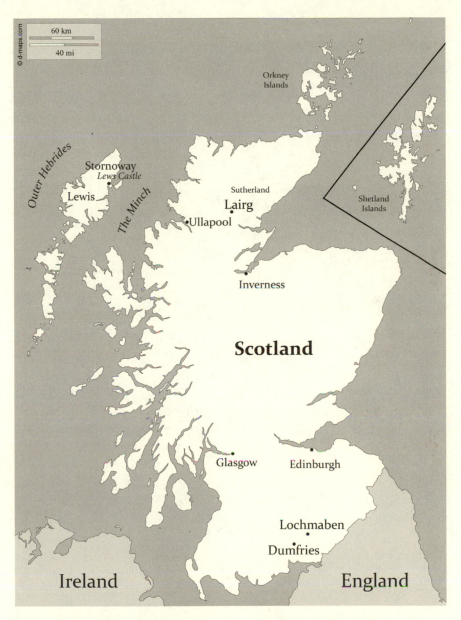

(Courtesy of d-maps and Michael Gallucci)

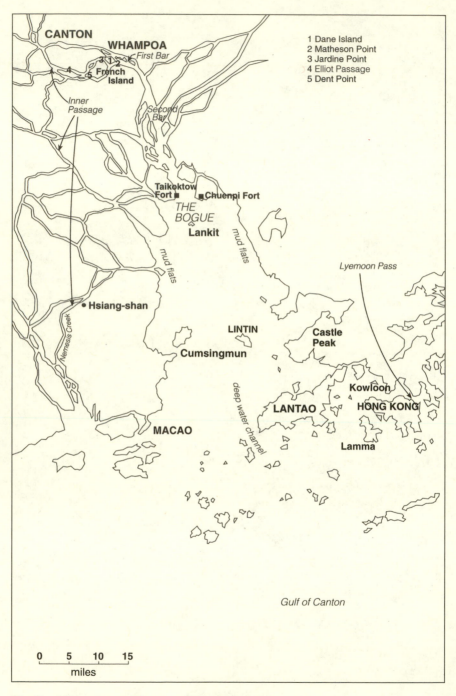

The Pearl River estuary (Courtesy of Mystic Seaport)

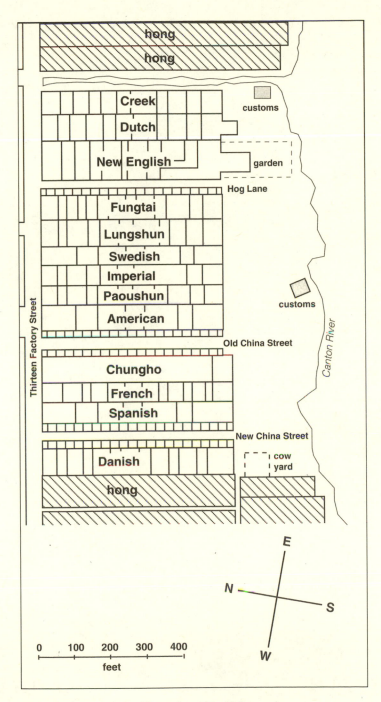

The Canton waterfront (Courtesy of Mystic Seaport)

# OPIUM AND EMPIRE

# THE SCOTLAND OF THEIR BIRTH

The cannons were long silent when William Jardine and James Matheson were born in the final decades of the eighteenth century. Yet, for them as for many contemporary young Scots, events in a Highland field many years before their births influenced the direction of their lives and led them to seek their fortunes far away from the graves of the clansmen who died on that field.

It was on a sleet-swept wasteland known as Drumossie Moor, near Culloden House, that the Jacobite army of Prince Charles Edward Stuart confronted impending disaster at noon on 16 April 1746. The field, a short distance from Inverness, had been selected by the Jacobite quartermaster, an Irishman named John O'Sullivan, whose choice of this lumpy terrain for battle was hardly suitable for the Highlanders' most effective tactic – a direct charge at the enemy line. O'Sullivan, who was trying to make the best of a bad situation, actually favoured retreat, for he thought that the Jacobite army's one chance of victory had disappeared with their exhausting march on the previous night.[1]

A few hundred yards to the northeast, the English and Lowland troops commanded by William Augustus, Duke of Cumberland and son of King George II, enjoyed great superiority of numbers in foot soldiers, cavalry, and artillery. The handful of Jacobite cannons began firing at about one o'clock, and within an hour the battle was decided. What John Prebble has called "the long brawl of Scottish history," which had been going on for centuries, reached its bitter climax in the dismemberment of the Jacobite army.[2]

Encouraged by manifold Scottish resentments against the 1707 union with England, the Jacobite rebellion sought the restoration of Stuart rule in Great Britain. Proclaimed in July 1745 in the name of the Old Pretender, James (III) Stuart, the military campaign had enjoyed a meteoric success in its early months, when England's military commanders were primarily concerned with the war against France. The rebels reached Derby, just one hundred and thirty miles from London, by early December; but the stark prospect of trying to hold the British capital with a force of only five thousand compelled Prince Charles to turn his army back toward Scotland in a prolonged retreat. They enjoyed some notable military success in January, but by 16 April the Jacobite forces were exhausted, desperately underfed, and without funds. The prince, in a foul mood that day, insisted that the battle be fought there and then; he took command of the troops and appointed O'Sullivan deputy commander.[3]

When the centre and right sectors of the Jacobite line charged across the moor, their courage was doomed by murderous fire from the English artillery. The Highlanders' usual tactic was to fire their muskets once, then toss them aside and dash straight at the enemy with swords drawn, hoping to catch the enemy reloading their muskets. Fifteen hundred men from eight clan regiments hurled themselves forward "in a wave of unleashed kilted fury."[4] In response, Cumberland's artillerymen changed from round-shot to grapeshot (lead balls and canisters of nails), to shower the advancing Jacobites with the small bits of metal while the government infantry maintained a steady fire. Although some of the clansmen did break through the left side of Cumberland's line, the Jacobite ranks fell into disorder on the boggy terrain that was obscured with smoke.[5] Charles was driven from the field by fire aimed close to him, and by that time the rout was irreversible. Remnants of his army reassembled at Ruthven in Badenoch, but Charles sent them a message to disperse for the sake of their own safety.[6]

What ensued was such savagery by the government forces that Cumberland came to be permanently known in the Highlands as "The Butcher." The Hanoverian cavalry pursued the retreating left side of the rebels' line along the road to Inverness, shooting the Jacobites as they rounded them up, and making an inferno of a barn in which about thirty had taken refuge. On the battle moor, blood-drenched tartans filled the field, as wounded Jacobites were bayoneted or shot by the victorious army and left unattended for two days. Even before Culloden, the standards for treatment of war prisoners were collapsing in Scotland. One recent assessment of the battle's aftermath asserts that the government forces may well have been moved by anger as they went about killing the defeated rebels, "but the men who killed at Culloden did so deliberately, and not in a blind rage."[7] Men, women, and children who had no direct role in the battle were taken captive and killed or sent off to jails and prison hulks. Knowing that a substantial number of enemy troops had regrouped at Ruthven, Cumberland determined to destroy the fighting spirit of the Jacobites once and for all. His initial impulse was to have all the clansmen transported to the colonies, but he ultimately resorted to a scorched-earth strategy of terrorizing the Highlands.[8]

The Jacobite army suffered 1,500 deaths, as compared to 50 dead and 259 wounded among the government troops. Although Prince Charles evaded capture and eventually escaped to France five months after the battle, three Scottish peers were beheaded, 120 common men were hanged, perhaps close to 700 persons died in prison, and nearly a thousand were transported in bondage to the American colonies.

The battle was fought not very distant from the town where James Matheson would be born (about forty-five miles), and reports of it reverberated through Clan Sutherland in the surrounding countryside. The news took a bit longer to reach the town where William Jardine would be raised, about a hundred and seventy miles to the south. The victory was completed by Parliamentary legislation aimed at destroying the Highland culture which had nurtured the rebellion. In the aftermath of an earlier Jacobite rising, in 1715, Parliament had passed a Disarming Act, intended to strip the clans of their capacity for independent military action. Fines were established for those convicted of possessing arms. But clansmen evaded the law by handing in old weapons and hiding their best arms. Now, in 1747, the Disarming Act was renewed and extended.

Parliament's design was to accomplish by legislation what Cumberland's brutality could not: the destruction of the ancient Gaelic culture of the Scottish Highlands. The wearing of kilts, tartans, and plaids was forbidden, as was the playing of the great Highland pipes and the speaking of Gaelic. Conviction for a second offence was punishable by transportation to any of the colonies for seven years. The mountain clans had only their tartans and their kilts, and they had no funds for purchase of replacement wardrobes. Therefore, in their desperation they resorted to vats in which they dyed their tartans black and brown, before sewing the kilt fabric up the middle, the result being ridiculous-looking breeches.[9]

The clan chieftains were stripped of their traditional authority, and the whole structure of barons' courts and clan councils that had long constituted the foundation of Scottish law was dismantled. The lands of rebel chieftains were forfeited, whereas the unattainted chiefs began to treat the clan's land as their own. Parental concern for members of the clan waned as crofters were cleared from their farms in order to facilitate leasing the glens and braes for raising sheep. Where clansmen had kept their crofts, the new people were often sheep farmers from the Lowlands or England.[10]

Scotland came to be routinely designated as "North Britain" as the eighteenth century wore on, and the formerly independent kingdom took on many appearances of being a compliant province of England's empire. With more sons surviving into adulthood by the late eighteenth century, the Scottish landed classes needed to find socially acceptable employment for their non-inheriting young men. London became the destination of some career-seeking Scots, but English suspicions of crypto-Jacobitism lingered for years after the 1745 rebellion was put down.[11] At Westminster, meanwhile, Scottish peers and MPs did not generally focus their primary attention on concerns of their Scottish constituents. Nonetheless, by the early 1760s, when Lord Bute had become the first Scottish-born prime minister since the Union of 1707, signs of Scotophobia were evident in London, where the press ran cartoon caricatures of Scots that depicted them as greedy opportunists, enriching themselves on English resources.[12]

Among the ideas put forward for the suppression of the Highland clans and their culture was a proposal to raise regiments of government troops among the clansmen. This was initially rejected as risky. However, with the onset of the Seven Years' War in 1756, both the Duke of Cumberland and William Pitt recommended the scheme of raising Highland regiments. Implicit in the proposal was the possibility that potential Jacobites might be killed in combat with the French.[13] The project bore abundant military rewards: over the next half-century, twenty-seven line regiments and nineteen battalions of fencibles. One remnant of the old clan structure served the Crown handsomely: the levies by which chiefs and their "tacksmen" – principal tenants – persuaded or forced young crofters to agree to service in the king's forces. The expenditure of these Scottish troops in wars against the rebellious American colonies or against France has prompted John Prebble to write with undisguised bitterness that "the last tragedy of the clans may not be the slaughter of Culloden, but the purchase and wasteful expenditure of their courage by the southern peoples who had at last conquered them."[14] While Scots constituted 15 per cent of the British population at the end of the century, the number of Scots who had volunteered for military service represented 36 per cent of the volunteer soldiery in 1797.[15]

By 1782, the Disarming Act was a dusty relic of "the '45" and the prohibition of wearing the kilt was removed. But few Highlanders resumed the old clan dress, apart from those serving in the government regiments. The clans were dying, and the role of the kilt became in many instances an affectation for some of the clan chiefs – now turned city gentlemen. In 1784 the lands that had been forfeited because of Jacobite associations were restored to their former owners upon payment of moderate sums of money. In the changing rural economy of the Highlands, the chiefs now came to act as landlords demanding rent of their tacksmen. In turn, the tacksmen, whose prior obligation had been the military organization of the clan, either emigrated or began to exact rent from their subtenants.

William Jardine and James Matheson were born in the last two decades of the eighteenth century, when the passions of the Jacobite rebellion were being relocated from the battlefield to the poetry of Robert Burns and the nostalgic remembrances of those who still drank to "the king across the water." By that time, a general European romanticization of the Highland Scots had emerged, as sympathy for their endangered culture was combined with a characteristically Romantic vision of the Highlanders as being in some ways akin to the "noble savages" whom the Romantics admired.[16] It was a transitional Scotland, not securely rooted in its prior traditions and somewhat ambivalent about its future. For Matheson's region in the north, changes in the life of the agricultural population were more dramatic than was the case with Jardine's neighbourhood of farms near the English border.

For several generations, extending from the last Jacobite rebellion into the second half of the nineteenth century, the Highlands experienced an agricultural revolution which coupled the destruction of the old clan culture with the displacement of its people. Known as the "Highland Clearances," the population changes often meant forced eviction of clan families and the introduction of sheep farming in place of subsistence agriculture.[17]

The earliest substantial clearances occurred in the 1770s and 1780s. Some peasants left of their own accord, recognizing the gulf between their welfare and the economic interests of the landlords; others were forcibly evicted. Some people left the Highlands to work in the newly emerging industrial areas of Lowland Scotland; many emigrated to America; some stayed in northern Scotland and moved to the coast to gather kelp. By the turn of the century, Highland society was composed of landowners, sheep farmers, and small tenant farmers trying to survive.[18]

Paralleling the uncomfortable transformation of the Highlands, the expansion of the Lowland industrial and agricultural economy in the late eighteenth century was a story of great promise realized with the help of English money. Glasgow was at the heart of the thriving textile trade, with banking and shipping resources to support the new industrial vitality, while Edinburgh was reshaping itself into a beautiful modern city, based on James Craig's 1767 plan for the New Town, a grid design of streets, with squares and crescents and gardens, constructed to the north of the old medieval town dominated by the castle.

In this new Edinburgh, the Scottish Enlightenment would establish its main camp. Voltaire regarded the city as an intellectual centre that was the equal of Paris, London, and Vienna, and Thomas Jefferson declared that in the realm of science "no place in the world can pretend to competition with Edinburgh."[19] A special coherence marked the intellectual society of the Scottish Enlightenment, which enjoyed a climate that did not generate expectations that intellectuals stand apart from the church (David Hume excepted) or quarrel with the government. Nor was there any need to posit hostility between revealed religion and natural science or natural philosophy. While there was much vitality in Scottish literature, painting, and architecture, the driving forces of the Scottish Enlightenment were to be found in the fields of science and philosophy, and those fields had special influence on the professions of medicine and law.[20]

In both Glasgow and Edinburgh, medical faculties had a long history, with qualification being normally established by years of apprenticeship to a practitioner coupled with some measure of academic instruction.

However, contemporary with the scientific elements of the Scottish Enlightenment, the medical faculty and facilities at Edinburgh, with encouragement by the town council, developed formal university instruction more quickly than the school at Glasgow. In the second half of the eighteenth century, medical studies at Edinburgh attracted large numbers of students.[21]

In many respects, Edinburgh was a magnet for young men from the distinctly changing regions of Scotland. From the Lowland area east of Dumfries, where new concepts of agriculture were taking hold, William Jardine was drawn to the medical school at Edinburgh, and from the unsettled agricultural region of the northern Highlands James Matheson was attracted to Edinburgh for university studies and thence to London for the beginnings of his career in commerce.

There were firm limits to social mobility in Scotland, in spite of the transitional character of the national experience in the late eighteenth century. The most influential and financially rewarding professions, such as the law, were in effect reserved for aspirants from socially established families. Moreover, boys whose education began in village schools, as did that of William Jardine, usually arrived at the universities too late to break into the mainstream of intellectual life as professors or scientists.[22] Thus, it happened that, in the latter part of the century, many young men took their education in Scottish academies and universities but set their ambitions on careers outside Scotland. Among the opportunities away from home, the India trade was a major lure for venturesome young men from all over Scotland, including Jardine and Matheson.

The man who exercised the most influence in Scottish politics in the 1770s and 1780s was a lawyer named Henry Dundas, sometimes called "Henry the ninth" because of the powerful political lineage from which he came. A close associate of William Pitt the Younger, Dundas held a seat in Parliament for a quarter of a century and, over the last three decades of the eighteenth century, gained the positions of lord advocate for Scotland, privy councillor, treasurer of the navy, keeper of the signet of Scotland, home secretary, and secretary of state for war in the cabinet of William Pitt. His place on the Board of Control, which oversaw the policies of the East India Company (EIC), provided the opportunity for him to tie together his patronage in Scottish affairs and his interests in the various channels of the Eastern trade.

In the aftermath of the loss of much of Britain's North American empire, some of Parliament's attention was focused on the development of its Eastern empire. Eighteenth-century India had been the venue of wild profiteering by officials of the EIC, some of whom were Scots who returned to Britain as wealthy "nabobs." The Board of Control had been created by the India Act of 1784 to superintend the government and revenues of British territories in the East Indies. In 1793 the salaried office of president of the Board of Control was created for Henry Dundas, who gave much encouragement to the export of Scotsmen to India. A few years after the Dundas era, Sir Walter Scott would refer to the Board of Control as "the corn chest for Scotland."[23]

During the early stages of war against revolutionary France, while president of the Board of Control and simultaneously secretary of state for war, Dundas was able to convince the directors of the EIC to convert ten of their great ocean-going ships to service in the Royal Navy as sixty-four-gun warships, and to raise three hundred men to serve on each of those vessels. In due course, the Company was reimbursed quite substantially for its wartime services.[24] By the 1790s, Dundas was the most powerful Scottish politician at the national level since the Act of Union 1707, and he was able to provide Scots with an impressive measure of official patronage within Britain and in the empire. Although Dundas lost his cabinet position when Pitt's government fell from office in 1801, he was raised to the peerage in 1802, as Viscount Melville.

In that same year, William Jardine entered the service of the Company as a ship's surgeon's mate. If Dundas was not directly involved in preparing the way for Jardine's appointment, the umbrella of patronage influence that he had been exercising with the EIC surely would have worked to Jardine's advantage. In fact, Scottish influence within the EIC had been growing over the course of the eighteenth century, and that expansion of Scottish influence at East India House, the Company's headquarters on Leadenhall Street in London, meant that younger relatives and sons of Scottish families with connections were regularly being brought into the Company's service.[25] Even among the Scottish gentry and some peers' families, the traditional prejudice against mercantile careers was set aside. T.M. Devine's study of the Scottish diaspora reveals that, as the empire became more British and less English in the eighteenth century, the transformation was dramatically manifested in the bureaucracies of the Company, where the number of Scots seeking career opportunities had the effect of sparking some of the Scotophobia of the years after mid-century.[26] In the period from 1777 to 1813, Scots accounted for 28 per cent of the men who were first appointed to command of East India ships, and this development was made possible in part by former commanders who, upon becoming shipowners, gave preference to Scots when ships' officers were appointed.[27]

For those who did not secure appointments to the Honourable Company, there were possibilities of obtaining permission from the EIC to engage in the "country trade" – that is, private trade among the Company's settlements along the coast of Southeast Asia and eastward to Canton. At the time, Dundas was being pressed by various parties to establish reliable access to the Indian products which were necessary to the conduct of trade with China. In response, as part of his economic strategy, he promoted the country trade, which enabled persons in the Company's service to invest their private resources as "free merchants" in enterprises outside the Company's monopoly.[28] With the British appetite for Chinese tea being encouraged by the younger Pitt's policy of reducing the import duty on that product, and with Company officials prohibited from engaging in private trade, the free merchants established – under licence from the Company – "houses of agency" in the various EIC settlements and handled diverse business ventures involving the capital of investors at some remote distance.[29]

Within this network of free merchants stretching from Bombay and Calcutta to Bencoolen and Canton, the proportion of Scots was fairly high, owing in part to the links of kinship among the Scots in the Company and among the free merchants in the country trade. To a considerable degree, the Scottish agency houses in India and elsewhere were family concerns, bearing the names of Mackintosh, Fairlie, Fergusson, Reid, Mackillop, and such.[30]

Hence the Eastern trade opened up one major road of opportunity for young Scots in a century which had seen the destruction of the ancient Scottish kingdom and the death of the Stuart claims to lead that kingdom. A half-century after the debacle at Culloden, and less than a generation after the loss of the Thirteen Colonies in North America, the Highland clearances were in progress. For many young Scots, emigration to Canada or other colonies was a route of escape; for others there was suffering on the old clan lands and little expectation of a better life. Some young men gambled on survival in the ranks of the Highland regiments, while others sought their opportunities in the shires of southern Scotland in modernized agriculture, or linen, or iron, or shipbuilding. For the adventurous and ambitious, the EIC and the private trade of the free merchants held the allure of sirens of fortune. Of those who did go out to the East, many never returned to Scotland, some returned with a few shillings, and a few came home, after many years in the East, with spectacular wealth and with family business empires to be perpetuated.

William Jardine and James Matheson left their homeland as soon as they could, neither being attracted by a life of farming in the Lowlands or the Highlands. To these young men on the make, the transitional Scotland of their youth offered less promise than the possibilities of careers connected in one way or another with the Eastern trade. They did not aspire to the status of landed gentry in Scotland; nor did they set themselves career goals in the manufacturing sector of Scotland's economy. As ambitious young participants in the British diaspora, they were destined to become "gentlemanly capitalists," a term that P.J. Cain and A.G. Hopkins use to describe the individuals who supplied the dynamic force in the expansion of the Victorian empire.[31] Yet neither of these young Scots could foresee that career track as they took their separate ways eastward early in the nineteenth century.

# 1

# ORIGINS

Eight years after the 1776 publication of Adam Smith's formidable theory of self-interest and natural economic liberty, William Jardine was born near Dumfries, fifty miles south of Glasgow where for a time Smith had held the position of professor of moral philosophy. While Smith may have had in mind a different model of self-interest from that which took shape in the career of William Jardine, his ideas of economic liberty, free from mercantilist advantages and chartered monopolies, came to be a kind of economic gospel to Jardine and his partner, James Matheson. Those economic beliefs would take Jardine halfway around the world from his origins in the southwest region of Scotland.

In the years of William's youth, that region was experiencing a phenomenon called the "Lowland Clearances," a term invented by historians to describe the consolidation of farms in southern Scotland. Parallel with the evictions of crofters in the Highlands, a transformation of tenant farming was occurring in the Lowlands, but the conditions of the change varied from region to region and estate to estate. The changes involved conversion to large pastoral farming and a consolidation of agrarian capitalism. Apparently, the Jardine family's farm survived the transition intact, at a time when the "Lowland Clearances" were threatening the livelihood of many small farmers and destroying that of many subtenant farmers. In general, the phenomenon produced few of the classic symptoms of peasant alienation. In contrast to the severe psychological dislocations associated with episodes of collective resistance to the Highland Clearances, the reactions of southern rural Scots tended to be less violent and more nostalgic, in keeping with the regard for old traditions of simple peasant life which was embodied in the verses of Robert Burns, himself a farm boy from nearby southwest Scotland.[1]

The Jardine family maintained a small farm called Broadholm, at Applegarth, a hamlet on the outskirts of Lochmaben, in Dumfriesshire. Situated on the flat plain adjoining a branch of the River Annan, the land today appears as a desirable piece of farm property. William Jardine was born at Broadholm on 24 February 1784 to Elizabeth (Johnstone) and Andrew Jardine. He was the sixth of seven children born of their marriage. Their wedding, which had taken place on 23 August 1772, was recorded as "irregular," for which they were officially rebuked by Kirk authorities. Precisely what the irregularity was remains unknown, but both Andrew and Elizabeth were older than the usual age of marriage at that time.[2] They were both then around thirty years old, and Elizabeth (who was to outlive her husband by thirty-two years) was forty-three when she gave her own name to the last of her children, in 1786. William's eldest sibling, Robert, was born at the Castlemains in 1773; all of the remaining children, four girls and two boys, were born at Broadholm.

Lochmaben is one of the three towns that claim to be the birthplace of Robert the Bruce in the thirteenth century. The ruins of Bruce's castle constituted the most dramatic part of the local landscape during William Jardine's youth. Since local farmers used the castle ruin as a quarry for stone for their farmhouses, it is quite possible that the Jardine farmhouse shared that pillage with its neighbours.

Along the banks of the River Annan the fertile farmland was held by tenant farmers according to a peculiar form of land tenure known as the "udal," by which the right to occupy the land was granted without written documents. The lord of the barony of Lochmaben was the Viscount of Stormont, to whom Jardine's father and his neighbours paid a modest annual rent. Substantial quantities of flax were grown along the river, since the land was so suitable for it; and many of the farm women, likely including William's mother and sisters, produced their own linen and took in foreign flax for spinning. The town produced about sixty thousand yards of flax annually, most of which was sold in England.

Young William would have fished for salmon in the river, and would have helped the family raise its swine. The border with England was a relatively short distance from the Jardine home, and the Jardines, like everyone else in town, would have bought swine that were born in England, bred them on their farms, and sold them back to the English market. It was a ready money commodity, bringing a significant amount of cash into the towns of southern Scotland.[3] He would also have cut peat for his family's fuel, but, as the mosses wore out at the end of the eighteenth century, it became necessary to import coal about thirty miles, from England, at considerable expense.

The population of Lochmaben numbered 1,395 at mid-century; of those, about thirty persons lived on the charity provided by the parish, but that was a pittance drawn solely from the church collection. The parish minister, the Reverend Andrew Jaffrey, reported that there was some competition among the locally resident poor and the itinerant poor for the available charity: "Those that are able are allowed to beg from door to door; and many strollers and idle vagrants are suffered to travel in the country, with which it is greatly oppressed, and by this means the poor of the parish are robbed of that charity which properly belongs to them."[4] These factors of town life no doubt helped to shape the disposition of William Jardine toward considerations of personal economics. His own hard work on the farm, plus the images of itinerant beggars, have to be factored into his later articulations of contempt for idlers.

He was fortunate to live in a town with a legally established grammar school, which had been endowed in 1726 with a bequest of £200 from James Richardson of Reading, England. The interest from that sum was to pay the salary of a schoolmaster who would teach English, Latin, writing, and arithmetic, without fee, to ten poor students. Additional bequests by the same donor provided for a library, a house for the schoolmaster, and an additional school at Hightae, for the benefit of all the children in the "Four Towns" of Lochmaben.[5] This, then, was the source of William Jardine's early education, a model of charity from a benefactor whom he would never know, and perhaps an example for his own philanthropy in China.

Among his siblings, his closest and longest attachments were to his sister Jean, ten years older than William, and his brother David, eight years his elder. When their father died in May 1793, at Broadholm, William was but nine years old; and compounding his grief over the loss of his father were the new burdens he had to shoulder on the farm, which would compete against any ambitions he might have for extending his education. When Andrew Jardine died, his widow, Elizabeth, was fifty years old and had three children yet shy of their teenage years. The oldest children, Robert and Jean, were twenty and nineteen, of marriageable age, and not certain to be around the farm for a predictably long time. Those considerations meant that, when William had finished his basic course of Latin and English and writing and arithmetic with the Lochmaben schoolmaster, the family faced a crucial decision regarding his future. How was the son of a poor farmer's widow to pay the cost of his tuition at the next stage of his schooling? Apparently, he remained at home at Broadholm until he was sixteen, at which point he enrolled in studies at the Royal College of Surgeons of Edinburgh. His brother David provided the monetary assistance necessary for his studies at Edinburgh, as William revealed much later in life: "The small sum due me from my mother's property I have always considered as belonging to my brother – he having supplied me with money when I had little or none of my own."[6]

Boys who attended the more advanced burgh schools could move on to university by their early teens. For the upper-class students, a solid early start could lead to a career in the legal professions, or to the type of scholarly development suitable for university teaching. However, the bright lad from a village school might obtain a scholarship to university in his later teens and proceed to ordination or prepare to be a schoolmaster. The other major option in Scotland was medicine, for Scotland was highly regarded for the level of instruction in medical science at its universities and colleges.

Edinburgh enjoyed a reputation as the centre of medical study in the English-speaking world, with its College of Physicians and its College of Surgeons, both antedating the establishment of the medical school at the University of Edinburgh. Moreover, the teaching hospital was the Royal Infirmary, held up as a model of clinical instruction. In a 1792 guide for prospective students, one professor asserted: "The Infirmary of Edinburgh is much superior to any similar institution in Britain for the purpose of medical education. The cases of patients are all regularly registered, and an account of their situations is given daily by the attending physicians."[7] Competition for the Royal College had developed at the end of the century when an Extra-Mural School of medical studies, offering rival independent teaching facilities, emerged in a cluster of buildings around the College of Surgeons building.[8]

The number of students pursuing medicine in "Auld Reekie," as the Old Town of Edinburgh was called, had grown steadily through the course of the eighteenth century, and in the time of Jardine's attendance, during the years of warfare against revolutionary and Napoleonic France, the student population of Edinburgh had nearly doubled, to

a total of 420 registered students as of 1800.[9] Career opportunities
formed the basis for the popularity of medical study in Scotland, for
there were few other professions offering such demand for their services. No doubt this type of opportunity helped draw the bright lad from
Applegarth to Edinburgh.

Medical qualification was usually achieved by serving a number of
years of apprenticeship to a practitioner; in addition, the corporations of
physicians and surgeons offered instruction in anatomy, medical practice, obstetrics, and related areas. The professors who lectured in medical theory and practice at the university also treated patients at the
teaching ward of the infirmary and delivered lectures on clinical procedures. Students had access to the teaching ward by virtue of a ticket of
admission (tuition payment) allowing them to attend clinical lectures
and to observe physicians and student surgical assistants (known as
"dressers") who had responsibilities for examining and dressing wounds
and sores.

Surgeon's apprentices like young William normally lived with their
masters but had an ill-defined status in the household, somewhere between family member and servant. Typically, apprentices would receive their room and board, but no clothing, in the terms of indenture.
Practising surgeons took on apprentices because they were a form of
cheap labour and because of the fees paid by the apprentice for the indenture. Much of the drudgery in the surgeon's practice could be assigned to the apprentice (sweeping out the shop, preparing medicines,
cleaning bandages, preparing bills, and running errands). As competence was gained, the apprentice would assist his master in tending to
patients, because many operations required two men to perform them.
In return for this work, the surgeon was expected to teach the apprentice the skill of surgery.[10] The name of the surgeon with whom Jardine
apprenticed is not recorded.[11]

Class fees were generally modest. As late as the second quarter of the
nineteenth century, classes at the university level in Scotland generally
did not cost more than three or four guineas. Admission tickets for the
teaching ward cost medical students ten guineas per year in the late
eighteenth century, but surgical apprentices paid a lesser fee than medical students. The range of expenses for a six-month academic season at
Edinburgh in the early nineteenth century has been estimated at fourteen to twenty pounds for the students on a tight budget.[12] Ten pounds
was about the least a student could skimp along on for the winter

session. William Jardine was much closer to that end of the scale than to the wealthy students who could afford a lively social life.

Different levels of apprenticeship involved indentures for five years, for those preparing to enter the guild of surgeons, or three years, for those simply seeking surgical training. From 1778 on, the Royal College issued two types of diplomas for students who had not served a regular apprenticeship for three years. One declared the candidate "sufficiently qualified to practice the arts of surgery and pharmacy." The other acknowledged that the student was "sufficiently qualified to act as a surgeon's mate in His Majesty's Service." The latter required class attendance for at least one year, and the former, known as a "full diploma," required two years of classes.[13]

Increasingly, toward the end of the eighteenth century, as liberal education became more important for surgeons, students spent the years between age fifteen and age eighteen learning mathematics, Latin, and natural philosophy (as well as medical subjects)[14] rather than simply doing the work of indentured servants. Training simultaneously in medicine and surgery was pursued by a growing number of students by that time, and John Bell, who established his own school of medicine and surgery in 1790, maintained that every young man studying medicine or surgery should be acquainted with the usual types of traumatic problems, including wounds, fractures, and dislocations. Periodically, surgical and medical students would be notified of scheduled surgical procedures so that they might observe these operations in the teaching amphitheater at the Royal Infirmary.[15]

The daily bedside instruction in the teaching ward, when combined with the regularly scheduled lectures every two weeks, gave the students an overall experience combining practicum and medical theory. The fact that medical students and surgical apprentices studied side by side, in an atmosphere of mutual tolerance and even collegiality, meant that the ancient barriers separating them socially and professionally were beginning to break down.[16] By the 1790s, surgical students were being educated in keeping with the model of a liberally educated gentleman, as was the case with medical students. Nevertheless, at the end of the eighteenth century, surgeons continued to be assigned a rank lower than physicians; theirs were the untidy, manual jobs among the healing professionals.[17]

The clinical lectures were organized primarily for the benefit of the medical students, and the patients admitted to the teaching ward were there as medical cases. Nevertheless, William Jardine would have had ample opportunity to observe the full range of ailments treated in Edinburgh, thereby acquiring knowledge that would be very useful to him in his years of service on board East India Company vessels. Although the Royal Navy contracted for the treatment of sailors at the Royal Infirmary, there was no sailors' ward, since there would not have been a large naval squadron at Edinburgh. However, a soldiers' ward had existed since the time of the Jacobite rebellion of 1745, because there was a sizeable military garrison at Edinburgh Castle. The regimental surgeon at the Castle supervised the treatment of the soldiers at the infirmary, but the physicians for the soldiers' ward consulted with the military surgeons when the nature of some soldiers' complaints required surgical attention. In these circumstances, Jardine would have observed the types of complaints common to military personnel. Those most common illnesses among men admitted to the ward were respiratory ailments and venereal diseases.

The spectrum of illnesses observed by students at the infirmary would also have included "fever," a catchall term for a broad variety of infectious diseases, "pectoral complaints" (often meaning respiratory infections), rheumatism, stomach complaints, diseases of the skin such as scurvy, and various forms of surgical infections. The two groups most susceptible to infectious diseases were female servants and seamen. While the skin lesions signalling scurvy were common among poor people admitted to the infirmary, owing to poor dietary habits, Jardine probably saw few cases of the disease among the seamen patients because the North Sea Squadron took only brief voyages and because of the regimen of citrus juice introduced by the Admiralty in 1795.[18]

After diagnosis, the forms of treatment offered at the infirmary ranged from simply defending people against the cold, to baths, dietetics, and various types of surgical intervention, such as bloodletting, leeching, blistering, electrical stimulation, and paracentesis (removal of fluid accumulations from the abdomen). But the most frequent articles of therapeutic treatment at the infirmary would have been drugs (both herbal and chemical). The categories of drugs administered included cathartics, emetics, diuretics, antacids, tonics, expectorants, and anodynes.

Of the anodynes (described then as "medicines which ease pain and produce sleep"), the most important was opium, generally administered by drafts of liquid laudanum or paregoric elixir. Almost certainly it was during his two years at Edinburgh that William Jardine acquired his first detailed knowledge of opium. The drug was employed for sedation and as an analgesic; it was used for arthritis relief, for controlling convulsions, to relax the bile duct when stones were detected, and for gout, hemorrhoids, diarrhea, fevers, and severe coughing. It was also administered topically, to decrease sensitivity to pain (such as toothache or chest pain), and it was available in the form of pills as an alternative to laudanum for internal administration. When taken internally, the effect of opium was to induce serenity and drowsiness; it would dilate blood vessels, retard the pulse, and reduce bowel activity. Opium was generally regarded as the ideal painkiller during the time of Jardine's surgical training, and hospital practitioners prescribed it with great frequency, since there was yet no clear understanding of its addictive qualities.[19] The commerce by which dried exudate from the seed pods of the opium poppy (*papaver somniferum*) was obtained for medical use at Edinburgh could hardly have been a major point of interest or concern for William Jardine, at age sixteen, as he set about learning the skills of a surgeon.

With few resources of his own, but some important monetary assistance from his brother David, and with his maintenance as an apprentice to a practising surgeon, the young Jardine managed to obtain two years of surgical training in Scotland before setting his designs on a wider world. Like 20 per cent of the surgical students at Edinburgh, William spent two years in apprenticeship. He entered upon his studies in 1800 and obtained a "full diploma" from the Royal College of Surgeons of Edinburgh on 2 March 1802. His diploma was more akin to a modern university degree than a traditional guild licence.[20]

Usually, after their apprenticeships the surgical students did extensive travelling in England and perhaps abroad, to gain acquaintance with different surgical techniques and ideas, before returning to Edinburgh to take three qualifying examinations for admission to the Royal College of Surgeons. Jardine lacked the financial resources for such foreign study. Doubtless, the need to scrape by on a thin purse added forcefully to the conviction that he held throughout his life that thrift and industry were essential virtues. It was also the likely cause for his relatively short apprenticeship.

Although numerous young men of Jardine's generation left Edinburgh without a degree, quite a few returned after the end of the French wars to pursue additional qualifications.[21] This was an option that would have been open to William Jardine, who by 1815 had sufficient resources to return to the university, had he been so inclined. But the intervening years had changed the course of his ambitions so decisively that resumption of medical schooling was not on the chart for the next stage of his life.

Far to the north of Dumfries and Edinburgh, indeed close to the top of Scotland, Jardine's future partner was born in somewhat more privileged circumstances. The Mathesons had served the Hanoverian kings since the Jacobite rising of 1715, when John Matheson was chief of the Lairg Mathesons. Their property, West Shinness Lodge, lay on the northeast shore of Loch Shin seven miles outside the town of Lairg, Sutherlandshire. It was there, at Shinness, that James Matheson was born on 17 November 1796; so he was a dozen years younger than William Jardine.

His father, Donald Matheson (1744–1810), who was fifty years old when James was born, had served in the regiments which the Hanoverian governments had organized to take advantage of the military resources of the post-Jacobite Highlands. During the Seven Years' War (1756–63), Donald Matheson was appointed ensign of a fencible regiment raised by the Earl of Sutherland, and he served in that unit from 1759, when he was fifteen, until 1763. His military career resumed at the time of the American Revolution, when the earl raised another fencible regiment; he served as captain-lieutenant in that unit until the Treaty of Paris in 1783.

Donald Matheson had been just a little boy when his own father died. Eventually he inherited the property of his grandfather (in 1775), and that land, likely rented from the Earl of Sutherland, gave him the economic footing to marry and begin raising a family in 1783. Subsequently he acquired the role of tacksman for the earl; in that capacity he paid an annual sum to the lord and retained the rents which he collected from the earl's tenants, whose livelihood was from cattle. In the end-of-the-century parish account he is said to be one of the four proprietors of surrounding lands and is referred to as "Captain Mathison, wadsetter of Shinness."[22] As a wadsetter, he held mortgages usually of lesser landholders within the parish. The farm at Shinness was wadsetted to Captain Matheson in 1779 by the Sutherland family, for a loan of £15,733 (Scots), which meant that he did have substantial resources. It took thirty years for the estate's proprietors to redeem the wadset, but the money was not paid until after his death, at which time it was received by his son Duncan. His annual rental of the farm cost £400

(Scots), but it would have risen substantially had he accepted the Sutherlands' proposal that the farm be augmented with neighbouring property to establish a large sheep farm. In 1808 he was sufficiently attracted to the idea that he gave notices to his own tenants that they would have to leave the property, and each family was paid £2 in "removals money," but the clearances did not take place at that time since the project was beyond his resources. The captain was still operating the Shinness farm when he died, in 1810, at age sixty-three.[23]

Although one might assume that James Matheson began life with certain economic advantages, it is reported that his father was not adept at managing money and that he had significant debts. The other important thing to note here is that the Mathesons did not take part in the harsh clearances of the crofters from the lands around Lairg in the next decade, when the Duchess of Sutherland oversaw the removal of much of the farming population, who were replaced by sheep. The clearance of the Shinness tenants did not occur until 1819, by which time the farm had passed from Matheson hands.

The parish of Lairg was not a region of rich farmland. Apparently the land was unsuitable to raising crops, on account of the stretches of heath and the coarse grass that grew there. Consequently, the rents of the district were small. Nor was the climate more generous than the land, being customarily rainy and damp. The anonymous writer of the Statistical Account of Lairg for 1791 remarked impishly that "the inhabitants, having great abundance of peats, take care to keep a good fire without, and as often as they can get at spiritous liquors, they will kindle a fire within, nor do they apprehend more danger to their conditions for the one than from the other."[24]

The young woman Donald married was Catherine MacKay, daughter of the minister of the parish of Lairg, the Reverend Thomas MacKay, a poor but saintly man. The MacKays were the dominant clan in the district. Captain Matheson and his bride made their residence in a substantial lodge at Shinness, near the loch, and in the course of their marriage Catherine bore eight children – three sons and five daughters – of whom James was the second son.[25] His roots were, therefore, in touch with both the Kirk and the clan system in the north, and while the clan system had been weakened, the Kirk had not. The religious dimension of his early life, in the Church of Scotland, was established both within the family and by his schooling at the academy in Inverness.

There was a schoolhouse at Shinness, but it is unlikely that James's education began there. He enjoyed a better opportunity for elementary education than William Jardine had known. The Inverness Royal Academy, established four years before his birth, offered five years of instruction for a fee schedule ranging from six shillings per term in the first year to eleven shillings and six pence in the fifth year. Young James was a student at the academy probably from July 1805 until June 1808, with the years divided into two terms. During the months of longer daylight (from early spring though mid autumn), the rigorous class schedule required the students to be in class from seven in the morning until six in the evening, with two breaks along the way. The daily sessions in the winter months were mercifully shorter, stretching from nine until four, with a two-hour break starting at noon. The subjects taught at the academy included English grammar, Gaelic, Latin, Greek, French, writing, arithmetic, bookkeeping, mathematics, geography, fortification, history (natural and civil), natural philosophy, chemistry, and astronomy. Music and dancing were taught at a separate school building under the same patronage.

At the academy, James's school day began and ended with prayers led by the rector, who also led the masters and scholars to church on Sunday morning and met with them again from five to six on Sunday for instruction in the principles of religion and morality. As one of the younger students, James was allowed playtime on Saturday afternoon, and in succeeding years he and the other older students could have playtime for all of Saturday. He and his schoolmates were expected to assist the school janitor, and they had to pay for the coal to heat their classrooms. Reports of the students' progress were made by the master to the academy's directors.[26] Presumably James received good reports, given his subsequent advancement to the Royal High School and thence to university. The transition from Inverness to Edinburgh came for James with the academic season of 1808–09, when he was enrolled in the fourth year class at the Royal High School, with George Irvine as his master.

Captain Donald Matheson died in 1810. Whether James returned from Edinburgh to attend his father's funeral is unrecorded. If he had, he would have witnessed, and perhaps taken part in, the farewell toast that was drunk to his father by the assembled Mathesons and MacKays and friends on 1 February 1810. The ledger for Shinness Lodge reveals that the captain's whisky smuggler, William MacDonald, supplied the mourners with the funeral whisky (eleven pints) free of charge. At more than a-hundred-proof strong, the illegal whisky likely was a powerful solace to some of the mourners.[27]

Family genealogy records indicate that Donald's wife, Catherine, died at a young age, but the actual date of her death seems to be undocumented. Therefore, it seems possible that, by the time of James's third year at the Royal High School, he was an orphan, albeit a well-educated one. James's brother Duncan inherited the Shinness farm after their father's death, but he had little interest in farming and instead attained the position of sheriff depute in Edinburgh. For that reason the farm passed into the care of Catherine's brother John MacKay, who had little success with it. Three years later the family sold the property.[28] Thus, by 1818, the ancestral home in which James had spent his childhood belonged to others, but by then he was not looking back toward Loch Shinness.

The Edinburgh where this young lad was to reside for about five years was a city of many faces. It had to be exciting for a boy of twelve to have a certain measure of freedom in the old, medieval buildings and alleys and streets of the "Athens of the North." The principal road in the Old Town was the thoroughfare known as Canongate at its eastern end and then High Street, running uphill to Edinburgh Castle. Off High Street ran the wynds and closes that connected the streets and courts of the Old Town. In their excursions around the Old Town, Matheson and his schoolmates, scurrying through tunnelled entrances to the closes and thence on to the next wynd, would encounter water carriers, coal sellers, rummaging pigs, piemen with bells, barbers in transit, ragamuffin "caddies" (public messengers), and advocates in gowns. Under the dominating presence of the Castle atop the great mound, they would pass famous churches, the old Parliament House, the Royal Exchange, open-air markets selling fish and meat and all manner of things, the shops of watchmakers and jewellers, the booths of hosiers and hatters and drapers and glovers, and houses hallowed in the city's history.[29]

Yet the picturesque town was also dirty and crowded, ridden with soot and peopled by numerous hard-drinking men and women. Moreover, it was, with all its sunless, narrow lanes and wynds, its open sewers, and its refuse-strewn courts, decidedly unhealthy. The quaint designation "Auld Reekie" was bestowed on the Old Town by the housewives of Fife, across the Firth of Forth, who could tell when it was dinnertime in Edinburgh by the layer of smoke which sat upon the city from the forest of chimneys.³⁰

A world apart from Auld Reekie was the thriving New Town, on the northern side of North Loch (now Princes Street Gardens). The elegant regularity of the streets and squares of the New Town, offering comfortable residences to the upper classes of Edinburgh, had taken shape starting in 1767 according to a town plan prepared by the young architect James Craig. But the students of the high school and the university found their home amidst the convoluted twists and turns of the Old Town.

The Royal High School was located in a simple, barnlike building just below the eastern end of Cowgate which had been built in 1777.³¹ Class size was quite large (eighty or more), which forced the masters into pedagogical compromises. Nevertheless, the level of education at Edinburgh was regarded throughout Britain as being the best in the kingdom. The curriculum was heavily concentrated on mastery of Latin, with up to six hours a day being devoted to that subject, the lessons emphasizing grammar, translation, and prose. Mathematics and Greek were also in the program of studies. In addition, families generally supplemented the basic curriculum by engaging private tutors, who could be hired by the hour for instruction in French, German, geography, drawing, music, and engineering.³²

The boys were seated in class according to their level of attainment, with the "dunce" at the far end of the back bench in a place reserved for the dullard, and the ranks proceeding up to that of "dux," the leading member of the class. By family report, young James was among a group of boys who competed for the position of head of the class.³³ Henry Cockburn, who entered the high school twenty years before James Matheson, remembered it as being notorious for the severity of its teachers and the riotousness of the students. In his unflattering recollection, the tone of the school was "vulgar and harsh," and he claimed that in a later period some of the masters could have been sentenced to transportation as violent criminals for the extent to which they whipped their students.³⁴

Young Matheson would have dressed like all the other boys at the high school. The typical attire included a round black hat, a shirt fastened at the neck with a black ribbon, a double-breasted waistcoat and a single-breasted coat with tail, corduroy breeches tied at the knees by a knot of brown cotton tape, worsted stockings (in winter), and clumsy shoes intended to be worn on either foot (necessitating that they be worn on alternate feet from day to day). The coat and waistcoat were always made of fabrics in glaring colours such as bright blue or grass green or scarlet.[35]

Hence the boys of the high school were easily recognizable in the streets, and this may have helped to generate the "bickers" or street fights which pitted them against boys of the lower classes. The students seemed to take readily to this "rough mode of play," which was without malice, according to Matheson's contemporary, J.G. Lockhart. When one side charged against the other, which sought to hold its ground, stones and sticks and fisticuffs were the means of combat.[36] Was Matheson scuffling in the streets like the others? We know that he was an adventurer, and so we cannot easily imagine him at age twelve or thirteen simply standing on the sidelines of a free-for-all between his schoolmates and some robust and tough young fellows from the Grassmarket or the wynds of the Old Town.

In the academic season 1809–10 James advanced into the fifth-year class at the high school conducted by the rector, James Pillans, who invented the blackboard for use in that building to instruct his geography class with coloured chalks. Caesar, Livy, Virgil, Sallust, Terence, and Horace were among the ancients encountered by students in their Latin lessons. At the same time, young Matheson's mind and imagination were turning to more exotic interests, as his library record reveals. Among the books he borrowed in the winter of that year were both volumes of *Captain Cook's Voyages*.[37] Eighteen hundred years separated Matheson and Virgil, whereas only thirty years separated Matheson's reading from the actual voyages and tragic death of Cook on a beach in Hawaii. Understandably, the accounts of the Royal Navy's most famous explorer would have appealed to the thirteen-year-old, and such interest anticipated his own extensive travels in the South Seas before a decade would pass.

To begin college, as most people still referred to the University of Edinburgh, his travels were minimal; in fact, he was able to remain in the same neighbourhood south of Cowgate when he enrolled. At the time of his matriculation in the fall of 1810, the college was in a state of transition from the "ancient shabby place of small courts and dingy classrooms"[38] to the splendid new classical building for which the

foundation stone had been laid in 1789. The inability of the city to finance the project by itself meant reliance on royal patronage, but the
huge costs of twenty-three years of warfare against France precluded
any such support for the university until the defeat of Bonaparte in
1815.[39] The design for the new university structure was the work of
Robert Adam as modified into its final state by William Playfair. Their
handsome conception took material form in instalments through the
first decades of the nineteenth century, and many students like James
Matheson saw parts of the plan realized. By the time the whole project
was completed in 1833, Matheson was conducting business with his
partner at Canton.

It was normal for students to begin university studies in their early
teens, with fourteen being the usual starting age. Matheson was a month
shy of his fourteenth birthday when he matriculated in the Faculty of
Arts in the fall of 1810. By the following November, his academic direction had changed; he was then matriculating in the Faculty of Medicine.
However, like so many young men who undertook university studies in
that era, he did not complete the course of studies for a degree.[40]

To gain a degree in the Faculty of Arts, attendance through four academic sessions was required, but there were no standard written examinations. The curriculum included Latin, Greek, rhetoric, belles-lettres,
history, logic, metaphysics, moral philosophy, and natural philosophy;
but mathematics was slighted.[41] Most students were content to take
those courses in which they had an interest rather than those from
which they expected to benefit, for the model of liberal education was
more prominent than the pursuit of a degree. The standard fee for matriculation in both the arts and medicine courses was three guineas per
course. As graduation became less important as a feature of the course
of studies in the Arts Faculty, students did not subscribe to a fixed sequence of courses, and many tended to avoid unpopular professors.[42]

In contrast to their counterparts at Oxford and Cambridge, students
at Edinburgh did not wear gowns, nor did they live within the walls of
the college. They attended lectures once or twice a day, often in large
classes (seventy or more), in an atmosphere of better discipline than
that of the High School. Critics of the quality of education at Edinburgh
in the early nineteenth century pointed to the disparity in the situation
"where world famous professors lectured to lads of thirteen and fourteen."[43] The Reverend Michael Russel complained in 1813 that the

philosophical lectures at Edinburgh were fit only for grown-up gentlemen, because "a very extensive and brilliant display of knowledge, so
far from being useful to lads who have still to learn the rudiments of
mental science, only dazzles and bewilders them."[44]

Students attending the university for professional development had
more compelling reasons to remain enrolled for a diploma or certificate or degree than did the students following a liberal course of
studies. In fact, those students seeking professional qualification were
more numerous than the young men following the liberal arts.[45]
Although Matheson moved after his first year from the Arts Faculty to
Medicine, that did not lead him to extend his stay at the university
beyond two years.[46]

In Matheson's time, "professional development" did not include the
field of commerce, which would in time become his career. Aristocratic
landowners, lairds who congregated in Edinburgh, and members of the
gentry with extensive estates dominated Edinburgh society in those
years, and their disposition toward people in trade was condescending.
Henry Cockburn reported, concerning Edinburgh, "There was no class
of the community so little thought of at this time as the mercantile ...
They had no direct political power, no votes; and were far too subservi-
ent to be feared."[47] Nevertheless, there were some younger sons of the
landowning class who went into trade. The eminent philosopher David
Hume serves as an example, having gone off to Bristol as a young man
to work in the office of a sugar merchant.

We have no clear evidence about James Matheson's decision to leave
the university halfway through his seventeenth year, but he may have
already had in mind a career in commerce, after turning away from
the liberal arts and from medicine. If that were the case, another academic season or two would probably not have advanced his practical
ambition much further. He was not about to become a minister or
theologian; nor was he about to enter the law; nor did medicine or
surgery command his sustained interest. Neither was he directing his
learning toward a life of scholarship in the teaching ranks. Perhaps the
death of his parents played some part in his decision not to continue
his formal education.

Whatever the reason may have been for the suspension of his studies, he did leave Edinburgh with an interest in ideas that would persist through his commercial career, and with skills in argumentation.

Certainly, the debating societies at Edinburgh – the most famous being the Speculative and the Academical – encouraged young men to be "keen doubters" and to be effective speakers, as they learned to "talk the sun down."[48] He may have learned social graces such as dancing, in order to be at home in polite society, since that was considered an essential polish for people who would be involved in public life at some professional level.[49]

One other bit of knowledge that he likely took with him from Edinburgh was an appreciation of the effects of opium as a narcotic. During his year in the Faculty of Medicine he studied chemistry,[50] and he may also have studied *materia medica* (the study of substances used in remedies), which was one of the standard courses for medical students. Like any other medical student, he would have been aware of the properties of the opium drug and the extent of its use as prescribed by professors of medicine and other practitioners.

James remained in Scotland for another six months or so, and sometime after his seventeenth birthday, probably early in 1814, he headed to London to enter the employ of a mercantile house.[51] Thus, his business career began in a more direct way than that of William Jardine, who was still serving as a ship's surgeon for the East India Company at the time when James Matheson took his classical education and his medical training into the financial and commercial precincts of the City.

# SAILING FROM LONDON TO CANTON

Eighteen years old by a week, William Jardine packed his things at Edinburgh and left the familiar surroundings of his Scottish youth permanently in the past. Whether he saw Broadholm or his mother before setting out we do not know, but within two weeks of receiving his diploma he was at London awaiting embarkation for his first journey to China in the capacity of a ship's surgeon's mate.[1]

The speed of his transition from student to ship's officer suggests the influence of an intermediary on his behalf. Whether that point of contact with the East India Company was a physician or surgeon whom he had known in Edinburgh or whether it might have been a member of Henry Dundas's circle of prominent Scots is a fact hidden from view two hundred years later. The striking thing is that no time at all was wasted on celebration over gaining the diploma or extended leave taking or making the rounds of London as a job seeker. He received his certification at Edinburgh University and passed down the Thames en route to South Asia within the same month.

Given the expense of travelling overland from central Scotland to southern England, it is quite probable that William sailed on one of the Leith smacks, which carried freight and passengers between Edinburgh and London and took upward of seven days to make the journey. That schedule would suggest that he had did not take the time to cross Scotland all the way over to Dumfries and then recross the Borders region in order to meet his sailing time at Leith.

Appointments for service on the vessels of the East India Company were not established by applying directly to the Company. Rather, ship's officers and surgeons were engaged by the managing owner of a vessel chartered by the EIC, which did not generally own the big ships that carried its people and goods between England and India. These very large vessels, plying the months-long ocean route for the Company, were custom-built to its specifications and chartered for a specified number of voyages. The investors who had such an Indiaman constructed would entrust the handling of their ship to an experienced partner, who selected the crew. The captain and the first, second, third, and fourth officers were presented in person to the directors of the Company. If approved, these officers would take an oath of loyalty to the Company and henceforth be known as "sworn officers." Similarly, surgeons and surgeon's mates who served on the Company's "Indiamen" had to be chosen by the managing owner and presented at the EIC's London headquarters. Prior to his first service on an Indiaman, a junior medical officer was required to present a diploma from the Royal College of Surgeons and to satisfy the Company's chief medical officer of his competence.[2]

Upon arriving in London, William Jardine sought out Thomas Newte, a veteran managing owner of EIC ships, to whom he had an introduction. An opening existed for a ship's surgeon's mate on the HCS *Brunswick*,[3] one of the Indiamen in which Newte held a partner's interest. After presenting his credentials to the Company's principal medical officer, Dr Hunter, who would have questioned the very young man about his experience and knowledge of surgery, Jardine was found adequate to the shipboard tasks of a surgeon's mate. Following that, Jardine and Newte proceeded to the Company's headquarters at Leadenhall Street in the City.[4]

With extensions on the rear of the building, East India House now reached more than three hundred feet back from the street. There were offices, a grand room for the court of directors, and a General Court Room, as well as warehouses well masked by the palatial new façade, just six years old when William Jardine first saw its imposing classical front, with a columned and pendimented porch in Ionic design. To a teenager from Scotland, the building, its exterior and interior appearance alike, spoke of command, solidity, assurance, and polish. If he were not awed, he had to be very impressed.

There William presented his credentials and the medical officer's endorsement, and his name was entered in the records of the Honorable Company as being accepted for service as surgeon's mate about HCS *Brunswick*. In the next few days, while awaiting the call for embarkation, he would meet his medical superior, Henry Everingham, ship's surgeon for the coming voyage, and he probably would have become acquainted with the Jerusalem Coffee House at Cowper's Court, Cornhill, the favourite meeting place of merchants, captains, and officers in the East India trade.[5]

Beginning in the late eighteenth century, the size of East India vessels was gradually enlarged, eventually reaching about twelve hundred tons; and, with the introduction of copper sheathing, the number of voyages for which the Company chartered the new ships was increased from four to eight. Many of the sturdy large Indiamen would still be sailing well into the nineteenth century. The shipowners received assurances from the Company that the vessels built for the Eastern trade would be employed for a specific number of voyages, because they were not suitable to other kinds of employment.[6] The *Brunswick*, one of these new twelve-hundred-ton Indiamen, had come into service in January 1793, and was about to make her fifth voyage to China.[7] Downriver, the *Brunswick* rendezvoused with HCS *Royal Charlotte* and HCS *Glatton* before heading out to sea. Among the last visitors to the ship before it left its anchorage at Lower Hope was an official of the Company's Pay Department, who distributed two months' worth of advanced wages to the entire crew. For many of the crew, this was a routine experience at the start of a long voyage, but for Jardine, it was the first earnings of his career, and it had to be exciting as he stepped forward from the mustered crew on deck to receive the sum of £5 for two months as surgeon's mate at £2 10s per month.[8] H.V. Bowen notes that "men of ambition" were drawn to service on Company vessels not "by the meager monthly wages on offer" but by the prospects of adventure and the opportunity to profit from the legal "privilege trade" (space in the ships' holds allotted to officers for private business ventures) or from smuggling enterprises.[9]

On 30 March 1802 the three ships weighed anchor and headed down the English Channel unaccompanied. It was the first time in years that captains commanding vessels bound for China had not been escorted by warships of the Royal Navy. The war against France had necessitated armed protection for the Company's vessels. The Indiamen were armed; in fact, ships in the twelve-hundred-ton class, like the *Brunswick*, were very well armed, normally carrying thirty-eight light eighteen-pounders, mostly on the middle deck, with a smaller number on the upper deck and a couple of stern-chasers.[10] Nevertheless, the French threat was sufficiently dangerous to make movements in convoy advisable.[11] However, when Jardine first saw the White Cliffs of Dover to his right and France's Cote d'Opal receding on his left, England and France were no longer at war.

Although dominant in the sea lanes, with nearly five hundred ships of the line and frigates in service, Britain was without allies on the continent, since the latest coalition against France had collapsed. Consequently, it was eager to negotiate a suspension of the hostilities. Delegates of the two nations signed a peace accord at Amiens in northern France on 27 March 1802, but the agreement was more an armed truce than a stable peace and lasted only fourteen months, just long enough for Jardine and his shipmates to complete the round trip from England to China.

The ships of the EIC were divided into two fleets, one outward-bound, the other returning. A certain number were designated to sail to China with stops in India at Bombay, Madras, and Calcutta, while the other fleet was dispatched directly to China. Given the length of time required for a round-trip to China, the two fleets were sent out in alternating years.[12] The *Brunswick* and its sister ships were among those sailing straight on to China in 1802.

Within three days of the diplomat's signatures at Amiens, the ships were underway. By 2 April, they were out past the Isles of Scilly and heading south through the great swell of the Atlantic. The new class of Indiamen could handle the seas with more authority than the Company's ships of just a generation earlier. For the most part they carried China trade cargo and passengers, but sometimes they would also carry troops.

The maritime routes of Indiamen were determined to some extent by factors such as currents and monsoons, but they also had predictable layover places in their journeys to India. Outward voyages normally sought ports of call and safe moorings at some of the following locations: Madeira, the Canaries, Cape Verde, Rio de Janeiro, the Cape of Good Hope, and the island of Johanna (in the Mozambique Channel). While few of the stopping places, outward or homeward, were British possessions, they did provide essential ship's services, for repairs and replenishment, and afforded opportunities for naval intelligence and commercial information.[13]

Usually, speed was not urgent. According to one historian, "they ploughed through the oceans in leisurely fashion (often heaving to at night) with their cargoes of silks, muslins, tea, and chinaware, and ambitious young men, starting their careers in the east, or families returning from home leave."[14] Nevertheless, it was an uneven match between the great ocean and the big sailing vessel. Prior to the growing popularity of the Suez route by the 1830s, most people regarded the Atlantic voyage as a very unpleasant experience. One young Company officer, on his first passage to India, confided his discomforts to his diary: "Ports all down. Ship labouring much … Sea very rough … A great scrambling at dinner, puddings, ducks and a large round of beef tumbling about, not able to save them, being so much occupied with seats … Unwell."[15]

Trouble with the *Brunswick*'s rudder forced the trio of ships to put into a Brazilian port early in May for repairs. By early June, they were at sea again, "rolling deep" through a heaving ocean in the South Atlantic. When they reached the latitudes of the "Roaring Forties," the weather on deck was wild and the young surgeon's work below the battened hatches was an education in itself. Captain Williamson writes: "We may picture him [Jardine], lantern in hand, groping his way forward along the reeling gun deck in company with his senior to examine any sick or hurt seamen, noting the surgeon's diagnoses, assisting in making up the prescribed potions and staggering forward again to administer them."[16]

The young surgeon's mate enjoyed the warm weather of the East Indies for the first time in August 1802 when his ship anchored in the Sunda Strait to take on food and water before rounding Singapore. Then, with the aid of monsoon breezes, the *Brunswick* steered a northeasterly course toward China. In early September the Portuguese colony of Macao was a welcome sight. Located on the tip of a peninsula jutting out into the South China Sea, Macao was the "maritime gate to China," where vessels stopped at the outer reaches of the Canton estuary.[17] The *Brunswick* picked up a Macao pilot and gradually proceeded upriver to the Whampoa anchorage, where the big ocean-going ships were moored, having completed their long journey. Whampoa was twelve miles downriver from Canton, and cargoes would be transferred to smaller vessels under the supervision of EIC supercargoes from Canton. (The supercargoes were on-board agents of the EIC, responsible for the security and sale of the cargo.) The captains would travel upriver by cutter and report their arrival at the East India factory along the waterfront at Canton, where they would take up residence.[18]

Surgeons customarily joined the captains in residence at Canton, so Henry Everingham would have entrusted William Jardine with full responsibility of attending to the ship's company at Whampoa. However, William would be allowed an opportunity to visit Canton, at some time when the teas were being loaded on the *Brunswick*. Not only did he survey the foreign commerce at Canton, as organized in the various "factories," but he had the chance to become acquainted with two men who would be of great importance in his career as a China merchant. One was a senior member of the Company staff at Canton, Thomas Weeding, who would eventually return to London to establish a clearing house which would do much of the Jardine, Matheson banking. The other acquaintance, Charles Magniac, was just eight years older than Jardine and had arrived in Canton less than two years before their meeting. Magniac had recently become a partner in the private firm of Reid, Beale and Company.[19]

The mention here of a private trading firm at Canton necessitates a digression in order to explain the unique circumstances of British trade in China. The operations of the EIC had taken two very different directions. In India the Company had assumed a major role in the collection of revenue and in the administration of extensive territories. In effect, the EIC had become the government of much of the subcontinent. But in East Asia the Company had little interest in acquiring territory; there it concentrated on commerce. Canton was the terminal point for that trade, which began at the East India docks on the Thames.

In 1757 the Qianlong Emperor had decreed that all foreign trade (except Russian and Japanese) be confined to the port of Canton. The terms by which China allowed trade were established by 1760, with amendments added twenty years later. The regulations were confining and annoying to foreign merchants, but there were fortunes to be made by venturesome and shrewd businessmen.[20] By the early decades of the eighteenth century, the EIC had already established itself at Canton, and under British law it enjoyed a monopoly in all commerce pursued by British subjects between the Cape of Good Hope and the Straits of Magellan. However, the monopoly was relaxed in certain respects. Ships' officers were allowed specified volumes of cargo space for their own business enterprises. This was known as "privilege tonnage" and it gave experienced officers personal incentives to remain in the service of "John Company" without jeopardizing EIC profits. Moreover, land-based servants of the Company were permitted to engage in private ventures between Eastern ports, though not between East Asia and England. As already noted, this compromise in the rule of the monopoly was known as the country trade, and it actually encouraged the extension of the Company's interests into new markets. Distinctions between the legal monopoly of the EIC and the private business of the country traders were often blurred, and in practice strict enforcement of the monopoly was applied only in cases of clear abuse, such as the misuse of Company funds. The tea-trade monopoly was closely guarded by the Company, but the country traders could speculate in many other commodities, including opium. So the effect of these flexible policies was to create a network of interconnected Company and private interests in the trade east of India.[21]

At Canton, a resident group of Company officials, known as the Select Committee of Supercargoes, had the responsibility of supervising the commercial activities of all British traders on the coast of China. "The Select" were headquartered in the English Factory on the waterfront. Their principle concern, after 1813, was the management of the Company's tea trade, with only twenty-two supercargoes and writers on hand to accomplish that function.[22] The factories (or *Hongs*) were places for transacting business, situated along the Pearl River and clustered in one district as a way of confining the movements of foreigners, who were not permitted freedom of travel within or beyond Canton.[23] The term "thirteen Hongs" refers to the Chinese Hong merchants who were authorized to conduct trade with foreigners, but there were seldom thirteen licensed in any single year.

Jardine's first experience of China would have been limited to Whampoa anchorage, the town on the island of Whampoa; and the section of the Canton riverfront along which the various European commercial operations were allowed. When he travelled upriver on the ship's cutter to join the other officers for a brief stay, he would surely have been fascinated by the exotic scene of all the river people with their small craft buzzing around the waterfront of the European community. One American merchant described his own first approach to the city in this way: "A low rumbling sound commenced and soon increased to a loud-heavy, humming noise, which never here ceases during day and night. This buzzing sort of serenade is caused by the beating of gongs, firecrackers, etc., etc., mostly among the river craft constantly on the move up and down the river."[24] Along the north shore of the river, Jardine would have found various other European traders, possibly including Dutch, French, Swedish, "Imperial" (Austrian), Spanish, Danish, and American. [25] (In spite of the traditional European names attached to various factories, the grandest of which was the EIC's New

English Factory, the original structure having been destroyed by fire in 1822, the resident European trading companies were not all represented every year at the start of the nineteenth century.) River passengers generally disembarked at Jackass Point, just in front of the Swedish Factory, and from there it was a short walk to the Company's establishment, where Jardine would have met the supercargoes and staff of the factory, numbering twenty-six persons, the largest European community resident at Canton.[26]

Foreign merchants were allowed to reside temporarily in these factories, during the trading season between September and March, when teas were being sold and loaded aboard the Indiamen. Edicts were issued at Peking each year, requiring foreigners to leave Canton as soon as the trading season was finished, but that regulation was rather easy to evade, although most foreign merchants preferred to make the seasonal exodus to Macao where there were women! The foreign community at Canton was all male, because the Chinese government did not allow wives or daughters or mistresses within the foreign resident community. The intent of that prohibition was to prevent the foreign merchants from establishing any permanent settlement in China. Not only was that regulation strictly enforced, but the floating brothels known as "flower boats" were officially off-limits to foreigners.[27] Nevertheless, "loose women" were on occasion sneaked into the factories by Hong merchants as a way of encouraging favourable trade arrangements.[28] Downstream, Whampoa provided other opportunities for foreigners to find prostitutes.[29]

The whole district of the factories was only about twelve acres in area, and was divided by two streets and an alley. The frontage of the factories, on the river side, averaged a bit less than a hundred feet apiece, but the properties were long and narrow, and stretched side by side back from the shore about five hundred feet to Thirteen Factory Street. Each factory was a collection of buildings of varying height (two or three storeys) with archways or passages connecting them as if strung together. Typically, the upper floors of a factory were devoted to counting rooms, a dining room, individual bedrooms, and a parlour – which might contain a library. Some of the factories had verandas facing the river as well as rooftop terraces, and the English Factory even had a garden on the riverside. But the greatest area of the ground floors was used as *gowdowns* (warehouses), where goods were stacked on platforms raised about a foot off the floor.

Among the factories and along the city side of the compound there were crowded, narrow streets, filled with small shops, selling all manner of things from porcelain and lacquered goods to grocery stores offering not only fruits and vegetables but cats, dogs, and skinned rats. Jostling for space in the narrow confines of the streets were street barbers, mobile street restaurants, beggars, soothsayers, and a broad array of peddlers. Along Hog Lane were the sailors' bars, serving up dangerous hooch known as "Mandarin gin" and "first chop rum."[30]

EIC officials were relieved of the burden of actually running the household of their factory, for the Company (like all the other factories) employed a *comprador* who oversaw all the details of operation, with the exception of personal servants employed by the supercargoes and other staff members. All exchanges of money passed through the hands of the compradors, and in each instance a little of the money remained in their hands. It was a lucrative position, but not a dishonourable one, for the *cumsha* (tip money) was a ubiquitous expectation in Canton and was acknowledged by the foreign traders.

Freed from those domestic concerns, the Company officials worked very diligently during the trading season, especially in the early stage of that season when supercargoes and the clerks might be kept toiling in the counting house deep into the night. Most of the clerks received their appointments as a matter of patronage arranged back home in Britain. The jobs were financially rewarding; the salary of a clerk (called "writer") might start at £100 per year but rise to £1,000 annually within a few years' time. More dramatically, a supercargo might be receiving as much as £9,000 in salary and commissions, which would allow him to return home within a relatively few years to enjoy a comfortable retirement.[31]

EIC men enjoyed the highest standard of living among the foreigners resident at Canton.[32] At the factory, living expenses were underwritten by the Company, and its staff dined very well. The residents held elaborate dinner parties on festive occasions, and their concerts of instrumental music on the veranda eventually became a weekly ritual for the whole foreign community. In Jardine's time at Canton, the English Factory gradually built the best library among the foreign residents. There were also billiard games and card games and an occasional game of cricket, but rather understandably, with the river immediately at hand, the most popular of the competitive recreations was boat racing.[33]

More genteel leisure was to be found in the river trips, allowed by the government, to the Fa Ti flower gardens, about two miles up river. Of course, the all-male picnic lacked the graces of female company, so the traders and Company staff were more than glad to retreat to Macao once the tea season was concluded. Described as "the Ascot, the Monte Carlo, the Riviera" for foreign merchants, Macao was year-round home to the families of the East India traders. Some had wives there, others kept mistresses, and more than a few enjoyed less permanent arrangements with women of Macao.[34]

The EIC maintained an elegant factory at Macao, and for half the year it was the scene of a round of balls, plays, formal dinners, and concerts that enlivened the social life of the mixed company which distinguished Macao from Canton.[35] The "Macao Passage" of the foreign merchants occurred each year at the close of the northeast monsoon, when the teas had been loaded and cleared and the Indiamen had left Whampoa, homeward bound.[36] That timing meant that, on his first trip to China, William Jardine would not have seen this grand parade of fifteen or twenty chop boats (licensed sampans) downriver on their two- or three-day journey to the Portuguese colony. Nor would he have had a chance to stroll on the beautiful Praya Grande esplanade or to get a sense of the very comfortable private residences of the colony. However, at Canton he would have observed the style of the Hong merchants, who were the Chinese counterparts of the Select Committee.

Just as the EIC exercised a monopoly over British trade in China, a committee of thirteen prominent Chinese merchants, known as the Cohong, acted as the obligatory filter through which all foreign trade had to pass.[37] Presiding over them and the foreign ships and merchants was the *hoppo*, who regulated the foreign trade of Canton and served as the superintendent of customs collections, enriching himself while extracting revenues from the foreign traders as well as the Hong merchants on behalf of the Emperor.[38]

Every ship that anchored at Whampoa had to be secured by one of the Hong merchants. Such a merchant, known as a *fiador*, was responsible for the foreign ship he secured; and in return he expected the commercial benefit of providing the bulk of the export goods (such as tea, porcelain, silk, or food commodities) being supplied to that ship.[39] The security pledge guaranteed the government that its customs fees would be paid and made the particular Hong merchant responsible for the orderly behaviour of the foreign personnel. Although there were rarely thirteen such merchants, they were collectively referred to as the "thirteen hongs," or sometimes as the *Cohong*. They were required to be the intermediaries for all communications between the

foreign merchants and Chinese government officials, such as the governor of Canton or the viceroy of the provinces of Kuangsi (Guangxi) and
Kuangtung (Guangdong). Such correspondence had to take the form
of petitions, a form that emphasized the inferior status of the foreign
merchants. Only the Hong merchants held licences authorizing direct
trade with foreigners. While the EIC conducted some trade with non-
Hong merchants, there were private English traders who negotiated
more deals than the EIC through non-Hong "shopmen," of whom there
were many.[40] In certain instances these "outside merchants," who had
shops near the factories, were permitted to deal directly with foreigners,
while such dealings were at other times sharply restricted.[41]

Some members of the Cohong acquired great wealth, but the role of
middleman was risky and some went bankrupt. Their chronic indebtedness was due in part to cash-flow problems which led to dependence on
cash advances from foreigners. As a group they accepted the principle
of collective liability, which meant that the guild of Hong merchants
would cover the failed debts of individual Hong merchants. For that
reason they maintained an insurance trust, known as the Consoo Fund,
supported by duties imposed on foreign merchants. The fund, established in 1779, was intended to establish joint responsibility for the
debts of merchants who had gone bankrupt.[42]

The Hong merchant who secured a vessel might assist the supercargo of that ship in finding a "linguist" (translator) who could facilitate
the foreigner's business with the Chinese customs house. The linguists,
licensed by the government, were also known to assist their clients by
bribing customs officers, lying, and keeping commercial secrets.[43] They
communicated in a bizarre "pidgin English," a language devoid of syn-
tax and reliant on simple parts of speech. It was a Chinese invention
that employed elements of their own language, words adapted from
Portuguese and some Indian languages, and, by the nineteenth century,
a great deal of English influence. Since foreigners were prohibited from
learning the Chinese language and the Chinese showed little inclination to learn English, it should not be surprising that as late as the 1820s
only three foreigners at Canton were fluent and literate in Chinese.
(Neither Jardine nor Matheson ever achieved fluency in the language.)
On the other hand, there was not a single Chinese person at Canton
who could read or write English. Hence the two sides came to rely on
pidgin as the standard medium of commercial discourse, sometimes involving transactions of enormous value.[44]

On first acquaintance with the Canton system and its myriad eccentricities, Jardine must have thought that Auld Reekie's peculiarities and problems were but child's play compared to the bizarre world of commerce, society, graft, language, and government regulation that he was observing in South China. Nor had he ever seen in Edinburgh's Old Town anything like the pitiful poverty he found among the beggars of Canton. Nothing suggests that he was so attracted to this exotic and harsh world of south China that his first visit led to ambitions for a career in trade there. Yet he did spend nearly three months on the Pearl River, between Whampoa and Canton, and his education now included many things no one had taught him during his time at his old college, then only nine months in the past.

While his ship was anchored at Whampoa, in the midst of a vast forest of masts, Jardine had plenty of work to attend to. Waterborne brothels enticed sailors from the EIC ships, while ashore there were bamboo bankshalls (temporary storage buildings by the docks) which illegally served fearsome alcoholic concoctions. No doubt there were clanging headaches suffered by the crewmen who drowned their boredom in such potions. But, more importantly for Jardine, there were bones to be set and lacerated skulls to be mended from the fights which the sailors got into after they had lost their senses and from the falls they had taken in their stupors.

Most ships could not escape the tropical diseases such as malaria and dysentery which lingered in the environs of Canton. Stomach disorders and liver ailments including yellow jaundice (hepatitis) and intestinal cramps were also common, due in large part to the low standards of cleanliness in the kitchens and to the state of the bacteria in the water supply.[45] With problems of this sort to deal with aboard ship, Jardine and Everingham could hardly share the crew's complaints of boredom during the months at the Whampoa anchorage.

The *Brunswick* began loading teas and other cargo, such as chinaware, in October.[46] Lacking sufficient depth of water to remain at Whampoa, they moved downriver to a deep-water anchorage and continued loading until the end of November. Although Chinese junks were watertight, Western-constructed sailing ships tended to be leaky; so the EIC masters had to take pains to prevent the teas from getting damp and thereby being ruined. For that reason, the bottom tier of an Indiaman would be loaded with cargo that could not be harmed by bilge water. Chinaware suited the purpose admirably, being "washed" almost constantly from the Pearl River to the Thames. Below the porcelain, ballast was loaded, including Macao stones, which provided a flooring level for the chests containing porcelain items. The EIC permitted speculation in this and other non-monopoly cargoes by the officers of a vessel, a practice that gave the captains and their officers an opportunity to supplement their Company wages for a voyage.[47]

Having arrived at Whampoa early in September, Jardine could observe the return of increasing numbers of the foreign commercial community in October, which occurred at just about the same time that the teas began arriving via the system of portage and river transport from their provinces several hundred miles north and west of Canton. The autumn months were very busy for the Hong merchants and their foreign customers, as the largest shipments arrived at Canton during the last months of the year and the very beginning of the next year.[48]

There were two basic categories of tea, black and green, with the Company adjusting its supplies according to the demand in the British market (which was drawn in the direction of cheaper varieties as the home government's duties on tea imports rose).The green teas were more delicate and their flavour would decline after a year; this led the Company to caution its supercargoes repeatedly about the risks involved in their purchases of green teas. Nevertheless, a green tea like Twankay was popular in the British market. Bohea (black) tea, an inferior grade of winter tea, was not much favoured until duties rose in the early years of the nineteenth century; but it could be blended with the preferable Congou black in order to achieve a better flavour. The basic principle of the EIC directors' policies was to set prices according to quality, while providing a wide variety of teas to serve the popular demand and to meet special tastes.[49]

The Company was required by British law to keep on hand a one-year supply of teas. Consequently, it could take as much as three years for a shipment of tea to make its progress from the interior of China into the hands of English consumers.[50] Company exports of tea from China doubled in the period 1786–1833, growing from nearly sixteen million pounds in 1786 to more than thirty million pounds in the year when the EIC monopoly was terminated.[51] Over those decades, a quarter of the net profits of the EIC was derived from its Canton tea trade.[52]

Inland shipments of tea took from four to eight weeks to reach Canton. Having passed about seven customs stations en route from Fukien (Fujian) or Kiangsi (Jiangxi) or other remote provinces, the teas escalated in price at each stage of their journey to Canton. Samples were taken to the factories where tea inspectors could assess the quality of teas being offered by the Hong merchants, and, after the inspectors were satisfied and the teas passed muster, deals were closed.[53] Foreign shippers wanted assurances that they would be able to sell the cargoes they had brought to Canton and to purchase. Accordingly, there were written contracts incorporating terms agreed between the foreign merchants and the Hong merchants, even though the terms of the contracts did not always conform to the laws of China.[54]

By the start of the nineteenth century, the EIC was importing more than twenty millions pounds of tea per year. H.V. Bowen maintains that "the whole point and purpose of the Company's trade between 1765 and 1833 was to provide a means of transferring wealth from India to Britain." The tea trade was a channel for remitting funds through commerce from India, but the EIC also had to resort to shipping home chests of bullion.[55] Nevertheless, that one commodity produced more revenue than the whole of the Company's regime in India.[56] In contrast, the other goods being carried by the Indiamen paled in significance. Vessels like the *Brunswick* normally left the Canton market with cargo such as silks, carved ivories, Chinese wallpapers, lacquered furniture, and chinaware in addition to the major cargo of teas.[57]

After Captain Hughes had signed the bills of lading for his ship's cargo and had secured the canvas letter bag for transport to England, he left Canton and returned to the *Brunswick* waiting for him and the surgeon at the Second Bar of the Pearl River. With all the cargoes loaded, the Grand Chop (clearance document) was given by the Chinese customs officials and Captain Hughes and Dr Everingham boarded the *Brunswick* for departure on 28 November 1802. Two days later, the convoy of four Indiamen set sail at Lintin Island, dropped off their pilots at Macao, and began to run southward with the northeast monsoon, unfurling the red-white-and-blue ensigns of the EIC.[58] Within two months they were passing the Cape of Good Hope and heading out into the South Atlantic, with St Helena fixed on their charts as the next destination, seventeen hundred miles to the northwest. There, the *Brunswick's* officers and crew found the HMS *Romney* awaiting the convoy's arrival, and learned that renewal of the war with France seemed imminent. Within three days, a new convoy, consisting of seven Indiamen, two whalers, and the warship, had formed and embarked for Britain.[59]

On Captain Hughes's orders, the *Brunswick* was prepared for service as a warship, but the voyage home was uneventful, although Everingham and Jardine had to make arrangements for the after-end of the lower hold to be used as a surgical ward, should casualties result from a hostile action with French warships. In the long run, the only "hostile" action occurred when the ships had reached home waters. Prior to parting company with the Indiamen, the HMS *Romney* sent a press crew aboard the *Brunswick* and seized thirty-six men for service in the Royal Navy. Just that abruptly, sailors who were within sight of England after a journey of thirteen months found themselves impressed rather than discharged.

The *Brunswick* proceeded with its reduced crew upriver to Long Reach, above Greenhithe, and anchored there on 25 April 1803, thus ending the young surgeon's mate's first trip to China. He and Dr Everingham reported to Thomas Newte, managing owner of the vessel, and then delivered their medical log to the principal medical officer of the Company; after that they were free men.[60] Three weeks later, the war with France resumed.

By then, William Jardine was home in Dumfriesshire. He had not remained at London long enough to collect his pay, which he had the third mate collect for him. It amounted to £27 13s 4d, hardly a significant amount for more than a year's service by a surgeon with a diploma from Edinburgh; but William had observed that senior officers in the service of John Company were able to supplement their income handsomely by engaging in a bit of trade on their own.[61] Among the items being unloaded from the *Brunswick*, after the teas, were the commodities that officers were allowed to ship as private commerce. Their "pidgin" chinaware was not included in the cargo known as "privilege tonnage" because of its lowly function of filling the hold below the level of the teas. Freight-free privilege tonnage allowed EIC officers to speculate in luxury and bulk items, in outward and homebound sailings.[62] By the terms of the Charter Act of 1793, the EIC was directed to make three thousand tons of shipping annually available to private individuals, at the rates of £5/ton outbound and £15/ton homebound. The effect was a dramatic increase in the value of imports being carried by returning vessels.[63] The actual privilege tonnage allotted officers was apportioned according to rank, with captains being allowed free outbound freight of fifty-six tons and homebound freight of twenty tons.[64] At the other end of the scale, skilled tradesmen were allowed a few cubic feet.[65] In the late eighteenth century, shrewdly investing captains averaged £4,000 to £5,000 of income per voyage from their privilege tonnage.[66] At the other end of the hierarchy, a surgeon was allowed three tons homeward and a surgeon's mate two tons.[67] An eighteen-year-old surgeon's mate, on his first voyage and just learning the ropes, would probably have been content to sell his cargo privilege to one of his seniors, for a reasonable supplement to his wages and perhaps a box of chinaware. But he could anticipate, upon elevation in rank, the prospects of profitable speculation in small luxury items purchased on commission for people in England or even for expatriate friends in India.[68]

Jardine's next opportunity to obtain that type of profit occurred in 1804 when the *Brunswick* was again chartered by the EIC. While the ship was being refitted at Blackwall, Thomas Newte had to reconstitute his list of officers. Captain Philip Hughes, who had resigned, was replaced by James Ludovic Grant, who had commanded the ship on earlier voyages. There were other changes, but the one most affecting Jardine was the resignation of Henry Everingham as ship's surgeon. Although yet only nineteen, William was apparently well recommended by Everingham, because Newte offered him the position of ship's surgeon.[69] After just one journey as surgeon's mate, Jardine had achieved a major advance in rank, raising him to a significantly higher level.[70] One venerable naval historian maintained that the EIC ships were at their very best during the first thirty years of the nineteenth century, and that, in this period, "to be able to get into the company's service was about as good as a commission in the Navy."[71]

The resumption of war against France made it imperative for an able-bodied young man like William to have his status as ship's surgeon certified immediately. Otherwise he was liable to be impressed into naval service aboard one of the king's warships, for the only men of military age who were immune from impressment were serving officers. Young men who had been discharged from one of the Company's ships or who were looking for new work aboard an outward-bound vessel were in danger of being carried off to the "press tender" near the Tower of London. The process for obtaining protection from the press gangs necessitated an Admiralty certificate, which Jardine obtained at the start of January when he was presented at East India House and signed an agreement which led a formal notation on the ship's record and an advance of two months' pay.[72]

Among the other great liabilities of maritime service in wartime one was the regulation that receipt of wages by members of the ship's company was dependent on safe return of the ship's cargo. One of the major complaints of the seamen was that they lost all their wages if a ship were captured. The Company was notoriously tight-fisted, and its concession to dependent families at home was slim: before a ship set out from Blackwall, each member of the crew designated their next of kin (or a friend) to receive a single month's wages for every six months that the ship was absent.

Normally, a twelve-hundred-ton Indiamen carried a total crew of about one hundred and thirty,[73] plus some passengers. However, the *Brunswick* was to be crowded for this trip, since the EIC had chartered that vessel and two others to transport the 66th Regiment of the King's Troops to Ceylon (Sri Lanka). Three hundred and fifty officers and men of the 66th boarded the *Brunswick* at Spithead, and on the first day of spring 1804 three Indiamen – *Brunswick, Canton,* and *Marquis of Ely* – sailed as troopships, in a convoy with five other Indiamen and the frigate *HMS Lapwing* as escort.[74]

With this huge number of men aboard the *Brunswick,* Jardine had his hands full and had to be very glad that, two weeks before his ship set sail, he had acquired an assistant in the person of William Rae, surgeon's mate. Having reached the age of twenty just three weeks before the convoy sailed, Jardine was now the senior medical officer on a ship carrying nearly five hundred people. The anticipation of such a large number of troops on board meant that Jardine had to spend a fair measure of time before embarkation ordering and supervising the loading of medical and surgical stores, and undoubtedly consulting with veteran surgeons in the Jerusalem Coffee House about the medical situations he should expect and the traditional ways of addressing them.[75]

The *Brunswick*'s crew slung their hammocks between the guns on the main deck and ate their meals in the same spaces, whereas the royal troops were situated in the steerage. The ship's mates, purser, and surgeon had canvas cabins in the steerage. For Jardine this was an improvement from the accommodations of his first voyage; now he had a cubicle partitioned off by sheets of canvas lashed to the decks above and below by cleats.[76]

As a way of preventing the incidence of scurvy among crew, troops, and passengers, the EIC Court of Directors had recommended in 1803 that China-bound ships carry one gallon of lemon juice for every four men both outward and homeward. Given the unusual number of people aboard, Jardine needed to ensure that the vessel was stocked with about a hundred gallons of lemon juice. That would eliminate most cases of a traditionally devastating ailment, but the water provision would create a different problem by causing ongoing intestinal disorders for him to attend to throughout the first stage of the journey. As was the customary practice, tons of water for the voyage had been drawn straight out of the Thames River. It was foul smelling and filthy. So the Court of Directors required that every vessel chartered by the Company for a trip to China carry its own water-filtering machine. Curiously, the organic matter that the water contained would set off a process of fermentation, which discharged gases and left a residue of salts, thereby cleaning the water and sweetening its taste considerably over the course of the long journey. Unfortunately for many persons who drank the water in the early stages of the journey, its bacterial qualities were as yet unfriendly and many a digestive tract was sent into spasm by the effects of the impure water.[77] Jardine's best treatment for this ailment, apart from counselling people to drink something other than water, was to prescribe a tincture of opium as a way of relaxing the intestines and arresting the spasms. Some of the travellers might have begun the journey with their own commercially prepared medicines containing opium, such as Godfrey's Cordial, Mother Bailey's Quieting Syrup, or Batley's Sedative Solution; but undoubtedly the young surgeon had brought aboard a quantity of alcohol and opium to be mixed into mild tinctures.

With his new surgeon's rank, Jardine enjoyed the right to walk on the weather side of the quarterdeck, but, more importantly, he also received the privilege of a place at Captain Grant's table in the cuddy. James Ludovic Grant was apparently a character, and the dinners with him were apt to be lively. Moreover, East India captains traditionally sought to have some musicians in a ship's company. Liberal amounts of wine and brandy would have been loaded aboard for the captain's table, as well as dozens of wheels of Double Gloucester and Cheshire cheese. So Jardine dined more agreeably than he had on his first voyage, when he had taken his meals in the steerage.

No hint of any epidemic among the ships of the convoy is to be found in the surviving logs. Thus, Jardine and his mate were most likely kept busy with routine shipboard medical matters – broken bones and lacerations from falls or fights, burns in the galley or at the forge, toothaches, digestive complaints from tainted food or water, and other such predictable kinds of distress. Four months after leaving England, the troops ships arrived at Trincomalee, Ceylon, no doubt carrying many men edgy from the unwanted intimacy of such close quarters for so many weeks and a surgeon and his mate tired out from dealing with the bruisings of hundreds of short-tempered men.

Madras, on the southeast coast of India, was but a short journey for the three Indiamen, whose supplies were thin after four months at sea. The vessels spent three weeks in the Indian port, taking on cotton for sale at Canton and recruiting Lascar (East Indian) sailors to fill some of the vacancies in their crews. Escorted by two frigates, the *Brunswick*, *Canton*, and *Marquis of Ely* resumed their progress toward China on 30 August, and rendezvoused with other Indiamen and country ships in the Malay Straits. Eighteen trading vessels sailed from the Straits at the start of September, with the armed protection of five naval escorts including the *HMS Russell*, mounting seventy-four guns, to offset the formidable firepower that the French had recently displayed in eastern waters.[78]

Given the presence of French and Dutch warships in southern waters, Jardine had good reason to expect his second trip through the seas of Southeast Asia to be far more dangerous than his first. However, the *Brunswick* escaped French attack on this last leg of her outward voyage. Instead, the convoy was menaced by a violent typhoon in the South China Sea, scattering the ships and wreaking extensive damage on them. Nevertheless, no ships were lost, and the Indiamen arrived at the mouth of the Pearl River on 13 October 1804, seven months after catching a northeast wind in the English Channel.

Although the *Brunswick* and two other ships ran aground in the dark, just short of Whampoa, they soon floated free and reached their anchorage safely. They unloaded their cargoes, paid their customs duties and cumsha, prepared to receive consignments of tea, and awaited formation of the homeward-bound convoy. As ship's surgeon, William Jardine was now entitled to travel with Captain Grant up river to the English Factory and enjoy the high standard of dining which was to be found in the Company's Canton quarters. Part of his time was spent lining up the cargo to fill his three-ton allowance, as well as some of the chinaware that would be deposited in the ship's holds below the tea chests. He could come to know the factory settlement on different terms this time, since the work of tending the ship's seamen, back at Whampoa, was entrusted to the surgeon's mate, William Rae.

When the Grand Chop for departure was issued and the *Brunswick* moved downriver to join her convoy, it was with a crew very different from the one that had set out from the Thames in March 1804: the impressment of crew members at Ceylon and India had necessitated the hiring of additional thirty sailors at Canton.[79] A convoy, consisting of fifteen ships, with naval escort, left Lintin Island on 8 January 1805, expecting to be home in England by early summer. Having reached Penang, a British-held port in the Malay Straits, after two weeks sailing without sight of any French threat, the convoy split, with the country traders steering toward Bombay and the Indiamen, including the *Brunswick*, setting out for England.[80]

Now the *Brunswick* began to struggle in the heavy seas of the Indian Ocean. Previously undetected damage from the grounding in the Pearl River was worsening as the ship's hull strained against the motion of the seas. The convoy ships sent Chinese seamen to assist with pumping, but the problem became critical, and the commodore had to convene the ships' captains aboard the *Brunswick* to assess her seaworthiness. She could not make it home, they concluded, and Bombay became her destination for docking and repair, while the convoy continued on its way homeward. Under escort by *HMS Winchelsea*, the crippled Indiaman struggled into Bombay at the start of March 1805.[81]

Jardine had time on his hands, since dock facilities for repair were not available until mid-May, possibly because of demands on the dockyard by the Bombay Marine, which was the Company's own formidable navy. The good teas that had been unloaded from the *Brunswick* were shipped home to Britain on another Company vessel and the teas that had suffered damage from water in the holds were sold at auction. Jardine sold his privilege cargo at Bombay and likely planned another speculation as plans for the *Brunswick*'s journey homeward were being worked out.

The Company officials at Bombay released the vessel from its charter and allowed Captain Grant to make arrangements for a private shipment of cotton to Canton, with the understanding that the *Brunswick* would then be engaged once again by the Company for shipping teas to Britain. Grant's opportunity for profit in this venture was considerable, since he had accidentally fallen into a situation that would make his vessel the first of the year to arrive at Canton.

Grant's cotton cargo was almost certainly secured through the agency of Parsi merchants, Indian Zoroastrians who were effective commercial brokers trading on relatively equal terms with the English, in contrast to the subordinate position of Indians elsewhere.[82] Among the foreign merchant communities that had settled in Bombay, the Parsis were "the most visible and enterprising group to engage in overseas trade, shipping, banking, and remittance" and they eventually became the most influential sector of Bombay society, with an eye toward modernization

of cultural and civic institutions.[83] The Parsi traders had a good sense of
the commercial opportunities available at Canton and eventually were
engaged in banking and insurance there and became members of the
Chamber of Commerce. Their presence in Canton was larger than the
English community; as of 1835, there were fifty-two Parsis as compared
to thirty-five English. According to Western sources, the Parsis constituted one-third of the total number of foreign traders at Canton prior
to the Opium War.[84] Along the waterfront, they were situated principally in what was known as the "Chow-chow Factory," also unofficially
called the Parsi Factory.[85] Such Parsi merchants marketed the two great
staples of the trade eastward from Bombay to China, opium and cotton.[86] They had the reputation of being aggressive traders, who annoyed both the EIC and the Chinese authorities by money-lending
operations so as to get the Hong merchants indebted to them. Beyond
their interests in shipping management, they were substantially invested
in shipbuilding, with their huge ships reportedly lasting as long as sixty
years in the country trade.[87]

Among the Brunswick's passengers bound for Canton was a young
Parsi named Jamsetjee Jejeebhoy, who was making his fourth journey to
Canton since 1799, though he was only twenty-one. Lacking any formal
education and barely literate, he had gained his only business training
by working in his uncle's bottle shop from the age of seven. His first
venture was profitless, and his second effort was notable principally for
his presence on one of the English vessels at the battle of Pulo Auro. He
and Jardine, one year his junior, became acquainted on the Brunswick's
voyage to Canton in the summer of 1805; they would remain lifelong
friends and business associates.[88] In fact, Jejeebhoy would in time become the major trading partner of Jardine, Matheson at Bombay.[89]

They sailed out of Bombay on the first of July 1805 aboard the newly
repaired Brunswick, which had no escort because Captain Grant chose
not to wait for the convoy of country ships going to China in late July. His
intent was to be the first arrival at Canton that season with a shipment of
raw cotton, thus gaining a good price for his cargo before the market
became glutted when the country ships reached Whampoa. By the time
of their departure from Bombay, Jardine had lost his surgeon's mate to
an impressment ordered by Sir Edward Pellew, who, with Admiralty
authorization, impressed as many sailors as possible at Bombay and depleted the Brunswick's already diminished complement of English seamen. Among other things, this meant that the trained gun crews of the

*Brunswick* were drastically reduced in number, since there were only about twenty British seamen left on board. (In fact, some of the Brunswick's guns were now stuck down in the hold as ballast.)

At Bombay the impressment of British sailors had forced Grant to hire some French sailmakers who were prisoners of war to assist in repairing the *Brunswick*'s sails. However, at the end of June those prisoners were paroled as part of a prisoner-exchange agreement. They left Bombay on a country ship named the *Prime*, headed for Mauritius under a flag of truce, for the prisoner exchange; however, the *Prime* was intercepted by the French warship *Marengo*, seventy-four-gun flagship of Admiral Charles-Alexandre Linois, who violated the agreement by removing seventy-five of the French prisoners and simply giving the captain a receipt. The Frenchmen were immediately put into service aboard the *Marengo* and the *Belle Poule*, bringing the French warships up to full complement as they prepared to pursue English merchantmen.[90]

Among the French sailors illegally repatriated by Admiral Linois were some sailmakers who had been working on the *Brunswick*'s sails only a few days earlier. Thomas Addison, midshipman on the *Brunswick*, recounted that "the [French]men, of course, told their tale about us as to our time of sailing, &c., &c., making it an easy business for Johnny Crapaud to catch us."[91] Linois learned that the *Brunswick* would be without naval escort and his new crewmen could identify her from a distance. In company with a country ship, the *Sarah*, the HCS *Brunswick* sailed right into Linois's trap off Point de Galle on 11 July.

Grant prepared his ship for battle, and Jardine prepared to deal with casualties; but the surgeon had none to take care of, since the battle lasted but two shots, one from a French frigate and one from the *Brunswick*. With the *Marengo* closing in, Grant knew that he was defeated and hauled down his colours. Summoned to the upper deck, Jardine found it occupied by French sailors.

The *Sarah* escaped and outran her French pursuer by virtue of setting every square yard of sail she had; but her success was her undoing, for she ran ashore on the coast of Ceylon and died there as a wreck. Her crew was rescued and her cargo was salvaged, and her escape enabled the English at Madras to know within days that Linois and his squadron were lurking in wait in the seas nearby. With his presence detected, Linois sailed away southward, his prize in hand.[92]

Grant and the rest of the English officers and crew were transferred to the *Marengo*, while the Brunswick was left in the hands of a prize crew,

with the Lascars and Chinese on board as the working crew. Jardine and
the first mate, Hugh Scott, were ordered to remain aboard the *Brunswick*,
to assist the French prize crew in running the ship and to take care of
the Asian working crew.[93] A prisoner of war now, the young Scot had
plenty of time to reconstruct the peculiar sequence of events starting
with the grounding below Whampoa and leading to French capture of
his ship. Having begun the long voyage tending to English troops and a
mostly English crew of seamen, now he could not predict where the trip
would end nor how his surgical skills might be needed by the French
occupiers and their Lascar/Chinese workforce.

While Grant sulked aboard the *Marengo*, which he called a "hulk of
insubordination, filthiness, and folly,"[94] his own ship sailed out of sight,
for the French admiral had sent the *Brunswick* ahead when he encountered an convoy of Indiamen headed for Madras. Before long, Linois
sailed toward the Cape of Good Hope, anticipating a rendezvous there
with the *Brunswick* and the frigate *L'Atalante*. The admiral released
Captain Grant and his officers at Simon's Bay. From shore they watched
the destruction of the *Brunswick*. "Early on the fourth morning after
landing we heard much firing out in the offing, supposed from a ship
in distress. It had blown hard all night. Between 9 and 10 a.m., saw the
poor old Brunswick running in with all her sails split to ribbons, everything adrift; obviously had parted from her anchors, and evidently reduced to the last alternative of running the ship on shore."[95]

The *Brunswick* had been mishandled by her prize crew, and Jardine
and Scott could only observe helplessly and fear for their lives as the in-
ept French crew drove the ship ashore on the Cape. In this catastrophic
way, the *Brunswick* came to the end of her days in early September 1805,
wrecked on the shore of South Africa, her cargo of cotton afloat in the
pounding waves. All hands were rescued from the doomed ship and
Jardine was reunited with Grant within sight of the wreckage.[96]

The English prisoners were transferred to Cape Town (then held by
France's Dutch allies) and treated well there for several weeks while the
French ships were refitting for sea. Jardine and most of the *Brunswick*'s
crew were soon sent to St Helena on an American whaler, the brig *Eliza*.
When they arrived there, the HMS *Howe* was riding at anchor.[97] The warship had been delegated the duty of transporting home to Britain the
recently retired governor-general of India, Marquess Wellesley. Jardine,
his fellow officers, and the remnant of the *Brunswick*'s crew were taken

aboard the *Howe* for the homeward voyage, and the frigate set sail for England on the twentieth of November.

Jardine and his fellow "orphans" provided Marquess Wellesley and Captain Cockburn with dramatic eyewitness accounts of the *Brunswick*'s capture and foundering as well as descriptions of the character of life in the newly egalitarian – if somewhat undisciplined – revolutionary French Navy. Dining in such elevated company and laughing at their impressions of *les nouvelles forces navales francaise* likely caused the men of the *Brunswick* to observe Christmas 1805, at sea, in a much improved frame of mind. Aboard the *Howe* their carols were all the brighter for their consciousness that England was just two weeks ahead and Scotland but a few days beyond that.

Almost certainly Jardine had learned, before leaving St Helena, that a month earlier, on 21 October, the combined French-Spanish fleet had been destroyed by Horatio Nelson's British warships near Cape Trafalgar, south of Cadiz. Early in the new year, British forces captured the Cape of Good Hope, thus depriving Admiral Linois of his base and prompting him to sail home to France. On 13 March 1806, Linois's two warships encountered a British squadron. In a fierce exchange of fire, the *Marengo* was pounded to a shattered hulk, and the *Brunswick* was thereby avenged.[98]

On 8 January, moving up the Channel in foul weather, the *Howe* arrived at Spithead, below Portsmouth. When better weather prevailed the next day, the ship proceeded proudly into Portsmouth harbor as a seventeen-gun salute greeted the retiring governor general of India. Jardine and his fellow officers and midshipmen were discharged later in the day and made their start toward London.[99]

The surgeon and first mate wrote to the directors of the Company, reporting their arrival in London on 11 January 1806. Jardine had no medical log to deliver to the chief medical officer, because of the loss of the ship. And the loss of the ship had meant the loss of most of his pay. But the EIC did make some merciful allowance for the crew of the *Brunswick*, granting them two months' allowance (beyond their initial advance of two months). For Jardine, this meant that he received a skimpy £6 10s *ex-gratia* after his sixteen months and fourteen days of service on the *Brunswick*. The ill fortune of that vessel cost him about £40 in wages. However, he had other sources of income: for tending to the troops of the 66th Regiment, he received about £175; moreover, the cargo he had acquired for private tonnage was transshipped at Bombay and sent home aboard the *Bridgewater*. Whatever his arrangements for sale of the cargo, the private trade did nevertheless offset his loss of wages even further.[100]

James Ludovic Grant was not so lucky. A court of enquiry convened by the directors of the East India Company blamed him for the loss of the *Brunswick*, especially since it was determined that he had moved six of the ship's guns into the lower hold in order to make extra room for loading cotton on the gun deck. The Company fined him £40 for each of the unmounted guns but meted out no additional penalties other than the loss of wages. The loss of his private cargo taken on at Bombay was very painful; however, his ultimate distress came with the court actions brought against him by the *Brunswick*'s owners, for he suffered the loss of his master's status and never again commanded a vessel.[101]

If, after that wild voyage, Jardine was having second thoughts about continuing as a medical officer for the East India Company, the opening for a surgeon on the HCS *Glatton* helped to resolve his doubts not long after he was released from his duties upon reaching London. The *Glatton*'s surgeon, Thomas Weeding, whom Jardine had met at Canton in 1802, was abandoning the sea in favour of a new career in the City. With Weeding's recommendation, the young man was approved as surgeon for the ship, which would sail in the spring of 1806.[102] Having secured his next position, he was free to visit the Jardine homestead at Applegarth, which he had not seen in two years. Whether he made it home in time to celebrate his twenty-second birthday there at the end of February is not known, but for at least for a few weeks of the raw winter season in Dumfriesshire he would have been the local hero of the little village. There they sang few songs of the sea but they knew well the songs of a local fellow named Robert Burns. And one can easily imagine that they sang "Wandering Willie" as they welcomed him home, or "Willie Brewed a Peck o' Maut" as they raised their glasses of malt whisky to the well-travelled young Dr William Jardine.

# 3

# THE SIRENS OF COMMERCE

Carrying out ashes for the janitor, learning second-declension Latin nouns, saying prayers with the rector, coming to recognize the major constellations, scraping a knee on the playground, and adulating the late heroic Nelson – these were the kinds of things James Matheson was doing at Inverness Academy in the spring of 1806 while his future partner was supervising the loading of medical supplies for the *Glatton*'s coming trip to China. Their lives were not to intersect for another fourteen years, during which the gap in their ages would seem to contract. For the moment, our course continues to be charted with William Jardine as he serves the East India Company and becomes gradually attracted by the lucrative private trade between India and China.

When Jardine went aboard the *Glatton* at Lower Hope late in April 1806, the vessel was all prepared for the voyage but for one consideration: she was not yet filled with troops. Chartered, as the *Brunswick* had been, to carry troops to India, the *Glatton* left the Thames with Spithead as her first destination. There, off the Isle of Wight, the 1,417-ton Indiaman took on board 322 officers and men of the 30th Regiment (with twenty-two wives and nineteen children accompanying the troops).[1] In the early, quiet days of the journey, Jardine had a chance to become acquainted with the *Glatton*'s purser, Henry Wright. Little could he have suspected while sailing down the coast of Kent and Sussex that Wright would become his business associate at Canton in the 1820s.[2] In stages, Jardine was meeting people like Wright, Weeding, and Jejeebhoy who would play significant roles in the commercial enterprises he was to pursue after leaving the service of the EIC.

Under the command of Captain James Halliburton, the *Glatton* sailed from Spithead in mid-May 1806, carrying a total of 540 souls. As the convoy of eleven Indiamen and three warships began making its way down the Channel, it passed an incoming squadron of five men of war showing signs of combat. As it happened, two of the vessels were prize ships captured in the South Atlantic and well known to William Jardine, for they were the *Marengo* and the *Belle Poule*.[3]

Nevertheless, French threats in the Indian seas persisted. One month after Jardine's convoy encountered the captured Frenchmen, the twelve-hundred-ton HCS *Warren Hastings*, sailing unescorted in the Indian Ocean southeast of Madagascar, was intercepted by the French frigate *Piemontaise*, which was literally armed to the teeth. With men in the tops armed with swivel guns and rifles, the forty-six-gun *Piemontaise* attacked no less than five times, over the course of four and a half hours, before the Indiaman hauled down its colours.

The casualties aboard the *Warren Hastings* totalled seven dead, including the surgeon's mate. In addition, while the surgeon was performing an operation during the combat, a French shell crashed through the operating cabin, destroying all his surgical instruments. When the vessels collided, French troops armed with daggers leaped aboard the Indiaman, stabbing the captain, the surgeon, and three other crewmen. Such news had to be sobering to the twenty-two-year-old Jardine, reminding him of the immediate danger to Company medical officers in naval combat situations.[4]

For the time being, the *Glatton* was well defended and in good company. Simon's Bay at the bottom of Africa had changed hands since his last visit there, when he was a French prisoner, shipwrecked on the shores of the Dutch colony; now in the possession of British authorities, having been seized back from the Dutch earlier in 1806, Simon's Bay received a good number of the troops which the convoy had been transporting. After the convoy resumed its voyage in mid-August, violent storms in the Indian Ocean scattered the ships, and the *Glatton* was alone once the weather abated. She sailed into the Malay Straits by herself, anchoring at Penang in mid-October, and there the convoy reassembled. Once the troops were disembarked, refitting proceeded for all the ships and repairs to the *Glatton*'s damaged rudder caused a long delay in the resumption of their voyage. The convoy was finally able to sail from Penang on 12 November but could not follow the direct route to China because of the northeast monsoon. Consequently, the ships sailed south of Borneo and eastward of the Philippines, prior to reaching Lintin on 19 January 1807, eight months after leaving Portsmouth.[5]

Upon the *Glatton*'s mooring at Whampoa, Captain Halliburton, Purser Wright, and Doctor Jardine moved up river to the Company's quarters in the factory compound at Canton. However, they had to return to Whampoa at the end of each week to comply with Company requirements that all members of the crew be aboard their vessel when in port on weekends. The captain was obliged by regulations to hold muster and inspection on Sunday morning, followed by a religious service.[6] This meant that Jardine was travelling back and forth regularly from Whampoa to Canton, alternately looking to the arrangements for his private trade and to the medical necessities of the *Glatton*'s officers and seamen. The off-loading of teas and other cargo on the *Glatton* and its sister ships in the convoy should have been over by early March, but a large-scale disorder along the Canton waterfront led to a disruption of trade in late February. Some crewmen from the *Marquis of Ely* and the *Neptune*, on shore leave, became embroiled in several fights with Chinese men, with one death resulting among the Chinese.

After two days of riotous disorder, there were more wounds to be sewed and ribs to be bandaged than a single surgeon could handle and Jardine must have been called into service to assist the other ships' surgeons and the factory's surgeon. In the aftermath, the hoppo suspended all trade and the Chinese authorities demanded that one or more English sailors be held responsible for the death of the Cantonese man. For days the matter was debated, but eventually the Chinese justices fabricated a compromise – reducing the nature of the crime to accidental killing and assessing a small fine (£4) – that avoided a rupture of trade for the season. The consequence was a delay of two months in the EIC ships' departure from China, which finally took place in early May 1807.[7]

Rumours of French naval and military units reinforcing the Dutch in Java led the homeward-bound convoy of Indiamen to alter its route, with the laborious journey to Penang taking two months. Consequently, the convoy did not reach St Helena until 14 October. Two weeks later, they began sailing the last leg in combination with a convoy from India, and Jardine had, as some compensation for the slowness of this return journey, the enjoyment of a spectacular sight of two fleets of Indiamen, plus naval escorts, under full sail making their way northward toward home waters.

When the huge, merged convoy reached the English Channel in late December, the weather was terrible. At three o'clock on 28 December the *Glatton* ran aground barely ten miles from the coast of France. Jardine was once again in jeopardy on the homeward voyage, as in 1805. Darkness fell upon the stranded ship as a passing bark responded to a distress signal from the *Glatton* and removal of the women and children passengers was accomplished. But good fortune came with the change of tide and in a few hours the *Glatton* floated off the shoal and resumed its progress toward the English coast.

A week later, Jardine and his shipmates were in the calmer waters of the Thames, moored at Greenhithe. The final stages of a journey were tediously slow, and it was early spring 1807 before the *Glatton* was finally cleared by customs officers and the crew was paid and discharged. Jardine's third voyage to China had lasted two whole years, for which he received £57 18s 8d as the balance of his surgeon's wages. Beyond that he was entitled to £180 for his medical services to the troops transported on the outward voyage. The privilege tonnage, which made it home safely on this voyage, was a further source of significant revenue for him, but the exact amount remains unknown. However, it is safe to assume that the private trade was providing a very comfortable cushion to his Company wages, for he did not bother to collect the wages due after his next voyage for a full three months after the crew was paid.[8]

Beyond the Thames and home waters, the larger world had become more aggressively hostile to British trade since Jardine left England on the *Glatton* in 1806. In October 1806 the Prussian army was smashed by Napoleon's forces at Jena and Auerstadt. Then the Russians were defeated decisively at Friedland in June 1807. Under this succession of blows, the Third Coalition against Napoleon collapsed and Britain once again found itself alone against the economic warfare of the French emperor, who prohibited the import of British goods into any part of the European continent under his rule or in alliance with France. His intent was to undermine the "nation of shopkeepers," as he called the English, by destroying their export commerce. One consequence of his "Continental System" was the reduction of Indian goods exported to Europe by the East India Company. American private traders rushed into the vacancy; however, the British and French strategies of economic warfare eventually led the United States to restrict trade with Britain and France. Simultaneously, the EIC was experiencing very serious internal disorder over its shaky financial condition and its attempts to retain the monopoly over trade with India.[9]

In these turbulent years, Jardine was securing a continuous sequence of appointments to Company service aboard Indiamen and he was profiting from the private trade he was allowed. For the moment, in the unsure circumstances of wartime commerce, he was content to remain with the Company, providing medical services on direct voyages to China; he would continue serving in that capacity until the conclusion of the wars with France.

Jardine's fourth voyage to China was unremarkable, but for the speed of the return journey and the menace of pirates in the estuary of the Pearl River. The "stationing"[10] of the *Glatton* for a new journey to China occurred in January 1809, and the intention of Jardine to engage in private trade required that he submit details of his venture within four days of the ship's arrival at Gravesend. Accordingly, the surgeon would have been back in London by mid-January and ready to sail with the ship in March when the advances were paid to the ship's company. His pay had been raised to £5 per month, but without supplement since the *Glatton* was not carrying troops on this voyage.

In a convoy of seven ships, with a warship chaperone, the *Glatton* sailed from Spithead at the start of April and reached Penang, Malaya, by late July. Upon arriving in China, the ship landed its few passengers at Macao and proceeded to Lintin, where the smooth progress of the journey was disrupted by the presence of swarms of pirates in the estuary. Bandit junks numbering upwards of two thousand in the waters at the mouth of the Pearl River made it impossible for the small boats used by the Company personnel to function normally.[11]

Piracy in the Indian Ocean, the Malay Straits, the South China Sea, and the Pearl River estuary was an ongoing threat to Western as well as local trade. Jardine's years as a ship's surgeon coincided with the last major wave of pirate activity in the history of imperial China, between 1780 and 1810, which was marked by the organization of several pirate leagues consisting of thousands of vessels and upward of seventy thousand predatory seafarers.[12] While petty piracy was an ongoing enterprise, many of the smaller gangs of local pirates were reorganized as more formidable fleets of "ocean bandits."[13] The pirate junks were often heavily armed, and their commanders were murderers who were inclined to throw into the sea, whether alive or dead, those persons for whom no ransom might be collected. Witnesses who could identify the pirates were in danger of elimination, because the Chinese authorities were committed to a policy of swift execution of the criminals.[14] Although pirates seldom challenged the sizable, well-armed East Indiamen, they frequently struck the smaller vessels operating between Macao or Whampoa and the factories along the river at Canton.[15]

The Chinese rule that escorting warships of the Royal Navy could proceed only as far as Lintin meant that Indiamens' cutters were vulnerable while proceeding to Whampoa and beyond there to the factories at Canton. Even the factories in Canton were not completely safe from pirates who lurked in the precincts of the river.[16] In 1804 the EIC officials at Canton reported that pirate activity was preventing them from supplying their vessels anchored near Lintin Island, and in 1805 British observers took note of the large number of villages between Canton and Macao that had been overwhelmed by pirate raids of rape and looting. Just two months before the arrival of the *Glatton* at the Pearl Estuary, the Black Flag Fleet leader undertook a major campaign in the Pearl River, lasting six weeks, which led to the death of approximately ten thousand people. By the second week of August, they had burned the customs house at Tzu-ni and had set up a blockade just sixteen miles from Canton.[17]

The *Glatton*'s convoy was riding at anchor at Lintin by 20 September 1809, apparently safe after their five-month outward voyage, but the EIC supercargoes reported on 26 September, concerning the pirates, that "tho' they have now been some weeks in the river, they seem to have met with no opposition from any but the people of the towns and villages they have attacked."[18] As Jardine's vessel waited for the right moment to move up to Whampoa, cannon fire from the pirate ships could be heard daily in Canton, and panic gripped the city. The pirate chieftain, Chang Pao, posted a notice that he intended to attack Canton, leaving British merchants temporarily helpless as they watched the market for foreign goods collapse.[19]

The pirates had already moved against Macao, driving American vessels to seek safety below the guns of the Portuguese settlement, and seizing a brig belonging to the Portuguese governor of Timor. In desperation, the Chinese provincial government sought help from Portuguese, American, and British vessels. A British country-trade vessel, the *Mercury*, was enlisted to assist provincial war junks in clearing the Inner Passage, which was accomplished by the end of September; however, negotiations for further British assistance foundered when Captain Francis Austen of the *HMS St Albans* insisted upon a written application from the Chinese for such help.[20]

Just one day after the *Glatton* had arrived at Lintin, an officer and six crewmen from the *Marquis of Ely*, while fetching a pilot, were seized by pirates and held for ransom (which was paid eleven weeks later – a hundred thousand dollars, Spanish). This episode delayed the *Glatton's* arrival at Whampoa by seven weeks. Members of the foreign factories who had been residing at Macao and needed to return to Canton for the beginning of the trading season were afraid to hazard the journey. It became necessary for the Indiamen to serve as armed ferries for the factory members wishing to return to Canton from Macao.[21] But British protection of Macao itself was a touchy subject with the imperial government. The viceroy was insistent that the British must guarantee that they would not repeat their earlier action (1808) of sending troops to Macao to defend the colony against any French attempt to take possession of Portugal's overseas territories.[22]

For a time, the boldness of the pirates became so alarming to the Chinese war junks that they actually sought cover among the foreign trading vessels at Whampoa, while a large fleet of the pirate junks was anchored nearly within gunshot of the foreign ships. In the absence of an agreement with Captain Austen, the viceroy struck a deal with the Portuguese to equip six small ships to combat the pirates. Although the outlaws eluded capture, the Company ships were able to move up to Whampoa on 6 November, and Jardine was finally able to proceed, with some risk, upriver to the English Factory. (The risk was dramatized in late January – six weeks before his ship sailed for home – when pirates seized a boat belonging to the country ship *Sir Edward Pellew* en route from Canton to Whampoa, threw the crew overboard, and took possession of three chests of treasure.)[23]

The pirate wave crested in late 1809, and just as spectacularly collapsed early in 1810, after the emperor had enlisted a former provincial governor, Bai Ling, to undertake a forceful campaign against them. By mid-December, two of the foremost pirate leaders were fighting between themselves, a feud that produced heavy casualties in their ranks. In January, after Portuguese mediation, the commander of the Black Flag Fleet surrendered to Bai Ling; by April, the leaders of the Red Flag

Fleet had surrendered; and, like dominoes, the Yellow, Blue, and Green Flag Fleets toppled in the following months. Thus, by mid-1810, the enormous pirate empire was a thing of the past.[24]

In spite of all the disorder in the river and its estuary, the trade at Canton had moved along smoothly that season and the loading of the ships was going so well that Jardine was expecting the convoy to sail by 1 February 1810. However, the death of a Chinese man from stabbing, near the factories in mid-January, led to an investigation which focused on English sailors. The Chinese authorities proposed that the English *taipan* (the president of the Select Committee) should determine who the culprit was and hand him over for trial and nominal punishment, following which he would be returned. But the English authorities refused, citing the conflict with English law, whereupon the hoppo declared that he would not issue the Grand Chops, meaning that the ships could not leave.[25]

Once again, Jardine was forced to cool his heels while the wheels of Cantonese justice moved slowly, paused, and stopped. Eventually, Captain Austen, as commodore of the convoy, informed the viceroy that he intended to take the fleet out, with or without the Grand Chops. However, he waited three weeks before ordering the thirteen Indiamen to prepare for departure. Then, suddenly, the Grand Chops appeared, with expressions of high regard from the Hong merchants. Jardine saw the *Glatton* weigh anchor on 1 March 1810 and the convoy finally moved away from Whampoa the next day.[26]

The voyage home was unremarkable for its speed, with the convoy anchoring in the Downs at the mouth of the Thames on 28 July, just slightly less than five months after leaving Whampoa.[27] As usual, the business of ending a voyage was painfully slow; it was not until the final week of October that the Company distributed wages to the crew. Jardine's impatience to be away from the ship is revealed by his long delay in collecting the wages due him (£73 10s 3d). Most probably he took the earliest allowable opportunity to leave the *Glatton*, after completing arrangements for the unloading and sale of his own cargo, and hastened over the road north to Lochmaben for the first sight of home and family in nearly two years.

The privilege tonnage that the Company allowed its officers was for Jardine the source of his greatest income from the China voyages. It was very carefully regulated by the EIC, which required that the cargo be consigned to a Company warehouse for weighing and measuring and other checks to be certain that the goods conformed to the specified allowances. Thereafter they were sold at public auction, with duty and other charges being assessed before the balance was remitted to the account of the officer. In many instances these sales would take place while the officers were at sea on a new voyage. For that reason, the Company maintained a list of merchants who were authorized to represent the officers for the transactions involving privilege tonnage.

In the matter of William Jardine's private trade, the agent was Thomas Weeding, then a London merchant but formerly the surgeon of the *Glatton*. The two men had first met at Canton in 1802. Undoubtedly, Weeding understood Jardine's situation thoroughly, knowing his allowances, his cargoes (tea and various other Chinese exports), his anticipated income from the auctions, and his way of investing the income. From observing Weeding's business, Jardine gained some sense of the profits available to him once he elected to retire from practising medicine at sea.[28] Given their business relationship and their knowledge of the China trips, Weeding and Jardine could speak a common language about shipboard medicine, about the factories at Canton, about the way the *Glatton* handled the seas, and about the prospects for profit in certain commodities.

Another person with whom Jardine could speak familiarly of medicine and trade was the new managing owner of the *Glatton* (the ship's "husband," as the managers were called in dockside parlance) since 1811, Sir Robert Wigram.[29] Wigram had also become one of the co-owners of the giant East India Dockyard at Blackwall in 1810. A former Company ship's surgeon himself, he was the founder of the Wigram family fortunes. It is reasonable to conclude that Jardine's close associations with these two former EIC surgeons, both of whom left the practice of medicine for the practice of business, set before the young man – now in his late twenties – an alluring model of financial success.[30]

Jardine spent the year 1811 ashore in Britain, because the *Glatton* was required by EIC regulations to undergo a sweeping overhaul after her sixth trip to China. This lost season meant that Jardine could accept an offer to serve as surgeon on another vessel or he could await the next "stationing" of the *Glatton*. Apparently no position was available for him on another Indiaman. So he was home in Britain for the whole calendar year, most likely practising medicine or studying business practices with Thomas Weeding or perhaps doing both things.

When the vessel was ready for sea again, he rejoined Captain Halliburton, and an otherwise entirely new crew took the ship to sea in January 1812. The seventh and eighth trips to China would be the last voyages of the formidable *Glatton*, and Jardine would be aboard for nearly three years, with but a short intermission in the fall of 1813. For the medical officer, these two voyages were marked by the notable incidents of death and birth aboard the vessel. On the round trip, which lasted from January 1812 through September 1813, eleven members of the ship's company died – from disease or from accident. Although the occurrence of death on the long ocean voyage was not unusual, the high number deaths among those other than seamen was quite uncommon. The second mate, the boatswain, the boatswain's mate, and one of the midshipmen all died, along with seven seamen.[31]

No sooner had the *Glatton* arrived at Whampoa in late September 1812, after a journey of six months, than the ship was beset with extensive illness among the crew. Jardine was required to spend a great deal of time aboard tending the sick members of the ship's company, and he had the sad duty of officially pronouncing a young midshipman dead at the start of November. James Clark succumbed to sickness aboard ship while it was anchored at Whampoa, and he was buried ashore on the evening of his death, far from the English country churchyard where his family might have visited his grave.[32]

For Jardine, as for any ship's doctor, the remedy was not always adequate for the disease. There were inevitably those instances of peritonitis or heart attack or falls from the rigging or knife wounds to the lung which no surgeon at sea could address successfully. His melancholic duty, certifying the end of life, as in the case of James Clark, was repeated on every voyage but never more dramatically than when the dying person was the captain of the vessel.

The last voyage of the *Glatton*, commencing in February 1814, was to be the last voyage of her commander as well. The ship sailed, in convoy, from Spithead on 22 February, two days before William Jardine's thirtieth birthday. Among the passengers were two expectant mothers (wives of sergeants) accompanying their husbands to St Helena. In mid-April, while the ship was taking the swells of the South Atlantic, Jardine assisted one young woman in delivering a healthy baby boy. A week later, he attended the second mother as she gave birth to a girl, but the baby was premature and lived just a few hours. Burial of the infant at sea would certainly have been a wrenching experience for the woman and her husband, but also for the doctor who had been unable to sustain the new life.

After an uneventful season of loading the tea and other cargoes in China, the convoy of six Indiamen left Whampoa, without need of escort, early in February 1815. Their sails full, the convoy was cruising briskly across the Indian Ocean, about fifteen hundred miles away from Capetown when, on 8 April, Captain Halliburton suddenly became ill. Jardine was perplexed by his patient's condition and called for another surgeon to be transferred to the *Glatton* for consultation. Dr Rolfe, surgeon of HCS *Thames*, joined Jardine aboard the *Glatton*, but their combined medical knowledge and experience were unavailing as the captain died just three days after falling sick. The first mate, Henry Upton, assumed command and determined that Captain Halliburton should be taken to St Helena for full funeral rites with honours appropriate to his rank. On 16 May, as the ship's guns fired a final salute to their deceased commander, the body of James Halliburton was taken ashore for burial on the Company's remote speck of an island in the South Atlantic.[33] Within six years, his silent neighbour in the earth would be the deposed emperor of France.

En route home from St Helena, Jardine and his shipmates learned from a passing ship that a great battle had occurred outside Brussels and that the day had belonged to the Duke of Wellington. Little could they have guessed that the victors were about to confine the defeated Frenchman to the island that the *Glatton* had just left. A week later, as the convoy made its way north, the commodore entertained his fellow captains at a dinner celebrating Wellington's triumph. No doubt, Jardine and his fellow officers took the occasion to celebrate in their own fashion aboard the *Glatton*. A month later, the great Indiaman was moored in the Thames above Greenhithe, her final voyage to China completed, and in effect her life's work done.

Jardine received £84 6s 4d as the balance of his wages as well as £78 for medical services to the military personnel.[34] The income from his private trade would follow, once the auctions were held. We do have some sense of the scale of the trade he was handling, for the details of his Canton ventures on that voyage were specified in a statement by Jardine testifying to the innocence of Henry Upton against accusations of smuggling. Jardine explained that only four persons from the *Glatton* were engaged in private trade during the recent voyage (Captain Halliburton, mates Henry Upton and Alexander Lindsay, and Jardine himself). Their business was conducted under his "immediate inspection," he asserted, and their funds were passed through his hands. (So it is evident that he was already getting a feel for the "agency" business while serving as an East India surgeon.) Nothing was taken on board at Canton except what appeared on the manifest, he said, and nothing was landed before he left the ship at its Thames anchorage. He invested a sum exceeding 28,000 dollars (Spanish) for nankeens and sundries purchased for the group of four private traders named above (including himself), but he also invested on his own an undisclosed amount for teas and chinaware and other merchandise.[35]

Once the ship's log was closed, the medical log – with its notation of the captain's death – was delivered to the Company's chief medical officer; and the career of the *Glatton* was at an end. The career of William Jardine was about to change. He had the options of adjusting his life to the new political and economic circumstances of British trade, of giving up shipboard medicine for surgical work at home, of continuing to serve the Company at sea on another ship, or of changing careers and taking up a new life. For the short term, he chose the least dramatic option. He would continue to practise medicine for the East India Company. But things were no longer the same at Leadenhall Street. The giant Company that would continue to employ him was now a faltering giant.

"The United Company of Merchants of England trading to the East Indies" (its official title), which he had been serving for twelve years, had been struggling to maintain its monopoly against increasingly strong pressures from manufacturers, merchants, and shippers who wanted shares of the commerce with the East. Moreover, there were private merchants and Company officials who had become wealthy in India and needed a way to transfer that wealth home to Britain, but the transport of goods from India and China to Britain was the Company's monopoly. The illegal use of foreign vessels, principally American, to accomplish this transfer of wealth had come to be known as the "Clandestine Trade." This meant that the carrying trade between India and England was being lost by the English.[36]

The Napoleonic Wars had generated a groundswell of anti-monopoly sentiment in Britain because the Continental System was causing severe hardship to manufacturers in the English Midlands and in Scotland. Particularly after 1810, merchants searching for new markets renewed the long-standing demand that the Eastern trade ought to be opened to all private traders. Petitions were prepared in Glasgow, Edinburgh, and Liverpool, and members of Parliament were lobbied to terminate the Company's monopoly.[37] One recent analysis maintains that the company was fighting a losing battle in the early nineteenth century, since "governance and regulation of British interests and subjects in Asia had become a project of an increasingly global imperial system, and the Company reduced as it never had been to an agency of the British state."[38]

When the charter of the EIC came up for renewal in 1813, the Company's directors were bitterly divided among themselves with regard to economic strategy, and the Company's finances were in extreme disorder. In fact, the EIC was in the awkward position of attempting to borrow two and a half million pounds from the government.[39] The bill for renewal of the charter was considered by the House of Commons in 1813, but the Company's monopoly was doomed when confronted by a ministry which did not favour renewal. Though the EIC was entrusted with administration of the Indian territories for another twenty years,[40] its monopoly on British trade with India was ended. Indian trade was to be open to all licensed British merchants, but the Company retained for another twenty years its monopoly on trade with China.[41]

By then, China was easily the largest market for British trade, and tea was the most lucrative Chinese export commodity, generating profits amounting to £30 million per year. The Company was actually managing the China trade rather effectively, and the Exchequer's revenues from tea duties amounted to about £3 million per year, nearly 10 per cent of its entire revenue from the whole of England. The export of Indian opium to China had so effectively reversed the balance of trade with China that by 1804 the value of British and Indian exports to China surpassed the value of imports from China (largely tea).[42] Although the Company oversaw the entire production of opium in India, it took no part in the transport or sale of a drug that was officially illegal in China. To avoid jeopardizing its trading rights at Canton, the Company sold the opium crop to agency houses in India, which shipped the drug to China and resold it to smugglers along the coast.

Within a couple of years, the new situation for trade with India would prompt Jardine to reconsider his whole relation to the Eastern trading enterprises. With the *Glatton* retired, his first attractive opportunity came along within a few weeks of his return in 1815, when he was offered appointment as the surgeon for the *Windham*, an "India wallah" of

850 tons. The coming voyage would be his first complete round trip in peacetime and his last as a ship's surgeon.

The *Windham* was a ship with a dramatic history, having passed from English to French hands no fewer than four times during her fifth voyage (1809–11). In the autumn of 1815, Joseph Andrews, sole owner of the *Windham*, nominated himself to command the vessel (for he had sailed as mate on four voyages to China aboard the *Bengal*) and began to assemble his officers and crew for a journey to China to begin in the spring of 1816.[43] The Jerusalem Coffee House, in Cowper's Court, London, was the favourite haunt of the Company's senior officers, and it was most probably there that Joseph Andrews and William Jardine became acquainted. The offer was made to the surgeon, now thirty-two years old, and Andrews acquired a medical officer. If Jardine was thinking "just one more time," we have no privileged information revealing his intent.

Two months before the *Windham* sailed down the Thames, a small convoy of three ships had left Spithead, bearing the latest English embassy to Peking to petition for broader and more regularized trade as well as diplomatic relations between the two nations. Led by Earl Amherst, the English delegation hoped to succeed where its predecessor had failed in 1793. The objectives of that earlier expedition, headed by Lord Macartney, included the relaxation of trading restrictions at Canton, the extension of British trade to China's northern ports, and the establishment of a British enclave on Chinese territory. Intending to impress the emperor and his mandarins by their dramatic spectacle, the Macartney party approached Jehol, the empire's second capital, in a formal procession. The emperor, though civil to the visitors, was not impressed by their splashy arrival. His reply to the British overture reveals the essential reason for Macartney's failure: China saw itself as self-sufficient, without need for British manufactured goods, and therefore had no reason to make concessions to foreign merchants beyond allowing their presence at Canton, which assured the country an export market for teas. And so, in the end, the Macartney mission's sole success was in being received by the emperor. The British government could comfort itself in the knowledge that the EIC footed the bill for the extravaganza, which cost £80,000.[44]

For Jardine as well as all Company officers and private merchants, Amherst's embassy would have generated new expectations, especially among those businessmen who saw the end of the Company monopoly over Indian trade as a signal that free trade was about to become the gospel of English commerce. When Amherst and his retinue arrived at Peking, they were informed that the audience with Emperor Jiaqing would take place at midnight and that just four of the party were to be admitted. Alain Peyrefitte recounts the ensuing scene: "An extraordinary row then broke out, as a horde of mandarins seized the British and tried to drag them bodily to the throne room. The ambassador resisted, citing his exhaustion, the state of his dress, and the unseemly hour. He protested the violence, reaffirmed his refusal to kowtow, and asked to withdraw. His resistance was reported to the emperor, and a furious Jiaqing demanded the embassy's immediate departure. The mission was ordered out of Peking that very night."[45]

By the time the Amherst expedition arrived home in Britain in October 1817, word of its failure had preceded them. The vivid descriptions of his expulsion from Peking cannot have failed to impress Jardine and Matheson, both of whom would have been in Asia when hearing stories of the recent diplomatic debacle. Their impressions of Chinese haughtiness and resistance to diplomatic cooperation would colour their attitudes toward the Chinese authorities, and would eventually influence their attitude toward transactions with Chinese clients.

The *Windham* sailed down the Channel, bound for China, on 21 April 1816. By then, Jardine had developed two skills, medicine and the China trade. The latter was soon to replace the former, but at this moment he was primarily a ship's surgeon, tending to his medicine first and his trade ventures second. By late May, the ship had crossed the equator and was being tossed about in heavy weather as it passed through the "Roaring Forties." Jardine had long since acquired his bearing in heavy weather, but the *Windham* was so much lighter than the *Glatton* that he would have had to resort to the sea-sickness remedies he had long been giving to passengers and crews.

By 12 October, the *Windham* was anchored at Whampoa. A day later, Captain Andrews and Surgeon Jardine went upriver to the foreign factory district and took up residence there. Gossip and rumour among the Chinese reported the Amherst embassy to be returning in disgrace to Canton after the emperor's refusal to receive them. But the English merchants rallied around the ambassador.

When Lord Amherst reached Canton on New Year's Day, 1817, all the British commanders and officers, in full-dress uniforms, put on a lavish welcoming reception for him. Jardine likely was present at the dinner to hear first-hand the reports of the rough episode at Peking on that wild night in September. But the captain and surgeon had just a few days to digest the accounts of the diplomats, for they were back on the *Windham* before Twelfth Night, and the vessel sailed from Chuenpee anchorage on 11 January 1817.[46]

Just under ten weeks after leaving the Pearl River estuary, the *Windham* was anchored at St Helena, where it remained for four days. Did Jardine have a chance to meet the celebrity prisoner? It is quite possible that Jardine, as a member of Captain Andrews's party ashore, had occasion to be presented to the exiled emperor. If not, it is reasonable to assume that he would have ridden out to Longwood to observe Napoleon – now an historical curiosity – on the grounds of that estate.[47]

The *Windham* arrived at the English Channel in exactly two months after leaving St Helena. Jardine's seventh, and last, voyage as a medical officer for the EIC ended on 25 May 1817, at the East India Dockyard at Blackwall. Company regulations necessitated that all ship officers stand by until the cargo was unloaded and customs officers cleared the vessel.[48] So it was 25 June before the surgeon could leave the *Windham*. Six months later, he collected the £55 16s 9d due him as the balance of his wages.[49] His income from the private trade was surely much more significant, and by then he had reached his decision that commercial speculation was the direction he would take upon leaving the service of the EIC.

For the next year and a half, most of Jardine's time was evidently spent in London, where he was learning two things – the operations of the export/import trade and the processes of banking and finance employed in the City. The precise character of his business association with Thomas Weeding during these months remains cloudy, but he was learning from an insider, for Weeding had been appointed in 1815 to the Court of Directors of the EIC. Weeding maintained an office at the Old South Sea House, in South Sea Yard at the end of South Sea Passage, which was near the east end of Threadneedle Street. The ancient lanes and passages that had re-emerged from the reconstruction of London after the Great Fire of 1666 constituted a warren of channels which made business through personal contact the established method of pursuing advantage and profit. The seventeenth-century building – located about equally short distances from the Royal Exchange and East India House – had formerly housed the Excise Office; now it served as office space for several businessmen, one of whom was Thomas Weeding, advertised as "General Merchant and East India Company Agent." Whether transacting business on the floor of the Royal Exchange or striking deals with shipowners and captains in the Jerusalem Coffee House, Weeding was on familiar ground, professionally and physically. From travelling about the City with Weeding, Jardine came to know the business landscape of London extremely well.

Among other things, Jardine learned how to open doors of opportunity for members of his family, and the first was his nephew Andrew Johnstone, who had studied medicine at Edinburgh (1814–16) and now, age nineteen and medically qualified, was seeking a position.[50] No doubt it was his uncle's influence that secured him the interviews that led to his appointment as surgeon's mate on the HCS *Scaleby Castle*. At 1,242 tons, the ship was similar to the big Indiamen on which Jardine had spent most of his adult life to date. It was, however, not a chartered vessel, but one of the half-dozen ships that the Company had acquired outright, known as the "Company's Own Ships."[51] When the *Scaleby Castle* set sail for Canton in mid-October 1818, Jardine would likely have been among the last visitors to leave the ship at the East India Dockyard, after imparting a few final bits of advice on medicine and trade to the young man.

While Andrew Johnstone was preparing for sea, his uncle was engaged in his own preparations. Weeding had applied to the Company in August 1818 for permission to send Jardine to India as his agent. The request was denied. A private individual could proceed to India for commercial purposes only if the directors granted him "Free Merchants' Indentures," and a formal nomination was needed from a director. But each director was allowed just a limited number of nominations, and apparently Weeding had none remaining. Consequently, Weeding and Jardine had to search out a director who had a nomination available. The person who provided the necessary nomination was John Thornhill, a newly elected company director.[52]

Matters moved quickly after that. By mid-November, Jardine was engaged in a partnership, and by the spring of 1819 he was on his way to India. The partnership brought together Jardine, Weeding, and a Bombay merchant named Framjee Cowasjee as co-owners of a ship to be built by a Thames shipyard and named the *Sarah*.[53] While the vessel was under construction, Jardine proceeded to Bombay, on a private ship, likely the *Bombay Merchant*, which arrived at Bombay early in the autumn of 1819.[54]

It was a good time to get away from England, given the political tensions as well as the economic dislocation and worker discontent which materialized in the years just after Waterloo. Jardine's decision to go out to India as a businessman had surely been taking shape for months as he refined his commercial skills in Weeding's office. However, it was at the peak of the social and economic disorders of 1819 that he actually began preparing to leave England and return to the Eastern trade. At the same time, he was aware that business between India and China was growing, and he perceived an opportunity for his future at Canton.[55] The great staples of the Bombay trade were raw cotton and opium, and at least for a while he could superintend cargoes shipped between India and China while travelling as a supercargo and taking only limited risk to his own financial resources.

After looking up Framjee Cowasjee to begin making arrangements for the *Sarah*'s entry into the country trade, Jardine would surely have sought out his old comrade in adversity, Jamsetjee Jejeebhoy. They had not seen each other since they were captives of the French aboard the *Brunswick*, fourteen years earlier. Their re-acquaintance blossomed into a lifelong friendship and eventually a thriving business collaboration operating between Bombay and Canton. Just about the time of their reunion in Bombay, the *Sarah* was being launched at the Thames shipyard. Registered as the *Sarah*, of London, at 488 tons, with a draft of eighteen feet, she was given permission by the Company's Court of Directors to proceed to Bombay, Madras, Calcutta, Penang, and Bencoolen. The licence for trade with China would have to be granted by Company officials in India, because that commerce was formally part of the country trade conducted by private merchants between India and Canton. The *Sarah* sailed from England on 2 November 1819, and Jardine must have first seen the ship at Bombay in April 1820, at about the time when he first met James Matheson.[56]

Matheson had actually arrived in India several years before Jardine, in spite of being a dozen years younger than the former ship's surgeon. At the age of seventeen, after two years at the University of Edinburgh, James had proceeded to London to observe and learn the practices of a mercantile house, where he spent two years.[57] In a sense this was his apprenticeship, paralleling the time Jardine had spent with a surgeon in Edinburgh. The Mathesons had long since established themselves in the service of the East India Company; so it was through family influence that young James, by then nineteen, was able to secure Free Merchants' Indentures in March 1815, allowing him to proceed to Calcutta, where he joined his uncle's agency house, Mackintosh and Company.[58]

Within three years he had lost his job. Within the Jardine, Matheson ranks a legend developed about the cause of his unemployment. Unverifiable by now, the story holds that he was sent to the quay with an urgent letter for the captain of a homeward-bound vessel; but he failed to reach the ship before it sailed and his angry uncle directed him to arrange for passage home. The most elaborate version of this story appears in Basil Lubbock's *The Opium Clippers*: "His irate uncle declared that he was of no use to him and had better go back to England. Matheson took his uncle at his word and went off to engage a passage. Luckily for him, the first Indiaman commander to whom he applied for a passage was, like most East India skippers, a shrewd man, and he strongly advised young Matheson to make his way to Canton instead of England. Matheson took his advice."[59]

In the short term his dismissal might have seemed a great misfortune, for Macintosh opened a commercial bank at Calcutta in 1819. However, in the long run, this turn of events may have been good fortune, because Mackintosh and Company suddenly collapsed in 1833, along with several other British firms at Calcutta, leaving a morose community of private merchants in the wake of the financial disaster.[60] As things developed for James Matheson in 1818, he did leave Calcutta before long, but not to return home. Instead, he seized the chance to see what opportunities Canton might offer him. During his time of unemployment in Calcutta, he had become acquainted with an elderly merchant named Robert Taylor, a former EIC purser. Taylor, who had previously been to Canton, possibly as a supercargo on a country ship, invited Matheson to accompany him on a trip to China and to become associated with him in establishing an agency handling general commerce and insurance. What developed was an informal partnership which enjoyed some brief success in 1819 but drifted into trouble thereafter, owing to a risky venture that betrayed a youthful rashness on the part of the twenty-three-year-old Matheson.

Matheson was a passenger on the *Marquis of Hastings*, from Calcutta to Canton, in the spring of 1819, acting as travelling agent for cargo shipped by the Spanish firm of Larruleta and Company of Calcutta. He reported from Penang in the Malay Straits that his first business there was to ascertain the state of the opium market, so as to determine whether he might make an advantageous sale of some portion of Larruleta's opium shipment. His first view of Singapore, about to become a British bastion of commerce at the bottom of Malaya, impressed him with the potential of the site for trade.[61] He thought that opium could sell high in Singapore, were there some merchants to deal with. "A person settling here for a few months with a few thousand dollars circulating money might do very well."[62] The eagerness of the young trader was manifest in his eye for speculation, and it was that speculative risk that soon got him and his partner into deep water.

No sooner had he reached Canton than he was learning the tricks of skirting the law in the business traffic of the river – resisting Mandarin demands for a bribe (and planning to divert the burden of the bribe, if necessary, to the local opium holders), and scheming to avoid duties by smuggling British cotton goods upriver. Immediately upon arriving at Canton, he began catching on to the manipulation of prices in the opium trade.[63] He was bright, eager, and to some degree reckless in these early days of his career in the China trade.

Entertaining "the fairest hopes" of carrying on a successful business with Taylor, Matheson discovered, after arriving at Canton in June 1819, that "a most disastrous reverse had befallen Mr. Taylor." He learned that his friend had unwisely loaned a large sum of money (65,000 Spanish dollars) to an Armenian named Bahoom, who turned out to be insolvent and incapable of paying back the amount advanced to him. Some measure of the elderly merchant's distress might have been relieved by the proceeds of their joint operations in 1819, but they planned to reduce that distress yet further by investing their available resources in "an adventure to India."[64]

The venture that nearly sank Matheson's career in its dawn involved the brig *Hooghly* owned by Larruleta and Company (Calcutta) but sailing under the Danish flag (which allowed English merchandise to avoid the restrictions still imposed at Canton by the EIC). The *Hooghly* arrived at Canton in the late summer of 1819, consigned to Taylor and Matheson as agents for Larruleta. With the ship available to them, and Matheson dazzled by the profits of the opium speculation, the partners chartered the vessel for a period of ten months, to ship some Chinese export cargo to the Coromandel Coast (southeast India). However, their second – and secret – purpose was to sail the *Hooghly* around to the Portuguese enclave of Damaun, on the west coast of India (north of Bombay), in order to secure a cargo of opium at prices lower than the EIC's sales. To carry out this venture, Matheson sailed with the *Hooghly* as supercargo.[65] Apparently Taylor had great confidence in his young partner's business skills, and even entrusted him with a mission to resolve an account dispute while in Calcutta. ("Knowing your qualifications at inspecting books," Taylor wrote from Canton, "I have asked Scott & Co. to allow you to inspect their accounts while you are on the spot.")[66]

The circumstances of the *Hooghly's* voyage to Calcutta and Bombay brought our two subjects together for the first time. Matheson wrote from Malacca in January 1820 to inform Larruleta that a Parsi friend was arranging for the ship's arrival at Bombay. As it turned out, the arrangement was for Framjee Cowasjee and William Jardine to serve as charterer's agents for the *Hooghly*.

Matheson's conduct on this voyage was marked by a combination of naive enthusiasm about opportunities and clever scheming to evade laws and regulations. At Pondicherry he heard from a Frenchman of an inland region of northern India that was rather like a drug purchaser's El Dorado, with "large quantities of excellent opium uninquired for & unnoticed." Moreover, the official authorities in that quarter were said to be "completely dormant," so that opium could be brought to the coast "without risk, to almost any extent."[67] He engaged the Frenchman to do the buying for him, while Matheson himself sought to find speculators in Calcutta for whom he would obtain the opium, adding his own 5 per cent commission to the cost. Hoping to evade official detection lest the smell of the opium give away his packet's contents, the young Scot sent a sample of the drug to Larruleta in Calcutta, addressed to the Court of Requests, with instructions that Larruleta arrange to pick up the parcel at the court.

He was both cocky and self-righteous in his approach to sales and quality. Regarding himself as a "tolerably good judge" of the qualities of opium shipments, he assured his correspondents of his own reliability – in contrast to some of the other agents: "Where disappointment in quality has been experienced I would in almost every case attribute it to disintegrity on the part of the agent."[68] In his effort to buy opium at bargain prices, he took the brig north to Yanam (a French possession on the east coast) but discovered upon arriving there that prices were far higher than he had expected. So he left the ship at Yanam with instructions to the crew to load as much of the drug as they could procure, while he proceeded to Hyderabad to do some "arranging." Following the loading of opium, the ship was to sail round the bottom of India and stop at Bombay before continuing to Damaun. Matheson notified Larruleta: "I have directed Mr. Jardine at Bombay to advance the Captain's wages for this quarter. You are aware that the control of the ship rests with that gentleman on my behalf."[69] Although he had as yet never met William Jardine, Matheson was making use of Jardine's services in the course of this madcap pursuit of cheap opium in 1820. He undertook a four-hundred-mile journey overland from Hyderabad to Bombay, likely arriving sometime early in May, and at that point the two future taipans met face to face for the first time. Jardine would surely have been skeptical about any long-term collaboration with this young fellow Scot had he foreseen how badly things were to develop for Matheson in the coming months – owing in large part to his ill-advised opportunism and his inexperience in a world of sharks and rogues.

The *Hooghly* had proceeded to Dauman but could not load opium there on account of the interference of bribed local officers who were reserving the opium trade to Macao for vessels flying the Portuguese flag. Matheson rushed to Goa to seek relief from the Portuguese viceroy, but his appeal was rejected. Forced to sail from Goa after having failed in the main object of chartering the brig, Matheson moved on to the Danish port of Tranquebar to seek Danish help in protesting to the Portuguese authorities in Goa. (The *Hooghly* continued to sail under the Danish flag.) His request was denied, but a second petition – that he be appointed Danish consul in China – was approved, a momentous turn of advantage for him in the long run.[70]

By the summer of 1820, Matheson's venture was about to be washed up on the rocks, and with it his career as an Eastern trader. His partner, Robert Taylor, died on 4 August, quite unexpectedly. His brief illness gave no hint of grave danger, and he died without even being confined to bed.[71] This happened while the *Hooghly* was still at sea, and Matheson, upon arriving at Canton on 6 September, reported to a correspondent: "My affairs were in consequence [of Taylor's death] within an ace of going to utter wreck." But he was rescued by a sudden spike in the price of opium, with demand exceeding supply by a third. He was able to sell off a consignment of opium for the very high price of $1,420 per picul (133 1/3 pounds), and he escaped the jaws of financial disaster.[72] In the aftermath of the nearly catastrophic enterprise, Matheson was blaming the Portuguese government in India "to whose injustice the failure of the venture alluded to was owing."[73] It seemed that the young man had learned a painful lesson about bold speculation with his own resources, but he had not forsworn encouraging others to speculate in opium. He wrote to correspondents in Pondicherry that the price of the drug was very high in Macao. "It is an article which it may be worth your while to attend to."[74]

Although the association with Taylor was not the happiest possible start to his life in China, it did cause Matheson to remain there. He had intended to return to India, but by early December 1820 he was concluding that it was "very doubtful when I may next be able to visit India," and a few weeks later he wrote to a publisher in India countermanding his order to discontinue a subscription "as it is now my intention to remain in this country."[75] Through the winter of 1820–21, the fast-learning entrepreneur was moving back and forth between Macao and Canton, attending to the sales of opium for clients in India. The scarcity of the drug was causing prices to skyrocket ($2,500 for a picul of Bengal opium, $1,800 for Malwa). But Matheson was gaining skill as a judge of the quality of drug shipments, and as he inspected deliveries at Macao he was careful to inform his correspondents as to the marketability of their chests.[76]

A sign of his financial recovery involved Jardine's nephew, Andrew Johnstone, now serving as surgeon's mate aboard the *Scaleby Castle*, anchored at Whampoa. Apparently, young Johnstone was in need of cash for investment in privilege cargo, and Matheson was in a position to lend him the money, as we learn from Johnstone's note of late November: "Dear Uncle, Mr. Matheson having advanced me the Sum of one Thousand eight hundred and Twenty Spanish Dollars – be pleased to honor his draft for the same should he draw upon you." Jardine had apparently authorized Matheson to assist the nephew, and Matheson now sent along his own note asking that the sum be credited to his account with Larruleta in Calcutta.[77]

Partnership between William Jardine and James Matheson was yet a long way off, but the ties were becoming more intricate. Although Matheson's base in India was Calcutta and Jardine was operating out of Bombay, the point of contact for them was the Pearl River estuary, as they learned to manipulate the country trade to their mutual advantage. The business courtship had begun. There would be other suitors for both merchants, but their relationship seemed fated.

# 4

# THE HEIRS OF COX AND BEALE

"I would be grateful if you could send me a prime Surat goat (if pregnant so much the better) – also some Bumly fish and some Bombay onions," Matheson asked of a man in Bombay at the start of March 1821. He was then residing in what he described as "a decent house in Macao," where he might entertain friends. And he was clearly intending to remain on the coast of China and conduct agency business – alone for the time being, but with the privileges of Danish consul at Canton – and with the expectation of a partnership materializing soon.[1]

His new associate would not be his friend and countryman Jardine, but a Spaniard from Larruleta's firm in Calcutta, a man named Xavier Yrissari, who arrived at Macao in the latter part of June. Not only was Matheson thrilled to be informally associated with Larruleta and Company through his new arrangement with Yrissari, but he was excited at the "unexampled magnitude of the business with which he will enable us to commence our Establishment far exceeding the most sanguine hopes I could have formed." Taking the name Yrissari and Company, the partnership began on 1 July 1821, with Yrissari's wide commercial contacts and Matheson's consular appointment allowing them to evade John Company's continuing monopoly at Canton.[2]

His correspondence that year reveals that he was developing a brisk business in the sale of opium for parties in India and Singapore who were speculating in the drug.[3] His enterprises also included participation in a Bengal insurance partnership known as "Phenix Insurance Office," established in 1820 for a period of five years.[4] Far from Loch Shin and the Kirk and the classrooms of Auld Reekie, James Matheson, at the age of twenty-six, was settling down on the coast of China as an ambitious agent for distant constituents who trusted his skill at negotiating high profits for them from the volatile opium market.

Although the evidence is thin, there is good reason to assume that William Jardine continued to travel with the *Sarah* as supercargo; and there is solid evidence that he was simultaneously speculating in opium, for which Matheson served as agent at Canton. In the spring of 1822, Matheson, anticipating great success in the sale of their opium, adopted a most peculiar use of biblical metaphor in telling Jardine: "We shall I think have a greater share of the *loaves* & *fishes* than last year."[5]

The *Sarah* continued sailing back and forth between India and China as a country trader between 1820 and 1822, but the vessel returned to England in 1823. Jardine did not travel home with the *Sarah* but remained at Canton in the autumn of 1822. Without Company permission to set up a permanent office there, he would have been obliged to retire to Macao at the end of the tea-shipping season. In all likelihood, he retired to the comfortable house of James Matheson. Additionally, Matheson had come to like Jardine's nephew, Andrew Johnstone, who was continuing as ship's surgeon's mate aboard the *Scaleby Castle*. Auguring a place for Andrew in their future connections, Matheson had written to Jardine in April 1822, "I am happy to tell you that he is a great favourite of all my friends & also of his commander."[6] This fellowship of Scots at Macao was growing tighter year by year, but another five years would intervene before their business affairs merged when they became the latest heirs of the mercantile genealogy of Cox and Beale.

In the late eighteenth century, the well-known London goldsmith James Cox had found a market in China for elaborate musical toys, which the Chinese called "singsongs," as well as handsomely jewelled clocks. They were purchased on credit by the Hong merchants of Canton who gave them to mandarins and other Chinese officials as obligatory New Year's gifts. The items, manufactured in Birmingham, were supplied for that market chiefly by Cox, who maintained his shop at Shoe Lane, London, and Francis Magniac, of London's Clerkenwell district. When several of the Hong merchants failed in 1779, their defaults had the domino effect of causing James Cox's business to fail; and in an effort to collect the debts due him, in 1780 Cox's creditors arranged for his son to go out to China for two years with the permission of the EIC.

John Henry Cox was the sole English "free merchant" left in China after the Select Committee of Supercargoes at Canton had expelled all the private merchants seeking to bypass the EIC monopoly. Rather than confining himself to debt collection and the sale of singsongs, Cox began to conduct business as the Canton agent for Company officers with privilege tonnage; moreover, he started to serve as agent for country traders located in India.[7] By the autumn of 1783, John Henry Cox had joined in some kind of partnership with a Scot named John Reid who had appeared on the China coast in late 1780 carrying diplomatic papers that designated him as Austrian consul at Canton. To the Select Committee it seemed a patent absurdity, but that diplomatic status put him beyond their reach.[8] Meanwhile, the efforts of the Austrian "Imperial Company" to revive its trade between Ostend, in the Austrian Netherlands, and Canton were not succeeding. For that reason, Cox sought a partner who might enjoy more stable diplomatic rights at Canton. When Daniel Beale arrived as purser of the *HCS Walpole* in December 1783, Cox worked out the terms of a partnership with him, but the arrangement did not take effect immediately. In the latter part of 1787, when Beale arrived, bearing papers commissioning him to be consul for the king of Prussia, the firm of Cox and Beale was founded.[9]

The partnership was still young when John Henry Cox died in October 1791, and his position in the partnership was taken by Thomas Beale, who had arrived in the fall of 1790 with the protected status of vice-consul to his brother Daniel, the Prussian consul.[10] Mrs Daniel Beale arrived in September 1791 to set up house in Macao, where the Chinese law did not prohibit her residence; but she and her husband returned to England in 1797, while his brother Thomas remained at Canton as the new Prussian consul. At that point, Thomas apparently joined forces with three newcomers, including a Scot named David Reid, who had arrived a few years earlier with an appointment as the Danish consul. That partnership was of short duration, since David Reid left for home in 1800. Shortly thereafter, Thomas Beale was joined, in 1801, by Charles Magniac, the son of London goldsmith Francis Magniac.[11] Charles was sent to keep an eye on the family interests at Canton and quickly took up the post of Prussian vice-consul, since there was no end to the variations which could be played on the diplomatic theme that John Reid had invented. The firm of many names became Reid, Beale and Company on 1 April 1801.[12]

For the next fifteen years, while William Jardine was sailing on Indiamen and James Matheson was going to school in Scotland, the evolution of names for the agency house continued. Thomas Beale went bankrupt at the start of 1816 and retired to Macao for the last few years of his life. The only remaining partners as of mid-1817 were Charles Magniac and his brother Hollingworth, who had arrived in 1811 with the title of "secretary" to the Prussian consulate at Canton. The renamed firm of "Magniac & Co.," established in 1817, prospered not on singsongs but by offering a range of services that included marketing, banking, shipping, and insurance.[13]

Their most mercurial commodity was, predictably, the Indian opium which they sold away from Canton, because the trade was illegal in China. The drug reached boom prices in 1819, and at that point the Magniac brothers were very heavily engaged in the opium market. However, after watching prices soar between 1819 and 1821 – the increase was 100 per cent – Charles and Hollingworth sold all the chests of opium that they had, just as Chinese officials were attempting to interdict the drug traffic. Their profits from this heady speculation were tremendous. By this time, the pattern of forwarding the proceeds of China market sales back to India or on to England had been refined to a smooth business mechanism.

One skill that James Matheson was perfecting was the facility for negotiating bills drawn on London, since the Western traders in Canton had come to rely on an elaborate system of transferring drug profits from silver (coins or ingots), paid by the buyers aboard the depot ships, to instruments of paper negotiable in India or London. When William Jardine took up residence in China in 1822, the same type of financial competence would become one of the principal features of his reputation as the manager of a house of agency.

Just about the time that William Jardine had begun serving as a medical officer aboard EIC ships, the export-import balance of the China trade was shifting in favour of the English merchants. Until the end of the eighteenth century, the Chinese had showed little interest in purchasing English commodities. So the challenge to the EIC and to country traders was to find something that the Chinese would buy. The limited market for spices and furs was not significant enough to come anywhere near offsetting the cost of the teas and silks being bought from Chinese merchants. Consequently, the EIC paid for their purchases chiefly by means of specie – gold and silver coins imported especially for that purpose.

Shipping specie posed huge problems. One was pirates in the Eastern seas, for whom a cargo of coins was a prime catch. Another problem was the Chinese government, which prohibited ships carrying only money from entering the river at Canton. There was the additional danger of losing a ship in a storm at sea. And valuing specie constituted yet another difficulty, for the Chinese preferred Spanish milled dollars (with a hierarchy among the coins, depending on which Spanish king was represented).[14]

Each foreign factory at Canton maintained a heavily secured vault, with limited access. Nevertheless, fires and civil disturbances, which were increasingly frequent, made these treasuries vulnerable to looters. Each factory also employed a *shroff,* a Chinese assayer, to determine the weight and purity of the silver coins and ingots accepted as payment. In the instance of opium sales, when payment was made offshore, a shroff would usually go aboard the depot ship to examine the coins as buyers were making their purchases; and he would imprint his stamp of approval on coins or ingots which met expected standards.[15]

As tea consumption increased in Britain, so did the need for specie to pay for the tea. The only source of hard metal currency for the EIC's tea purchases was the country trade of the private merchants, whose principal cargoes from India were raw cotton and opium. Although the Dutch and Spanish sold some rice in the China market and the Americans brought furs to China, the aggregate of Western trade with the Celestial Empire was not enough to offset the one-way movement of silver into the coffers of the Chinese sellers of tea and silk.

At the start of the nineteenth century, China began buying greater quantities of Indian goods, particularly cotton. Simultaneously, the Chinese demand for Indian opium accelerated. In consequence of these shifts in the markets, the balance of payments was reversing by 1804 and within three years silver began flowing out of China and into the hands of the Anglo-Indian country traders. That change of fortune did not, however, eliminate the problems of shipping silver by sea; moreover, Chinese law prohibited the export of silver.

Opium was not yet the chief Indian product in the country trade, but it was one of the significant sources of the silver acquired by English private merchants, and it had to be "laundered," so to speak, for the traders to realize their profits without defying Chinese law any more than the contraband commerce was already doing. The solution for private merchants was to deposit their silver in the treasury of the English Factory at Canton, thereby providing the Company specie for tea purchases. In return, the merchants acquired bills of exchange, allowing them to avoid the costs of storing, shipping, and insuring the large quantities of silver, and giving them the benefit of interest-bearing notes which could be negotiated (cashed) in India or in London.[16]

Normally, bills of exchange enabled the seller of goods to obtain cash as soon as possible after the goods were dispatched, while allowing the buyer (importer) to defer payment until the goods arrived. When bills were issued at Canton, the seller of silver received a paper instrument which could be sold to a third party before reaching its accepting bank in London or Calcutta or Bombay. "Discounting" meant selling a bill, once it was properly accepted, to a bank or discount house in London (or one of the major Indian cities), and the "discount rate" was simply a rate of interest per annum charged for providing the money for the lifetime of the bill. (Thus, a discount rate of 3 per cent on a three-month bill would actually amount to a charge of .075 per cent.)[17] In the long run, the business started by Reid and Cox, which was inherited by Jardine and Matheson, would serve both ends of the exchange process, with its offices in East Asia and its headquarters on Lombard Street in London.

In the 1820s, the Treasury of the Select Committee at Canton was buying silver not only from British country traders but also from Spanish, Portuguese, and American merchants in the China trade. But the Select Committee would set limits to the amount of silver that it would accept. In these circumstances, the American traders recognized the possibilities of a new kind of trade. An American merchant who had established his credit with a London merchant bank could avoid travelling with large quantities of silver if he carried an interest-bearing document to Canton, where it could be sold for silver to a British opium dealer who was seeking a way to remit his earnings to London.[18]

While the financial mechanism of the opium trade was being progressively refined by Western merchants, the trade itself remained illegal in China. In contrast to the export trade of the EIC, in which tea was the central commodity, the country trade was based primarily on the importation into China of cotton and opium. The legal prohibition of opium excluded the Hong merchants from the most profitable element of the import trade; as a result, the country trade had very damaging consequences for the finances of the Hong members.[19]

Peking had issued its first edict against importing opium in 1729. Succeeding pronouncements prohibiting the trade were made in 1780 and 1796, and thereafter declarations of its illegality followed almost annually. By the early nineteenth century, opium smoking in defiance of Peking had spread deep into the interior of China and cut across all classes. There was evidence of drug use even among the emperor's palace guards and the eunuchs of his imperial household.[20]

In contrast to the Chinese prohibitions, the importation of opium into Britain was extensive and its use for medicinal purposes was normal and widespread. Until the beginnings of the public-health movement in the 1830s, there was virtually no established distinction between medical and non-medical use of opium.[21] To the British mind, opium was not a pernicious drug meriting proscription but an anodyne to be used as readily as aspirin or acetaminophen or ibuprofen would be at the beginning of the twenty-first century. Tinctures of opium were commonly used for relief of toothache, diarrhea, angina, arthritis, sciatica, menstrual discomfort, bronchitis, even tuberculosis and cancer, and for numerous other sedative or analgesic purposes. In Britain, people could obtain opium in the form of pills or powders, lozenges, suppositories, plasters, liniments, syrups, and seeds from the poppy itself.[22] For many adults, laudanum was the preferred way to ingest the drug – mixing a tincture of it with water or wine or beer.

Most opium entering Britain (80 to 90 per cent) was acquired from Turkey, and it had a much higher morphine content than Indian opium. But on occasion some Indian opium was available in England. The Ottoman empire purchased substantial quantities of cotton manufactured goods, which meant that a roughly balanced trade could be carried on between British and Turkish merchants, unlike the lopsided tea trade at Canton. Bristol, Dover, and Liverpool were all opium ports, but the centre of the European opium trade was in the City, concentrated around Mincing Lane and Garraway's Coffee House.[23] Matheson and Jardine, in their extended periods of learning business in that sector of London, would have been familiar with the character of the opium trade, its risks and its profit margins. Addiction to the drug was certainly known in England, but it did not account for the extent of imports (91,000 pounds as of 1830, and triple that in the next generation).

Some opium imports were sold at auctions held at Garraway's Coffee House near the Royal Exchange, but most transactions were private arrangements between the opium importers and the large London wholesalers. The Apothecaries Company, which had rights to inspect both medicines and apothecary shops, normally bought its supplies of the drug through brokers, and then had samples examined and evaluated by members of the Buying Committee ("medical gentlemen"). Prices for opium were influenced by the amount of duty charged (which was sharply reduced from four shillings to one shilling per pound in 1836), but in general the fluctuation in the price of good-quality opium was nothing like the sometimes wild variations in price along the coast of China.[24]

Once the deals were struck, imported opium became the property of wholesale drug firms, which sold to manufacturing druggists who then retailed the drug preparations. However, the wholesalers also manufactured their own preparations. The most prestigious of the drug wholesalers was the Apothecaries Company (one of the livery companies in the City), which manufactured numerous opium preparations of its own. Until passage of the Pharmacy Act in 1868, the stocks of the wholesalers were available for sale to anyone who wished to purchase opium, without limitation.[25] There was no special stigma attached to the sellers, which was an indication of how normal the drug trade was in British commerce. Opium was "just another commodity on the market."[26]

Until 1868, when Parliament regulated the sale of opium, it could be bought in most town shops, in pubs and bakeries, from tailors and street vendors, and even from country peddlers. The wholesale opium business was open to anyone willing to acquire quantities of the drug for retail sales. In the Fen district around Ely, families spent on average between eight pence and one shilling weekly on opium. The little market town of Wisbech was reported to consume the highest proportion of opium in East Anglia. Working men in the Fens preferred to have a beer with their opium pill, while laudanum was often substituted for doctors' visits, and many women relied on Godfrey's Cordial or Mrs Winslow's Soothing Syrup to keep their children quiet.[27] Even respected medical professionals endorsed the use of opium preparations for calming very young children.[28]

British medical theory did not accept the principle that a person could become addicted to a cure. Drug dependence, or "addiction," was not studied in a scientific way until well after mid-century, when medical administration of opium by hypodermic needle became more frequent. By the 1870s, some physicians had started using the term "morphinism" to describe the disease of addiction.[29] Nevertheless, earlier in the century there were famous persons who were habitually dependent on opium, and whose abuse of the drug was revealed in their writings, such as Samuel Taylor Coleridge and Thomas de Quincey. For Coleridge, the effect of opium was to produce vivid imagery. In "Kubla Khan," a poem attributed to an opium-induced dream-like trance, Coleridge refers to the drug as "the milk of Paradise." On the other hand, de Quincey's *Confessions of an Opium Eater* (1821) explains the use of opium in terms of pain-relief or pleasure or mood elevation. "Whereas wine disorders the mental faculties, opium introduces amongst them the most exquisite order, legislation and harmony." However, his confession proceeds to describe the tortures of addiction, which he was eventually able to escape only after Herculean efforts.[30]

The common English use of laudanum or paregoric did not generally threaten addiction. However, *smoking* opium involved a vastly greater risk of addiction, and the Chinese buyers of Indian opium were not risking their freedom and their lives for the sake of laudanum but for the mind-bending reveries which followed the inhaling of several pipes of opium vapours in rapid sequence.

Carl Trocki, in his book on opium and the global economy, argues that opium was the "keystone" factor in the development of the nineteenth-century British empire, describing it as "the one element in a larger system upon which the entire complex of relationships came to depend."[31] An editor of data for commercial handbooks, J. Phipps, who was a contemporary of Jardine and Matheson, claimed in 1836 that the opium trade could "scarcely be matched in any one article of consumption in any part of the world."[32] Certainly, it was a rapidly growing commerce at the time that Jardine and Matheson became established in the agency business at Canton in the 1820s. However, it was not simply the private agency houses and their constituents who were profiting from the trade; in a very considerable way the opium trade was sustaining the EIC in its governing of the Indian subcontinent. In the latter part of the eighteenth century, the British rulers of India had assumed a monopoly of the production and sale of opium, resulting eventually in one-seventh of the total revenue of British India; and the British House of Commons was keenly aware of the importance of that revenue to colonial stability in South Asia.[33] The profits from its opium business were so reliable that the EIC seldom made less than 100 per cent net profit annually.[34] Trocki maintains that, by the 1770s, opium began affecting every aspect of the European presence in Asia, and that the drug came to constitute the sole commercial advantage that the foreign merchants had over the Chinese through much of the nineteenth century.[35]

The opium crops of India were grown principally on the Ganges plain, between Patna and Benares, by peasant farmers sowing and harvesting the products of the *papaver somniferum* – to give the opium poppy its formal name. The growth and harvesting of the opium crops was exceedingly labour-intensive.[36] The poppy produces white flowers (sometimes crimson or pink or purple) which last only a few days before shedding their petals to reveal a pod that continues to grow until it reaches the size of a hen egg. At that point it must be scored so that its opaque, milky sap may drain and be captured by the farmers. Exposed to the air, raw opium becomes a dark brown, viscous, sticky substance which would be moulded into the shape of a ball or cake, after taking on the consistency of putty. It would then be wrapped in its own leaves and stored, hardening as it dried, resembling twenty-four-pound shot, said one observer. When sufficiently dry, the balls of opium were packed into mango-wood chests, each holding forty balls, totalling about forty pounds. The chests were then sealed with pitch and sewn into gunny sacks or hides to protect them in transit. Prior to auction or sales, the opium would be judged on factors such as weight, water content, granularity, density, and colour, in ways parallel to a wine taster's judgment on a vintage of Bordeaux.[37]

It was EIC policy to confine its opium business to the production and auctioning of the drug within India, because the Company feared disruption of its relationship with the Chinese government if it were "implicated in the charge of illicit trade."[38] Accordingly, Indiamen were prohibited from carrying opium to China, and the distribution of that cargo was left to the country traders who bought it at the Calcutta auctions, which began in January. When, in 1819, the Company considered increasing the supply of opium which it sold, it dodged any responsibility for increasing the drug's harmful effects in China: "For it is evident that the Chinese, as well as the Malays, cannot exist without the use of opium, and if we do not supply their necessary wants, foreigners will."[39]

Outside the control of the EIC, there was a private industry in opium production on the western side of India, in the Malwa region, which the Company did not govern. Frustrated in its efforts to suppress the competition, the EIC decided, by 1819, to purchase Malwa opium and then auction it either at Calcutta or Bombay, in order to prevent the Malwa from undercutting the prices of EIC Patna and Benares opium, and to regulate the supply of Indian opium headed for China. But the more Malwa that the Company purchased, the more Malwa merchants produced in order to ship some of it on their own accounts.[40] Eventually, the EIC had to be satisfied to collect revenue on the independent producers of Malwa by imposing a "pass duty" on every chest of Malwa that was shipped from Bombay. By the early 1830s, the total quantity of opium reaching China, from Patna, Benares, and Malwa sources, amounted to about seven thousand chests. Trocki observes that opium was by then doing for Asia what tobacco and sugar had done for Europe. "It created a mass market and a new drug culture."[41] The handsome profits of this business were realized in the difference between what the EIC paid the hard-working peasant cultivators of the poppy crop and the prices paid at auction by opium speculators. Once the chests of opium began their journey down the Hooghly, Calcutta's branch of the Ganges River, the EIC washed its collective hands of the drug commerce.[42]

Chests destined for Chinese smugglers contained a quality of opium that was suited to smoking, as opposed to the common Indian practice of chewing opium in its gummy state or the broadly used English form of opium drunk as a tincture in some kind of liquid base. The habit of smoking opium had developed in China at a time when tobacco importation was prohibited. For smoking purposes, opium had to be concentrated into the form of a pea-sized pill, which was heated in the enclosed bowl of an opium pipe until the drug began to vaporize. The reclining smoker would draw deeply through the main tube of the pipe, filling his lungs with the vapours and holding his breath as long as possible before exhaling. Many Chinese used water pipes, like hookahs, which drew the vapours through water or a scented liquid. The effect of the inhaled vapours was immediate, because the lungs assimilated the smoke instantly. An experienced smoker might take three or four pipes (with a new pill each time) in quick succession, which would cause him to fall asleep for an extended period before waking in a calm and languorous condition.[43]

The foreign merchants, marketing chests of opium to smugglers in the Pearl delta, adopted the position that the buyer's use of the drug was not their concern. Since their homelands were accustomed to using opium in mild doses for medicinal purposes, or sometimes in heavy doses prescribed by doctors, they were able to conceive of the drug in terms of its beneficial rather than destructive capacities. It is reasonable to assume, as Trocki does, that many upper-class Chinese used opium, or started using the drug, as a painkiller.[44] Nevertheless, the Chinese government declared that its prohibitions of the drug were intended to interdict its debilitating and addictive effects on the society. Given the illegality of the trade, much of the profit made by Chinese sellers of the drug was acquired by marginal elements of Chinese society – criminals, secret societies, pirates, and smugglers.[45]

In the decades just before the first Opium War, three smuggling networks operated in the region of the Pearl River delta, with operations based at Macao, at the Whampoa anchorage close to Canton, and at Lintin Island, about twenty-five miles south of the Bocca Tigris (the main entrance to the Canton River). By the early 1820s, the primary destination of the opium ships from India was the deep anchorage off the northwest tip of Lintin Island.[46] The opium trade at Whampoa, with the collusion of local officials, had become so visible that between 1819 and 1822 concentrated efforts were made to suppress it. Though more rigorous than earlier efforts, the actions were nevertheless somewhat superficial. However, at the same time, the compradors who supplied the foreign ships with provisions were staging a strike against the increasing fees that they had to pay the mandarins at Whampoa for every ship that they provisioned. They declined to continue provisioning ships arriving at Whampoa, but agreed for the sake of the ships to establish a provisions station at Lintin Island, where ships could purchase food supplies including vegetables and livestock.[47] This action led to the removal of much of the opium trade from Whampoa and the beginnings of Lintin's pre-eminence among the smuggling centres.[48]

By the second decade of the nineteenth century, the smuggling system had become so well organized that foreigners could arrange for opium to be stored in warehouses at Canton, with sales being conducted at the factories.[49] But when much of the opium trade was relocated from Whampoa to Lintin in 1821, the private foreign merchants, led by James Matheson, began stationing their opium-storage vessels at Lintin where the trade prospered.[50] The firms dealing in contraband opium sales would anchor depot ships there as permanent floating warehouses which were regularly resupplied with chests of opium from country traders' vessels. As long as they did not convey the goods ashore, the private merchants could argue that they were not actually engaged in smuggling.

Local mandarins had the authority to make business difficult for the warehouse ships, but they had no navy with which to enforce the law against the well-armed floating hulks of the English merchants; their only enforcement opportunity was to intercept Chinese boats smuggling the chests ashore. However, that threat to the trade was undermined by the susceptibility of the mandarins to "squeeze," bribes by which they were persuaded not to see the illegal traffic. On the other hand, the Hong merchants of Canton were more scrupulous about observing the law, and they let it be known in 1821 that they would not conduct business with any vessel that had chests of opium in its holds. Although not actively opposed to the trade, they would take action when their own safety required it. Accordingly, they specified four vessels by name, and this prompted the initial flight to the outer anchorages. One of the vessels was an American ship, while the other three were country traders consigned to James Matheson, who was storing opium in one of them. When he asked the Company's Select Committee of Supercargoes what he should do, it refused to be tainted by giving him advice about the opium trade. Relatively new to the Canton scene, Matheson was not prepared to defy the Hong merchants, the mandarins, and the Select Committee, and he decided to remove his ships from the river. From that moment in 1821, the greater part of the opium trade was moved toward the outer anchorages, where American, British, and Spanish firms anchored receiving vessels.[51] By the start of the 1830s, there were so many vessels stopping at Lintin that the island's villagers could not supply sufficient provisions to meet the requirements of the ships, and additional provisions had to be sent over from Macao.[52]

With their masts removed and their decks shaded by bamboo roofs or canvas awnings cut from the vessels' sails, the storage ships stocked various kinds of goods and supplies for the operation of the private merchant vessels; but, more dramatically, they also provided a place for silver to be smuggled out of Canton. It had been very risky to smuggle out sycee silver bullion at Canton, once the balance of trade had swung to the advantage of the English. However, after 1821 the export of silver was accomplished much more readily (for a monetary consideration) aboard the depot ships.[53]

The smugglers came up alongside the depot ships in brightly varnished, long, narrow vessels, known as "fast crabs," "scrambling dragons" or "centipedes," armed with cannons, swivel guns, and various small arms. Normally, the mandarin boats made little attempt to bother the business at the receiving ships, but had to lurk in creeks or inlets in order to attack the smugglers before they reached shore.[54] About thirty-five or forty such smuggling vessels were operating in the delta by the start of the 1830s. Paul Van Dyke reckons that "they carried contraband in and out of China with as much regularity as a postal service."[55]

Sales were not actually conducted aboard the depot ships, for the transactions were negotiated at Canton by brokers acting on behalf of the big Chinese wholesalers of opium. In this way, opium deals were realized at the factories in the same way that sales of Chinese teas and silks, Indian cotton, and English manufactured goods were transacted. Accordingly, when Lintin became the hub of the primary opium-smuggling operations, James Matheson was able to return to Canton and conduct his agency business, concentrated in opium, at the English Factory. There he would meet with Chinese brokers who paid immediately in silver. He received a fixed commission (initially 5 per cent, later 3 per cent) on the sale of the opium consigned to him; a delivery order (on a standard form printed at Macao) would be sent by means of a "fast crab" to the captain of a receiving ship. Unpacking, weighing, and repacking the opium of a hundred chests could be accomplished in just a few hours, and the captain of the receiving ship would be paid a cumsha of five dollars per chest. No one of the participants engaged in an opium sale saw the whole transaction through from start to finish.[56]

Matheson and Jardine arrived on the scene at Canton at a time when the spectacular boom in opium sales was the single most dramatic feature of a sweeping reconfiguration of the China trade. After recovering from the difficulties associated with the Napoleonic Wars, the old China trade entered into a period of prolonged crisis, which started in 1818 and lasted into 1827. One factor in the commercial instability was the arrival of newcomers – Matheson and Jardine among them. The result of this influx of ambitious young men was increased competition at Canton, accompanied by excessive inventory, price declines, and a general atmosphere of economic depression.

Another contributing factor was the financial instability of the Hong merchants, several of whom had gone bankrupt. As a result, there were just four Hong merchants trusted by Western businessmen to be financially safe. The great fire of 1822, which destroyed much of Canton, made their problems worse by consuming such a vast amount of property. In addition, market changes at Canton eroded some of the traditional commodities of the old China trade. "Singsongs," for example, were no longer in much demand, partly because Chinese craftsmen had learned to produce inexpensive copies. But it was cotton that worried the English country traders most of all, because sales of Indian cotton began to slide downhill starting in 1819. Until 1823, Indian cotton had been the most important commodity in the country trade; thereafter, opium became the foremost speculation, followed by rice, which went through phases of spectacular but irregular prosperity. The depressed state of the country trade reached its bottom in 1827–28, when the only commodity yielding substantial profits was opium.[57]

At age twenty-six, Matheson was riding the crest of the opium wave in 1822, declining to handle "shopman's goods" and defining the business of Yrissari and Company in terms of opium, cotton, and the remittance of proceeds in silver and bills. He retained the Danish consulship, which gave him protection from the EIC Select Committee at Canton, and he expanded his commercial contacts through the wide-ranging connections of his partner, Xavier Yrissari, who had relatives in Manila and Mexico as well as Calcutta.[58]

Early in 1822, all of the British subjects at Canton left the factories after a party of seamen from the frigate HMS *Topaze* was set upon by angry villagers at Lintin. The first lieutenant of the frigate ordered several shots fired toward shore and landed a force to assist the embattled seamen. Two Chinese were killed and several persons on both sides were wounded, which provoked the viceroy to demand that the "foreign murderers" be handed over for trial and to interdict temporarily all British trade at Canton. At that point, the English Factory's staff and most of its treasure were removed to ships which left the Canton River and anchored at Chuenpi for several weeks. Matheson was among the private British traders who left Canton in the immediate wake of the staff's relocation. Eventually, the *Topaze* sailed away to Macao and thence on to India, with its commander promising to submit the case to his superior officers for trial according to the laws of England. When the viceroy settled for this resolution, the Select Committee and factory staff returned to Canton; but Matheson remained away from the city until the early part of April, likely because of the severe edicts which Chinese officials had issued against the opium ships.[59]

While H.B. Morse's term "the Lintin System" implies that Lintin became the exclusive zone of the drug smugglers, more recent studies have determined that Whampoa remained active in smuggling activities. Local officials, eager to retain some profit from the opium traffic, encouraged smugglers to use the cover of rice shipments as a way of carrying their illegal cargo upriver, hidden in the rice or in other places on the rice ships. In fact, once the major smuggling operations were being conducted from Lintin, the number of rice ships concealing opium as they proceeded upriver toward Canton increased significantly. In fact, some of the rice was smuggled back down the river from Whampoa in order to be "rented" to smugglers who planned to return to Whampoa on rice ships.[60] By 1836–37, the various methods of corrupt officials at Whampoa were having such success that opium was being smuggled openly into Canton with almost casual frequency.[61]

Chinese brokers would purchase their opium chits in Canton at a counting house where they paid in silver. For delivery within a specified number of weeks, they would pay "bargain money" (a nominal deposit), with the balance due at the time when they went aboard the depot ship. All of the dirty work – the bribes paid to local officials, the actual delivery of the drug ashore, and the sales of the opium to individual buyers, including addicts – was managed by the Chinese.[62] Resident merchants handling the sales, such as Matheson and eventually Jardine, charged a commission fee to the owner of the cargo for every chest of opium sold (normally $20).[63] In this way the agency houses were able to profit from the sales without taking the risk of speculating in the cargo. Of course, any fluctuation in the trade would mean a loss of income for the agency house.

The "Lintin System" had taken shape quickly in 1822, with James Matheson being one of the private traders centrally responsible for engineering its design and operation. But William Jardine had yet to arrive on the scene as a permanent resident of Canton. While Jardine was still operating out of Bombay, Matheson was attending to the sale of Jardine's opium speculations, but some time early in 1822 Jardine chose to leave India and take up residence in China, occasionally staying with Matheson.[64]

Jardine's long stay of seventeen years on the China coast started in the late summer or autumn of 1822, when he was thirty-eight. He began managing cargoes assigned to him at Canton by merchants in India, but, without the protection of consular status, he could not maintain a permanent residence in the factory area of Canton, so he would have moved to Macao when the tea-shipping season was over. Most likely he lived at the home of James Matheson during the off-season of 1823,[65] when all the British merchants abandoned Canton because of the ravages of the fire which destroyed the Thirteen Factory area at the start of November 1822.

The blaze had flared up on the night of 1 November, among the flimsy bamboo and matting houses north of the factory area, and by nine o'clock the buildings of the English Factory were engulfed in flames, forcing the staffs of the factories to take refuge in the open ground along the riverfront. The contents of the factory's treasury, amounting to three-quarters of a million dollars, were removed when it was safe to approach the smouldering ruins.[66] Almost immediately the Hong merchants began rebuilding and the foreign factories, properties owned mostly by the Hong merchants, were soon replaced by more substantial and impressive edifices.

William Jardine and James Matheson would have been among the evacuees from the English Factory, since both were doing business at Canton during the tea season of 1822. Through the early months of 1823, while at Macao, Jardine continued to establish himself in the agency business for Indian constituents, and the association with Matheson was valuable for that purpose. During the summer of that year, when one correspondent in Calcutta wished to place all his opium cargo in the care of Yrissari and Company, the firm indicated that it preferred to act in union with Jardine.[67]

However, Yrissari and Company had undertaken a gamble that was excessively ambitious for Jardine at this moment. Matheson's firm had attempted to corner the market in Patna opium, and its inventory was too large. Accordingly, the partners chose to market some of their supply away from the Gulf of Canton, and planned an expedition along the coast in mid-1823. To make a first-hand assessment of the potential market, Matheson sailed, on 1 June 1823, aboard the small brig *St Sebastian*, flying a Spanish flag and under the command of his cousin, John MacKay. The expedition, which lasted for about two months, was not particularly successful, but eventually Matheson was able to sell about $80,000 worth of the drug, and that was enough to keep alive their hopes for a coastal market to reduce the glutted inventory.[68] Two further voyages of the *San Sebastian* proved commercially successful, and, when the *San Sebastian* returned in late January 1824 from its third expedition, it had sold all but one of the chests of opium that it had set out with. For a time, Matheson and Yrissari were inclined to think that the opium trade along the coast would eventually assume such importance that Canton's role as the trade's hub would cease.[69]

For William Jardine, the special opportunity that led to his long-term enterprise in China came in the course of 1824 when a crisis materialized in the firm of Magniac and Company, then the oldest of the private firms situated in the factory district of Canton. Together, the brothers Charles and Hollingworth Magniac had enjoyed the diplomatic status of consul and vice-consul for Prussia. Principal heir of the Cox and Beale enterprises, their firm was conducting agency business for correspondent merchants, and they were engaged in some private trade with their own resources. Hollingworth testified before a committee of the House of Lords at the end of that decade that his own trade at Canton "was principally in opium, almost entirely indeed."[70]

When Charles Magniac fell seriously ill at Canton in 1823, he was advised by the EIC doctor that he should return as soon as possible to England. Hollingworth, who had been sharing the burden of running the business with Charles, was already in England on holiday. Consequently, Charles sought out William Jardine, by then a Canton merchant of proven ability, and asked him to take charge of the Magniac firm until the return of Hollingworth. After Charles's departure for home, in January 1824, Jardine managed operations of the Magniac business until Hollingworth reappeared on the scene in October, whereupon Jardine wound up his interim management and proceeded to India where he closed out his partnership with Framjee Cowasjee, owing to some disagreement between them.[71]

Before winding up his affairs as a Bombay merchant, Jardine made the rounds of the principal Indian correspondents of Magniac and Company. His intention had all along been to return to Canton, and he was back there by August 1825, taking up permanent residence at Creek Hong, the easternmost factory; but even before Jardine's arrival, Hollingworth Magniac had circulated a notice that William Jardine was admitted as a partner of Magniac and Company as of 1 July 1825. Charles Magniac had died early in 1825, not long after returning home to England, and Hollingworth was eager to wrap up his career as a China merchant, after twenty years on the coast, and retire to England.[72] He was sure that he had found a reliable manager for the firm: "You will find Jardine a most conscientious, honourable and kind-hearted fellow, extremely liberal and an excellent man of business in this market, where his knowledge and experience in the opium trade and in most articles of export is highly valuable. He requires to be known to be properly appreciated."[73] The conclusion was a gentle understatement.

For Jardine, the partnership held a prospect of succeeding to full control of Magniac and Company. Hollingworth's intention was to have his

Cantonese wealth remitted to Britain, and Jardine must have seemed a reliable agent to accomplish that. The cordial quality of their relationship was manifested in Jardine's glowing description of Hollingworth: "honest and liberal beyond what we generally meet with, or even expect to meet with in the general intercourse of business transactions."[74] In January 1827, when Hollingworth bade farewell to Canton, William Jardine assumed complete control of Magniac and Company's operations, at the same time deciding to relinquish his share of ownership of the *Sarah*.[75] For the next twelve years the riverfront hongs of Canton would be the centre of his world.

Just before Hollingworth's departure, Jardine recruited an old friend to assist him in the capacity of junior partner. Henry Wright had been purser of the HCS *Glatton*, during Jardine's first two voyages on that ship (1806–10). When Wright arrived at Whampoa in October 1826, as purser of the HCS *Castle Huntly*, Jardine seized the opportunity to enlist him. "Old Wright," as he came to be known in the factory, would remain with Jardine's firm for about sixteen years.[76] According to one report, Wright became so securely ensconced in Creek Hong that he did not leave it for a stretch of seven years, and, upon finally deciding to go out, he discovered that he had no hat.[77]

While Jardine was becoming a principal in the house of Magniac and Company, the firm of Yrissari and Company was prospering at its location in the Imperial Austrian Hong. Orders sent to London suppliers for personal items reveal considerable success in their business ventures. For example, when requesting new coats from Hood and Son, London, James Matheson was very specific about his coat being altered according to the prevailing fashion of the day, with the skirts to be lined with silk rather than cloth. Yrissari's usual wine supplier was Gledstanes, London, from whom it ordered, late in 1824, a pipe of the best Madeira, double its usual quantity of sherry, a quarter pipe of Malmsey, and a variety of French clarets.[78]

Beyond bodily comforts, the needs of the mind were also addressed in Matheson's letters to the London supplier: flute music by Haydn and Mozart and Pleyel; a collection of favourite national airs; prints of Scottish towns; a continuation of *Nolan's Universal Grammar*; and two copies of a new translation of *Don Quixote*. Eager to print commercial circulars (as well as other things), Matheson requested that his London stationer send him a printing press (not to exceed a price of £60), with type that included Portuguese and Spanish accent marks.[79] It arrived safely in the fall of 1825 and within two years was printing the first English-language newssheet in China.

Known as the *Canton Register and Price Current*, the paper devoted much of its space to unembarrassed publication of the current prices of opium at Canton. Initiated in November 1827 by James's nephew, Alexander Matheson (but doubtless founded with his uncle's resources), the *Canton Register* was held up as "objective" news by James but functioned as if it were a house organ for Yrisarri and Company and eventually for Jardine, Matheson.[80] Until the 1820s, information about the China trade was circulated among foreigners by word of mouth, letters, and published journals. Now, for the first time in the operation of the Canton System, all the foreigners could have a clear idea of what everyone else was doing; moreover, the *Register*, and the other newspapers that were soon established, enabled the foreign community to know whether the Chinese authorities were adjusting their stance on smuggling.[81] William W. Wood was the first editor of the *Register*, but he lasted only six issues because of his less-than-delicate criticism of the EIC and the Chinese authorities.[82] In 1834 John Slade became the paper's editor and his editorial policies tended to reflect the thinking of Jardine and Matheson.[83]

Yrissari and Company prospered largely because of its handling of opium for Indian clients and its speculation in sales on its own behalf. With prices holding steady in mid-1825, the firm was expecting to have a total supply of about three and a half thousand chests by later that summer. The prosperous state of the opium market not only led Matheson and Yrissari to encourage their correspondents at Mackintosh and Company to resume operations in the drug in 1825, but also prompted their request that Mackintosh purchase opium to a moderate extent on the account of Yrissari and Company.[84] The stability and prosperity of their partnership allowed them to plan holiday leaves.

Xavier Yrissari left Canton on the *Snipe* just after the start of the New Year in 1826. He passed through Singapore and proceeded to India, with the intention of returning toward the end of the year so Matheson could take his own holiday. But his plans were never fulfilled, for he died at Calcutta on the last day of September.[85] It may be that his visit to Calcutta was linked to the shaky condition of Mendietta, Uriarte and Company, a firm in which he held a quarter-share, worth about $40,000, and that the stress of trying to salvage his investment contributed to his sudden death.[86]

For the second time in six years, Matheson was left with the remains of a partnership broken by the sudden death of his associate. However, he was financially secure this time, in contrast to his position at the time of Robert Taylor's death. The news of Xavier Yrissari's death did not reach James Matheson until early January 1827, at which point he had already made plans to travel to Bengal.

Xavier Yrissari had left two wills (the earlier made out at Calcutta, the later at Canton), with Matheson listed in both wills as the executor of his estate in China. Matheson began notifying clients that Yrissari's interests in the firm would be closed out as of 30 April, and he continued to make preparations for his Bengal trip while entrusting his business affairs to William Jardine, whom he referred to in correspondence as "my old & intimate friend." In its day-to-day operations, Yrissari and Company was being managed by James's two assistants, his nephew Alexander Matheson, and Yrissari's nephew, Jacquin Ybar.[87]

Overseeing the two young clerks, Jardine had overall responsibility for the firm's affairs in Matheson's absence, which was anticipated to last three or four months. No longer a simple holiday from Canton, the journey took on the character of a business trip to begin winding up Yrissari's commercial affairs. Before embarking, Matheson transferred, in four instalments, a total of $90,000 to his account with Magniac and Company, so that his funds might be secure in Jardine's keeping and not subject to claims against Yrissari's estate.[88] By the time he reached Calcutta, Mendietta, Uriarte and Company had collapsed, and it remained for him to protect the interests of Yrissari and Company against the demands of the failed firm.

The $40,000 of Yrissari's share in the collapsed Calcautta house was never recovered. However, the size of his assets at Canton was declared to be $17,000 – a very small sum, which Matheson explained bluntly, in a letter to Xavier's mother and sister, in Spain; he declared that Xavier had put no start-up funds into the partnership, except for his share of the property gained – minus the expenses of "liberal living" over the term of their association.[89] Matheson benefited more appreciably from the dissolution of the partnership, when his own account in the firm was closed out. He was able to remit to India, on his own account, $250,000, presumably his portion of the assets of the defunct partnership.

One dilemma Matheson moved quickly to resolve was the disposition of Yrisarri's premises at Factory Number 7 of the Imperial Austrian Hong on the Canton waterfront. Apparently, the partners had made significant improvements in the property (newly built after the big fire of 1822), and Matheson was not ready to write off that expense; instead, he proposed having the value of the improvements established by a neutral assessor. He offered the remainder of the lease (six years) to Magniac and Company (in effect, to Jardine), but even between "old and intimate friends" his business instinct required that assets, such as physical improvements to leased property, be carefully gathered in prior to the termination of Yrissari and Company.[90]

On the ashes of his old partnership, he had launched a new venture, calling the firm Matheson and Company in his circular announcements of September 1827. But he was acutely aware of his isolation as a single entrepreneur in an environment of well-established competitors, of whom the principal British houses were Magniac's and Dent's. Before leaving for India, he had made an inquiry about joining the firm of Dent and Company; however, he was turned down. It may be that he had never intended to join Dent's but had made the proposal to satisfy his Calcutta correspondents at Mackintosh and Company, who were associated with Dent's through their London house. The rejection left him free to move in any direction he chose, which had likely always been to seek association with Jardine.[91] He was, therefore, very receptive to Jardine's offer of a partnership in the house of Magniac, and so the firm of Matheson and Company proved to be but a shooting star in the fall of 1827.[92]

Manifestly confident that he had made a solid new beginning, within a few weeks of entering the firm of Magniac and Company he began preparing for a new trip to Bombay and Calcutta aboard his own swift barque, the *Jamesina*.[93] Although the partnership of Jardine and Matheson began at this point in time, the Magniac name continued to identify the firm because that family's interests had not yet been taken over by the new partners. The youngest brother, Daniel Magniac, remained a shareholder at Canton, while his brother Hollingworth continued as a sleeping partner until 1832.[94]

Matheson brought monetary resources, amounting to $60,000, and Yrissari's Spanish connections into the partnership; Jardine brought the experience of running an established, major agency house. Jardine was now forty-four years old and had been resident in China since 1822. Matheson, just past his thirty-second birthday, had been on the coast since 1820. The personal relationship of the two partners provided much of the formula for a successful partnership. Matheson, although the more intellectual of the two, generally deferred to Jardine's greater experience and sound business judgment. On the other hand, in the absence of any British-trained lawyers at Canton – the nearest being at Calcutta – Matheson was relied on for legal advice by members of the English Factory community. Their agency business was generally directed toward buying and selling for others on commission, but they would occasionally undertake "handsome adventures" in opium, rice, and silk with their own resources.[95]

One of Matheson's principles of business practice, articulated in a letter during his partnership with Yrissari, involved transparency and openness between associates. When the correspondent tried to keep an issue secret from Yrissari, Matheson remarked: "For my own part I disapprove of reserve in business matters there being nothing so conducive to a good understanding as the most perfect frankness and the free disclosure of even disagreeable truths."[96] This kind of open communication came to be one of the hallmarks of the relationship between William Jardine and James Matheson for all the years of their business association.

Where business ventures were concerned, Matheson was the bolder of the two men, Jardine the more conservative. To avoid disappointments resulting from funds lying unused in a trading season, owing to an apparent lack of opportunities in a specific field of trade, Matheson was willing "to stretch a point" and exceed a constituent's instructions. "Any expedient by which you can prevent disappointment to a constituent will generally be acceptable to him."[97] Both men had the capacity to be frank, even sharply frank, with clients, staff members, and dealers with whom they transacted buying and selling. Among those who might hear the honest communication of the partners' displeasure were relatives who were brought out to China on the condition that they work industriously. Both Jardine and Matheson were generous with their nephews, taking them into the firm and providing them with the opportunity to spend an indefinite length of time in China learning the methods of Eastern trade and accumulating some wealth. With the advocates of free trade on the brink of success in Parliament, it was becoming clearer that the East India Company's monopoly at Canton was soon likely to vanish, with a resulting boom in trade opportunities for private merchants. Well-positioned young men, such as Jardine's and Matheson's nephews, could gain great advantages from the predictable end of the EIC monopoly – if they passed muster with the uncles.

Jardine stood ready to provide monetary assistance to the extended family at home in Scotland, but he wanted Andrew Johnstone to let the circle of young cousins understand his distinction between genuine need and laziness. "You are aware I have a strong objection to extravagance & idleness; and I trust you might impress this on the minds of your young cousins – I never can consent to assist idle and dissipated characters, however nearly connected with me, but am prepared to go to any reasonable extent in supporting such of my relations as conduct themselves prudently and industriously."[98] James's nephews, Hugh and Alexander Matheson, joined their uncle at Yrissari and Company in the mid-1820s and followed the family business interests to the point of being founding partners in Matheson and Company at London in 1848. William's nephews, Andrew Johnstone and Andrew Jardine, both joined their prominent uncle at Canton in the first half of the 1830s. Other members of the two Scottish families became associated with the various Jardine and Matheson enterprises in the early years of the budding commercial empire.

Neither partner had children of his own to train in the ways of business. Matheson remained a bachelor until he returned to Britain in the 1840s, and Jardine never married.[99] In this respect, they were not unusual in their circle: at Canton, since foreign merchants were prohibited from having their wives live with them, the senior partners in most firms were not married. For their part, William Jardine and James Matheson had both left Britain early in life and had devoted their careers in China to developing their businesses. Neither went home to Britain with any frequency, and their opportunities for making the acquaintance of marriageable young women of their own social class were very limited.[100]

Although the Select Committee denied that concubinage existed among the English, it was in fact a common practice for foreign merchants at Canton to have mistresses and pensioners at Macao; but prevailing custom among the English merchant class there virtually forbade formalizing such relationships by marriage. Social and economic factors combined to establish this code – both the elevation of Asian or half-caste women to formal social equality within British circles, and the issue of inheritance for children of such unions, who might stand to take over the businesses of their fathers. Provisions were made for the pensioners and their children when the British fathers left China. Jardine and Matheson held powers of attorney for various kinds of businesses, including personal matters, and they were in many instances the local executors for wills. Frequently, trust funds were left for them to administer in order to maintain the pensioner women and their children in decent comfort and security for the rest of their years.[101]

Being at the forefront of British merchants at Canton and Macao, Matheson and Jardine were repeatedly looked to for help in relieving the distress of persons associated with the British community. And they were sensitive to the matters of economic justice for those women who were used and then left behind.[102] Matheson was willing to help offset the effects of inflation on the pensions of women abandoned by British men; he pledged company funds to underwrite the upgraded pensions of two women in Madras who were provided for by Captain Hugh MacKay of the 4th Cavalry, killed in combat in India.[103] Similar solicitude marked Jardine's response to the distressed circumstances of a stranded English widow. Although he regarded her late husband as being guilty of "reprehensible" business conduct, Jardine initiated a subscription fund for her among the English at Canton and Macao, to enable her to book passage to Singapore (where her sister lived) or to England, with provision of one or two hundred pounds for her, should she elect to proceed home.[104]

Daniel Magniac, youngest of the three brothers in the firm, had stayed on at Creek Hong as the remaining resident Magniac partner after Hollingworth retired home to London, but Daniel had a mistress at Macao, probably a Portuguese-Asian woman, by whom he had fathered two children. He defied convention by marrying her, and for that "scandal" he was forced by his brother to retire from the firm in 1827, with a severance gratuity. (His son, Daniel Francis, was to have been educated at Calcutta by arrangements provided by Hollingworth Magniac. But Jardine and Matheson deemed the boy's health too delicate for Calcutta and sent him to live with Alexander Matheson's mother at Inverness, where he was enrolled in the Academy.)[105] It was Daniel's forced retirement that left Jardine completely in charge of the firm's operations until Matheson was invited to join the partnership.[106]

James Matheson also kept a mistress, but he was much more discreet about that aspect of his personal life and her existence is veiled in mystery. Known generally by her Chinese name, Ayow, she was also called

Roza Maria Xavier, from which it may be presumed that her heritage was partly Spanish or Portuguese. The first mention of her seems to be in a letter of November 1825, but there is no solid evidence detailing when the relationship began or how long it lasted.

Nothing in the firm's records suggests that William Jardine had any similar long-lasting relationship with a local woman during his years in China. However, extended correspondence in the Jardine, Matheson letter books suggests that before going out to China he may have had a liaison with a woman named Mrs Ratcliffe who lived in Kent.[107] Their private correspondence is not available, and perhaps was not preserved. Mrs Ratcliffe, who was unmarried (or perhaps widowed early), had a daughter named Matilda Jane, and the extent of William Jardine's provision for this child suggests that he may have been her father.

Directions from Jardine to his nephew Andrew Johnstone (then in Britain) and to Thomas Weeding, his London agent, provide for payments to Mrs Ratcliffe on a regular basis. Weeding was authorized to increase her allowances as he saw fit, for Jardine wished her to have "every necessity and every reasonable comfort" – but none of the "unbecoming luxuries." There was an element of bitterness evident in his instructions to Weeding, for the lady's sisters had apparently behaved so badly toward her as to forfeit any claim for her aid through his money. He was convinced that some of the money he had been forwarding to her had been ill-spent, but he was willing to overlook that and wished for her to take care of her mother and father, as long as none of the money went to benefit her sisters.[108] Selection of a proper school for the girl was entrusted to Captain John Hine of HCS *Atlas*. Jardine instructed Hine that the education of the child should be a "useful education … suited to her situation in life – not a fashionable one."[109]

By 1834, Mrs Ratcliffe had received a proposal of marriage, to which Jardine gave his approval. He recommended that Weeding arrange a settlement for her daughter, to be made *previous to the marriage*. Writing to Mrs Ratcliffe in care of Weeding, he acknowledged her letters to him and extended his "full consent" to the marriage. He also sent Weeding the following instruction: if Mrs Ratcliffe had waited for his consent, he should make her a marriage present of £20.[110]

After her marriage, Mrs Ratcliffe faded from the correspondence, but concern for the well-being of "Tilly" (Matilda Jane) continued. By the late 1830s, when she wrote to him complaining of hardships, she would likely have been in her late teen years or perhaps twenty. Apparently her stepfather had fallen upon hard times and lost all his property. "No doubt she exaggerates their sufferings," Jardine told Weeding, "but we have sent her in the enclosed letter an order on you for Ten pounds, £10."[111] He had evidently made, or would make before his death, much more elaborate provision for Tilly's security, for in 1854 she wrote to Jardine, Matheson, Hong Kong, from her residence at Mile's End, London, explaining that her circumstances necessitated that she draw upon her principal, and requested that they remit to her £100 drawn from her account.[112]

The nature of Jardine's relationship to Tilly and her mother cannot be known with full confidence in the absence of the private letters between them, but Alan Reid's guess that Mrs Ratcliffe was Jardine's mistress at some time in his pre-China years seems a strong possibility for explaining his protective – even possessive – relationship toward them.[113]

In a certain sense, both William Jardine and James Matheson *were* married during their China years – *to their jobs*, in their offices at the factory at Creek Hong. They were hard working, often being at their desks deep into the night, and the firm prospered from their industry. The associates at Creek Hong, as recorded in the *Chronicles of the East India Company* for March 1829, were William Jardine, James Matheson, Francis Hollingworth (a cousin of Hollingworth), Alexander Matheson, Henry Wright, and Thomas Chay Beale. In this veritable genealogical summary of the firm's evolution, the Jardine standard of industry was obligatory, which is why young Francis Hollingworth soon found himself dismissed, with a generous severance allowance.

Having established themselves in the 1820s at Canton, where they developed networks of business contacts and clients in India and Britain, and now being positioned as the principal partners in the most prominent of the private English firms in China, William Jardine and James Matheson were prepared to capitalize on their experience, their business savvy, and their financial resources. They still had the Prussian flag which they had inherited from the Magniacs; but it would soon have diminished importance, once the free-trade forces in Parliament broke the East India Company monopoly. In the competition of free-trade rivals, their own skills would count for more than diplomatic privilege. In Maurice Collis's assessment, "they were the ablest men in the opium trade and, united in one firm, built up a selling organization far more efficient than any other."[114]

At the end of 1830, the private English merchants at Canton sent a petition to the House of Commons asking for relief from the "humiliating condition of British subjects, in common with other foreigners in China," caused by corrupt Chinese authorities at Canton. In forwarding the memorial to Westminster, the Select Committee appended a note that the document "bears the signature of nearly every respectable British subject in China unconnected with the [EIC] Factory." At the head of the names were the signatures of William Jardine and James Matheson, now the most prominent of private English merchants in China.[115]

# DOING BUSINESS AT CREEK HONG

In William Jardine's office at Factory Number 6, Creek Hong, there was but one chair – his. He had no use for idle chatter that would while away his precious work time, and his gospel of industry was proclaimed wordlessly by having callers stand while they transacted their business with him. In a similar no-nonsense way, his reputation in Canton was enhanced by an incident that occurred one day when he went to the city gate where foreigners were permitted to submit requests to the mandarin officials who governed the city. There he was struck on the head by a piece of lumber wielded by an unknown local who was apparently contemptuous of the "foreign devil." Jardine did not even bother to shrug off the blow, but simply continued on his way, disregarding the offence. For that he came to be known locally as the "Iron-headed Rat," an expression of regard for his toughness rather than a term of derision. Stories about the one chair and the blow on the head took on the character of legend among the Chinese and the foreign merchant community at Canton, but Jardine was far from a colourful eccentric. Indeed, his words were carefully measured and temperate, his financial skills were highly respected, and his reputation as a shrewd yet honest businessman was broadly recognized.

Matheson was a more outspoken man and more articulate in expressing opinion. He was also more inclined than Jardine to show sharp annoyance. While not flamboyant, he was more stylish than Jardine, which is understandable in view of the differences between their families' economic backgrounds. Matheson was more inclined to travel, whereas Jardine was more inclined to stay put in Canton and Macao. Moreover, Matheson was the greater risk taker of the two men. His work habits were sound even before he became Jardine's partner; but once they came together as the principals of Magniac and Company, the older man's discipline seemed to shape Matheson's approach to his work. After two years of their partnership, Jardine wrote to a friend in Britain: "I have been in better health for many months than I have been for years before, in defiance of hard work & late hours. Matheson has, from necessity I believe, fallen into my plan; and is very generally in the Office till past midnight; but he also enjoys good health; & we have quite enough to do to keep the business of the House up, which has increased a good deal since you were in the Celestial Empire."[1]

Late work at their waterfront office was a routine for the partners, as their correspondence occasionally revealed. William Jardine: "We are all tolerably well here; but sadly fagged. Matheson almost knocked up ... Young Jardine [nephew] quite well, and old Jardine [William himself] laboring under a severe Cold and Sore Throat – fitter for his bed than the office at ¼ past 1 o'clock."[2] James Matheson: "I am writing at 2 a.m. preparatory to starting a short excursion to Bombay."[3]

John Fairbank observes that the successful Canton agent was marked by "imagination, assiduity, and an eagle eye for profit and loss," and he finds all these features in James Matheson. For instance, after studying the Chinese buyers' tastes, Matheson reported that blue bandanas "with weaving white lines sell for considerably more than if marked with round white spots."[4] Commercial intelligence of that sort enabled distant clients to avoid futile shipments of unsaleable commodities.

Among the factory community of Canton, Jardine and Matheson became twin models of personal industry and carefully measured business judgment. Critically important to the success of their partnership was the element of trust between them. While Matheson was in Singapore in the spring of 1830, the partners were considering a loan of $20,000 to a client there. Jardine wrote to him: "Do as you please and I shall be satisfied."[5] Their combined energies were directed toward termination of John Company's monopoly, prying open the Chinese market to international trade, and establishing Magniac's dominance over competitors. Those three elements of Jardine's and Matheson's overall strategy were necessarily linked one to the other, but new commercial opportunity would be limited if China continued to deny foreign enterprise access to the major harbours along the coast.

Their standards of business conduct were shaped by a clearly conceived code of commercial and personal integrity. While the enterprise of opium trading could, and did, raise eyebrows and prompt moral criticism both in China and at home in Britain, there was in their own minds a propriety in business affairs that was more than a matter of good manners, and they endeavoured to adhere to the standard. Anticipating the possibility that the EIC's monopoly over the tea trade might be terminated, Jardine wrote to a London constituent that private merchants would be able to procure black and green teas from Hong merchants in quantities proportional to the particular foreign merchant's role in the tea trade – "always supposing them to be honest, reasonable, just, and honorable in all their mercantile transactions."[6] Jardine could be hard-nosed in his approach to certain business situations, but to call him ruthless, as Basil Lubbock does, is inaccurate in regard to both character and practice.[7] While he was shrewd at commercial strategy, Jardine was critical of conduct that seemed to him too crudely conniving.

In his own estimation, the "most gentlemanlike speculation" available was careful investment in the opium market. That was the substance of his advice to a young client in Essex. "The safest, and most Gentlemanlike speculation that I am aware of is this. Buy good bills on Calcutta or Bombay … Send the bills on to India to be realized, and the proceeds invested in the drug under such limits as may be advised from hence, which drug send here, to be made the most of, and the proceeds to be invested home, as directed, in Raw Silk, Nankeens, Sycee, or even broken coin."[8] To Jardine, this was a sensible business venture – untainted by anything slippery, and profitable if handled with discretionary power by experienced agents. In spite of prohibitions by the Chinese government, Jardine did not regard the opium sector of his agency business as a black-market operation run by shady figures; rather, he saw it as a sound commercial opportunity, pursued through normal business procedures (marketing, financing, accounting, shipping, quality control, etc.) in defiance of the official Chinese resistance. The ready cash of the buyers, the extent of demand, the complicity of local officials in the illegal trade – all these convinced him and Matheson that the formal position of the imperial government did not represent the actual wishes of the Chinese people. It seems, from their correspondence, writings, and behaviour that they reached the conclusion that they had a sound basis for evading the Chinese decrees against the drug, and this did not intrude upon their sense of honest business practice. Moreover, they were philosophically attached to the concept that free trade is the natural law of commerce, and that government-awarded monopolies and government-imposed obstructions to the free movement of commercial traffic were unreasonable intrusions upon the proper functioning of that natural law. In this respect, Matheson was the theorist, following the lead of Adam Smith.

Their sense of obligation extended to the point of scrupulous honesty in transactions, but not to the point of respecting unwarranted regulation of their business opportunities. Their resentment of the Chinese government's refusal to legalize or ignore the opium trade was aggravated by their feeling that the community of foreign merchants at Canton was treated abusively by the officials of municipal and provincial government.

In pronounced ways, Jardine's and Matheson's commonly held ideas of personal responsibility were manifested in their concern for the well-being of their blood relatives and close friends at home in Britain. Since neither of the principals in the firm was married, they imported nephews from Scotland to become their lieutenants in the agency business. In part this was a way of securing the services of trusted family members, and in part it was a form of avuncular patronage. Simultaneously, the partners were generous with their money in underwriting the economic well-being of branches of their families which were not independently secure.

Nephews from the Highlands and the Lowlands made their way out to China, some for a few years, some for a longer stretch. Among the Matheson nephews, the most prominent were Alexander Matheson, the son of James's sister Margaret, who had married John Matheson of Attadale, and Hugh and Donald Matheson, the children of James's older brother Duncan, who was an advocate in Leith. After Yrissari's death, Alexander managed his uncle's business in Canton, in combination with Yrissari's nephew, and remained with his uncle when James became a partner in Magniac's in 1828; eventually he became a junior partner in Jardine, Matheson as of 1835, and succeeded James Matheson as head of the firm when James returned to England in 1842. Donald Matheson went out to China with his uncle in 1835, as James was returning from a visit to England. The young man would in time come to manage Jardine, Matheson affairs at Hong Kong, but his discomfort with the opium trade eventually caused him to leave his role in the firm's operations. Decades later, he inherited his uncle's properties in northwest Scotland when Lady Matheson died.

Much more directly involved in the clandestine opium trade than most of the nephews was a cousin of James Matheson, named John MacKay, who commanded the *San Sebastian* during James's opium-selling voyage along the coast of China in 1823. In later years John MacKay would be captain of the brig *Laetitia*, which served as one of the depot ships at Lintin.[9]

Beyond James's compassionate concern for the immediate relief of friends in economic distress and widows of deceased friends, there was the occasional kindness of a box of teas (with duties paid) for many of the folks at home in Scotland. But there was also more systematic plan-ning for the security of his relatives in Scotland. He set aside a substan-tial amount of money (invested in opium for lack of a better opportunity to earn interest with security) as a fund for the support of his mother and sisters. And in 1833 he sent home bills amounting to £3,500 as a family fund to be managed by his brother Duncan.[10]

The Jardine clan began with thinner economic resources than the Mathesons and for that reason William Jardine seemed to be more fre-quently conscious of the need to send home some funds for one or an-other of the branches of the kin in southern Scotland. When his brother David died in 1828, William arranged for the security of David's family in Muirhousehead. He sent funds in care of Andrew Johnstone, his sister's son; further sums would be available as needed, he promised. Andrew Johnstone was Jean (Jardine) Johnstone's first boy and of all the neph-ews he was the closest to his uncle. Just fourteen years younger than William, he was but two years junior to James Matheson. In William's absence of nearly twenty years from Scotland, he trusted Andrew as a reliable agent for family affairs. The young man followed his uncle into EIC medical service (until 1831) and eventually took up residence at Canton in 1833. He became a partner in the firm in 1835; he was, how-ever, not as durable in the China trade as his uncle, and left Macao in 1836, after just fourteen months as a partner on site.

David Jardine's eldest boy, Andrew – who came to be called "young Jardine" to distinguish him from his uncle – was the oldest of Johnstone's cousins to go out to the East. Through Johnstone, William provided for the education of his nephews at Muirhousehead, and Andrew was the first of those boys to join the firm. "I have taken charge of [him]," William wrote to one of the nephews' neighbours, James Stewart. "He will no longer be a burthen to his Mother, and may ... make over his share of the family property to his Brothers and Sisters."[11] The long-remembered charity of his brother could now be repaid. "The small sum due me from my Mother's property I have always considered as belonging to my Brother [David] – he having supplied me with money when I had very little or none of my own – and I should prefer paying the sums due to [my brother-in-law James and my sister Elizabeth] myself, to having any deductions made from my Brother's family."[12] He told James Stewart that he continued to be anxious about them, since they were "left less comfortable than their other relations." He thought that it might be best for him to set up an annuity for the mother, which would provide for the boys' education "to allow them to get on in the world, at home or abroad."[13] To that end, William directed Andrew Johnstone to arrange that James and Elizabeth receive their portions of David's estate from funds that he would provide. In this way David's widow, Rachel, and their six children could receive the long-accumulated dividends of David's help to William when William was a medical student at Edinburgh.[14]

Apart from money, boxes of teas, with duties paid, were the easiest thing for Jardine to send from Canton to relatives and friends in Britain, and he did so liberally. There is no evidence to suggest that he ever sent them opium, in spite of its common use in Britain as an all-purpose analgesic. The trouble of taking it to a chemist for processing probably discounted its appeal as a gift, and it was likely that neither of the partners wanted to be known among their Scottish friends and neighbours for their largesse with such a commodity. In fact, little Indian opium made its way to Britain, that market being supplied largely from Turkey.

The pattern of protecting the kin reveals a strong residue of clan consciousness well after the time when English policies had attempted to break down the fibres of the clan system. Both Jardine and Matheson would spend more time in London than in Scotland in the years just after their retirements from China, but, as their shared sense of family responsibilities demonstrated repeatedly, their identities remained Scottish.

In the long run, the firm's future would lie with the collateral descendants of William Jardine. Andrew Johnstone's younger sister Margaret married into the Keswick family, and their heirs came to be the foremost ongoing presence of the Jardine family in Jardine, Matheson enterprises in the twenty-first century. The separate firm of Matheson and Company, established on the ashes of Magniac Jardine in 1848, would include the Matheson nephews and their descendants until the beginning of the twentieth century.[15] By the late 1820s, both Jardine and

Matheson were intent on remaining in China for an extended period of time while they built up their agency business. So their interests in the well-being of their relatives in Scotland were necessarily long-distance concerns that had to be addressed by people closer to home, and their practice of taking in nephews was a strategy to maintain control of the firm within their two families.

In day-to-day operations, the working capital of the firm was adequate for its needs because, as an agency house, they operated on the capital of their correspondent merchants who shipped goods to China. Rather than withdrawing his share of the capital, Hollingworth Magniac had retained his financial interest in his family's company, which meant that Jardine and Matheson were financially secure when they became the principal managing partners in 1828.[16] The primary activity of their agency house was buying and selling for correspondents on commission. A schedule of commission rates was established among the Canton agency houses in 1825 and it was confirmed in 1831. For example, 3 per cent was charged for sales of opium and cotton and a few other commodities, 5 per cent on most other goods, 2 ½ per cent on chartering ships, 5 per cent for obtaining outward freight, 1 per cent for negotiating bills of exchange, and 2 ½ per cent to guarantee bills, bonds, or other engagements. In practice, some of the agency houses undercut the rates regularly, and even the most respectable firms, such as Magniac's, made special concessions to correspondents with whom they had very close working relationships, such as Jamsetjee Jejeebhoy and Sons (Bombay).[17] Profits were divided among the partners each year, but usually they were reinvested in the firm, with each partner keeping a separate capital account. When they chose to speculate on their own account in opium and rice and silk, then Jardine and Matheson had to risk their own capital on the "adventures," as they called them.

The prospect of a more crowded field of competitors in the opium trade at Canton meant that the partners at Magniac's needed to consider using alternate sites for marketing the drug, dealing regularly in various other commodities to avoid exclusive reliance on opium, and engaging in other types of commercial activity. Their principal competitors at Canton were the English firm of Dent and Company and the American firm of Russell and Company. Relations with Dent were embittered from 1830 and remained so throughout the period of Jardine's and Matheson's careers in China. According to James Matheson, the bitterness began with a dispute about correspondence addressed to Dent and carried from Calcutta aboard one of Jardine's clippers. A letter that would have given Dent information about the failure of its Calcutta agents at Palmer and Company was allegedly withheld from Dent, who suffered a serious financial loss as a result of the failure and the lack of timely notice.[18]

According to James Matheson, the letters in question were aboard the barque *Jamesina*, on her experimental voyage in 1830, being towed from India to China by the steam towboat *Forbes*. Letters aboard the *Jamesina* were late in being delivered, because the steamer and the barque were separated on account of an inadequate supply of coal for the steamer. No one had anticipated that one ship might arrive at Canton before the other, but the steamer *Forbes* actually arrived two days before the *Jamesina*. Matheson asserted that Dent was upset because he did not receive his letters by way of the steamer, but he never approached Jardine to ask for an explanation. His principal complaint was that Jardine had not informed him of the failure of Palmer and Company, Calcutta, when early knowledge might have spared Dent some losses. Matheson insisted that Dent's agent in Calcutta had not applied for the right to have their letters carried by the steamer, that *Jamesina* carried letters only for consignees of opium shipped in her, and that the understanding was they be delivered in due course.[19] John Fairbank suggests that the bitter rivalry of the two houses, "which enlivened two generations of life on the China coast," reflected a pattern already established elsewhere in British commerce, because the Indian correspondent firms with which they had close ties were already bitter rivals (Fairlie and Company connected with Magniac's; Palmer and Company tied to Dent's).[20]

One of the firm's many enterprises was an insurance business actually shared with Dent's on a schedule of alternating years. The First Canton Insurance Office had been established by Reid and Beale in 1805, and its management alternated every three years between the partners of that firm or its successors and the houses that preceded Dent's. A complete settlement of the insurance firm's resources was made each time the management changed, and the company started up anew as the Second Canton Insurance Office, or the Third, or Fourth. Finally, after the Tenth Office was wound up in 1836, the Canton Insurance Office was permanently established as a subsidiary of Jardine, Matheson.[21] Thereafter,

Jardine's Canton Insurance Company and Dent's Union Insurance Company would run competing advertisements on the front page of the *Canton Register,* separated sometimes only by a victualler's promotion of beer, hams, and raisins.

For merchants risking the transport of rich cargoes, whether opium or silk or silver, against the dangers of violent seas and the threat of piracy, insurance was an essential cost of doing business. Having losses payable in China or in India was a huge convenience, which led to the establishment of the successive Canton Insurance companies and the close relationships between Calcutta houses and the Canton office. Upon re-establishment every three years, the Canton office normally had sixty shares, which were eagerly sought by prominent merchants in Canton and Calcutta and Bombay, for no cash deposit was required from the participants in the insurance plan, and the profits of the company generally yielded a dividend of $3,000 to $4,000 per share. As of 1829, Magniac and Company was acting as agent for at least six insurance companies. So profitable was the insurance business that James Matheson began his own private underwriting account in 1829. "J.M. and Friends" issued thirty-six shares, of which Magniac's held twenty, with an annual profit of about $1,000 per share being realized for each share.

Banking was yet another source of profit for Magniac's under the Scottish partners. In the absence of European banks at Canton, the foreign merchants there had to provide the necessary credit arrangements for distant commercial transactions. Lending was done, normally at 1 per cent per month, in the form of bills of exchange drawn on the lenders themselves or on their London agents. Moreover, Magniac's, like the other major agency houses, provided many of the services offered by modern banks, such as letters or credits to travellers, trustee and executor services, short-term loans to persons associated with the English Factory or the EIC, and investment brokering. One technique the company employed to take advantage of the shortage of capital at Canton in the 1820s was to accept monies from India on deposit, for which it paid rates as high as 10 and 12 per cent annually, while using those funds to make loans to the Hong merchants at even higher rates.[22]

The great expansion of the country trade during the 1820s created a problem in remitting funds to India and London. The solution that Magniac's adopted in the second half of that decade was to remit funds by means of American bills drawn on London banking houses, most notably Baring Brothers. By the end of the decade, a panic had swamped some of the major agency houses in India. When James Matheson went to Calcutta in the spring of 1830, he saw first-hand the early stages of the financial disaster.

After the rechartering of the EIC in 1813, the private agency houses in Bengal fell to alluring temptations of speculation in Indian exports, most particularly indigo, and the volume of money was abundant as their trade ballooned. They were able to borrow money at low rates and invest it recklessly in indigo enterprises. But the tremendous cost of the first Anglo-Burmese War (1824–26) caused the money market to contract severely; money became scarce at the same time that indigo prices were dropping and the major agency houses found themselves in jeopardy.[23] Palmer and Company, "the indigo king of Bengal," closed its doors in the first week of 1830. Scott and Company failed in January 1832, with Alexander and Company following suit at the end of the year.[24]

By early 1833, Mackintosh and Company – Matheson's first employer – had failed, bringing the financial panic in Bengal to full-flood stage; and by 1834 all of the major agency houses at Calcutta had also collapsed. The crash brought down houses with a total debt structure of about £15,000,000, and there were various explanations for the disaster. Matheson blamed it principally on the rash speculation in indigo, "that most treacherous of articles,"[25] whereas a writer for *The Times* attributed the crash to the greed of partners in the various Calcutta firms who would spend a few years in India enriching themselves and then retire home to England, leaving the affairs of their houses in disarray. But there were other issues, including intense competition resulting from the large number of new agency houses at Calcutta, and the Indian government's establishment of a bank of deposit which threatened to draw depositors away from the agency houses.[26]

Given the extent of the ties between Canton and Calcutta agency houses, the financial earthquake in India sent tremors through the waterfront establishments in Canton. Dent and Company suffered serious damage from the collapse of Palmer and Company. But Jardine and Matheson escaped fairly lightly because they had advanced warning of the downfall of the Calcutta firms and protected themselves by dividing their risk through adoption of the system of using American bills. When Fairlie and Company went down in 1833, Jardine and Matheson lost about £22,000 "which is getting off lightly – under the circumstances," Matheson thought. Their ability to sustain a loss of that sort and regard it as light reveals the solidity of their firm and the strength of their name. As the distress in Calcutta intensified, Hollingworth Magniac came out of retirement to support his old partnership and secured the protection of a powerful London financier, Timothy Wiggins, for the bills of Jardine, Matheson (as the firm had been called since 1832). As a result, friends of the partners informed them that their standing on the Royal Exchange was not only unimpaired but actually higher than ever.[27]

As a way to bypass India in remitting funds to London, Jardine and Matheson (while still using the title Magniac and Company) had come to rely initially on bills drawn by the Bank of the United States and soon thereafter on bills of John Jacob Astor of New York or Stephen Girard of Philadelphia. Matheson was of the opinion that bills of the Bank of the United States ought to sell as well as bills of the East India Company, because their security was better.[28] (The irony here was that Matheson – probably uninformed of American politics – must have been unaware that President Andrew Jackson, if re-elected in 1832, intended to destroy the Second Bank of the United States.)

Matheson wrote to his nephew Hugh, in Calcutta, that it was likely "that three-quarters of all the exchange business of Canton have passed through our hands this season." The firm's strategy was to diversify their acquisition of bills: "We think that we afford a stronger guarantee against the hazards by distributing the risk which is inseparable from doing business, among a number of good Houses, whose bills we purchase and pay for, rather than by relying on any single house.[29] However, when it came to the reliability of their own firm's name, Jardine and Matheson were determined that their endorsement be recognized as solid: "We never endorse any bills except such as we are morally certain will be duly honored."[30]

In 1831 Jardine and Matheson (still operating as Magniac and Company) notified Bombay firms that "it is generally in our power to remit funds to England on more advantageous terms than can be effected in Bombay."[31] Thereafter the strategy adopted by Bombay merchants was to send large quantitites of Malwa opium to China so that the proceeds of sales could be sent to London through the medium of American bills. Not only was the system profitable to all concerned in the China trade, but it also gave agency merchants a degree of financial independence from the EIC's rate for bills of exchange on London.[32] These transactions through American bills helped Jardine and Matheson to funnel the profits of Indian commerce through Canton for deposit in England.[33]

Shipping constituted yet another sector of Magniac's operations which Jardine and Matheson developed in innovative ways, always seeking to achieve an advantage over their competitors by trying new vessel designs and new technology, as well as employing combinations of vessels that would secure speed of intelligence and freight in addition to the benefits of relays among ships of different size and capacity. The firm's shipping-agency business was inseparable from its trading operations, and its ships that were engaged in the opium trade had to have the ability to contend with the tides and currents along the China coast, besides having the facility to beat to windward against the monsoon conditions of the China Sea.[34] The summer monsoon (May to September) blows from the southwest, while the tougher winter monsoon (October to March) rages from the northeast. "The iron logic of the monsoons" was a natural pattern that traditionally determined the shipping strategies of the foreign traders going to Canton. Traditionally, there were two principal routes from India to China – one through the Malacca Straits, and the other through the Sunda Straits.[35] However, by the late eighteenth century, some Spanish ships began developing a route that went first to the Philippines and then on to Macao, which allowed them to make multiple trips each year along that route.

There were disadvantages to arriving at Canton in the off-season, most prominently the fact that most of the best products available for export from Canton were bought up during the normal trading season between July and December. But the off-season arrivals enabled firms to keep someone at Canton throughout the year, which gave them advantages in commercial intelligence; moreover, the prices of opium rose during the off-season when there were fewer sellers in the region.[36] The arrival of foreign ships during the off-season also gave Chinese merchants an opportunity to dispose of leftover stocks.[37] By the early nineteenth century, the number of ships trading at Canton each year had risen nearly threefold in just four decades, and the China trade was becoming a year-round enterprise, even though the Chinese authorities continued to enforce the migration of foreigners to Macao at the end of the normal trading season. In effect the "iron logic of the monsoons" was waning.[38]

Thus, the fleet of vessels that served Magniac's agency firm and its clients had to be versatile, which helps to explain why some ships were owned and others were chartered. One of the strategies devised by the Magniac partners in the late 1820s was the system of unloading Chinese export cargoes at the new free port of Singapore and then reloading those cargoes on the same vessels for shipment to England. In this manner, the firm was able to evade the prohibition against private traders shipping directly from Canton to England, for that route continued to be a monopoly enjoyed – at least for a few more years – by the East India Company.[39]

In the early decades of Canton agency houses, the firms served as local agents for the country ships owned by trading companies in India. The agency houses were paid percentage commissions for handling freight arriving in China (1 per cent) and for obtaining outward cargo (5 per cent). Higher percentages were received for chartering or selling ships at Canton. Certain firms became the perennial consignees of the same ships owned by clients in India, such as Magniac's handling of the vessel *Ann*, owned by Leckie and Company (Bombay), and the *Good Success*, owned by Jamsetjee Jejeebhoy. These were the private trade ships known as "country wallahs," the private counterparts of the EIC's Indiamen. But the expansion of the opium trade forced the agency firms at Canton to become much more actively engaged in the shipping business. In many instances, the opium clippers would be owned jointly by the Canton agent and his principal Indian supplier of opium.[40]

There were two categories that distinguished ships engaged in the opium trade. Those of 200 to 300 tons carried the cargo of opium chests from Calcutta and Bombay to the island of Lintin, taking a month or more to make the journey. The receiving ships anchored there served as storehouses of opium for the ships that sold their chests along the coast. These vessels could also cruise the coast of China seeking markets. The second category was that of the smaller "running ships" which kept the selling vessels supplied with opium.[41]

By the late 1820s, the stocks of opium in Calcutta and Bombay were so considerable that the traditional mode of sailing them to Canton on leisurely "wallahs," making one trip per year, was no longer acceptable. The opium merchants wanted vessels that could deliver chests bought at the EIC sales in January to the coast of China by February, and then return to India for loading in May and again in July. Ships capable of defying the northeast monsoon for that February run up the China Sea might be able to make three round trips each year.

The advent of steamboats prompted the Calcutta agency house of Mackintosh to devise a plan for their new towboat, the *Forbes*, to tow a sailing ship from Calcutta to Canton. The brig *Louisa*, loaded with coal for the steam engines and opium for sale in China, left Calcutta on 26 July 1829, with the side-wheeler towing her down the Hooghly. Misfortune struck just a few hours later, when the *Forbes* ran upon a shoal. Before the tow-lines could be slipped or cut, the brig crashed into the steamer and lost her anchor; she then punctured herself on the anchor and lost most of her cargo.[42]

The disaster with the *Louisa* might have deterred most investors and agents from repeating the steam-sail experiment. But James Matheson was so impressed by the potential of steam navigation that he chartered the *Forbes* a year later to tow his barque *Jamesina* to China in thirty days or less. The venture was the basis for a lottery, with tickets sold at Calcutta. Among the ten ships consigned to Magniac and Company in 1829, the *Jamesina* was the only one engaged exclusively in the opium commerce, and it was carrying 840 chests of the drug when she left Calcutta on 14 March 1829. In her holds the *Jamesina* had 52 tons of coal to supplement the *Forbes* supply of 130 tons. But the coal supplies proved inadequate. With the coal depleted to the point of four days' supply, the ships parted company on 12 April, and the *Forbes* arrived at Lintin a week later, two days ahead of the *Jamesina*. The experiment was never repeated, because Captain William Clifton (sole owner of the ill-fated *Louisa*) had already demonstrated the virtues of a new design for vessels carrying opium.[43] *Red Rover*, the first of the opium clippers, had successfully defied the monsoon in the early months of 1830, and Matheson could see that she represented a better way than his lost bet on the steam-assisted *Jamesina*.

Clifton convinced the governor general of India, Lord Bentinck, that such a sleek clipper would be able to complete three round trips between India and China in the course of a year, and Bentinck agreed to underwrite the experiment. So the 255-ton barque was constructed at the Howrah Dock Company on the Hooghly and was launched in December 1829, having been christened *Red Rover*. The barque was flush-decked, with little or no sheer, so that her design minimized wind resistance when sailing into the monsoon. With raked masts that could deflect some of the force of the oncoming wind, she was capable of beating crisply to windward, a capacity not enjoyed by any of the other

British vessels in the China trade. Looking more like a privateer than a merchant vessel, *Red Rover* was named after the pirate hero of James Fenimore Cooper's recent novel, and her figurehead was an imagined likeness of the fictitious pirate. She left Calcutta on 29 December 1829 and, after knifing close-hauled through the northeast monsoon in the China Sea, reached Macao on 17 February. Ten days later the barque began her voyage back to Calcutta and completed the round-trip in eighty-six days, a feat no British trading vessel, whether private or Company, had previously accomplished. Two more round trips were accomplished before the end of 1830.

In succeeding years, Jardine, Matheson, as well as Dent and Russell and Company, acquired clippers that were designed specifically for the opium trade. The clippers constituted something of a revolution in naval architecture, as they had relatively small cargo space, sleek hulls, and as much canvas as it was safe to spread without risk of capsizing. They required sizeable crews and heavy armament, in order to fight off pirates or coastal authorities. There was nothing faster afloat, for they could make three trips per year from Bombay or Calcutta and did not need to stop along their route to India to drop off or acquire miscellaneous cargo, as was the case with the country ships of standard design.[44]

The speed of delivery, and the advantages of market intelligence provided by the swift clippers, meant that the quantities of opium being delivered to Lintin would grow enormously after the first voyages of *Red Rover*. The result of the sailing innovation was a steady stream of opium reaching Canton, with each clipper carrying between 500 and 1,000 chests of the drug.[45] Jardine's firm obtained 50 per cent ownership in *Red Rover* in 1833 and completed the acquisition in 1836 when Clifton retired.[46] Jardine and Matheson would build or buy other vessels of similar lines, in the categories of barques or brigs or brigantines or topsail schooners, and the other Canton agency houses would follow suit; but *Red Rover* could hold her own against all the others and continued to be the champion of the opium clippers even into the 1840s. (She disappeared in a gale in the Bay of Bengal in 1853.)

In the spring of 1832, Matheson wrote to John MacVicar, a Manchester piece-goods merchant who was a client of the firm, asking him to look into the acquisition of a fast sailing vessel for the purpose of conveying intelligence dispatches to India or elsewhere. His instructions to MacVicar were quite explicit: "Fast sailing and the power of making head against a heavy sea are the principal requisites." The more cargo it could hold, the better, as long as the freight capacity was compatible with the primary objectives. Sails, mast, sweeps, and other dimensions were all discussed in the letter, along with preferred accommodation. Even the crew was specified: "two good skates of Scotch Smacks, a Carpenter, and five good sailors of sober habits and character, and attached to each other, who would agree to serve for a certain number of years."

The going rate for new vessels was £12–13 per ton, but the firm was willing to go as high as £15–16 per ton in order to get the right ship to satisfy their needs. However, the firm wanted a form of guarantee. No doubt Jardine had a role in formulating, with Matheson, the contractual provision they would require: builders should agree to forfeit a certain amount of the price of the ship if she did not meet expectations. They cited American maritime precedent for such a practice, but one is inclined to perceive two shrewd Scots insistent on getting their money's worth.[47]

MacVicar was unable to find a suitable vessel for sale, and turned to the Liverpool shipbuilding company of J. Wilson and Sons for advice. Their experience of building fast vessels, including the famous Falmouth packets, led them to recommend a brig-rigged ship of no less than 160 tons to combine speed and power. Impressed with their recommendations and bearing Matheson's authorization, MacVicar placed an order with the Wilson shipyard for a vessel such as they had proposed. In addition, he secured the services of John Templeton, the partners' preference for commander of their new vessel on her maiden voyage out to China.[48]

With dimensions of 77 feet in length and 22 1/2 feet in the beam, the 161-ton brig was christened *Fairy* at the start of May 1833. Her cost was £4,000 when she was completely fitted for sea and ready to sail on the eve of the summer solstice. Carrying £15,000 worth of piece-goods as cargo, she also had a single passenger, Andrew Johnstone, en route to join his uncle's firm in Canton. The *Fairy* performed well on the voyage to China and reached Lintin by the end of November.[49]

Ironically, the firm had already secured a half-ownership of *Red Rover*, which gave them the speed of commercial intelligence which they sought to have, and the *Fairy* was no longer needed to serve that purpose. However, there was a different role for the new fast packet, and she was promptly put into service as a "running" vessel to maintain contact with the firm's "selling" vessel stationed off the coast of China. Not long before *Fairy*'s arrival, the firm had sent the bark *Colonel Young* to find an anchorage east of Amoy for the purpose of selling opium and other cargoes. The *Colonel Young* was owned by Charles Thomas of Singapore, who had mortgaged it to Magniac's in the amount of $8,707, which was less than the full value of the ship. Accordingly, Matheson proposed that Jardine, Matheson might take over the vessel and consider it as payment for the entirety of Thomas's substantial debt to them. The matter remained unresolved until 1833, just before the arrival of the *Fairy*, when Jardine and Matheson acquired the *Colonel Young* and put her to work as their "selling" vessel off the coast. The two vessels were therefore the first tandem in the new arrangement for retailing commodities, mostly opium, away from Canton.[50]

The appearance of the opium clippers on the China trade scene radically altered the circumstances of business for Jardine and Matheson as well as their competitors. The normal schedule for EIC Indiamen was to leave London early in the year, so as to be able to travel up the China Sea with the advantage of the southwest monsoon at their backs. In contrast, the private traders' country ships had operated year-round; but there was a always a quiet period at Canton between the last arrivals of ships that came up the China Sea and those that went through the East Indies and around by way of the Philippines. During this quiet period, a sellers' market would materialize at Canton, because the stocks of opium would shrink and prices would be forced higher.[51] The advent of the clipper traffic, beating against the northeast monsoon, meant that the advantage of the sellers' market was no longer secure, because shipments would be expected to arrive at different points in the year. Those that carried both cargo and commercial intelligence from India would enable their agents to shape strategies against the anticipated competition. Accordingly, rivalries would intensify and the market was sometimes saturated. At the start of the 1830s, less than 20,000 chests of the drug were reaching the China market annually, but by the close of the 1830s the amount was just over 40,000 chests.[52]

By the time the opium boom of that decade was well underway, the partners at Magniac's were ready to advertise the formal retirement of Hollingworth Magniac and therefore the end of the Magniac name on the firm. His name had been kept in the firm for an additional two years (to 1832) so as to allow financial provision to be made for the retirement of Francis Hollingworth, the last member of the Magniac family in China. Jardine remarked that Magniac was "having scruples about allowing us to provide for his relatives." So arrangements were made for the transfer of funds that Magniac had remaining in the firm, amounting to £30,000; and a settlement of £10,000 pounds (or about $50,000) was set aside for Francis Hollingworth to enable him "to get on comfortably at home."[53] Francis had been found unsuitable for a partnership in the firm, but initially he balked at the terms of severance. The new partners were not sad to see him board the *Larkins* bound for England in March 1832. Jardine wrote to Magniac that "Mr. Hollingworth's conduct, from first to last, has caused me so much annoyance; and turned out so completely opposite to what you and I both wished and expected." His regard for Magniac restrained him from adding "Good riddance!"[54]

After ten prior name changes, dating from the founding of a partnership between John Henry Cox, Daniel Beale, and John Reid in 1782, the firm finally arrived at the name it has carried all the way down into the twenty-first century. On 30 June 1832 the doors closed on the operations of Magniac and Company. When the offices opened for business on the first of July, the name of the firm was Jardine, Matheson and Company.[55]

After a dozen years of experience in private trade at Canton and Macao, Jardine and Matheson were at the forefront of the British merchants in China. Jardine had passed his forty-eighth birthday; Matheson was approaching his thirty-sixth. They were about to eclipse the importance of the members of the Select Committee, since the East India monopoly at Canton appeared to be doomed, and they exerted great influence at home in England with their financial services and their marketing skills. They had been the managing partners de facto since 1828, and now their names identified the firm. Formally, they were the heads of an agency house that provided merchandising, insurance, finance, and shipping services. Informally, they were a powerful combination that influenced the political climates of London and Canton.

Surprisingly little is made of the name change in the personal letters of Jardine and Matheson, and even *The Chronicles of the East India Company Trading to China* devotes only one sentence to the renaming of the firm. On 15 February the firm sent out a circular announcing Mr Magniac's retirement from the business as of 30 June,[56] and with little more fanfare than that the change was accomplished. In reality, Jardine

and Matheson *were* the firm from 1828 onward, so the change of title
did not affect the scale or manner of their business in any appreciable
way. Three years later, Alexander Matheson, Andrew Johnstone, and
Henry Wright were made partners in the firm, but there was never any
doubt while William Jardine and James Matheson were on the scene
that the whole operation revolved around them.

Hollingworth Magniac continued to be a close friend and associate
of his former partners, and he was eventually reunited with them in
business – first with Jardine and later with Matheson – once they were
all home in England. He emerged from his temporary retirement in
1837 to support Jardine, Matheson bills of exchange during a financial
crisis which crippled their London correspondent firm. Two years after
that, he helped to found a new agency house in London to correspond
with Jardine's. The new firm, Magniac, Smith and Company established
their offices at 3 Lombard Street and was eventually reorganized, in
1848, bearing the name of Matheson and Company, with Hollingworth
Magniac teaming up with Alexander and Hugh Matheson, Andrew
Jardine, and John Abel Smith as the first partners of that house.[57]

That would be sixteen years after the nameplate on the door at
Canton had changed to "Jardine, Matheson and Company," at which
time the private merchants were anticipating the end of the EIC's dominant role in the China trade. When the Company's charter had been
renewed by Parliament in 1813, its monopoly over British trade with
India was terminated, but an extension of twenty years was granted for
its monopoly at Canton. In the ensuing commercial boom for private
merchants at Calcutta and Bombay, thousands of new agency houses
were founded, many of them concentrating on the country trade to
China. However, most of the great agency houses at Calcutta went under in the commercial disaster of the early 1830s, when the market in
South China for Indian raw cotton collapsed. But the country traders at
Canton were able to weather the crisis, thanks in part to their financial
services, such as Jardine's practice of handling American bills drawn
on London.[58]

Nevertheless, the trade at Canton was unstable and unwieldy, and in
1829 the agency houses of Bombay demanded reform of the system.
In addressing the EIC monopoly, Matheson's newspaper, the *Canton
Register*, had declared in the summer of 1828: "It seems impossible from
the fettered state in which all mercantile operations pass here, that the
negotiations and intercourse can be pursued with any degree of mutual

satisfaction."[59] Most members of the EIC Select Committee at Canton were sympathetic to the complaints of the merchants, and proposed a reform of the whole system of trade with China. However, the president of that committee stood in opposition to such an initiative, and travelled to London to make his argument in person to the Court of Directors, which reacted by dismissing the members of the Select Committee. Jardine accused the court of making a "grand mistake" in dismissing the committee so precipitously, without knowing the facts of the situation. "They were the first Committee that ever took the British Trade of the port under their protection, or afforded the slightest protection to the property and interests of individuals."[60]

Nevertheless, Jardine, his colleague, and the other British traders in China understood that termination of the EIC monopoly would not bring about the establishment of a satisfactory trade relationship with China. In describing the makeshift commercial arrangements for private traders, Jardine lamented: "We are in a sad, stupid state, and I am afraid the ruling powers in England will not afford us the protection we solicit; but time will determine."[61] In February 1832 he told a London correspondent: "Great Britain never can derive any important advantage from opening the trade to China, while the present mode of levying duties, extorting money from the Hong merchants etc. exist ... We must have a Commercial Code with these Celestial Barbarians, before we can extend, advantageously our now limited commercial operations ... We have a right to demand an equitable Commercial Treaty, and to enforce it if refused."[62] He did not explain how such a treaty could be "enforced" but his tone was sometimes feisty – and loud; and his actions were occasionally as bold as his tone.

However, it was neither the country traders in China nor the Parsi merchants of Bombay whose complaints decisively undercut the monopoly of the EIC. Rather, it was the English manufacturers who lobbied Parliament with great success. The development of new export markets was perceived in the Midlands as an essential factor in the growth of the British industrial economy. Cotton piece-goods were at the forefront of commodities in need of new markets. The Indian market for such products had grown significantly in the years after termination of the Company's commercial monopoly there, and Manchester expected similar market growth in China.[63]

In April 1829, at a public meeting in the Manchester Town Hall, representatives of the commercial and manufacturing interests of the

district had voted to adopt several resolutions demanding that full freedom of trade with China be established. The meeting led to a broad
collaboration of deputies from Manchester, Liverpool, Glasgow, Bristol,
Birmingham, Leeds, and Calcutta, and their lobbying efforts in the
spring of 1829 resulted in agreement by the government to conduct
a full enquiry into the Eastern trade. The first national meeting of
delegates from the towns that were opposed to any extension of the
Company's China monopoly was held in February 1830, when it was
decided to raise of war chest of £1,000 to promote the cause.[64] The
campaign was pressed repeatedly through 1831 and 1832, with delegates presenting their case directly to the prime minister, Earl Grey, in
1831 in an effort to persuade him of the commercial benefits to be
gained by opening of China trade.[65]

On the other side of the controversy, the EIC could no longer take a
relaxed view of the traditional method of doing business at Canton. The
Company's profit from the China trade had averaged over a million
pounds annually since 1814,[66] profit that was being used to help offset
the deficit expenses of EIC operations in India. Tea was the very heart
of this profit, and it was the commodity over which the Company
exercised a jealously guarded monopoly. But the Company's Select
Committee at Canton was willing to allow an experimental venture
along the coast of China to test the market for English textiles. In 1832,
one of their junior supercargoes, Hugh Hamilton Lindsay, chartered a
bark named *Lord Amherst*, which he loaded with cotton and woollen
goods from Britain. After engaging a German Protestant missionary,
Karl Gutzlaff, to serve as interpreter for the anticipated transactions,
Lindsay sailed northward along the coast of China, landing numerous
times at cities such as Foochow, Ningpo, and Shanghai. While he succeeded in forcing his way into various locales, he did not manage to
market his whole cargo of woollens and cottons.[67]

When he returned to Macao with a portion of his merchandise unsold, the senior supercargoes were convinced that the experiment
served as evidence that the potential for the China market was being
vastly exaggerated in English manufacturing circles. Lindsay was given
no further encouragement.[68] However, Jardine and Matheson had
gained an idea that they might try a voyage like that of the *Lord Amherst*,
but with a different marketing strategy – to include English manufactured goods as a minor part of a cargo that was primarily opium.[69] Their
own exploration of the coastal markets for opium and English textiles

would be undertaken with the *Sylph*, hard on the heels of the *Lord Amherst's* return. While not a resounding success, the voyage of the *Sylph* had a profit, in contrast to the loss incurred by Lindsay's enterprise.[70]

In England, a drive for reform of Parliament had been paralleling the English manufacturers' pressure for reform of trade, and that political movement crested in 1832 with the passage of the great Reform Bill, which reassigned some seats in Parliament to the newly burgeoning manufacturing cities and expanded the voting franchise. The first Parliament elected after the adoption of that act would address such major issues as the abolition of slavery, the restriction of child labour, and the reform of the poor law. One of its early actions was the extension of the East India Company's charter, and in this instance the reform element represented the cause of free trade. The renewal of the EIC charter occurred in the late summer of 1833, but the legislation called for the termination of the Company's commercial enterprises as of April 1834.[71] Henceforth, the EIC would be the British government's agency for ruling India, but its long, storied history as a giant of international trade was at an end.

With the Company no longer an impediment to free trade at Canton, the shining new moment of the China trade had arrived – or so it seemed to the English manufacturing interests which had been lobbying so hard for years.[72] The reality differed radically from the rosy expectation, for the Chinese restrictions remained, even though the English monopoly was gone. The barriers were yet to be lifted by the Chinese authorities; in fact, not even the city of Canton itself was accessible to the foreign merchants, who remained clustered along the waterfront in the factories and at Macao during the off-season. Well before departing, the members of the Select Committee had speculated that military action might be the necessary corrective. They took the tough-minded position that the Chinese understood raw power and disdained moderation in political communications.[73] Jardine was less prepared to encourage recourse to cannon fire. "We require an equitable Commercial Treaty, with the power of appealing to the Emperor, when justice is denied us in Canton; and, I am convinced, this may be obtained without bloodshed, if properly demanded."[74]

The act of 1833, in abolishing the Company's authority at Canton, simultaneously replaced it by creating the position of a British superintendent of trade at Canton, with his mandate being to oversee the British community of merchants. In Jardine's mind, there was a fresh

problem, almost as troublesome as the Chinese contempt for foreigners, and that was the prospect of commercial disorder among the foreigners themselves. What recklessness might characterize the British
merchant community at Canton now that the restraining influence of
the EIC was at an end? The existing community of private merchants
there feared that a flood of new traders would result in intense competition and that Canton would be overwhelmed by British goods.
Moreover, Jardine worried that as long as foreigners, like slaves or beggars, were submissive to Chinese intimidation and extortion, there
would be little chance of securing a formal agreement with the Chinese
for acceptable terms of commerce.[75]

Pending the arrival of a superintendent of trade, Jardine and
Matheson were prepared to seize the day for experimentation. Peter
Ward Fay comments that, with the restraining influence of the Select
Committee about to disappear, the private traders began to anticipate
the Company's departure by conducting themselves "with an exuberance, a downright arrogance."[76] Jardine was among those who sought to
rewrite the rules of the game by reshaping the system of trade, the methods of shipping cargoes, and the geographical reach of the China
market.

It became obvious in 1833 that the Select Committee, although a year
from extinction, had lost its real authority to compel merchants to follow the old rules. When Jardine and Matheson elected to redo the voyage of the *Lord Amherst*, applying their own commercial instincts and
methods, they hired Karl Gutzlaff, fresh back from the Amherst's experimental journey, to serve as interpreter aboard the *Sylph*, which was
sent up the coast loaded with Patna and Benares opium and a lesser
quantity of British products. By the spring of 1833, the *Sylph* was back in
the Gulf of Canton, depositing a quarter of a million dollars into the
treasury of the Jardine, Matheson receiving ship *Hercules*.[77] The conclusion reached by Jardine and Matheson was that there were indeed major opportunities to be exploited northward along the coast.

The commanders of two ships in Jardine's employ, captains James
Innes and Alexander Grant, by their defiant and flippant behaviour, so
angered the Select Committee during that spring season that the committee lifted their licences. But the punishment was circumvented because the licences were reinstated by the EIC authorities at Calcutta.
The episode was evidence of the exhausted authority of the Company's
factory at Canton, and Jardine took careful note of that. Referring to

the reconstituted Select, he remarked, "They have committed many other foolish acts this season for which they are laughed at by all, despised by many. So much for the expiring efforts of the Select."[78] Jardine had even threatened the committee with civil action for recovery of any losses that the firm might sustain from their actions.[79]

The boldness that stimulated the Scottish partners to test the markets along the coast with the *Sylph* led to an even bigger enterprise in the autumn of 1833, when they entrusted the bark *Colonel Young* to a capable captain named John Rees, whom they directed to take the vessel to Chinchew along the coast of Fukien and have it serve as a relatively stationary store for the sale of opium and piece-goods. Shortly after the *Colonel Young*'s departure, the new brig *Fairy* arrived, freshly out from Liverpool.[80] She was promptly refitted and loaded with cargo, then sent up the coast to find the *Colonel Young*. Now the two ships became a team in the Jardine, Matheson fleet of depot and courier ships (or "selling" vessels and "running" vessels). *Fairy*'s job was to carry chests of opium, mail, and provisions from the Gulf of Canton to the *Colonel Young* and to transport silver back to the Gulf.

*Fairy* had arrived in the midst of a rather wild controversy that illustrated the virtual independence of action enjoyed by Jardine, Matheson and the increasing impotence of the Select Committee to restrict the behaviour of the firm's ship officers. In the late summer of 1833, a severe storm blew the Jardine, Matheson receiving ship *Samarang* ashore at Cumsingmun in such a way that refloating her was impossible. Captain Alexander Grant of the *Hercules*, another Jardine, Matheson vessel, was the ranking officer of the company's fleet, and he decided to salvage what could be obtained from the ship before it was a hopeless wreck. However, local islanders had the same intent, and the competition led to serious tensions resulting in bloodshed in October.[81] With Chinese authorities demanding satisfaction for the death of a Chinese man killed in the fighting, the Select Committee relied on Jardine to bring about a resolution of the incident. Captain Grant was sent to negotiate with the Mandarins, and the episode was quieted by the start of the English New Year.[82]

The meaning of the events at Cumsingmun was clear to the Select Committee as the sand ran out of its hourglass. Its humiliation came from two directions: the Chinese governor general and the Jardine, Matheson firm. Nonetheless, in spite of the latter's deviation from the old EIC rules of the game, the retiring officers of the Select Committee voted to order a piece of silver plate for Jardine as an expression of their gratitude for "a succession of kindnesses of no ordinary value or magnitude." At a public meeting at Captain Hines's factory, they told him that, as their departure approached, they felt obliged to acknowledge the many times that he offered the assistance of his firm, "without fee or reward."[83]

Although the governor general insisted that the Select Committee was responsible for the actions of the English private merchants, the actions of Grant and Jardine demonstrated that the committee no longer had that sort of authority. In fact, Grant brazenly informed the Select that, because the committee could not be relied on to protect the interests of the private merchants, his standard of behaviour would be determined solely by his responsibility to the owners of the property in his care, which was of course the opium that Jardine, Matheson was marketing.[84]

In the lame duck months of the Select Committee and before the arrival of a British superintendent of trade, Jardine and Matheson had come to exercise a significant measure of power and influence at Canton, Macao, and the Gulf of Canton; and that power extended well beyond commercial and shipping affairs. In mid-December Jardine wrote to Gutzlaff: "No more Comps ships expected in China." It was as if he were writing the last chapter of the EIC's story at Canton, while he was himself one of the principal figures in that chapter.[85]

# 6

# CHARTING NEW WATERS

Flying from the masts of Jardine, Matheson ships, a blue flag with a white diagonal cross (the company's adaptation of Scotland's cross of St Andrew) identified the most prominent fleet among the private British merchants in China as of the 1830s. With the colours of the East India Company withdrawing from the coast of East Asia, the standard of Jardine, Matheson unfurled above the decks of barks, schooners, brigs, and sloops which constituted a fleet larger than the navies of some small nations. The firm's clippers relegated to obsolescence the old India-built "country wallahs," old fashioned teak ships of five to eight hundred tons, some of which had been at sea for a hundred and fifty years.[1]

Among the vessels of the Jardine, Matheson fleet, some were owned outright, others were partially owned, and others were chartered – allowing the partners the flexibility of adjusting their shipping resources according to their needs. Their firm was poised to seize the opportunities for the expansion of markets, a greater share of the opium agency business, a central role in remitting funds to London, and chances to profit from regional trade in items such as cotton, silk, and rice. The fast clippers were to be essential to the commercial intelligence of the India-China trade, especially bearing on the quantity, quality, and departure times of opium shipments; Jardine, Matheson clippers gave the firm a huge advantage in such intelligence.

The country trade merchants of Canton spent little emotion on nostalgia for the departed East India Company. Jubilation was brief, however, for the giant that continued to stand across their path to new riches was the enduring Chinese refusal to regularize the commerce between China and the barbarians from over the seas. The rickety old system of mediated trade through the Hong merchants and the Celestial Kingdom's proud aloofness from diplomatic arrangements were to remain in place for years after the Select Committee had packed its bags. While persistently calling loudly for a commercial treaty between Britain and China, Jardine and Matheson shrewdly made the best of the old system, and bent the rules to their own advantage.

Both men articulated a canon of commercial integrity, but they were not reluctant to defy the laws of China with regard to limiting trade to the port of Canton. Decrees that seemed to them nonsensical or insulting were evaded by recourse to a coastal trade which relied on the willingness of the buyers to smuggle the goods ashore. From the autumn of 1832, the coastal business became a regular feature of the firm's trade, while the normal conduct of commerce at Canton continued, but with the uncertainty of impending changes related to the departure of the Select Committee.

In their willingness to be outspoken about trade relations, Jardine and Matheson were the vanguard of the British merchant community. A substantial minority of the community was not eager to follow the Scottish partners' demands for new commercial arrangements with the imperial government of China. The Select Committee had been traditionally reluctant to disturb the long-standing "unequal" relationship between the foreign traders and Peking, and a group of the Tory merchants did not want the status quo disturbed. Among them was Jardine's principal rival, Lancelot Dent.[2] "Our trading expectations along the Coast appear to have had a wonderful effect on the minds of the Emperor's Ministers who naturally enough inquire why we leave the comfortable and safe port of Whampoa to trade among the Ice and Snow ... at the risk of Life, and in disobedience of the laws of the Celestial Emperor." The answer was easily understood, Jardine told MacVicar: the Chinese authorities at Canton were imposing oppressive fees which foreign merchants felt justified evading.[3]

That the partners were aggressive in expanding their business operations is evident from the hours they had to put in, and from the difficulties they had keeping their accounts up to date. There is an almost comical sequence of letters to Hollingworth Magniac promising an accounting of his assets in the firm but conceding that such a report was not ready yet. When Magniac bade farewell to his associates at Canton in January 1827, he left a very considerable amount of liquid assets and real estate in Jardine's keeping. But the volume of work that they took on as the coastal trade burgeoned meant that it was not easy for them to maintain up-to-the-minute accounts for him or others. Early in 1830 Jardine wrote to Magniac about the *Red Rover* and other news but noted that he would have to decline comment on the account books until they had been closed for 1829. Fourteen months later he expressed regret that their clerk, Chay Beale, did not have the books closed – but everything would be up to the day within four months' time. Finally, in mid-November 1833, nearly six years after Magniac's departure, Jardine was able to write to him: "I have the pleasure to enclose your account current, with a balance in your favor (as of June 30) of 403,035 Spanish dollars."[4]

By then, with several vessels in operation on the coast, it was a wonder that the exhausted partners were able to deliver to their sleeping partner an accurate report of his assets at Canton. And it should have been no surprise that, within a rather short time, Matheson was beginning to experience some very serious eye trouble. "Old Wright" was still with them and would remain throughout the whole decade, but they still had more than they could handle. Jardine had to apologize to Thomas Weeding for not having Weeding's accounts ready: "I have found it impossible, though Matheson and I have seldom been in bed before two or three o'clock during the greater part of the season."[5]

Part of the difficulty involved the reliability of their help. Some of the nephews could be trusted to persist in the enterprise, such as Alexander Matheson, while others like Andrew Johnstone found that China was not their cup of tea after all. Chay Beale had been assisting with book-keeping, but he was not a model of diligence. He eventually left the firm in the winter of 1832–33. "I am not aware what he intends doing," Jardine remarked, "as yet he appears to be an idler." Being an idler was, of course, to the industrious Jardine a very serious vice.[6] Then there was the matter of another clerk in the firm, a man named Ullman, who seems to have suffered from a lack of clarity of mind ("alarming fancies" that he and his family were in danger). Matheson was forced to conclude that Ullman was no longer capable of doing useful work in the office. The old gentleman's head was so swirling with bargain money, forfeitures, advances on opium, and other accounting matters that Jardine genuinely pitied poor Ullman, who never said a word about his difficulties. Between Ullman's incapacity and Beale's indifference, Jardine was embarrassed by the internal inefficiency of the firm in the fall of 1830 – "a very annoying state of affairs for a public office," he grumbled.[7] The partners established a subscription fund to protect Ullman and his four daughters from starvation, and Matheson told some friends that the firm would try to find some useful employment to take up Ullman's time.[8] It was characteristic of both Jardine and Matheson to go out of their way to help a countryman in distress.

And it was equally characteristic of them to hold a shiftless fellow in contempt. When they were critical of someone, they did not hesitate to tell him so, quite directly. Jardine (to a client in Australia): "If you are not yourselves satisfied that you acted improperly in the affair, self-interest must have warped your reasoning faculties to a greater extent than I fancied." Matheson (to a commercial agent in Macao): "In a spirit of kindness I bring to your notice our dissatisfaction with your management – for lack of action, slowness in landing goods, overreadiness to part with clients' money, and unwarranted concessions at their expense." Again, Matheson (to a correspondent in Lisbon): "I have done my best to promote the interests of your protégé. But I must candidly tell you that I question much if he has sufficient acuteness to get on in the world. He is so incorrigibly vain as not to be the least aware of his shallowness of intellect."[9]

Nor were the partners reluctant to growl at a friend when they found cause for complaint. Jamsetjee Jejeebhoy was one of the great merchant princes of Bombay, with whom Jardine, Matheson did very substantial business and whom Jardine regarded as a rather close friend. Nevertheless, the senior partner would speak plainly: "We have acted with a view to your advantage, in preference to our own. I revert to the matter of your account with no other view than expressing to you the very great annoyance your letter ... has occasioned me. More particularly when combined with your peremptory instructions respecting remittance this season; as they have left us a choice of evils only."[10]

Even Jardine's old patron, Thomas Weeding, would feel the sting of his friend's sometimes acid-tipped pen. When a general financial panic prompted Weeding to decline to honour some Jardine, Matheson bills on London, Jardine scolded him quite sharply (while allowing a little wiggle room): "You know best how you were situated as to money matters, at the time you did us all the injury in your power if you had not the means you are not to blame, but if you hesitated, even out of prudence, you acted as I would not have done, were our situations reversed."[11]

While the partners did not shy away from such frankness when the occasion seemed to call for it, they were normally very even-tempered and even diplomatic in their correspondence. Both men kept vast letter books, mainly in English, but Matheson handled the correspondence in Spanish and Portuguese.

Once in a while there were touches of humour in the letters. Jardine, writing to a young friend in England who was contemplating marriage, promised a gift – but with strings attached. "Success to your matrimonial scheme – the commission for a handsome workbox being left unexecuted till I shall have heard of your having obtained the consent of the Lady and secured her heart and hand, by means of your own insinuating manners, and a few words from the Parson."[12] In fact, letters such as that one reveal Jardine to be the more complex personality of the two partners – stern, even dour, much of the time, but with a mischievous twinkle in his eye at other moments. As Magniac had remarked, "He requires to be known to be properly appreciated."[13]

Apparently, neither of the partners was especially proficient in reading or writing the Cantonese dialect of the Chinese language; perhaps they spoke enough to meet their needs at Canton.[14] But their coastal trade demanded the skills of someone adequately fluent in Chinese dialects to negotiate deals with the smugglers along the fringes of China. With more than a little irony involved, they found such a man in the Reverend Karl Gutzlaff, a Protestant medical missionary, originally from Prussia. An enthusiastic evangelist and a decidedly eccentric character, Gutzlaff had been sponsored by the Netherlands Missionary Society as far as Siam in 1827, but from then on he was on his own. An anglophile, he married three Englishwomen in succession, and upon the death of his first wife, he used the money she left him to make his way to North China, where he handed out religious tracts and medicines while becoming familiar with the coast and its dialects.[15] Gutzlaff maintained a little house in Macao, where he was a familiar figure with his broad brimmed straw hat shading his great round face. But he was a man of restless energy who was frequently on the move, earning his keep as translator. When the Select Committee allowed Hugh Lindsay to take the *Lord Amherst* along the coast in 1832, Gutzlaff went ashore numerous times with landing parties and used the opportunities to teach the local inhabitants about Christianity. At the same time, he proved his value for trading ventures.[16]

As soon as the *Lord Amherst* returned, as we have seen, Jardine was enlisting Gutzlaff for interpreting duties with the *Sylph* and the *Colonel Young*. The missionary was convinced that Western commerce was a suitable vehicle for the message of Christianity to reach the Chinese heathen, but Jardine, Matheson ventures depended on the ready money available through opium sales and that required Gutzlaff to consider the propriety of collaborating with such traffic. How did Jardine convince the evangelical missionary that opium sales could be reconciled with his conscience? Writing to persuade Gutzlaff in October 1832, Jardine acknowledged that the firm's principal reliance was on opium, but then added: "Though it is our earnest wish that you should not in any way injure the grand object you have in view by appearing interested in what, by many, is considered an immoral traffic, yet such traffic is so absolutely necessary to give any vessel a reasonable chance of deferring her expenses, that we trust you will have no objection to interpret on every occasion when your services may be requested ... You must be well aware that in the state of our intercourse with the coast of China no other cargo holds out a prospect of gain sufficient to induce any private merchant to engage in such an expensive expedition." Having made the point that Gutzlaff had little hope of continuing his missionary contact with the people of coastal China other than by travel on opium-selling ships, Jardine turned to the rewards that Gutzlaff might anticipate: "We have only to add that we consider you as surgeon and interpreter to the expedition, and shall willingly remunerate you for your services in that capacity, and the more profitable the expedition, the better we shall be able to place at your disposal a sum that may hereafter be usefully employed in furthering the grand object you have in view and for your success in which we feel deeply interested."[17] Beyond these terms, Jardine was willing to underwrite the expenses of Gutzlaff's Chinese-language magazine, begun in 1833, and to obtain from London high-quality medicines for the missionary to distribute during his travels.

Gutzlaff had doubts but overcame them: "After much consultation with others, and a conflict in my own mind, I embarked in the Sylph ... October 20, 1832."[18] He found receptive people in many places: "In the villages they inquired whether I had brought new books with me, and were eager to obtain them. After distributing a few, the demand grew more urgent, so that I could scarcely show my face in any of the villages without being importuned by numerous crowds."[19] By the spring of 1833, Gutzlaff was living with Jardine and Matheson at Macao, but he was anxious to undertake another such expedition. He set out again in November 1833 aboard the *Colonel Young*, another of the Jardine, Matheson opium vessels. Alan Reid remarks that these trips earned the firm a reputation for simultaneously distributing bibles and opium – "pouring a torrent of tracts over one side of the *Sylph* as the drug went over the other."[20]

Until such time as the sale of British manufactured goods, especially textiles, might find a sizable market at Canton and along the coast, and with the East India Company still holding a monopoly on tea shipments (until 1834), opium would continue to be the most important commodity handled by Jardine, Matheson. Chinese officials occasionally interdicted the drug, but the firm's greatest danger involved wild speculations in price brought on by the large inventories forwarded to China by speculators in India. The partners knew that they could be ruined by dangerous levels of speculation on their own part, whereas they could make substantial profits by providing steady service of high quality to the speculators who would willingly pay the firm well for its professional management of clients' cargoes. Nevertheless, they did indulge in a limited amount of speculation in opium on their own account, which naturally gave them a more intense personal interest in the success of the ships along the coast. Moreover, they invested on their own separate accounts as well as the firm's. On one occasion in 1831 James Matheson directed his nephew Hugh, in Calcutta, to credit an endorsed bill for £202 to "James Matheson's Trust fund" to be invested in opium, along with £2,200 remitted a month earlier.[21] In another instance that year, both Jardine and Matheson speculated with other English merchants in Canton as shareholders in a cargo of opium.[22] Such arrangements would distribute the risk, so that spoilage or backed-up inventory would not hurt any one of the investors severely. However, the partners were not at all inclined to entertain offers of mergers, for they were confident that they had the capital necessary for their purposes and they were disinclined to change their ways of doing business to accommodate the expectations of another party.[23]

The Scots partners were well known throughout the whole region of East Asia, Southeast Asia, Australia, and India. In fact, their counsel was sought out and relied upon by numerous parties involved in trading various commodities, but particularly opium. Their shrewd abilities to gauge the markets and to provide their clients with timely information made them invaluable commercial advisers. Time and again their letters convey either sound instincts or advanced information about shipments and sales prospects. And they had strategies to cover their tracks as they sought to play the market to their clients' best advantage. When they wanted competitors to be deceived about the extent of the Indian opium that their clients were buying in a given season, they would disguise their shipments: "It is occasionally of importance to conceal what we are doing in the way of sales; which is difficult to do unless the Opium to our consignment is mixed up with a considerable quantity belonging to others in the general returns [cargoes bound for China]."[24] The logic of this deception was to keep the competition guessing as to how much or how little opium might be advisable to have on hand at Lintin. In a season of difficult sales, the clients, especially those at Bombay, were warned to buy sparingly at the Indian auctions, because Jardine and Matheson did not want to be forcing their correspondents' opium into a dull market with low prices. What they were willing to disclose publicly was published in the *Canton Register*, for the commentary headed "Commercial Remarks" was invariably reviewed by either Jardine or Matheson for its accuracy. Similarly, the "Price Current" by which the levels of opium prices were reported – rather brazenly, given its contraband status – was confirmed by one of the partners.[25]

As of the early 1830s, the firm was sending out "Opium Circulars" to its constituents each month (sometimes more frequently), reporting the prices at which different types of opium were selling and indicating the amount of opium on hand at Canton; the circulars also commented on other major import commodities, such as cotton and rice, as well as exports such as tea and silk. Now that commercial information travelled between Calcutta and Canton in just a matter of weeks, the volatility of the drug market was increased, since a surge in opium buying in China would quickly affect the auction prices for new opium in Calcutta. Such information and the firm's market forecasts were valued highly by merchants throughout South Asia and gave the Jardine, Matheson partners a great edge in the highly competitive markets of the region.[26]

In 1831 the partners were contemplating the expiration of the EIC charter and the non-renewal of its commercial provision. They were appropriately worried about the chaos that might result with a horde of speculators and their agents entering the drug trade; and they expected that these "green" men-on-the-make would be so concerned with making sales for the sake of remitting funds to Bombay or Singapore or London that they would not be sufficiently attentive to achieving a good profit. In those circumstances, said Matheson, "it can hardly be worth pursuing [the drug trade] on the old plan, unless by operating on a large scale, and on the secure footing of being always before hand with one's neighbours in point of intelligence."[27]

Well before Parliament took up the question of renewing the East India charter, the new boys in Canton were doing precisely what Jardine and his partner anticipated. The subject of opium was painful, he told Jejeebhoy, because many persons holding inventories of opium were ready to run prices down, just to achieve sales – in spite of his firm's efforts to check them. They seemed ready to sell on any terms, he reported. So he advised the Parsi merchant sternly: "Whatever you do, do not attempt to touch next year's Indian opium crop unless you can buy at prices that will allow us to sell at prices as low as $400 a chest." In contrast to the sluggishness of their record keeping of clients' accounts, the firm's communications regarding shifts in the markets were very quick.

In turn, Jardine steamed at parties at the other end of the line when they were not equally careful. Misinformation from Bombay (with the implication that Jejeebhoy's firm was partly responsible) came up more than once in his letters through the second half of 1832. "We have buffered your losses last season by sharing in them," he told the merchant, but the loss on Malwa opium was due to incorrect information emanating from Bombay. Even as the year was ending he still thumped home that message to Jejeebhoy: we were "grossly misled" by advice from Bombay associates.[28]

Among the private merchants at Canton, Jardine and Matheson liked to play their cards close to the vest and not disclose their intelligence very generously. In some instances the major agency houses at Canton sought to cooperate in order to stabilize the market; but Jardine did not like being forced into confidential conversations of this sort and maintained that they hampered the market when the Chinese dealers learned of them.[29] On the other hand, when he was anxious to convey confidential intelligence to clients, he would go to great lengths in order to get the news to India in a timely manner. In one instance, in order to give Jejeebhoy a jump on the sales of raw cotton at Bombay, he dispatched the *Dansborg* to India in a hurry, with news of the prices being paid for cotton at Canton.[30] In another instance, when the market for opium soared dizzyingly, late in 1832, Jardine rushed to get the information to his client DeVitre at Bombay but cautioned that the market was frenzied and the high prices might not endure; he enjoined DeVitre to observe strict secrecy about that information, lest competitors get wind of "the mania" as he called it and rush in to profit from the overexcited market.[31] The partners were keenly aware that the comings and goings of their dispatches were observed by their competitors who did not have such advantages in communication as Jardine, Matheson had. James Matheson told a client in Singapore: "It seems almost impossible to land a letter with you, en passant, without exciting observation."[32]

Their opium sales and confidential messages were intimately linked to the promotion of their shipping business. Cargoes consigned to their vessels could be watched by them for the identities of shippers and receivers. "The more Opium stored in Ships under our charge, the better we are enabled to judge what is going on in the drug market," Jardine told DeVitre. Mixing their own cargoes with the cargoes of other parties on Jardine, Matheson vessels enabled them to conceal their own operations from the spying efforts of competitors in the trade. "This concealment is sometimes of very considerable importance," wrote Jardine, "particularly in difficult times when every sale is anxiously watched by the small holders, and strangers, who are too apt to follow the example of the established Houses, in place of being guided by their own judgment." That was what prompted the firm to begin chartering the *Dansborg*, a two-hundred-ton brig flying the Danish flag, as a way to confound the scrutiny of other traders.[33]

They were not only looking for ways to confuse the observers; they also wanted cargoes in their ships for the more traditional reason of making profits on storing opium aboard the warehouse vessels. They enjoyed a certain leverage with potential shippers because many of the clients were eager to receive advanced payments in anticipation of the sales. Jardine and Matheson had the financial resources to accommodate some of those requests, but they did not particularly like to do so, for it sometimes meant forcing the opium onto a dull market. Moreover, they were especially annoyed when clients consigned their cargoes to someone else's vessel and then requested advances from Jardine, Matheson on opium in someone else's possession. Eventually, the partners gave notice to merchants that advances would be given only on cargoes held on their firm's depot ships at Lintin. In that way, they were able to retain the fees for storing chests of opium belonging to clients who might seek advances, since they were simultaneously able to disguise the origins of the opium, thereby befuddling the snoopers. Jardine was blunt in his correspondence with the folks at Bombay, directing them to tell their friends to give explicit instruction to their Canton agents to use the *Samarang* and the *Jamesina* if they wanted the benefit of advances from Jardine, Matheson.[34]

To secure best advantage for their distant clients, Jardine and Matheson were constantly adjusting their strategies, like great military planners or talented athletes, in order to outwit the competition by manipulating the market in one way or another. To one correspondent in India, Jardine recommended storing opium in the countryside, so that there would be no public knowledge at Canton of the quantity of the drug that might be expected after the northeast monsoon.[35] To a ship captain, he pointed out the advisability of withholding the new opium for a month or six weeks in order to push prices upward.[36]

Timing the market right was based on shrewd guesswork, past experience, sound intelligence, and plain old luck; but these veterans of the agency business relied less on luck than on depth of experience and fair dealings with their clients, who came to value the advice emanating from the Jardine, Matheson quarters at Creek Hong. Jardine was frank and specific with John MacVicar about the types of English textiles which would sell in the China market and those for which there was little demand. (Longcloths and woollens would sell; chintzes and printed handkerchiefs would not.) His message was clear: we'll try to sell the cloth that is marketable; don't bother sending the other stuff. That was what MacVicar needed to hear, and for that reason he could rely on Jardine's advice.[37]

At the end of 1832, James Matheson wrote to his nephew Hugh, in Calcutta, that the agency's business was increasing and there was no need for reduced rates to lure new clients. We have an advantage over others, he declared, because we transact a large share of the commerce at Canton. So we can see further and sooner and we can *anticipate.*[38] Clients' satisfaction arose from the firm's avoidance of rash predictions; the partners' ability to negotiate advantageous prices; the good advice they gave about sensible investments; and their reputation for integrity. Matheson was manifestly proud of that reputation. He told Hugh that the philosopher William Paley once said that he could not afford to keep a conscience. "Now we *can* afford to do so – and this is probably the keystone of the preference given to us."[39]

There was, however, some element of flexibility to the matter of conscience when the partners sniffed out a good opportunity. Just a few weeks before Matheson's favourable look in the mirror just mentioned,

Jardine seized upon a chance to sell a cargo of rice in the Chinese market. For two years in a row, the rice crop had not been good. Jardine was
genuinely sympathetic with the population because of the hardships
brought on by such scarcity.[40] He was also sensitive to the commercial
ramifications of scarcity, and late in 1832, when he saw the prospect of
rising prices for rice over the next three or four months, he contacted a
man in Manila about securing permission to export rice to Canton. A
shipload of fifty to a hundred thousand peculs of rice was what Jardine
was looking for, and he hoped that J.H. Zobel would have enough political influence to make the arrangement. The potential profit had to
be alluring, because Jardine offered generous terms – a quarter-share
for Zobel and a quarter for the governor (at Manila) or any influential
party who could facilitate the export permission. "In the event of the
influential party preferring a sum of money to a share, you might after
having made your arrangement for the supply of Rice engage to pay in
Cash after having shipped off the last Cargo, a sum of $8,000 or even
$10,000 for 100,000 peculs, retaining a quarter share for yourselves."[41]
Some Western observers would certainly describe that way of approaching an official through an intermediary as a bribe; but Jardine was so
used to the kind of expectations for cumsha or "squeeze" that were common among Chinese authorities that this offer may not have ruffled his
conscience.

Just a few weeks later, Jardine told his friend Charles Majoribanks
(former president of the Select Committee) that the foreign merchants
at Canton needed some favourable change in the way duties were being
collected before trade there could be expanded significantly – "unless
we adopt the American system of bribing the Examiners of Cargo &
Linguists to defraud his Celestial Majesty of half the established duties
– which is not the most honorable mode of conducting matters."[42]
Apparently, he saw a clear distinction between facilitating a one-time
deal with some cash – as in the rice deal with Zobel – and systematically
bribing officials as the normal way of doing business.

Jardine and Matheson acquired a well-known reputation as good judg-
es of the quality of opium cargoes, the state of the market for it in China,
and the uses of opium. Clients in England, where the principal imports
of opium came from Turkey, were hopeful that Jardine might try to sell
some of their Turkish opium in China. But it was generally not a good
enterprise, and he told them so rather frankly.[43] On the other hand,
Jardine was interested in sharing in a speculation in Turkey opium for

the English market, in collaboration with Weeding, because he was aware of the large sums of money that had been made at home in Britain on the Turkish drug in 1829 and 1830. In effect, what he told Weeding was: if you find an opportunity for good profit in a speculation in Turkey opium, cut me in.[44]

At times, the partners would try to deflect the questions coming from all quarters about their knowledge of the drug and their forecasts for the coming season. Sometimes the questions were rather naive, but even then Jardine or Matheson might take the time to give a response, in brief or at length. When a fellow in Calcutta wrote to ask how opium was prepared for smoking, Matheson started to refer him to the "British Museum in China," a scientific society among the British residents of the factories at Canton. But the letter eventually became a somewhat detailed explanation of reducing the raw opium to paste, then toasting it over a fire, then cutting it again and boiling it and filtering it until an extract was obtained which had the consistency of tar. He even had statistics to offer, when the questioner asked what it was that the Chinese called the "touch" of a batch of opium. That, he explained, was the percentage of smokeable extract contained in a given quantity of the drug. Patna normally yielded 45 to 50 per cent "touch," whereas Malwa yielded about 70 per cent. Clearly, Matheson was quite familiar with the way in which the raw opium could be transformed into a hallucinogenic substance.[45]

Nevertheless, Jardine declared that he and his associates were not at all knowledgeable about the growing and harvesting of opium. When he learned that a client named McLeod in Bombay was intending to write a book on the culture and cultivation of the plant, Jardine offered to buy a half-dozen copies, saying that the book would deal with "a subject on which we are all most profoundly ignorant."[46] He showed no sign of irony in the letter!

Although the Scots partners were best known in their own day for their expertise in marketing opium, it would be misleading to suggest that their business skill ended there. Their enterprise was truly diversified, and their skills were applied to many commodities and services. Raw cotton from India and finished cotton as well as woollen products from England found their way to Chinese markets through the Creek Hong offices of Jardine and Matheson and in many cases on their ships. Rice reached China and tea reached England by their services. And there

were other commodities, which were handled with the firm's characteristic shrewdness. For example, Weeding wanted musk, and Jardine was
able to secure a cargo for him. But Jardine knew that their pecul of
musk would hit the market in England along with all the other musk
travelling on the *Mermaid* in 1832. Accordingly, Jardine hatched a plan
to ship part of his musk via the Danish ship *Syden,* by way of St Helena,
so that it would reach England long before the *Mermaid* with everyone
else's musk.[47] And the competition did not know that he was beating
them to market until it was too late for them to do anything about it.

Insurance was another element of their diversified enterprises. By the
time that the Dent-managed Ninth Canton Insurance Company completed its term at the end of 1832, Jardine and Matheson had organized
the distribution of shares to men willing to underwrite the new Tenth
Office. The Tenth would be the last of the three-year-term insurance
companies, for in 1836 the firm established the Canton Insurance
Company on a permanent basis (with two hundred shares). Writing insurance was a consistent source of profit for the firm, and apart from
the Canton Insurance Company the partners maintained their own private underwriting operation, "Jardine Matheson and Friends."[48]

In the operation of their business, Matheson spent far more time at
sea than Jardine did. Jardine moved back and forth between the Canton
riverfront and Macao, but that tended to be the extent of the small
world in which he lived for nearly twenty years. In contrast, Matheson
was on the move a great deal, with stops in India and Southeast Asia, as
well as a trip home to Britain in 1835. His journeys seem to have been
largely for commercial purposes, but there were medical issues involved
with his extended visit to Britain.

He began travelling to the two most prominent commercial cities of
India in the years after Magniac's departure from Canton. His first trip,
at the end of December 1829, took him to Calcutta where he stayed
until the spring of 1830. He was back at Canton by mid-spring, much to
Jardine's relief, for the routine management of the firm fell squarely on
Jardine's shoulders in the absence of his partner. All of the correspondence with clients and operation of the agency business had to be overseen (in an executive way) solely by Jardine in the months while
Matheson was travelling. The evidence that they could barely get to
leave their desks before the small hours of the morning, when both were
present at Creek Hong, suggests that the workload must have been very
taxing on Jardine in the seasons when he was managing on his own.[49]

By late in 1832, Matheson was at sea again, bound for Bombay. In troublesome financial times, because some firms in Calcutta were failing, Jardine and Matheson worried that the difficulties at Calcutta might cause a run on the agency firms in London. Accordingly, Matheson wrote to Magniac and Weeding from Singapore to authorize them (through power of attorney) to act on behalf of Jardine, Matheson and Company to protect their interests. As it turned out, 1832 was not a crisis year for Jardine, Matheson's solidity with London creditors; Magniac had in fact intervened to guarantee Jardine, Matheson's bills and to extricate Jardine's assets from Fairlie and Company, one of the India houses which did fail in that year.[50]

By the time of Matheson's return to Canton in mid-August of 1833, Jardine was so run-down physically that he was sick. "Excuse this confused letter," he wrote to Jejeebhoy. "I have caught a severe cold and sore throat, and can scarcely hold my head up." But he was still working at the office, even though he told another Bombay client that he was "very useless and very miserable."[51]

The pattern that had emerged in his travel schedule was for Matheson to spend the fall at Canton, while the teas were arriving from inland China, and then to depart for Singapore and India toward the end of the tea season and after the earliest clippers had arrived with the new opium shipments. In the spring of 1834, Matheson sailed for Bombay. The need for him to make this particular trip must have seemed urgent to the partners, because it was going to coincide with the end of the Select Committee's authority (therefore offering a window of vulnerability for British merchants at Canton until a new supervisor of British trade was appointed), as well as Jardine's entry into the tea-export business and the complex management of the firm's local and coastal marketing at the start of the new opium season. But, within a few weeks of Matheson's departure, a disturbance in the opium market was generated by the actions of some junior officials of the imperial government, acting on their own authority in the absence of the governor general. Ninety-six chests of opium were seized from a vessel at Lintin and with that the Chinese opium brokers ran for cover.[52] For Jardine, left to deal with the marketing problems on his own, the episode absolutely flattened the opium market at Canton, for the two principal dealers had been responsible for purchasing or negotiating half of the opium sales at Lintin in the most recent years. For a time, all contacts between the coastal selling vessels and the firms at Canton were interrupted, but the flexibility provided by coastal sales offered a way to compensate for the absence of a lively market at Lintin/Canton.

Jardine's correspondence during Matheson's absence reveals him to be a virtual wizard at the manipulation of company shipping according to the week-to-week, even day-to-day, needs of the firm's clients and the conditions in the markets where commodities could be obtained and those where they could be sold. (If the *Lady Hayes* does not visit Calcutta, we may send *Red Rover* ... In event of *Colonel Young* not returning in two or three days, we have determined on sending *Fairy* along the coast ... I hope the *Austen* will get any opium Lyall Matheson may have purchased for us ... Will send the *Colonel Young* to Singapore with Dr Gutzlaff to pick up a cargo of straits produce ... Hope to have the Doctor back by June, ready to start for Formosa.)[53]

To relieve the lack of sales in the Canton region, Jardine began diverting additional quantities of the drug to the coastal vessels, which were achieving a rather good price for opium. Moreover, he allowed prices of the commodity to fall, as they necessarily would, in the half-dead market at Canton/Lintin, and then re-entered the market as a buyer (no doubt through an intermediary) and began buying at higher prices so as to reverse the trend and elevate prices. Nonetheless, the summer of 1834 would have been a disastrous one for Jardine's opium trade had it not been for the success of *Fairy* along the coast, which caused Jardine to redirect significant quantities of the drug from the Lintin depot ships to vessels selling to smugglers farther north. In fact, he even encouraged Captain MacKay of the *Fairy* to contract with the buyers for delivery of specific quantities of opium at a fixed time with the price guaranteed at levels lower than the average prices for the most recent trip.[54]

Jardine did not frighten easily, as can be seen by the fact that he did not panic when the opium market temporarily collapsed at Canton. He kept his composure and manipulated the sales by exploiting his great advantage over his competitors through the coastal operations. At the same time, he initiated Jardine, Matheson's new role in the tea business and promoted, to the extent feasible, the merchandising of English textile commodities. Upon his return late in the summer of 1834, Matheson had many reasons to be pleased with the commercial shrewdness of his partner.

Like many of their competitors among the Western merchants of Canton, William Jardine and James Matheson were left in the dark, so to speak, about the precise terms of the future supervision of British trade with China. Consequently, they had to follow their own best instincts. "We are completely in the dark regarding the Tea Trade, though it is of the first importance for us to know when we can embark in Tea operations," Jardine told Thomas Weeding in November 1833; and two months later he told another correspondent: "We are still in the dark about the nature of the establishment to succeed the East India factory here. I anticipate some difficulties, but none that may not be conquered by firmness and prudent management."[55] Matheson anticipated sufficient business in teas to require the services of a tea taster; so in a manner not terribly unlike ordering a piano for the Creek Hong factory to be sent out from London, Jardine authorized Weeding to be on the lookout for a "respectable young man [who] can be procured on moderate terms"! The letter advised: "Sudden departure from England might be required."[56]

The EIC was not retiring completely from the tea business, but for a while its continuing interest in the trade would be focused on India, where the cross-breeding of Assam wild tea with Chinese tea plants would require years before shipments of Assam tea would be ready for the English market. The first twelve chests were not sent to Britain until 1839. Until then, China would remain the centre of the tea trade. While the British merchants at Canton were keyed up about the market being thrown open to them, they were also conscious of the need for a parliamentary revision of the duty on tea, lest English consumers find themselves paying a 100 per cent customs tax on the usual price of the commodity.[57]

Jardine determined, in the absence of his partner, to proceed at the earliest date possible in the spring of 1834 with shipments of tea to British ports aboard Jardine, Matheson vessels as well as aboard a vessel not under its flag. Jardine wrote to Matheson indicating that he had determined to send the *Camden* to Glasgow, the *Frances Charlotte* to Hull, and the *Georgiana* to Liverpool – "chop chop after the 23rd of April." In addition, Jardine had teas loaded aboard *Pyramus*, which was bound for Falmouth.[58]

He told Weeding that, superintendent or no superintendent, the firm intended to send ships out after the 22nd. There was a note of defiance in his assertion that the new officers of the Crown should have arrived at Canton well before then if their presence was necessary to legalize the new trade.[59] It was typical of Jardine not to scruple about such concerns when the British government had sent no clear regulatory provisions to

Canton in time to take effect as the Company's monopoly expired. So, overnight on 22/23 April 1834, Jardine and Matheson became tea merchants on a large scale. There was no gradual build-up to the new trade. Their ships were loaded and ready to go on the first tide after the East India's Company's tea trade ended.

Jardine held a low opinion of the "Tea Men," as he called the Chinese merchants who brought the green and black teas to market at Canton. The tea was delivered to Canton by inland merchants, of whom there were about four hundred men of small capital,[60] whose sales were sent through the Hong merchants. The inland "tea men" generally could not speak pidgin English, so they had to rely on the Hong merchants as intermediaries for their deals. And there were times when foreign merchants did not want direct transactions with the inland merchants. "Generally men of indifferent character," Jardine called them, and he suspected that they would pull tricks on the new parties to the trade, just as they had done to the EIC by holding back much of the best tea, in order to sell it to the Americans at higher prices.[61] Connivance seemed to bother him more in the tea trade than in the opium trade.

Shrewd in assessing the necessary course of finance for the new ventures at Canton, Jardine insisted that the funds for the tea trade needed to be provided from England in the form of bullion, bills, and letters of credit, because credit was too expensive at Canton to accommodate all the ships that were aspiring to the trade.[62] The number of British traders at Canton swelled from 66 in 1833 to 156 by 1837, which meant that – given all the new competitors – less profit was realized from British goods being imported and higher prices were being paid for Chinese exports.

The Darwinian sort of free trade that existed at Canton after the EIC's authority over British commerce expired was hardly what Jardine and his partner had in mind when they had called for the end of the Company's privileges. After the termination of the Select Committee, there followed months of uncertainty about how the British commercial community was to maintain its collective discipline in dealing with the Chinese government, the Hong merchants, and the tea men. A superintendent had been designated by the British government, but he did not arrive at Macao until mid-July 1834, three months after the Select Committee had closed its files.

The expectations of many members of the British merchant community had been articulated in an unsigned article which had appeared in the *Chinese Repository* in December 1833. The piece asserted that the Select Committee should be succeeded by a Crown officer who was authorized to speak and act vigorously. Although the writer recognized that such a change was not without difficulties, he contended that, if the Chinese government resisted formalizing trade arrangements, the threat of war could be very useful, and the presence of British cruisers offshore would be sufficiently alarming to the Chinese. The author concluded that a sound commercial relationship between Britain and China could not be possible until the whole Chinese empire was opened to free trade. Whether Jardine wrote the piece or not, these were Jardine's views and he would urge the Crown's representative to adopt a "forward" position.[63]

The prime minister, Earl Grey, initially offered the job of chief superintendent of trade to Lord Auckland, but Auckland, hoping for an appointment in India, turned down the position at Canton, which he called "perhaps the least pleasant residence for a European on the face of the earth."[64] In contrast, a Scottish peer, Lord Napier, who had lost his elected seat in Parliament, was actively seeking the chief superintendent's position and enlisted the support of King William IV, which smoothed the way for his appointment at the end of 1833.

William John Napier, Lord Napier of Merchiston, was almost entirely unprepared by experience for conducting commercial diplomacy with China. At age forty-eight, Napier was a naval veteran and a sheep raiser. After the Napoleonic Wars, he had left the Royal Navy and spent nearly a decade farming in Scotland, but eventually he re-entered the Navy as commander of a frigate. Earl Grey and his foreign secretary, Lord Palmerston, regarded Napier's role at Canton as a consular position and not as a diplomatic mission. For that reason they declined to give him extended authority, and Grey cautioned him to act with forbearance should any point of difference arise with the Chinese authorities: "Persuasion and conciliation should be the means employed."[65]

In addition to his lack of acquaintance with matters of Chinese law and commercial practice, Napier was further handicapped by a confusing and ambiguous set of instructions from Foreign Secretary Palmerston, who directed him to supervise English commercial interests at Canton but also to look into the possibility of extending British trade to other Chinese ports and to pursue the possibility of normal relations with the Chinese government. However, he was not to do anything that would awaken the fears or offend the prejudices of the Chinese. Opium was a topic that required "peculiar caution," he was told; for, while he was to avoid encouraging the traffic, he had no authority to interfere with it. He would have a naval frigate at his disposal, but he was directed not to order it to enter the Pearl River except in the most extreme circumstances.[66] Burdened with these instructions, which Collis calls "perhaps the most ill-considered ever drafted for the guidance of an officer of the Crown sent on an important mission overseas," Napier set out from England aboard the frigate *HMS Andromache* in the winter of 1834, accompanied by his wife and two daughters.[67] In the course of their long sea voyage, Napier reviewed several documents which had been provided him by the Foreign Office, dealing with the history of Britain's relations with China. He concluded that the best way to deal with the Chinese authorities was to adopt a stern disposition and to press his instructions to the limit.[68] Priscilla Napier, writing of her husband's late kinsman, maintains that "before ever he laid eyes on Jardine or stepped ashore in China, his readings of the story had made him form much the same conclusions" as Jardine, regarding free trade and the need for respect from the Chinese. "But whatever he thought, he had not the wherewithal, let alone the authority, to take a firm line."[69]

At Canton, the viceroy,[70] the mandarins, and the Hong merchants all awaited the arrival of the new official, whom they referred to as the "Barbarian Eye," and made plans to frustrate any British design for revising commercial relations between the two nations. Napier was not welcome at Canton, but he was determined to push his way forward and deal only with the viceroy rather than through the Cohong. This possibility alarmed the more conservative merchants, like Lancelot Dent. Because their business was largely confined to Canton and its environs, they regarded a stoppage of trade – which might result if the new superintendent pursued a "forward" policy –as a truly bleak prospect. They therefore were inclined to accept a continuation of the old system of conducting business through the Hong merchants and tacitly accepting their lack of recognition from the Chinese government. To Jardine, Dent's bitter rival, appeasing the viceroy and the imperial court was a kind of denigration that he was no longer willing to abide. For Jardine and Matheson, an interruption of trade was not likely to have dire consequences, since their firm had expanded its markets along the coast. Hence, Jardine was prepared to encourage Napier to be resolute.[71]

Had Napier known what was in store for him, caught as he would be between these cross-currents, he would likely have remained at home in southern Scotland, breeding sheep and waiting for his daughters to marry and make him a grandfather. The few months he spent in China were to be filled with frustration, controversy, vice-regal contempt, and debilitating illness. Moreover, more than a few members of the British community were not especially grateful for his strenuous efforts to carry out Palmerston's instructions, as confusing as they were.

For all that Jardine and Matheson and many of their compatriots were glad to see the Company departing from Canton, there were functions that the Select Committee had performed which would now be left unattended. For one thing, there would be no regulator of British trade with Chinese merchants until the newly appointed official arrived. In addition, there was the matter of financing the trade. Once the Company treasury at Canton was closed, there would be difficulty for the British merchants in making their remittances to India and England.

Speculation about the new official began well before the end of 1833, with Jardine expressing the hope that Westminster would not appoint one of the veteran members of the Select Committee. We do not want to start a new system, he told Weeding, with people who were accustomed to being abused by the Chinese.[72] Napier's appointment relieved his anxiety that the new superintendent would be a Company man, but Jardine was concerned that Napier was (by Palmerston's instructions) to be advised by former Company men. He did not object to Napier, but he insisted that the merchants' opinion was that it would be better for Napier to stay home than to arrive at Canton and take up negotiations through the Cohong. The Chinese authorities, uncertain how to receive Napier, assumed that they would send the Hong merchants to deal with the new superintendent. In contrast, Jardine maintained that Napier should be prepared to take his frigate to the Yellow Sea and proceed to the imperial court, "there to state our grievances to the 'Son of Heaven' himself, and demand redress. If this is done and done in good manly style I will answer for the consequences. It may do good, but can not do harm. Enough of this subject. I seldom touch politics as you are well aware."[73] In spite of this ingenuous disclaimer, it is abundantly clear from his letters and from his influence on Napier that, once the peer arrived, Jardine hardly shied away from politics.

Greeted at Macao Roads by a salute of Portuguese cannons, Napier had good reason to believe that he was being accorded the respect due an officer of the British Crown. Hoping to establish a good relationship with the first superintendent, and to encourage him to follow a tame approach to his new duties, several former members of the Select Committee offered him accommodations at the Company's rather splendid residence on Macao's waterfront. However, Jardine had beaten them to the punch. The competition to influence Napier had begun even before he arrived. While he and his family were en route, Napier received a letter from Captain James Innes extending the offer of a spacious house "as a loan from Jardine & Co." and begging him to keep it as long as he liked. "This was a very great catch," Napier reported to his kin at home in Scotland. He was quick to recognize the terms of competition between the Company men and the free traders: "I am inclined to think there was a struggle on both sides into whose hands I should fall. Jardine-Innes and the like are Free Traders, but to be free of all parties I preferred going into an unoccupied house ready furnished and thus kept from contamination of party."[74]

The next morning, the "tall raw Scotchman with light hair" met with members of the former Select Committee and took on the new assistants Palmerston had designated.[75] This retinue of persons with Company connections was not likely to advise Napier to adopt a tough policy toward the Chinese authorities, for the Company's policy had been to avoid confrontation. Their advice was more probably to caution the new superintendent about the troubles that might ensue if he were to insist on direct communication with the viceroy.[76]

"Your Lordship will announce your arrival at Canton by letter to the Viceroy," was one of the instructions Napier received from Palmerston.[77] Accordingly, Napier allowed himself little more than a week to settle his family at Macao, gather his staff, purchase the Company's armed cutter *Louisa,* and prepare for his journey from Macao to Canton, which took fourteen hours. Rowed upriver from Whampoa in a small boat which laboured through a series of heavy thunderstorms, Napier finally reached Canton at two in the morning on 25 July. When he stepped ashore at Jackass Point, he found William Jardine waiting there in the darkness to escort him to his accommodations in the New English Factory. As their association developed in succeeding weeks, Jardine would become confidant, adviser, and intermediary with the Hong merchants for Napier.[78]

The Chinese authorities and merchants were aware of the arrival of "the Barbarian Eye" at Macao, and the viceroy, Lu K'un, was determined to prevent the foreigner's advance toward Canton. Lu told the Hong merchants: "I, the governor, having examined, find that a barbarian *eye* is not on a par with barbarian merchants … he can not have permission to come of his own accord to Canton."[79] He had issued an edict to the Hong merchants on 21 July, directing them to warn this Barbarian Eye that he was not to approach Canton until he had submitted a petition requesting permission to enter China.[80] As directed, a delegation of the Hong merchants set out for Macao by the inner passage, but Napier was already on the *Andromache* making progress toward Canton by the outer passage.

What ensued bore resemblance to theatrical comedy, although the stakes were high and the players were intensely serious. Neither Lu nor Napier would agree to receive the other's communication, and their messengers seemed to keep bypassing each other. Lu resolved that his edict should be delivered to Napier at the New English Factory. While preparations were made for that delivery, Napier was composing his letter to Lu, with translation help from Protestant missionary Robert Morrison and his son John. At three o'clock that Saturday afternoon, Napier's secretary, John Astell, as well as the younger Morrison and a small group from the New English Factory, set out for the city gate, where foreigners normally submitted their requests to the Chinese authorities. However, Napier's communication was not headed "petition" but bore the designation "letter," which was regarded by the mandarins at the Gate as unacceptable.[81] In the meantime, two prominent Hong merchants, Howqua and Mowqua, had arrived at the factory bearing Lu's edict, but Lord Napier refused to receive it. He treated the merchants courteously but informed them that he had been sent to initiate a new system of trade and that he intended to communicate directly with the viceroy.[82] That evening Napier had dinner with Jardine.[83]

During the weekend, the health of Robert Morrison, who was already ill at the time when he was translating Napier's letter to Lu, declined severely, with EIC surgeon Thomas Colledge and Jardine prescribing opium for the stomach pains he was suffering. By the end of the next week, Morrison was in the grip of a severe fever, which took his life on Friday, 1 August. His death deprived Napier of one of the finest English experts in the Chinese language, one of only three foreigners at Canton with that kind of scholarly expertise.[84] John Morrison accompanied his father's remains to Macao, and Karl Gutzlaff was away on a trading expedition; so Napier had no one with him through whom the Chinese authorities could communicate precisely.[85]

In August the viceroy directed a series of edicts to Napier, reminding him that there were formal regulations by which foreigners were allowed to conduct trade at Canton. He ordered Napier to return to Macao. In insultingly crude translations of Napier's name, the edicts referred to him by the designation "hard, labouring, vile beast," which Napier took to mean, in one syllable, "ass."[86] Defiantly, Napier not only intended to remain in the New English Factory but quickly began to plan for the construction of an additional storey in order to allow room for a large dining room, bedrooms, and other spaces, above which he wanted to have a flat terrace "for evening walks like jolly old King Davie."

In the contest of wills, the viceroy could not determine exactly who this Barbarian Eye was, because he refused to receive and read Napier's letter. At the same time, Napier was not aware of the content of Lu's edicts until the Hong merchants passed them on to Jardine, who had John Morrison (lately returned) translate them from Chinese to English. Napier remained firm in his refusal to present a petition which would concede that he held subordinate status, and he steadfastly refused to leave Canton. In letters to English merchants at London and Manchester, Jardine complained that the British government had badly mismanaged the Napier mission by not giving him authority to approach Peking directly and by not giving the commander of the *Andromache* permission to enter the Bogue (the main entrance to the Pearl River).[87] Almost certainly Napier's resolve was reinforced by his frequent meetings with Jardine, who was firmly opposed to resuming the old system of doing business through the Cohong.

Caught in the tangle of conflicting British sentiments over the proper response to Lu's position, Napier came to rely more on the advice of Jardine and Matheson than on the more reserved counsel of the former Company men. Matheson was back from his travels by late August, and the two Scots partners bolstered Napier's determination to remain at Canton and force the issue with Lu. Sixty members of the British community, gathered at the New English Factory to celebrate the king's birthday on 26 August, heard Napier proclaim his intent. After toasts honouring King William IV and Princess Victoria, Captain Charles Elliot proposed a toast to Lord Napier, which was greeted with exuberant cheering. When the assemblage had quieted, Napier remarked that he "would glory in having his name handed down to posterity as the man who had thrown open the wide field of the Chinese Empire to British spirit and industry."[88]

He had already written to Westminster urging the government to authorize him to use the threat of force against the resisting Chinese authorities. In a long dispatch to Lord Palmerston (who was in fact no longer foreign secretary, since the Grey Cabinet had fallen in July), the superintendent asserted that Lu's edicts manifested the obstinacy of the Chinese government. Napier called for an ultimatum demanding that Britons be given the same commercial privileges as Chinese. If the Chinese response was unfavourable, then British naval actions should destroy the Chinese forts and batteries along the coast, without harming the people. "Three or four frigates or brigs, with a few steady British troops, not sepoys, would settle the thing in a space of time inconceivably short."[89]

Equally intemperate was Napier's decision to respond to the edicts by posting copies of a notice on street corners in Canton, criticizing the "ignorance and obstinacy" of the viceroy and regretting that thousands of industrious Chinese would be ruined by the perverse behaviour of their government. Napier had the idea that Chinese opinion would support him. However, he not only miscalculated their support but also found himself losing some support within the British community when the Hong merchants were ordered, on 16 August, to begin preparing for a stoppage of trade. Once British trade with China was all but suspended, Napier was forced to reconsider his strategy. In a postscript to his dispatch, he told Palmerston that if he found a prolonged stoppage of trade causing the British merchants to suffer, he would retire to Macao.

Napier's posted notice provoked the viceroy so sharply that Lu responded with a notice of his own, denouncing the British superintendent for trying to incite the people. Within a few days there followed an edict proclaiming that the Barbarian Eye was "stupid, blinded, ignorant" and declaring: "There can be no quiet while he remains here. I therefore formally close the trade until he goes."[90] Two days later, Napier was informed by alarmed servants that soldiers were surrounding the New English Factory. The whole Chinese household staff disappeared, and Napier concluded that he was being detained in a state of house arrest. His response was to order the two frigates *Andromache* and *Imogene* to move up river from the Bogue to Whampoa. The message was carried by one of Jardine's schooners, and on Saturday, 6 September, a small detachment of Royal Marines, led by a lieutenant from the *Andromache*, managed to make their way up to the New English Factory and joined Napier and the small group of Englishmen confined there.[91]

Palmerston's instructions had cautioned Napier not to move the *Andromache* into the river unless the most extreme sort of emergency required it. Although British merchants had generally been very safe at Canton, Napier chose to interpret the presence of the Chinese soldiers as a dire emergency. He had told Mark Napier two weeks earlier that the viceroy had ordered him away "at the point of the Bayonet," an action that the superintendent regarded as being "equal to a Declaration of War."[92]

Observing all this from Creek Hong, Jardine wrote to Jejeebhoy, explaining that a resolution of the dispute might take forty days, now that the viceroy was in the process of referring the matter to the emperor. In the meantime, the authorities were allowing commercial deals struck before 16 August to be fulfilled, which – in Jardine's judgment – meant that there would probably be plenty of trade going on while the emperor's response was awaited.[93] But if firing began, the complete cessation of trade was inevitable.

As this drama unfolded, persistent rains and extensive flooding plagued Canton from the middle of August.[94] Eventually the unhealthy climate got to Napier – whether from airborne bacteria or waterborne germs, he was not feeling well as August ended. No doubt his physical condition was sapped by the stress associated with the movement of the two frigates upriver. On Sunday, 7 September 1834, the HMS *Andromache* and the HMS *Imogene* began to sail into the channel which serves as gateway to the Pearl River.[95] Chinese war junks trained their guns (without much success) on the Royal Navy's warships; and they were soon joined by the cannons in forts on either side of the bay, pounding away at the frigates as they tacked across the water. "Thus happened the first collision between the British and Chinese Governments in modern times," wrote S. Wells Willliams, an American missionary living at Canton.[96]

The scale and duration of the military engagement were limited. Casualties among the English crews were not severe – one man killed and a few wounded. But the ships of the Royal Navy were served adequate notice that Napier was not to be rescued readily. Lu had made extensive preparations to block the river above Whampoa, and it was going to be extremely difficult for Napier to make his way downriver to the security of the frigates.[97]

By Monday, 8 September, at about the same time that the frigates were advancing toward Whampoa, Napier began feeling feverish. A day later he was seriously ill, and his condition would continue to deteriorate as the week wore on. When the ships had reached Whampoa, the superintendent was intending to remain in his residence at the factory in Canton. But the discord within the English community over the suspension of trade, in combination with the poor state of his health, forced him to consider withdrawing. Back in Canton by September, Matheson was among the voices of the British community urging him to adhere to his firm resolve; in fact, Matheson was decidedly hawkish, for he wrote that the Chinese would need to be given "a further demonstration of force on a larger scale."[98] Actually, his attitude was militarily unrealistic, for the shallow depths of the river above Whampoa meant that the frigates were unavailable to help Napier fight his way out of the city, if things came to that.

After seventeen days of trade disruption and blockade of the factory, Napier decided to withdraw. Jardine seems to have had the strongest influence on Napier in reaching this decision. However, Jardine was not motivated by commercial urgency, for much of his firm's trade took place at the outer anchorages where Lu's embargo did not affect it. He may have been prompted to counsel retreat by his medical concern for Napier's worsening condition.[99] The superintendent reached his decision on Sunday, 14 September, but extracting himself from the blockaded factory was not as readily accomplished as he anticipated.

Now able to walk after getting some good rest in an apartment that James Innes had made available to him, Napier expected to board the cutter *Louisa* and proceed downriver to the frigates at Whampoa, where he planned to sail on a British vessel to Macao. However, the viceroy intended that Napier's trip have the appearance of expulsion.[100] The *Register* reported contemptuously that on the eighteenth the Chinese had made "a childish parade of their ridiculous fire-rafts" on the river in front of the factories.[101] Napier would be required to proceed on a Chinese houseboat via the inner passage, once the frigates were gone from Whampoa. These were Lu's terms. So the days drifted on without a resolution to the standoff, and in the course of these days Napier's health declined precipitously. Ultimately, his "release" was secured by

Jardine and Dr Colledge, who met with Howqua and Mowqua and managed to obtain a departure permit. Napier yielded and signed the order directing the frigates to sail away from Whampoa. On the evening of 21 September, he finally walked, with help, to the English Factory's wharf and boarded a chop boat, which was escorted by a flotilla of armed Chinese escort vessels.[102]

At this point, and not knowing the tragedy that lay ahead, Jardine was ready to concede the "disastrous failure of the first attempt to raise our country from the degraded state in which the lust of gain of the E.I. Company was content to retain it." He blamed the failure on "the miserable ignorance of the British government" regarding the China trade, and on the duplicity of the EIC whose "finance committee" constituted an obstacle to free trade. His letter, signed "A BRITISH MERCHANT," was printed in the *Register* while Napier was en route to Macao.[103]

Colledge accompanied Napier on his journey, which was laboriously slow and noisy, with long delays punctuated by gongs, firecrackers, and people poking their heads into his compartment. His fever rose, but Colledge did not have medicines to relieve Napier's symptoms. It was Friday before they reached Macao, after suffering what must have seemed to a sick man an interminable trip of five days.[104] He was carried up the hill to the house where his wife and daughters were residing, and lingered, feverish but conscious, for two weeks. During his final days, the churches of Macao silenced their bells so as not to disturb him. By the second week of October, Matheson was still holding out hope, but Jardine's assessment was more sober: "Lord Napier is very seriously ill at Macao, and doubts are entertained about his recovery."[105] Indeed, the doctor's instincts were accurate, for the beleaguered peer passed away on the night of 11 October 1834, two days short of his forty-eighth birthday.[106]

His funeral, four days later, accorded him the formal dignity that he never had enjoyed in China. Following the honour guard, the pallbearers, and the bier came the family and the second and third superintendents. Immediately behind them in the cortège was Napier's recent confidant, William Jardine, while James Matheson marched with the main body of merchants in the rear of the funeral procession. As the procession went toward the grave, the guns of the *Andromache*, then anchored in Macao Roads, fired a final salute to Lord Napier.[107]

The story of Lord Napier's short tenure as first superintendent of trade has many of the characteristics of a classical tragedy, yet contemporaries rather unkindly characterized it as "the Napier Fizzle." His brief tenure had two major consequences: it caused the Chinese authorities to conclude that the British merchants could be rendered defenceless by a blockade of the riverfront factories; and it made succeeding British superintendents aware of the dangers in forcefully challenging the existing terms of trade at Canton without a contingency plan for military action.[108] The time required for London-Canton communications had precluded advice and instruction from Whitehall to Napier during the crisis. Months after the superintendent's death, the Duke of Wellington, during his short period as foreign secretary in 1835, while unaware of Napier's fate, wrote to remind him that British policy was to sustain commercial privileges at Canton by peaceable means rather than by force.[109]

The Chinese had reached the conclusion that British pressure could be successfully rebuffed and that the Barbarian Eye had been humiliated by his expulsion. But for merchants such as Jardine and Matheson, the Napier affair had opened an issue that would not be denied a clearcut resolution, however long it might take to achieve that. Looking back on his first impressions of Canton in the early 1830s, Gideon Nye remarked: "The actual situation of foreigners at Canton was aptly likened to the condition of the Animals in the Zoological Gardens of London." Nye observed that the authorities wanted the foreigners confined because they did not expect barbarians to act with the decorum characteristic of Chinese society.[110] To Jardine and Matheson and a number of like-minded British merchants, opium was not the central consideration; rather, the primary questions involved reciprocal respect between Chinese and British, based on diplomatic recognition and formal documents establishing the terms of trade.

Among scholars familiar with these events, there is broad agreement that William Jardine had the most influence on Lord Napier's strategy as first superintendent. Matheson was away from Canton for the first stretch of Napier's tenure, and by the time he returned Napier had already carved out his policy. Jardine had succeeded in swinging Napier over to his side of the policy debate. The two men dined together, saw one another frequently, and gradually came to think alike. Jardine acknowledged at a year's distance from the events that he had been Napier's intermediary with the Cohong. "Every effort of reconciliation through them was conducted privately by your humble servant."[111]

To what degree does all this make Jardine responsible for "the Napier Fizzle"? It does appear that Jardine must bear some of the burden for

the outcome of the standoff between Napier and Lu. He encouraged
Napier to persist in his refusal to submit to the terms of the old "Canton
System" and he served as an intermediary through which Napier and
the Cohong could communicate without Napier acknowledging that
this was the proper line of contact between himself and the viceroy.
Weeks before Napier arrived, Jardine had conceived the probable sce-
nario: the Chinese authorities would likely send the Hong merchants to
the superintendent; in response, Napier should be courteous but not
say a word to them regarding business.[112] Having counselled Napier
along those lines, Jardine was eventually the one to advise him that this
round of the contest was lost and that withdrawal from Canton was necessary. He recognized that this episode between the superintendent and
the viceroy was but the start of a campaign to convince both London
and Peking that a new set of rules had to be drawn for their commercial
relationship.

Priscilla Napier argues that Lord Napier was seen in his own day as a
good man and an intelligent person, who largely escaped the censure
that was subsequently heaped upon him by later historians who have
represented him as bad-tempered, light-headed, and downright stupid.
She reiterates that he was not seen in 1834 as a tool of William Jardine,
"as some historians have since seen him."[113] There is nothing to suggest
that Jardine saw Napier as an expendable figure to be used for the cause
and then left to his fate. On the contrary, his letters convey a genuine
concern for his fellow Scot and a feeling of real loss at Napier's passing.
He told Weeding: "His death is severely felt by most members of our
small society – and doubly so because of the treatment he received from
the Chinese Government when he was too much reduced by disease to
be capable of negotiations."[114] Not long after the Barbarian Eye was
committed to the earth at Macao, the Iron-Headed Rat returned to
Canton, determined to continue the campaign that had recently
claimed his fellow Scot's life.

Through the early 1830s, Jardine and Matheson had taken the lead
in shaping a new pattern for British commerce in China, through their
coastal ventures and their aggressive approach to the tea trade once the
EIC monopoly was finished. Beyond that, they had become the most
vocal proponents of a new relationship between the British and Chinese
governments. The "Napier Fizzle" was a defeat, but their determination
to see things changed foreshadowed further trouble. When the decade
began it was not their design to become agitators, but, as it turned out,
the Napier episode was their apprenticeship.

# 7

# THE PARTNERS APART

The Napier affair and its aftermath helped to clarify the roles of William Jardine and James Matheson in the merchant communities of Canton, London, and the English Midlands. Like a smooth, behind-the-scenes operative, Jardine had manipulated the Napier mission along the lines favoured by the more liberal free traders among the British people at Canton. He managed this without proclaiming his position from the rooftops of Creek Hong.

In contrast, James Matheson was the more publicly articulate of the partners, not only in his influence on the English press at Canton, but even more dramatically in his statements while at home in Britain in 1835–36. He was also concerned that the merchants of India know of his views on the differences among the factions at Canton. Writing to Robert Lyall in Calcutta, Matheson asserted that he did not want the other side (Dent, Daniell, et al.) to dominate the public mind. So he asked Lyall to find a newspaper that would print an extract from a letter he (Matheson) had written to the new chief superintendent, but not to identify the writer.[1]

As Lady Napier and her daughters packed their belongings at Macao for the long, sad journey home to the Scottish Borders, the British community of Canton/Macao was subscribing to a fund for a monument to the late peer. The fund and a commission to carry out the memorial were given over to Matheson, who travelled home to Britain in the spring of 1835 for medical treatment. During his extended stay in the homeland, he published a lengthy statement of economic philosophy applied to the China trade, presenting the sentiments of the dominant voices at Canton as expressed through the Chamber of Commerce there (established in 1834). With the declared purpose of "giving form and efficiency to the British mercantile community,"[2] the Chamber proceeded to elect James Matheson as its first president and to campaign for the elimination of the existing Canton commercial system and the Finance Committee which survived as a residue of the EIC presence at Canton.[3]

In the wake of the Napier mission, business-as-usual did not revive at Canton. Markets for cotton and opium were both dull, and the emperor had issued an edict so severe that the drug brokers would not even enter the European factories. It was not Peking's first effort to obstruct the drug trade, but none of the prior campaigns had been effective. In this instance, the governor general sent the hoppo a message to be passed through the Hong merchants: pilots and compradors who expedited the drug trade were to be punished without mercy.[4] As late as Christmastime, Jardine was noting that a recent, extensive seizure of opium chests had frightened the Chinese drug dealers from appearing in daylight.[5] "I have never had so much anxiety in China as this season, nor ever had so little satisfaction in transacting business," he confessed.[6] After the two-month stoppage of trade, he and his partner helped secure a resolution from the Chamber of Commerce asking the British cabinet for a tougher policy toward the Chinese government. But a more immediate response from the foreign merchants was a determination to move away from Lintin, where government patrols could harass the drug trade. By 1837, the opium sellers had begun moving their vessels to Hong Kong, which seemed to offer a safe harbour.[7]

In his history of Jardine, Matheson, Robert Blake poses the question: "But where did the Canton foreign merchants want to get to? They were already making vast profits from opium smuggling. Was there much to be gained by a row with a regime under which they flourished? The answer, oddly, was yes."[8] If they could realize a formal change in the terms of trade, and thereby open a larger Chinese market to British wares and British transport of Asian commodities such as rice and cotton, the heavy reliance on opium as a way of offsetting the costs of tea could be overcome. They recognized that there was little chance that they themselves could persuade the Chinese government that it made good business sense to modernize their commercial relationship. Consequently, in spite of the passivity of the superintendents who followed Napier, the Chamber of Commerce elected to press London for a new policy.

Just two months after Napier's death, the stronger faction within the Chamber drew up a petition, addressed to the king-in-council, maintaining that the most unsafe policy would be to submit quietly to insults such as those imposed on Lord Napier. The petitioners urged the appointment of a plenipotentiary empowered to demand compensation to British merchants for the interruption of trade; the opening of northern Chinese ports to foreign commerce; and termination of the requirement that all foreign trade pass through the Cohong. They advised that the new official be supported by a naval expedition which would have the power to interdict Chinese revenues, to interrupt China's internal and external commerce, and to take possession of all of China's armed vessels, should the imperial court disdain his mission.[9]

Eighty-eight signatures represented thirty-five of the approximately forty-five individuals comprising the British trading community, and all the commanders of EIC ships who returned to Canton after the opening of the trade. At the top of the list the first two signatures were those of Jardine and Matheson. In due course, they were joined by the signatures of Andrew Johnstone, Andrew Jardine, Alexander Matheson, Robert Thom, Henry Wright, and James Smith of the firm's office.[10] Only two firms, Dent and Whiteman, declined to have their members sign the petition. However impressive the list may have seemed to the signers themselves, the new superintendent, John Davis, chose to undermine the petition by urging the foreign secretary to ignore the document, which he described as "crude and ill-digested."[11]

Jardine was particularly annoyed by the continuation of the EIC Finance Committee at Canton. The members of that body enjoyed the privilege of having priority in clearing bills and advancing credit to members of the British commercial community. Jardine insisted that the senior members of the committee were using their position to feather their own nests, by appropriating available funds to accomplish the loading of two vessels under the management of Daniell and Company. (Daniell was the senior member of the Finance Committee.) He was not averse to employing very hard-nosed business practices, as we shall see; but he deeply resented his competition taking advantage of their privileged opportunities to go one up on him.[12] This bad residue of a bad system, as Jardine saw it, was described in the complaints addressed to the king, and he made quite sure that the business communities of London and Manchester were well aware of the financial shenanigans at Canton.

For both Jardine and Matheson, the fall and winter of 1834–35 constituted a difficult period in their lives, for various reasons. One or the other was going to return home for an extended period or perhaps for good. The other was to be left on site as the managing partner in an unstable business situation. Their primary commodity, opium, was under pressure from Peking and from competitors, and the market for it was behaving in a skittish way. Moreover, the financial condition of several of the Hong merchants, on whom they were still necessarily reliant for business connections, was rickety, at best.

As matters evolved, Jardine's plans to return home were shelved in deference to Matheson's medical needs. So Jardine was left on his own for a year and a half, running the whole operation with the assistance of Matheson's nephew, Alexander, and the new hand, young Mr Smith, their tea taster. Newly arrived from London, James Smith was immediately set to work selecting teas for the Indian and English markets. Jardine put a premium on Smith's discerning taste, for he anticipated the need to get the valuable tea cargoes home should the British government adopt a tough policy which might lead to another disruption of trade.[13]

In his correspondence Jardine reveals that he was deeply disappointed not to be going home that season: "I had fully made up my mind to proceed to England in one of the ships of this Season ... but Mr. Matheson having for some time past suffered a good deal from an attack of inflammation of his eyes, we have determined on his proceeding home."[14] Matheson's ocular ailment was sufficiently serious to prevent him from working. He admitted to Robert Lyall that he had neglected the problem in the first instance and was now obliged to have someone else do his writing, as he was "prohibited by the Doctors from myself using the pen."[15]

Nor was Jardine in the best of health, as indicated in letters written in mid-1835. He recognized the risk he was taking by not addressing his own health problem, but seemed to accept staying on as his fate. He told an old friend in Scotland that Matheson's departure "fixes one in China till he returns unless driven away by sickness."[16] However, there was no hint of bitterness toward the partner whose trip home forced cancellation of Jardine's own plans.

Part of the pain of his disappointment stemmed from the necessity of turning down an invitation from his old partner, Hollingworth Magniac, to join a new firm in the City. Magniac had joined with John Abel Smith and Oswald Smith to establish an agency house in London in 1834, with the name Magniac, Smith and Company. Magniac had raised the "probability" of Jardine's wishing at some future time to become a member of the firm, and Jardine was touched by the generosity of his former senior partner in extending the invitation. His response admitted the attraction of the offer but included a quiet reference to his personal worry: "It is impossible to foresee what my wishes may be on my return to England; but I should certainly prefer having the option of joining an establishment of so much promise should I live to return home in a state of health equal to undertaking a share of the labors of the Firm."[17]

Prior to Matheson's departure for Britain, he and Jardine had agreed to place some of their business in London with the new firm; and Jardine entrusted his partner with making the arrangements. Within a few weeks' time, he was authorizing Andrew Johnstone to draw upon the Jardine, Matheson account with Magniac Smith.[18] In the estimation of Jardine and Matheson, the combined resources of the new agency house made it financially more powerful than either Thomas Weeding or Timothy Wiggins, who had been handling most of the Jardine, Matheson affairs in London.

The long-time friendship and business association between Weeding and Jardine made it a ticklish matter for Jardine to convey his firm's wish to diversify its financial relations in London. In April 1834 (before the organization of Magniac Smith), Weeding had offered a tactful evaluation of his business relationship with the Scottish partners. In replying, Jardine once again empowered James Matheson to act on their behalf in reworking the connection with Weeding. "As Mr. Matheson and I are in the habit of communicating, most freely, on all subjects, public or private, connected with our interests and failings, I at once laid your letter before him, and must now leave it to you and him to discuss the subject on which it treats." Jardine delicately suggested that Weeding would feel less pressure in handling a portion of Jardine, Matheson financial matters than would be the case if he were their sole agent.[19] This episode reveals an aspect of Jardine's personality that prevented him from letting business sense be trumped by sentiment. Nevertheless, when circumstances demanded, he could pick his words so carefully that he spoke or wrote like a career diplomat. Yet it was not simply diplomacy that was on display in this case, for he was mindful that the feelings of an old friend and associate ought to be respected and not handled roughly. Moreover, he did not intend to remove all of their business from Weeding.

The *Orwell*, taking James Matheson homeward, sailed from Macao in
March 1835. Lady Napier and her daughters had left Macao in December, but the remains of her late husband were being transported home
aboard the vessel Matheson was sailing on.[20] By the time Matheson arrived home, the British cabinet had reverted to Whig leadership, but
neither the Whigs nor their Conservative predecessors were inclined to
make a case for military action against the Chinese.

Upon arriving at Portsmouth on 8 July, exactly four months after leaving China, Matheson travelled to London post-haste on the outside of a
stagecoach. He went immediately to Weeding's office, and to Magniac's,
Wiggins', and Lloyd's Bank, before settling in at the Burlington Hotel.
Though the Whigs had regained power in April 1835, Matheson quickly
learned that their policy was as cautious as that of the Conservatives,
who had shown no interest in the Canton merchants' petition. He
promptly concluded that the ministry of Lord Melbourne had no intention of lending any muscle to the cause of the British at Canton. In a
personal letter to his partner, written two days after arriving, Matheson
complained: "The fact is, Jardine, people appear to be so comfortable
in this magnificent country, so entirely satisfied in all their desires, that
so long as domestic affairs, including markets, go right, they cannot really be brought to think of us *outlanders*. Until therefore there is a stoppage of trade, or something to touch the pockets of the merchants &
ship-owners, expect no sympathy here. The more successful you are in
China in keeping things quiet, and getting tea no matter at what sacri-
fices – or in what manner – the less sympathy you will have here. Lord
Palmerston means to do nothing."[21]

Less than a week after reaching London, Matheson joined a deputa-
tion of tea merchants imploring Lord Melbourne for relief from the
duties on tea. On the outside of a letter to Jardine he jotted an adden-
dum describing the frustration of waiting to see the prime minister.
"Tell [James] Innes that going to the Prime Minister is very much like
going to the City Gate at Canton – We wait in the street, at his door, until
he is disengaged."[22] He persisted in his political lobbying and managed
to get an appointment with Palmerston, but learned that the foreign
secretary was not disposed to do anything about Chinese affairs at the
moment.[23] The explicit and implicit messages Matheson was hearing
from the government meant that his various tasks at home would include an appeal to the manufacturing interests of England, whose influence on the Whig ministry was significant.

There seems to be no documentation for his eye treatments. He was absent from Canton for a year and a half, during which the composition of his rather long tract on the future of trade with China was accomplished after the relief of his ocular complaint. To improve his health he went to the attractive Regency town of Leamington Spa, in the Cotswolds, soon to be designated "Royal" Leamington Spa by the queen in 1838. The mineral springs that had been discovered there were being used for hot and cold baths to treat gout and rheutmatism, joint stiffness, and various kinds of paralytic illnesses. Drinking the mineral waters was known to have a mildly laxative effect. The length of Matheson's stay there is unknown, but he told Andrew Johnstone that he emerged feeling much better. He gave great credit for his recovery to a physician named Henry Jephson, a much-celebrated figure in the development of the spa treatments. "With me he was most successful – as he is generally with nearly all his patients, and I strongly recommend him."[24]

He also devoted some time to visiting his family in Scotland. After spending a month at London, he travelled by steamer to Edinburgh, where he stayed for a week, and then worked his way north by way of Inverness to visit his mother and other members of the family at Lairg.[25] By the early weeks of 1836 (perhaps even sooner), he was back in London, living at Hanover Square and preparing the *Present Position and Future Prospects of the British Trade with China*, a forceful eighty-page tract advocating major reform in Britain's commercial relationship with China. He evidently had access to a good library and to the records of the EIC, for the piece is laced with citations from Company reports as well as references to English legal authorities, parliamentary committee reports, and writers on the Chinese people and the China trade.[26] As published by the London booksellers Smith, Elder and Company in 1836, it was packaged with a brief history of the China trade, statements (called "memorials") addressed to the prime minister, Lord Melbourne, from merchants in Manchester, Glasgow, and Liverpool, and the Canton merchants' petition to the king-in-council. The production was a slick piece of propaganda, which suggests that Matheson spent a fair bit of his time consulting with men who had strong stakes in the manufacturing communities of the Midlands, Liverpool, and Glasgow. The assertions of the several documents build upon one another, creating a cumulative pressure on the Whig cabinet to adopt a new policy.

The treatise begins with an unfavourable portrait of the Chinese people before it proceeds to elaborate on the evils of the Canton system: "It

has pleased Providence to assign to the Chinese, – a people characterized by a marvelous degree of imbecility, avarice, conceit, and obstinacy,
– the possession of a vast portion of the most desirable parts of the
earth, and a population estimated as amounting to nearly a third of the
whole human race. It has been the policy of this extraordinary people
to shroud themselves, and all belonging to them, in mystery impenetra-
ble, to monopolize all the advantages of their situation. They consequently exhibit a spirit of exclusiveness on a grand scale."[27] It should be
noted that his use of the word "imbecility" is rather casual and means
something like "foolishness," for he applies it to his own people as well
at later points in the work.

He moves quickly from this jaundiced characterization to a more focused declaration that foreign trade is barely tolerated by the Chinese
because of a general policy which draws a sharp distinction between
China and the "barbarian" world. Consequently, foreigners, limited to
trading at Canton, are constantly exposed to "the most ignominious
surveillance and restrictions."[28] Thus, he has within a few pages established one of the major themes of the treatise – his assertion that British
merchants in China are, as a matter of local government policy, treated
with a lack of respect, are subjected a regular pattern of insults, and are
forced to suffer a corrupt system of extortion just to keep the trade running. Most specifically, he points to the contempt and dishonour that
were heaped on Lord Napier, who was "speedily destroyed" by the indignities and injuries he experienced, while the whole trade was "ruinously
suspended" for a month. "All [that] seems now utterly forgotten," he
complained, a theme brought up repeatedly in the treatise and the accompanying memorials.[29]

Two lines of development form the main structure for Matheson's
argument: first, that the abolition of the East India Company's monopoly created an opportunity for British merchants in China to escape
from demeaning subservience to the Chinese authorities; and second,
that the Canton system was now placing the British merchants – forced,
by lack of any commercial treaty with China, to deal with the Cohong
individually – in a gravely precarious position, not simply for the stability of their businesses but also for their personal safety.

Having described the unhappy situation at Canton, Matheson proceeded to a new line of argument by declaring that China had invited
English commerce and had tacitly sanctioned it by acquiescing in its
presence. That behaviour meant that China ought now to be bound by

principles of justice and the law of nations to allow the trade to continue under terms of mutual respect.[30] "Is it excusable ... that our ships, laden with most valuable cargoes, after a six months' voyage, should suddenly be prohibited from entering the Canton river, and when on the point of return, freighted with tea, after having paid all the enormous and dishonest duties exacted from them, should be forbidden to leave it, at the mere caprice of the local authorities, on grounds the most ridiculous and wicked?"[31] Moreover, the mutually beneficial features of the trade made it obligatory for the Chinese authorities to maintain the established trade for the sake of their own people. He insisted that "removal of our trade would be followed almost immediately by infinite disorder in China," given the reliance of so many people on that commerce.[32]

What policy should the British government adopt in keeping with the honour of the British nation? The treatise turns a corner with that question, for it begins to build a demand, quiet but insistent, that the government needed to formulate a new policy; else, Britain would look foolish before the world.[33] Matheson hammered home the details of the Napier affair in order to impose a burden of neglect on the Foreign Office for letting this ugly episode pass unacknowledged.[34] Risky as it was to imply that the cabinet was being pusillanimous, Matheson was ready to offer the government an escape by identifying a course of action not likely to produce deep trouble. "The Emperor of China has, in truth, neither the inclination nor the power to resort to hostile measures, in order to destroy our trade or banish us from his territories, *if he saw us disposed to offer a serious resistance.*"[35]

What, precisely, was Matheson suggesting? He recommended that any effort to renew negotiations at Canton be abandoned, because "the establishment of the Hong merchants is one of the most artful and successful engines of oppression and extortion ever devised." Therefore, Matheson advises that a plenipotentiary be appointed to deal with the imperial government at Peking, and that his list of desiderata include the following: that the Chinese drop their arrogant and offensive language in speaking of the British king and his subjects; that they make reparation for the fatal insults directed at Lord Napier, as well as provide remuneration for losses incurred during the stoppage of trade; that the full protection of Chinese law be extended to British subjects at Canton; that extortions and impositions be prohibited; and that a formal arrangement be agreed upon for the mutual benefit of Chinese and British commerce.[36] Working himself up to a rhetorical flourish in conclusion, Matheson declared that "we must, at once, make up our minds either to abandon for ever our dear-bought commercial intercourse with China, or take effectual measures for securing its continuance, and that upon a safe advantageous, honourable, and permanent footing."

The treatise is a very revealing window into the person of James Matheson, his talents and his ideas. It is examined here at length because it is given no similar exposition in any work dealing with him or the firm, and because it shows him to be in his own right as forceful a commercial leader as his senior partner, who was normally accorded pre-eminence among the merchants at Canton.

His strategy in constructing the treatise and its appended memorials into one carefully orchestrated argument was to capitalize on British sensitivity about the respect and honour due to the British monarch, the Union flag, British subjects wherever they might be resident, and their property. In his legal and moral case about the implicit approval that the Chinese authorities had bestowed on the foreign trade at Canton, Matheson evaded the question of opium smuggling as a contraband trade that the Chinese were legally entitled, on a natural law basis, to suppress. In a sense, however, Matheson was right to keep the two issues distinct, for the question of Britain's trade relation with China was not the same as the question of country traders' sub rosa dealings in smuggled opium. In fact, the goal he was promoting, if reached, would have led British merchants to concentrate on other commodities and free themselves from such heavy dependence on opium (especially now that there were so many competitors in the coastal trade). Nevertheless, he was vulnerable if someone were to challenge him on opium's place in a new commercial relationship, for it constituted a glaring hole in his moral argument.

He buffered himself shrewdly against such criticism by the way in which he lined up the memorials from merchant groups in Manchester, Liverpool, and Glasgow, for none of them had a role in the illicit opium trade, yet all of them were strenuously urging that Melbourne's government summon up the courage to defend the British trading community in China. The directors of the Manchester Chamber of Commerce and Manufacturers anticipated great extension in the China trade, and declared that the existing trade was already employing one hundred thousand tons of British shipping.[37] As if coached in their language, the

Liverpool petitioners and the Glasgow East India Association decried the two great evils of the Canton system: the imposition of unauthorized and arbitrary duties by corrupt local officials, and the restriction of trade to the Hong merchants, "most of whom are in embarrassed circumstances."[38] This concert of complaints about the Hong manifests a single guiding hand among the petitioners, and that hand seems most likely to belong to James Matheson.

In the long run it was the Scots businessmen of Glasgow who made the boldest suggestion. Their memorial called for a "treaty of amity and commerce" which lifted the existing disadvantages and restored trading privileges at Amoy and other ports on the east coast of China. However, they were not satisfied to entrust these goals to a plenipotentiary, and proposed acquiring territory: "It would be of the greatest advantage to British trade in that part of the world, were his Majesty's government to obtain one or more islands near to China, as an emporium for carrying on commerce free from the exactions, control, or annoyance of the Chinese government."[39] The same proposal would become a central feature of Jardine's advice to Palmerston during the Anglo-Chinese crisis of 1839. Whether Matheson channelled this idea to Jardine, or whether Jardine had arrived at such a proposal independently, remains unknown. Nevertheless, it seems quite clear that Matheson had carefully assembled and synchronized his arguments with the statistics gathered by the British manufacturers and the Glaswegians' call for British-held territory as a haven for British commercial interests in China. The propaganda campaign, although never explicitly identified as a main purpose of his trip home to Britain, became one of the most important activities of that fortieth year of his life.

Matheson asked Jardine when he was expected back in China, and Jardine replied quite patiently that he was content to let his partner be the best judge of that. "I have enough to do, and am often very much knocked up, but if we manage to keep our health I hope to be able to manage matters for ten or twelve months longer."[40]

While home, Matheson found himself engaged in some commercial diplomacy, for one of the firm's major British clients, John MacVicar, was in a bad frame of mind, upset that he was not receiving commercial intelligence in a timely way, and annoyed that Jardine, Matheson had sent his remittances in the form of bills rather than silk. Matheson had to explain to MacVicar that the price he was willing to pay for silk was too low and that the firm had been waiting to see if silk prices would fall. In the process, Matheson had to do some delicate mediating to keep Jardine and MacVicar from severing their relationship.[41]

When Matheson sent word to his partner that he had arrived at a full understanding with MacVicar, Jardine told Matheson he was glad that the air was cleared, but two days afterwards he blasted MacVicar with grapeshot: "Unwilling as I am to carry on a useless controversy, I cannot refrain from remarking on your observation, on the spirit in which your letter of the 10th of May 1834 had been received here. You must have fancied us to be callous indeed, and extremely wanting in due regard for our own characters as honest men, had we not felt and expressed our indignation at being falsely charged with acts that must have been at variance with every principle of common honesty. Having said so much I shall drop the subject I trust forever."[42]

Although Jardine had it in his nature to be quite sharp-tongued on occasion, this outburst seems to have been symptomatic of a crabbiness that he manifested once the work piled up on him during Matheson's absence, for there are other instances of such sharpness with people he had known well for years – even Hugh Matheson and Andrew Johnstone. The letters from the last week of the year make no mention of Christmas (which is understandable for a Scottish Protestant), and neither do they mention Hogmanay (which one might expect a man from Burns country to be anticipating on the next-to-last day of the year). The stress of recent work probably helps to account for this dourness. He was still writing letters at two o'clock on the morning of 31 December, but was not disposed to add a New Year's greeting (perhaps because the letter would not reach England until springtime).

Managing the firm's opium trade was the most stressful work for the senior partner, but now that the tea trade was in the hands of private traders, that also demanded much attention, as did silk, cotton, rice, and other commodities. Beyond the commodities and the financial management, which was becoming much more complicated, there was the Jardine, Matheson fleet to worry over, as he certainly did in the year and a half that Matheson was away.

As ever, opium was the biggest worry, with mercurial prices offering the biggest potential source of profit and an equally great chance for a collapsed investment. So Jardine was constantly in touch with speculators in India, purchasing agents there, and ships' captains along the coast; and he was always assessing the extent of the competition, and the psychology of the buyers, who had to take the risks of smuggling the chests ashore. He wanted his ships' captains to be in frequent communication, not only with him but also with each other so as to have a clear understanding of how much opium was being sold, what the prices were, and how much more of the drug to send to the selling vessels from the depot vessels. He allowed his captains extensive discretionary authority but expected good sense of them and gave them detailed advice. "On your falling in with the *Colonel Young*," he told Captain MacKay of the *Fairy*, "you must be guided by circumstances, but we should prefer your returning with from 60,000 to 80,000 [dollars] treasure on board to remaining on the station for a larger supply." If the competition were to force their opium on the market by dropping prices, the *Fairy* was to follow suit, in spite of the diminished profit.[43]

If anything, in 1835 Jardine was showing more concern about the competing opium-selling vessels, such as Dent's *Aurelia*, than about the Chinese authorities. When it became clear in March that there would be no lack of competition among opium sellers along the coast, Jardine advised Captain John Rees of the *Colonel Young*: "If you could manage matters so as to make the mandarins[44] attack every one but our own party it would have a good Effect." "My principal fear," he acknowledged, "is that numbers may bring down the displeasure of the Government Authorities on the dealers and Boatmen, while competition among the sellers will reduce the price very much."

He was not being at all ironic in his reference to bribing the mandarins to go after the other opium vessels, for he directed Rees that, if he could not bribe the mandarins, an alternative plan would be to undersell the competing vessels by such a painfully descending rate that they would abandon the competition. The plan would be "to place one of your vessels alongside of or on the same station with each of the strangers and by taking the first of the sales, following prices down to the lowest rate ... say 40, 30, or even 20 [dollars] per chest beyond the Lintin prices, you might possibly sicken them of the trade, as you would ... always have the latest intelligence from hence."[45]

The principal competitors in opium sales along the coast were Dent and Company, some American firms, especially Russell and Company, Parsi merchants such as Heerjeebhoy Rustomjee, and individual British entrepreneurs, such as James Innes.[46] As Peter Ward Fay observes, if Jardine, Matheson did not move the chests that were consigned to them, their clients in India would switch their business to one of the other houses or individuals, for there was a two-year pipeline from the time money was advanced to peasant cultivators until the sales were accomplished in the China market. There was too much money tied up in this pipeline for the constituents in India to be casual about the pace of sales at Canton and along the coast.[47]

The opium market in China was sluggish in the early 1830s. Sales surged in the season of 1832–33, which is when Jardine, Matheson began its new operations along the coast,[48] but tapered off in 1833–34 by more than a million dollars (almost seven thousand chests less than the previous season).[49] The mercurial sale prices of all three types of Indian opium meant that speculators who committed themselves substantially when optimism fed the market in the winter of 1832–33 were hard pressed to realize profits by the summer of 1833.[50] Consequently, by the winter of 1834–35, Jardine was determined to pursue sales aggressively, telling Captain Rees, "If two vessels are deemed necessary on the coast, and two to keep up the intercourse with Lintin, say so."[51]

In all its many dimensions – Chinese politics, Indian purchasers, vessels shipping and selling, sales arrangements at Canton and along the coast, inventory on the depot vessels, remittances to clients near and far – the drug trade demanded vast amounts of Jardine's time. The strain was evident in his correspondence, and in his deteriorating health, and his resolve to leave China was a strong theme in his letters during the spring of 1836.

Beyond his function as agent for clients far afield, Jardine was, by the mid-1830s, also conducting a more adventurous speculation in the drug than had been the firm's policy in previous years. He did not consider himself a gambling speculator, for he relied on solid intelligence and expeditious transactions. He knew how to ride the market like a rough sea, without getting overwhelmed in the troughs that followed the crests of opium waves.

The firm's purchases were sometimes quite large, for he acted decisively once he was determined to move on an opportunity. He was even prepared to have the drug shipped on vessels not belonging to the firm, if that could gain an advantage in the Chinese market.[52] However, his business instincts demanded reciprocity from the other shipowners, as he told Captain Clifton early in 1835: Clifton, he said, might ship 100 to 150 chests by any clipper leaving before he did, provided he could arrange a similar amount for *Red Rover* from the parties in charge of the other vessel.[53]

The more his firm chose to take risks in the opium market, the more testy Jardine became about the expected efficiency of the vessels carrying the drug. In mid-March 1835 he gave Captain Clifton broad authority to strike a deal at Calcutta, telling him that he was authorized, after consulting with Johnstone, to enter into any arrangement he deemed advisable for the benefit of *Red Rover*.[54] Johnstone was authorized to draw £8,000 on Magniac Smith for investment in opium. "You are fully aware of our views on the subject of opium; and we have perfect confidence in your discretion in keeping any purchases you make within prudent limits," the uncle told his nephew.[55] Before long, Jardine concluded that his confidence had been misplaced, and he growled to Hugh Matheson about it: "The unfortunate delay of the *Red Rover* in your port has annoyed me so much that I am afraid to trust myself with a single remark on the subject," he fumed. "We have been disappointed; – most grievously disappointed." As if another exclamation point were needed, he indicated that the firm's G.T. Gordon, travelling on the *Water Witch*, would explain Jardine's disappointment in full detail upon arriving at Calcautta.[56] Three weeks later, his complaint was still echoing along the China coast, as he vented his anger to Captain Rees of the *Colonel Young*: "The Red Rover has not yet made her appearance, to my great annoyance, as you may suppose."[57]

This matter was eating at him so obsessively that, six weeks after his first letter to Hugh Matheson, he resumed punching: "I have not written to you for a long while, and, as this letter is not likely to be one of the most pleasing description you will say I might well have kept silence till my bile had evaporated … How Mr. Johnstone and you could keep the Rover lying at Calcutta, laughed at by everyone, I cannot fancy, particularly after receiving instructions to invest all our funds without limit."[58] He reported to his partner, still in London, that the nephews had bungled things at Calcutta by adhering too strictly to normal price limits. "After receiving instructions to buy at prevailing prices they sent the *Falcon* back [to China] without a chest on our account."[59] One can just imagine the blistering reception that Andrew Johnstone had from his uncle upon returning to Canton that September.

Beyond his management of the firm's shipping strategies, Jardine had to contend with the unpredictable troubles that vessels have –

groundings, sick captains, weather-related damages, government restrictions. The headaches were numerous and frequent. At the end of January 1835, the *Sylph* ran aground sixty miles beyond Singapore while en route from Calcutta bearing 1,115 chests of opium. The EIC's sloop *Clive* appeared on the scene the following day and took on board 680 rescued chests but most of them were damaged. Jardine was among the merchants to whom the opium had been consigned, and he was mightily distressed by the accident (among other reasons, because the cargo had been insured for fourteen lacs of rupees, and he was likely one of the underwriters).[60] Moreover, he held Captain Wallace of the *Sylph* largely responsible for the disaster. He declined to seek prosecution of the captain, but he did want the consignees to unite in pursuing legal redress for their losses.

About the same time as the *Sylph*'s misfortune, the *Austin*, another of Jardine's opium clippers, also ran aground; it managed to regain its freedom of movement but had to stop downriver from Canton to be hove down.[61] Not many weeks later, the *Governor Findley*, while selling opium along the coast, was caught in a typhoon and had to cut away her masts in order to survive. That took her out of service for remasting. Simultaneously, one of Jardine's captains resigned because of bad health and another returned temporarily to Lintin owing to an attack of bilious fever. In the absence of Matheson, Jardine had to devote vast amounts of time to troubleshooting these transport problems, and concurrently manage the buying and trading of vessels that were a normal part of his conduct of maritime commerce in numerous commodities.

By the spring of 1835, he was busily engaged in the maritime equivalent of horse trading, securing the bark *Falcon* (once a warship) from Captain David Ovenstone for £8,000 and in return selling him the *Lady Hayes* for £17,500. Within a few years the *Falcon* would become the "flagship" of the Jardine, Matheson coastal fleet, then numbering about a dozen vessels. And by April 1836, the fleet operations and personnel of the firm had become extensive enough that Jardine needed to acquire a hospital ship to be stationed at Whampoa.[62]

Early in her existence, the *Falcon* had been fitted with two twenty-four horsepower engines, but when Jardine, Matheson bought her in 1835, he had the engines removed and renovated her for service in the opium trade as a full-rigged ship (the only clipper so fitted).[63] That transformation did not mean that the firm was giving up on steam power. Undeterred by Matheson's mixed luck with the steamship *Forbes* in

1830, Jardine chose to give steam navigation a second chance in 1835 with a schooner appropriately named *Jardine*. Built in Aberdeen, the *Jardine*, with a twenty-six- horsepower engine and paddle wheels, arrived at Lintin in September 1835. Its proud owner, hoping to use the steamer for better communication with his vessels in the estuary, gave a demonstration of the *Jardine*'s abilities for the local Chinese authorities, including the admiral. In spite of its versatility, the *Jardine* was banished from the Pearl River by an edict from the vice-admiral, who declared that "the 'Smokeship' should spread her sails and begone." Bowing to Chinese jurisdiction, Jardine sent the vessel to Singapore in the hopes of selling her. Instead, the engine room caught fire and in the aftermath of that accident the engine was removed. Later renamed the *Lanrick*, the vessel returned to Lintin as a small running ship, and Jardine and Matheson abandoned, at least for the moment, their modern ideas of steam navigation in Chinese waters.[64]

William Jardine had carefully and skilfully expanded the firm's opium fleet. The company's operations in teas, silks, raw cotton, rice, and British manufactures, when combined with Jardine's shipping and insurance operations, may have outweighed the value of the opium trade.[65] Nevertheless, through the 1830s nothing displaced opium at the top of the list. However, Jardine and Matheson were very sensitive to the volatility of the drug trade, not only at Canton and Lintin but along the coast as well.

Indeed, the whole Canton system was unsteady by the time Matheson returned from England. The financial condition of the Hong merchants was so fragile that the old way of doing business, left over from the EIC days, was no longer secure. Moreover, the Chinese court was hearing arguments promoting legalization of the drug as well as countering arguments urging elimination of the trade. Either way, the long-established patterns of opium commerce were to be undermined. By the second half of the 1830s, Jardine and Matheson had to be commercially agile for their firm to survive in a scene so fraught with uncertainty.

The British government's new approach to overseeing trade by their nationals at Canton was not a resounding success, since the superintendents tended to be unsure of themselves. Their "policy of quiescence" was a source of annoyance to Jardine and Matheson and other merchants who were looking for a "forward policy" from the ministry of

Lord Melbourne.[66] But no such "forward policy" was signalled from London, and superintendents took no strong initiatives on their own authority.

Superintendent John Francis Davis maintained his office at Macao but had little sense of what to do. Trade drifted back into its normal channels, the legitimate tea trade at Canton and the illegal opium trade at Lintin, and Davis simply signed papers (payrolls, ships' manifests, and the like) without demanding or commanding much notice from the Chinese authorities.[67] After several months of this minimalist superintendence, Davis retired quietly to England in the early part of 1835.

The Melbourne ministry directed his successor, Sir George Robinson, to press for direct communication with the viceroy, but it did not give him any authority to do so. Accordingly, for nearly two years he observed the comings and goings of British ships as quietly as his predecessor had done. In November 1835 he moved his office to the *Louisa*, anchored off Lintin Island among the opium ships. And if, as he attended to his routine duties of signing documents, he were to look up from his papers, he saw the clippers unloading chests of opium onto the depot ships and watched those chests make their way onto Jardine's coastal schooners or onto the boats of the Chinese buyers who had paid in advance at Canton.[68] Jardine informed his partner that the superintendents had been residing at Macao, "doing nothing," until Robinson moved to the *Lousia*, for the purpose of signing port clearances, "which affords general satisfaction." But he found the superintendents to be so useless that his preference was to have their positions eliminated: "The sooner something is done from home the better, were it only to remove them all & save the larger expenditure."[69]

Officially indifferent to the opium trade going on before his eyes, Robinson was personally offended by the smuggling that surrounded him, and he wrote to Palmerston in February 1836 that he was well placed to take measures against that activity. Yet, not only was he not given instructions to take such measures, but Whitehall reduced the significance of the chief superintendent's post by cutting his salary in half and abolishing the office of third superintendent. Robinson elected to retire from China in December 1836, closing out his long career in the China trade and bequeathing his meagre authority to Captain Charles Elliot of the Royal Navy, who had served as Lord Napier's aide.[70]

Elliot was an intelligent and self-confident individual with strong connections to influential people at home in Britain. Although he acted decisively at the outset in leaving the *Louisa*, with the intention of taking up residence among the factories at Canton, he was at a disadvantage in having no clearly defined, official British China policy to rely on. Moreover, when he wrote to Foreign Secretary Palmerston, the journey of his letter to Britain and the return journey of Palmerston's reply took up to eight months of travel time, which meant that he was sometimes left to his own devices and then left to take the official scolding for his initiative.

After a while, the viceroy, Teng T'ing-chen, was willing to receive sealed letters from Elliot (without an intermediary reading them), but his communications to Elliot were sent via the Hong merchants, who read them and explained their contents to the superintendent. His dilemma was to be caught between a home government that gave him little policy guidance and a Chinese authority that would not communicate directly with him. Collis concludes that Elliot seemed to understand that London expected him to promote the legitimate trade in tea and to close his eyes to the opium smuggling. In the end, his vacillations pleased nobody.[71]

His creative efforts to communicate effectively with Teng eventually led the viceroy to make such a ruckus about the issue that Elliot took down his flag and withdrew from the factory waterfront at Canton. He left a clerk to look after affairs there and removed his own headquarters to Macao.[72] Consequently, he was no longer resident at Canton when some of the bolder British merchants, bothered by the viceroy's crackdown on smuggling but attracted by the prices Canton addicts would pay, decided to force the drug up the Canton River in armed cutters flying the British flag. Elliot wrote Palmerston in alarm that the "great and hazardous change in the mode of the opium trade" was threatening to disrupt all of the British commerce with China.[73] The superintendent understood from Palmerston that he was neither to protect nor to discipline British merchants such as Jardine or Innes or Dent who were selling opium. He lamented "that the conduct of a great trade should be dependent upon the steady continuance of a vast prohibited traffic in an article of vicious luxury, high in price, and liable to frequent and prodigious fluctuation."[74]

The number of speculators had indeed increased significantly, and Jardine was much annoyed that his firm, having pioneered the coastal sales, now found the imitators, dreaming of fortunes in opium, to be legion.[75] He had correctly anticipated that the spasms of official pressure on drug sales at Canton would lead the new speculators to assume that the opium sales were thriving in distant markets which would likely be bare of the drug. As early as the spring of 1835, Jardine was authorizing Captain Rees to explore selling locations farther north, including one called the "Buffaloe's Nose," as a way of intercepting smuggling boats headed south with cash ready for purchases. Not only was Jardine coaching his captains daily regarding their strategies about selling to smugglers and about dodging the mandarins, but he was also giving advice about how to deal with the competition (roughly if necessary) and how to cultivate a market for Malwa opium, which was not immediately popular among the smugglers.[76] He was also looking for market information about articles that might be saleable in the coastal bays. In fact, he advised Captain Francis Jauncey in mid-summer 1835 to load the *Austin* with rice and other articles, with Malwa being the last item loaded aboard. "What we so anxiously wish for," he told Jauncey, "[is] a steady market for Malwa at from 50 to 100$ per chest beyond the Lintin prices." And those higher prices would be likelier the farther north Jauncey took the *Austin*.[77]

If one holds in suspension for the moment any judgments about the morality of this drug trade, Jardine's agility as a trader is impressive. While dealing with correspondents in Britain and India, negotiating through the Hong merchants with the tea men and dispatching cargoes of tea to Britain, handling silks and rice and raw cotton as well as British manufactures, chartering ships and underwriting insurance on those ships and their cargo, and financing the remittances of funds to India and Britain, he was simultaneously directing in minute detail the firm's traffic in opium both at Lintin and along the coast.

By the mid-1830s, Jardine, Matheson was operating seven ships along the coast. A summary of his instructions to Captain MacKay of the *Fairy* in August 1835 serves to illustrate the close personal attention he gave to the coastal vessels and their opium cargoes. "Capt. Parry [aboard *Hercules*] is taking 100 chests of Malwa, which should suffice for the *Fairy* and the *Austin* until Captain Rees [aboard *Colonel Young*] returns. You may take up to 40 chests, which should be sold for $665 near Amoy or $700–750 near Ningpo. You must occupy the ground *Austin* will be leaving until Rees [*Colonel Young*] joins you or you are out of Patna and wish to bring treasure to the *Hercules* [at Lintin]."[78] He was equally explicit about delivery instructions when deals had been struck at Canton for delivery of the drug on the coast. Jardine wanted to be sure that a ship's voyage expenses would be met, lest the Chinese dealer disappear with the whole shipment, having put up in advance only a portion of the purchase price. This would be accomplished by holding back part of his opium until full payment had been made.[79]

He reported the drug market at Canton to be "astonishing" in September 1835, with prices rising far beyond expectations of even the most sanguine individuals.[80] A year before Matheson set foot on China's earth again, Jardine wrote to tell him that the firm's drug speculations that season were likely to wind up to their advantage, but prices were too high at Canton to expect low sales prices at Calcutta for the next season. So, in planning for that next season, he told his partner, "we are ... too deeply engaged in the Coast Trade to trust to the chance of purchasing on the Spot. We must have a supply from both sides of India." Hence the *Governor Findlay* would be sent to Bombay (for Malwa), while *Red Rover* would be dispatched to Calcutta (for Patna and Benares).[81]

Well before Matheson's return in the fall of 1836, an extended debate had materialized within the hierarchy of Chinese officials. Taking the form of "memorials," or what we might now call position papers, these documents were a means of arguing major questions of governmental policy before the emperor and his court. The future of imperial policy toward the opium trade – whether to legalize and regulate it or to suppress it – was the urgent question before the court in the course of 1836.[82] The emperor was given a comprehensive report which accurately detailed the extent of opium smuggling and the way in which [it] was affecting his empire.[83]

In the eyes of certain high officials, known as the "moralists," dependence on opium was corrupting the governing class at a much greater rate than the general population. Their advice was to suppress the trade completely. Arguing for continuation of the trade as a state monopoly was another group of high officials referred to as "legalists," because they advocated legalization of the trade. The latter bloc insisted that a complete ban on opium smoking was next to impossible, and they made the persuasive argument that a regulated commerce in opium would decrease the outflow of sycee silver and bring in revenues for the imperial government which was then getting nothing from the smuggling trade. One formula on the "legalist" side proposed admitting opium to the port of Canton as medicine, but only on terms of barter, with no cash transactions. The foreign merchants sent word to the viceroy that such a plan was unworkable.[84]

Complicating the debate was the known connivance of prominent Chinese officials with the illegal trade. Prior to 1839, the opium trade was always tolerated by some of the authorities, because it was the source of revenues that stimulated the legal commerce.[85] To facilitate the tea trade, the hoppos found it better to put up with the drug smugglers than to rout them.[86] Over the years, many Chinese bureaucrats had come to regard the laws against opium as opportunities to squeeze the dealers.[87] The great weakness of the Ch'ing administration lay in the corruption within the mandarin establishment, as with the viceroy of Canton, Teng, and his subordinate officials, who were profiting handsomely from the illegal trade. When Peking directed him to suppress the trade, he ordered his river police to be aggressive about apprehending smugglers operating in the waters below Canton. But Teng himself then chartered a fleet of boats flying his own flag, to deliver quantities of opium to Canton.[88] According to Van Dyke, "the Canton System was incapable of cleaning up its own house."[89]

Superintendent Elliot concluded that legalization of the opium business would draw the centre of the trade away from Lintin and into Whampoa, closer to Canton. Jardine was not favourably inclined toward legalization, for he recognized that his firm would gain no advantage from a government-regulated opium trade at Canton. Jardine, Matheson was better served by the competitive edge that it held over other dealers along the coast, given the size and speed of the firm's opium fleet. Once the Hong merchants learned of the debate going on at Peking, the foreign merchant community knew about it through their Hong contacts. Jardine was well aware of the ongoing argument at Peking. His response was "annoyance" that the debate was introducing uncertainty into the market. After extended consideration, the imperial court concluded that it would be impossible to control the drug smuggling and that legalization would create more problems than it solved.[90]

Van Dyke points out that, because opium was regarded as a legitimate item of commerce at other ports in Asia, it was not difficult for foreign merchants and Chinese officials to justify marketing it in China.[91] Jardine was unconcerned about the moral terms of the discussions at Peking, for his interests were purely commercial and he understood that prohibition of the trade would undermine the ways of remitting funds acquired by opium sales, whereas legalization would prompt new levels of speculation, thereby forcing up prices at the drug sales in India.[92] Whichever way the debate was to turn, he was convinced that any prohibitory edicts emanating from Peking would be, like earlier versions, futile. But, forever shrewd, he spotted a commercial advantage in the local smugglers' fear of a stoppage in the opium trade. Such a feeling "may prove favorable to our operations on the coast," he told Captain Rees.[93]

In September 1836 the emperor directed Teng to investigate accusations that the foreign poison was being sold right within his jurisdiction at Canton. To cover his own complicity, the viceroy issued repeated warnings to the Hong merchants and targeted nine foreign merchants for expulsion, as a way of showing the severity with which he would punish opium traders. At the top of the list was "Jardine, alias the iron-headed old rat." [94] The Hong merchants were instructed to conduct an investigation of the charges against the nine, in response to which Jardine defended himself with some elusive prevarications in a letter to Howqua at the start of November. He acknowledged receipt of the viceroy's chop dated 28 October and proceeded to describe his activities as follows:

I am a British Subject, having resided in the Creek Factory upwards of ten years, transacting Agency business, in the course of which we have been in the habit of selling Cotton, Sandalwood and other articles the produce of India; Woollens, Cotton piece Goods, Metals, etc. from Europe, on which we have paid duties to a large amount every year. We have also for several years imported upwards of 100,000 peculs of Rice annually, & exported Teas & Silk to a large extent. We have now at Whampoa Nineteen Vessels – not one of which has any Opium on board; and we never heard of the Hong Merchants dealing in that article, nor have we any means of ascertaining exactly the quantity imported.[95]

The nine individuals cited by the viceroy consisted of five Britons (Jardine, Dent, Innes, Turner, and Whiteman), three Parsis (Merwanjee, Dadabhoy, and Framjee), and one American (Gordon). Jardine was convinced that the fuss was all noise: "Foreigners are in no danger, though some of the Censors have advised the Emperor to decapitate a few of them, if necessary." However, a week later, the nine named individuals were ordered by Teng to pack up and leave Canton within a fortnight. The Cohong reported that one of the Parsis, Merwanjee, could not be found. The other eight foreigners all claimed that they were expecting the arrival of ships with cargoes that demanded their attention, but promised to leave eventually, with their dates staggered across the first half of 1837. The governor's annoyance at their non-compliance prompted yet another edict, on 13 December. Clearly, Jardine was the primary target, since his name was cited first in all references to the nine. The edict even quoted Jardine as replying: "I myself have now many ships lying at Whampoa; it is necessary for me to purchase raw silk, teas, and other goods to load and send them away; the teas of this year have, compared with those of last year, been late in their arrival; I earnestly entreat permission to remain and finish my affairs and send all my ships away; and in the fourth moon of next year I will go down and dwell in Macao."[96]

Jardine declared that he had upwards of twenty ships to unload and load, and their cargoes to sell and purchase. He insisted that it would be illogical to expect the Hong merchants to sell and buy select teas for him, for they had business interests that conflicted with his. Dent promised to be gone by April and Jardine by May, but the provincial edict of December 1836 insisted that they both be gone by March.[97]

In the months that followed, some of the nine merchants left for a short time but returned to Canton. Jardine sashayed around the order by sending his nephew Andrew to Macao in his stead. Predictably, nothing happened to those who defied the viceroy's directive. Elijah Bridgman, editor of the *Chinese Repository*, a very respectable English-language magazine published at Canton, offered this summary of the little drama: "At a distance all this fulmination may look terrific," yet upon closer examination it was simply "a shower of rockets in a mild summer's evening."[98]

In fact, the two Scots partners had gotten used to thinking that the proclamations of the imperial court were windy rhetoric, and that many inconveniences could be dealt with by oiling a few palms with some money, a normal business expense. When small captures of opium cargoes were being made frequently and a Portuguese vessel carrying opium was seized in March 1835, Jardine remarked to Jejeebhoy: "I presume … some arrangement will be entered into between the dealers and the Authorities in the course of a week or two."[99] Near the end of 1835 Jardine had casually remarked to one his captains that the only new development in the trade was an imperial edict against foreign vessels frequenting the coast.[100] It did not seem to be much cause for alarm.

Nevertheless, there were moments when Jardine had to wait to see just how the wind was blowing. He had to tell Jejeebhoy that there was nothing doing in drug sales in early March 1836. The smuggling boats were all in hiding "until it is ascertained if the new Viceroy intend any measures against the dealers in the drug."[101] At that point not even the mandarins knew the direction in which government policy would be headed. He was careful, however, to avoid antagonizing the Chinese authorities. He had made provision for arming the coastal vessels, but he did not want them firing on government junks. When Captain William MacKenzie did just that, Jardine told him: "You appear to have done no harm, no edict having been published or outcry made about it, but the policy is questionable … You should on all occasions avoid giving offence or rendering your ship conspicuous."[102]

James Matheson arrived back in China just in time for the "shower of rockets" that Bridgman described. Appropriately enough, the last leg of his return journey was accomplished aboard the *William Jardine*, which arrived on 14 November. Although the journey from Batavia to Canton was a tedious passage of thirty-six days, Jardine reported his partner to be in "tolerably good health, but not very stout." Within a few days Matheson was once more immersed in the operations of the firm.[103]

He must have been able to recognize immediately what a toll his long absence had taken on his partner. Jardine had written to Matheson a year before the latter returned: "If we keep our health I hope to be able to manage matters for ten or twelve months longer."[104] He did that, but he was worn out, and would have readily booked passage home were it not for the unsettled state of affairs at Canton, particularly the fragile financial state of the Hong merchants. There had been few holidays for him in the course of Matheson's time away, and the single-handed management of the firm had exhausted him. What is more, while Matheson was away, Jardine had to bid farewell to the nephew of whom he was so fond. According to his uncle, Andrew Johnstone took his leave of the firm early in 1836, to go "home to rusticate" at his estate of Halleaths, near Dumfries in southwest Scotland.[105] Another nephew, Andrew Jardine, sailed home on the *Camden* in the spring of 1836, suffering from ill health (but he would return to China and become a partner in the firm in 1839).[106]

The senior partner, now age fifty-two, had intended to follow Andrew Johnstone home to Scotland in short order. "On Mr. Matheson's return

I shall endeavour to take leave of the Celestial Empire," he wrote to a Scottish client.[107] His intention to return home seems to have become firm during or shortly after a stretch of poor health in the early part of 1836. His desire to retire to Britain in the near future was well rooted, for he mentioned it in several letters. He wrote to an old chum, James Jardine: "Having made up my mind to return to my native country soon after the arrival here of my friend (& partner) now in England, I look forward to shaking you by the hand in the Land of Cakes, not many months after this reaches you."[108]

However, not long after Matheson returned, Jardine wrote to Howqua that he had been intending for some time to leave Canton at the end of that season, but the actions of the black tea sellers had held back sales for so long that his departure would be delayed until the end of the third Chinese Moon (about mid-spring), "when I shall be too happy to find that it is my power to go."[109] But he returned from Macao in 1837 and did not sail homeward until January 1839.

Ill health beset him in November 1835, when he wrote to Matheson, "I have got a severe cold, and, being past midnight must go to bed, and if possible sweat it off."[110] It was typical of Jardine to try to stick with his office routine while trying to overcome an infection: as a doctor he was not his own best counsel. The infection recurred in January 1836, when he was utterly knocked down by what he described as "a severe attack of cold and fever" that started on the twenty-fifth of the month. He was confined to his room for more than two weeks and was not back at his desk until the tenth of February. (Characteristically, the tough "iron-headed rat" returned to work a week before he was able to return to the dining table.)

Glad as he was to have received a portable shower at the start of the year, he informed the sender, a friend named George Moffat in London, that he had been unable to make use of that "life prolonger" because he was "in the Doctor's hands for a very severe attack of cold and fever; which prevented me from using the bath." By the end of February, he was reporting himself to be "nearly recovered."[111] Yet in May he admitted to Thomas Weeding that the poor health had left him "in so debilitated a state that I have been incapable till lately of exerting my faculties as formerly." He asked Weeding's understanding for "the languor & aversion to business which accompany bad health." This in itself would be most unusual for the workaholic Jardine to admit, but it would be understandable in view of his run-down condition.[112]

More ominous were the symptoms that emerged toward the end of May. He begins to mention in his letters a severe "bowel complaint" which had left him "too restless to write a connected letter." He admitted to suffering a good deal from this "bowel attack" at that point in the year, but apparently the symptoms subsided, since he was able, in December, to describe his episodes of illness as "occasional indisposition" which he ascribed to being overworked during Matheson's absence.[113] But the ominous factor in this "indisposition" was not the fatigue that may have predisposed him to his cold and fever; rather it was the bowel complaints that were the first signs of a condition that would prove fatal not many years after his return to England.[114]

A year after returning to China, Matheson judged his partner to be in very good shape. Assuring Andrew Johnstone that his uncle was healthy, Matheson declared: "Mr. Jardine is quite well, and failing in nothing that I can perceive, except his eyesight – being constantly obliged to use spectacles in reading and writing. He seems really made of Iron, as I often remark to him."[115] From these comments one might conclude that Jardine did not speak much about his discomforts, and Matheson, being twelve years younger, had not yet reached the stage of life when aches become routine.

There is no record of who attended him when he was sick, although there was a small circle of physicians and ships' surgeons among the British and American residents of Canton. When the EIC closed its factory at Canton, the senior surgeon for the Company was Thomas Colledge, who had also maintained a small public clinic at Macao. It is likely that it was either he or the medical missionary Peter Parker, who arrived in 1834, who looked after Jardine when he was ill. Jardine had not abandoned his own interests in medicine altogether after leaving the Company's service. (He is reported to have written a pamphlet concerning surgical instruments.) When in 1835 Parker opened a clinic called the Opthalmic Hospital among the factories along the waterfront, Jardine assisted him in the first major surgery, to remove a tumor from a girl's face.[116]

Not until 1836 was there permanent medical care available to British and American residents and sailors in China.[117] Moreover, great numbers of the local Chinese population put up with ailments that could have been addressed by routine surgery in Edinburgh or London. Peter Parker's little hospital on Hog Lane in Canton attracted so many patients that he needed additional physicians and help with his expenses.

Initially he depended on the charity of his friends, but eventually Jardine and Matheson, as well as Charles King and several other foreign residents, organized the Medical Missionary Society to help pay the bills and to recruit more doctors.[118] Gideon Nye, Jr, reports in his memoir of Canton that Jardine took a great interest in that society and assisted Dr Parker with surgical procedures. Nye recalls that Jardine paid one of Parker's Chinese patients $50 to agree to an amputation, because the man had been afraid that foreign doctors were performing surgeries simply for monetary gain.[119] The Society established a clinic in Macao and secured the services of another missionary doctor. Thereafter it was possible for the Medical Missionary Society to provide year-round treatment both at Canton and at Macao.[120]

There is, of course, a huge irony in the contrast between the public charity provided by Jardine and Matheson and the medical problems resulting indirectly from the opium they imported. Their generosity for good causes has been largely overlooked because of all the attention given to their very successful opium marketing, and the addiction of many Chinese to the drug. Moreover, the legitimate medical uses of their imported opium in relieving pain and providing a makeshift pre-ether anesthetic have been overshadowed by the debilitating effects of the illegal trade.

Their charity was not confined to medical philanthropy. Jardine is known to have been among the merchants who raised a fund to help create the Morrison Education Society at Canton. Although the purpose of the fund was to establish a school providing Christian education for young Chinese students, the project did not immediately attract a teacher from England or the United States, and directed some of its funds monthly to support an institution for blind and orphaned Chinese girls at Macao. In the course of the late 1830s, a young American named Samuel Brown arrived, fresh from Yale, to establish the school that Jardine and the others had envisioned.[121]

With reserve typical of their relationship, neither Jardine nor Matheson manifested any excitement over the resumption of their collaboration at Canton. Matheson was back and Jardine was glad to have his help in managing the firm's operations. Beyond that there is no reference to any special celebration at Matheson's return nor any great sigh of relief on Jardine's part that his burdens might be eased. Perhaps that says enough about the terms of their friendship and the tone of their office. Both men were in reasonable health as the rigours of the tea season and the worries of the expulsion crisis confronted them. Nothing much is said of the eye problem which prompted Matheson's journey to England, so one assumes that it was cured or at least eased. And Jardine's ill health of the first half of 1836 had passed, although he was clearly fatigued.

Their roles had been dramatically different for more than a year and a half, while Matheson was in Britain, and now the partners could not simply resume where they had left off when Matheson sailed home, for the ground was shifting beneath their feet. The Cohong was a less viable financial intermediary. The future of the remittance system was unpredictable. And the debate at Peking was threatening to destabilize the agency operations of Jardine, Matheson and the other houses selling the drug.

Yet, when Teng made no effort to force the expelled merchants to leave China, Jardine and Matheson concluded that the whole affair was but another instance of hollow imperial proclamations. So they gave no thought to abandoning their opium operations and remained optimistic about ongoing profits from their extensive trade.

# 8

# APPROACHING THE SHOWDOWN
# IN CHINA

Although Viceroy Teng failed to enforce the expulsion order against William Jardine and the other designated merchants, Teng was sending other signals that should have indicated to them a change in the wind of imperial policy. Severity in the threats of punishment for smugglers was accompanied by examples of the sort of treatment the government intended to impose. Along the Canton River, Teng smashed the circle of smugglers and destroyed the "fast crab" boats by which they had dodged enforcement of the law. Moreover, to impress the imperial court as well as the local people, he gave a statistical report on the amounts of opium that had been seized and burned as well as the trials and sentences of the smugglers and brokers who had been apprehended. However, Jardine and Matheson and the other foreign merchants were more inclined to think that the officials of Teng's administration were simply retailing the confiscated opium for their own profit.[1]

Teng's order for the public strangling of an opium broker near Macao and the construction of a gun emplacement overlooking Cumsingmoon sent other signals in the early months of 1837. Opium boats still operated in the river, but the mandarins squeezed out of them a crooked "duty" of about 15 per cent on each chest of smuggled opium.[2] Van Dyke asserts that, as the Canton trade became more dependent on opium income to finance the growth of the tea trade, the hoppos concluded that it was better to tolerate the smuggling than to put an end to it.[3] Major importers of opium were now caught up in a strange three-cornered competition, which pitted them against each other and against the government. The rules of the game were ill-defined, for the government spoke one policy and followed another.

The opium market had been particularly flat at the start of 1836, with Jardine reporting the season to be "as unsatisfactory ... as ever I saw in China."[4] The competition moved away from Lintin and intensified along the coast. "The trade in the Bays now generally known and resorted to by parties who had neither public spirit nor energy equal to the task of establishing a new station is now nearly ruined, as I always expected it would be sooner or later, but did not expect it to have been so suddenly & unnecessarily rendered worse than the Lintin trade."[5] Jardine had no taste for the use of guns, although the firm's ships were armed (for last-resort protection against pirates or government junks, not against business competitors).[6] However, he was not loathe to resort to bare-knuckles trading competition.

The competition included the *Volunteer* (belonging to Framjee Pestonjee) and the *Lord Amherst* (belonging to Dent and Company). The commander of Jardine, Matheson's *Colonel Young*, Captain John Rees, was allowed to arrive at pricing agreements with both of them to avoid cutthroat competition. But, in a moment of aggravation, Jardine had been prepared to allow Rees to play rough with Dent's ship. Captain Thomas Rees of the *Lord Amherst*, who was a brother of Jardine's John Rees, had devised a way to secure some of the coastal sales. He sold opium on board at a price agreed upon by the rival vessels; but, once the opium was ashore, Dent's Chinese collaborators there were rebating as much as ten dollars per chest to the smugglers.[7] Jardine was disgusted at his rivals' behaviour and expressed his disdain that "such mean Arts should be resorted to by men placed in a respectable situation in life, a situation of great trust and responsibility, for the petty consideration of selling a few additional chest[s]."

The remedy would be nose-to-nose competition between Jardine's coastal fleet and Dent's barque. He had a suggestion for Captain Rees aboard the *Colonel Young*: "As you now have more vessels than your Opponents how would it answer to place one of them alongside the Amherst and run prices down as low as they may think fit to go, while you keep prices up in the distant Bays? Cured they must be of such evil practices even at [our] sacrifice of reducing prices."[8] Rees took a more conciliatory approach to the rivalry and reached an agreement with his brother to fix their price for opium chests. Jardine allowed the agreement to stand but doubted its long-run durability. Moreover, he would not agree to any bargain about equalizing the proportion of sales.[9]

Throughout the spring of 1836, Jardine had been hammering out a theme like a mantra in his correspondence: we need to open another market. He suggested to Rees that they explore the possibility of sending a vessel to the Chusan group of islands, much farther north, where opium prices were high and bribes to the mandarins might allow the ship to hang around for as long as six months. This would put Jardine, Matheson operations far beyond the reach of their competitors.[10]

The firm had been using the brig *Fairy* as a running vessel, carrying opium from the warehouse vessels at Lintin to the *Colonel Young* along the coast. However, just as Matheson was arriving back at Canton, ominous stories about the whereabouts of the *Fairy* were reaching a climax. Jardine had heard "unpleasant reports" from Macao, as early as September, about the fate of the *Fairy,* which had been returning to Lintin with gold and silver.[11] By the end of that month, he was in a state of "extreme anxiety" because of conflicting stories that reported the ship having been attacked, possibly by pirates who murdered the crew, possibly by mandarins. Jardine was left to sift blindly through hearsay accounts. In his growing anxiety, he began to fear for the safety of his other ships and their captains, and he offered to provide Captain Mackenzie of the *Governor Findlay* with more men and arms if they were needed.[12]

As late as the third week of November, Jardine was still hopeful that the *Fairy* would turn up, but reports reaching Canton from the *Jardine* and the *Harriet* were discouraging, and when Matheson finally reached Canton he was greeted with the news that his cousin, Captain MacKay of the *Fairy*, might be dead.[13]

MacKay was indeed dead, the victim of an insurrection among the crew of his vessel. Six crew members from Manila had mutinied on 21 August, in reaction to some harsh treatment by the first mate. They killed him on deck in the dark of night, then burst in upon the cabin where they murdered the captain, second mate, and gunner, and proceeded to throw them overboard. The rest of the crew – Lascars, Portuguese, and Chinese – was sent away in the longboat and reached the coast of China after about eight hours. (Some drowned when the longboat capsized near the beach.)[14] The mutineers sailed the *Fairy* to Subic Bay, northwest of Manila, where they scuttled it off the island of Luconia. By January 1837, Jardine and Matheson had learned that the mutineers had been identified, and by April Matheson was able to report to a friend that they had been apprehended and executed at Manila.[15]

Jardine had received a full report of the weight and appearance of the stolen gold bars, which he estimated to be worth seventy thousand dollars. While the firm had the vessel and its cargo insured, the real pain for Matheson came from the loss of his kinsman: "The sad fate of my poor cousin Capt. Mackay of the Fairy is but too truly confirmed ... My uncle and Aunt succeed to about £15,000 by the melancholy event."[16] Of all the risks incurred by the coastal trade, this was a consequence the partners would never have imagined.

As of 1836, the annual sales of opium in China amounted to about 1,820 tons.[17] For Jardine, Matheson, beyond its share of that market, there was also the prospect of securing silks from ports at the mouth of the Yangtse if the firm sent a ship to Shanghai and Ningpo and other northern ports.[18] By the time Matheson arrived back at Canton, the firm was poised not only to defy the mandarin moralists but also to enter a new stage of market development that would stamp William Jardine as the boldest of Western entrepreneurs on the coast of China.

Two ongoing headaches for the partners involved the financing of East-West commerce at Canton. One problem concerned a surviving remnant of the EIC, in the form of the Finance Committee that served as a source of money for private merchants, while the other problem was the financial fragility of the Cohong houses.

The Canton Committee in effect had become a financial agency, an activity that was specifically against the terms of the parliamentary legislation which had ended the Company's commercial charter. It continued in operation, much to Jardine's annoyance, until the exodus of British merchants in 1839. Not only did the availability of the Finance Committee's funding encourage the new rivals, but it also led the Chinese merchants to raise their prices, especially for teas, since they knew that the Committee's treasury assured the operations of their British buyers. And the respondentia agreements[19] had the effect of making the East India Company, at least in the short term, the regulator of a great proportion of the privately shipped China trade goods entering Britain. As Cheong explains it, the private merchants had succeeded in breaking the East India Company's dominance of the homeward-bound cargoes, but almost immediately handed back the effective control of a large part of that commerce.[20] While the Finance Committee's exchange operations at Canton did fill the needs of many private traders in China, additional sources of credit and exchange for Western commerce in the country were found among the major Anglo-American financial houses, most notably, Wilson and Company, Wiggin and Son, Wildes and Company, and Baring Brothers.

In the financial disaster that hit the British agency houses in Calcutta during the early 1830s, Fairlie and Company had suspended payments in November 1833, costing its Canton agency, Jardine, Matheson, a loss of £22,000, a relatively small amount given the scale of the Calcutta failures. But Fairlie's bankruptcy temporarily left Jardine's endorsements unprotected. With the help of Hollingworth Magniac, Jardine's bills were immediately protected by the established banking house of Timothy Wiggin and Son, and the firm's reputation for financial stability stood untarnished.[21]

In negotiating a reliable connection with the new London house of Magnaic Smith in 1835, James Matheson made it clear that his firm did not intend to make Magniac Smith its sole London agent but rather would continue to carry on business with other London houses. Nevertheless, the good relationship established with Magniac Smith would pay a huge dividend within a relatively short time, for the big Anglo-American exchange firms were in mortal distress within a matter of months after Matheson's return to Canton.[22]

The major financial crisis of 1837 was a huge distraction from the Jardine, Matheson emphasis on drug sales along the coast. In a sense, the two issues could not be separated, for the firm's financial operations were intimately tied to its available cash, which was derived principally from the trade in opium. The two partners were taken by surprise, blind-sided by the phenomenon that has come to be known as the Panic of 1837, originating in the United States and extending to British financial markets and the Continent.

After President Andrew Jackson vetoed the congressional renewal of the charter of the Second Bank of the United States, Americans, who had previously paid for imports of Chinese goods with silver bullion, now began to use bills of exchange provided by British buyers of American cotton. As American importers were no longer sending silver bullion to China, the quantity of Mexican silver in the United States continued to accumulate and swell the money supply. However, in 1837 the financial policies of the American government caused the financial climate to shift from inflationary to deflationary. Businesses failed from unwise investments; commercial stagnation occurred; the crisis spread internationally.

For Jardine, Matheson, the financial quake coincided with the bankruptcy of Hengtai, a Hong merchant who was indebted to them for about $2 million. In August 1837 Jardine acknowledged the prospect of a big loss in a letter to a Manila agent, John Shillaber. The times were so trying, he said, that many firms were going to be ruined before the commerce of England and America regained a firm footing: "Our friends have been wild beyond anything in their orders for Tea and Raw Silk, & much money must be lost; we are fortunate in having little interest in either article this season, & still we do not expect to escape a loss in some way or other ... but unlike your neighbours in this particular we shall have no satisfaction in seeing our friends or even our enemies (as we appear to have some) suffer with us."[23] He was referring to some of Shillaber's neighbours, who were apparently gloating at the prospect of Jardine, Matheson's loss from Hengtai's bankruptcy.

At the end of 1837, Matheson projected that the firm's losses would be comparatively light, even though it could not hope to escape unscathed. Even if its American bills failed, the company's losses would be easily met, he predicted, by its safe earnings of a single year.[24] As it happened, the crash stung Jardine and Matheson more than either anticipated. Nevertheless, the company survived the financial contagion, in part by the caution of avoiding speculative cargoes that might be refused at their destinations, and by the discretion that Jardine and Matheson exercised in their choice of London agents.

Jardine's foresight in declining to rely on Wiggin alone was keen, for Wiggin's firm was among those that failed as a result of the collapse of the American bill system in 1837. The protection offered by Magniac Smith made it possible for Jardine, Matheson to weather the crisis. In this instance, for endorsing bills issued by the houses of Wiggin, Wilson, and Wildes, the firm would suffer a loss of £100,000, five times the sum lost in the Calcutta crisis of 1833; but the firm's signatures were honoured by Magniac Smith, leading Matheson to conclude that the loss would fall lightly on his partnership because the integrity of their name had been preserved.[25]

Matheson assured Smith that Jardine, Matheson would use the earliest practicable, safe means to restore the funds that Magniac Smith had advanced on its behalf.[26] In a similar tone, Jardine told Hollingworth Magniac rather philosophically: "In times like these we must expect to suffer along with others; but we have no reason to apprehend anything that can materially inconvenience us; as we have every reason to believe that nearly all the Bills we have drawn or endorsed will be ultimately made good, if not paid when due."[27] Gideon Nye remembers Jardine as being "calm in the darkest moment" of the crisis.[28]

There was a vast amount of money tied up in the bills of credit that Jardine and Matheson (and Dent) had been moving through the Anglo-American houses, and it had not been possible for them to redirect their business abruptly away from Wiggin, Wilson, Wildes and the others without causing a scare that would risk harming the reputations of some respectable businesses. To a certain degree, it was a matter of honour not only for Jardine, Matheson but also for Dent to swallow some of the losses rather than provoke a public uproar by hastily abandoning their connections with the Anglo-American houses.[29]

As it happened, the Canton agency houses did not hear of the American bankruptcies until August 1837, and it took even longer for them to learn that several of the major Anglo-American banking houses had stopped payments as of the first week of June. Upon hearing of the crisis, Jardine hastened to assure Jejeebhoy that Jardine, Matheson was not in any danger. It was the firm's good fortune, he indicated, to have less than £5,000 at stake in tea and silk that season, commodities where a great deal of money was going to be lost as a result of the panic.[30] By October 1837, the whole commercial scene at Canton was becalmed: no ships loading for England or America, not a chest of tea or a bale of silk being purchased; nothing doing in the financial exchange market. Canton was never so dull at this time of year, he lamented.[31] On the eve of a brief trip to Macao early in September, Jardine wrote to a Bombay client: "We are, for the present at a stand as regards Exchange operations; and all we can do is to accumulate Cash in our Treasury and keep it ready for anything that may offer." Not only was it difficult to estimate the exchange rates between Canton and England, but it was even more difficult to determine whose bills were safe to be taken.[32]

By year's end, Matheson was still apologizing for being a burden on Magniac Smith because of the remittance problem.[33] There was also a distressing revelation in Matheson's correspondence with Smith: the old relationship with Thomas Weeding was in tatters. During the crisis, Weeding had declined to advance funds to cover bills drawn or endorsed by Jardine, Matheson, thus leading Matheson to tell Smith: "On Mr. Weeding's conduct I shall make no comment, further than that it greatly enhances our estimation ... of your kind aid, – It will of course prevent our having further recourse to his agency."[34]

For Jardine, the falling-out with Weeding was especially painful, for it was in Weeding's office at South Sea Yard, London, back in 1817–18 that Jardine had learned the skills of export-import trade and international finance. Now, twenty years later, he waited many months before articulating his unhappiness with his old business tutor. In the spring of 1837, before the dam burst, Jardine had assured his erstwhile patron that the firm's bills were reliable: "Make your mind easy respecting your advances on our account, we being flush of Cash, while it is a scarce article generally." Similar reassurances were contained in a letter late in the summer.[35] Nevertheless, in the course of 1837, Weeding declined – for the second time in a decade – to honour bills bearing the signatures of Jardine and Matheson. Six letters from Weeding had gone unanswered when Jardine finally vented his spleen to his former London banker. There were two reasons for the long delay, he declared: one, the uncertainty of his own return to England, and the other "a certain feeling of discontent, not to say disgust, at your conduct in dishonouring the Bills of JM & Co.; which nothing but time can wear off."

Unless the firm's copyist was drunk or overtired when writing out the letter, the extent of William Jardine's ire toward his long-time friend and associate can be gauged by the ungrammatical and confused state of the "sentence" which followed his expression of disgust: "When I contemplate the position in which we now stand, in comparison with that in which we should have stood had you been our sole Agent in England, as you were desirous of being, I cannot but feel highly grateful to MS & Co, who evinced such determined confidence in their protection of our drafts, and endorsements, when dishonoured by you and others – though J.A. Smith is a Gentleman I never saw to my Knowledge – the contrast I wish to forget for many reasons, the feeling of gratitude I should despise myself did I forget it. Enough on this to me very disagreeable subject."[36]

Upon reading this barbed declaration of lingering resentment, Weeding must have been astonished when the next part of the letter contained Jardine's nicely phrased expression of congratulations to Weeding upon the occasion of his marriage, with best wishes for the happiness of Weeding and his bride as well as Jardine's hope of meeting the lady upon his return to England. However, the correspondence books make it clear that Weeding had ceased to be the friend, even confidant, upon whom Jardine had depended for years: the letters from Jardine to Weeding simply stopped.

To a certain degree, Weeding's reticence is understandable, for Jardine, Matheson seemed to be living inside a circle of failures – first the collapse of the British houses in Calcutta in the early years of the decade, then the ruin of the Anglo-American houses in the 1837 disaster, which overlapped with the failure of Hengtai in 1837. To a London financier, it might have seemed that sooner or later Jardine's luck was going to run out and that the firm was going to be burned severely in one of these bankruptcies.

In reality, the textile market at Canton was not a balanced and stable commerce. Jardine's had a substantial trade in raw cotton imported from India, but it also had a speculative venture, or one might say "forced," trade in English finished textiles (woollens and cottons) which was precarious. The Manchester connection was a difficult one for Jardine, given the irascible temperament of John MacVicar who had great expectations for the China market as an outlet for English piece-goods. Hengtai, Jardine's "favorite" Hong merchant, had been persuaded to undertake retail sales in British piece goods, although the known market for such items did not justify strong optimism about this new enterprise. Nevertheless, in the mid-1830s, MacVicar had about £400,000 in cargoes and instruments of finance invested in the China market under Jardine's management.[37]

His prominence among Lancashire textile manufacturers and his role as political lobbyist for merchant interests overseas gave MacVicar a high visibility both in the English Midlands and in London. Anxious to take advantage of the new circumstances of free trade for British merchants at Canton, MacVicar pressed Jardine to market piece-goods for him. Jardine had warned him to regulate his shipments sensibly, in view of the competition from American cotton-goods exporters. He had informed MacVicar at the start of 1836 that the foreign merchants at Canton were buying silk at "most extravagant prices," far beyond MacVicar's instructions to buy at low or moderate prices.[38] Nevertheless, when Jardine followed his client's instructions, MacVicar complained to other merchants about the way Jardine and Matheson were remitting funds. He wanted silks, but he specified a price that was too low, so they had to send MacVicar bills rather than silk, thereby causing their grumbly client more dyspepsia. In the midst of the international crisis, when Jardine, Matheson was being so careful about the reliability of its name, both Jardine and Matheson finally found MacVicar's abrasiveness intolerable.

Piece-goods was a "forced trade," as Jardine observed, but MacVicar was eager to reinvest his cotton-sales earnings in cargoes of tea and silk bound for England, and he wore down Jardine and Matheson with his complaints. By the end of 1836, Jardine had suffered enough of MacVicar's spleen, and handed over his accounts to Magniac Smith with directions to close down that commercial relationship.[39] "Our final dispatches respecting your various complaints are in progress," wrote Jardine to MacVicar, "and should be completed before ... the end of the month."[40]

MacVicar, of course, was in a category of his own. Not only did he communicate with Robert Thom, a member of the Jardine, Matheson staff, about business matters, but he also addressed Thom confidentially about the character and management styles of the firm's partners. Beyond that, he accused Jardine of "humbugging" a ship captain named Marshall over the purchase of silk.[41] Over several months in 1837, both Matheson and Jardine informed various people in Britain and India that they were able to look forward with "complete indifference" to the dissolution of the connection.[42] Although Matheson declared to another English correspondent that "we are ... right glad to be quit with MacVicar and his querulous gang," he had not actually seen the last of MacVicar's firm.[43] Before the year was out, MacVicar and Company was itself operating in Canton, established there as agents for the Bombay Commercial Insurance Society.[44]

For the Hong merchants who were handling both tea and textiles, there was a simultaneous problem caused by a scheme among the so-called "Black-Tea men," who were attempting to force up the prices paid by the Cohong for black tea, the main type exported to Britain. In 1836 this faction of tea producers refused to deliver their teas to market, even though they were under contractual agreement to do so, unless the Hong merchants provided advanced payment in cash or provided security for the tea shipments.[45] The merchants waiting to ship teas were all disappointed, but they had no redress for the Tea men's violation of their contracts. Everyone at Canton understood that the Tea men were holding back their teas, knowing that if they were left with the teas on hand they could pledge them to the Company's Finance Committee for two-thirds of their value and receive that amount of money at once, in cash or in Company bills.[46]

As a monopoly of middlemen dealing with the foreign merchants, the Cohong were nevertheless powerless to stand up to the bullying tactics

of the Tea men. The Hong merchants were manifestly incapable of acting with unanimity for their own protection, so Jardine was prepared to
ask Howqua to appeal to the Chinese authorities – a curious reliance on
the government for which he traditionally showed contempt – for enforcement of the tea contracts. The Tea men had received big advances
from the Hong merchants, whose funds were tied up in this game of
commercial extortion, but the English merchants at Canton were showing the same lack of unity as the Cohong, angering Jardine by their
willingness to pay exorbitant prices for whatever chops (parcels) of
tea were reaching Canton.[47] Jardine, Matheson contracted, through
Howqua, Mowqua, Hengtai, and other Hong merchants, for a large
quantity of good-quality tea in the spring of 1836, but Jardine acknowledged that the wholesale suppliers of tea were "slippery characters,"
whose success during the first two seasons of free trade had made them
"as saucy as possible."[48] When the Tea men did bring forth teas, enough
for three vessels, in the spring of 1836, virtually all the cargoes were
committed to the EIC for the funds that the Finance Committee made
available to the Tea men, who thereby managed to bypass the Cohong.
Clearly, the English parties at Canton were fouling each other's lines, by
playing for private advantages in such ways that the ruthless tea merchants were the beneficiaries.

When Jardine, Matheson, along with other European merchants, undertook direct negotiations with the "slippery characters," the effect on
the Cohong was to undermine their credit. Jardine admitted that the
outcome of the struggle between the Cohong and the Tea men could
determine the continued existence of the Hong merchants as a public
body.[49] Matheson knew that all the Hong merchants, with two exceptions, were in precarious situations, but he predicted that Hengtai's
business was not likely to fail.[50] He was wrong. Hengtai did indeed fail,
late in 1836, at which moment eight of the eleven Hongs were hope-
lessly indebted. The unsafe ventures in English piece-goods had contributed significantly to the distress of these Hongs. To acquire ready money
they had been discounting English piece goods at from 5 per cent to
7 per cent in their sales to Chinese merchants in the city of Canton, and,
as a consequence, they built up staggering debts.[51] Ready money was so
scarce among the Hong members that as early as 1835 Jardine had reported to a Bombay client: "We have not received $150,000 in Cash
from the Hong Merchants during the whole season."[52]

When Hengtai failed in 1836, his Hong owed Jardine, Matheson sixteen lacs of dollars ($1,600,000). He attributed the collapse to overtrading, interpreting the markets wrongly, and misusing his Hong's funds for family expenditures. Jardine was angry: "The failure is, I am convinced, a dishonest one; the money has not been lost in trade." Yet he described his firm as being ready to ride out the crisis, for the large sum of money that it lost had been tied up for some length of time, during which it had not had difficulty making remittances to clients.[53]

Jardine was fearful that if he and other creditors applied too much pressure to the indebted Hongs, they would all break; and if that happened, he forecast, the hoppo would simply create six or eight more, each of which would collapse within a few years. "This is a gloomy picture," he told Jejeebhoy. "I see no mode of remedying this evil, but by coming to cash sales, or barter; in the latter case the goods to be handed over at the same instant." Yet he understood that the consequence of such a policy would be to bring down prices dramatically in the short run.[54] To some degree, the financial suffering was to be buffered by the Consoo Fund, established by imperial decree for the reimbursement of foreigners should insolvency overwhelm debt-ridden Hong merchants.

In planning his departure from China, William Jardine was more concerned about the stability of trade than he was with the debts of the Chinese merchants.[55] He told his friend Magniac that the troubles caused by the Tea men had revealed such weakness among the Hong merchants that he could not think of leaving until some arrangements had been made for the settling of their accounts and for the stabilization of trade at Canton on a safe and solid basis. "Our outstanding claims would not detain me a day; but I am well aware of the time and trouble required to gain the object we have in view; and am unwilling to leave Mr. Matheson such an unpleasant task at a time when the general business of the Firm requires constant attention."[56] Consequently, Jardine would not pack his trunks in the spring of 1837, for he was resigned to spending more seasons in what he sometimes referred to playfully as "Cheapside China." Matheson appreciated his partner's grit: "He speaks of going home this season; but I shall never believe him serious in this till he is actually off."[57] As things played out, it would be a full two years before he embarked on the first leg of his journey homeward.[58]

Although opium remained the most volatile and most profitable of his agency's commodities, it was not opium that kept Jardine in China.

The financial security of his firm was something that he and his partner would have to devote long hours to protecting; and the general trade of the firm in various commodities and services would be a heavy burden for Matheson alone to manage while simultaneously shielding the firm's assets against the defaults of merchants indebted to them.

There can be little doubt that the advent of free trade was a problematic development for William Jardine and James Matheson. Having lobbied for an end to the dominance of the EIC in the China trade, the two partners were resentful of what they saw as the reckless behaviour of johnny-come-lately types who had leapt into the commerce as opportunists: "We are ... almost sighing for a return of the Company's monopoly," Matheson wrote to a man in Philadelphia, "in preference to the trouble and endless turmoil of free trade."[59] Jardine continued to blame the Company's ghost, the Finance Committee, for fuelling the wild speculations by extending too much credit.[60] The partners found themselves thinking that they were stuck with the worst of both worlds – the remnant of the Company's monopoly and the onrush of more new entrepreneurs than the China trade could reasonably absorb. This was not the brave new world of China trade that Jardine and Matheson had envisioned; moreover, they continued to be saddled with the unwieldy system of the Hong merchants as intermediaries for the newly opened free trade.

Fortunately for its partners, Jardine, Matheson was formidable enough to handle diversified cargoes on a scale that the recently arrived speculators were not capable of undertaking. This factor gave them leverage against the risks of concentration on a single commodity. Among the crops that Jardine, Matheson marketed profitably, rice was very prominent. The Chinese market for rice was especially large in seasons when rainfall was insufficient to produce a good crop in China. Jardine would arrange for rice or "paddy" (rice shipped with its straw) to be transported from Manila; and for this he relied on John Shillaber, who was personally liked by both Jardine and Matheson even if he was not always an effective business manager. The firm that he operated, as a partner, was named Otadui and Company. Jardine and Matheson were sometimes so eager to have Philippine rice shipped to Canton that they would even send the bags for packing it, in addition to the money advanced for purchase.

Jardine's correspondence with Shillaber opens a window on his estimation of the Chinese instincts in business: "The Chinese, generally speaking, are extremely sanguine & speculative, so much so, that many of their mercantile operations are reduced, unnecessarily, or to all appearances intentionally, to gambling transactions, & in no article of commerce does this occur so generally as in Rice. A few wet days, or a week or two of dry weather seldom fail to produce a Spirit of Speculation among the dealers in rice. They are far too sanguine, & too much under a gambling influence to be prudent merchants."[61] Hence Jardine's reluctance to retire to an estate in Scotland while the Cohong members were struggling with credit problems and teetering on bankruptcy.

Cargoes that Jardine, Matheson was not handling directly might nevertheless be put up as security for debts to the firm, and among such cargoes rice was prominent. When an English merchant at Canton, A.J. Keating, was unable to settle his debts to the firm in 1835, Jardine blasted him for withholding payment when his rice, pledged as security to Jardine, Matheson, could very well have been sold to pay the debt. After threatening to invoke his legal right and direct that his agent sell the rice, Jardine, in one of his finer moments of pique, concluded: "I refrain from making any observations on your conduct, or your neglect of my notes." Two weeks later, while Jardine's and other firms were selling rice to a receptive market, Keating was angling for the best bargain with a broker to sell his rice. Jardine did not care who sold the rice (and thereby received a commission), he just wanted the firm to be paid: "We have sold many thousand peculs, on account of ourselves, as well as other parties, while you have held on; and kept us out of funds which we have been desirous of receiving for many months; and now you complain of our not being satisfied with your thanks for our long continued forbearance – really, Keating, this is too much of a good thing."[62] As in so many instances, Jardine's bark was worse than his bite. He could have foreclosed on Keating, but his forbearance was actually rather liberal.

There was a soft spot in Jardine under the tough talk. It appeared again, in a way that resembled his restraint with Keating, when the firm was threatened with legal action by an Indian merchant named Shapoorjee Maperwanjee for alleged inaccuracies in its accounts. Jardine and Matheson reacted by suing him for the balance that he owed them, and the court in India decided in favor of their firm. However, after the favourable judgment, Jardine was reluctant to press the case. He wrote to Jejeebhoy asking whether he knew of any reason for leniency: "However bad his conduct has been, it is very contrary to our feelings to pursue him with anything like undue severity."[63]

This is the private side of Jardine, seldom seen in public during his long career, and it reveals to us a dimension of the man not immediately recognizable in the gruff entrepreneur who contested with the East India Company, competed with rival opium dealers, complained loudly to the British government, haggled with Hong merchants, and handled a complex list of commodities and services for clients in Europe and Asia.

When rice is added to the list of cargoes, inbound and outbound, including tea, silk, raw cotton, finished textiles, and opium, in addition to the financial services, shipping, and insurance that Jardine, Matheson was managing as an agency house serving clients in Britain, India, Southeast Asia, and South China, the complex sweep of the firm's affairs becomes evident. James Matheson, in writing to a correspondent in Chile in 1837, was more forthright than his partner had been when describing (indirectly to the viceroy) the firm's commercial enterprises in 1836. Matheson explained to Robert Young: "We confine ourselves chiefly to the sale, on commission, of the opium and cotton of India, of British manufactures, on a limited scale, and to the shipment of Teas and raw Silk for the home Market; very seldom shipping on our own account and never dealing in silk manufactures, unless as Agents."[64] Of all their ongoing business affairs, however, opium remained the most volatile issue on their agenda in 1837 and the following year, both for commercial and political reasons. It is the prevailing concern in their private letter books from the time of Matheson's return in 1836 until Commissioner Lin's confiscation of the firm's opium stocks in 1839.

The panic of 1837 had not only endangered the assets of Jardine, Matheson, but it had strained, and in some instances destroyed, relationships that the firm had relied on for its network of commercial activities. Even before the flood broke, Jamsetjee Jejeebhoy had complained that Jardine, Matheson was neglectful and inefficient, but the tensions between the firm and its foremost Bombay client increased in 1837 when word of the Anglo-American commercial crisis reached India. W.E. Cheong estimates that the value of Jejeebhoy's account with Jardine, Matheson was as much as a million dollars a year.

Normally, the firm would receive Jejeebhoy's shipments from Bombay, immediately notify his London agent, Forbes and Forbes, and then draw as much as one-third of the value of the cargo for investment in goods bound for London. The remaining two-thirds would be forwarded to

Forbes and Forbes in the form of Jardine, Matheson bills or cargoes consigned to Forbes and Forbes and that agency would direct the proceeds into Jejeebhoy's account. In effect, this meant that Forbes was advancing to Jardine's the one-third that was employed for investment in China-produce headed for London.[65]

In the troubled financial climate of 1837, Forbes complained widely and loudly that Jardine, Matheson was failing to cover the drafts that it had taken and was not remitting covering consignments. This meant that the arrangements were working to Jardine's advantage and Forbes's disadvantage, given the heavy advance from Forbes that was the result of such methods. Jejeebhoy, who was an icon of wealth in India, was both angry and embarrassed, and aired his grievance with Jardine regarding the firm's clearance of bills as well as the specifics of Forbes's complaints. When he responded to Jejeebhoy, Jardine insisted that there were no bills on London available in 1837, but he soon dispatched a covering cargo of teas to Forbes and Forbes. Jardine's relationship with Forbes and Forbes was terminated soon thereafter, but the episode had been a challenge to the honour of the firm, and both Jardine and Matheson devoted significant effort to explaining their modus operandi to various interested parties. [66]

In his study of Jardine, Matheson and Company, Cheong reports that there were many other complaints against the firm during the crisis period of 1837–38 which the partners worked hard to refute. They referred some of the troublesome cases to Magniac Smith for arbitration.[67] Cheong estimates that, in the troubled seasons of 1837 and 1838, Jardine, Matheson lost the agency business of more clients than in all its prior commercial experience. Most of these severed relations were due to the firm's reluctance to engage in extended bitter correspondence, for Jardine and Matheson generally followed a conciliatory policy in their dealings with other houses and were prompt in expressing their thanks to those houses that displayed continuing confidence in them.[68]

The dreary sales of tea and silk, as well as the Peking government's pressure on opium sales, had made the British clients of Jardine, Matheson testy to say the least. On top of that, the problem with the American bills and the ensuing difficulty of remitting funds to London led to even greater anxieties among the firm's correspondents. When Henry Templer wrote to Jardine at the end of 1836, complaining about the lack of profit on his cargoes, especially his teas, Jardine responded with considerable tact, thanking Templer for the "friendly feeling" that pervaded his letters. After expressing regret at the lack of a better outcome, Jardine offered to meet Templer "on fair and honorable terms after a calm and deliberate view of all the circumstances connected with the transactions." Templer had implied that the "strong pecuniary position" he should enjoy from the funds he was allowing Jardine to manage should have earned him better treatment than other merchants from Manchester and Liverpool "in bartering for opium and cotton."

While Templer's letter reveals the competitive jealousies of the British merchants whom Jardine, Matheson was representing at Canton, Jardine's candid response offers us an extraordinarily clear window on his method of conducting business with the Chinese buyers. He explained that opium was the only ready money article sold in China, and that the firm never bought or sold on barter terms. "Our plan is to fix the true market value of the articles, without reference to the circumstance of one being given in payment for the other. But for this system we should never be able to do justice to our friends, which is our first wish."[69]

Jardine's tone with Jejeebhoy in September 1837 was conciliatory: "I am aware, as you observe, that we have friends and enemies. We are proud of the former and forgive the latter; being unconscious of having done anything to provoke the enmity of any man." And he stressed the preservation of their good relationship, emphasizing his gratitude for "the warm friendship you have for many years evinced toward me individually."[70] And, in the absence of bills and good cargoes, he shipped bullion to Jejeebhoy early in 1838, to pacify his important client and friend.

Since it was not in his nature to be unctuous, Jardine's earnestness in his remarks to Jejeebhoy can be taken as genuine. Certainly, as a sharp businessman, he recognized that his firm's ties with Jejeebhoy needed preserving far more urgently than Jardine, Matheson's agency for MacVicar did. Similarly, in contrast to the sorry conclusion of the firm's dealings with MacVicar, great sympathy was displayed by the partners for the troubles suffered by Charles Thomas, their principal agent in Singapore, during the panic year of 1837. During his absence, his partner, Mr George, had brought the firm to the brink of collapse by mismanagement. James Matheson warned Thomas in January of 1837 that the poor management had built up increased debts to Jardine, Matheson, but Matheson offered assurance that he was trying to promote Thomas's interests when opportunities arose. The Singapore firm did in fact crash during 1837, but Jardine, Matheson declined to hasten its demise by refusing to honour its drafts, "though but well assured that we should never see our money again." Even prior to that time, Thomas had owed Jardine, Matheson a great deal of money, "which we had long since given up the hope of recovering."[71] In spite of his debts, Thomas had always acted with probity in his relations with Jardine, Matheson, which led Matheson to remark that "we cannot divest ourselves of sympathy for his destitute situation, at his advanced age."[72] And this was at a time when Jardine, Matheson itself was losing £100,000 from the Hong failures and the international financial crisis.

Although he was advanced in years, Thomas proceeded to London in 1838 to seek a declaration of bankruptcy in order to obtain discharge from his debts. Matheson and his partner promised to send him whatever agency business they could direct his way, if he should be allowed to resume business in Singapore, and they even encouraged their friends in London and Singapore to employ the old man. Thomas reported that Magniac Smith was contemplating employing him, and Matheson told them that he and Jardine would be glad to see him provided for in any way. They also appealed to John Purvis in Singapore to take Thomas into his firm, by indicating that they would direct their agency business in Singapore to Thomas, with the resulting advantages to Purvis's firm.

As the international financial scene recovered in 1838, Jardine, Matheson was unwilling to add its endorsements to American bills, and as a consequence it was forced in the short term to rely on bullion, which it called in from the firm's opium ships on the coast. In February 1838 Matheson was confident that the company had weathered the storm: "I am glad to say we shall have suffered comparatively little, as far as we can judge from present appearances."[73] A month later, Jardine, Matheson learned that much of the value in its American bills would be eventually recovered, but in fact William Jardine was long dead by the time the last of those accounts was closed some twenty years later.[74]

If his letters are any true measure of the focus of his attention through the last two years of his time in China, William Jardine devoted more attention to the opium trade than to any other business matter. It is understandable that this should be the case, given the government's resolve to clamp down on the trade, the competition that had developed with British and American firms trading along the coast, and the moral criticism of the trade both in Britain and among the foreign merchants in China.

In the fall of 1836, Elijah Bridgman published in the *Repository* a pamphlet by an anonymous author who was strongly critical of the opium business. Bridgman printed it immediately after an article on temperance in alcohol consumption, which managed to set the ensuing discussion in the framework of comparisons of alcohol and opium. The piece concluded: "How long is a British Government to be seen drawing revenue from this source?" And it asked how long a whole community of British merchants would be justifying their blood money with the argument that if they did not do so, others would in their stead.[75]

Bridgman was an American missionary whose monthly journal was financially supported by the American firm of Olyphant and Company. He believed it to be the duty of the press to speak boldly about the drug trade, but he allowed the respondents an opportunity to rebut the arguments in the anonymous pamphlet because "the subject ought to be thoroughly examined." Accordingly, he printed a rejoinder from an anonymous "Reader." The fingerprints of the Jardine, Matheson partners seem to be all over the letter (from arguments that they made elsewhere during the decade). Which one actually composed it may be undiscoverable, but it surely appears to be their work. The writer objects to the timing of Bridgman's publication of the pamphlet, coinciding as it did with the expulsion order for the nine designated merchants. But he moves past that complaint quickly, to present his opinion that "opium is a useful soother, a harmless luxury, and a precious medecine [*sic*], except to those who abuse it." Using population statistics to estimate the number of Chinese using opium, he presented the figure of 1 out of every 326, with the vast majority of those not being abusive smokers but "well regulated families that present a pipe of opium to a distant neighbor visiting them" as an English yeoman might offer wine to a visitor. His defence of the sellers is that any commodity that can stimulate the passions ought to be retailed by respectable people, who provide important revenue to India, lest the supply fall into the hands of "desperadoes, pirates, and marauders."[76]

Two strong countering responses were printed in the next issue, with Bridgman leaving his other readers to form their own conclusions. "Another Reader" began punching the "traffickers of this poison" from the very outset of his argument, and "V.P.M." accused the "Christian gentlemen" dealers in opium of obstructing the propagation of the gospel in China.[77]

As 1836 was drawing to a close, Jardine and Matheson had to feel pressures accumulating on them from different directions – the continued weight of the moral arguments appearing in the most respected English journal at Canton, the arrival of a new superintendent who was unsympathetic to the opium trade, and the edicts expelling known opium merchants. From their perspective, the opposition was unreasonable, because opium was regarded as a legitimate commodity at the other major ports in Asia, as well as at home in Britain. For that reason, says Van Dyke, it was not hard for both foreigners selling the drug and Chinese buying it to rationalize the sale of opium in China.[78]

When the imperial government at Peking had opted in late 1836 for suppression rather than legalization of the opium trade, it moved to stop the means of paying for the illegal commerce by prohibiting the export of silver.[79] As these decisions were being reached at the Chinese court, the new British superintendent of trade was officially taking office. Captain Charles Elliot succeeded to that office on 14 December 1836.[80] He had not been instructed by Lord Palmerston to abet the opium trade of British merchants. However, it was difficult for him to promote the well-being of British commerce if he watched the termination of their most profitable item of trade.

J.Y. Wong has argued that the suppression of the opium trade in China would have had disastrous consequences for the global economy. The national budget of Great Britain would have had to be revised downward, the revenue supporting British India would have collapsed, and some of the textile mills in the English Midlands would have had to close.[81] Wong applies this analysis to the situation existing prior to the Arrow War, but the same projections might be applied to the intertwined elements of international commerce and finance in the late 1830s.

Elliot had the bad luck of arriving at his station just at the time when the viceroy was pronouncing the expulsion of Jardine and the eight other banished merchants. The superintendent had concluded that legalizing opium would draw the drug traffic to Whampoa, which was something that by now did not hold much appeal for Jardine.[82] Elliot thought that legalization was the best short-term resolution that the British merchants could hope for, but he suspected that it would be the source of future conflict, as the corrupt local officials and smugglers would lose their sources of income too quickly.[83] Any prospect of the drug's legalization disappeared during the first half of 1837; "buried in oblivion" was Matheson's assessment.[84] Nevertheless, both he and Jardine were anticipating that the failure of government interdiction efforts would eventually lead to legalization.[85] Jardine expected that, at some point in the future, the import of opium would be legalized, under the category of medicine, with duty charged on it.[86]

Simultaneous with the cessation of talk about legalizing opium sales, a precipitous drop in the drug sales prompted Matheson to send warnings to their clients in India to be wary of adventurous speculations in a market that was both oversupplied and outlawed.[87] Still, unprecedented quantities of opium continued to arrive in 1837. The glutted market and the official crackdown on sales meant that, while there were more than 5,000 chests unsold after the 1836–37 season, there were more than 10,000 unsold in 1837–38.[88] Moreover, storage locations became problematic after the Chinese authorities erected a gun emplacement overlooking Cumsingmoon to intimidate the receiving ships from anchoring there. Eventually Jardine and Matheson elected to remove their depot ships to safer waters at Lyemun and Kowloon Bay.[89]

Toward the end of 1836, Jardine and Matheson had instructed the firm's opium buyer at Bombay, T.W. Henderson, to invest the whole of the funds it was sending on to him in opium, barring severely high prices. No doubt they were second-guessing themselves within a few months' time, for the Chinese opium brokers had disappeared by January 1837. The firm sent a ship to the coast with 200 chests, hoping to be able to dispose most of the drug belonging to their constituents. "Our own must take the chance." Jardine declared, meaning that he and his partner were committed to giving priority to the sales of their clients' opium rather than rescuing their own speculations.[90] He was aware that "the drug dealers," as he called the Chinese wholesale buyers, were trying to bribe the government "preventive boats," but with little success. Adding further discomfort to the firm's business operations in 1837 was the series of maritime disasters, including the loss of its own *Fairy*, and other ships, among them the *Bannerman* and the *Pascoa*. The costs of these losses to insurers, which would include Jardine and Matheson, were heavy. "This has been a severe year for the Insurance offices both in India and in China," the senior partner commented to a client in Bombay.[91]

The firm's coastal vessels were following different strategies to achieve sales. "We trust there will be no lack of zeal on your part," Jardine told Captain Jauncey of the *Governor Findlay*; and he instructed Captain Edward Parry of the *Hercules* to be especially hospitable to Chinese smugglers' assistants who were sent to accompany the ship to its selling locations. "Receive on board such Chinese as may be sent, and treat them kindly – giving them a place to sleep, and plenty of chow-chow." Facing a tough market, the man who would not keep an extra chair in his office at the factory was not beyond cultivating the customers with some public-relations gestures.[92]

In spite of Peking's determination to clamp down on the drug dealers, the mandarins, both civil and military, expected to split what amounted to an illegal duty on the smuggled opium. Every chest coming up the Pearl River in the spring of 1837 was being charged a "tax" of $75 ($20 for the owners of the smuggling boats and $55 for the mandarins). As a result of their quarrels with the mandarins over the charge, the drug dealers were reluctant to make purchases (at $550 to $600 per chest, plus the $75 tacked on by the risk-taking boat owners and the extortionist mandarins). Jardine had to concede that the firm's hopes of delivering and selling the drug among the islands and in the bays along the coast had not been realized, and he reported to Jejeebhoy: "We must find some other mode of evading the $75 per chest now charged." His business skills were being put to a rough test by the Peking government on one side and the crooked local officials on the other.[93] Innovation was required, and Jardine eventually found a way to dodge the heavy "tax," by sending the opium to Namoa, where for $25 or $30 Jardine's ships could deliver their opium cargo without paying the standard $75 demanded by the boatmen and the mandarins.[94]

Charles Lyall, husband of Jardine's niece and partner of Matheson's nephew, who was their buying agent at Calcutta, made things worse by purchasing excessive amounts of opium at extravagantly high prices. Matheson complained that Lyall was "saddling us with a heavy loss" and gave the young man a sternly avuncular scolding: "I intend all the lecturing I have given vent to, in utmost kindness, in order that you may endeavor to be more successful on future occasions."[95] With financial panic abroad, depressed opium prices and limited sales in Canton and on the coast, insurance woes, and unpromising markets in tea, cotton, and silk, Matheson was relying on his relatives for assistance rather than distress.

By the middle of 1837, many of the smuggling boats had been destroyed by their owners to avoid criminal prosecution, which meant that opium smuggling in the vicinity of Canton was at a standstill. The price of Malwa opium fell, rather than rising owing to scarcity, and even at reduced prices the drug dealers were afraid to buy. Still, the major importers, including Jardine, Matheson, felt that they could not abandon their commerce in opium, for it was the only ready-money commodity that could be used to acquire funds for exporting teas.[96]

Jardine was certainly worried about the potential for violence between the selling ships along the coast and the cruising vessels deployed by the Chinese authorities. An incident in June involving the viceroy's rowboats and a junk that had purchased about a hundred chests of opium led to a small-scale battle during which the junk was destroyed, with the loss of most of its cargo, crew, and passengers. Jardine was unsettled by reports that one of Dent's vessels had fired a warning at the war junks and had unintentionally sunk one of them, and he was concerned about the menacing placement of war junks near his firm's *Governor Findlay*.

In this troubled market, his business instincts dictated that he play every angle possible. One ploy was to propose a bribe to the Chinese admiral in the Namo Straits. The design of the scheme was to have the admiral allow one of Jardine's vessels the privilege of staying permanently on location, while the admiral had his cruisers prevent any other vessels from delivering or transshipping their opium in the vicinity. His logic was that one ship might pass unsuspected, while many were certain to be noticed and interfered with. As scrupulous as he was about fair dealing with his clients and even with the smugglers, Jardine was not above taking advantage of the corruption among the mandarins if a "gratuity" could buy an advantage in sales.[97]

Recognizing the difficulties that sellers were having, potential Chinese buyers of opium were proposing very low prices for Malwa. Jardine was unwilling to sell at those prices and held out for better deals.[98] Still, he was anxious to receive new shipments of Patna from Calcutta, and delays made him especially irascible. He protested loudly to Charles Lyall and Captain Rees about Lyall's handling of the new purchases at Calcutta. "Our friends on that side of India appear to have taken leave of their senses; and are keeping our Opium back, while we are obliged to buy for the Coast."[99]

He hoped to sell by pre-arranged transactions rather than simply by having the firm's vessels cruising the coast. Deals were struck at the firm's offices at Creek Hong, and the vessels were loaded in the Gulf of Canton, with designated delivery points along the coast. His ship's captains were instructed to signal the receiving junks by hoisting a red flag on the main mast so that the smugglers could recognize the Jardine, Matheson ship.[100] When contact was made, duplicate copies of the sale order would be compared, and the chests of opium would be exchanged for silver.[101]

Business conditions were so stressful by the fall of 1837 that there was no sign of celebration when the *Red Rover* arrived from Calcutta with newspapers carrying reports that an eighteen-year-old young woman had succeeded to the British throne in June.[102] There would be time enough for celebration when Victoria's coronation came around in 1838, but now the partners were focused on the financial crisis and the stagnating opium market. Jardine refused to be alarmed by the viceroy's edict ordering Captain Elliot to drive away the opium ships or face a complete cessation of trade. "We have no disposition to move the ships so the trade must take its chances, a stoppage for two months would do a great deal of good, but I have no expectation of such a measure being resorted to."[103] Even in the depths of the financial crisis, Jardine and his partner felt confident that their firm could endure a winnowing of the cluttered competition in the opium trade, for some of the competitors would be ruined by a two-month stoppage.

Elliot was using varied strategies in his effort to protect British trade. On the one hand, he had petitioned Governor General Teng for permission to take up residence at the factories in Canton and eventually received a favourable response. That he had addressed Teng in the form of a *pin* (a petition presented through the Hong merchants) was an implicit admission that the British representative stood in a relation of inferiority to the Chinese government. This was hardly the message that Lord Palmerston wanted his chief superintendent to convey to the Chinese government, but, as we have seen, exchanges of letters between Canton and London took about seven or eight months.[104]

The decrees that Chinese authorities had issued in the late summer of 1837, directing Elliot to send the opium ships away from the coast of China, carried the threat that failure to do so would lead to a stoppage in the entire foreign trade of Canton. Elliot did nothing, which led the local authorities to declare him "unfit" to be superintendent. Elliot responded that he was authorized by his government to deal only with the legal trade.[105] It was an uncomfortable pose to adopt, in view of the

British boats that were landing the drug. He had to face the strong possibility that the preventive boats might attempt to seize one or more of
the private British smuggling boats. If a Chinese were killed in such an
encounter and demands were made for the surrender of a British sea-
man, Elliot would be in very difficult straits.[106]

Elliot's other strategy was to seek a demonstration of British naval
strength from the East Indies squadron in order to relieve the British merchants of Chinese intimidation. He appealed to Rear Admiral Sir Thomas
Bladen Capel early in February, and seven months later Lord Palmerston
sanctioned the visit of a British warship to China.[107] The foreign secretary's instructions directed the vessel's commander to protect British
property from pirates and to restrain the behaviour of rowdy seamen
serving on British merchant ships.[108] On the one occasion when he did
address Elliot about opium, he was quite explicit in stating the British government's refusal to intervene in defence of any of the British firms engaged in illegal opium sales. "With respect to the smuggling of opium …
Her Majesty's Government cannot interfere for the purpose of enabling
British subjects to violate the laws of the country to which they trade. Any
loss, therefore, which such persons may suffer … must be borne by the
parties who have brought that loss on themselves by their own acts."[109]

Long before that policy statement was composed at Whitehall, Elliot
had hauled down his flag and left Canton. He had received instructions
from Palmerston to avoid the subservience of the *pin* and to discontinue
communicating with the viceroy through the Cohong. The superintendent tried other methods of contacting Teng, but the viceroy reacted
badly to the initiatives. Consequently, early in December Elliot moved
his headquarters to Macao, where he could live with his wife and newly
born son.[110]

Jardine and Matheson realized that they were "on their own," so to
speak. With the regular Chinese opium boats bullied out of their function of smuggling the drug ashore, Europeans and Americans were taking the risk of landing their opium sales with their own boats. The
long-established channels of connivance were breaking down, and
Jardine recognized that the improvised system and the evolving uncer-
tainties were making the opium trade very precarious both for the distant investors and for the on-site sellers.

Even though Malwa was selling for as low as $380 dollars per chest, the
prospects of a "very handsome return" such as the schooner *Jardine* delivered in the last days of 1837 prompted Jardine to deny her captain's

request to lay over for repairs. He was eager to have his vessels working the coast as far away as Chinchew Bay and Shanghai in order to establish contacts with distant buyers. Moreover, he was willing to have his captains reduce the prices of their opium in order to dispose of their cargoes, and achieve a profit by volume sales.[111]

When opium was purchased by Chinese buyers in advance, Jardine wanted his captains to be aggressive about delivering the drug, so that purchasers would not begin complaining that Jardine, Matheson was disappointing them. He had the *Red Rover* delivering hundreds of chests to different stations along the coast, with the *Jardine*, the *Austin*, the *Hercules*, the *Harriet*, the *Omega*, the *Governor Findlay*, and the *Colonel Young* all participating in wholesale storage or selling or delivering to other vessels. Three more ships were added to the firm's fleet in the first half of 1838 – the *Hellas* (from England), the *Omega*, and the *Coral* – to ensure that there were enough vessels to maintain the connections between Lintin and the coast. Indeed, Jardine was working the available markets and the shipping resources so assiduously that he must have found his marketing job to be exhausting. Other cargoes might be involved. For example, Captain Rees was instructed to establish communications with "the Chusan group" in order to obtain raw silk in return for opium, with the silk being loaded directly aboard one of Jardine, Matheson's vessels in the vicinity of Poo-lo.[112]

Arrangements were made on specific contractual terms for sharing the risks.[113] The buyers could not drag out transactions for long without incurring additional costs. For instance, Jardine gave Captain Parry explicit orders to charge an extra $10 per chest if the 200 chests ordered by a buyer named Woking in July were still on board more than a month after the *Hercules* left Hong Kong.

The distress of the winter of 1837–38 seemed to pass when the viceroy left Canton for a military-inspection tour. Sales were brisk, even as close as Whampoa, with the mandarins taking advantage of the viceroy's absence to use their preventive boats for drug deliveries and thereby make a few thousand dollars smuggling opium for customers who formerly relied on the regular opium-smuggling boats. Jardine called the Whampoa trade "disgusting" because of the losses incurred when swindlers paid in bad sycee silver bars or fake copper dollars. Nevertheless, trade was brisk at Whampoa even after the viceroy's return, and along the coast demand continued "unabated." By spring, it looked as if Jardine's opium fleet had gotten past the doldrums.[114]

"The Coast trade flourishes to a wish," he reported exultantly to his friend Captain Alexander Grant, back in England. Not only were prices up, but competition was diminished. Beyond the bright prospects he had for every type of opium, his firm had virtually cornered the market in silk purchases and was in possession of most of the new Malwa reaching the depot ships in the estuary.[115] By June 1838 it was boom time. Jardine was in a bright frame of mind. Smuggling was brisk, he reported to a friend in Ceylon, and the pretended opposition, in the shape of edicts, was being disregarded as if the edicts were waste paper. It certainly seemed that the reformists had lost the fight, and that prosperity had returned to Jardine, Matheson.[116]

Charles Elliot apparently had little influence on the course of events. Jardine described him as being in "a state of non-intercourse" with the Chinese government. But his long-standing request for a visit by British naval vessels was about to be realized, as a formidable ship of the line, the *Wellesley*, accompanied by a corvette and a brig, sailed past Macao and anchored in Chinese waters, near Lintin, in July 1838, on the visit Palmerston had authorized. Aboard the *Wellesley* was the commander of the Royal Navy's East Indian station. He notified Elliot that he wanted the Chinese to understand that his visit did not signal any hostile intent, but their communications were returned unopened.[117] So Admiral Frederick Lewis Maitland moved his warship up to the Bogue when both he and Elliot perceived an insult by Chinese who had detained a vessel on the suspicion that Maitland was trying to make his way upriver to the factories. The towering presence of the *Wellesley* was sufficient to overawe the Chinese admiral, and Maitland remained in the vicinity until October. "The admiral has alarmed the Chinese not a little," Jardine told Captain Rees, "but his visit is a peaceable one unless they drive him to use his guns in self defense."[118]

While Maitland's visit was giving Jardine and Matheson encouragement to think that their government had not abandoned them, the Scots partners were excited by the renewed vigour of the opium market. Matheson chided his nephew, Hugh, resident in Liverpool, for not gambling on the recovery of sales. "Let me impress upon you generally ... that the best of all periods for speculation is in the midst or termination of such a panic as we have escaped from, when the minds of most men are disheartened and many are disabled from competing with you." He advised: "You cannot go far wrong in authorizing purchases at such rates as we may consider safe."[119] At least for the short term, that was bad advice. The exuberance did not survive the summer, as panic gripped buyers in August 1838 and sales dropped off severely. The imperial court had resumed deliberations early in the summer. Much of the discussion concerned the need to prosecute the users of opium, while much attention was also given to the drain of sycee silver that was being used to pay for the smuggled drug.[120]

Numerous severe edicts did not initially cool down the roaring market, which was selling Malwa for $700 per chest by the third week of August. But the arrest of several retail dealers led other buyers to sacrifice as much as $100 per chest in order to clear their stocks. Some were forfeiting their bargain money (down payments), while many others who had placed orders simply absconded without paying anything. Jardine remained calm. He had seen this happen before, and he was confident that the fright would pass within ten days and the firm would begin to dispose of its inventory while prices moved upward again.[121]

Doubts set in by October 1838, and with buyers absent and prices declining, he began to worry that the summer's optimistic predictions were going to lead to a big supply of Malwa arriving in February 1839. His business instincts were thrown into turmoil, as he now faced the disquieting "threat" of a glut in the market, which was once again being menaced by government efforts at suppression.[122] He hastened to reassure Jejeebhoy that Jardine, Matheson was seeking to secure the Bombay business mogul $600 per chest for his opium. While Matheson maintained his confidence in the long-term future of the drug trade, the short-term inventory issues bothered Jardine tremendously, as the firm outfitted six ships to sail for Namo and Chinchew Bay to make an effort to dispose of the supplies on hand. "Adopt every possible means to get rid of it," he told Captain Jauncey.[123]

It was extremely difficult for Jardine to maintain his resolve to leave China that winter, when the trade that had been his mainstay for years was eroding with such speed. Just a few months earlier he had been able to contemplate sailing away from Canton with confidence that business was brisk. Now, in the fall of 1838, even the sanguine Matheson had to concede that the opium market was "in a complete state of stagnation." The general gloom was making it "impossible to sell a single chest on any terms," he lamented. There were many people who wanted to buy opium, including local dealers seeking a profit and addicts driven by their habits. However, they were all afraid of the consequences, should they be caught either buying or selling or smoking.[124]

Nevertheless, Jardine was proceeding with his plans to retire from Canton. He went down to Macao on the first of November, and spent two weeks there, in all likelihood winding up his affairs in the Portuguese colony. Matheson confirmed with the estate agent there that Jardine's rent would continue to be paid as usual, but it was clear that a major change was imminent.[125] Matheson was given a brief preview of what it would be like to manage the firm in the absence of his partner.

By December, Jardine was informing his clients and his ship captains that the prisons were full, with upward of two thousand in confinement in Canton on charges of smoking, selling, or shipping opium. The viceroy of the two provinces had received a severe reprimand from Peking for leniency, and in consequence he was now "seizing, trying, and strangling the poor devils without mercy." Jardine understood that some of those dying in prison were casualties of total and immediate withdrawal from the drug. "In some instances those found smoking the drug have been arrested & placed in confinement without the possibility of procuring the article, and in some instances death has ensued." This statement, to Jejeebhoy, reveals that he recognized the lethal potential of opium deprivation to addicts. It was not common for American and British opium merchants to make such an acknowledgment.[126]

Even the Hong merchants were being harassed with enquiries and threats. "We have never seen so serious a persecution or one so general," Jardine testified soberly. Not an opium pipe was to be seen, nor a vendor; and as a result the tea trade was being neglected – no shipping, no delivering – because the merchants were so preoccupied with the government's campaign against opium.[127] With seizures, strangulations, and tortures impressing the public vividly each day, the market for everything was depressed. "The storm may blow over," Jardine remarked limply to a Bombay client. "We know similar storms have blown over; and so may this; but appearances are at present unfavorable, probably more so than ever we saw them."[128]

Things got worse. By Christmastime – with Jardine's departure just a month away – Howqua was predicting that the coming season's opium sales would not exceed one- fifth of the 1838 season. Jardine concurred and he cautioned Jejeebhoy gravely: at all costs, he should avoid purchasing opium for the present. Never, in all his years in China, had he felt obliged to give such an absolute warning.[129]

And he was annoyed at Elliot for "doing much mischief" to make life difficult for British traders at Canton. The melodrama began with James Innes, the long-time maverick British merchant who had been attempting to land opium right at the Creek factory where he was a neighbour of Jardine and Matheson. On 3 December, two coolies apprehended in the act of unloading the opium confessed that they were working for Innes and that they named the vessel at Whampoa from which the twelve chests had come. The Canton authorities wrongly identified that ship as the *Thomas Perkins*, which was consigned to an American name Talbot. The *Thomas Perkins* (which in fact carried only rice) was ordered to sail away immediately and both Innes and Talbot were given three days to leave town. Thereupon, the Hong merchants threatened – no doubt to protect themselves against government accusations of connivance – to burn down the Creek factory if Innes did not comply with the expulsion order. Then the Cohong members appealed to the Chamber of Commerce to stop the smuggling of opium into Canton and to supervise the furnishing of good-conduct bonds by British merchants. The alternative to compliance with their terms would be a cessation of trade.

In response, the chairman of the Chamber of Commerce, Hugh Lindsay, explained that he could not discipline Innes, for Innes was not a member of the body, and that the Chamber could not regulate the passage boats coming to Canton from Whampoa because it was simply a commercial association without legal authority over the boats.[130] In these circumstances, the governor general summarily ordered the suspension of all foreign trade at Canton.[131]

This is how things stood, unresolved, on the morning of 12 December, when a much wilder episode transpired. In front of the Swedish Factory, a Chinese officer and some coolies were preparing to erect a cross for the strangling of a convicted opium dealer named Ho Lao-chin. The location of the strangling was clearly meant to signal the complicity of the foreign merchants in the drug trade. When several American and British residents objected vociferously to the site of the strangling, and then to a second site near the factories, a Cantonese crowd gathered and jostling between them and the foreigners led to a fracas, much to Jardine's dismay. Soon the Cantonese crowd had put the foreign residents to flight, with Matheson taking refuge at the home of Peter Snow, the American consul.[132] The editor of the *Canton Register* blamed the incident on "the rash behavior of various individuals who struck and drove back the Chinese crowd with sticks." There would have been no disturbance if the foreign residents had retired to their houses once the implements of the execution had been removed.[133]

Eventually, Chinese soldiers were sent to disperse the crowd, and the episode subsided without serious bloodshed, although some people fell into the river and drowned. Word was sent to Captain Elliot, who hurried upriver from Whampoa to the factories and concluded that he had to intervene to obstruct the movement of opium by British smugglers along the Canton River. Apparently, Elliot linked the violence near the factories with the presence of British-owned schooners in the river, and believed that if the vessels that were engaged in opium smuggling did not leave within three days, he would communicate with the local government that his own government was in accord with the perfectly admissible punishment of the smugglers. John Slade reckoned: "Thus it appears to be the intention of Captain Elliot to offer himself as a kind of chief of the Chinese preventive service."[134] In explaining his action to Palmerston, Elliot asserted: "It has become clear to me, my Lord, from the origins of this peculiar branch of the opium traffic [inner-river smuggling by foreigners], that it must grow to be more and more mischievous to every branch of the trade, and certainly to none more than to that of opium itself."[135]

Elliot recognized that the big houses, such as Jardine, Matheson, were not apt to do anything about the issue: Jardine had made it clear that he did not propose to police the conduct of the other British merchants. Nor was the Chamber of Commerce to be relied on to exercise any control. So Elliot determined to take action himself, and he gathered the British community together and instructed them to remove their small craft from the river. Then he notified Governor General Teng, through a *pin*, that British boats carrying opium that were seized above the Bogue would be given no assistance from him. The merchants were warned that "Her Majesty's Government will in no way interpose if the Chinese Government shall think fit to seize and confiscate the same," and that any British subject involved in opium smuggling who caused the death of a Chinese person would be subject to capital punishment.[136]

Although Jardine maintained that the viceroy had "acted like a madman," he still placed much of the burden on Elliot for letting things get out of hand. Jardine accused the superintendent of attempting to gain a point of diplomatic etiquette, at the expense of his countrymen's trade.[137] In his eyes, Elliot had acted very foolishly. On 22 December he wrote: "My own opinion is that Trade would now have been opened, had he been quiet." As ever, Jardine was quick to recognize the implications of a situation: "Capt. Elliott & his friends, if he has any, assert that the *inside* or *river trade* was the cause of the late severe proceedings against opium smokers etc. which is incorrect." Viceroy Teng's recent vigorous prosecution of dealers and smokers was his reaction to the emperor's characterization of him as being of no more use than a piece of wool. "The Viceroy was well aware of the extent of the inside trade and encouraged it – while issuing threatening Chops [decrees] in Canton, his officers at the Bogue were granting papers to the Schooners coming in." In Jardine's assessment, the large issue was not the river trade but the campaign against the drug throughout the whole empire, and Elliot had made a huge concession to the Chinese based on a wrong interpretation of the problem.[138]

The long shadows cast by the Napier incident in 1834 gave a certain tint to the 1838 riot and Elliot's response. In Frederic Wakeman's judgment, the Napier affair had convinced Chinese officials that the foreign merchants were vulnerable to a blockade of the factories. Moreover, the superintendents who followed Napier had to recognize that they could not challenge the Canton system without being prepared to go to war if push came to shove. Elliot had asked for a demonstration of British naval muscle, but he had no thought of allowing the rough treatment of opium sellers and smugglers to become a *casus belli.*[139]

Jardine understood that the British merchants trading in opium were going to have to protect themselves with their wits and their capacity for brazen defiance of imperial edicts and local authorities. If he waited for the Cohong to become fiscally more reliable or for the legalization of the drug, he might have to spend the rest of his days in Canton. He was not prepared to do that, for in spite of the troubles of December he was firmly resolved to proceed homeward in January. He had received more than one invitation to enter partnerships at London, and he was entertaining various options for life after China. Long before his departure date drew near, John Gledstanes had written, asking Jardine to consider joining a partnership. Jardine's response was non-committal but cordial: I hope to have a chance of talking this over with you – over a glass of your oldest and best port.[140]

Jardine had his itinerary worked out at least ten months before leaving – first to Bombay, then to Europe via the Red Sea, and eventually to

Scotland – and he began informing people of his intentions. His plan was to accompany a couple named Crawford as far as Bombay. So his departure came as no secret, and the British residents of Canton began planning their farewells as soon as the name of his departure vessel was known.[141] Strangely enough, he was also being threatened at this time with arrest by his partner in ownership of the *Sarah,* Framjee Cowasjee, over a disputed claim involving that vessel. Unalarmed, Jardine delegated T.W. Henderson to negotiate a settlement and promised to be satisfied with whatever settlement Henderson arranged.[142]

We have no account of whether he packed methodically over the course of weeks or frantically at the last minute. But we do know that he did not take his attention off trade until he was virtually at the dock at Whampoa. Reprimanding a trusted ship's captain was not something that Jardine did often, but he had enough energy and focus left to scold Jauncey just two weeks before departure. The captain had apparently trusted Chinese drug dealers along the coast and had been burned in a swindle. The firm had taken a heavy loss, and Jardine attributed it to Jauncey's violation of instructions. As if it needed to be said, Jardine insisted that without full payment the "low characters" along the coast should not receive the opium they sought. "Lay it down as a rule, not to be denied pray, to keep your accounts square, and obey your instructions – Never trust one of the low fellows who accompany you along the coast, one dollar; if you do, it is a dollar lost to your employers … The men sent in the ships are generally low unprincipled characters, not to be trusted." That was apparently the last big blast of Jardine's irritability after nearly twenty years in China.[143]

That he still had a countervailing gentleness to his temper can be seen in a letter sent on the same day as that reprimand. Shroffs served as authenticators of metal currency aboard ships. The shroff aboard the *Harriet* had made an error and cost the firm a bit of money, but trifling in Jardine's assessment. Let the man have his pay, if his error was honest, said Jardine: "We have an aversion to cutting wages."[144] Tough-nosed businessman that he was, he had an abiding sense of fairness.

The opium market was virtually dead as he made his final arrangements for departure from Canton. He and Matheson had given up any expectation of legalization, and the best they could hope for was a rebellion against the opium prohibition. "An insurrection in some of the Provinces is the only chance I see of any great relaxation," he remarked in his dejection about the market.[145] He knew that was unlikely, and would have thought it equally unlikely that any new severity by Chinese authorities was impending. Peking had other thoughts.

On the last day of 1838, the emperor appointed a special commissioner to extirpate the drug trade at Canton. Lin Zexu had made the greatest impression on the emperor in the course of the renewed debate about opium policy in 1838. Scholarly, honest, and persuasive, he had gained the emperor's confidence to such a degree that he was given nineteen private audiences in the fall of 1838. He took the position that the opium trade should be attacked on the Chinese side of the traffic, with provision being made for smokers to withdraw from the addiction and severe punishment for those persisting in the habit. That approach, coupled with crippling pressure on the barbarian suppliers of the drug, including even execution by strangling, would be sufficient to break the back of the opium problem, Lin argued.[146]

Lin left Peking on 8 January 1839, with a small entourage, and arrived at Canton twelve hundred miles and sixty days later, on 10 March. His appointment as special commissioner conferred on him extraordinary powers, surpassing even those of the viceroy. Teng issued a proclamation on 23 January, addressed to the foreign community (an unprecedented communication), alerting them to the anticipated arrival of a special commissioner. It was widely printed and all the factories had copies of it.[147] But, at the time of Jardine's leave taking, the foreign community at Canton had no clear idea of the extent of Lin's powers or the depth of his determination. If they had, it might have spoiled Jardine's farewell party.

# 9

## JARDINE'S FAREWELL AND
## MATHESON'S GREAT HEADACHE

The banquet to honour and bid farewell to Jardine began at 7:30 on the evening of 23 January 1839; it ended eight hours later in a jolly uproar of drunken revelry echoing through the streets and buildings of the foreign settlement along the riverfront at Canton. The entire community of foreign merchants, 132 in all (minus Dent and Daniell), had gathered in the British Consular Hall, the biggest space available among the factories, with a grand verandah that looked out upon the river. About a hundred and forty people were assembled for the "magnificent fête" (Matheson's term), with endless rounds of toasting and speeches, during which the Parsi merchants gave Jardine an extraordinary service of silver valued at a thousand guineas.[1]

The evening evidently made an especially vivid impression upon the young Americans present, since they left detailed accounts. Gideon Nye and Robert Bennet Forbes mark this as one of the most memorable occasions in their recollections of Canton before the Opium War. Among the speakers, Dr Peter Parker expressed his gratitude for Jardine's medical help and monetary aid at the hospital, and Mr Elijah Bridgman, the American missionary, declared that he hoped that Jardine's name would be transmitted to posterity not simply by virtue of his honoured reputation but also by children, and conveyed his wish that, upon arriving home, Jardine might meet the "fairest of the fair" who would smooth his path through life. "I give you then the future Mrs. Jardine," he said in proposing a toast, at which the whole throng cheered and the band of musicians from one of the ships at Whampoa struck up the tune "Willy he'd a peck of malt."[2]

It was about one in the morning when Jardine rose from his seat and replied that he doubted that someone who had first seen China in 1802 was likely to go home to find the fairest of the fair waiting for him. The best he could hope for was "fat, fair, and forty," to which the assemblage roared its approval. He expressed embarrassment at the lavishness of the testimonial dinner and indicated that he was deeply touched by the sentiment they were showing.[3] In a serious vein he indicated that his joy at the prospect of seeing his native land again was mingled with regret at leaving Canton where he had enjoyed a good deal of comfort and security. He had felt safe at Canton, where "a foreigner can go to sleep with his windows open, without being in dread of either his life or property" thanks to an excellent and watchful police. He asserted that neither he nor any of the other foreign merchants were smugglers. "We are not smugglers, gentlemen! It is the Chinese government, it is the Chinese officers, who smuggle, and who connive at and encourage smuggling, not we." An audience receptive to that message responded with applause and cheering, and turned back to merriment.[4]

"Then was seen what had never been seen at Canton before," wrote Gideon Nye years later: "Mr. Jardine himself and Mr. [William] Wetmore attempting a Waltz to a simple Negro melody by two Messrs. Tiers of Philadelphia."[5] Nor were Jardine and Wetmore the only ones dancing. The verandah, decorated with coloured lights and evergreens around the pillars, and flowerpots around the balustrade, was nicely fitted up for dancing. Fuelled by sherry, champagne, and strong, hot punch, a large number of the banqueters took to dancing, singing, and shouting that became "very uproarious." In the process of attempting a waltz, young Warren Delano, Jr (Franklin D. Roosevelt's grandfather) "was let go of by his partner & tumbled headlong against a flowerpot & cut a gash in his head an inch long." "But he came home in better order than I did," Robert Bennet Forbes confessed in a letter to his wife.[6] Jardine had sensibly slipped away before the party slid into collective inebriation.

After the numbers had thinned, the candles had dwindled to stumps, and many glasses had been broken, the last of the revellers quitted the hall at four in the morning, but not quietly. Forbes recorded the afterglow: "After leaving the hall we marched in a body & gave three more cheers under Jardine's window and various others elsewhere & at 4 AM I bolted from the very small remnant of the riotous party & got home

– first calling into Mr. Snows [the elderly American consul] room & *awaking him up* to enquire how he was & if the noise had disturbed him!!!"[7]

One may safely assume that little work was accomplished within the factories that morning. Two days later, Will Jardine (as Forbes called him) was gone from Canton, in the company of Mr and Mrs Alexander Robertson. After twenty years in China, like his long-time friend Jardine, Robertson also was returning home with a handsome fortune, estimated at 2 lacs of dollars (200,000).[8] Jardine had a royal send-off, according to the *Register*: "He was attended to the beach by about eighty gentlemen, English, American, and Parsee, and stepped aboard amidst huzzas, hurrahs, [and] the deafening noise of long strings of crackers." John Slade could not resist crowing: "Such a triumphant exit from Canton ... has never before been made by any private merchant, with such a display of respect and esteem."[9] They sailed for Bombay aboard the *Bolton* from Macao Roads on 29 January 1839, with silver from the coastal opium sales travelling along with Jardine for remittances to Bombay clients.[10] Matheson estimated that they would not reach Bombay until late March, and that they would have to spend about a month there before moving on to Suez. The length of time for a journey from India to Britain using this route was about two months. Once the paddle steamer from Bombay arrived at Suez, the passengers would travel eighty-four miles by horse-drawn wagon to Cairo, and then board a small paddle steamer, the *Jack O'Lantern*, for a trip down the Nile. The final stage of the journey would be accomplished aboard a barge on the Mahmoudieh Canal, with Alexandria as the Mediterranean terminus. Since Jardine was not in a hurry, and had some tourist plans for the eastern Mediterranean, such as visiting Istanbul, Matheson asked Magniac Smith to address mail to Jardine at Alexandria, including provision for his travel expenses on the homeward journey.[11]

On the day he left Canton, Jardine had taken the time to write a letter to Matheson, in effect conferring the mantle of senior partner on him. "One thing I beg to assure you of: I am thoroughly convinced that you will carry on the business of the House quite as well as ever I did. You only require confidence to be fully equal, if not superior to me, in managing the business of the House. Time will be required to gain the confidence of the Chinese. I mean a short time. In the meantime I have perfect confidence in your management and feel quite easy on that subject."[12] The letter constitutes the closest thing we have to an expression of affection from the older partner to the younger.

Matheson would be assisted by his nephews Alexander and Donald, as well as Jardine's nephews Andrew and David, who stayed on in China. Matheson's elder brother, Duncan, had died in 1838, leaving a vacuum in the management of James's financial interests at home. He thought of Duncan as his "only near relative in the least acquainted with home business," but Duncan's executors had nominated a man whom James regarded as incompetent. As a consequence, just as he was taking up the senior leadership position, he had to write to Magniac Smith asking them to provide "safe custody" for his funds invested in Scotland.[13] That he was intending to stay on in China for a lengthy period was evident in the clothing orders he dispatched that month to a tailor on Sackville Street, London. He wished to be both stylish and warm.[14]

In the week that Jardine departed, the opium market at Canton was utterly dead. There was, however, a new way for the firm to earn some money in the slow market: it began allowing venturesome independent operators to charter Jardine, Matheson ships for speculations in coastal sales. Apparently the firm had made the decision, before Jardine left, that the coastal trade was so overrun with new risk takers that this was one way to take advantage of the situation. The only limitation specified in these arrangements was that chartered vessels were not to intrude upon the area of the coast occupied by the *Austin* (Jardine, Matheson) and the *Lord Amherst* (Dent).[15]

By the end of January 1839, Matheson was hearing reports that only 20 per cent of the opium smokers in Canton were continuing to use the drug – so severe was the fright among consumers. Yet within a matter of weeks opium was pouring in from India – a ship with 1,480 chests, another with 1,750, and yet another expected with 1,200 – for a market that was, in his assessment, "totally inactive."[16] The state of affairs at Canton had caused Matheson to think broadly on the whole question of the ethics of opium sales, the illegitimacy of the trade, and the role of the Chinese and British governments in relation to the opium merchants. He disclosed his thinking in an especially revealing letter to the governor of Ceylon, written on the day of Jardine's departure. It is worth citing at length here:

The introduction of Opium into this country is the point of contention at issue and however much philanthropists may justly lament the immoderate and hurtful use of the Drug in China, as of Gin in England and America, it is clearly the exclusive province of

the Chinese Government alone to enforce its prohibitory laws on
the subject. Capt. Elliot the Chief Superintendent has however adopted the novel course of assisting the Government in this, against
his own Countrymen and it is probable some embarrassing discussion will be the consequence; of a nature seriously detrimental to
the EI Coy's Opium Revenue on which they chiefly rely for the
means of paying the dividends on their Stock. A proclamation
about to be issued ordering off all the Opium ships from the
mouth of the River, and threatening to suspend all foreign trade,
if they should persist in remaining [sic]. This however will probably be obviated by the obnoxious vessels disappearing for a time,
and none will be more ready to welcome them back than the
Mandarins themselves, on account of the fertile source of emolu-
ment derived to them from conniving at the prohibited trade.[17]

The final idea in this statement would become a major assumption in
Matheson's predictions as the whole province awaited the arrival of Lin
Zexu. Matheson vacillated in telling some people that the market was
showing slight signs of improvement and others that the trade was at a
standstill. But he was quite consistent in forecasting (no doubt from his
high hopes) that there would be a reversion to the old complicity of the
local authorities with the opium traffic. In contrast, the *Register* anticipated, with some sarcasm, that Lin intended to take the most dramatic
measures.[18]

In the days before the big party for Jardine, Matheson began relaying
to his clients the news that a special commissioner was soon expected
from Peking, and that the viceroy, to parade his zeal for prohibition of
the drug trade, had issued a proclamation requiring the depot ships to
leave or face the consequence of a complete stoppage of foreign trade
at Canton. He was sure that the document was "a make-believe" but
tended to think that the Hong Kong fleet of opium ships might be
obliged to put out to sea or take shelter somewhere for a few days to let
the storm blow over. He was confident that "affairs will no doubt in due
time return to the old system of venality and connivance."[19]

Keeping his ear to the ground, Matheson learned that the fifty-five-
year-old commissioner was a native of Fokien, a man of mild disposition,
and "not likely to act with harshness." His reputation as incorruptible
was encapsulated in his nickname, "Blue Sky," meaning as clean as the
unclouded skies.[20] As Fokien was said to be a district heavily addicted to

opium, the speculation among the factories was that Lin might be disposed to report preventive measures to the emperor and then let the prohibitions be relaxed. Nevertheless, Lin was en route with powers that had been delegated only three times by emperors of the Qing dynasty.[21]

An episode at the end of the month led to a flurry of precautionary activity among Americans and British. Late in the afternoon of 26 February, a group of soldiers brought a prisoner to the street in front of the American Factory and quickly tied him to a pole and strangled him. It was eventually determined that the man was associated with the opium business. The foreign merchants were incensed at this pointed demonstration of local police authority, staged for their benefit in view of the factories. English and Parsi merchants pressured Elliot to take down his flag until an apology was received, and he did so. The Americans, Dutch, and French struck their flags as well.[22]

In the aftermath of that incident, for which there was no apology forthcoming, Howqua appealed urgently to Matheson to send the opium ships away from Hong Kong. In response, Matheson gave orders to his ships' captains to move their vessels to a station south of Lantao, which would be outside China's "inner waters."[23] The other British and American houses followed suit. Russell and Company, the large American firm, sent its ships to Lantao but simultaneously renounced the opium trade at the end of February. The company wrote to all its constituents to notify them that Russell's would no longer accept new shipments of the drug. Moreover, it notified its vessel on the coast, the *Rose*, to terminate sales and come back in. "And thus perishes one of our most important sources of business," Forbes declared in a letter to his wife.[24]

Matheson was hardly ready to abandon opium. He was aware that the smokeable extract of opium was being prepared at Macao and smuggled into Canton "chiefly by women" (who were less strictly searched). He knew that many Chinese would crave the drug and reached the conclusion that "all classes will be happy to revert to the long established system of connivance," once the new commissioner had had his moment in the sun. He thought that the great number of persons "who have all their lives been habituated to the daily use of such a stimulant" would not be able to forsake their dependency, but deliveries would have to be accomplished with greater secrecy and caution, the result being reduced consumption.[25]

Where would that leave Jardine, Matheson? Matheson himself was not worried about financial disaster. Cash would keep coming in, he assumed. Even if the depression in the opium trade were not relieved, he said, regular dividends from the Consoo Fund would return to the firm about $250,000 per year. In fact, he was so confident in the security of the firm's financial position that he wrote this remarkable statement to John Abel Smith: "We are of course extensively interested in Opium both as principals and Agents, but the heaviest loss that could occur, even in the improbable event of [the opium market] not recovering from its present depression, would not be materially felt by us."[26] Given the size and diversity of his firm's business, Matheson could afford to be more relaxed than many other merchants at Canton.

All concerned parties were positioning themselves for the anticipated crackdown: the Cohong, the viceroy, the American and British merchants, the local Chinese drug buyers, the British superintendent of trade, and, of course, the new commissioner. As he came closer to Canton, Lin issued secret orders, on 24 February, addressed to the judicial authorities at Canton, calling for the arrest of a number of persons known to be associated with the illegal trade, most of them being complicit government officials.[27] The anticipation was clearly weighing heavily on the British superintendent. On the day before Lin appeared, Elliot issued what Matheson called a "furious proclamation" ordering unlicensed schooners in the Canton River to withdraw beyond the Bogue and threatening to call their presence to the attention of the Chinese government.[28]

Lin Zexu arrived, very noticeably, at Canton on the morning of 10 March 1839. His formal procession of boats, carrying blue button and red button mandarins, passed the factories, and he disembarked at the water stairs not far away from the factories. One observer, William C. Hunter, reported that, along both sides of the river, every window and door was thick with people eager to see Lin's entrance into Canton. After he was greeted by the governor general and other prominent local authorities at a pavilion prepared for the occasion, he was carried away in a palanquin and spent the remainder of the day making courtesy calls before retiring to his residence at the Yueh-hua Academy, relatively close to the foreign factories.[29]

Lin set right to work ordering the arrest of various local persons connected with the drug trade, including mandarins, and he focused much of his attention on Lancelot Dent, now the most prominent figure among

the foreign opium merchants. Within the first week of the commissioner's pursuit of drug dealers, Matheson escaped that prominence because
the Chinese had been using Jardine's name alone to designate the firm
and they knew that he was gone. Lin had intended to arrest Jardine,
whom he described to the emperor as a particularly unscrupulous foreign merchant, with a sly and crafty disposition. "Before I set out from
Peking I sent a confidential agent post-haste to Canton to inquire about
this Jardine's movements. He heard that it was generally rumored in
Canton that the new Commissioner's first act would be to arrest Jardine.
That was why he got a pass to Macao and at once took ship to England."[30]

Matheson persisted for the first few days in thinking that Lin would
be making noise to impress Peking: "He must of course for the sake of
effect make a great noise and splutter at starting."[31] Yet, within a week,
he was inclined to think that Lin was achieving success in suppressing
the opium trade at Canton, "nor is it likely to revive in the open manner
that we have witnessed for some years back."[32] Lin's intent was manifested in many ways, including communications with the Cohong, the
foreign merchants, and even Queen Victoria (although that letter was
never delivered because he could not establish a channel through which
to send it).[33] Late on the evening of 18 March, Robert Thom entered
Matheson's office bearing two documents given to him by Howqua. The
first was a denunciation of the Hong merchants for countenancing the
extensive commerce in "foreign mud," for conniving in the export of
silver, and for protecting the foreigners (with Jardine being named specifically). The twelve members of the Cohong had to listen to this ha-
rangue on their knees, and were confronted with the threat that Lin
would ask the emperor for permission to execute one or two of them if
they did not immediately arrange for the surrender of the opium stocks
aboard the foreign vessels.[34]

The second communication, addressed to the foreign merchants, put
them on notice that the death penalty for opium offences would come
into force shortly and would be applied equally to foreigners as to
Chinese. Then the hammer struck: "I now call upon you to hand over
for destruction all the opium you have on your ships and sign an undertaking that you will never bring opium here again, and that you are
aware that if you are found to have done so your goods will be confiscated and you yourselves dealt with according to the law."[35]

Given his facility for putting the best face on a bad situation, Matheson
immediately began to think about compensation if the opium were

surrendered. Surely, the British government could not afford compensation for the twenty thousand chests of opium estimated to be on hand. So he speculated that it might be possible to surrender some and seek compensation for that portion, while sending the rest away temporarily. Nevertheless, he tried to accept the reality of Lin's determination and admitted the urgency of the predicament: "The Crisis is most important and we fear considerable sacrifice of property will be unavoidable; but as far as our firm is concerned, this will not materially affect us and we have already made up our minds to endure it with a good grace." Little could he have suspected how much good grace would be required within such a short time.[36]

In the company of five other merchants, Matheson met with Howqua and other Hong merchants at the Consoo Hall less than twenty-four hours after first hearing of the surrender demand. They were informed that the hoppo would prohibit any foreigners from leaving Canton for Macao, and they had Commissioner Lin's ultimatum read aloud to them. Although they refused to promise a reply within three days, they did assent to a general meeting of the Canton Chamber of Commerce on Thursday, 21 March. Matheson was inclined to think that the merchants would agree to surrender part of their stocks of opium for burning, if compensation were guaranteed and the remainder of their stocks could be sent away to someplace like Singapore.[37] He had considered sending the Jardine, Matheson stock of opium to Singapore, but hesitated when he found no sympathy for that course of action among his neighbours at the English Factory, and when "Dent's usual dilatoriness" delayed insuring vessels.[38] Meanwhile, from Lin's perspective, there could be no question of monetary compensation for surrendered opium, which he considered to be forfeited contraband. On the other hand, he was committed to continuing trade in legal commodities, but he apparently failed to understand that the suppression of the opium trade would immobilize the very funds by which the foreigners paid for their purchases of teas and silks.[39]

Forty members of the Chamber met twice on that Thursday, with Dent being the foremost speaker. They drafted a reply to Lin but pleaded the need for more deliberations before sending their formal response. However, they informed the Cohong that "unanimous feeling exists in the Community of the necessity of foreign residents at Canton having no further connection with the Opium trade." The Hong members retired from the session, knowing that the foreigners wanted at least six days to frame their formal response, and they returned that same evening with the news that Lin was getting angrier and was planning to select two of them for execution in front of the foreigners on the following morning. They asked for at least a token surrender, say, a thousand chests belonging to the agency houses themselves rather than distant speculators. So the Chamber assembled once more in extraordinary session at 10 p.m. and, to save the Hong members from arrest, subscribed 1,037 chests of opium for immediate surrender "under solemn protest." A quarter of the total was put up by Matheson in the name of his firm.[40] Although some merchants declared that their action was prompted by fear for their lives, Matheson denied any such motive "but submitted to the sacrifice as a measure of expediency calculated to produce a compromise and accelerate the return of quiet to the trade."[41]

The "Kin-chae," as Lin was called, deemed the gesture unsatisfactory, and proceeded to turn the screws on the foreign merchants by placing a complete embargo on the foreign trade of Canton and by suspending all communication between Canton and Whampoa one day after the thousand-chest offer by the opium houses. All ships' boats arriving from Whampoa were prevented from making the return trip downriver.

With Jardine gone, Lancelot Dent became the lightning rod for the foreign merchants as far as Lin was concerned. Not long after the Chamber of Commerce adjourned at two in the morning on 22 March, Lin sent word to the factories that he wanted to speak directly with Dent. Initially, Dent was willing to enter the city; however, other merchants discouraged him from going without a safe-conduct guarantee from Lin himself. Howqua and Mowqua reappeared at Dent's residence the following morning, wearing iron chains (signs of degradation, but lightweight, like necklaces) and lacking the buttons of rank on their caps. Some members of the Chamber were appalled by the pathetic appearance of the prominent Cohong members. But Matheson thought it a ruse – "the most complete exhibition of humbug ever witnessed in China." In spite of their fear that Lin might subject some of the Cohong to execution, the entire community of foreign merchants concurred that Dent should not go without a guarantee of safe conduct from Lin. Matheson was even more resolute about resistance; he urged "that Dent be placed in the Superintendent's Hall, guarded by the whole foreign community and that we should dare the Chinese to take him." He was, however, bolder than his neighbours. "But will you believe it? There was scarcely one to second me!"[42]

Robert Inglis, Dent's partner, was persuaded to go into the city to meet with some officers and he assured them that Dent would meet with one of the officers at ten the next morning; but, as he remembered that the next day was Sunday, he secured a delay of one day so residents of the factories could attend church. Meanwhile, James Matheson sent word to Captain Parry and the other commanders of Jardine, Matheson vessels that the firm had promised the Chinese government that it would abstain from the opium trade. In fact, however, his intention was really to circumvent the promise, in a very brazen way. The captains were instructed that "all future orders for delivery will be granted by Mr. A. Matheson at Macao. Should we have occasion to issue any orders here, they will have the signature 'Alexander' simply annexed to them." He explained to Jardine, "We thus in a manner divested ourselves of control."[43] It was a devious scheme that might have had perilous consequences for the members of the firm and for the whole foreign merchant community, had it been implemented and discovered.

That Sunday unarmed guards in the employ of the Cohong surrounded the factories and the riverfront in front of the foreign residences was sealed off by war boats. "We were really prisoners," Forbes told his wife. He was walking in front of the factories with members of his firm late Sunday afternoon when a "tremendous hubbub" began on the river. In a moment they could see that the uproar was about a small boat, approaching the factories, with four mandarin boats in pursuit. In the stern of the boat stood Captain Charles Elliot in full uniform, having run the blockade to take charge of the besieged British community at Canton.[44]

The superintendent had little naval strength with which to protect British nationals and their property. The eighteen-gun sloop *Larne* was the only British warship in Chinese waters, and it was hardly sufficient to challenge the numerous armed junks that had been assembled. On 22 March, Elliot had the melancholy parental duty of seeing his two young children off on the *Melbourne* as they sailed for England, entrusted to his sister's keeping. That very same day he received word of Lin's demands. He set out the next day aboard his own cutter, the *Louisa*, with the *Larne*'s gig in tow. At the fort four miles below Canton he moved into the gig and proceeded up the river unmolested, finally nosing his boat into the stairs below the English Factory at about six o'clock on Sunday, 24 March. Seeing no flag above the factory, and having no Union Jack at hand, he took the ensign from the gig and ran it up the flagpole, generating great approval from the residents.[45]

The superintendent went directly to Dent's residence in the Paoushun Factory, and took the English merchant into his protection, declaring that he would not allow Dent to go into the city to meet Lin. They proceeded to the Company's Hall, where Elliot addressed a large assemblage of British, Parsi, and American merchants as well as Howqua and Mowqua, there as quiet observers. He spoke with great intensity as he informed the crowd that he had directed the British merchant vessels to take up defensive positions at Canton, and that he was advising all British subjects to move their property out of the Canton River and be prepared to take leave of Canton themselves. Those applauding him included James Matheson, who thanked Elliot for a brave and heartening speech.[46]

The foreign merchants there feared that if Lin could intimidate Dent into surrendering all of his opium, estimated at six thousand chests, the same procedure could be used to isolate every one of them, including Matheson, and to browbeat each into surrendering all of his chests. In reality, Lin did not want to provoke an incident that might lead to war. So he did not move to seize Dent. But Elliot's actions convinced Lin that the superintendent was planning to help Dent and the other opium traders escape from Canton. To prevent that from happening, the commissioner chose to confine the whole lot of them within the factories.[47]

During the night that followed Elliot's arrival, Chinese guards surrounded the factories and a double line of ships in the shape of a half moon blockaded the waterfront, to prevent any of the residents from escaping. In addition, all of the Chinese servants were ordered to leave the factories, which meant that the *fan kwae* were not only besieged but left to fend for themselves. Incompetent at cooking and unaccustomed to doing their own cleaning and laundry and provisioning, they were thrown into considerable disorder. "You would have been much amused," Forbes told his wife in a letter that day, "to see me making fire, splitting wood & boiling the Tea Kettle this morning ... our poor cows have had to be sent away as we could not well act [as] servants and grooms."[48] Others in the firm who never set foot in the kitchen were conscripted into cooking eggs, rice, and ham – all quite badly. Getting fresh produce and meat, as well as fresh water, was a major problem.

On the other hand, Matheson came to terms with the inconvenience quite well, as he told Jardine some weeks later: "By kindness of Heerjeebhoy in lending us his Indian Servants, with the assistance of some sailors who happened to be up, we have not only lived comfortably all along but have entertained the remaining inmates of the Hong."[49]

In their forty-seven days of confinement, the residents of the factories were not seriously deprived of food or opportunities for entertainment, or even shared conversations over beer with some of their guards. Although the beating of gongs and blowing of horns through the night hours by parties of guards did deprive some people of sleep, no one suffered from lack of nourishment. Matheson would later remark that the hostages suffered more from lack of exercise and from excessive eating than from any actual want of the necessities of life.[50] Much the same situation prevailed among the ships detained at Whampoa, where discreet provisioning of the ships allowed by Chinese authorities enabled the ships' captains to host a round of dinner parties.[51]

That Monday morning, 25 March, while the residents were contending with their laundry and meals on their own, the Chinese authorities had been busy plastering posters in various locations about the factories. The message, written in large letters, was addressed to the *fan kwae* and came from Commissioner Lin. He repeated his demand for surrender of the opium, and explained in a patient tone that he would rather avoid harsh measures.[52] Elliot's position was quietly being undermined, since there was no longer any way for his valour to trump Lin's strength of will. The factories were under siege, and there was no relief at hand, short of submission. Elliot had rushed from Macao to Canton, running the blockade, precisely to interpose himself between the merchant community and the Chinese officials. Indeed, in the placard notices Lin had put him on the spot by asking: if the superintendent was not able to stop the British merchants from importing opium into China, "what is it that Elliot superintends?"[53]

On Tuesday afternoon, the superintendent notified Lancelot Dent that he had decided to call for the surrender of all the opium in the possession of British subjects. The drug was to be surrendered to him, and the British government would compensate the merchants for their losses. He communicated that decision to the rest of the British residents on Wednesday morning, explaining that he was "constrained by paramount motives affecting the safety of the lives and liberty of all the foreigners here present in Canton." Acting in the name of the queen, he demanded that all of Her Majesty's subjects in China surrender to him by 6 p.m. that evening, for delivery to the government of China, all of the opium in their possession or under their control. He declared British ships engaged in the opium trade to be subject to his direction. The British agency houses were ordered to provide inventories of their opium supplies, and upon his receipt of those lists he would assume responsibility in the name of the Crown for the value of the drugs surrendered. If an agency house were not honest regarding its supply of opium, the British government would deny responsibility for compensating that house. After adding up the import entries of the various agency houses, he arrived at a total of twenty thousand chests, and informed Lin that he was prepared to turn over that amount, which he believed to be the entirety.[54]

In writing to Foreign Secretary Lord Palmerston, he justified his action on the basis of protecting the lives of his countrymen and the avoidance of commercial disaster. Had the "forced and separate surrender to the Chinese of all immensely valuable property by individual merchants, without security of indemnity" occurred, the consequence would have been a commercial convulsion in England and India.[55] In a letter to his wife, who was at Macao, Elliot wrote with bolder strokes: "It was obviously [Lin's] purpose to bully the merchants into forced and separate surrenders of their property ... But I burst in upon Him, and his measures met an officer with all the train of consequences that his treatment of me has produced ... They [the Chinese] will have to pay for everything, 50 shillings to the pound sterling, and be you assured that trade at Canton is finished forever."[56] Elliot saw himself as achieving a far different result from Napier's embarrassment four years earlier. There was no possibility that he could wait for instructions from Whitehall, so he had to make a decision on the spot.

The superintendent's conclusion that there were 20,283 chests of opium on hand at Whampoa or at the outer anchorages was inaccurate. In his haste, he had not consulted the houses whose books he was using, and had not taken into account recent sales of the drug; nor had he realized that mortgagor and mortgagee would be including the same item in their accounts and thereby duplicating some of the listings. That shortsightedness caused him to promise Lin more opium than he could actually collect and surrender, with the result that he found it necessary to purchase new amounts of opium to complete the promised total. It was fortunate for him that a new consignment arrived for Dent and Company, which he purchased at inventory price in order to meet his promised total of chests.[57]

For Matheson and many other foreign merchants, the huge "purchase" of the drug inventories was a godsend, for it relieved the glut in a market that was already being squeezed out of existence by Lin. After Elliot's decision to surrender the drug supplies, Matheson wrote: "I cannot but feel sanguine on mature reflection, [that it] will prove far more advantageous than if we had to work off so large a stock in an overburdened and persecuted market." The British government had become, in effect, the customer of last resort. Referring to the shipments coming from clients in India, Alexander Matheson later testified that "the opium was deposited in our hands to dispose of it, and the money of the British Government was as good as any other money we could get."[58]

Delighted with Elliot's assurance, James Matheson planned to ask a jolly good price for the surrendered goods: the January prices current in Calcutta, plus interest and carrying charges. On those terms, Matheson and all the other merchants would be eager to surrender every chest they could. The estimated value of all the opium surrendered to Lin eventually amounted to £2,400,000.[59] Of the 20,383 chests surrendered to Lin, 5,315 belonged to Parsi firms.[60]

As of Good Friday 1839, at the end of that turbulent week, Jardine, Matheson alone had already surrendered 7,141 chests; two thousand of them belonged to the firm. James wrote to Alexander: "If you have sent merchandize away we shall now have the expense of bringing it back again *as it must all be given up.*" He was glad now not to have sent the ships away at the first sign of danger, because that would have placed them outside the scope of Elliot's surrender/compensation policy, and that would have meant selling off the huge inventory in a depressed market.[61]

Lin must have been astonished at the quantity of opium that was promised for surrender. We do know that the Hong merchants were flabbergasted, according to Matheson's account of their reaction: "What for he pay so large? No wantee so much, Sir. Six, seven thousand so would be enough."[62] Lin did not respond by relieving the siege upon receipt of the promise. In fact, the confinement became more tightly sealed, as Chinese workmen were sent to brick up all the outer entrances to the factories except for the one at Old China Street, which was guarded constantly.

The commissioner sent a present of food to the hostages, but refused to lift the siege until the chests were actually being delivered, and that took weeks to accomplish. Lin was convinced that Elliot was dragging his heels. His diary for 29 March reads: "Elliot is now inventing reasons for delaying the surrender of opium, insisting that liberty of movement must first be restored to the foreigners in the factories." Negotiations for the delivery of the opium continued until 2 April.[63] For a time, communications with Macao were not allowed, so the bolder ones among the hostages resorted to ruses. Matheson paid $50 to get a message to his nephew Alexander by sending it rolled up inside a cigar.[64] To hasten the deliveries, Lin set up a four-stage schedule, with incentives to take effect as each quarter of the total was landed. Servants could return after the first quarter had been delivered; communications with Macao and Whampoa could be restored after the second quarter; the embargo on trade would be lifted after the third quarter; and the "normal" status of relations prior to the March disruption would be resumed upon conclusion of the deliveries.

The deliveries were slow and not completed until the third week of May. Matheson's tactic of telling the coastal vessels' commanders to pay attention only to directives from Alexander had to be countermanded, and the vessels had to be brought in from considerable distances. The message they all received from him in mid-April was straightforward: "Having surrendered all the opium under our control ... we request you will all return immediately to Lintin and deliver the drug you have on board to the Chief Superintendent's order."[65] Still, some captains stopped long enough to make sales during their return trips to Chuenpi. The *Lady Hayes* and *Governor Findlay* never appeared at Chuenpi at all. Matheson bought seven hundred chests newly arrived from India to replace the chests not delivered by the *Lady Hayes* and *Governor Findlay*. The last of the chests from the opium fleet were unloaded on 21 May, and Commissioner Lin finally had the vast number that was promised to him.[66]

Early in the crisis, Matheson was already looking far into the future, and planning rather calmly to wind up the firm's business before any military reckoning might take place. "I suppose War with China will be the next step," he told Jejeebhoy in a letter written before full communication with the outside world was restored, "but not probably till we have had time to get through with next season's business."[67] It seems that he was planning to stay on as long as possible, but Lin would call the tune in that regard. The commissioner demanded that the merchants sign a bond promising never to sell opium in China again, or submit to being tried for their lives if they were apprehended doing so. Matheson had no intention of making such an unconditional pledge, having already sent Andrew Jardine to Manila to establish the new base of operations for the coastal trade in opium.[68] The first of the hostages to be released left the factories on Monday, 6 May, with most of the others having their liberty restored over the next ten days.

However, on Lin's orders, sixteen persons connected with the opium traffic were held in confinement until the delivery of the 20,283 chests was completed. Among the sixteen so designated were four members of the Jardine, Matheson firm: James Matheson, his two nephews – Donald and Alexander (the latter not actually among the hostages) – and his partner's nephew, David Jardine. Of the notorious sixteen, those who were actually present in the factories during this drama were finally released from detention on 24 May and expelled from China forever. They were required to sign a bond declaring that they would not return to China. Led by the superintendent, Matheson and his rival Dent, as well as the other members of their firms, departed from Canton by the Whampoa passage, not knowing where they were going to make their abode. Matheson doubted that he would be allowed to reside at Macao. He assured Jardine, "If not, we shall go afloat & on no account desert our post."[69]

Elliot had actually made an overture to Governor Pinto of Macao to take the British evacuees and their property under Portuguese protection, but the request was denied. Lin had managed to neutralize Macao by assuring that the colony would remain undisturbed as long as Macao cooperated in the suppression of the opium trade and in expelling the English.[70] Actually, Matheson had been hoping that for the coming trade season the Chinese would patch up some arrangement for English vessels to go up to Whampoa, but now that was clearly not going to happen, and Lin's naive idea that "normal" relations could resume after the final opium deliveries was likewise lost.

Before the end of March, Lin had obtained signatures of all the foreign merchants on a pledge not to sell opium in the future. James Matheson did sign, but his signature would not be binding for Alexander Matheson and Andrew Jardine who were not at Canton. However, the commissioner was not satisfied that the pledge was sufficiently ironclad, so he issued a new version of the bond at the start of April, while the foreign merchants were confined. It was sent to Elliot through the Hong merchants and required that, whenever a vessel entering the Canton River was discovered to be carrying opium, the drug and vessel would be confiscated and the offenders would be subject to trial in a Chinese court, with a sentence of execution for the guilty. Elliot refused to sign such a bond, and the English merchants followed him in refusing, as did the Americans initially. He perceived the danger that the Chinese would apply the principle of collective responsibility in the instance of violations, and that would subject innocent parties to trial and execution. Elliot was so angry when the bond was presented to him again on 20 April that he tore Lin's document into a thousand pieces and pitched it into the fireplace.[71]

Given the danger of British merchants and captains and seamen facing trial under Chinese jurisdiction, on 19 May Elliot issued an order that no British ships were to enter the anchorage at Whampoa. A few days later he issued a notice insisting that the English residents of Canton leave with him, or risk grave trouble. Nearly all complied.

The English departure from Canton took on the appearance of permanence. "A whole fleet sailed," says Peter Ward Fay, with many people taking their furniture, business ledgers, and their supplies of wine. Matheson made arrangements to have the office records, and the furnishings of No. 1, Creek Hong, follow him and the other members of the firm within a few days' time. There would be no need for Jardine, Matheson to retain their property there, for their operations at Canton were being closed down, and Matheson was taking permanent leave of the city that had been the site of his rise to fortune.[72] By the end of May, barely a handful of English subjects remained at Canton.

No sooner had the English left Canton than the Americans began drifting back into town. In effect, the foreign system of trade there was reinvented, with the American ships carrying British goods in the absence of British merchants and shipping.[73] And no sooner had James Matheson arrived at Macao than he was back in the opium business, directing the movements of his fleet along the coast of south China. Less than a week after being released from confinement at Canton, he sent both the *Lady Hayes* and the *Hellas* to Manila to await instructions. Since the *Lady Hayes* had not needed to surrender its opium, owing to Matheson's purchases of newly arrived chests, he elected to run the risk of sending her back to the coast. At about the same time, he sent Jejeebhoy a message saying that the coastal prospects were good, and that the Bombay merchant should send on his vessel *Mahommedie*, with a full cargo of opium. He told Jardine, almost gleefully, "The coast trade promises fair. [Captain] Rees and his gang are at work again."[74]

While Matheson was making arrangements for Rees to resume selling on the coast and for Otadui to begin handling the opium storage at Manila, Commissioner Lin was preparing to have the twenty thousand chests of opium destroyed. Elaborate preparations were made near the village of Chen-k'ou, about five miles above Chuenpi, with the construction of three trenches, each about twenty-five by fifty yards. An aqueduct to the rear and exit gates to the seaside provided a way to introduce water into the pens and to expel the watery slush of destroyed opium into tidal waters that carried the mixture out to sea. Coolies brought the cakes of opium to platforms over the pens, crushed the cakes, and pushed the pieces into the fresh water. Salt and lime were added to the mixture, and the opium decomposed into a vile-smelling concoction that was released into the creek.

It took three weeks of intensive labour to destroy the two and a half million pounds of opium that Lin had acquired, and the coolies employed on the project were stripped and searched every night to make sure that they were not pilfering for their own use. A few of the Americans who had returned to Canton actually ventured out to the village to observe the destruction, among them Charles King, the severely anti-opium member of the Olyphant firm. The destruction was complete by 25 June.[75] Yet, as real as Lin's satisfaction was at that moment in the summer of 1839, it was premature, for Lord Palmerston would eventually have other thoughts about resolving the episode, and Matheson was, as already noted, at work circumventing the commissioner's achievement.

When Captain Elliot reported the surrender of the opium to Palmerston, he called for an armed response: "It appears to me, My Lord, that the response to all these unjust violences should be made in the form of a swift and heavy blow unprefaced by one word of written communication."[76] After their release from captivity six weeks later, a number of the British merchants, led by Dent, composed a memorial to Palmerston, in which they allowed that the Chinese government had the right to stop the import of opium but argued that lax enforcement of existing laws amounted to implicit sanction of the trade. Hence they regarded the "recent acts of aggression by Lin as unjustifiable."[77] Matheson declined to sign Dent's memorial, because it linked the opium trade and the demand for compensation. Matheson thought it better not to open a public discussion of the opium traffic and thereby allow the "High Church party" in England to join in Lin's condemnation of the trade.[78]

The foreign secretary did not learn of the drama at Canton until 1 August, when an inflamed account appeared in *The Times*. The first accounts from Elliot did not arrive until the end of August, but the cabinet of Lord Melbourne did not let the initial rush of emotion carry them into a decision for war. As for Matheson, he was not eager to see a war take place; he was insistent on compensation for the confiscated opium, but he was also keen on resuming commerce in teas and silks and other commodities from the outer anchorages through the agency of Americans who had returned to Canton. After Matheson's expulsion the firm was represented at Canton by the American merchant James Ryan; and when Ryan expressed his intent to sail home in August, Matheson made plans to engage another American, John Shillaber of Manila..[79] The rather wild irony of enlisting Shillaber to handle Jardine's business in legitimate items at Canton lay in the fact that Shillaber's firm, Otadiu, was being recruited to serve as the Jardine, Matheson opium-receiving agency in Manila.

While still in confinement Matheson had reached the conclusion that Elliot's policy constituted a "large and statesmanlike measure, more especially as the Chinese have fallen into the snare of rendering themselves directly liable to the British Crown." It seemed to him that war would be inevitable, and he was hoping that the outcome would be the gaining of a territory to be under the British flag, from which "safe and unrestricted liberty of trade" could be conducted with the major markets of China.[80] In the meantime, he was ready to resume both the legitimate trade through the Americans and the opium trade in the coastal markets. But the fleet needed attention. The *Colonel Young* was "too tender," so Matheson had sold her; and the *Findlay* was condemned as unserviceable. Jauncey had taken over the *Hellas*, and Baylis was commanding a new arrival, the *Kelpie*. All this buying and selling of vessels for use by the opium commanders reveals that Matheson had firm intentions of staying in the drug business.[81]

With extraordinary logic, Matheson declared to a Singapore merchant: "We consider our pledge to the Chinese [not to sell opium again]

not merely as null and void because given in durance but as wholly ab-
rogated by their faithless conduct in expelling the majority of our Firm
in violation of their pledge not only of oblivion of the past, but [to tender us] a reward for the surrender exacted."[82] Having resolved that obstacle to his own satisfaction, Matheson managed to justify the resumed
drug sales as an obligation to long-time clients in India: "As many of our
friends to whom we are endebted for extensive business have probably
opium on hand, in India without any means of realizing it, since being
excluded from the China market, it has occurred to me as a sort of duty,
in protection of their interests to extend a Branch of our Firm to Manila
for drug business, and *no other*, as a mere temporary arrangement till
times mend."[83] There was no local market for opium at Manila, so the
drug sales there would be for vessels selling along the coast of China.

Manila offered a better option of operating quietly than did Macao.
Hence, James could afford to relieve his nephew Alexander of his emergency managerial position at Macao, and send him home to London to
promote compensation from the British government.[84] No long-term
security could be anticipated at Macao, though the British community
in exile from Canton did spend the months of June and July there. By
July, Matheson was efficiently reorganizing the agency business in legitimate cargoes sent to Whampoa. He was confident that the Americans
provided a legal way to circumvent Elliot's order prohibiting British
ships from going to Whampoa, and he encouraged John Abel Smith to
expect "considerable shipments of Tea ... until the Port of Canton shall
be regularly blockaded by a British squadron."[85]

The improvised arrangements for continuing trade were to be disrupted before long as a result of a night of drunken disorder involving
British and American sailors who went ashore. On 7 July their fracas
with local villagers at Chien-sha-tsui left one Chinese man dead and resulted in demands by Commissioner Lin that the guilty party be turned
over to Chinese authorities. Although Elliot conducted an investigation
which led to the conviction of five men for rioting and mayhem, the
trial of a sixth man on a charge of murder was inconclusive. The Chinese
idea of community responsibility conflicted with the British idea of personal culpability that had to be proved against the individual charged.
So Elliot could not meet Lin's demand. As a consequence, the situations
both at Macao and at Hong Kong deteriorated quickly and steeply.

When it began to seem that Lin would move against Macao, the British
population there became alarmed, especially when their servants began

disappearing. On 15 August, Lin moved two thousand troops to within forty miles of Macao, which had never formally been ceded by China to Portugal. Elliot asked Matheson to leave Macao, as a way of calming Lin, for the residence of expelled British at Macao was one of the commissioner's chief complaints. Temporarily, Matheson found sanctuary aboard the small schooner *Maria*, anchored in front of the Baya Grande. His nephew Donald and Jardine's nephew Andrew accompanied him, but Andrew proceeded on to Manila to oversee drug operations. As unruffled as ever, Matheson assured clients in India that he did not anticipate an interruption in business: "Whatever happens our Firm will endeavour to maintain a floating position in this vicinity and we are now writing to Manila for provisions, etc." He intended to live decently during the inconvenience, for his order for supplies included bread, pigs, poultry, beer, and "some moderately good French claret."[86]

Elliot advised the British subjects resident at Macao to leave, and three days later, on 24 August, the Portuguese governor, complying with an edict from Lin, directed the British population to depart. Elliot, his wife, and their young son were among the fifty-seven English families taking leave of Macao.[87] Just as the last of the English merchant vessels were leaving Macao, a twenty-eight-gun frigate, the HMS *Volage*, arrived from India, and a smaller frigate, the *Hyacinth*, mounting eighteen guns, was expected shortly. So the migration to Hong Kong began on 26 August and soon enjoyed the protection of the *Volage*. Within a week the Britons were accommodated among the nearly seventy merchant ships at anchorage off Hong Kong, under the surveillance of Chinese war junks.[88]

Matheson explained to Otadiu that Andrew Jardine was being sent to Manila for the purpose of "carrying on under the name of our Firm, at your place." Although it was not essential that Andrew have a place of his own, Matheson said it would be beneficial in case he and all the firm members had to go to Manila. However, as it turned out, James Matheson would not settle in Manila. For the next several months he would be afloat most of the time, but occasionally he would be ashore at Hong Kong, and by February 1840 he would be back at Macao.

No sooner had the English merchant fleet anchored off Hong Kong than they were "thrown into the greatest alarm" by loud and protracted gunfire near Kowloon at the start of September.[89] Commissioner Lin had urged the mainland population near Hong Kong to prevent food and water supplies from reaching the English merchant ships. Elliot determined to challenge the embargo and attacked the three Chinese junks at Kowloon with the cutter *Louisa*, the brigantine *Pearl* (a hired opium vessel), and the pinnace from the *Volage*. The two sides fired at one another furiously for a time, and when the ammunition ran low on the English ships, some smaller English boats came up to support them. Although the brief fight was inconclusive, partly because Elliot persuaded Captain Smith not to polish off the junks and their shore battery with the firepower of the *Volage*, Elliot's point had been made. Access to the supplies of water and food on the mainland was achieved and the rest of September was uneventful for the vessels at Hong Kong.[90] By the end of the month, Lin was tolerating the return of a few English persons, including Elliot, to Macao.[91]

The opium business was proceeding rather favourably. Lower prices along the coast had prompted significantly increased sales. Matheson was not too concerned about the price reductions for they allowed the firm to work down the stock at Manila at what he called "fair rates" and this made it possible to take on fresh supplies from India.[92] Those conditions prevailed through September, with Matheson gratified to report that the firm's treasury was "well replenished" from the coastal sales and that it possessed a virtual monopoly on ready money among the merchant vessels anchored at Hong Kong. When he had the leisure to reflect on the events of recent months, he composed a broad statement of his perspective on the drama that was being played out in south China. Not only is this document Matheson's most candid acknowledgment that there was a moral controversy surrounding the opium trade, but it is also his most extended defence of his personal moral position on the issue. It reads:

> [Lin's] great object is to annihilate the Opium trade, on which he has staked his official character, most probably his life, and he perhaps knows enough of what I must be excused for terming the senseless clamour of the High Church party against the traffic, to hope for the cooperation of our Govt in his designs. You I think will not be led away by the mis-statements, which are so industriously circulated on the subject and as you have access to accurate information from so many of our friends who have lately gone home you will I hope give the benefit of your powerful influence to the right side – During 21 years that I have passed almost entirely in China, I can conscientiously declare that I have never seen a native in the least bestialized by Opium smoking, like

drunkards in Europe, nor any Chinese with his faculties more impaired from excessive indulgence in the habit, nor indeed so much so as Gluttons & topers in our own Country, while of this the instances are far from common, and much of the Opium smoked, used to be on convivial occasions of the upper classes as in England Champagne & costly wines. Forgive this little digression which I shall sum up satisfactorily by adding that our operations in that line go on well.[93]

Matheson could not have known that, as he was writing to John Abel Smith about Commissioner Lin's desire to avoid military conflict, his partner was in London conferring with the foreign secretary about an appropriate British response to the seizure of the opium and the taking of merchant hostages.

As Jardine travelled homeward, he was always a short distance ahead of the news from India – until it caught up with him at Naples. He had stopped at Bombay to visit with Jamsetjee Jejeebhoy and other old friends among the Parsi merchants. But he was not there long enough to receive the news of the great drama at Canton, which had reached Madras on 13 May via Jamsetjee's vessel *Good Success*.[94]

Jardine and his travelling companions took the overland route through Suez and spent some time sightseeing in the eastern Mediterranean. Writing to Matheson from Istanbul at the end of May, Jardine was entirely unaware of the ongoing drama at Canton.[95] When they reached Naples early in August, they heard the startling news that Lin had seized all the opium stocks and had banished Matheson and the other opium merchants from Canton. Abandoning their leisurely itinerary (even though Jardine had lost their passports), the travellers purchased a coach and horses and hastened across Europe, cutting through the Alps by way of the St Gotthard Pass. They arrived at London early in September.[96]

Jardine immediately set to work shaping public opinion and seeking an opportunity to advise the foreign secretary. The City was in a state of great agitation, since the tea trade was endangered. Lin's expulsion of British subjects and impounding of their property was seen as an outrage. Well before Jardine gained access to Palmerston, the foreign secretary was under pressure from the China lobby. Jardine adopted their strategy as articulated in a petition sent to Palmerston by the London

East India and China Association. That body argued that the EIC, overseen by a cabinet minister, was encouraging the opium trade, and that
the merchants should not have to shoulder the blame for a trade that
was sanctioned by the highest authorities.[97]

The appeals to Palmerston were arriving at an unfortunate time.
While the drama of hostage taking and opium destruction was transpir-
ing at Canton, the Foreign Office in London had been unaware of the
emergency in the Far East, but it was keenly aware of threats (whether
perceived or real) in the Near East and Middle East. It was France and
Russia, rather than China, that concerned the Whig cabinet in the
spring of 1839. Things would get so bad that there was even some
chance that Britain and France might have gone to war in 1840 over
tensions in the eastern Mediterranean.

Within the Ottoman empire, an Albanian opportunist named
Muhammad Ali had been appointed by the sultan to the vice-regal position of pasha of Egypt, but he then turned renegade. Having used his
French-trained army to take control of Ottoman Syria in the early 1830s,
Muhammad Ali, with French backing, sent his son Ibrahim Pasha to
repel Turkish forces attempting to reconquer Syria in 1839. Palmerston,
deeply concerned about his country's interests in the region, determined to undermine French influence on Muhammad Ali by proposing
that the Great Powers guarantee the territorial integrity of the Ottoman
state. However, France balked at what it saw as British effrontery, and a
serious deterioration of Anglo-French relations occurred by 1840.[98]

What seemed like accord between Britain and Russia over the eastern
Mediterranean was by no means a global accord, for Russophobia per-
meated British politics in these years. Suspicious that Russia had designs
on northern India, Baron Auckland, the governor general of India, con-
spired with the Sikh ruler of Punjab, Ranjit Singh, to install a compliant
ruler at Kabul, to keep the Russians away from the passes that protected
India. To achieve the installation of Shah Shuja, units of the Bengal and
Bombay armies were sent to Kandahar in the spring of 1839, and it
seemed that the Afghan campaign was succeeding fully.

The scope of these foreign-policy concerns in 1839 was so sweeping
that news of yet another crisis, this one in China, could not command
Palmerston's full attention that autumn.[99] Nevertheless, John Abel
Smith, who was a prominent Whig MP and a friend of Palmerston, ar-
ranged for Jardine to see the foreign secretary. After dashing across
Europe to get home as quickly as possible in order to make his case to

the government, Jardine was anxious to see Palmerston, but his patience was tested. He wrote to Matheson in mid-September: "His Lordship appointed Saturday at the Foreign Office. We went there and found many people waiting, but no Lord Palmerston. Parties connected with India and China are becoming very impatient ... We prefer doing the thing quietly if possible, though the delay is very provoking."[100] To his mind, it was important to have the receipts for the surrendered opium before opening up a full-scale public debate, which would spill across the pages of the newspapers and into the House of Commons. "The question is very little understood here," he informed Matheson, "and many people are for doing nothing; they very foolishly mix up the insult & violence with the illicit trade, & are for remaining quiet, pocketing the insult, and refusing to pay for the opium."[101]

So Jardine bided his time, but none too placidly, as befitting one to whom leisure was a foreign concept. With September nearing an end he wrote again to Matheson (by then aboard the *Hercules* off Hong Kong): "You will be surprised to hear that we have heard nothing from H.M. ministers respecting their intentions, nor have I seen Lord Palmerston. Mr. Smith had an interview with him three days ago, when he told him I was anxious to leave town for Scotland, and would not be back for some time; his Lordship said he was desirous of having an interview; as he has many questions to ask and added: 'I suppose he can tell us what ought to be done.' He proposed a day in town in the end of the week ... and begged I should not leave Town until we had met."[102]

In the last days of the month, Palmerston finally received Jardine, but even then he kept his visitors waiting for two hours. It was 27 September when Jardine, Smith, and Captain Alexander Grant, until recently the firm's fleet commodore in the China seas, called on Palmerston and bore with them maps and charts of the waters and islands off the China coast. They commenced by spreading out the maps and charts "in order that his Lordship might have a clear idea of the country with which we must cope, should Her Majesty's Ministers determine on redress." The conversation moved past general and theoretical issues to consider specific details of a punitive expedition, if such a course of action were decided upon. It was typical of Jardine to get right down to brass tacks, and apparently Palmerston was willing to entertain such particulars. "The extent of armament, number of troops necessary, number of shipping etc., were all described, but no direct avowal made of a determination to coerce."[103]

After the session, Jardine wrote to his partner that Palmerston retained the charts, in anticipation of a cabinet meeting the next Monday, and that the foreign secretary expressed the hope of seeing him again in the ensuing week. "It is difficult to form an opinion as to the real views of the Government," Jardine commented, "though it is still more difficult to believe they can remain quiet, pocket the insult, and purchase a continuation of the legitimate trade at two million sterling."[104] He left the meeting somewhat unsettled but not terribly discouraged. "All this is unsatisfactory enough, but we must wait patiently," he told his partner.[105] He was at least gratified that Palmerston was more communicative with his little group than with other deputations, to whom the foreign secretary kept saying, in effect, "My ears are open but my lips are sealed."[106]

Just days later, at the Windsor cabinet meeting of 1 October, the Melbourne government concluded that military action against China had to be undertaken. Once informed that the Chinese had taken the merchants' opium by force, the cabinet members were in general agreement that an armed response was necessary. The more complicated questions for the cabinet involved the precise objectives of the expedition and the problem of dealing with Elliot's promise that the British government would compensate the merchants for surrendering their opium.[107] Palmerston, encouraged by Secretary of War Thomas Babington Macaulay, thought that the Chinese should be made to pay for the confiscated opium and for the costs of the expedition. Upon hearing that the cabinet had decided to demand reparations, Jardine saw the chance to influence Palmerston's next move. "We intend sending his Lordship a paper of hints tomorrow," he informed Matheson.[108]

After the cabinet's decision, Palmerston wrote a secret letter to Captain Elliot alerting him to the impending military action.[109] Jardine offered to have the letter carried aboard the *Mor*, a brand-new full-rigged clipper ship, owned jointly by Jardine, Matheson and Jamsetjee Jejeebhoy, which was at Plymouth preparing to sail for China. Palmerston composed the letter on 18 October; the *Mor* sailed on 23 October; and after a swift journey of 114 days, the ship arrived at the Gulf of Canton on 15 February 1840.[110] Thus, even before Jardine's second meeting with Palmerston, the decision had been made for war, and elements of his advice to the foreign secretary were being implemented.

When they met again, on 26 October, Jardine gave Palmerston a more complete idea of the needs and wishes of the merchants trading with East Asia. The list included a commercial treaty, a blockade of Chinese ports as pressure for reparations, the occupation of some Chinese islands, and the opening of several new Chinese ports to British commerce. A month later, Palmerston wrote to Elliot with additional, more detailed, instructions regarding future negotiations with the Chinese government.[111] By mid-December, Jardine was informing Matheson that he had that day sent Palmerston "a paper of hints."[112]

Apparently at the request of the foreign secretary, Jardine prepared a specific set of recommendations for the Melbourne government to consider. The long memorandum was completed in early December and forwarded to Palmerston by the Scottish MP for Aberdeen, Alexander Bannerman, on 17 December 1839.[113] In it, Jardine made it clear that he was not anxious to have a British military expedition blockade and bombard the coastal cities of China, for such actions would be expensive and would result only in an unreliable agreement with the Chinese. Rather, he wanted the British government to authorize the seizure of a territory where British merchants could be secure. "Prompt, vigorous, & Decisive Measures for acquiring a permanent & commanding position in the China Seas, for British Subjects & Property under the national flag, are what the present Crisis demands."[114] At the bottom of the whole controversy, he said, was the "probable claims on the part of the British Govt. for Injuries inflicted on, & losses sustained by its Subjects." National honour might rally votes in Parliament for war, but Jardine's call for the government to fulfill Elliot's promise of compensation was the uppermost thing in the minds of the China traders who had lost their investments in opium. He urged a settlement that he summarized in these terms:

1st    Reparation for the Insult inflicted on the national Honor, by the Detention & Captivity of British Subjects.
2ly    Compensation for the opium extorted from the British merchants outside the Port of Canton and afterwards confiscated by the Chinese Govt.
3dly   The Establishment of a Commercial Treaty upon fair Principles of Reciprocity, & whereby the Persons and Property of British Merchants shall in future be protected from Insult & aggression.[115]

The Chinese had set the model of conduct in these matters, he claimed, so the British response could follow suit. In reaction to the Chinese

seizure of £3,000,000 (Jardine's figure) worth of British property without ceremony, the British government could "return the compliment"
by quietly laying hold of the "tight little Island of Lantao" as a place of
refuge for the expelled British merchants and as an "emporium" for
British enterprise. "No doubt the *fee simple* of Lantao (or such like)
might in the first Instance appear an inadequate equivalent for the
large Sum at which the Confiscated opium has been estimated," he
wrote, but the actual value would warrant the British government's
redemption of Captain Elliot's pledge to the opium owners, for the island's long-term worth would outweigh that purchase price (compensating the merchants) within a short time.

This was far from being a modest plea for the Whig Government to
bail out the merchants by covering their losses. It was a tough-nosed
argument for the acquisition of a permanent British territory that would
be enormously advantageous for the China traders. Jardine bared his
teeth in the climactic paragraph of the memorandum:

> No formal Purchase, – no tedious negotiation, – is required, nor
> while British Property to an immense amount is daily going to de-
> struction from the exposure to the winds & the waves of the
> Chinese Seas does the Case admit of either. – *A Firman insistently* is-
> sued to Sir F. Maitland authorizing him to *take & retain* possession
> is all that is necessary, & the Squadron under his Command is
> quite competent to do both, until an adequate naval and military
> force, accompanied with requisite material for setting the Colony
> agoing, could be sent out from the mother Country.
>
>    When all this is accomplished, – but not till then, a negotiation
> may be commenced in some such Terms as the following – "You
> take my opium – I take your Islands in return – we are therefore
> Quits, – & thenceforth if you please let us live in friendly
> Communion and good fellowship. You cannot protect your
> Seaboard against Pirates & Buccaneers. I can – So let us under-
> stand Each other, & study to promote our mutual Interests.[116]

Jardine's realpolitik quietly and efficiently cast aside all considerations
of the moral question about the opium trade and drilled home his
version of an eye for an eye with bonuses attached. It was, in Jardine's
summary analysis, far preferable to adopt this strategy of grabbing
one or more islands and then proceeding on the basis of virtually

unchallengeable commercial strength than it would be to send an expedition which imposed by force of arms a commercial treaty that the Chinese would cease to observe once the expedition had left. He concluded: "Such at least are the sentiments of one very incompetent to give an opinion upon such a subject, but nevertheless deeply interested in the Result."[117]

If Jardine had shark's teeth, they were clearly on display in this line of argument. Moreover, he convinced Palmerston that the strategy outlined in his memorandum was the appropriate one for the Melbourne cabinet to adopt. With Palmerston having a great many things on his mind, it was a rich opportunity for Jardine to recommend a forceful line of conduct that seemed to have a compelling logic. The foreign secretary retained the memorandum for months, returning it only after the parliamentary debate in the spring of 1840 on the military response to the events at Canton.[118]

Lord Palmerston was convinced that, even though Elliot's promise had been unwise, the British government should honour it by paying the merchants for the confiscated opium and that the Chinese government should be required to provide compensation for that outlay. Moreover, he had determined that there had to be a permanent resolution of Britain's commercial and political relationship with the Celestial Empire, and that the seizure of a suitable island would be the way to insure the stability of that settlement.[119]

Among other things demanding the foreign secretary's attention in December 1839 was his wedding. Just one day before Alexander Bannerman forwarded Jardine's long memorandum, Palmerston had turned his attention to marrying his long-time mistress, Emily (Lamb) Cowper, sister of Prime Minister Melbourne. Their liaison had begun thirty years earlier, and her marriage to Lord Cowper had not deterred Palmerston from fathering three of the five children born during her marriage to Cowper. After her first husband died in June 1837, Lady Cowper observed what was a minimally decent interval of mourning by Victorian standards, before she and Lord Palmerston, ages fifty-two and fifty-five, legitimized their long relationship by marrying on 16 December 1839 at St George's Church, Hanover Square. They went to his estate of Broadlands in Hampshire for a Christmas honeymoon of ten days, but the boxes of official papers followed them, as did the representatives of Austria and Russia who worked with him through Christmas to patch up an agreement on the eastern Mediterranean.[120] Small wonder, then, that Jardine's great concern was competing for attention among the "avalanche of other foreign troubles"[121] and the high point of Palmerston's middle-aged romance.

By that Christmastime, Jardine was in Scotland, spending the season in Dumfriesshire. Since arriving at London in September he had been eager to see his family and the countryside of his youth, from which he had been absent for about twenty years. Alexander Matheson, recently returned from China to promote the case for compensation by the British government, joined him in Dumfriesshire that winter. Jardine's four siblings had a total of fourteen children, some of whom had been born after he took up residence in China, and who were by now adults whom he had never met. So he had a great deal of catching up to do. (Jardine's mother, Elizabeth, of whom little is known, was likely dead by the time of his return, since the eldest of her children would have been nearly sixty; his father, Andrew, had died when William was a little boy.) While in China, he had been mindful of the needs of his relatives, especially the widow and children of his deceased brother David (the Muirhousehead Jardines). Now he had the chance to renew his connections with them all. But the length of his stay in Scotland was limited by his need to return to London.

When he met Palmerston on 6 February 1840, Jardine used the occasion to appeal for the government's assistance in collecting the debts owed by the Cohong to British merchants resulting from the interruption of trade at Canton.[122] This appears to have been Jardine's last meeting with Palmerston, but it seems to have had strong influence in solidifying the intent of the cabinet to carry out its earlier decision for military action. Two weeks after that interview, Palmerston sent instructions to Lord Auckland, governor general of India, to make ready sixteen warships, mounting among them more than five hundred guns, as well as transports to carry four thousand troops.

Jardine had likely conceded in his own mind the reality of Palmerston's resistance to having Parliament shell out the £2 million sought by British merchants as recompense for the surrendered opium. In fact, Palmerston told the House of Commons early in the year that he had no intention of asking it to appropriate funds for that purpose. Of central importance in this matter was the vulnerability of the government to derision at Westminster should it appeal to British taxpayers to advance compensation for the Chinese commissioner's destruction of British property.[123]

With rumours of the plans for war circulating in England, the Tory opposition insisted that the government provide Parliament with papers relating to China policy, and at the start of March 1840 Palmerston submitted a sanitized compilation of "Correspondence Relating to China." Not long thereafter, the *Times* drew its own conclusions. "EX-PRESS FROM INDIA: DECLARATION OF WAR AGAINST CHINA," the paper proclaimed, citing newly arrived intelligence from Bombay.[124] Responding to Tory pressures for clarification, Lord John Russell, leader of the Whigs in the House of Commons, revealed the government's aims for the expedition: first, to obtain reparation for insult and injury; second, to obtain compensation for lost property; and third, to obtain security for the future of British trade with China.[125]

The Tories prepared to introduce a motion of censure for the ministry's handling of the China crisis. They accepted war as a necessity now that matters had reached such a crisis point, but contended that the Foreign Office had bungled the management of British policy regarding China for years, particularly in Palmerston's instructions to Elliot.

A three-day debate in Commons opened on 7 April, with Sir James Graham leading the attack for the Tories. He was countered by Secretary of War Macaulay, who declared that the flag should protect all Englishmen wherever they might be, and that the Chinese actions in 1839 demanded retribution. Macaulay granted that the government of China had the right to prohibit the opium trade, but he maintained that it had resorted to measures that were unjust against British subjects.[126] In response, Macaulay's young counterpart, William E. Gladstone (then a Conservative), characterized the opium trade as an embarrassment to the British nation. In contrast to Macaulay's waving of the flag, Gladstone asserted that the flag had always been associated with the cause of justice, "but now, under the auspices of the noble lord [Palmerston], that flag is hoisted to protect an infamous contraband traffic." While he conceded that a display of force would now be necessary to demand equity, he blamed the ministry for creating such an unfavourable situation. Gladstone characterized the coming war as a national mortification: "A war more unjust in its origin, a war more calculated in its progress to cover this country with permanent disgrace, I do not know and I have not read of."[127]

And so it went for three days and nights, with Palmerston calling on all his political skills to deliver the final speech for the government. He concluded by citing a recent letter from the American merchants at

Canton to the American government, sympathizing with the British merchants and observing that military force leading to bloodshed would probably not have to be used because a demonstration of naval power would likely be adequate. As dawn approached on the third night of the debate, Palmerston sat down to thunderous applause.[128] Graham's effort to respond was cut short by weary members calling the question. When the House divided, the vote favoured the ministry, but only by nine votes.[129]

A similar fate awaited the censure motion in the House of Lords, where there was actually a Tory majority. Although Lord Stanhope elected to pursue the condemnation of government policy on moral grounds, similar to the argument advanced by Gladstone, the Tory position was undercut by one of their own, when the Duke of Wellington declared that in his fifty years of public service he had never known of such insults and injuries equal to those inflicted upon the English at Canton.[130] After that, the Tories withdrew to lick their wounds.

As Tory pressure on the government had been mounting, the China lobby took advantage of Palmerston's discomfort to push for relief for the merchants whose property had been seized. Jardine had temporarily become an observer, and so the case was made to Palmerston by John Abel Smith and William Crawford. They pressed the cabinet to establish a parliamentary committee with the authority to investigate the reimbursement claims. When the Tories announced their intent to challenge the government on its handling of China policy, Palmerston acceded to the proposal for a committee of inquiry. It was a political concession that the Melbourne cabinet needed to make in order to retain the loyalty of Smith's friends in Commons during the coming debate.[131]

One of the star witnesses before the committee of inquiry that May would be none other than William Jardine, whose experience and status among the British at Canton gave him a unique voice among the committee's witnesses. But there was to be little more debate on the sending of an expedition. The issue was resolved with the drama of 7–9 April in the House of Commons. The *Times* referred to the coming action as an "opium war," and the name stuck. In spite of the term's negative cast, the *Times* concluded that the war had to be fought.[132]

On 18 May, the second day of Jardine's testimony before the committee, the frigate *HMS Alligator* weighed anchor at Singapore and sailed northeastward for the Gulf of Canton, with the main force of the expedition to follow in short order. It had been barely fifteen months since William Jardine had left Canton. In that span, the homeless James Matheson had managed to keep out of range of the Chinese authorities while steering the firm's business on a zigzag course that kept it running as an agency business.

If, on the eve of the war, either partner reflected on his role in the origins of the war, he left no record of those thoughts. In the spring of 1840 Jardine was largely concerned with the reparations issue, and Matheson with sustaining the firm's business as long as possible if a blockade of the China coast were imminent. If, on the other hand, we were to ask how much they had to do with the origins of the war, the answer would have to be: plenty.

Their long-term evasion of Chinese law and their collaboration with the drug smugglers had been a provocation to Peking that eventually brought on the tough measures of Lin Zexu. Their determination to draw China into the world of free trade and to open that vast nation to British entrepreneurial activity was a matter of economic philosophy which set them in opposition to Peking's policy of narrow access. Their perennial appeals to the British government and complaints to the British public argued that British merchants needed to receive better protection from their political leaders and security achievable through a commercial treaty with China; and they were not quiet about the indignities visited upon British officials and merchants by the Cohong system and by the inaccessible remoteness of mandarin officialdom. Now Jardine favoured a show of force and seizure of an island, but he did not want a blockade that would interrupt commerce. Matheson was determined to keep the opium trade moving even as the prospect of hostilities loomed.

Seen from the Chinese side, the foreign merchants were criminals who corrupted the population of south China and beyond by their traffic in a mind-bending narcotic. Although morphia had been isolated at the start of the nineteenth century, the opium from which it came was regarded at the imperial court not as an analgesic but as the source of debilitating addiction. Moreover, the drug merchants were held responsible for the vice of bribery, which was rampant among Cantonese local officials who winked at the drug deals. Beyond that, their sales were draining the country of its sycee silver. Its export was prohibited, but the smugglers used it to pay Jardine, Matheson for its opium.

Many other merchants, of various national origins, were engaged in similar operations. But Jardine, Matheson was "the princely Hong," and its principals were the taipans who stood out among the foreign merchants. Although they conducted a great deal of legitimate business, Peking saw them as drug peddlers, and Lin's imperative was to crush that business.

Neither William Jardine nor James Matheson had foreseen the extraordinary chain of events that would be initiated by Lin's siege of the factories and destruction of the impounded opium. In the long run, to many British minds, the issue was not opium but insult to persons and property. The thought of actually going to war over the opium trade was never expressed by Jardine or Matheson, though Jardine had occasionally spoken of the need for London to flex its naval muscles within sight of the Chinese. In the spring of 1839 neither Chinese nor British leaders could have anticipated the hostilities that materialized in 1840, nor the enormous long-run consequences for both the Chinese and British empires.

Unquestionably, Jardine and Matheson played a great role in the development of a situation that led to the Opium War of 1840–42. However, the specific occasion of the war and the very fact that there was a prolonged war were largely outside their initiatives.

# JARDINE'S AND MATHESON'S ROLES IN THE OPIUM WAR

"P.S. My sisters advise a small purchase of land for me which I shall immediately remit you for," James Matheson wrote, in concluding a letter to John Abel Smith on Boxing Day 1839.[1] After living aboard one vessel or another, in one bay or another, for half of that year, his thoughts were often directed toward following Jardine homeward and putting his feet down on dry land in friendly surroundings.[2]

Although the Chinese authorities and his countryman Captain Elliot had kept him on the move through the second half of 1839, Matheson's opium business was thriving; all the same, he had concluded that renewed opium sales would need to be conducted as secretly as possible, without the former boldness of publicly listing the "Prices Current" for opium as formerly published at Canton. For that reason, the firm used code in corresponding with its distant clients, and many of the firm's letters were left unsigned.[3]

Further, Matheson now viewed Manila, rather than Macao, as the most secure base from which to conduct operations; he wrote to Charles Lyall, in Calcutta, "We think the Trade can be carried on much better & more quietly at Manila than here [Macao]."[4] It did not hurt that the Philippine government had elected to encourage the trade by reducing its import duty on opium designated for re-export and by agreeing to make warehouse space available.[5]

Whatever sense of duty Matheson actually felt toward his Indian clients, it did not involve a tremendous self-sacrifice on the firm's part, for the revived opium trade was enormously profitable for Jardine, Matheson. It had about five hundred chests left in its possession after surrendering six thousand to Lin, but its vessel *Hellas* was waiting at

Singapore with a thousand chests of the new crop. Once ordered to Manila, the *Hellas* provided young Andrew Jardine, then in charge of operations there, with enough opium to distribute among his six coastal vessels, which then set out for the coast of China. The firm used its receiving vessel *Hercules*, anchored at Hong Kong, as the treasury for the resumed transactions and as a post office for internal correspondence. Initially, the demand along the coast was small, but the profit ratio was dramatic (upwards of 300 per cent), given the low prices that dealers were able to pay for the new opium being placed on the market at Singapore.[6] Guessing at increased demand once the coastal smugglers regained their nerve after the fright Lin put in them, Matheson resolved to purchase opium on the firm's own account. In June 1839 he invested £30,000 in chests available at Singapore and ordered another £8,000 worth of the drug from Calcutta.

For about nine months, extending up to the spring of 1840, Jardine, Matheson enjoyed a virtual monopoly over the opium business operating out of Manila. The bulk of it was on behalf of other parties, but the firm did carry and sell opium on its own part for a few favoured clients, under a new form of arrangement. Once the re-export took place at Manila, the drug's owners were credited with an estimate of the proceeds, minus the charges that Jardine, Matheson assessed for its shipping flotilla and a "reasonable allowance" deducted for the heavy risks run by the firm and the commanders of its vessels.[7] Matheson's strategy led to average profits of 200 per cent through that period, but he had to revert to the firm's normal methods by April 1840.[8] In that month Matheson told Jardine that "the golden days of the [opium] trade are gone by."[9] The reappearance of competitors along the coast and the recovery of prices at the auctions in India led him to fall back on the safer practice of marketing on commission for distant clients. The firm dispensed with its Manila operations and Andrew Jardine was recalled.

In those months of thriving opium sales, the legitimate commerce of the firm prospered as well, because of Matheson's arrangements with American merchants to carry the firm's goods up to Whampoa. Its net profits for 1839–40 were more than four times greater than the figures for the previous season. That was in keeping with the general increase in legitimate commerce for the uneasy season before the war. Nearly three dozen British merchantmen were anchored at or near Hong Kong, transshipping their imported goods by pacts with the neutral American merchants, and obtaining tea regularly through them.[10]

Matheson informed his partner in November 1839 that, by transshipping through American merchants all the cotton consigned to it, the firm had been able to discharge nearly all its inventory, so as to make the way clear for further consignments. Tea was a different story. Unable to make a satisfactory arrangement with the firm's tea agent at Tongku, Matheson remained aloof from the tea market that fall. However, he recognized that his hard bargaining might turn out to be regrettable, should war break out before the firm could acquire a supply of tea at better prices. He confessed that "of my whole policy, since you Jardine left us, there is no point which I am [more] doubtful of meeting your approval than this."[11]

For a stretch of time in late 1839, Matheson's strategies were designed to counteract the anti-opium sentiments of Superintendent Elliot. In September, Elliot had directed all vessels with opium aboard to leave the outer anchorages; and in mid-October, he notified the British merchant fleet that they would have provisional liberty to trade at Chuenpi, outside the Bogue, as long as they paid the port charges and agreed to be searched for opium (with the penalty being confiscation). Moreover, he offered Lin the concession that no British firm should be allowed residency in China until its members and ship's captains had declared that they had nothing to do with opium.

It was hard for Matheson to believe that an officer of the British government would act against its own subjects "to enforce the fiscal regulations of a foreign power."[12] Nonetheless, he notified Jejeebhoy, his biggest shipper of opium, that it was not safe to send any opium to Hong Kong, and advised the Parsi merchant to ship the drug to Singapore for transshipment to Manila.[13] Elliot insisted that Matheson leave the Hong Kong anchorage in mid-October, but the crafty merchant took to sea on the Manila-bound *Good Success* intending to transship himself to another vessel and "hover on the coast" for a couple of weeks. Indeed, after a fortnight's absence he slipped quietly back to Hong Kong.[14]

For the time being it seemed to Matheson that Elliot was virtually allied with Lin in their determination to suppress the opium trade. Although it was true that Elliot did not approve of the opium traffic, his reason for wanting to keep opium away from the Gulf of Canton was to promote the resumption of British trade in legitimate commodities. However, a very serious naval incident involving Chinese war junks and two British naval vessels occurred on 3 November, and negotiations for resuming British trade at Chuenpi foundered later that month when Lin declared that no English ship would be allowed to enter the port of Canton. In January he issued a proclamation stating that English trade was to be forever excluded from China.[15] That development and the arriving news of Palmerston's directives for the military expedition en route to the area brought about a transformation in the relationship between Elliot and Matheson, who became almost chummy by the eve of the war.

They both had reason to be glad that many of the American merchants had returned to Canton. Matheson had arranged in the summer of 1839 to have two Americans, James Ryan and Joseph Coolidge, serve as his firm's agents in Canton, with authority to buy teas and silks and to sell cotton at a fixed commission of 1.5 to 2 per cent. They regularly received detailed instructions from Jardine, Matheson's floating post office regarding purchases, and they profited greatly from serving as sub-agents for the big British agency house. The lucrative freight charges for transshipping British-managed goods between Lintin and Whampoa prompted the Americans to "talk with contempt of the sort of business done formerly." It cost as much as $18,000 to move a shipload of goods from the outer anchorages to Whampoa. Nevertheless, Elliot was grateful to the Americans for keeping the lines of trade open for British merchants.[16] But the Americans had no tea tasters! So, naturally enough, Matheson found a tea taster who could go to Whampoa to assess the teas being purchased by Americans for the firm. The Chinese were not particularly stringent in their exclusion of British goods.

As the year neared its end, Matheson wrote to Charles Lyall that foreign vessels, with goods transshipped at Hong Kong, were being admitted to Whampoa as before the spring crisis, as long as they avoided deck loads which would betray what was happening. That precaution had the effect of "enabling the authorities to shut their eyes with good grace."[17] Matheson's resourcefulness was also demonstrated in his manipulation of the available shipping, as the Americans, upon discovering that they did not have enough bottoms to contend with all the freight they were asked to carry, sought to purchase more vessels. Matheson was glad to oblige, selling the old warhorse *Hercules* to Robert Bennet Forbes of the American firm Russell and Company for $25,000, since the vessel was deemed too notorious for its opium service and it was getting old.[18] Beyond that, Matheson resorted to the old device of using foreign flags on vessels that could carry English freight to Canton. He had retained his status as Danish consul at Canton, and he used that to fly the Danish flag on vessels that had formerly born British names.

Living aboard ships for such a lengthy stretch of time meant that Matheson was missing some of the comforts of life that he had become accustomed to. He asked Charles Lyall to send out "our old servant Ibrahim and one or two others." He wished to be entirely independent of Chinese domestic servants, so he was seeking to recruit new help from India. By December, he was calling for a good cook, "a first rate Artist, accustomed to cook for a large family." He was so eager to have a talented chef that he told Lyall, "to secure this I do not care how liberal his wages" – so long as they would not encourage social pretensions in the man. He was prepared to pay fifty rupees a month, if necessary – "or even double"![19]

Monotonous and carelessly prepared food must have seemed to him a poor reward for his labours during these months at sea. He found the cumulative effect of his many burdens as the managing partner to be exhausting, and he openly criticized some of his neighbours at sea who were less inclined to push themselves. "God knows the responsibilities and inconveniences of all kinds under which we have done business since leaving Canton have been so weighty as most people would have shrunk from; and several of our neighbors have been looking on idle, with their goods lying on hand, rather than incur any responsibility at all." He could not resist adding: "But such never has been nor shall be our principle of action."[20]

Six months at sea was enough to make Matheson sufficiently bold to return his "Establishment" to Macao at the start of February 1840. Whether the firm would be allowed to remain there unmolested seemed to him doubtful, nor could he predict how long its indirect trade through neutrals could continue. His big concern in that regard involved tea exports. He relied on the British government keeping the channels of the tea trade open, given the demand for tea at home in England. His opinion, in letters to Jardine and Smith, was that the British cabinet's credibility with the public would be endangered if the shipments of tea were cut off, so he expected the government to connive at continuing the tea trade even in the event of hostilities.[21]

In late February, Matheson learned that the Portuguese governor of Macao had sent word to Commissioner Lin that an advance on the colony by Chinese troops would probably provoke an English seizure of

Macao. By mid-April, he was amazed that no action had been taken against him and the members of his firm: "We are entirely free from molestation at Macao, & the Chinese remarkably quiet, considering that war is so near." Not only did Macao give him a base of operations on terra firma, but it allowed him the comforts of home in his residence at Macao. At least until hostilities began, he was snug in his familiar surroundings.[22]

Tea was a legal item for the British to buy and ship, through American intermediaries, but the supply was a matter of concern, in view of the impending military actions. Opium, on the other hand, had to be traded outside the pale and the worries about that trade in the spring of 1840 involved competition rather than supply. There seemed to be little concern on Matheson's part that the drug trade would be interrupted by hostilities.[23] Just a year earlier he had been uneasy about the chances for marketing his clients' opium, and tea had been virtually taken for granted as an export item. Now the situations were dramatically reversed – so much so that Matheson wrote to his most trusted correspondents: "I am glad to say our Chief Superintendent seems completely weaned of his hostility to the drug trade, and does not think it will be interfered with by the Men of War."[24]

Charles Elliot had learned of Palmerston's intentions when the *Mor*[25] arrived from England in February, but the foreign secretary's letter to Elliot instructed him to keep word of the expedition from leaking out, lest the season's trade be disrupted. Elliot's first cousin, Sir George Elliot, was to command the forces assembling from various parts of the empire.[26] Palmerston named Charles Elliot plenipotentiary, in joint authority with his cousin to negotiate with the Chinese.

By the first day of spring 1840, it was evident to Matheson that the news from England was creating an alarm at Macao. The American merchants of Russell and Company were declining to accept any further consignments from British parties.[27] Soon many of them would be making plans to depart from China. But Matheson had no intention of letting the coming hostilities cause him to abandon the established trade of Jardine, Matheson.

The superintendent was on such good terms with Matheson by mid-April 1840 that he allowed the merchant to read some of his private correspondence with Palmerston; and Matheson returned the favour by acceding to Elliot's request for the use of an opium clipper to reconnoiter the mouth of the Yangtze River. Captain Jauncey took the *Hellas* north along the coast for that purpose, with instructions from Matheson to sell some Malwa opium en route. During this mission, pirate junks attacked the *Hellas*, which was becalmed, and for four hours poured musket fire on the schooner and tossed flaming pitch onto its deck. When the wind eventually rose, the *Hellas* was able to sail away, but with extensive casualties aboard, including Jauncey himself, who had to be treated at Macao for a broken jaw and a badly wounded eye.[28] In the weeks after *Hellas* returned from its battle, the Americans were abandoning Canton, just before a Chinese mob sacked the factories.[29] Matheson made arrangements with Robert Bennet Forbes to take Jauncey aboard the *Niantic*, which was about to sail for New York. Forbes agreed and Jauncey was treated en route by Dr Peter Parker, the Protestant missionary who had left Canton along with the American merchants.[30]

Matheson was touchy about the interpretations which might be put on the episode that led to Jauncey's injuries, lest anti-opium parties construe it as fighting provoked by forcing opium on the coastal markets. He described the incident to the firm's client Thomas Scott in Singapore, and he asked Scott to "kindly communicate the foregoing particulars to your newspapers by way of anticipating the distorted account which our friends the missionaries may perhaps try to get up."[31]

Matheson was increasingly sensitive to expressions of disapproval. In the first specific reference to one of his family denouncing the trade, he told Willliam Lyall, a London correspondent, "I have omitted to thank you for receiving my Nephew Thomas into your office. I hope he gives satisfaction. I have a letter from him abusing the opium trade. But if such is to be his way of thinking he had better leave off business & turn Parson."[32] Maurice Collis tells of a similar comment by Matheson about one of his captains: "The *Gazelle* was unnecessarily detained at Hongkong in consequence of Captain Crocker's repugnance to receiving opium on the Sabbath. We have every respect for persons entertaining strict religious principles, but we fear that very godly people are not suited for the drug trade. Perhaps it would be better that the Captain should resign."[33]

Matheson was especially annoyed by the public denunciations of the trade which were made by Charles W. King, head of the American house of Olyphant and Company. That firm's quarters in Canton were known as "Zion's Corner" because of its friendship toward the Protestant missionaries, and it was also sometimes called "Humbug & Co." because of its righteous condemnations of the merchants who were engaged in the illicit opium trade.[34] Matheson concluded that the missionaries were being egged on by King, and that occasioned one of Matheson's finer tirades, turned loose in a letter to Jardine: "The Chinese Government appear to be allowing themselves to be misled to their ruin by Missionary Cant; of which I am heartily sick & tired; and I begin seriously to think of discarding our friend King, whose business subsisting as it does, exclusively by his extensive negotiations with us, would be extinguished were we to drop him. Let him then try how he could get on without the aid of the drug, against which he is waging so unfair a crusade making a tool of Bridgman [the American missionary], to a far greater degree than consistent with Christian principles."[35]

These instances of sensitivity about references to the opium trade and irritation about anti-opium attitudes are more pronounced than previous statements of the kind from Matheson, and reveal that he was increasingly worried about the future of trade once hostilities were over. He did not want people in Britain thinking that the war had been fought for the opium trade, nor did he want to be the scapegoat for people whose pious posturing, as he saw it, belied their dependence on opium for some portion of their income. There was also the matter of compensation, which might become a tarnished cause if the anti-opium voices were able to persuade the British public that the origin of all the troubles in China was the drug business.[36]

At home, Jardine was continuing to be the strongest voice advocating reparations, and his best forum was the hearings of the Select Committee on Trade with China. The committee hearings in May 1840 coincided with the gathering of the expedition forces and gave Jardine a platform from which to insist that China be made to pay for the destruction of British property. But the government was elusive about a commitment. Two years later, Jardine would still be arguing for compensation, now in the House of Commons as an MP himself, but with the same lack of sympathy from the government (now Tory). In fact, the merchants' claims would not be paid off until August 1843, six months after his burial at Lochmaben.

Matheson could not do much to make the argument for compensation during those tense days at Westminster in the spring of 1840, but he was situated in a spot that could enhance his firm's standing with the Crown's officials by making his house at Macao available to naval officers and by putting the resources of the firm at the disposal of the superintendent and the expedition commander. The first sign of the fleet off Macao was the arrival of *Alligator* on 9 June 1840. By the end of the month, seventeen men-of-war had arrived at the Gulf, but Canton was not Rear Admiral Elliot's destination. The transports reportedly carried five thousand troops, a relatively small number given the plan to compel Chinese atonement. Matheson expressed the disappointment of all the interested parties at Macao upon seeing such a small force, because he thought that revealed a course of action which was bound to lead to protracted, long-winded negotiations.[37]

Nevertheless, Matheson and his staff and their neighbours felt secure in Macao because of news that the Portuguese government of the colony had worked out a deal between the Chinese and the English, providing that the English would not attack native Chinese small craft and that the Chinese would not disturb the English residents of Macao or hinder them from being provisioned. Matheson saw the arrangement as temporizing but recognized that it would "tend greatly to our comfort "and that it would allow for the safe landing of cargoes for sale.[38]

Calm and safe in his well-appointed home, he was impatient for the military action to begin, since the hostilities were not to be on his doorstep. He told his friends at Bombay that the state of affairs at the Gulf was "more pacific than any of us would wish."[39] Nevertheless, he was thinking of personal precautions, for he wrote to William Lyall in London, "Oblige me by sending me out a couple of neat slender Sword Sticks, as much disguised as possible, so as not to be distinguishable from a common walking cane."[40] Where and when he had learned to use a rapier-like weapon remains a mystery.

Admiral Elliot wasted little time lingering at the Gulf when the troop transports began to reach Macao Roads on 21 June. The admiral, without even stopping at Macao, declared a blockade of the Gulf and sailed his fleet northward so as to deliver Palmerston's letter to the emperor. Nor did Matheson waste any time angling for financial advantage should the Chinese capitulate soon. He told John Abel Smith: "I lost not a moment in using my influence with Elliot to have M.S. & Co. nominated as Agent for any property that may be got from the Chinese in payment of the compensation." Naturally, Charles Elliot could not give him any definite assurance at that time, but Elliot was even thinking that the claims should be traded off in favour of acquiring an island that could serve as the home of British trade. On the other hand, Matheson was convinced, from his private conversations with Elliot, that the superintendent was prepared to relax the blockade, which began on 2 July, for the sake of continuing trade, and that meant that the war's commercial hardship might be limited.[41]

In fact, when Admiral Elliot sailed north, he took with him several local interpreters. Among them, on loan from Jardine, Matheson, was Robert Thom, one of the firm's long-time office staff who was fluent in Chinese. Thom was instructed by Matheson to use this golden opportunity to acquire commercial intelligence where the fleet paused and to communicate that back to his boss at Macao.[42] No sooner was word received of Chusan's capture on 5 July than Matheson was arranging to send Andrew Jardine there, but word from Chusan revealed that Admiral Elliot had prohibited opium vessels from entering Chusan's harbour. Matheson was distressed by that news, reading into the admiral's directive a disaffection toward the drug trade resembling that of his cousin a year earlier. But he felt that he had a trump card up his sleeve: "As the drug sales here form [the] only source from which they can obtain money for the war in China it is some consolation to think that they cannot do without us, & must therefore tolerate us in some shape or other."[43] Without the silver obtained through the opium deals, the British fleet would not be able to obtain the cash needed for its operations, and it would not be able to sell its bills to obtain cash if the opium vessels were not selling their chests in return for sycee silver.[44]

Palmerston had been expecting the capture of Chusan to produce such alarm within the Chinese government that it would be prepared to surrender. Such was not the case, because the Chinese remained unconvinced that the English, so good at naval warfare, were at all competent on land. As a result, the Elliots elected to move north toward the Peiho, following Palmerston's instructions, in hopes of finding a mandarin to accept the letter and pass it on to the emperor. Their departure from Chusan was delayed by naval problems. The seventy-four gun *Blenheim* had not yet arrived to join the expedition, and the *Melville* had been damaged when it struck a rock.

With the energy of the expedition being turned toward the north, and with Chusan under British occupation, Matheson kept sending people from his staff to the captured island. By early October, he reported that the firm had a small family there – actually five men, including Donald Matheson, David Jardine, and Andrew Jardine. They had hoped to market British goods on the island but found the local populace unreceptive.[45] Moreover, the place was decidedly unhealthy.

Palmerston's instructions to the Elliots followed the plan of action that he had drafted late in 1839 to inform the peers in the House of Lords of the measures to be taken. In it he declared that the interests of the British nation and the honour of the Crown required "vigorous measures" for demanding and exacting from China full satisfaction and reparation.[46] Following Jardine's advice (which he did not reveal to the peers), Palmerston directed the plenipotentiaries to blockade Canton and deliver a copy of his letter addressed to "The Chinese Minister" to the governor of Canton for transmission to Peking. He told the Elliots to proceed to occupy the island of Chusan and to send another copy of the letter ashore along the coast of China adjoining Chusan. Their next steps should be to blockade the Yangtze and Yellow rivers and to move north to the Peiho River and deliver another copy of the letter there. Palmerston directed them not to end the hostilities until they had succeeded in negotiating a treaty; he provided a complete draft of the treaty he had in mind, and advised them to use minimal force to achieve the agreement.[47]

The foreign secretary's letter to the Chinese stated that the British government had no intention of trying to protect British subjects abroad against the consequences of their violations of local laws. However, the Chinese had not enforced their laws in an even-handed way, he said, and they had looked past the connivance of their own officials in the opium trade. The letter narrated, presumably for the sake of the emperor, the dramatic episode of the surrounding of the factories and the confinement of the English merchants, and it accused the Chinese authorities of subjecting a Crown officer to insult and of unjustly confiscating the property of English subjects.

In compensation, Britain was demanding compensation for the "ransom" extorted from the British merchants, as well as restitution of the value of that confiscated property. Moreover, Palmerston demanded satisfaction for the insulting treatment of Superintendent Elliot and a guarantee of the security of British merchants. For that purpose, the letter stipulated that an island be surrendered to British control for use as a base of British commerce. Palmerston articulated an expectation that China should not only reimburse the merchants for the opium seized but should also compensate Britain for the expense of the expedition.[48]

While the expedition made its way northward, Matheson was comfortable at Macao, doing his best to sustain elements of his firm's trade in spite of the blockade of the coast. He wanted his family to know of his safety, and wrote to Jardine: "Send for my young nephew at Lyall's, and tell him to write home that I am well. Chin Chin to all around you."[49] He even felt secure enough to move about the Gulf a bit, and in late October he travelled across the outer anchorages to Tongku.

The great irony of the new situation was that Matheson, having long skirted China's trade restrictions by dealing with smugglers, was now skirting Admiral Elliot's blockade order by conducting business surreptitiously in order to sneak tea and silk out of the Pearl River estuary and to sneak opium in. Moreover, the argument long used by him and his partner – that the Chinese officials had connived at the illegal opium trade – now seemed to be vacated by the apparent consent or inattention of the British superintendent of Trade, who wanted to avoid ruining British merchants in the region by the cessation of commerce during hostilities and who was also intent on providing England's home market with the teas which were so much in demand there. The absence of both Elliots made it possible for merchants such as Matheson to accomplish their evasions of the blockade without making the Crown officers seem complicit.

Despite his newly affable relationship with Charles Elliot, Matheson was suspicious that Elliot might soften the British position: "From what I have observed of Captain Elliot's character, I have fears of his agreeing to some truce, that may enable trade to resume."[50] What Matheson feared in particular was that Elliot would not persist in negotiations for legalization of the opium trade but would instead sacrifice that commerce in order to rescue the tea trade because of the revenue that it generated for the British Treasury.[51] He was cheered by hearing reports that British blockading vessels had destroyed sixteen or seventeen war junks near Chinchew, because that had the effect of reviving the sluggish opium trade in that region.[52]

While drug smuggling had continued in spite of the hostilities, it had become a roughneck trade. Most of the opium business had been controlled by agency houses at Canton in the past, but by the fall of 1840 the trade was dominated by the commanders of ships among whom an intense rivalry prevailed.[53] Nevertheless, Jardine, Matheson continued to be the foremost dealer in opium. Matheson estimated that, of the 6,500 chests of opium aboard vessels along the coast, 3,700 – far more than half – were under the management of his firm. (The next largest opium firm, Dent, had only about 800 chests.) Matheson had the resources and the boldness to intimidate the rival firms and ships. For example, when a brig belonging to Hughesdon Brothers intruded upon a coastal locale where Jardine, Matheson's *Ann* was stationed, Matheson directed the captain of the *Ann* to offer to buy the entire cargo of the other ship.[54]

Two developments of enormous consequence affected the whole prospect of British commerce in the late summer of 1840. Within a matter of weeks in August and September, the Chinese government agreed to negotiations with the representatives of the British Crown and Commisssioner Lin was dismissed from his post.

Reports of the British fleet's progress up the coast of China had caused great agitation within the emperor's council and there was even fear that the foreigners might be preparing to attack Peking. On 9 August, Qishan, the governor general of Chihli, went down to Taku to receive the letter from Palmerston and agreed to forward it to the emperor. After taking more than a week to digest the foreign secretary's letter, the Chinese court directed Qishan to invite the English plenipotentiaries to meet him on shore.[55] The Chinese insisted on holding the negotiations at Canton, and the Elliots agreed, because their ships were not suited to blockading the Peiho effectively. The plenipotentiaries reached Canton on 20 October, and ten days later Admiral Elliot resigned on account of heart palpitations.[56] In fact, the emperor was furious at what he considered Lin's mishandling of the opium crisis at Canton, and blamed him for having provoked the English campaign, after Lin had predicted a quick and easy solution of the opium problem.[57] On 1 October, Lin had received notice that Qishan had been appointed high commissioner at Canton. Two weeks later, Lin learned indirectly that he had been sacked as governor general.[58]

Lin's initial target, William Jardine, was by now becoming a remote bystander to the drama in China. Less than six months after he left Canton, Jardine's firm advertised his retirement. Dated 30 June 1839, the notice announced that "the interest and responsibility of Mr. William Jardine in our Establishment cease this day."[59] The remaining partners were announced as James Matheson, Alexander Matheson, Henry Wright, and Andrew Jardine. Retired or not, Jardine was hardly becoming disinterested in the matter of compensation.

After testifying before the Select Committee of the House of Commons in the spring of 1840 regarding the merchants' compensation claims, he took part in private deliberations on whether to press the issue in the full House, and when the decision among interested parties was to wait for a better moment, he left London for several months. His first destination was Cheltenham, presumably for its health benefits as a spa town. His partner had had such good things to say about his time at Leamington Spa and the good effects of the spa regimen that Jardine was prompted to go there as soon as he could extract himself from the remuneration issues. He remained there until some point late in the summer, then returned to London briefly before making his way to northern Scotland, where he spent the early weeks of the autumn of 1840, in all probability enjoying the Perthshire countryside of his new estate of Lanrick. He would have preferred to purchase the estate of Castlemilk, in the old familiar surroundings of southern Dumfriesshire, but Lanrick proved to be a better buy.[60]

By October, he was enjoying the hospitality of his bachelor nephew Andrew Johnstone, at Halleaths on the River Annan, not far from his birthplace at Lochmaben. If he enjoyed the good fishing of the River Annan, famed for its salmon and trout, he left no account of it. But he might have sought the quiet of the riverbank to escape his preoccupation with the compensation issue, which had been dogging his steps and his thoughts for a year. Even in the stillness of the Annan, however, he could not escape that disquiet, though he was following the practice of cabinet ministers and MPs in resorting to the countryside or the continent to get refreshed between sessions of Parliament.[61] He was bitter toward the government for not supporting the claims of the China merchants, yet he hoped that good news from China might induce the Whig cabinet to change its policy on that issue. "But they are a vile set," he fumed to Jejeebhoy, "and I fear that the Tories would be no better."[62]

He returned to London at the start of November, with plans to seek an interview with the Duke of Wellington in the hope that the fragile old soldier would aid the cause. Wellington had certainly given Jardine reason to regard him as sympathetic when he spoke in the House of Lords during the April debate. Nevertheless, Jardine's efforts to gain an ally in Wellington were unavailing, and he was left to grumble about the Whigs, the Tories, and Elliot, whose strategy he derided. From his perspective, British manifestations of anxiety about preserving the trade at Canton were bound to let the Chinese manipulate the negotiations to their advantage. "Such conduct on our part," he wrote, "must tend to confirm them in their belief that we cannot exist without their Tea and Rhubarb."[63]

Matheson, on the other hand, was trying to steer the firm through the troubled waters of commercial and political uncertainty. He was forced to make intelligent guesses at the probable direction of the military actions and the negotiations, in order to notify his distant clients whether it was safe and sensible to ship their commodities to the Gulf of Canton. Moreover, Matheson was highly suspicious of the Chinese strategy, for he thought that the removal of Lin was a way of "humbugging" the negotiations in order to slow them down.[64]

In the strange interlude between Elliot's first conversation with Qishan and the resumption of their talks at Canton in January, teas and silks began arriving from the interior of China. Matheson, with his usual efficiency, had his finger on the pulse of the trade whether it was through normal channels or by indirect routes. By mid-September, tea was being smuggled out of Canton in small quantities, and Nankin silk was bypassing Canton en route to India. Timing the market was a major priority in Matheson's mind. He was arranging for cotton headed for Canton to be smuggled past the blockade, and he had Coolidge, the American merchant, fronting sales of cotton at Canton on behalf of Jardine, Matheson.[65]

Late in the fall he told William Jardine that he was convinced some fighting lay ahead, and he revealed his intent to wait until then in order to purchase teas. For the moment he was not venturing to buy. He was speaking with Elliot with some regularity, and he informed Jardine that the chief superintendent was sure that the British merchants would not be able to return to Canton under the old terms of trade. So, to Elliot's mind, the Chinese authorities would have to devise a new system in order to keep Chinese traders in business. "This mode of speaking shows you how backward & unsettled everything is," Matheson told Jardine in exasperation.[66]

As business intelligence was precious, Matheson communicated very cautiously. As far as he was concerned, the more mystery the market had to contend with, the better advantage he would have. With a good assortment of teas purchased by Coolidge at Canton, Matheson sought to maximize his advantage by chartering the *Charles Kerr* and other vessels to set out for England as soon as possible with the new teas.[67] And if capitalizing on the advantage meant working on Boxing Day, so be it! The teas had been brought out by the American vessel *Kosciusko*, one of the ships that Elliot let through the blockade. The opportunity for getting that cargo home ahead of rival tea shippers was so good that

Matheson wrote to Jardine stating that he was hoping to invest up to $25,000 of the firm's money in the teas being carried to England on vessels hired to take on the cargo of *Kosciusko*.[68]

As that autumn progressed, Matheson seemed to grow increasingly distressed by the inaction of the negotiators and what he saw as stalling by the Chinese authorities. By Christmastime he was smelling fraud: "And it would be quite Chinese like, should it hereafter be found that they are now deceiving us & that we shall have to fight after all."[69] The commercial situation in south China was so changeable from day to day that Matheson's strategy was necessarily makeshift. Elliot told him that he would not mind the firm sending vessels up to Whampoa, "as a temporary arrangement" in order to load teas. With that possibility open, Matheson joked with his former partner, "Do not be surprised ... if we should be soon again writing to you from Creek Hong" (their former location in the riverfront factories).[70]

The uncertainty led to wild fluctuations of pessimism and optimism on Matheson's part. On 28 December, fighting seemed imminent. A day later, Elliot used Matheson and Dent to spread the word that the British plan to attack the Bogue forts was shelved.[71] Matheson was sufficiently buoyed by that news to tell Jejeebhoy, "I have a strong impression that we shall arrive at a settlement in a few weeks without a general war."[72]

Neither Matheson nor Elliot were aware of the extent to which the British withdrawal from the Peiho had encouraged the war party at Peking. Moreover, the mandarins at Canton were eager to resume the hostilities. On 6 January 1841 the British commanders learned of a Chinese edict calling for the destruction of the British ships.[73] Their reaction was to attack the Bogue forts two days later, with the assistance of a new, well-armed ironclad paddle steamer, the *Nemesis*, belonging to the East India Company.[74]

The British attack on the inner forts had barely commenced on that Friday morning when a small Chinese vessel slipped in among the big British ships announcing Chinese agreement to the ceasefire that Superintendent Elliot had suggested. Elliot was distressed by the extent of the slaughter, but he was additionally concerned about the extraction of the *Kosciusko*, which was headed downriver when the action began. The vessel was loaded with more than a million and a half pounds of teas, and Elliot wanted it to clear the estuary safely and transship its cargo.[75]

Not content to sit out the action while so much tea was at risk, Matheson hastened into the turbulent scene at the Bogue once the truce was declared. The *Kusciusko* had gone aground at the second bar and Matheson was deeply concerned for the fate of the vessel, caught in the midst of the hostilities. He arrived at the ship on the ninth, and once satisfied that the vessel would be capable of sailing freely away from the trouble, he moved over to Chuenpi on the tenth. By the thirteenth, the *Kosciusko* was at the outer anchorages transferring its teas to the three vessels hired to carry them to England. Within ten days Elliot had reached an agreement with Qishan.

When Matheson heard that Elliot had secured Qishan's consent to British possession of Hong Kong, he was delighted and immediately began thinking of what the firm would need to do business there. It would require a season of preparation to get adequate warehouses and other facilities ready at Hong Kong, so he presumed that "this season's business ... will have to be conducted as before at Canton *for this year only*."[76] Apparently, he also presumed that any peace settlement would cancel his expulsion from China, and that Lin Zexu's disgrace would amount to a restoration of James Matheson's trading privileges at Canton.

The terms of the Convention of Chuenpi were published on 20 January 1841. Hong Kong was ceded to Great Britain; an indemnity of six million dollars was to be paid to the British government; direct official diplomatic relations would be established between Great Britain and the Chinese empire, on the basis of equality; trade at Canton was to resume within ten days of the Chinese New Year.[77] Nothing was said of opium, nor were the Hong debts mentioned in the settlement, nor were any additional ports opened for trade. In the conversations between Elliot and Qishan, the subject of opium came up only once. Matheson concluded that their intention was, for the moment, to connive at the same trade as existed before Lin's arrival; nonetheless, he was convinced that, if Qishan were to remain in power, opium trading would be legalized.[78]

Matheson was disappointed that there was no provision for a northern port, but on the whole he was satisfied with what Elliot had achieved and he was inclined to defend him when loud complaints were heard from Dent and some of the merchants under his influence. They complained that Elliot had let two American vessels slip through the blockade, while their other grievance involved the sailing of the *Enterprize* for

Calcutta with the dispatches about the peace agreement but without mail from the merchants. Matheson felt obliged to support Elliot against his critics: "For this purpose," he told Jardine, "I authorize your paying liberally any lawyer or other qualified person who will defend him in the newspapers."[79]

Matheson had his own arrangements in place to speed news of the settlement to Bombay and Calcutta. When his own clippers were urgently needed elsewhere, he arranged for the *Moulmein,* owned by his old friend Heerjheboy Rustomjee, to take his special insider's knowledge to the few close associates in India who could profit from early news of the Convention of Chuenpi. Such previews would give them an opportunity to buy cotton before a rise occurred in prices as a result of the convention.

When he heard that the Union Jack was to be hoisted at Hong Kong as of 26 January, Matheson calculated the advantage straight away. Until Westminster's reaction was known, there would be great freedom of action for the British superintendent and merchants at Hong Kong. With manifest excitement, tempered by discretion, he told Jardine: "So independent will be our tenure, Elliot says, that he sees no objection to our storing opium there. And as soon as the [Chinese] New Year holidays are over, I shall set about building – but of course with every caution & on a small scale till the pleasure of the home Govt is known. Nor shall we remove the drug from the good security of our own vessels, until we see the most undoubted security for it on shore."[80] Matheson was present at Hong Kong for the raising of the British flag, and subsequently sailed completely around the island with the commodore of the British fleet, Sir Gordon Bremer. Without waiting for the first land auction, Matheson selected a spacious area at East Point and began building; it was not long before he had some mat-sheds constructed on the island to store the raw cotton consigned to the firm by Jejeebhoy. But for the moment, the firm's manager at Hong Kong slept aboard the *General Wood* where he – and the opium – were more secure.[81]

The cession of Hong Kong was a mortification to the influential men of Canton, and their reaction was duplicated at Peking when the notice of Qishan's agreement with Elliot arrived. The emperor issued a blistering edict, repudiating the Convention of Chuenpi; he also ordered that Qishan be deprived of his post and sent to prison.[82] Matheson was embarrassed; he confessed to Jardine: "I fear you will put little value on my opinion as to the future, after having allowed myself to be humbugged into a belief in Elliot's fallacious hopes for a peaceful settlement."[83] Of course, they were Matheson's fallacious hopes as well. The war resumed in late February, and Matheson was forced to tell his partner that trade was at a complete standstill. He was contrite, not about the resumption of hostilities as much as about encouraging Elliot. However, his contrition was compromised by the self-justifying contention that he had the responsibility of encouraging peace for the sake of his firm's clients. The letter with those sentiments reaches this extraordinary conclusion: "In listening to him [Elliot] I was further influenced by the consideration that in managing for others, we were not authorized from merely speculative notions, to run the risk of disregarding the opinions of the only one among us who had information and official documents inaccessible to the rest of the world – preparation for peace having been moreover the *safer* course, *under any circumstances* for ourselves & friends interested in the Tea market."[84]

With teas en route to London and more fighting in the Gulf of Canton imminent, Matheson was in an awkward position when it came to offering advice to his English associates. Should the hostilities interrupt the tea trade, the firm's teas would dominate the English market in the short term. But, if trade were to resume, competition within the tea markets of England could be expected to develop rather quickly upon that news. When the fighting broke out late in February, he went to great expense to hire the *Folkestone* to carry the news as quickly as possible to India, with instructions for forwarding it to England so as to gain the advantage of selling the teas at prices lifted by anticipated scarcity.[85]

The renewal of fighting on 26 February led to British seizure of the inner Bogue forts. Three weeks later, British sailors and marines finally stormed the riverfront factories and captured the factory square. On 20 March, Superintendent Elliot used the great hall of the New English Factory to make his announcements of another ceasefire and the resumption of trade.[86]

Once the factories were in British hands and foreign merchants began scurrying back there, Matheson sent Andrew Jardine and one of the firm's tea inspectors as far as Whampoa. By early April, Matheson himself was doing business at Canton. He was buying teas in substantial quantities, for he thought that, if the truce endured, as much as thirty-five million pounds of tea could be shipped during that season. If his thinking was right and the war turn out to be prolonged, teas would be more scarce in the following year. So he was very active while the suspension of fighting lasted, with teas for Scotland being high on his agenda as soon as he arrived back in the old familiar surroundings of the Canton waterfront.[87]

William Jardine had asked his partner to invest in teas for him, so Matheson began by giving Jardine a 50 per cent share of his own shipment of superior congo tea headed for Leith, Scotland. He was uncomfortable with the situation at Canton; he told Jardine that the sense of personal security and the security of property necessary for commerce did not exist just then at Canton. He stayed at Canton for two weeks, bringing in Indian cotton tentatively, so as not to glut the market, and then returned to Macao. [88]

In spite of the evidence of Chinese troops gathering at Canton by the beginning of May, Matheson risked returning to the city briefly in the early days of the month.[89] He was anxious to get rid of the cotton consigned to the firm by Jejeebhoy, but he could not sell it all and left Canton once again on 9 May. As the latest crisis developed, he remained at Macao, though Andrew Jardine continued to conduct business for the firm at Canton while the people of the city were escaping in droves.[90]

Elliot returned to Canton, where tea was being shipped at the frenetic pace of a half-million pounds daily, and notified the English and American merchants that they should be prepared to evacuate Canton if necessary. On 21 May, Elliot warned the British merchants and other foreigners at the factories to leave Canton by sunset; nearly all did so by six o'clock.[91] Andrew Jardine had left on 20 May but did not reach Macao for seven days as the Gulf became a chaotic war zone shortly after he quit the factory area.[92]

In the darkness of midnight, 21/22 May, the waterfront at Canton exploded with cannon fire and fireboats chained in pairs, as the Chinese forces launched a surprise attack. The attack was a dismal failure. However, it provoked preparations for a full-scale assault on the city by General Hugh Gough, newly arrived from India. In the disorder of the night attack by Chinese forces, the factories had been ransacked. One of the casualties was Creek Hong, where William Jardine and James Matheson had lived and worked for so many years. The prospect of resuming trade was bleak, Matheson concluded, as he directed Jejeebhoy not to send any more goods for sale, except opium.[93] In the midst of all the chaos of troop movements, brief but intense fighting, and truces followed by unsuccessful agreements, one thing remained fairly stable

– the opium trade. Matheson reported "our usual progress with the sale of your drug" to Jejeebhoy, while sending him large remittances on drug sales and encouraging him to use the *Mor* for three round-trips per year between China and Bombay, with opium in her hold.[94]

The superintendent announced the terms of a provisional settlement on 5 June. The character of the settlement was local and temporary, an expedient arrangement to avoid slaughter and destruction within Canton. The Chinese authorities achieved the sparing of Canton by agreeing to pay the six million dollars (about £1.4 million) immediately, as well as providing compensation for the damage at the factories and promising to withdraw their troops. In return, Elliot consented to removing the British warships from the river and to abandoning the forts and anchorages they had seized. No mention was made of opium or of the resumption of trade or of the transfer of an island to Britain. So anxious were the Chinese authorities to escape the British assault that they agree to pay the six million within six days, and immediately began delivering sycee silver to the British warships.[95]

Dent and Company served as the agents engaged by Elliot to remit Canton's ransom money to England. It discounted the six million by some sixty-three thousand pounds, which they claimed was the value of the five hundred chests that Elliot had "bought" from them in 1839 to arrive at the total number of chests that Commissioner Lin had demanded. It was a slick manoeuvre, by which Lancelot Dent got his compensation long before any of the other opium merchants and at a much higher rate.[96]

In the aftermath of the fighting at Canton, Elliot acted on the assumption that Hong Kong was a British possession. On 7 June, two days after publicizing the terms of the Canton settlement, he announced the process of selling parcels of land on Hong Kong, and he encouraged British merchants to establish their firms on the island.[97] Matheson needed no encouragement, for he was present at Hong Kong when Elliot initiated the sales, and by that time Jardine, Matheson had already made substantial progress on construction of a large stone warehouse. At the first public auction on 14 June, Jardine, Matheson acquired three prime lots with three hundred feet fronting on the water.[98] But the government belatedly announced that it wanted to hold on to those lots, so the firm surrendered them. All advantage was not lost, however, for the broker acting on the firm's behalf had also bought East Point during the first day of auctions, and there Jardine, Matheson

would build its permanent home in a wooded, pleasant area of the island.[99] Never one to miss a business opportunity, Matheson launched a
trade in construction materials. By August, the firm was advertising in
the newspapers the establishment of a floating lumberyard. The *General
Wood* was stationed at Hong Kong, with "a quantity of Timber and Planks
fit for Ship and House Building."[100]

In the strange interlude between the siege of Canton and the planned
expedition northward, commerce resumed in the Gulf of Canton – with
the emperor's sanction! Matheson continued to use the Americans
Coolidge and Ryan to buy silks and teas. Although not in direct contact
with the Hong merchants, Matheson was willing to be generous in assisting them to complete sales if they needed funds, in spite of the Hong
debts being a great point of contention in Elliot's negotiations. It was as
if the old spirit of commercial amity had bounced back.[101]

In the meantime, he continued to market opium very successfully, in
part because there was little chance of Chinese interdiction and because
the British authorities were not opposing the drug trade. In time of war,
it was the one item of trade that could be relied upon for regular sales.
In fact, the drug trade was so good that the investment opportunity was
irresistible for Matheson. He instructed T.W. Henderson to invest whatever Jardine, Matheson funds the Bombay merchant was holding, as
long as prices were favourable.[102]

However, commercial uncertainty increased dramatically at the end
of July, when bad news and bad weather arrived simultaneously. In the
fourth week of the month, two fierce typhoons struck the Gulf within
the span of five days, piling wrecked ships on the rocky coastline and
heaving big vessels into each other. Hunkered down at Macao, Matheson
sat out the storm in the security of his home, not even going to the office between storms because of distressing news from Scotland that reported the deaths of his uncle and his niece.

After a harrowing experience aboard the *Louisa*, which was wrecked during the first typhoon, Charles Elliot reached the safety of Macao on 24 July.
There he was given the dispatches from London carried by the *Good
Success*, which arrived between the storms. The mail told him that he had
been sacked.[103] The Convention of Chuenpi was his undoing; it had
prompted a chorus of complaint directed at him from London.[104] Even
the young Queen Victoria joined the chorus, writing to her uncle Leopold,
king of the Belgians: "*All* we wanted might have been got, if it had not been

for the unaccountably strange conduct of Charles Elliot ... who completely disobeyed his instructions and *tried* to get the *lowest* terms he could."[105] For his part, Elliot saw things in a far different light. His concern for the promotion of trade had prompted the truces that he had negotiated in the first half of 1841, which had led to the export of thirty million pounds of tea, gaining the Exchequer £3 million in duties. Moreover, he was appalled at the prospect of needless slaughter in the conduct of the military operations. The basic purpose of the expedition, he maintained, was to protect and preserve British trade, not to kill people.[106]

Whether Jardine had ever heeded Matheson's request to hire a lawyer to defend Elliot against the complaints of Lancelot Dent and his associates is unknown. Although Matheson was clearly sympathetic toward the superintendent, Jardine would have known long before his partner and Elliot did that the Chuenpi agreement had received a scorching reception at Westminster. In fact, Jardine had a private conversation with Palmerston about the terms of the settlement. In that session Jardine had complained that the opium compensation negotiated at Chuenpi was only a half of the amount due, and grumbled that if Elliot had put such a high value on Hong Kong in the settlement, then he (Jardine) and his fellow merchants would be glad to consider the government indebted to them for the other half. "His Lordship laughed & said he supposed we would." It was a rare moment in a somber season, for the sharp-witted merchant had truly tickled the dour foreign secretary.[107]

Elliot's replacement, Sir Henry Pottinger, arrived at Macao in August bearing a letter of introduction from Jardine, the implication being that Jardine was endorsing Palmerston's decision to replace Elliot as superintendent.[108] Matheson received Pottinger warmly, welcomed him to his house (where Sir Hugh Gough, commander of the British armed forces, was staying), and set out his linen and china so that the commercial community could have an opportunity to meet the new superintendent over dinner. Indeed, Matheson's place was the first house that Pottinger visited. The significance of Matheson's prominence on that occasion cannot have been lost on the rest of the foreign mercantile community at Macao. With Jardine's introduction in his pocket upon arrival, and Matheson's dinner party to welcome him, the new superintendent began his tenure on good terms with the principal partners of Jardine, Matheson and Company.

Pottinger had met with Jardine in May, prior to departing for China. "I have had two or three conferences with him of a very satisfactory nature," Jardine wrote Matheson, "and he has spared no trouble to gain information. He had a conversation with Captain Rees on Saturday last, and on Friday he dined with me, no one present but Alexander Matheson until John Abel Smith joined us about ten p.m. We had the chart of the coast of China before us, and discussed many knotty points no doubt most ably. I intend to send him a few hints on paper through the foreign office tomorrow."[109] If Jardine had for a while become something of a bystander in the Anglo-Chinese drama, he had emerged from that status to bear a serious influence on the new direction of the war.

As much as Matheson sympathized with Charles Elliot, he could not afford to let that colour his relationship with Pottinger. Nevertheless, in private, he revealed a soft spot for the cashiered ex-superintendent. He admitted to Jardine that Elliot's unpopularity among the English at Macao was due in part to his adopting measures that had the effect of benefiting Jardine, Matheson. Matheson even went so far as beseeching Jardine to give Elliot his assistance "towards making good his case in the eyes of the people of England."[110] That was probably asking too much of Jardine, for it would require offsetting *The Times*' contemptuous declaration regarding Captain Elliot that "to rely upon the representations of such a man would have been as foolish as it would be mischievous to follow out his views."[111]

Matheson's conduct in this change of superintendents revealed a solid strain of personal loyalty in his character, for he declined to join the chorus deriding Elliot. As the *Atalanta* would be stopping at Bombay, with Elliot among its homeward-bound passengers, Matheson asked Jejeebhoy to repay Elliot's help by giving him a friendly reception and showing him respect. Fearful that Elliot's unpopularity would descend on his pet child, Hong Kong, Matheson begged Jardine to lobby for its retention. While its future was uncertain, Hong Kong could not prosper, he acknowledged, but once under British protection, roads and houses and godowns would be built, and "it could hardly fail to become a considerable Emporium." And there was the consideration of Matheson's new lumber business at Hong Kong. The fact that Pottinger departed from his instructions to negotiate for the retention of Hong Kong suggests very strongly that Matheson was persuasive in laying out that case. He informed his old friend and partner that "our outlays in building an extensive Godown etc at Hongkong will bye & bye amount to perhaps $20,000 – so that I am not disinterested in advocating its retention."[112]

A shrewd, tough Irishman from Belfast, striking in appearance because of his well- curled moustache, Pottinger made a favourable impression on the merchants gathered at Matheson's house. He had retired from EIC service in India just a year before this appointment. The government now granted him a salary of £6,000, twice what they had been paying Elliot.[113] Fairbank describes Pottinger's policy as "putting diplomacy before trade and force before diplomacy."[114] In that frame of mind, Pottinger sailed from the Gulf of Canton with a well-provisioned expedition on 21 August 1841, bound first for Amoy.

At just about the time that Pottinger's expedition set sail for Amoy, Matheson's nephew Alexander had arrived back in China, after two years at home in Britain. He had married his Ross-shire neighbour, Mary Macleod, in 1840, but the marriage was tragically brief, as his bride died in 1841. A widower at thirty-six, Alexander turned his attention back to China. To his uncle James, this was cue for changing the guard: "Mr. A. Matheson having returned from England about six weeks ago, I contemplate proceeding home early next year," he told James Adam Smith. During that year he had been transferring large sums of money to Scotland for his retirement plans and for the needs of his family, and he was sending home personal items in care of his friends on Lombard Street.[115]

What he described as a "smart attack of influenza" in October 1841 seemed to strengthen his resolve to leave China. The strain of contending with the fluctuating circumstances of wartime commerce was taking its toll on him. "I have to apologize for the irregularity of my correspondence with you," he confessed to young Smith, "which is owing to an impaired state of health, not so well able as it used to be, to cope with the cares and fatigues of business."[116]

By mid-November he was shipping home gifts for his sisters, as well as Chinaware items that he wished held for him in a warehouse or cleared through customs for his retrieval upon reaching Britain. He had already sent some furniture, in hope that Jardine would mind the pieces for him, and some months earlier he had shipped a pony home aboard the *Kyd*, much to the entertainment and admiration of his family in Scotland.[117] Signs of his serious intent were his cancellation of subscriptions to several periodicals, and directions to his London bookseller not to send any more books to him. Still, his departure was hostage to a small army of anxieties that were not easily driven away, and in the last days of the year he admitted, "It is still uncertain whether I shall go home this season."[118]

The delay was not owing to reluctance to hand over the reins to his nephew, for Alexander was just nine years younger than James and had plenty of experience in the trade at Canton as well as in the politics of Westminster. Moreover, Andrew Jardine had had years of on-the-job training. More pressing concerns for James included the future of Hong Kong as the firm's base of operations, the ongoing worry about the debts of the Hong merchants to the firm, the lull in the war and therefore the uncertainty of commercial relations between Britain and China, and the distressing turn in the firm's relationship with its Manila agents at Otadui and Company. Additionally, the guesswork connected with their large-scale operations in tea and opium during wartime preoccupied his mind whenever there might have been a chance for relief from the catalog of other problems. When could he pack his bags and leave the bundle of worries to the nephews? Could he sail away from China with the war unresolved? There was no one to give him the signal or hand him his discharge, but his body was telling him.

In that fall and winter of 1841, when the war seemed moribund, trade took on the same complexion. Opium sales were lethargic, and sometimes barter (for teas) had to be conceded. What is more, to do business in commodities apart from opium, foreign firms had no choice but to let the Hong merchants run up big debts to them. With prices for Malwa opium as low as $340, Matheson found that some of his clients were beginning to desert his firm's agency in hopes of doing better with others. Nevertheless, he kept Jardine, Matheson to its usual course, confining it mostly to agency services for others and striving to sell in quantity even if it had to settle for low rates.[119] In Matheson's view, there was no way to bypass the drug trade if cash were to be secured: "It is the command of money which we derive from our large Opium dealings and which can hardly be acquired from any other Source, [that] gives us important advantages."

However, apart from the safety of Hong Kong, the drug trade in wartime was rather dicey in the Gulf of Canton, so Matheson tried to disguise his firm's identity there. He had the name *Jardine* removed from that selling vessel and replaced it with *Lanrick*, the name of his partner's newly acquired estate in Scotland; and he inverted his own name in order to create a fictional operation named "Thomasen and Company" for the delivery papers needed when chests of opium were handed over.[120]

The Manila operations that Matheson had established through the agency of Otadui and Company had been useful after his expulsion from Canton and during the early stages of the war. However, the American partner in the firm, John Shillaber, proved to be reckless in his speculations and in his depictions of that firm's prospects. Jardine and Matheson had both been willing to keep him afloat because of personal sympathy for his interests. As early as 1836, Shillaber had run up a significant debt to Jardine, Matheson, and by the start of 1841 Matheson was angry that Shillaber was borrowing money (for his firm) from the account of Jardine, Matheson – "*money taken from us without our knowledge or consent.*"

James Adam Smith had been sent to Manila to succeed Andrew Jardine as liaison with Otadui and Company, and had become a lesser partner in that house. A very messy situation had developed between Otadui and the Yntendente (the civil governor of Manila), who was apparently receptive to a bribe and wanted the money being held to his credit ($18,000) to be invested in opium. Shillaber had framed a commercial venture which relied on the governor's influence, but the scheme collapsed when the governor was removed from office in 1841. When that venture crashed, Matheson conveyed his embarrassment and discomfort to Smith: "In short it must be well known to you, we were averse to [the plans] from the beginning, from a systematic dislike to all plans depending on corrupt influences and corrupt agents, which carry in them the seeds of disappointment, and it was merely to please you and him [Shillaber] that against our own conviction, we gave a reluctant & qualified consent to them."[121]

As reluctant as Matheson was to bring down the Manila agency, he was nevertheless forced to acknowledge that the connection with Otadui was a disaster. As he went about clearing up his affairs before leaving China, clearing up the debt of Otadui and Company was "a truly painful subject," partly because he continued to regard Otadui and Shillaber as friends. When it came time for him to write "a line to say good-bye," he told Otadui that, if he followed Jardine, Matheson's advice, it would see him through to recovery.[122]

Matheson's effort to put things in order with Otadui was certainly not due to any shortage of cash resources on his part as he prepared to leave China. In a most generous gesture, he sought to relieve the demands of creditors on George Chinnery, the famous painter who had lived in Canton for many years. A good friend of both Matheson and Jardine, Chinnery had painted their portraits and entertained them at dinner

with his garrulous conversation and eccentricities. Chinnery had arrived at Macao in 1825, leaving behind in India a wife and a trail of
debts, and his expensive tastes ensured that his indebtedness was chronic. Just a few months before sailing homeward, Matheson contributed a
credit of sixteen thousand rupees to the care of a lawyer in Calcutta to
alleviate the weight of debt on his old friend.[123]

An even greater outlay of personal funds was directed by Matheson
toward the purchase of land in Australia. In the spring of 1841 during
the awkward interlude between the English recovery of the factories at
Canton and the resumption of fighting in the Gulf, Matheson focused his
attention at least temporarily on the acquisition of a large tract of land in
Australia suitable for arable farming and sheep grazing. Within the span
of three weeks, he forwarded bills totalling more than £11,000 to M.D.
Hunter and Company of Sydney, New South Wales, for land that would
be likely to increase in value while also serving as an outlet for emigration
of tenants from Matheson lands in the Highlands of Scotland "whose
clannish feelings will lead them, when I go home, to look to me for assistance in getting on in the world." The terrible mid-century famine was
still a few years off, but he was conscious of the hardships caused by the
Highland Clearances, which had driven many crofters to the margin.

With astonishing naïveté, he asked the members of Hunter and
Company "whether you see any feasibility in this plan, where you would
propose buying land, and what sum would be sufficient for the purpose? Would ten thousand pounds be enough?" He intended the land
to be named "Shinness," after his deceased father's estate in Scotland,
and he was interested in a fertile, uncleared tract – "the larger the better," he added. He had in mind two possible managers, Alexander
Mackay and Mitchell Scobie, both already resident in Australia. In a letter to Scobie, he sought advice about proceeding with the enterprise.
"You will much oblige me by letting me know, what you think of this
scheme for benefiting a part of our Sutherland tenantry, & at the same
time making a profitable investment for myself. Six months later, with
Pottinger biding his time and doctors urging Matheson to go home, the
thought of eleven thousand pounds unemployed in Australia prompted
him to write again to Hunter, explaining that he was not impatient
about the land purchase but would be glad if Hunter could invest the
funds in "any good security" until they were needed.[124] If ever there
were a project that certified Matheson as being more romantic and dar-
ing than Jardine, this was it.

Before anything was realized of that plan in Australia, Matheson was gone from China. In January 1842 he told R.W. Crawford of Bombay that he expected to be there in about two months, for "relaxation," but his ultimate destination was uncertain: "On reaching Bombay I shall determine whether or not to proceed home." By the start of March he was ready to sail for India aboard the *Tartar*, hoping to reach Ceylon in time to catch the steamer that would be headed to Suez by way of Bombay. "Tho' not very seriously ill, I am summarily ordered off by the Doctors to avoid the risk of getting worse should I remain over the hot weather." He expressed regrets to Jejeebhoy that he could not long remain in Bombay (because of the steamer's schedule). "But the Doctors' orders are not to be resisted, & I can only hope that I shall very soon be able to return to you from England." Whether he really intended to return to China or whether his remark about seeing Jejeebhoy again was just formulaic politeness is not clear, but he did say that "Alexander Matheson will supply my place while I am away" and thereby implied that he did have thoughts of returning.[125]

He did have time for goodbyes to some of his old broker friends from Canton who went to visit him at Macao at the start of 1842. Otherwise, his last weeks in Macao were relatively quiet, as Coolidge and Ryan conducted the firm's business at Canton, which continued to be the central location of Jardine, Matheson transactions while the future of Hong Kong remained tentative. Matheson had one last opportunity to speak with Pottinger on the day before he embarked on the *Tartar*, as Pottinger had made the short trip from Hong Kong to attend a magnificent fête at Macao.[126]

Matheson had to miss the ball, for he sailed from Macao on the morning of 10 March, with the sole purpose of the *Tartar*'s journey being to transport the departing taipan. Matheson acknowledged that such private accommodation was an extravagance, but he hoped that his Indian friends would secure a profitable return freight for the vessel.[127] Whatever his intentions really were at that moment, his view of the Praya Grande bay, as the *Tartar*'s sails filled, was the last he would ever see of Macao and in fact the last he would ever see of the Celestial Empire where his fortune had been made. Not only was he leaving China, but he was also leaving the unfinished war, which became more remote with every mile of his journey down the South China Sea.

# THEIR LIVES AFTER CHINA

In the splendid surroundings of Sir Jamsetjee Jejeebhoy's home, a hero's reception awaited Matheson upon his arrival at Bombay, where the Parsi merchants assembled to cheer him on his leave taking.[1] Though he continued to hint that he might return to China one day, the wealthy Parsis who assembled there on 13 June 1842 spoke as if they were seeing off a benefactor for the final time. The elite Bombay merchants were paying tribute to the "Merchant Prince" as they described the man they regarded as their champion during the crisis at Canton and their protector during the war that was still in progress.

On behalf of the group, Bomanjee Hormusjee read a formal address, signed by eighty merchants, declaring: "After the affair of the opium trade in 1839, which deprived India of two millions sterling, the Bombay trade was completely paralysed, and the most fatal consequences might have ensued; but you generously came to the rescue of our country and sustained our commerce, helping us carry it on under foreign flags. All this was done at your own risk and on your own responsibility for the public welfare."[2] In gratitude, they had requested Magniac Jardine to present him, upon his homecoming, with a silver service valued at £1,500. Matheson was, understandably, "quite overwhelmed" by the extravagance of their words and their gift. Acknowledging their "splendid token of gratitude," he said, "I shall preserve it all my life, and it will be preserved by my heirs," and added solemnly "this present was not necessary to make me always remember you in my heart."[3] It was a deeply emotional farewell, both for Matheson and for his Parsi friends, and while different in mood from the grand party held for Jardine at Canton, it corresponded to the excitement of that famous send-off.[4]

Upon leaving China, three years apart, the two Scottish tai-pans retired to the "House of Lords," as the Hong Kong members of the firm would refer to 3 Lombard Street in London. Not far from South Sea Yard, where Jardine had apprenticed with Thomas Weeding, Lombard Street was the home of Magniac, Smith and Company, the London banking affiliate of Jardine, Matheson.

In the few years that remained to him after returning, Jardine was not essentially a hands-on banker, doing day-to-day financial operations; his role was more that of an associate, whose name enjoyed exalted status in the City. He was important to the firm for referral of business to them, as well as for his governmental connections and political influence. In contrast, James Matheson was much more directly involved with the firm, which eventually came to bear his name, and he played a central part in the reorganization of the company. The powerful duo had few days for collaboration on Lombard Street. By the time Matheson arrived home from China, Jardine was losing ground to the disease that had been bothering him for a long while.

Jardine had returned home a hero to the East India merchants in London. His close friend, John Hine, formerly captain of the *Sarah*, organized a grand public dinner in his honour at the London Tavern in 1840. By then he had settled into an office at 3 Lombard Street. In time he would buy out John Abel Smith's interest in Magniac Smith, which would be renamed Magniac Jardine in 1841. He maintained his London residence in the fashionable neighbourhood of Upper Belgrave Street, but, having no family obligations to keep him at home, he spent many of his weekends with Smith at Blendon Hall in Bexley (southeast London) or with Hollingworth Magniac, at Colworth, near Bedford.[5]

He joined the Oriental Club, which had been founded in 1824 as a retreat for members of the East India Company. The club's members included the Duke of Wellington, so Jardine may have had casual contact at the club with that powerful Tory who was sympathetic to the English merchants in China. He surely must have been comfortable in the company of so many old EIC officers and old China hands. Eventually, a second home away from home was added when in February 1841 he was elected to Brooks's, a club on St James's Street which was a stronghold of Whigs. The men who proposed him for membership were both prominent Whigs, E.J. Stanley and Edward Ellice.[6] There he could take his meals, if he wished, and enjoy the fellowship of men with similar political views. It seems that he had entertained political ambitions prior to leaving China, ambitions that were encouraged at Brooks's, for he was a candidate for a seat in the House of Commons at the general election of 1841, four months after he was received into that circle of Whigs.

He arrived at a moment when Whig control of the House was precarious. Lord Melbourne's majority had been a scant twenty-four members after the general election of 1837, and that number was reduced to an insecure nine when the vote was taken at the end of the China policy debate in 1840. In the general election of July 1841, the Tories won a decisive victory. Melbourne resigned, and Peel formed a very strong cabinet, including five past or future prime ministers. But in the election a free trader had slipped in here and there and some of them were China traders, including William Jardine.

Jardine had been nominated for the seat representing Ashburton, an ancient stannary (tin-mining) town in Devon, located about half way between Plymouth and Exeter, and situated along the little River Ashburn. A town with interests in the textile trade, especially the production and export of woollen goods to China, Ashburton was suffering as a result of the interruption of trade at Canton, and unemployment was a serious concern there. While this borough on the edge of Dartmoor was a long way from Jardine's estate in Perthshire and his home on Upper Belgrave Street in London, it was a good prospect for the Whigs, because Jardine was capable of voicing their economic concerns at Westminster.

His ideas of standing for Parliament had been ridiculed by Dent's people at Canton prior to his departure from China. But the 1841 general election silenced their derision, since his Tory opponent was a London associate of the Dents. Apparently, Jardine campaigned very effectively, for his rival withdrew from the contest just before the voting, and Jardine won unopposed.[7] He reported gleefully to Matheson, still at Macao, "Thomas Dent laughed at the idea of my ever expecting to be returned ... You will be glad to know that we have maintained our position here as well as in China."[8] Subsequently, as it turned out, Peel's ministry was less a cause of distress to the free traders than they might have anticipated, for he sponsored a series of reforms in the 1842 budget that would lead to the reduction of tariffs on hundreds of imported articles. As a free trader, Jardine could applaud many of Peel's initiatives, for he too was a vigorous opponent of tariffs.

With the realignment of the House, Jardine took his seat behind the opposition leaders, Lord John Russell and Lord Palmerston. Though he spoke infrequently in the parliamentary debates, there was one notable occasion when his voice was raised against Peel's government. In 1841, after Canton had been ransomed for six million dollars, the money was shipped home in the form of silver, with sixty-five tons arriving at the London terminus of the Southampton Railway, headed to the Mint. Its arrival generated hope among China interests that the Treasury would use some of that money to provide at lease partial recompense for confiscated opium. Hugh Hamilton Lindsay, like Jardine a newly retired China merchant, introduced a resolution calling for use of the Canton ransom to repay the merchants for the opium surrendered upon Elliot's order. On 17 March 1842 Jardine spoke forcefully to the House.

He was at a loss, he said, to understand how the government had any claim upon the money that took precedence over the claims of the merchants. If the East India Company had any claim, the government would hurry to settle the dispute, he argued. Melbourne's government would have settled the matter, but it was constrained by its budget woes. Now, however, it was "the cupidity of the Chancellor of the Exchequer" which held back the money, for nothing could be clearer than that the merchants ought to be compensated before the ransom money was used to defray expenses of the expedition.[9]

In the last extended speech of the debate, the Whig leader, Lord John Russell, remarked that "there was great force in the observations which had been made by the hon. Member for Ashburton." Nevertheless, a short while later the House voted, with the ayes gaining only 37 votes to 87 for the nays. Jardine, Lindsay, John Abel Smith, and their associates had lost resoundingly. Even their leaders admitted that the payment claimed by the China merchants was not a right but would be a reasonable relief offered by the government to alleviate their economic distress. Peel had successfully contended that the previous government, with Palmerston as foreign secretary, had declined to fulfill Elliot's guarantee of payment until China had been defeated and forced to pay for the opium. Peel argued that the money that had arrived at the Mint belonged to the Crown by virtue of the unexpected ransom of a Chinese city. He was not rejecting the claims of the opium traders; it would be better, he said, for the government to admit the claim conditionally, to establish an inquiry, and to pay the compensation afterwards.[10]

The Chinese, in paying the ransom for the city of Canton, were under the impression that they were settling the claims of the British opium merchants. The merchants were of like mind, but the Treasury Board disapproved of the way that Elliot had allowed Dent to deduct £63,265 from the silver being shipped to Britain. Accordingly, the remaining money was designated a *droit* of the Crown and a reward for the troops who had besieged Canton.[11]

The cabinet had made its decision and the House had supported it. The merchants would have to wait until the conclusion of the war for their reimbursement. The treaty ending the hostilities was signed in August 1842, but the opium merchants had to wait for another year before the Tory government dispensed payments to those holding opium scrip. It had taken so long for the reimbursement to occur that the receipts for the surrendered opium were being traded like bills of exchange. In August 1843 Matheson and the other merchants received about $300 for each confiscated chest, which was far below the price that they had originally claimed to be due them. However, many people reminded them that their compensation was better than the prices they would have been able to realize in the Gulf of Canton in the flat market of 1839. Most observers concluded that the government's reimbursement rate was fair.[12]

While Jardine was arguing the case for compensation and Matheson was travelling homeward, the war was in a state of suspension, and no one could predict with any assurance when it might be concluded; first it had to be resumed. The new superintendent, Sir Henry Pottinger, had decided, late in February, to transfer the British superintendent's headquarters from Macao to Hong Kong. The news would have been a source of great satisfaction to Matheson, for it meant that his gamble in acquiring land and constructing buildings there for the firm had paid off.

In the early summer of 1842, the British expedition's Yangtze campaign had led to the capture of Woosung, Shanghai, and Chinkiang. By 5 August, the seventy-four guns of the *Cornwallis* were positioned before the walls of Nanking, and it appeared that a fearsome assault on the city was imminent. In these circumstances, Chinese negotiators rushed to satisfy the British demand that they show proof of their plenipotentiary authority. They wrote to the emperor: "Should we fail to take advantage of the present occasion, and to ease the situation by soothing the barbarians, they will run over our country like beasts, doing anything they like."[13]

When Pottinger went into the centre of Nanking for a long working session with the Chinese negotiators, they spoke off-the-record about the issue that had provoked the conflict. The Chinese asked why the

British did not terminate Indian cultivation of opium. In response, Pottinger advised the Chinese to legalize the drug and place a tax on it in order to benefit their treasury. In the end, the treaty said nothing about opium.[14] Pottinger concentrated on establishing by treaty law a system of commercial rights which would facilitate the expansion of British trade in China.[15]

Four silk-bound copies of the Treaty of Nanking were signed aboard the *Cornwallis* on 29 August 1842. It was the first treaty that China had concluded with a foreign government in more than a century and a half. Harry Gelber argues that, given the decisive defeat suffered by China, the terms imposed by the British were remarkably moderate and limited.[16] On the other hand, Arthur Waley records that, after the Treaty of Nanking, the feeling of self-respecting Chinese was "one of implacable hatred towards the English."[17]

Those terms called for an indemnity of $21 million, including compensation for seized opium, for the costs of the expedition, and for the debts of bankrupt Hong merchants; in addition, five ports were to be open to British residents and commerce – Canton, Amoy, Foochow, Ningpo, and Shanghai – with British consuls permitted in each port. Future relations between Britain and China were to be based on perfect equality (the demand for an ambassador at Peking was quietly dropped); the island of Hong Kong was to be transferred to Great Britain in perpetuity; and the monopoly system of the Hong merchants was to be abolished.[18] News of the settlement reached London on 22 November 1842.

The small, rocky island of Hong Kong was already becoming a centre of Anglo-Chinese commerce.[19] Matheson's instincts were vindicated; and Jardine's demands for compensation and for open commercial opportunity, free from abusive treatment, seemed to have been achieved. True, the early days of the new colony, not yet officially British until ratification of the treaty ending the Opium War, were inauspicious. The indigenous inhabitants were peacefully disposed toward the Westerners, but the new arrivals from the Chinese mainland included brigands and pirates. One English resident of China (later to be the colony's treasurer) declared as late as 1844: "It is a delusion or a deception to talk of Hongkong becoming a commercial emporium."[20] But Matheson had been willing to take the gamble, as were Dent, and Framjee Jamsetjee, and even MacVicar. Following suit, most of the Parsi firms moved their operations to Hong Kong not long after the war.[21] What is more, the Morrison Education Society moved its school from Macao to Hong

Kong in 1842, three months after the treaty was signed and the island was securely British.[22]

The two Scots partners had been members of the original cast of the Opium War, so to speak, Matheson as a hostage and Jardine as a consultant for the government. In the long run the war turned out very much as they would have wanted, except for its duration and human costs and the delay in compensation. Afterward, Palmerston acknowledged Jardine and Smith as being his principal sources of strategy for the war. Three months after the treaty signing, the former foreign secretary and future prime minister wrote to John Abel Smith: "To the assistance and information which you, my dear Smith, and Mr. Jardine so handsomely afforded us, it was mainly owing that we were able to give to our affairs, naval, military and diplomatic, in China, those detailed instructions which have led to these satisfactory results."

As Smith was not familiar with the British situation in China firsthand, it is fair to conclude that Smith's role in this drama was largely that of bringing Jardine to see Palmerston. That Jardine was the mover and shaker behind Palmerston's policy is established further in that letter. Palmerston told Smith he found it "remarkable" that the information supplied by them "and which was embodied in the instructions we gave [to Elliot] in February 1840, was so accurate and complete that it appears that our successors have not found reason to make any alterations in them." That remarkable insider's knowledge had to have come from Jardine. In concluding his tribute to Jardine and Smith, Palmerston waxed prophetic: "There is no doubt that this event, which will form an epoch in the progress of the civilization of the human races, must be attended with the most important advantages to the commercial interests of England."[23]

It is tempting to imagine Jardine grinning in disbelief that his role in the Anglo-Chinese hostilities was destined to have such world-changing consequences, but it is certainly true that his influence had transformed the dynamic of British commerce in East Asia. Matheson was not accorded such lavish praise for his role in the first Anglo-Chinese War, but his hard work in sustaining the firm during tempestuous times would make him a giant among British traders in early Victorian times, and his foresight in gambling on the future of Hong Kong was evident straight through to the return of the colony to China in 1997.

Once home, Matheson recognized that it was futile to try to defend the opium trade in an English environment that was increasingly hostile to the drug trade, even though it provided the money to sustain the tea trade, which generated 10 per cent of Britain's customs duties. Matheson needed to keep the opium trade out of the public eye because, like his partner, he had political aspirations. When Matheson had arrived in England in the summer of 1842 he found his old friend to be in serious pain, but his own health was steadily improving.

He travelled home to Scotland in the fall of 1842, and from Glasgow wrote to Jejeebhoy about the steep decline in his partner: "I am deeply grieved that Mr. Jardine's symptoms are becoming more unfavourable and it is feared that he cannot hold out long."[24] The enemy in this instance was cancer of the bowel. By January, he was confined to a water bed, after weakness had forced him to abandon the standing and kneeling positions that he had been using to obtain relief from the pain. The water bed was allowing him to get some sleep, and that gave his friends reason to think that he might survive for a few more weeks. The resilient spirit he displayed amazed those closest to him, and he defied the attendant doctors by refusing to give up. His mind remained clear and his disposition was even cheerful at times. He was, to the last, "the iron-headed rat," as defiant of death as he had been of the menacing streets of Canton. Special arrangements were made for him to take his meals in the company of friends and attendants; and Matheson noted that "he still precides at his breakfast and dinner table which he enjoys with his wine and beer as usual."[25] According to John Abel Smith, who apparently saw him regularly in the last stages of his illness, he was uncomplaining, even when in pain, and never expressed disappointment at being deprived of the anticipated enjoyment of his retirement. He was, according to Smith, free from acute pain in the final weeks of his life, but to obtain that relief he had to lie face-downward in the waterbed for most of every day.

The end came on Monday, 27 February 1843, at his home on Upper Belgrave Street, London. The immediate cause of his death was recorded as "effusion of water on the lungs," which usually involves symptoms of shortness of breath, coughing, and chest pain. Yet Smith described his passing as quiet: "His end was so easy & gentle that it was difficult to believe that the last struggle was over."[26]

William Jardine died three days past his fifty-ninth birthday. He was buried in the family plot at the churchyard in Lochmaben on 14 April 1843. He had no wife to mourn him, and some of his nephews were serving the firm in south China; but he was likely seen to the grave by his sister Jean's son, Andrew Johnstone, who had close ties to Uncle William.

Andrew survived his kinsman by fourteen years; now their names appear together on the tall obelisk that marks the grave site. Inscribed with an "IHS" identifying them as Christians, their monument rivals in scale the statue of Robert the Bruce, another son of Lochmaben, which dominates the town square barely a hundred yards from the cemetery. After all the drama of his life, half a world away from Scotland, his final resting place was barely two miles from Broadholm, the farm where he was born.

By the time of Jardine's funeral, James Matheson had already stood successfully to retain his old friend's seat in the House of Commons. The by-election was scheduled for Tuesday, 7 March 1843, a mere nine days after Jardine's death. So Matheson had to hasten down to Ashburton, introduce himself, and call on all of the electors. Armed with numerous assurances of support, he announced his candidacy the following day. His campaign statement pledged to promote every measure of practicable and progressive reform. "I profess myself the zealous and ardent friend of Civil, Religious and Commercial Freedom," he told the electors, assuring them that his mercantile experience enabled him to promote the town's staple trade. Five days later he was elected to be Ashburton's MP. He maintained the same political affiliation as Jardine (except that the designation "Whig" was being increasingly supplanted by the term "Liberal").[27]

Just a month after Matheson's election, a motion was introduced in the House of Commons by the eminent Anglican evangelical, Lord Ashley, aimed at suppressing the opium trade. His argument was framed along moral and practical lines, contending that the ongoing opium trade would jeopardize the whole range of British commerce with China, as well as the future of Britain's political relations with China. In support of his motion, petitions were submitted by committees of the Wesleyan, Baptist, and London missionary societies. Although the motion was eventually withdrawn by Ashley, at Peel's request, so as not to affect tariff negotiations in progress with the Chinese, it was sufficient to alert the new member from Ashburton as to the direction of public feeling. He could see that the event had been a moral victory for the anti-opium forces in England.[28]

The motion prompted Matheson to caution his firm's fleet captains in China. An eager British naval officer at Shanghai had tried to expel opium traders along the coast early in 1843, but he was reprimanded and the Navy was given to understand that it had to overlook the opium trade. Matheson wrote to Captain McMinnies, senior among his opium ship commanders, urging him "to make every effort ... to please the mandarins, such as moving from one anchorage to another when they require it, and not approaching too near their towns." He had reached the conclusion that "the opium trade is now so very unpopular in England, that we cannot be too cautious in keeping it as quiet and as much out of the public eye as possible."[29]

Matheson's direct involvement in the coastal operations of Jardine, Matheson was now diminishing, as his nephew Alexander became the managing partner at Macao. The firm would continue to pursue the profitable commerce in opium vigorously. After Peking declined to legalize the opium trade, in 1843, the implicit agreement of the two governments was that the opium trade would continue and that the two governments would act in such a way as to ignore the facts of the trade. By the end of that summer, Alexander would declare rather cynically, "All hopes for legalization of the drug trade are ... at an end and you may rest assured that if ever it is legalized, it will cease to be profitable from that time. The more difficulties attend it the better for ... us. We shall always find ways and means to carry on despite every obstacle."[30] In March 1844 Alexander would direct the relocation of Jardine, Matheson's central office of about twenty members to Hong Kong, though he would continue to spend part of his time at Macao. Even though the foreign secretary, Lord Aberdeen, had directed Pottinger to keep Hong Kong from becoming a base for British smuggling activities, that was indeed its primary function in 1844. For the time being, opium dominated the commerce of the new colony, which served as the first port of call for vessels arriving from India and as the hub of British drug shipments to the mainland coast of China.[31]

Although he was present when the British force occupied Hong Kong, James Matheson would never manage the firm's operations from the new colony. He had commented to Jamsetjee Jejeehoy that Alexander would be filling in for him temporarily until he could return. However, he never did return to China, nor is there any indication that, after arriving back in Britain, he ever seriously considered returning. If he had such ideas, the events of 1843 in his own life finalized his intent to remain in Britain.

The death of his partner and his election to Parliament were the first dramatic changes in Matheson's life in early 1843. Another change, more personal, followed in the autumn when, a week shy of his forty-seventh birthday, James Matheson took a bride, Mary Jane Spencer Perceval. Twenty-four at the time of the wedding she was the daughter of the late Michael Henry Perceval of Spencer Wood, near Quebec, once a member of that colony's Legislative Council. Her mother, Ann Mary Flower Perceval, was the daughter of Sir Charles Flower, who was at one time lord mayor of London (1809).[32]

The marriage ceremony was performed by the Very Reverend E.R. Ramsay at St John's Episcopal Chapel, Edinburgh, on Thursday, 9 November 1843. The chapel was crowded with the prominent people of Edinburgh and following the ceremony a lavish luncheon was held at Charlotte Square where the mother of the bride maintained her home. The band of the 26th Regiment provided entertainment for the luncheon guests; and in the evening a ball was given in honour of the newlyweds, with "all the rank and fashion of the city" in attendance.

Not only at Charlotte Square but up and down the island of Great Britain glasses were raised to James Matheson and his bride, and seemingly endless quantities of wine and whisky were consumed in toasting the couple. At Tain, where the Academy was generously supported by Matheson, a dinner party was held in their honour. And at Dingwall, about fifty gentlemen gathered at the Town Hall to drink to the royal family and then to the newly married couple. The simultaneous celebrations in many locations ranged from very formal, as in Edinburgh, to decidedly folksy, as at Ashburton, Devon.

Perhaps the liveliest was the public holiday at Ashburton, where Matheson's constituents celebrated from dawn until dark. He had sent a purse of £100 to be distributed to the poor folk of the town on the occasion of his wedding, and the townspeople took that as their cue to live it up for the entire day. Guns firing on the nearby hills awakened the people at an early hour, and at seven o'clock the bells of St Andrew's Church tower began pealing. Overlapping with the bells, the sounds of the town band carried through the principal streets of Ashburton. At mid-morning, clergy gathered at the Church of St Lawrence for the distribution of the alms money left a few days earlier by Matheson. A local journalist recorded the afternoon's festivities: "Through the liberality of Mr. Matheson numerous poor persons enjoyed themselves with their children, and drank, with joy and gratitude, long life and every blessing to their excellent member and his lady." Late in the afternoon, a hundred people sat down to a splendid dinner at Honywill's London Inn, and after more toasting the assemblage was entertained by madrigal singers. At about ten o'clock a lighted tar barrel led people through the streets to the market place, where a bonfire was lit and a grand display of fireworks illuminated the sky. Just after midnight a large fire balloon made its ascent over the town, bearing the name of James Matheson.[33] Then the weary celebrators made their ways home to bed. No doubt there were many headaches in Ashburton on Friday morning.

From this time on, the merchant adventurer evolved into a Highland laird, spending three-quarters of every year in northern Scotland and the Hebrides. His land acquisitions would eventually make him the second-largest landowner in the United Kingdom, with vast properties in Sutherland and Ross as well as his estate on the isle of Lewis. His marriage was childless, but the domestication of his personal life was in marked contrast to the often hectic character of his existence for all those years in south China.

In the fall of 1839, well before his return from China and more than three years before his marriage, he had purchased from Hugh Ross of Cromarty the estate of Achany near Lairg. He also exchanged with Sir George Munro the estate of Udale in Cromarty for the barony of Gruids, also near Lairg. The combination of Achany and Gruids gave him all the lands along the west and south shores of Loch Shin, just across the loch from his birthplace. Together the two estates totaled about 42,000 acres.[34] Matheson had also inherited the Ross-shire estate of his uncle, John Matheson of Rockfield, who had died in 1841.[35]

In the year after his marriage, James Matheson acquired the island of Lewis in the Outer Hebrides for a price of £190,000. The island had belonged to the Seaforth Mackenzies for more than two centuries. Stewart Mackenzie, who had fallen into considerable debt, died in 1843, and the island was sold by his widow to Matheson.[36] Three years later he purchased the port of Ullapool from the British fishery commissioners for a price of £5,250. Located on a peninsula stretching into Loch Broom, Ullapool is the principal port of northwest Scotland for vessels sailing to Lewis. Barely thirty miles (as the crow flies) from Achany, the pretty little town of white buildings, quays, and wharves is dwarfed by mountains which surround it dramatically on three sides. The crossing from Ullapool to Stornoway covers about fifty miles, most of it across an Atlantic strait called The Minch, which can be very rough or surprisingly calm in any season. Matheson's acquisition of the port was a shrewd purchase for it assured him of substantial control of the traffic between the mainland port and Stornoway, the major town on Lewis, where Matheson would maintain his residence.

In addition to the properties in the Highlands and the Hebrides, Matheson acquired the estate of Rosehall in Sutherland by exchanging for it the Estate of Benholm in Kincardineshire in 1844. To achieve this swap, Matheson engineered a private Act of Parliament. Bit by bit he was building his own real-estate empire in Scotland. In London he made his home at the very fashionable address of 13 Cleveland Row in the St James district of Westminster, adjacent to Green Park and just a few hundred feet away from Buckingham Palace. The house at Cleveland Row was within easy walking distance of his clubs, Brooks's on St James Street and the Reform Club on Pall Mall.

Halfway around the world, his speculations in Australian sheep runs were prospering. He relied on the managerial skills of two fellow Scots to obtain for him these properties in New South Wales. Alexander MacKay, a young man who apparently had been working for Jardine, Matheson at Canton until 1839, was engaged by James to manage sheep runs in the district around Sydney. The other young Scot was Mitchell Forbes Scobie, a native of Sutherland who had a sheep run of his own in the area of Port Philip.

Matheson's original design of encouraging emigration of impoverished Highland crofters to Australia was supplanted in the famine years of the 1840s by a more practical arrangement to send the migrating families to Canada. Nevertheless, he shipped Merino and Southdown rams to Australia to improve the breeding stock. He owned estates in Sydney and Port Philip and held two sheep runs (together called Lewis) outright in his own name, while joining in partnership with Scobie to operate two more sheep runs. He maintained his interest in sheep farming until the mid-1850s. Alexander MacKay returned to Scotland to wed, in 1856; and at that time, Matheson offered one of his sheep runs to Mackay, possibly as a wedding present but perhaps for purchase. From that time, his interest in the Australian projects seemed to decline, as he concentrated more and more on being a Hebridean laird.[37]

Nearly half his life lay before him upon his return to Britain in the spring of 1842. He was forty-six years old, and he would live to the age of eighty-two. Hong Kong was more than three months' sail away, and Sydney even further. His direct interests in that part of the world would become subordinate to his political life at Westminster, his business interests in the City, and his attention to his estates in Scotland. He had left Jardine, Matheson in the hands of his nephew Alexander, and his properties in Australia were being managed by MacKay and Scobie. It was time for James Matheson to begin a new life – as a husband, a Scottish land baron, a member of Parliament, the chairman of a steamship company, and a banking director on Lombard Street. His new role in British society would confer on him a respectability that was more secure and less controversial than his career as an eastern trader. But detaching himself completely from the opium trade was not possible just yet.

Although his active partnership in Jardine, Matheson came to and end with his departure from China, James still had $1,200,000 invested in the firm as of November 1843, the time of his marriage. While his returns on that investment could be remitted in bills on London, the firm continued to accord him the privileges of a senior partner, writing to him that season to say that it proposed to "appropriate to you part of our early purchase of fine congou [teas], as those most likely to yield a better result than bills."[38] When partners retired, this was one way of remitting their share money. Accordingly, the same procedure was followed with William Jardine's estate, which received the entire cargoes of two vessels dispatched to Britain that year.

Not long after James Matheson retired from China, his rivals, Lancelot and Wilkinson Dent, followed suit. But the rivalry between their firms continued in China, where they became parties to a duopoly in the opium trade. The British government would not allow ships carrying any opium to enter the five ports opened by the Treaty of Nanking; nevertheless, the Chinese authorities did not attempt to interdict the trade, and the opium clippers were unmolested by either government as they anchored at their usual spots offshore. Hong Kong was now the principal depot anchorage for the opium trade.

The five treaty ports, plus Hong Kong, held forth promise that Matheson's vision of the opening of China to a broad range of Western commodities might be realized. Nevertheless, in spite of his new reluctance to defend the opium trade publicly, opium consignments continued to be Jardine, Matheson's foremost source of profit. The firm had Indian constituents, fast clippers, receiving vessels at Hong Kong, and coastal schooners with experienced captains. Moreover, there was an ongoing demand for the drug in China.[39]

In spite of their dislike for each other, Jardine, Matheson and Dent's would collaborate against third-party interlopers. In this way, the two firms dominated the coastal drug trade until the 1850s, when the Peninsular and Oriental Steam Navigation Company (P&O) entered the coastal trade and the duopoly disappeared.[40]

When the new British residents and officials at Hong Kong found it difficult to get along among themselves, a Select Committee of the House of Commons was appointed in 1847 to investigate conditions in the new colony and the state of the China trade. As an old China hand, Matheson was not only a well-informed member of the committee but also a party with significant interest in the prosperity of the recently acquired island. Among the Hong Kong traders whom the committee heard, the most important witness was none other than James's nephew Alexander, newly home from Hong Kong. In keeping with his new caution, Matheson had to allow the committee's report to disapprove of the opium trade, but it did so tersely and without heavy censure. The monetary effects of the opium trade "would be diminished by [any future] legalization of the traffic," the committee's report said; but then it admitted that "we are afraid" that the drug's demoralizing influences on the population "are incontestable, and inseparable from its existence."[41] To be party to such a committee report, James Matheson had to be prepared to mute his argument, made in the fall of 1839, that he could conscientiously declare that he had "never seen a native in the least beastialized by Opium smoking."[42]

After the Second Opium War (Arrow War, 1856–60), once the drug was legalized in China, Jardine, Matheson and the other European traders faced heavy competition; but Jardine, Matheson, in collaboration with Jardine Skinner (an independent correspondent firm) of Calcutta, managed to dominate the Calcutta market for export of government-controlled opium production. In the first half of the 1860s, the firm was doing nearly £300,000 of commissioned business in opium annually, and simultaneously investing heavily on its own account. But it withdrew almost completely from the opium business by 1871, owing to the effect of P&O steamships and the powerful rivalry of the Bombay organization of David Sassoon and Company.[43] The competition from Sassoon was ultimately more telling in Jardine, Matheson's shift of focus than the moral arguments against the trade. By the 1870s, the firm was concentrating more on diversified enterprises – in banking, insurance, shipping and docks, railways, mines, cotton mills and commission services – than on sale and purchase of commodities.[44]

Nevertheless, the state of British disapproval of the opium commerce was mirrored in Matheson's own family, which began to turn its back on the firm's drug business in the 1840s. Hugh and Donald, two of the sons of Duncan Matheson, James's brother, repudiated the opium trade. Duncan was a lawyer and deputy sheriff of Leith, Edinburgh's seaport; his family was deeply committed to evangelical Christianity. Hugh, who was convenor of the English Presbyterian Church for a half-century, was a senior working partner at Magniac Jardine. His uncle James offered him a position with Jardine, Matheson in China in 1843, but Hugh declined, in order to avoid becoming associated with the opium trade.[45]

However, Hugh did make an extended visit to Hong Kong in 1845–46, when his brother Donald was managing the firm's offices there. Donald, a kind and charitable man, was involved in the construction of the first permanent church building in the new colony. At about the time of his brother's visit, Donald began suffering a troubled conscience about the opium traffic he was engaged in. After making this known to his cousin Alexander (then at 3 Lombard Street), he was warned that resignation from the partnership would cost him all financial interest in Jardine, Matheson. Undeterred, Donald resigned his position in 1848; he was the last Matheson to serve as taipan for the firm. He returned to England soon thereafter, and many years later, in 1892, he became the chairman of the Executive Committee for the Suppression of the Opium Trade.[46] Donald's resignation effectively terminated the Mathesons' role in directing the affairs of the firm. The leadership of Jardine, Matheson would be assumed by the collateral descendants of William Jardine, specifically his nephews, sons of his brother David and his sisters Jean and Margaret. Jean's daughter Margaret married into the Keswick family, and the Keswicks eventually dominated the firm's hierarchy.

Alexander Matheson, contemptuous of the "absurd" complaints of the "saints" against the drug trade, remained the senior partner until 1852, but he left East Asia in 1847 and arrived home just in time to shore up Magniac Jardine against the banking crisis looming over the City. Upon examining the private ledger of Magniac Jardine, Alexander concluded that John Abel Smith's investment policies had left the house vulnerable. The central difficulty was that the firm might be defenceless against bankruptcy, given the number of calls that could be made on its financial reserves, unless it received a boost of new capital. The resources to accomplish a reorganization came from James Matheson, Andrew Jardine (using William Jardine's legacy), and Alexander Matheson. Through their joint efforts, Magniac Jardine experienced a metamorphosis, emerging as Matheson and Company in 1848, quartered at the same premises on Lombard Street. Hugh Matheson became the senior working partner, while the lion of the previous generation was known in the halls of 3 Lombard Street as "Uncle James," though he was not among the first partners of the revivified business.[47]

"Uncle James" was "otherwise engaged," one might say – but not always far away. A leisurely twenty-minute walk from the Lombard Street offices, past the Bank of England and Royal Exchange, would take him to the brand new headquarters of the P&O at 22 Leadenhall Street. In 1847 Matheson was invited to become chairman of the expanding new shipping enterprise (ten years old at that time) but his appointment was not without controversy.[48]

The office of chairman had been vacant for a year when Matheson was recommended by John Abel Smith to Brodie McGhie Willcox, one of the three managing directors of the P&O. Matheson accepted their offer, and took up the position of chairman early in 1849.[49] While the P&O was still a young firm, the managing directors had not established methods of making all critically important decisions within the framework of directors' meetings. Matheson's appointment had something of the character of a private arrangement, made apart from consultation with the stockholders.[50]

Nonetheless, the managing directors and many shareholders held the opinion that the P&O needed a close tie to Parliament, and Matheson fitted their needs for a prominent figurehead splendidly. Moreover, he was not likely to get in the way of the managing directors by seeking to exercise strong executive authority. He was offered the position not so much for energetic policy shaping as for his status among London merchants, his secure place at Westminster, his business contacts, and his extensive experience in shipping ventures. Additionally, he could offer the P&O managing directors expert advice in the transport of opium, at a time when their firm was beginning to ship the drug from India to China. He had not "gone over to the enemy," that is, to Jardine, Matheson's rivals; rather, he had become chairman just at the time when the steamship was overtaking the clipper ship as a means of conveyance between India and China. The introduction of the opium-carrying steamship was inevitable, once the P&O vessels began operating in south Asian waters. The older firms, such as Jardine, Matheson and Dent, introduced steamships into service as soon as practicable, but they could not compete as shipping firms with the likes of the P&O.[51]

Was there a potential conflict of interest in Matheson's dual loyalties? Possibly. But nothing suggests that he was disloyal to either party. He could retain his financial interest in the profitability of Jardine, Matheson and simultaneously be a source of valuable advice to the P&O directors.

Fred Harcourt maintains that "opium played such a significant part in P&O's history and prosperity in the nineteenth century that the company's expansion in the Far East needs to be placed in the context of the opium trade."[52] After the Treaty of Tianjin (1858, ratified 1860), anyone could purchase opium in India and ship it on P&O steamships to the open treaty ports in China. This undercut the advantages of the long-established British agency houses, because it meant that Chinese buyers could make arrangements directly with the Indian suppliers.[53]

Five years before Matheson became chairman, the P&O was awarded a government contract to carry mails in Eastern waters, and the Ceylon-China line began operations in 1845. The government contract made it possible for the P&O to begin using steamships to transport chests of opium to China, and that traffic started up in 1847 with shipments of Malwa opium from Bombay. However, the Calcutta trade continued to be controlled by the EIC and it travelled by sail until steamships were established in that market in the 1850s. The transit time for steamers from Bombay to China was twenty-three days, a speed that made the sailing clippers virtually obsolete for Bombay exports.

In 1851 the promoter of a rival steamship company misjudged the P&O's capacity for shipping from India when he declared "I do not find a single name [on P&O's board] that has anything to do with the India trade at all ... excepting the chairman, Sir James Matheson, who, I believe, has a mere honorary appointment but who has nothing to do with the direction of affairs." That opinion was utterly wrong, for it was the policy of the P&O directors that there should always be one man on the board who had some personal experience of the opium trade.[54] Matheson could fill that advisory role for them, even if he were not a policy maker.

There is evidence in the P&O archives that a Matheson affiliate facilitated the insuring of cargo and specie aboard P&O steamers in Eastern waters by establishing connections between a London house and its

Calcutta link for open policies, effected at Lloyds, to be filled in upon arrival in Calcutta. Given his extensive experience with shipping insurance in the East, it is very likely that James Matheson was party to the initial conversations about such insurance arrangements, whether or not he had any hand in the final agreements.[55]

By the time of the Second Opium War, Jardine, Matheson was sending at least some of its Malwa opium from Bombay to China aboard P&O steamers, specifically the *Ottawa* and the *Aden*. This would mean that, in the months following James Matheson's resignation as chair of the P&O board, his old firm and his new firm were collaborating in the drug trade between the west coast of India and Hong Kong.[56]

His signatures on board of directors' minutes testify to his frequent attendance at those plenary sessions of the company. The pattern seems to have been for him to attend meetings in the first half of the year and not the second. He is recorded as chairing meetings in the early months of the year, particularly in the spring and early summer. On the other hand, his signature is usually missing on minutes from August through December. The inference from this pattern is that Sir James and Lady Matheson likely moved from Scotland to their London house for the social season that brought so many prominent members of British society and continental guests to the imperial capital for the glittering round of balls and regattas and similar events of the high season. As he was in London in the summer of 1853, it is quite likely that he and Lady Matheson joined the other directors and guests aboard the P&O screw-propeller steamer *Cadiz* for the Royal Naval Review in the Solent off Spithead. Retaining the P&O position was sufficiently important to him that he wrote, from Edinburgh, to the directors in 1853, expressing regret at missing their annual meeting and requesting that his name be submitted for re-election to the board.[57]

From the time that James Matheson began serving as chairman of P&O until the year after his retirement, the company's fleet grew from twenty-two to fifty-five steamships, among them the world's largest merchant ship, the *Himalaya*, launched in 1853 (later sold to the government). In his first year, the company's net profits were reported at £107,630; for his final year, the net profits were £241,080. Moreover, the firm's insurance fund had grown from £123,589 to £323,000.[58] By the 1850s the company had proven itself an asset to the nation, by moving troops quickly and reliably (Crimea, 1854; India, 1857) and by extending its fast mail routes to the farthest reaches of the empire.[59]

As of the late 1850s, both Arthur Anderson and Brodie McGhie Willcox, two of the three managing directors, held seats in the House of Commons; so it was no longer quite so important for James Matheson to be guarding the firm's interests at Westminster. His resignation as chairman was announced to the directors at the end of May 1858.[60] While he was not responsible for the managerial decisions which spurred the firm's growth, he was their veteran China hand. Moreover, he gave the firm a presence in Parliament at a time when its competition for mail contracts was subject to recommendations by parliamentary committees. For a "ceremonial" chairman, he had brought a wealth of experience and a host of connections to the P&O.

His letter of resignation cited duties in Scotland which were making it difficult for him to pay adequate attention to the affairs of the P&O.[61] At age sixty-two, he was hearing in his mind the music of the Highlands, as his attention was now concentrated more on the ancient lands of the Shinness Mathesons which he had brought back together and on the Hebridean property which he had added to them.

# SIR JAMES MATHESON,
# LAIRD OF LEWIS

Just before stepping into the role of P&O chairman, Matheson had ended his ties with Ashburton in Devon when he stood for a Scottish constituency in the election of 1847. (The Ashburton voters next chose another Matheson – James's brother Thomas – who served as their MP from 1847 to 1852.) James was elected in 1847 to represent Ross and Cromarty, a single constituency which included the Isle of Lewis, thereby enabling him to represent his own properties in Parliament for more than twenty years (1847–68).

The 1847 election was uncontested after Matheson's opponent withdrew. Consequently, the Liberals in that district could save all their energy for celebrating. On the day of the election, Matheson was greeted on his way into the county town of Dingwall by a group of electors from the south, accompanied by a band; and upon reaching Conon Bridge, he was welcomed by yet another group of electors, from the north, who had with them a piper. Amid loud and enthusiastic cheering, with plenty of flags waving from windows, the two groups formed into a parade, led by one band, followed by electors marching, then pipers, then electors on horseback, then another band, and finally the carriage conveying James and Mary Jane Matheson to the site of the election formalities. One is tempted, on reading the *Courier*'s report, to think that not even Macbeth (born in Dingwall) had ever entered this ancient town with such triumphal pomp.

At the hustings, Matheson's name was placed in nomination and duly seconded; and, there being no other nominations, he was declared elected, to the delight of the assembled crowd. After his victory speech – in which he derided his erstwhile opponent, proclaimed both his allegiance to the Church of Scotland and his support for the Free Church, and defended his vote for a grant to Maynooth College (a Catholic college in Ireland) as a way to redress the effects of the penal laws – he led the crowd in giving three cheers for the queen. Next he was chaired through the town (borne triumphantly aloft in keeping with a traditional kind of victory lap for successful candidates for the House of Commons).

That evening the large dining hall at the Caledonian Hotel in Dingwall was bursting at the seams for a victory dinner. There followed the customary sequence of toasts, until it seemed the guests could think of no one else to toast, at which point the gathering broke up and the small town (population 2,300) resumed its quieter ways.[1]

At the next general election, in 1852, Matheson had to campaign for the seat against a Conservative, Hugh Ross of Cromarty (what could be more appropriate?), the previous owner of Achany, who had made a fortune provisioning the Royal Navy in the West Indies. Following a spirited campaign, Sir James (by now a baronet) won by a margin of only 70 votes out of 500 cast.[2] Thereafter his seat was secure for the next sixteen years, until in 1868 he passed the mantle to his nephew Alexander.

The Palace of Westminster, to which Sir James was returned in 1852, was nearing completion, according to the designs of Sir Charles Barry and A.W. Pugin for replacing the Parliament complex that perished in the fire of 1834. The House of Commons chamber, with its striking neo-Gothic ornamentation and its characteristic green benches, was newly finished in 1852. Matheson's seat there gave him the opportunity not only to promote legislation favouring his district, and particularly Lewis, but it enabled him to testify, with the knowledge of an insider, at hearings held by select committees of the House, and to lobby for relief appropriations for the impoverished population of his district.

In fact, Matheson had become laird of Lewis at just about the worst of times. A year before he purchased the island, the Church of Scotland had been rent by a schism that came to be called "The Disruption," caused in part by civil government's intrusion in Kirk affairs and by the excessive influence of wealthy patrons on the appointment of ministers. About one-third of the Kirk membership broke away to form what they called the Free Church. This was a serious blow to the Presbyterian community of Lewis, many of whom declared themselves adherents of the new Free Church. The Free Church had to provide itself with new church buildings and schools, as well as homes for the ministers and new colleges for training clergy. On Lewis, this turn of events placed a financial burden on the new proprietor which he did not shy away from; it also affected his estates in Sutherland.

When the House of Commons established a committee to investigate the need for new church buildings in Scotland, in 1847, Matheson testified that a considerable portion of the population of Lewis now adhered to the Free Church. In answer to a question about whether he had provided sites for schools and parsonages, he explained that he had learned from an episode in Sutherland that if he refused sites for new churches, people would "surely not" drift back to the Established Church. "When I came into possession of Lewis, which had a large population, I found that there was no means of giving them either religious or secular instruction, except through the Free Church ... I therefore made up my mind at once to grant sites, contrary to what I had done in the previous instance" (Sutherland).[3]

Almost simultaneously, he had to address an emergency of even larger proportions. A year after Matheson bought the Lewis estate, he had to deal with the beginnings of the catastrophic failure of the potato crop which was to blight Ireland and western Scotland through the second half of the "Hungry Forties" and beyond. His plans for improvements to the economic infrastructure of the island were undercut by food shortages that necessitated relief projects and by emigration plans that sidetracked his grander vision of the island's future.

For the span of eleven years prior to Matheson's purchase of Lewis, the island had been administered by the Seaforth Trustees, who were in Edinburgh. J.A. Stewart Mackenzie, whose wife, Lady Hood, was the Seaforth heiress, held the post of British high commissioner in the Aegean area of the Ionian Islands. With absentee proprietors and trustees, the island had not enjoyed progressive development plans, and virtually nothing had been spent on improvements in recent years.[4]

To prevent the Seaforth Trustees from dunning his new tenants for arrears of rent, Matheson bought up all the arrears as of Whitsunday 1844 and paid the Seaforths a total of £1,417 18s 1d. He did not seek reimbursement from the tenants, except in certain cases where permanent tenants who were in arrears could afford to pay their feu duties. The agricultural lands of his Lewis estate had an annual rental value of £9,800 at the time of his acquisition, but he immediately set out to make improvements to the island's roads and harbour facilities, with the result that any expectations of profit from his huge investment had to be deferred.[5]

In the early years of his proprietorship, Stornoway prospered, with new gas and water works being built, new houses constructed, a jail established as well as a ragged school, and a series of new quays created along the harbour. His decision to build a castle on the site of the Seaforth Lodge was unpopular with local people who had been used to pasturing their cows on the lands where the castle grounds were to be developed. Nevertheless, those stretches of land were enclosed and afforestation was undertaken. Work on the castle, designed by the renowned Glasgow architect Charles Wilson, commenced in 1847 and continued for the next seven years, at a cost of £60,000.[6] Through those years, coinciding with the worst times of the famine, Matheson simultaneously expended considerable money of his own for relief of the local population.[7]

Just as the famine was about to strike, he had undertaken a land-reclamation project to improve the agricultural value of Lewis, on the advice of one James Smith of Deanston. Nearly a thousand acres were targeted for reclamation to be used for arable farming, and the work continued until 1850 (the year Smith died), but the whole project was finally given up as a failure.[8]

The famine that afflicted the Scottish Highlands in the 1840s seemed to its victims like a vicious caprice of nature, but its effects were intensified by the chronic weaknesses of the Highland agrarian system. Consequently, the impact of the crop failures in the northwest Highlands and the Western Islands was much more harsh than the distress in the south and east areas of the Highlands.[9] The crofting society was particularly vulnerable to the wavering behaviour of annual growing seasons, since the crofters were land tenants whose properties were generally worth an annual rental of £10 or less. Lower on the scale of farming society were the cottars, who had no legal claim to any land at all and subsisted in many cases simply as squatters.[10]

Dependence on the potato was inevitable for smallholding farmers, who found that they got more for their efforts from the potato than other crops on their meagre plots of land. Not only could the potato be grown in all types of soil except for stiff clay, but it was tremendously productive. (Earlier in the century Sir John Sinclair had reckoned that an acre of potatoes could support four times the number of people that an acre of oats could sustain.)[11] Accordingly, in parts of the Hebrides, more acreage was devoted to potatoes than to grain crops. In northwest Scotland and the outer islands, the vulnerability of the crofting system lay in the inadequate size of many crofts (with ten acres being regarded as the minimum for a family's subsistence). By the 1840s, meal was commonly imported, given the half-century of increasing dependence on the potato and the woefully small plots of land the crofters scratched at (averaging two to five acres in the northwest).[12]

Moreover, the fishing industry at Lewis (for whitefish and herring) fluctuated unpredictably and produced small income; additionally, the price of cattle fell, thereby removing another prop from the crofters' livelihood. Hence the potato blight coincided with a serious downturn in the traditional economy to produce a crisis that strained the rescue resources of landlords even as wealthy as Matheson.[13]

The worst suffering occurred among the crofter and cottar elements of the population in the Hebrides and the western coastal areas of mainland Scotland in 1846 and 1847, when famine began threatening lives. The distress, which persisted until the mid-1850s, was particularly severe in the Outer Hebrides, where 71 per cent of the population was named on the relief lists.[14] On the estates of James Matheson, on the mainland and on Lewis, the extent of severe poverty was dramatic. For example, in the parish of Lochbroom in Wester Ross, when the food supply collapsed, 95 per cent of his tenants held land with less than £10 rental annually. On the Isle of Lewis, the parish of Uig lost more than half of its population (to death, migration, or relocation) in the two decades from 1841 to 1861. However, many people on Lewis were resistant to emigration, and the total population of the island actually increased in the depression years, meaning that relief assistance was necessary for a greater number of people. Yet nothing like the vast numbers of famine-related deaths that occurred in Ireland took place in northwest Scotland. Demographic records are sketchy for northwest Scotland for this period, but available sources suggest that significant increases in mortality in the northwest and the islands were confined to the later months of 1846, the early months of 1847, and to a lesser extent 1848.[15]

For the first three years of the famine, Matheson avoided requesting assistance from the Highland Relief Board and provided employment to his tenants through projects such as building and repairing roads, construction of quays, raising up dykes to protect cultivated land from animals, and moving forward with the land-reclamation project. He purchased quantities of oatmeal and sold them to his tenants at 25 per cent of the market price. Additionally he imported seed potatoes and distributed them to the crofters, with the cost being added to their rent bills, which they could repay in labour or in cash.[16]

Tom Devine asserts that "in their scale and comprehensiveness, the efforts of the Duke of Sutherland were only surpassed by James Matheson, the proprietor of Lewis." His expenditures for meal and seed, over the span of five years, 1846–51, amounted to £30,000. Using evidence from the Napier Commission (1884) and Scottish newspapers from the famine years, Devine offers the astonishing figure of £259,248 for the total of expenditures by Matheson on various projects and emigration aid during the 1840s and 1850s. Among these forms of aid, one of the most dramatic was the free transport aboard his private yacht, *Mary Jane*, for seasonal migrant workers from the Hebrides travelling to the labour markets of southern Scotland in 1847. In this endeavour, he had the backing of the Free Church, which gave families reason to believe that families would be sustained while the men were away from home working in the Lowlands.[17]

Between 1845 and 1850, Matheson spent £107,767 on "extensive improvements," and that amounted to nearly £68,000 more than the entire revenue obtained from his Lewis estate during those years.[18] When testifying before a House of Commons committee, in 1847, he was asked by the chairman whether he had made great efforts to mitigate the suffering of the population on his estates? The question seems like an invitation to self-praise, but his answer was restrained and clarified his disposition toward relief expenditures. "Yes," he said, "I have made considerable efforts; but I have endeavoured to avoid giving charity. What I have done has been chiefly giving work to the people to avoid gratuitous distribution."[19]

In assessing the performance of the landowners during the famine and depression, Devine notes that there was broad agreement among contemporary independent observers, whether from the press, or the government, or destitution committees, about those proprietors deserving of praise.[20] James Matheson falls into the category of those praised most consistently, though he was not without critics.

In 1848, during the worst stages of the depression, Mary Jane Matheson established a school for young women at Stornoway, first called the Female Industrial School (later changed to "Lady Matheson's Seminary for Young Ladies"). The intent was to provide poor girls with skills which would enable them to acquire suitable employment. On the whole, the two-storey school enjoyed considerable success, with four teachers overseeing two classes on each floor. It was a favourite project of the Mathesons; they visited frequently and offered prizes to its students, who began their schooling at a very young age. Enrolment eventually reached more than two hundred and thirty students, and the school was considered to be ahead of its time, for it eventually educated the girls in music, physical training, needlework, proper deportment, religious knowledge, and geography, as well as providing foundational learning in reading, writing, and arithmetic. Lady Matheson, who is remembered locally as a forceful woman who was willing to spend money, often gave treats to the children and distributed clothing to the poorer pupils.[21] In its origins at the time of the emergency, the seminary was a capital investment that was very much in keeping with the thinking of James and Mary Jane Matheson that long-term improvement of the condition of the population was preferable to a band-aid type of charity that helped briefly but risked encouraging indolence.

Beyond that special project at Stornoway, James Matheson built schools throughout the island in districts where there were no parochial or Free Church schools; moreover, he appointed and paid the salaries of the teachers at the Free Church Normal School. He was disappointed that the rural schools were not well patronized and that there seemed to be little appreciation of the value of schooling among some elements of the island population. Accordingly, he put the rural schools under the direction of the Edinburgh Ladies Association, though he continued to grant them an annual payment toward the salaries of the teachers. His expenditures on the Ladies Seminary and the other schools amounted to more than eleven and a half thousand pounds.[22]

At the start of 1847, the Central Relief Board was established for the purpose of assisting any party ascertained to be destitute, willing to work, and without employment. Most landowners immediately accepted the benefits of the Relief Board for their tenants; but a few, including Matheson, continued to provide for their destitute tenants without seeking the aid of the Relief Board in 1847 and 1848. However, by 1849 even Lewis and Sutherland were receiving help from the relief committees.

The population of the island in 1848 was 18,359, of whom more than fifteen thousand lived in rural districts outside of Stornoway. In 1849 more than forty-seven hundred people on Lewis were included on the relief rolls. When Matheson's land- reclamation program was given up in 1850, the number of Lewis inhabitants receiving help from the Relief Board jumped to 12,829. However, the resources of the Relief Board were exhausted well before the emergency had passed. Accordingly, four of the parochial boards of the island sent a memorial to the prime minister, Lord John Russell, asking for government assistance to promote "a judiciously conducted emigration" to the colonies, and for relief aid to sustain the remaining population.[23] Matheson forwarded their memorial in January 1851, with his endorsement of their proposal.[24] Even if people were not dying in battalions from the famine, as was the case in Ireland, there were, in the view of the proprietor, too many mouths to feed and not enough regular jobs available on the Isle of Lewis.

As long as the landed classes in Scotland enjoyed a status that amounted to legal omnipotence, the vulnerability of the crofters was severe. For the land that tenants held, their tenure was subject to annual renewal; and the cottars were altogether lacking in legal security. Although some of the landlords suffered serious losses during the mid-century depression years, most of them survived the crisis securely intact.[25]

Matheson had offered the tenants themselves contracts for improving their crofts. Even though they were in most cases getting paid more than the rent due on their property, food costs and the depressed economy meant that many were continuing to fall in arrears on their rent. By 1851, over five hundred families were two years or more in arrears on their rent. Matheson's estate manager (factor), John Munro Mackenzie, reached the cheerless conclusion that capital expenditures on agricultural improvement would never allow for fair rental return nor provide stable subsistence for the crofters as long as the potatoes continued to fail. Adding to that pessimism were the feelings of disappointment and annoyance shared by Mackenzie and Matheson at the lukewarm response of the island's population to their strenuous efforts at relief works and agricultural improvements.

To encourage relocation in Canada, Matheson offered to pay the passage of all destitute persons wishing to settle in Ontario or Quebec. As further inducement he offered to forfeit all arrears of rent for those migrating, to give up his legal claim to the cattle of families in arrears, to buy up those cattle at a fair price, and to provide clothing for those needing it.[26] When the landed proprietors began to employ more rigorous policies regarding evictions and forced immigration, that reaction was spurred in part by their fear that the government would demand steeply higher assessments of them to pay for temporary relief for able-bodied persons who were utterly destitute. Such an extension of the Poor Law of 1845 would have had serious consequences for even the wealthiest landowners, such as James Matheson. Those steeply higher assessments were averted when local destitution committees generated greater private relief efforts.[27]

While no one was physically compelled to leave the island for Canada, there was, to be sure, plenty of arm-twisting involved in Matheson's program of "assisted emigration." Having expended so much of his own fortune on projects to relieve the famine and improve the lot of the island population, without much success, Matheson adopted the emigration plan as one element of a larger policy intended to achieve financial stability for his Lewis estate. In a strategy approved by Matheson and implemented by his factor, Mackenzie, certain sectors of the Lewis population were to be evicted from their plots of land and "encouraged" to accept Matheson's offer for help with the costs of relocating.

At the start of 1851, Mackenzie visited the various townships, selecting those families that should be evicted and pressed to emigrate. He specified two classes of residents who should be pressured to leave the island: those who were two years behind in rent payments and who were able-bodied and without acceptable reasons for the arrears; and the populations of whole townships which were generally in arrears, whose land could be used more profitably for grazings. Even in his fair-minded evaluation of Matheson's estate policies, Devine is prompted to conclude that "the policy of the estate swung decisively from one which reflected considerable concern for the welfare of the people to a strategy in which the well-being of the inhabitants was rigorously subordinated to efficient economic management."[28] Ironically, the shift in policy occurred at precisely the time when Matheson was receiving notice that he was to be honoured with a baronetcy, with the public understanding being that this honour was for his great efforts to relieve the effects of the famine on his estates.

The residents selected for emigration were notified of the terms of Sir James's offer in February 1851. In addition to paying for their passage, cancelling their debts, and offering to buy their livestock at a fair price, Matheson specified that he would provide free passage for a Free Church minister to accompany the emigrants and attend to their spiritual needs. He indicated that he would pay the minister's salary for two years. Those who refused the offer would be tendered summons for eviction at Whitsunday that spring, which was the usual date for renewal of tenancies.[29]

The emigration offer met a cool response from those whom Mackenzie had selected. Many contested the total amount of arrears that they were assigned. However, their protest was offset by support for the plan coming from the ministers of the Kirk, and by the Free Church nomination of the Reverend Ewen MacLean to accompany the emigrants to Canada. Sir John McNeill, after visiting Lewis for the Board of Supervision, came to the conclusion that emigration had become, by 1851, an essential element of the economic recovery of the island. In his judgment, emigration was a merciful way to relieve the distress of those who were starving and unemployed.[30]

The majority of people in the Highlands invested a good deal of their trust in the Free Church. Consequently, with the support of the Presbyterian clergy and the recommendations of Sir John McNeill, the Matheson estate was in a position to apply strong coercion to the selected families who declined to go. They were to be denied work on the estate; their cattle were subject to confiscation; they were to be ineligible for grants of seed or food; and, of course, they were subject to eviction. The weight of these sanctions was made heavier by the fact that the Central Relief Board had run out of funds.

Initially, less than 250 persons had agreed to leave Lewis; however, before the end of 1851, Matheson had assisted 1,554 persons in relocating in Canada; an additional 453 followed in 1852, and three years later the *Melissa* carried 330 to new homes in North America.[31] To accomplish this migration of 2,337 persons, Matheson spent nearly £12,000.[32] Those who had sailed away in 1851 had their Free Church minister with them, and they were offered free passage from Quebec to any place in the interior of North America that the emigrant family might designate before leaving.[33]

The Matheson estate was more considerate about relieving the distresses of passage than most of the landlords seeking to promote emigration. Mackenzie excluded from designation for emigration families whose heads were too old for the journey as well as those who had several small children. Overall the emigration was well organized and managed carefully. Quebec authorities complemented Matheson for the good conditions of emigrants from Lewis and contrasted them with the burdens borne by migrants from elsewhere in the Hebrides. And closer to home, Matheson was singled out for praise by the *Inverness Advertiser*, which declared that "the terms were liberal and such as in every way accorded with the character for distinguished munificence which the proprietor of this island has won."[34]

In spite of such praise, long-term assessments of the Matheson estate plan see it as failing to achieve its goal of relieving the pressure of population on the land. There was no redistribution of land to the advantage of those who stayed on Lewis, and it seems that acreage available for families actually decreased owing to the persisting growth of the island's population. Those who remained on the island baulked at any further efforts to promote assisted emigration.[35] Matheson's plans to rescue Lewis from population pressure and to restore some stability to the finances of his estate there had provoked a bitterness among some of the residents which diminished their regard for him. Having spent lavishly on material improvements and on relief projects, he had eventually determined to stop the bleeding and to pursue what he saw as responsible fiscal policies. But this perspective was not theirs.

The view from London was different. In recognition of his efforts to relieve the suffering of the people of Lewis during the famine years, James Matheson was honoured with a knighthood and baronetcy by Queen Victoria in her New Year's list for 1851. The announcement was made on 31 December 1850 in the *London Gazette* that the queen had that day directed that Letters Patent be passed under the Great Seal, granting the dignity of "Baronet of the United Kingdom of Great Britain and Ireland to James Matheson of the Lews and Achany."[36] At the other end of Britain, an announcement appeared in the *John O'Groat Journal* ten days later. It was not the practice for Letters Patent to specify the queen's reasons for granting an honour; however, it was universally accepted that the prime minister's aim in nominating Matheson was to recognize his benevolence and generosity toward the people of his island during the emergency brought on by the potato crop failure.[37]

A public celebration was held at Stornoway on 8 January, when the steamer *Marquis of Stafford* (owned by Matheson and the Duke of Sutherland) glided slowly into the harbour with ensigns streaming, cannons roaring, and fireworks illuminating the water. When the crowd on the quay was informed that the display was being staged to honour their proprietor on his elevation to the rank of baronet, "a general shout rent the air" (according to the exuberant reporter for the *Inverness Courier*, which was already disposed to cheer for the landlords as a class). One night later the celebrations continued with a general illumination of the town, with even the most humble buildings taking part in a contest of inventiveness. Outdoing all the other buildings was the Lews Castle, as viewed across the waters of the bay, whose waters reflected the elaborate lighting of the Mathesons' home.[38]

One day after the illuminations at Stornoway, the skies over the baronet's Sutherland properties were alight with bonfires that had been constructed over the course of many days by men hauling barrels of tar, mounds of peat, and bundles of wood. The *Courier* reported that estates tried to outdo each other in a gala observance of Sir James's good fortune. The newspaper report attributed their excitement to a sense of gratitude among the people of his Sutherland estates for his protection against the famine; and their elaborate festivity was ascribed to feelings of "the happiness they felt at the present mark of royal favor extended to a kind and benevolent landlord." Achany, Gruids, Sallachy, Rosehall and other locations north and south of his birthplace at Loch Shin lit their fires at dusk that Friday, initiating a chain of town and village celebrations which blasted away the quiet of the winter's night. The *Courier* raved about the merriment: "Refreshments were bountifully served out to the people, who toasted in overflowing bumpers the health of her Majesty, the worthy baronet, his amiable lady, and all the branches of their respective families. Dancing to the exhilarating tunes of the national bagpipe followed, and afterwards each township had a separate ball which was kept up till morning dawned."[39] The newspaper accounts offer reason to think that among those with cause to be particularly grateful to the queen were the distillers of northwest Scotland.

No doubt Matheson's testimony about famine relief before the Select Committee on Sites of Churches (1847) strengthened his chances for a knighthood. And it would not be unlikely that his membership in the Reform Club had some influential Whigs encouraging Russell to make the nomination. However, the honour could not be attributed to political cronyism or to self-advertising, for his relief efforts were widely applauded in Scotland. The fact that there were so many examples of negligent or slow-moving landlords during the famine may have made his endeavours seem all the more notable. Moreover, his seasonal patterns of movement between Stornoway and London indicate rather clearly that he was far from being an absentee landlord.

He did spend less time at Lairg, but he was not negligent of the families on his estates in Sutherland. The famine had not hit the areas of eastern Sutherland, where Matheson's mainland properties were located, with the same severity as it brought to the Hebrides. Their situations differed strikingly because of earlier Highland clearances.

By the time he returned to Britain in 1842 and began purchasing property in Sutherland, there was little to be seen of the old Highland way of life, except for the ruins of cottages, barns, and the byres where the crofters had kept their black cattle. The suppression of the clans had been severe in the three generations after the decisive battle at Culloden. As early as 1793 the *Old Statistical Account* had indicated that the best Lairg parish could do in a good year was to produce enough bread for eight months.[40] When James Matheson retired from China, the hill townships of the crofters and cottars were gone. So arable farming was not the mainstay of that part of Sutherland and the district around Lairg was not as badly afflicted as the lands along the northwest coast when the famine struck in the 1840s.

The properties he acquired in the 1840s had been largely cleared of their small-holding farm tenants by the early 1820s. There were no more evictions once the property was in his hands. He had purchased the Barony of Gruids, including Achany (south of the town), through a London estate agent, a couple of years prior to leaving China. He renamed the whole property "Achany."

When Queen Victoria developed a fondness for the Highlands, wealthy elements of English society followed suit and took to spending weeks in the Highlands for hunting and fishing vacations. The Mathesons rented lodges, such as Sallachy on Loch Shin, to Victorian gentlemen who enjoyed trout fishing or deer stalking or simply hiking in the Highland scenery.

The most gracious of the Matheson houses in Sutherland was the country house at Achany, which he would renovate handsomely. Achany had been the home of his great-great-aunt in the seventeenth century, and after his renovation it would become the residence of his siblings. Thomas, who had risen to the rank of lieutenant-general in the Welsh Fusiliers and served in the House of Commons, lived there (when not in London) with his unmarried sisters. Thomas died in 1873, but Elizabeth and Johanna both outlived James.[41] Though the Mathesons were generous in the benefactions to Lairg, their presence there was less dramatic than the role of laird that Sir James filled for the Isle of Lewis. When the Mathesons took up residence at Achany, they became the great benefactors of the parish school at Lairg, and Sir James and his sister Johanna were especially admired and respected for their generosity to the school.[42] In addition to his private charity as a landlord, he served the county of Sutherlandshire as deputy lieutenant and as justice of the peace. He also held the offices of lord lieutenant and sheriff principal of the county of Ross, as of 1866.

His benevolence as landlord in the estates around Lairg was quiet when compared with the strenuous efforts he made to improve the conditions of life on Lewis. In addition to his land-reclamation undertaking and the school support on Lewis, a number of other important capital projects for the benefit of the island were underwritten by James Matheson in his early years as proprietor, including several efforts to improve communication between Lewis and the mainland of Scotland. However, his three attempts to establish steamer service between Stornoway and Glasgow failed to turn a profit, and when a competitor, John Ramsay, entered the traffic, Matheson and his partner (the Duke of Sutherland) gave up the Glasgow steamer route. His losses on these shipping enterprises amounted to £15,000.[43] Given his success in chartering and owning ships in his days with Jardine, Matheson at Canton and Hong Kong, it must have been a shock for him to find that his business instincts were not as reliable when it came to Scottish shipping.

His determination to have a dependable and efficient mail service between Stornoway and Poolewe in Wester Ross was yet another expensive and frustrating experience. After much negotiation, the Royal Post eventually agreed to grant Lewis the same arrangement as the Orkneys and offered a subsidy of £1,300 for carrying the mails. However, most shipowners found the subvention inadequate. Hence, Sir James agreed to take on the mail service for a period of ten years, beginning in 1871, but the arrangement was a money-loser and it cost him £16,805, an even bigger loss than that suffered with the Clyde steamer ventures.[44]

As his sense of efficiency demanded a regular, frequent mail service (which would have been needed for his connections with the P&O and Matheson and Company, as well as for his duties in the House of Commons), similarly his assessment of the needs of travel on his island estate led to plans for road improvements. At the time when he purchased Lewis, there were about forty-five miles of rutted, ill-planned country roads and tracks. He spent more than £25,000 to improve travel and transport on the estate, so that there were more than 200 miles of excellent roads, including bridges, by the time of his death.[45] Within Stornoway, he had streets developed so that visitors landing at the ferry dock would go up James Street to Matheson Road, a nice broad avenue with substantial houses, which cut across town while avoiding the squalid housing by the waterfront.

Among other improvements in the town during his years, one involved the elimination of the sleazy drinking holes offering illegal whisky. Some of these taverns belonged to the lowest class of shebeen, and their suppression may have been as much a result of public displeasure with them as of the laird's effort to clean up the town.[46] There is, of course, a bizarre irony in the suppression of smuggled whisky during the tenure of a proprietor who made his original fortune by selling opium to smugglers along the coast of China.

The unprofitable undertakings he had withstood – Lewis land reclamation, Clyde-Stornoway steamers, Lewis mail steamers, the road construction – give some indication of the extent of his resources, for he could at the same time keep up and extend the Lews Castle, underwrite the Ladies Seminary, provide work relief projects for his estate residents, and maintain residences at Lairg and in London, in addition to the costs of living according to the standards of wealthy Victorians. It is undeniable, however, that these losing endeavours did drain away a significant portion of his fortune. He was hardly a spendthrift, for that would have meant turning his back on all that he had learned of personal economy during his days in China, when he enjoyed personal comforts but avoided extravagance. On the other hand, he understood that, in taking on projects like the land reclamation or the mail contract, he was not dealing with calculable profit margins such as he and Jardine would have reckoned at Creek Hong.

Ventures such as the Gas Works and Water Works at Stornoway were undertaken for the improvement of the town. The Chemical Works was an industrial project that would have provided work to some of the country people who migrated into town, but it failed. In contrast, Sir James's investment in a patent slip at Stornoway (an inclined plane for removing ships from the water for repairs) more than paid for itself, and the fish-curing houses turned out to be a profitable enterprise.[47]

One writer on the history of Lewis asserts that Matheson's career of trade in East Asia had not fitted him "for the leadership of a people accustomed in spite of dire poverty, to considerable freedom."[48] If that assertion of being ill-prepared for his ambitious program to transform the island was true of James Matheson, it must have been just as true of Lord Leverhulme, the English philanthropist. After the Matheson family finally sold the Lewis estate to Lord Leverhulme in 1918, the co-founder of Lever Brothers discovered that his grand enterprise for advancing the economy of the island was as expensive and as frustrating as the experience of Sir James. He had long dreamed of converting the population of Lewis from agriculture to industry. He had envisioned a great fishing industry, with organization along the lines of factory work. But he could not convince the country folk to break with their past as crofters and cottars. So he abandoned his plan after five years, and left the island forever in September 1924.[49] Like Matheson, Leverhulme learned the expensive lesson that some visions of a better life are unfeasible, in spite of all the philanthropic good will behind them.[50]

By far, the biggest construction endeavour undertaken by James and Mary Jane Matheson was the building of the Lews Castle, on the site of the Seaforth Lodge. Their marriage was childless (though she was certainly of child-bearing age when they married); however, Mary Jane's mother, Ann Mary Flower Perceval, lived with them at Stornoway. (She was just six years older than Sir James, and she was admired as a gracious hostess in her own right, having served in that capacity while her husband held high offices in Quebec.) So one might say that the Castle was an indulgence of the rich, a splendid big home with vast gardens and forests, to accommodate a family of three. However, staffing the castle and its grounds provided regular work for a sizable number of servants and gardeners. Moreover, the construction project itself, beginning in 1847, furnished work for a great many carpenters, masons, glaziers, and other workmen in the midst of the economic crisis.[51] The cornerstone was laid on 30 November 1847, St Andrew's Day. In the cavity of the stone were included coins, books, and documents, as well as the names of the officers of local Masonic lodge, whose members had marched through the streets and along the main avenue on the Matheson property to take part in the laying of the cornerstone with Masonic honours.[52]

Tudor Gothic was the style chosen by the Mathesons for the mansion, which bears strong resemblance to a castle because of its four towers and its castellated roof line and projecting parapets. Charles Wilson designed a handsome building, which he organized as a series of asymmetrical blocks of differing elevations. The window design, different for every level of the Castle, tied together the various blocks of the structure by serving to identify each floor of the three-storey mansion. Built of local stone, with yellow ashlar veneer, the mansion was clearly unified by a single design idea. On the north side, the main entrance was enhanced by the projection of a porte cochère, and above the main entrance the Matheson arms carried the inscription "Heart and Hand." Carved stone bosses, gargoyles, and griffons were added to the exterior walls in keeping with the Victorian fancy for neo-Gothic decoration.[53]

Sitting dramatically on a rise that overlooks the inner harbor at Stornoway, the Lews Castle offers a striking visual welcome to those approaching the town from the sea. The Bayhead River separates the Castle grounds from the town itself, but the distance is slight so that travel on foot between between Stornoway and the Castle does not take long. The immediate cost of the building was £60,000, but additional expenditures on the Castle, its grounds, and its associated offices brought the total figure to £109,000 in the years of Sir James and Lady Matheson. Most of the additional cost of £49,000 was associated with developing the surrounding grazing land into forest and gardens.

Suits of armour, with lances in hand, guarded either side of the entrance to the long hall running northeast to southwest from the main entrance to the kitchen. The hall, with its low Tudor-gothic arches, constituted the axial line of the Castle, with the drawing room and ballroom to the east and across the hall a grand staircase leading to the upper storeys. Elaborately carved wood panelling decorated the walls and furnishings of the large public spaces, with the dining room reaching for added splendour in its tapestries and large paintings.

The intricate parquet floor of the ballroom was more than a showpiece, for the news accounts of fetes at the Castle suggest that many dance patterns were hammered out on that floor by the feet of distinguished visitors as well as local friends. It appears that the Mathesons and Mrs Perceval were fond of entertaining and that they were good at it.

Among the celebrated nights at the Castle, one of the most memorable was the occasion when young Prince Alfred, the fourth child of Queen Victoria, visited Lewis not long after being appointed lieutenant in the Royal Navy. The HMS *Racoon* arrived at Stornoway in the middle of July 1863, and the town showed its excitement with guns firing, flags flying everywhere, and a great bonfire on the Castle grounds at dusk. The next evening the Mathesons' ballroom resounded with dancing, while undoubtedly the townsfolk looked on and listened from across the harbour. The tired feet did not stop thumping the parquet until shortly after midnight when the band concluded the event with "God

Save the Queen" and the whole company cheered the prince as he tod-
dled his way back to the ship.[54]

Even more splash was connected with the ball held at the Castle in
the autumn of 1868, when Sir James and Lady Matheson celebrated
the twenty-fifth anniversary of their marriage. The festivities started on
9 November, the actual day of their wedding a quarter-century earlier.
The town held an artillery competition, cheered Mrs Perceval as she
formally presented a new fountain and water trough for the community,
and witnessed the charity of the anniversary couple as Sir James and
Lady Matheson contributed food and clothing to labourers and other
estate workers, totalling 160 persons (a tradition they observed every
year on their anniversary). In the evening the whole town was illuminated, with lights in the windows of all the houses, as well as bonfires on
the quay and Goat Island, which were topped off by fireworks. After a
night's rest for the Mathesons and the town, the merriment resumed
the following day, with a grand ball at the Castle, attended by the officers and men of the Ross Artillery Volunteers and ladies and gentlemen
from the town.[55]

The fountain given to the town by Mrs Perceval on that anniversary
day was the third such gift of that type that she had given to the town.
She was seventy-nine at the time and immensely popular with the people of Stornoway for her kindness. Her fondness for James Matheson
was revealed in the anniversary gift which she gave him, a wall along the
waterfront of the estate, with a monument and a tablet dedicating it to
"the best of sons-in-law." She lived with them at the Lews Castle for another eight years, until dying at age eighty-seven in November 1876. No
doubt her interest in the beautiful grounds of Spencer Wood left a lasting impression on her daughter Mary Jane, for it was Lady Matheson
who was principally responsible for laying out the woods at the Lews
Castle, with a deer park and an amazing variety of trees.

The conservatory that guests saw on the evening of the silver anniversary ball was to be superseded within a few years by a more magnificent
glasshouse complex, which housed an Edenic variety of exotic plants,
including palms and ferns from remote parts of the world. Although the
climate of Lewis was not perfect for plants from tropical climes, the conservatory made it possible for the Lews Castle to gain a reputation for
being second only to the gardens at Kew for its huge number of plant
species. Some of the trees and plants were thought likely to have come
to Lewis from Asia aboard Jardine, Matheson ships.[56] The property had

woodland paths, and closer to the Castle there were carefully mani-
cured gardens with a grand horticultural diversity of trees, shrubs, and
flowering bushes that was not to be seen anywhere else in the Highlands
and Islands.

To accomplish the transformation of the Castle grounds, running between the Glen River (to the north) and the Creed River (to the south),
the Mathesons had to remove and relocate the crofters who had been
living on that portion of land. Although the proprietors made an effort
to resettle them on better land than the peat surfaces they had been
working, the tenants were nevertheless resentful at being displaced and
relocated. Their resentments toward the proprietors would increase
when John Munro Mackenzie retired from the position of factor in
1854 and was replaced by Donald Munro, who already held a number
of official positions on the island.

Munro held the position of factor for twenty years, until he eventually
brought the house down on himself, so to speak, by provoking the crofters to the point of angry resistance. He was called "The Shah," a nickname given him by the crofters for his domineering and autocratic
manner. Sir James, however, seemed to be blind to the distress caused
by his factor, for Munro was a loyal servant of the Matheson estate. In
consequence, many of the island's inhabitants directed their bitterness
ultimately toward Sir James and Lady Matheson who were seen to be
endorsing Munro's tactics.[57]

Donald Munro held so many offices at Stornoway and throughout the
island that there were multiple conflicts of interest in his overlapping
jobs. He was a solicitor, whose legal roles were entangled in an amazing
feat of pluralism. All told, he held nearly thirty public offices.[58] One
writer of local history calls him "the most hated man in the island's history" but concludes that "he was carrying out the settled policy of the
proprietor, Sir James Matheson."[59]

Five years before Munro became the estate factor, Sir James had published a set of rules and regulations for his crofting population, who
were tenants at will and had no security of tenure on land that they
farmed. Their continued use of the land that they rented depended
on their compliance with the terms of these regulations. The "Conditions of Let" were prepared by Matheson's Edinburgh agents and they
corresponded generally to the standard terms of land use in the mid-
nineteenth century. They were stern, and sought to impose a discipline

on the crofters' behaviour. The final condition stipulated that Sir James was very desirous of advancing education on the estate, and that he would look with "grave displeasure" on parents who could not give adequate reasons for extended absences of their children from school.[60] By the tone of their document, the Edinburgh drafters did their client no favour, for it implied a rather Olympian distance between the proprietor and his crofting tenants. And it set the wrong tone for Munro, who could use it with decisive muscle to intimidate the unlettered crofters.

The reports on Munro's conduct as factor are broadly similar, and generally quite unfavourable. He was reliant to some extent on his ground officers, who dealt more immediately with the crofting population and were considered to be tough and unsympathetic. Munro had an advantage over the Mathesons in the sense that he knew Gaelic and thus had a capacity to speak with many of the crofters in a direct way that Sir James and Lady Matheson did not. He is remembered as having dispensed fines liberally for matters as venial as unintentional breaches of courtesy, and for threatening crofters with evictions for non-compliance with his decisions.

In the instance of the big confrontation between Sir James and the townsfolk of Stornoway in 1863, it seems that Munro did not play a pivotal part. The inflamed issue at that time was the regulation of Stornoway Harbour. Instead of promoting an act of Parliament, Sir James elected in 1862 to petition the lords commissioners of the Treasury to allow him to purchase the entire waterfront of Stornoway. The question was referred to the commissioners of woods and estates, and they decided that Matheson could, by a payment of £400 in order to forego the cost of a harbour survey, establish his ownership of the foreshore (which right he claimed was actually contained in the grant of a charter to the barony of Lews in 1845).[61] Within a month of the commissioners' decision, Donald Munro had notified the tenants who had built piers extending over the foreshore that they were no longer entitled to rent them during herring season or use them for curing fish or building boats as they had in the past done as a matter of right. In effect, Sir James Matheson would henceforth regulate the use of the piers.

When he did agree to meet with a committee representing the distressed townspeople, his formal letter included a demand for transfer to him (as trustee) of the funds that had been collected by a pre-existing quay committee. When the committee protested, he took the matter to the Court of Session.[62] This time the concerned townspeople responded in anger when they met again at the Masonic Hall on 1 June. They felt that a fast trick had been pulled on them and they cheered as the chairman derided Sir James for departing from common justice.[63]

Apparently, Sir James wanted to create a beautiful esplanade along the shore below the Castle, because his expenditures on the Castle grounds were compromised to some degree by the herring fishermen's use of that shore for drying their nets. He did favour regulation of the harbour, but he wanted it on his own terms, as proprietor of Lewis.[64] The dispute dragged on until February 1864. Sir James eventually consented to the creation of a Harbour Commission of seven members (three appointed by him, three elected by the townspeople, and one nominated by the sheriff).[65] The compromise quieted "the Big Quay case," but it was a costly episode for Matheson. He had forfeited the good will of some of his neighbours at Stornoway in order to make his legal rights secure, and his standing with them was significantly lower once the episode was closed.

The harbour dispute had not directly involved the crofters who were distant from Stornoway, but their insecurity on the land was an ongoing source of discontent among them, and their habit of subdividing the crofts, so as to make room for married children, was an ongoing aggravation to the proprietor and his estate officers.

An incident provoked by Donald Munro in 1874 caused the crofters of the island of Bernera to focus their ire on the now elderly Sir James even more dramatically than the harbour question had alienated some of the Stornoway people. It is often referred to as the "Bernera Riot," though it was not much of a riot. It resulted from some arbitrary shifting around of the crofting population on that island, which is barely off the west coast of Lewis, and it needs to be viewed in connection with the preferences given to land use for sporting grounds ("shootings and fishings"). For generations, the small tenants of Bernera had been taking their cattle to the mainland (by having the animals swim across the small strait that separates Bernera from Lewis proper) for summer grazing.

Having relocated their grazing animals at mid-century to accommodate a new deer park, in the early 1870s they were again compelled to relocate their animals because of the development of new sporting grounds. They complained but agreed to abide by the order of the ground officer. They were required to build a dyke, about seven miles long, at their own expense, to keep their animals off the sporting grounds, before they were allowed to put any livestock on the assigned moorland. After signing (or putting their crosses to) a document which they believed granted them some permanence on that grazing land as long as they paid their rents, they set about building the dyke.

Less than two years later, Donald Munro sent instructions with a ground officer telling the Bernera crofters that they would no longer be allowed to use the mainland grazing space, and that they were to be confined to the island of Bernera, on which he would allot them the Hackleit farm. Furious, after building a seven-mile dyke and then being evicted from that sheiling-moor,[66] the Bernera folk refused to abide by the order. Munro subsequently went out to meet the Bernera crofters at Earshader (on the mainland side) bearing a new agreement, and, by alternately wheedling and threatening, he sought to get them to sign the new agreement, but they dug their heels in and stubbornly resisted. Munro told them that they would not be allowed to move their cattle to the mainland after Whitsunday 1874.[67] Nevertheless, their resistance disturbed him so much that he decided to evict them from their crofts on the island of Bernera in addition to denying them the grazings on the mainland.[68]

Three of the Bernera men were accused of assaulting a sheriff-officer in the course of his duties and warrants were issued for them. On 8 April 1874 one of the accused, Angus MacDonald, was spotted in Stornoway and was seized by two constables. A large crowd surrounded them, which resulted in the sheriff being summoned. When ordered to disperse, the crowd failed to do so, and the sheriff read the Riot Act, after which the man in custody was finally taken away to the jail, four hours after the episode began.[69]

Although there had not really been anything like a riot, word of these happenings caused alarm when it reached Bernera. About a hundred and fifty men from Bernera marched across the island to appeal directly to Sir James. They slept outside of town after their night march and in the morning enlisted a piper and proceeded to the Porter's Lodge of the Castle, where they presented their petition to speak with Sir James.[70] He listened to what they had to say and replied that he was not aware of the land changes that Munro was attempting to implement and promised to take the matter up with the factor. With that, the Bernera contingent marched back into town and within a couple of hours they were on their way home.

Sir James did not make public any formal response to the Bernera petitioners, but he did sack Munro. It was done in a quiet way, and not with the intention of disgracing his long-serving factor.[71] But before that happened Munro was taken over the coals when called as a witness at the trial of the three Bernera men. Though the accused men were acquitted, in effect Munro was convicted – not formally, of course, but in the eyes of the public – of having abused his authority.

At one critical moment in the lawyer's questioning, Munro admitted that he was acting on his own authority: "I did not consult Sir James Matheson about removing the people, and I issued all the summonses of removing against them without receiving instructions from him so to do. I am not in the habit of consulting Sir James about every little detail connected with the management of the estate."[72] Although the crofters' lawyer, Charles Innes, conducted his case in a way that distinguished Donald Munro from Sir James Matheson, he did at one point in his remarks to the jury indicate that the proprietor was negligent: "The proprietor of this and the neighbouring islands might be a little king. He lives and entertains, I hear, in a princely style, but it appears to me he has, so far as the management of his realm is concerned, absolutely abdicated in favour of the … man we had before us today."[73] Criticism along these lines would follow Sir James virtually to his grave, though the conclusion of the Bernera trial did not cause an uproar against him.

The trial of the "Bernera rioters" may be seen as a milestone in the land agitation which led to reform of the land laws. Perhaps it was a "victory for the Island crofters against officialdom," as Donald Macdonald has written.[74] The passage of the Crofters' Act in 1886 provided the crofters with security of tenure as long as they paid their rents, and also established a Crofters' Commission to set fair rents. Devine rightly observes that social and economic conditions in the Highlands and Islands could never be the same after that legislation, for the state was now intervening as an arbiter in the relationship between landlord and tenant.[75] After the death of her husband, Lady Matheson would repeatedly be asked to consider the requests of crofters to resettle farms that had been leased for sheep raising. She was, however, very distressed by threats, whether implied or open; so she would refuse the petitioners' requests if she detected any sign of intimidation. The agitation carried through the 1880s and into the 1890s. Her relations with the island's inhabitants were not ruined by the agitation, but the pleasure of being the landlady of Lewis must have been compromised greatly.

Over the last two years of his life, Sir James was subjected to some rather nasty criticism from letter writers in the Glasgow press, who accused him of living extravagantly while his crofters subsisted in poverty. From London, Hugh Matheson sprang to the defence of his uncle, with a letter to the *Glasgow Weekly Mail*. He described his uncle's generosity, carefully employing statistical evidence, and condemned the person or persons who would attack him at this stage of his life: "But I very much mistake the character of true Lewsmen if they will, on reflection, give countenance to attacks upon a venerable proprietor, who has ever been proud of them to a fault, and has unceasingly sought their good, and who, having passed fourscore years and fallen into bad health, is now quite unable to defend himself."[76]

Even the *Glasgow Daily Mail*'s "holiday correspondent," writing from Stornoway in the summer of 1877, joined in the sport of bashing the baronet. The debate about Sir James and his accomplishments as proprietor spread to papers in Edinburgh and London, with somewhat more sympathy and civility than the "holiday correspondent" showed. But the fact was that in the last months of his life, when he was incapable of responding, James Matheson was being measured by anonymous writers in Glasgow, Edinburgh, and London.[77] Whether he was aware of all of this inky fuss is impossible to say, but it certainly did not let him depart in peace.

Discouragement must have sat heavily on Sir James as his eightieth birthday came and went. Not only were there infirmities of old age; but he also would lose his mother-in-law and close friend, Mrs Perceval, in the fortnight after he turned eighty; and he had to live with the lingering dismay that the people whose lives he had hoped to transform had blamed him to a great extent for the harsh treatment they received from Donald Munro.

He had long since given up his seat in Parliament (1868), which meant that he had less reason to use his house in London. Nor did he have an active role in Matheson and Company or in the P&O; so there was even less need to be in residence at Cleveland Row. Also, his brother Thomas, who had had a neighbouring residence in London, was now dead. So his place was in the Highlands and the Hebrides, but his world was clouded, in spite of the beauty that surrounded him at the Castle. The splendid new conservatory might protect his plants against the gales that churned the seas seen from his windows, but the harsh winter in the Western Isles was more than he could endure. He departed the Lews Castle in July 1877, travelling to England that season. Although he spent the following summer at Lairg, he never did return to Lewis, on account of declining health.[78]

Toward the end of 1878, in order to avoid the cold and dampness of an English winter, he chose to spend the winter abroad. He and his wife crossed the Channel late in the autumn and made the long journey to the French Riviera in easy stages. His ultimate destination was the spa town of Menton, situated just inside France, barely more than a mile from the Italian border. Whether he had been there prior to 1878 is uncertain, but he was reported to have gone there that winter for reasons of his health.

An English physician named James Henry Bennet had long been promoting Menton as a health resort and had established a permanent winter practice there as of 1861. He maintained that the town's subtropical climate was beneficial to patients suffering from lung diseases, especially tuberculosis. When Dr Bennet first wrote of Menton, it was a sleepy little place, but by 1869 a rail line from Nice had reached the town and the community of foreign visitors began to swell; by the mid-1870s there were thirty hotels and four times that number of villas, with exotic gardens.[79] As a warm refuge from the cold of Scotland in winter, Menton would have been attractive to the octogenarian James Matheson, even if he did not have some serious medical reason for wintering there. In all likelihood, James Bennet was his attending physician.

Sir James nearly made it into the New Year 1879, but not quite. He departed this life at two o'clock in the afternoon of 31 December 1878. He was eighty-two when he died. An Inverness newspaper reported that he died unexpectedly; but the cause remains unknown. The death certificate issued by the Ville de Menton does not state a cause of death.[80] The *Inverness Courier*, announcing his death, said that the news would scarcely surprise its readers, for the fragility of his health had been well known.[81]

Lady Matheson took her husband's remains home to Scotland for burial, and his funeral was held at Lairg on Thursday, 6 February 1879, with a Church of England ceremony at which Dr E.A. Sanford, rector of the church at Combe Florey, Somerset, presided. (His Presbyterian connections eventually seem to have yielded to Anglican affiliation by the time of his death, perhaps through the preference of Lady Matheson.)

Sir James was laid to rest in the Matheson family plot at the cemetery in Lairg, alongside his kin.[82]

By the time of his death, his wealth was not as extraordinary as it was when he purchased his Scottish estates in the 1840s, since he had spent so much in attempting to improve the conditions of life on the Isle of Lewis; however, he was still a tremendously wealthy man. An assessment of his real estate in Ross and Cromarty, made just five years before he died, estimated his property at 406,000 acres, with a gross annual rental value of £17,676; an additional 18,490 acres in Sutherland, with rental value of £1,812, was listed in his name. He left an English will (1853) and a Scottish will (made out at London, in 1872).[83]

Prior to his wedding in 1843 he had created a marriage covenant of £160,000 to provide his wife with an income of £3,000 per year after his death. The interest that this amount was drawing was attached to his Scottish estate. He left all of the contents of his properties, as well as all of his stock (much of it in Scottish railroads), all the debts owed to him, and all of his Scottish estates, except Achany, in life rent,[84] solely for her use. The beautiful estate at Achany was to be her possession, subject to provision for his brother Thomas and his sisters Elizabeth and Johanna who were entitled to reside there during their lifetimes. Upon the death of Lady Matheson and his brother and sisters, all of the Scottish properties were to pass to the heir of entail, his nephew Duncan Matheson. The total value of his estate in Scotland was assessed at £169,685.[85]

By the English will, Mary Jane Matheson received all the contents of the mansion at 13 Cleveland Row, London; the house itself was entrusted to his trustees for her use until her death (and thereafter it would follow the entail). The London house was partly freehold and partly leasehold. The property bequeathed by the English will was assessed at £25,000; but there were also properties in Australia, specifically an estate of 1,100 acres, a wharf at Sydney, and four sheep runs, and the value of those properties had not been determined as of May 1879, when the other two wills were presented. Adding together the figures indicated in the two wills does not come close to giving a clear picture of Matheson's total wealth. When one considers the marriage-settlement fund, the value of the castle, gardens, conservatory, and the whole estate of Lewis, plus the Sutherland properties, the property of Ullapool, the London property, the Australian property, the railroad stocks and other stock, and the debts that various parties, including renters, owed to him, he must be deemed a very wealthy man at the time of his death, and Lady Matheson a very well-provided-for widow.

His death occasioned tributes from far and wide, countering the tarnished reputation that the Bernera episode had caused. The *Inverness Courier* declared it no exaggeration to say "that a more kind-hearted and generous landlord never owned property in the Highlands."[86] The word "kind" or versions of it occurred often in the public testimonials. The large assemblage gathered at Stornoway upon news of his death applauded when Dr Charles Macrae stated "that Sir James Matheson had just and enlarged conceptions of the duties as well as the rights of property ... Personally, as we know, he possessed a native courtliness and dignity of demeanor, and a grace and kindliness which fitted him to entertain, as occasion offered, peer and peasant with true inbred courtesy and suavity."[87] In the weeks following his death, various school boards on the island and the Stornoway Town Council adopted resolutions remembering James Matheson for his generosity as a landlord, his liberal support of education, and his efforts to promote the well-being of his tenants. They expressed a sense of loss to the parish and to the whole community of Stornoway. There was no sign of lingering bitterness.[88] The positive remembrance endured well into the twentieth century, when most of those who had known him were long gone. The *Stornoway Gazette* published a pair of articles in 1950 honouring the memory of the man who was reported to have been affectionately called "Sir Seamus" in his own day. The writer maintained that Matheson's purchase of Lewis had led to "the first era of prosperity in that island," even if his improvement schemes did not all succeed. In spite of some hyperbolic praise, comingled with some factual errors, the tone of the two articles, and a response from a reader, reflects an enduring respect for Sir James.[89]

The absence of personal letters from his marriage, or diaries by himself or Mary Jane, or memoirs by close friends of the Mathesons screens us from knowing much about the bonds of their relationship. In that respect they were rather typical Victorians, sharing their affections very privately or hiding the strains. For that reason, the remarks of Sheriff Charles Grey Spittal at the Stornoway meeting are as revealing as we can hope to find. "The married life of Sir James and Lady Matheson was long, and as it was long so also it was happy. In the truest sense she was a helpmeet to her husband ... We in Stornoway know well how assiduously and at the sacrifice of her own health she devoted herself to tending Sir James in his latter years when his health was failing, and it was not too much to say that, humanly speaking, it is to Lady Matheson's watchful care that Sir James owed the last years of his life."[90]

In the aftermath of her husband's death, Mary Jane arranged with a French sculptor, A. Vicyl of Menton, to create a monument to Sir James on the grounds of the Lews Castle. The graceful figure of an angel, which tops an inscribed stele, was installed at a prospect overlooking the harbor of Stornoway in July 1880. The sides of the monument recount the principal facts of his life, with expressions of Lady Matheson's esteem for him personalizing the cold stone. The south side of the column bears the gospel citation: "Well done, thou good and faithful servant ... Enter now into the joy of thy Lord" (Matthew 25: 21). On the north side, an inscription acknowledges her benevolence, and it too incorporates a gospel verse: "She hath done what she could" (Mark 14: 8).

Mary Jane Matheson survived her husband by seventeen years. Death caught up with her, at age seventy-seven, in London at their Cleveland Row home on 19 March 1896. A week later she was laid to rest alongside her husband in the Matheson burial plot at Lairg, where their graves are sheltered by a raised vault that resembles a tented structure of imperial India, recalling the years Sir James spent as an Eastern trader. Sculpted flowers surround the base of the vault, guaranteeing that, however harsh the wind or hail may blow across Sutherland, the Matheson monument will be permanently garlanded with opium poppies.

# GENTLEMANLY CAPITALISTS?

It is not the function of a biographer to erect a statue or to conduct a trial. On the other hand, it is quite appropriate for the biographer to make some assessments of his subject's life and to ask how that person used the opportunities life presented, how he or she dealt with the moral choices that had to be made, how the person addressed the difficulties that arose at various times, how the subject treated others, and how he or she related to the historical patterns of that era.

Assessments involve values, and such values deny the biographer the shade of neutrality. Nevertheless, the writer's imperative is to be even-handed in making the assessments. With this self-admonition, then, we venture into a concluding assessment of the uses that William Jardine made of his fifty-nine years and James Matheson made of his seventy-eight years. And we attempt to measure them against the thesis of "gentlemanly capitalism" set forth by P.J. Cain and A.G. Hopkins as a way of interpreting the driving force in nineteenth-century British imperial conduct. Accordingly, this conclusion uses two scales – one to weigh the personal values and ethical consciousness revealed in Jardine's and Matheson's words and actions, and the other scale to measure their historical importance.

Jardine and Matheson were not identical in behaviour or personality or experience, so we cannot ascribe to them the same exact values and thoughts and decisions. In some respects they were as close as their names on the firm's nameplate, yet in other ways they differed in temperament, conduct, and goals. So our judgments steer away from assumptions that the partners in business were necessarily partners in mind and spirit.

Jardine's nickname among the ordinary Chinese of Canton, "the Iron-Headed Rat," offers one perspective on the man's perceived toughness. It is very fitting to see him as tough-minded. He was a shrewd businessman who understood the balance sheet of advantages and disadvantages in the China trade. He did not like being outdone by his rivals. The fact that he came from relatively poor origins in southern Scotland's farmlands and had to depend on his brother to support his higher education gives some clue as to why he met economic challenges aggressively. He took on the hard life of a ship's surgeon but learned of the profitability of Eastern trade from his years on EIC ships. When his turn for commercial opportunity came round he was ready to seize it and quit medicine for trade. This departure from the healing arts did not, however, mean that he shelved his concern for people in order to concentrate on profit. There are plenty of examples of his charitable activity, for British and for Asians, both monetarily and in personal efforts. Behind the mask of the "Iron-Headed Rat" and the "official" gravity of his business mien there was a vein of kindness. He showed little soft emotion in his letters or speech or actions, but he took care of his family members back in Scotland, he encouraged his nephews (at least the industrious ones), he showed a genuine interest in medical services for the Chinese population of Canton, he provided help for down-on-their-luck British seafarers, and he showed a tender concern for friends among the Chinese and Parsi business communities who had come upon hard times.

Jardine was not a ruthless businessman, but he was gruff and he was vigorous in pursuit of commercial reward. He was not driven, but he was enterprising; and his sense of timing in the market was acute. Matched with that instinct for opportunity was his personal industry, which kept him in China longer than he had intended and kept him at his desk until two in the morning on many occasions. All this cleverness in the arts of commerce has to be set against a characteristic of patience. He did not jump recklessly at chances or make rash decisions. Sometimes his judgment was wrong, as in the case of the Napier affair, but even then he did not act on impulse. He was deliberate; for example, his fifteen years in the service of the EIC gave him a long time to weigh the prospects of prospering in the private trade of the Eastern seas, and he waited for the right moment, which came with the end of the French wars.

However, he was a risk taker when he sensed good prospects or when he saw that a competitor might beat Jardine, Matheson to the market advantage. Moreover, his skill as a commercial agent for Indian merchants earned him admission as a partner in the house of Magniac. In the early stages of his Canton career, he was reluctant to speculate with his firm's funds and preferred to rely on the income from his various services. But, by the time Jardine, Matheson was well established in the 1830s, he was willing to take a risk on sale of opium for the firm's profit and not simply for the distant clients' benefit. He was generally cautious in that respect, but certainly not timid.

Of his spiritual life little can be said, since he was very private in that aspect of his interior life, though it was clear that he was a Christian. He was encouraging to Gutzlaff in his missionary efforts to distribute bibles and tracts, but there was a reciprocity for the firm in Gutzlaff's ability to serve as translator for the opium deals along the coast. Jardine did have a strong sense of personal moral responsibility and a willingness to help people in need and those in distress. Apart from that, however, he kept his religion pretty much to himself. Whether religion meant anything beyond morality to him was and shall likely remain an opaque pane in our views of him. Here and there we get a glimpse into a private self that is softer than the public face that is better known. Hollingworth Magniac said of his friend Jardine: "He requires to be known to be appreciated." Even then, it seems, there were certain corners of his soul that he simply did not choose to reveal.

Did a sense of purpose govern his life? Hard work is the best answer to that question, for he applied himself diligently to his duties right down to the time of his final illness. He was not frivolous in his use of his wealth, nor did he seem to be concentrated on converting his resources to pleasure, though he lived rather comfortably. The example he gave to his nephews and his staff was that of a man who had an idea of social and economic justice which was tied to the thoroughness with which he applied his energies to the tasks before him, whether they be marketing his clients' commodities, sending home monetary assistance, promoting the cause of free trade, or advising the government on China policy. We can observe this not only in his own conduct but in the standards he demanded of those he dealt with both in Britain and in Asia. Jardine sought to conduct himself as a gentleman, and he had his own clear idea of what it meant to be such.

In personality, Matheson was cut from a different cloth, but he was very much in tune with his associate's concept of gentlemanly conduct. He came from a privileged background and he returned to northern

Scotland more a squire than a nabob. In the intervening years, spent largely in south China, he bore himself with a sense of dignity and style which were in some contrast to Jardine's rather more flinty type of gentleman. Matheson was more intellectually curious, though he had spent no more time than Jardine at university. The aspects of the Scottish Enlightenment that influenced him were likely to be the economic and moral thought of Adam Smith and the applied science of figures such as James Watt, rather than Francis Hutcheson's aesthetics or David Hume's ideas on religion. He became a fellow of the Royal Society, and he was receptive to new ideas for engineering and agriculture. And in his Canton years he was a source of legal advice to the English factory community, which did not have the benefit of British lawyers on site. He was very intelligent, and his mind was inclined more to practical applications than to philosophical speculation, which may help to explain why he was more engaged by the mechanisms of the opium trade than he was by the debates at Peking and at London over the ethics of that commerce.

Matheson was very good at dealing with people – better than Jardine, probably because his demeanour was less peppery. If he had an overriding goal for his life it would be describable as "improvement," for he did have a progressive vision that applied to ways of doing business, introducing new modes of transportation on sea and land, freeing the British overseas economy from traditional regulation, opening up opportunities for his nephews, and bettering the conditions of life for the people whose laird he became in the 1840s. He was more inclined than Jardine to savour the refined pleasures of life, such as stylish clothing and very nice homes, but he did not flaunt his wealth in vulgar show. He was not afraid to spend his money for other people's improvement, as his expenditures on Lewis demonstrated.

His generosity went hand in hand with his religious tolerance. Like Jardine, he had little to say about his faith, or so it seems. Nevertheless, his attachment to the Church of Scotland did not prevent him from giving substantial assistance to Free Church communities in northern Scotland and on Lewis. And eventually, as we have seen, he seems to have left Presbyterianism behind to become an Anglican. Nevertheless, his theological tenets were not much more visible than Jardine's.

The wealth gained by their commerce, with the dramatic profits due mostly to opium, made possible a beneficence that characterized Jardine's and Matheson's conduct both in China and in Britain. They

seem not to have been conflicted by the collision between their generosity, kindness, and principles of hard work and improvement, on the
one hand, and the deleterious effects of their opium sales on the even-
tual users of the drug, on the other. What Reinhold Niebuhr said of
politics might aptly be applied to their commercial behaviour, which we
can see as "an area where conscience and power meet, where the ethical
and coercive factors of human life ... interpenetrate and work out their
tentative and uneasy compromises."[1]

   Their candid denial of responsibility for the ruined lives that resulted
from opium abuse by some of the Chinese purchasers of the drug is
perhaps shocking to observers of a later age who conceive of drug merchants as sleazy criminals with wanton disregard for the people who buy
their illegal narcotics. One needs to be cautious about applying such a
stereotypical image of the modern drug lord to the merchants who sold
opium in Britain and Asia in the nineteenth century. Laudanum, a tincture of opium produced by mixing the drug with alcohol (or even just
water), was the most common of analgesics in the age before aspirin
(which was not generally available until the early twentieth century). It
was widely used in Victorian Britain, and both Jardine and Matheson
would have been aware of its therapeutic qualities from their medical
studies. Opium was not subject to international regulation and it was
not a substance limited to dispensing by chemists in Britain until 1868.
Its sale was, consequently, quite legal in Britain and India while it was
simultaneously quite illegal in China. Twenty years after the Opium
War, American troops in the Civil War used upwards of ten million opium pills, which were distributed routinely as a painkiller. Not until 1914
would the Congress of the United States pass legislation regulating the
use of all opium derivatives. Nothing like Commissioner Lin's seizure
and destruction of opium ever happened in Britain or America in the
nineteenth century.

   Jardine was not a naive man. He knew that the Chinese emperors'
edicts prohibiting opium sales were prompted by the debilitating effects
of addiction to the drug, but he maintained that drug abuse was the
buyer's fault rather than the seller's. Once the money was delivered and
the buyer got his opium, then it was his affair, Jardine told a parliamentary committee. He and his partner took the position that they were not
in business to regulate how the buyer dealt with the drug he had purchased. Matheson even declared that he had never seen a Chinese person "bestialized" by opium smoking, in contrast with the degradation

suffered by drunkards in Europe. But he did have to acknowledge, by 1843, that the trade had to be conducted quietly, because of the moral complaints being raised about it in England.

They saw the commodity as morally neutral, and chose not to become the avant- garde of regulation, since they were without influence at Peking to lobby for a policy of regulated sales, nor was their firm interested in such a policy. The two had become partners to pursue the opportunities that the China trade held out. Free trade offered many such opportunities, among them the chance to gain a large share of the tea trade. Banking and insurance provided other opportunities for major income, as did shipping. Opium was the greatest opportunity for their marketing skills, and they seized the opportunity without worrying any more than their British or American competitors did about the possibilities of addiction among the buyers. When responding to a young Mr Rolfe who wrote from Essex, Jardine maintained that careful investing in opium was "the most gentlemanlike speculation available." In writing that, he was not misrepresenting his actual belief.

In effect, Jardine and Matheson played by two sets of rules. By one standard they were men of integrity in their business relationships with Indians, Englishmen, and Chinese. By the other standard they were engaged in a sort of commercial warfare with the imperial government of China, and opium was a major factor in that struggle. If Peking was determined to prohibit opium imports, the Scots partners were equally determined to force chests of the drug onto the Chinese black market.

Jardine argued repeatedly that the Chinese government treated the foreign merchants with condescension and refused to engage in even-handed negotiations with a representative of the British nation, when such conversations might have led to the expansion of trade in general and to the regulation (or even suppression) of the opium trade by mutual agreement. Moreover, his experience convinced him that the local Chinese authorities connived in the smuggling of opium. Such resentments seemed to validate his perseverance in the illegal trade, in spite of the dangers of addiction that menaced the people at the end of the drug retail chain.

He did contend that the drug could be a useful soother, a harmless luxury for social occasions, and a precious medicine, as long as people did not abuse it. Perhaps he genuinely believed that to be a strong defence of his drug sales. But it rang hollow to many of his contemporaries. Matheson could maintain that he had never seen anyone bestialized by the drug. Perhaps he had not. But the statement suggests that he preferred not to know if the drug was wrecking people's lives. However, if we place these two men in London as opium brokers handling a legal commodity, they cease to be drug sellers in the darkest sense, and likely go unnoticed by history. Their defiance of the Chinese authorities was the issue that led to their centrality in the drama of their time. In the introduction to their anthology on opium regimes, Timothy Brook and Bob Tadashi Wakabayashi assert that China's focus at the time of the Opium War was "less on the addictive consequences of opium than on the hemorrhaging of the Chinese economy through the rapid outflow of silver to pay for the opium imports."[2] From this perspective, Jardine and Matheson may have seemed in their own day more like aggressive businessmen than drug lords.

Those same authors acknowledge that "it is not surprising that opium has inspired more in the way of strong reactions than dispassionate research," and that "a popular historiography targets foreigners as morally culpable for having used opium to intoxicate, impoverish, and demoralize the Chinese people."[3] For some writers, this makes it possible to identify Jardine and Matheson as one-dimensional villains, labelled as ruthless, ignoble, and wickedly irresponsible. But such labelling does little to give us a fully rounded portrayal of the two individuals. It has been the aim of this study to follow the course of dispassionate investigation, but not to the point of indifference.

Theirs are the most readily recognized names among the opium merchants in China in the nineteenth century – and therefore the names most easily invoked for moral condemnation – even though there were brigades of merchants similarly engaged. In the eyes of some writers, that prominence has meant that Jardine and Matheson get to carry the heaviest moral baggage of all the drug sellers. They indeed deserve to carry some of the burden, but they cannot do it all by themselves. Concerning the Parsis engaged in the trade, one recent author states: "Moral reservations associated with the trade in opium, addiction, and with cultural and political questions concerning the penetration of imperialism in Asia only entered the traders' calculations inasmuch as it affected their trade, if at all."[4] And the Parsis had plenty of company among British and American traders – but none of their names resonate as loudly as those of William Jardine and James Matheson. In part, the explanation of their prominence lies in their skills as business leaders and as vocal advocates of free trade when Britain was turning in that direction and China was resisting it. Those who would assess their lives have to deal with a conundrum: How does one account for their standards of integrity in business practices in combination with their aggressive pursuit of an illegal drug trade? That enigma impedes any facile labelling.

No careful accounting of their lives can be reduced to opium trading as a provocation of war. One author calls them "sinophobe warmongers."[5] But the record shows that Jardine repeatedly indicated that he did not want to see war happen. He was willing to encourage some display of muscle by the Royal Navy, in order to coerce the Chinese into accepting a commercial treaty that would establish a respected status for foreign merchants. Nonetheless, his disposition was against provoking hostilities (which would, among its effects, disrupt trade): "We require an equitable Commercial Treaty, with the power of appealing to the Emperor, when justice is denied us in Canton; and, I am convinced, this may be obtained without bloodshed, if properly demanded."[6]

Jardine is sometimes regarded as the architect of Britain's strategy in the Opium War. Wong asserts that Jardine "literally masterminded the government's approach toward China and the Opium War."[7] There is ample evidence to demonstrate that Jardine had a strong influence on Palmerston's war strategy, but there is also evidence to mitigate the term "mastermind."[8] Jardine was not eager to see an expensive blockade undertaken; he did encourage the acquisition of an island near the coast, but that idea had been proposed in the merchants' petition to Parliament at the end of 1830; he had not specified Hong Kong, but had suggested Lantao; and the strategy of imposing a commercial treaty by force of arms was something he did not favour. So he was neither a warmonger nor the mastermind, but he did have a persuasive influence on the foreign secretary's thinking, as Palmerston later acknowledged.

To think of Jardine and Matheson only as opium merchants and political strategists would be exceedingly inaccurate. Their agency business was multifaceted, and they handled a great variety of cargoes for export and import. Their services included market intelligence, discounting of bills on London, shipping food and textiles into China while sending silk and tea to Britain, and maintaining a fleet of vessels for transporting various kinds of cargo (among which opium was the foremost) as well as travellers and mail.

To the populace of Canton and to local and imperial officials, Jardine and Matheson were "barbarians," aggressive Western merchants peddling "foreign mud." But to the great majority of their British contemporaries in China, they were respectable gentlemen. Although they were disliked by a few of their competitors and by some people at home in Britain, they were respected by many more, and genuinely admired for their business integrity, their skills at identifying and pursuing profitable opportunities, and their management talents. In her study of the firm and the Hong Kong trading industry, Carol Matheson Connell repeatedly stresses the importance of the reputation Jardine and Matheson enjoyed for financial probity and trusted business behaviour.[9] This study provides numerous examples of their canons of fairness and commercial integrity. To most of their peers they were the antithesis of robber barons.

Jardine had been feted both at Canton upon leaving and at London upon arriving. Matheson was honoured by the Parsi merchants of Bombay. Both were elected to Parliament and while serving in the House of Commons pursued careers as influential businessmen in the City. Matheson was raised to the peerage by Queen Victoria, and he was applauded by mainland Scots for his efforts to relieve the distress of his island population. Opium notwithstanding, they were regarded as gentlemen by most who knew them. And they were venturesome capitalists.

Our second scale weighs their historical importance. Cain and Hopkins use the term "gentlemanly capitalists" to describe a sector of British society with influence in political and economic matters, and particularly as the dynamic force in the expansion of the British empire in mid- and late Victorian times. They do not mean to endorse the actions of the gentlemanly class by applying the term as a form of commendation (nor do they employ it in an unsympathetic way). It is for them a descriptive designation that accounts for much of the energy in British overseas economic policy and practice between 1850 and 1914.[10] The authors maintain that the landed aristocracy constituted a form of gentlemanly capitalism that prevailed in Britain during the eighteenth and early nineteenth centuries, dominating political and economic policies until such time as free trade became the guiding economic code of British government in the middle decades of the nineteenth century. According to their argument, the rise of British industrialism did not produce a class of gentlemanly capitalists to supplant the landed interests. Rather, with the gradual decline of the landed aristocracy, power devolved upon the service sector of British society – the prominent individuals and firms, centred in London, which provided financial, shipping, and insurance services on such a scale that their influence was global. Cain and Hopkins assert that this non-industrial gentlemanly elite conducted their businesses on principles that were closer to the ideals of the previously dominant landed aristocracy than to the patterns of industrial ownership.

Hence, according to Cain and Hopkins, the aristocratic ideal survived because it was adopted by the service sector concentrated in the City, where the most prestigious financiers could handle vast sums of other people's money without venturing anything like such amounts of their own resources. The transfer of authority could be seen developing after the end of the Napoleonic Wars, but it became especially noticeable after 1850. The new gentlemanly elite came largely from the leading public schools and the ancient universities, and was linked by assumptions of personal integrity, membership in certain London clubs, and ties of church affiliation. It absorbed and adapted the manners and strategies of the old class of landed wealth, and kept its distance from the world of everyday work associated with manufacturing interests.[11]

When applying this analysis of social-economic change to Britain's interests overseas, Cain and Hopkins connect the "British diaspora" with the values of the landed interests at home and the political goals of mid-century leaders such as Palmerston, who aimed to tie overseas trade to national security and domestic political stability.[12] As an example of his mindset, they cite his endorsement of the war against China in 1840 as a way of addressing domestic problems through overseas actions. They find support for that conclusion in his statement that "it is the business of government to open and secure the roads for the merchant."[13]

In this context, a prominent aspect of the imperial mission of Victorian Britain was the export overseas of the gentlemanly order. "The refurbished gentlemen who played the game overseas both expressed and reinforced the new forces emerging at home during a period of profound transformation."[14] Not only did they share the values embraced by the service sector in London, but they applied to their endeavours the reforming principles of the politics associated with free trade. To Cain and Hopkins, the empire became "a superb arena for gentlemanly endeavor."[15]

In their interpretation, the distinguishing feature of imperialism was "an incursion, or an attempted incursion, into the sovereignty of another state." In general, they say, agents of imperialism usually believe that they are representing a superior power. Within Victorian imperialism, representatives of the service sector "formed the advanced guard of capitalism abroad."[16] Not only did their banking operations facilitate the financial operations of large overseas firms, but their shipping resources moved goods vital to the lifeline of imperial trade, and their insurance firms wrote guarantees for the physical security of those goods in transit.

In their understanding of the reality of Victorian imperialism, Cain and Hopkins distinguish the existence of a vast formal empire from the hegemonic influences connected with British trade. Beyond territorial possession, there was the matter of the extent to which a foreign country became an "organic portion" of Britain's overseas economic network.[17] In the period after 1815, Britain countered the new protectionism practised by continental powers and the United States by extending its trade and its financial operations in areas that were outside its formal control. In this context of informal empire, William Jardine and James Matheson recognized the opportunities which enabled them to gain commercial prominence and eventually a good deal of political influence.

Do they fit the Cain-Hopkins description of "gentlemanly capitalism"? Chronologically, William Jardine and James Matheson anticipate the time frame that Cain and Hopkins use for the maturing of gentlemanly capitalism in the service sector. However, that is not a major problem in identifying them with that phenomenon, for they were actively promoting the cause of free trade in the decades before Britain's conversion to that set of trade policies. And they did so while conducting the very type of service sector business that is identified by Cain and Hopkins as typical of the new gentlemanly capitalism in the imperial field.

They were never involved in the world of manufacturing, but they rode the service-sector train to commercial success and political influence by providing marketing functions, market intelligence, shipping facilities, bill-discounting services and currency transactions in precious metals, commercial insurance, and shrewd business advice to clients in Britain, India, Australia, Malaya, the Philippines, and, of course, South China (especially Canton and Macao, prior to the acquisition of Hong Kong). For the most part, their marketing services involved other people's investments rather than their own. In the process they helped to carve out an enlarged area of influence for British trade in the Celestial Empire, which had been resisting the inroads of foreign commerce and hoping to use tea exports as a way to maintain a greatly favourable balance of trade against the Western commercial group at Canton.

It seems beyond dispute that Jardine and Matheson were members of that "British diaspora" which promoted incursion into the sovereignty of a foreign power. Their economic incursion involved efforts to market various commodities sent from Britain and India, but the most confrontational incursion involved the prohibited substance of opium, with which they defied the authority of the imperial court at Peking. They were agents of informal empire, achieved partly by their own commercial and financial efforts and partly by the naval forces which they called for when their defiance led Commissioner Lin to apply a radical cure to the problem of "foreign mud." Ultimately, they were tied to Palmerston's policy of protecting British interests abroad, and in fact their pressures and advice helped shape that policy.

In some ways they do not match up precisely with the Cain-Hopkins model of "gentlemanly capitalism," for they seemed to have to grow into the role rather than simply stepping into it after university and some apprenticeship. Jardine came from a relatively poor farming family in Dumfriesshire, while Matheson came from a Sutherland landed family in better circumstances (but hardly landed magnates). Jardine's early education was unremarkable, while Matheson had the advantage of attending Inverness Academy. Neither stayed at university long enough to secure a degree. The point here is that neither had the sort of educational pedigree which virtually entitled one to entry into the ranks of the younger gentlemanly capitalists. Both men spent time in London learning the ways of international commerce and finance, Jardine after his EIC service as ship's surgeon, Matheson more immediately following his departure from Edinburgh.

James Matheson spent two years with a London firm learning commercial practices, and then obtained free merchant's indentures from the EIC which allowed him to join an agency house in Calcutta in 1815. William Jardine was a few years behind his younger partner, having parted company with the EIC in 1817 in order to learn trade operations from a London merchant who was a Company agent. By 1818, he was back at sea again, learning the business of a supercargo sailing between India and China; but in 1820 (the year he met Matheson) he settled into commerce in South China.

Their graduation into the gentlemanly class of China merchants was a slow process, but they rose to be the most prominent members of the

British community in China and over the course of nearly two decades framed for themselves a commercial philosophy which matched that of the great houses of the City. And in practice they echoed the service-sector gentlemen of London by providing the kinds of marketing, shipping, banking, and insurance which extended British economic power into non-British territories. To borrow a nicely turned line from Cain and Hopkins, we might say of Jardine and Matheson that "being on the make, they were also gentlemen in the making."[18]

When they retired from China, Jardine in 1839 and Matheson in 1842, both men entered the company of gentlemanly capitalists in the City. Jardine served in the House of Commons while acting as a consultant and partner in the banking house of Magniac Jardine. Matheson settled into Parliament for the next quarter-century, while helping to reorganize Magniac Jardine into the financial giant, Matheson and Company, housed at 3 Lombard Street in the City. For nearly a decade he was chairman of the Pacific and Oriental Steam Navigation Company, during a period of dramatic growth for that firm. Moreover, he began what amounted to a second life when he purchased the Isle of Lewis, organized relief for the famine of the late 1840s, and received a baronetcy from Queen Victoria for that charity. Both men owned estates in Scotland but also maintained houses in London (Jardine on Upper Belgrave Street, Matheson nearby the palace at Cleveland Row). They became members of prestigious clubs, frequented by the fraternity of London's "gentlemanly capitalists." (Jardine was a member of the Oriental Club, as well as Brooks's; Matheson also belonged to Brooks's and to the Reform Club.)

For the moment, let us temporarily set aside their lack of pedigreed education, their need to put a certain amount of sweat into building their prestigious firm, and the fact that their China years preceded the Cain-Hopkins time frame (1850–1914) by a couple of decades. With these exceptions noted, Jardine and Matheson serve as fine examples of what those authors refer to when they speak of the gentlemanly capitalists who provided so much of the energy of the Victorian empire. They were aggressive in their free-trade strategies, their opium trade was indeed an incursion into the sovereignty of the Chinese empire, and they were insistent on having the strength of the British Navy for their protection, as they pursued and promoted an informal British economic hegemony along the coasts of East Asia. Their historical importance is not due principally to their opium commerce. Many Western merchants sold opium in China. Hardly as many had the same level of impact as Jardine and Matheson on the growth of Britain's empire through the dynamics of vigorous free-trade practices.

A younger Victorian, Arthur O'Shaughnessy, who died just a few years after Matheson, gave us the term "movers and shakers" in his 1874 "Ode" ("We are the music makers ..."), a term that has become a cliché stretching far beyond the poets and musicians he was extolling. In a more muscular application, the term suited the gentlemanly capitalists of O'Shaughnessy's time. William Jardine and James Matheson belonged to that race of movers and shakers.

# NOTES

PRELUDE

1  Duffy, *The '45*, 512–13.

2  Prebble, *The Lion in the North*, 301.

3  Kybett, *Bonnie Prince Charlie*, 205.

4  Magnusson, *Scotland*, 620.

5  Kybett, *Bonnie Prince Charlie*, 207.

6  Devine, *The Scottish Nation*, 45.

7  Plank, *Rebellion and Savagery*, 45.

8  Devine, *The Scottish Nation*, 45; Magnusson, *Scotland*, 623.

9  Prebble, *Culloden*, 328–9.

10  Somerset Fry, *The History of Scotland*, 198–9.

11  Devine, *To the Ends of the Earth*, 5–10.

12  Ibid., 10–11.

13  Lenman, *Integration, Enlightenment, and Industrialization*, 65–6.

14  Prebble, *The Lion in the North*, 302. In the course of the wars against revolutionary and Napoleonic France, the Highland units supplied the British army with what amounted to seven or eight divisions.

15  Devine, *To the Ends of the Earth*, 11, citing J.E. Cookson, *The British Armed Nation, 1793–1815* (Oxford: Oxford University Press 1997), 128.

16  Trevor-Roper, "The Invention of Tradition," 25.

17  Lenman, *Integration, Enlightenment, and Industrialization*, 71.

18  Mitchison, *A History of Scotland*, 375–8.

19  Somerset Fry, *The History of Scotland*, 205–6.

20  Mitchison, *A History of Scotland*, 352–3.

21  Lenman, *Integration, Enlightenment, and Industrialization*, 90–1; Mitchison, *A History of Scotland*, 352–3.

22 Mitchison, *A History of Scotland*, 351.

23 Lenman, *Integration, Enlightenment, and Industrialization*, 82.

24 Bowen, *The Business of Empire*, 50–2.

25 Parker, "Scottish Enterprise in India," 194.

26 Devine, *To the Ends of the Earth*, 20–1.

27 Bowen, *The Business of Empire*, 272–3. For example, in 1805 (three years after Jardine's initial appointment), twenty of the forty-seven East India ships dispatched to Asia were under the command of Scottish captains.

28 Fry, "Dundas," see *ODNB*, http://o-www.oxforddnb.com.helin.uri.edu/view/article/8250?docPos=1 (accessed 5 June 2013).

29 Lenman, *Integration, Enlightenment, and Industrialization*, 83; Parker, "Scottish Enterprise in India," 198–9.

30 Parker, "Scottish Enterprise in India," 199–201.

31 Cain and Hopkins, *British Imperialism*.

### CHAPTER ONE

1 Devine, "Social Responses," 152–6.

2 Three types of "irregular marriage" were recognized by Scots law: exchange of promises before witnesses; betrothal and consummation; and cohabitation and "repute" (being recognized as husband and wife). Such marriages bypassed the publication of banns in the local parish church. The wedding did not take place before officiating clergy; however, such marriages could be legally registered.

3 Sinclair, ed., *The Statistical Account of Scotland*, 4: 385–95. This extraordinary accounting of the demography and landscape of late-eighteenth-century Scotland was accomplished by questions put to the local parishes by Sir John Sinclair. In the case of Lochmaben, the responses were prepared by the Reverend Andrew Jaffrey.

4 Ibid., 395.

5 Ibid.

6 Williamson, *Eastern Traders*, 51–2.

7 Alexander Hamilton, professor of midwifery, quoted in J. Johnson, *A Guide for Gentlemen Studying Medicine at the University of Edinburgh* (London: Robinson 1792), 45, as cited in Risse, *Hospital Life in Enlightenment Scotland*, 240.

8 "The Faculty of Medicine at Edinburgh," http://www.med.ed.ac.uk/history/history3.htm (accessed 13 February 2001).

9 Risse, *Hospital Life in Enlightenment Scotland*, 245.

10 Rosner, *Medical Education in the Age of Improvement*, 30, 89.

11 Traditional guild rules allowed a surgeon to have one apprentice every three years, with the consequence that most surgeons had only five or six apprentices over the course of their careers. However, three surgeons consistently accepted more than one per year, and, during Jardine's years at Edinburgh, they seemed to be functioning as a partnership for the purpose of training apprentices. Benjamin Bell, Andrew Wardrop, and James Russell, in the years prior to and during their partnership, took on 154 apprentices (36 per cent of the total in Edinburgh) between 1780 and 1815 (Rosner, *Medical Education in the Age of Improvement*, 88, 97). It is quite possible that William Jardine received his surgical training from a member of this partnership.

12 Risse, *Hospital Life in Enlightenment Scotland*, 242; Williamson, *Eastern Traders*, 51–3; Lenman, *Integration, Enlightenment, and Industrialization*, 90–4; Mitchison, *A History of Scotland*, 35–41; Ferguson, *Scotland 1689 to the Present*, 207–8.

13 Rosner, *Medical Education in the Age of Improvement*, 143–5.

14 In Jardine's time, nearly all apprentices at Edinburgh registered for courses in anatomy and surgery, medical practice, and chemistry. Other courses available to them included medical theory, botany, *materia medica*, midwifery, and clinical lectures. Ibid., 96.

15 Risse, *Hospital Life in Enlightenment Scotland*, 268.

16 Ibid., 277, 294.

17 Horn, *A Short History of the University of Edinburgh*, 96.

18 The range of diseases treated at the infirmary is described well in Risse, *Hospital Life in Enlightenment Scotland*, chapter 3.

19 Ibid., 193–4, 379. A study of the drugs prescribed by one physician in the teaching ward during the winter of 1795 reveals that nearly 85 per cent of his patients received opium in one form or another. J. Worthes Estes, M.D., "Drug Usage at the Infirmary: The Example of Dr Andrew Duncan, Sr.," Appendix D in Risse, *Hospital Life in Enlightenment Scotland*.

20 Rosner, *Medical Education in the Age of Improvement*, 97, 144; Williamson, *Eastern Traders*, 53.

21 Information provided by Jo Currie, assistant librarian, Special Collections, Edinburgh University Library (letter to the author, 17 October 1997).

22 Sinclair, ed., *The Statistical Account of Scotland*, 18: 385–95. The unnamed author of the section on the parish of Lairg regarded the local residents as lazy, and commented wryly, "Respecting their character, in general, it is not much in its favour, that they seemed to entertain a particular dread of

these statistical inquiries, and would not permit the minister of the district to draw up an account of it, as if conscious that it could not turn out much in their favour."

23  Ketteringham, *A History of Lairg*, 57, 158.

24  Sinclair, ed., *The Statistical Account of Scotland*, 18: 453. As of the 1780s, the Highlands region was distilling about 700,000 gallons of whisky annually.

25  Some details of his early life may be found in Mackenzie, "A History of the Mathesons," 489–90; and Alexander Mackenzie, *History of the Mathesons*, edited and rewritten by Alexander McBain, 2d ed. (Stirling: E. MacKay, and London: Gibbings and Cay 1900), 141–5.

26  Inverness Royal Academy, *The Inverness Academical*, War Memorial Number (Inverness: December 1921), 48–9.

27  Ketteringham, *A History of Lairg*, 148.

28  Ibid., 179–80.

29  For an excellent, vivid description of the streetscape of the Old Town, see Johnson, *Sir Walter Scott*, 1: 35–40.

30  Daiches, *Sir Walter Scott and His World*, 14–15.

31  The school moved in 1828 to a building of classical design at the foot of Calton Hill. In 1832, thirty years after William Jardine had received his surgeon's diploma, James Matheson's Old High School building was re-opened as a surgical hospital. (It now houses the Department of Archeology at the University.)

32  Johnson, *Sir Walter Scott*, 1: 31–4; Sutherland, *The Life of Walter Scott*, 21–2.

33  Inscription on the memorial to Sir James erected by Lady Matheson on the grounds of the Lews Castle, Stornoway, Lewis, July 1880.

34  Cockburn, *Memorials of His Time*, 3–10. Henry Cockburn (1779–1854) was a Whig lawyer who became solicitor general for Scotland in the 1830s. An anecdote by Walter Scott buttresses Cockburn's report of the temper of the school. Scott pulled a humiliating prank in class on one of the masters, pinning a distorted quote from Virgil on the man's coattail in revenge for that teacher's physical assault on the revered rector of the school, Alexander Adam. Lockhart, *Memoirs of the Life of Sir Walter Scott*, 5 vols., 1: 95.

35  Cockburn, *Memorials of His Time*, 12.

36  Lockhart, *Memoirs of the Life of Sir Walter Scott*, 1: 86. John Gibson Lockhart, eventually Walter Scott's son-in-law, was two years older than James Matheson.

37  Extract from Class Lists in Library Registers and from Library Ledger of Books Borrowed by Pupils, 1809–10, Archives of the Royal High School, Edinburgh.

38  Buchan, *Sir Walter Scott*, 36.

39  On the same day in the summer of 1815, the town council, in separate motions, thanked the lord provost for helping to obtain the government's first annual grant of £10,000 to complete the university construction and for sending news of Wellington's victory at Waterloo. Horn, *A Short History of the University of Edinburgh*, 122.

40  Extracts from the Matriculation Album for 1810 and 1811, Manuscripts Division, Edinburgh University Library, courtesy of Charles P. Finlayson, keeper of manuscripts (in correspondence with Margaret Pamplin, Cambridge University Library, 17 August 1977).

41  Daiches, *Sir Walter Scott and His World*, 35; Horn, *A Short History of the University of Edinburgh*, 120.

42  Horn, *A Short History of the University of Edinburgh*, 60.

43  Buchan, *Sir Walter Scott*, 36.

44  Michael Russel, *View of the System of Education at Present Pursued in the Schools and Universities of Scotland* (1813), cited in Horn, *A Short History of the University of Edinburgh*, 120.

45  Horn, *A Short History of the University of Edinburgh*, 46, 68.

46  The Faculty of Medicine continued in session until July. So the change in area of study may have caused Matheson to remain at the university three months longer than would have been the case had he remained a student of the Arts Faculty, whose courses would have ended in April.

47  Cockburn, *Memorials of His Time*, 164–5.

48  Horn, *A Short History of the University of Edinburgh*, 68; Buchan, *Sir Walter Scott*, 39.

49  Horn, *A Short History of the University of Edinburgh*, 68.

50  Matriculation Album, 1811, Edinburgh University Library. The record does not list all of his courses, because the entries in the matriculation album are meagre and do not necessarily include all the courses a student took. Nothing like the modern college transcript existed.

51  Burial monument, Lairg Cemetery.

### CHAPTER TWO

1  The contours of his career as a medical officer for vessels of the EIC are set out best in Williamson's *Eastern Traders*.

2  Ibid., 52–3.

3  The abbreviation HCS stand for "Honourable Company Ship."

4 Ibid.; Wild, *The East India Company*, 71; Gardner, *The East India Company*, 128.

5 Williamson, *Eastern Traders*, 53.

6 MacGregor, *Merchant Sailing Ships*, 171–2. The twelve-hundred-ton rating of the ships referred not to their actual tonnage but to their capacity for cargo. Through the latter part of the century the largest ships at Canton were Danish and Swedish.

7 Farrington, *Catalogue of East India Company Ships Journals and Logs*, 84–5. The 1,244-ton *Brunswick* was launched in 1792.

8 Ibid., 54.

9 Bowen, *The Business of Empire*, 270. Men seeking command of East India vessels were prepared to lay out substantial sums for their commands in order to secure the private-trade opportunities that senior officers enjoyed. A resourceful commander could gain profit of as much as £10,000 on one round-trip voyage to Asia.

10 Ibid., 174, 187. Sometimes the Indiamen had false gun ports painted on the lower deck to deceive the enemy about their actual strength.

11 In wartime outward-bound fleets of the EIC sailed in convoy while in hostile waters. MacGregor, *Merchant Sailing Ships*, 174.

12 Hunter, *The "Fan Kwae" at Canton*, 103–4; MacGregor, *Merchant Sailing Ships*, 174. Hunter was employed at Canton by the American firm of Russell and Company. The term *fan kwae* was a Chinese designation for "foreign devils."

13 Bowen, "Britain in the Indian Ocean Region and Beyond," 55. Fewer options were available for homeward-bound vessels, so St Helena served as the main location for refitting and refreshing Indiamen returning to Britain.

14 Gardner, *The East India Company*, 98.

15 Ibid., 180–1.

16 Williamson, *Eastern Traders*, 56.

17 Downes, *The Golden Ghetto*, 19.

18 Williamson, *Eastern Traders*, 56.

19 Ibid., 56–8.

20 Van Dyke, *The Canton System*, 16; Hsü, *The Rise of Modern China*, 150–1; Pritchard, *Anglo-Chinese Relations during the Seventeenth and Eighteenth Centuries*, 126–7; Blake, *Jardine Matheson*, 16.

21 Wild, *The East India Company*, 79.

22 Bowen, "Britain in the Indian Ocean Region and Beyond," 54.

23 Reid, "Sealskins and Singsongs," 51.

24 Downes, *The Golden Ghetto*, 27, citing Bryant Tilden, "Father's Journals," 2: 32 (Fifth Voyage, 1 August 1833), Peabody and Essex Museum.

25 Blake, *Jardine Matheson*, 22.

26 Wild, *The East India Company*, 34.

27 Blake, *Jardine Matheson*, 23; Downes, *The Golden Ghetto*, 62; Downing, *The Fan-Qui in China*, 1: 242–3, 298–9.

28 Van Dyke, *The Canton Trade*, 61.

29 Downing, *The Fan-Qui in China*, 1: 245–6.

30 Downes offers a detailed and vivid description of the environs of the factories in *The Golden Ghetto*, 25–37.

31 Wild, *The East India Company*, 34.

32 In 1830 a parliamentary investigating committee learned that the expenses of the English Factory at Canton totalled about £90,000 a year, which indicated a very lavish style of life. Downes, *The Golden Ghetto*, 36.

33 Ibid., 47.

34 In many instances British naval and government officers were accompanied by their wives and families. The same held true for missionaries, ship captains, and some members of the Select Committee of Supercargoes, who had houses at Macao. However, the senior partners in most private firms were bachelors. With few opportunities for meeting unattached and socially acceptable young women in China, many private merchants maintained homes in Macao that were occupied by their Portuguese or Chinese mistresses. Reid, "Love and Marriage," 39.

35 Downes, *The Golden Ghetto*, 49–51.

36 Hunter, *The "Fan Kwae" at Canton*, 81. The seasonal migration of foreign merchants to Macao had been an enforced policy of the Chinese government since the mid-eighteenth century. Passengers were transported on specially prepared sampans by the West River passage, so that the hoppos could keep track of the number and identity of the foreigners trading at Canton. Passenger traffic via the Bocca Tigris was forbidden. Van Dyke, *The Canton Trade*, 111, 115.

37 Fairbank, "Ewo in History," 247.

38 Cheong, *The Hong Merchants of Canton*, 193; Blake, *Jardine Matheson*, 22.

39 Van Dyke, *Merchants of Canton and Macao*, 7–8.

40 Van Dyke, *Merchants of Canton and Macao*, 9; Blake, *Jardine Matheson*, 22–5. The number of Hong merchants at a given moment during the time of the Canton system varied between six and thirteen.

41 Van Dyke, *Merchants of Canton and Macao*, 10–11. In Jardine's time there were about one hundred "outside merchants" who were overseen by the Cohong.

42 Cheong, *The Hong Merchants of Canton*, 274; Van Dyke, *Merchants of Canton and Macao*, 7; Downes, *The Golden Ghetto*, 76. However, by the end of the eighteenth century, the Consoo Fund was being drawn on to pay for expenses associated with military, naval, public-works, and welfare expenditures. Consequently, the function of covering Hong merchant debts became just one of many types of claims on the fund. Cheong, *The Hong Merchants of Canton*, 232.

43 Downes, *The Golden Ghetto*, 22. The linguists were to a considerable extent the foreigners' "shadows, guides, and factotums." Among other things, they helped to arrange for lighters to transship cargoes from Whampoa to Canton. Smith, "Philadelphia Displays 'The Flowery Flag,'" 36.

44 Hunter, *The "Fan Kwae" at Canton*, 44, 60–4; Downes, *The Golden Ghetto*, 22. "Pigeon" was a round-about corruption of "business." Broad use was made of words like "chop," meaning "document," and "chow-chow," which was elastic in its usage but often meant "mixture," among other things.

45 Downes, *The Golden Ghetto*, 25, 60. Jardine himself would suffer from stomach complaints in the years after his return from China. In his fourth year home he would die from a tumour in the bowel.

46 Williamson, *Eastern Traders*, 59.

47 Ibid., 58–9.

48 Downes, *The Golden Ghetto*, 71.

49 Hoh-cheung Mui and Lorna H. Mui, *The Management of Monopoly*, 92–4, 96, 117.

50 Hunter, *The "Fan Kwae" at Canton*, 91; Downes, *The Golden Ghetto*, 65–71; Fay, *The Opium War*, 18–19.

51 Gardella, *Harvesting Mountains*, 37

52 Ibid., 34.

53 Van Dyke, *Merchants of Canton and Macao*, 13; Hunter, *The "Fan Kwae" at Canton*, 97; Wild, *The East India Company*, 34.

54 Van Dyke, *Merchants of Canton and Macao*, 31. Because Chinese merchants were prohibited from communicating with foreign governments or engaging in direct trade with Europe, they could not appeal to European (or Indian) courts for help in collecting debts owed to them. Ibid., 217.

55 Bowen, *The Business of Empire*, 258–9.

56 Wild, *The East India Company*, 40.

57 Downes, *The Golden Ghetto*, 71–2; Wild, *The East India Company*, 44–6. Private traders were apt to accept British orders for fine-quality finished silk cloth, but the EIC handled the bulk of the trade in raw silk.

58 The ships of the EIC were authorized to fly their ensigns in Eastern waters (beginning after passing St Helena). The EIC ensign in use after 1801 consisted of thirteen alternating red and white stripes, with the United Kingdom's new Union Jack of 1801 in the canton (upper left corner). See "Flags of the World," as well as the illustration of "Whampoa in China (1835)," after a painting by William John Huggins, in the exhibition catalog of the Hong Kong Museum of Art and the Peabody Essex Museum, *Views of the Pearl River Delta*, 128–9.

59 Williamson, *Eastern Traders*, 59.

60 Ibid., 60–2.

61 Ibid., 62.

62 Bowen, *The Business of Empire*, 247.

63 Ibid., 252–3. Bowen observes that the serious challenge of private British merchants operating in the Indian trade was not fully acknowledged by the directors of the EIC until the Company lost its monopoly on trade with India in 1813.

64 This tonnage was restricted to a specified list of goods, and it was subject to duties assigned by the Company. Certain exports from England, such as woollens, metals, and military items, were excluded from the privilege tonnage.

65 Bowen, *The Business of Empire*, 270.

66 Gardner, *The East India Company*, 97; Bowen reports that a captain's profit would range as high as £10,000. Bowen, *The Business of Empire*, 270.

67 Gardner, *The East India Company*, 97–8; Blake, *Jardine Matheson*, 31.

68 Williamson, *Eastern Traders*, 58–9; Reid, "The Steel Frame," 14.

69 Williamson, *Eastern Traders*, 62.

70 Letter from David Scott to Sir William Grant, 29 August 1800, cited in Sutton, *Lords of the East*, 79.

71 Chatterton, *The Mercantile Marine*, 104–5.

72 Williamson, *Eastern Traders*, 63. At the rank of surgeon, his advanced pay for two months was £6 10s.

73 In addition to captain, six mates, surgeon, surgeon's mate, purser, boatswain-gunner, master-at-arms, and midshipmen, the twelve-hundred-ton Indiaman carried the whole range of tradesmen: carpenters, cooper, sailmaker, caulker, armourer, butcher, baker, and poulterer, as well as officers' servants and stewards. Seamen accounted for about half the ship's company. Sutton, *Lords of the East*, 79; Chatterton, *The Mercantile Marine*, 106; Bowen, *The Business of Empire*, 269.

74  Chatterton, *The Mercantile Marine*, 106; Williamson, *Eastern Traders*, 63.

75  Williamson, *Eastern Traders*, 63.

76  Ibid., 64.

77  Sutton, *Lords of the East*, 88.

78  Ibid., 64–5.

79  EIC regulations required that three-quarters of the crew of an Indiaman be Englishmen. However, impressments and desertion necessitated replenishing the ranks with Lascar and Chinese seamen. Bowen concludes that a reasonable estimate would be that during wartime two-thirds of the crewmen of the EIC ships were British. Bowen, *The Business of Empire*, 269.

80  Addison, *The Journals of Thomas Addison*, 351–2; Williamson, *Eastern Traders*, 66.

81  Williamson, *Eastern Traders*, 66.

82  Wild, *The East India Company*, 53–4.

83  Subramanian, "Seths and Sahibs," 320–1.

84  Deyan, "The Study of Parsee Merchants," 54.

85  Thampi, "Parsees in the China Trade," 19.

86  Shalini, "Parsi Contributions to the Growth of Bombay and Hong Kong," 27; Reid, "The Steel Frame," 16.

87  Thampi, "Parsees in the China Trade," 20. As of 1840, the Banaji family was operating upward of forty ships in the country trade. In several instances, Jardine, Matheson owned many shares (sixty-fourths) in ships that were nominally under the ownership of Parsis, such as the Banajees and the Camas; and Parsis sometimes owned shares in Jardine, Matheson vessels. Deyan, "The Study of Parsee Merchants," 64.

88  Shalini, "Parsi Contributions to the Growth of Bombay and Hong Kong," 26–7, 29–32; Reid, "Jamsetjee Jejeebhoy," 17. By 1807, he had established business connections in India, Southeast Asia, China, and England. He then settled down in Bombay to oversee his wide-ranging commerce. His foremost commodities were opium and cotton, and beyond those enterprises he eventually built an extensive commercial fleet to save on the freight charges which were consuming much of his profit. He was known and respected in Bombay for his generous philanthropy, especially in medicine and education, and he gained the respect of Queen Victoria, who designated him Knight Bachelor in 1842 and elevated him to baronet in her birthday honours list of 1857.

89  Thampi, "Parsees in the China Trade," 20.

90  Parkinson, *War in the Eastern Seas*, 266.

91  Addison, *The Journals of Thomas Addison*, 353.

92 Williamson, *Eastern Traders*, 67–8. Shipping losses for the EIC were heavy at certain times in the Napoleonic Wars, most notably 1808–09, when the Company suffered the loss or capture of eighteen ships. Bowen, *The Business of Empire*, 155.

93 Williamson, *Eastern Traders*, 68.

94 Parkinson, *War in the Eastern Seas*, 271, quoting HEIC Proceedings Relative to Ships, appendix 4229. In his journal, midshipman Addison comments: "We soon discovered the looseness of their discipline, officers and men mingling, hail well met. Liberty and Equality was a motto indeed stamped on their guns." Addison, *The Journals of Thomas Addison*, 359.

95 Addison, *The Journals of Thomas Addison*, 362.

96 The wreck and what was salvageable of its cargo were sold for 3,500 rix-dollars to an American captain. Ibid., 363.

97 Ibid., 364. Captain Grant, two of his officers, and two of the ship's boys were allowed to travel home from Cape Town in a neutral vessel. With great difficulty, Jamsetjee Jejeebhoy secured passage on a Danish ship that was headed toward Calcutta. Thampi, "Parsees in the China Trade," 19.

98 Parkinson, *War in the Eastern Seas*, 273–5.

99 Williamson, *Eastern Traders*, 71.

100 Ibid., 72. Jardine was entitled to 10 shillings per head for the soldiers travelling on the *Brunswick*.

101 Williamson, *Eastern Traders*, 72; Sutton, *Lords of the East*, 65–6. Chapter 5 in the latter work gives an excellent summary of the pay and perquisites for commanders of East India ships.

102 Williamson, *Eastern Traders*, 72–3.

### CHAPTER THREE

1 Williamson, *Eastern Traders*, 79.

2 Ibid., 73–6; Reid, "The Steel Frame," 18.

3 Williamson, *Eastern Traders*, 79.

4 Chatterton, *The Mercantile Marine*, 109–10; Sutton, *Lords of the East*, 46.

5 Farrington, *Catalogue of East India Company Ships Journals and Logs*, 277. The *Glatton* sailed from Spithead (Portsmouth) on 14 May 1808. After leaving Penang in mid-October, it proceeded south of Borneo, through the Straits of Macassar, north of Celebes (Sulawesi), and into the Pacific. After sailing eastward of the Philippines, the *Glatton* took the Bashi

Channel between Taiwan and Luzon and "squared away before the N.E. monsoon for China." Williamson, *Eastern Traders*, 80.

6  Williamson, *Eastern Traders*, 80.

7  The incident is described at length in Morse, ed., *The Chronicles of the East India Company Trading to China*, 3: 40–9.

8  Williamson, *Eastern Traders*, 81–2, 84.

9  Philips, *The East India Company*, 156.

10  The term refers to the Company's chartering of the vessel for a specific voyage.

11  Williamson, *Eastern Traders*, 83.

12  Antony, *Like Froth Floating on the Sea*, 19–20.

13  Ibid., 19.

14  Antony reports that the cruelty of the pirates went as far as cannibalism, and that the reciprocal cruelty of Chinese authorities sometimes involved painfully slow dismemberment of the pirates – "veritable theaters of horror meant to impress the public." Ibid., 115–17.

15  Ibid., 44–5.

16  Wild, *The East India Company*, 78; Blake, *Jardine Matheson*, 34; Morse, ed., *The Chronicles of the East India Company Trading to China*, 3: 8–9. One family, the Zhengs, dominated piracy in the Canton delta for a century and a half. Antony, *Like Froth Floating on the Sea*, 43.

17  Murray, *Pirates of the South China Coast*, 126.

18  Ibid., citing Consultations and Transactions of the Select Committee of Supercargoes, 16 August and 27 September 1809.

19  Ibid., 131–2.

20  Ibid., 133.

21  Williamson, *Eastern Traders*, 83.

22  In September 1808 a British fleet commanded by Admiral William Drury had landed troops at Macao to prevent a French occupation of the Portuguese colony. After three months of diplomatically awkward occupation, the troops were withdrawn because the Chinese emperor, who maintained that he could defend Macao should the French try to seize it, was threatening to prohibit British trade at Canton. Parkinson, *War in the Eastern Seas*, chapter 16.

23  Morse, ed., *Chronicles of the East India Company Trading to China*, 3: 117–23; Murray, *Pirates of the South China Coast*, 140.

24  Antony, *Like Froth Floating on the Sea*, 51; Murray, *Pirates of the South China Coast*, 144–5.

25  Morse, ed., *Chronicles of the East India Company Trading to China*, 3: 123–5.

26  Ibid., 123–6; Williamson, *Eastern Traders*, 83.

27  Farrington, *Catalogue of East India Company Ships Journals and Logs*, 277;
    Williamson, *Eastern Traders*, 83–4.

28  Williamson, *Eastern Traders*, 90–1. Weeding had served as ship's surgeon
    for the first three voyages of the *Glatton*.

29  Ibid., 85.

30  Parkinson, *War in the Eastern Seas*, 123, 211.

31  Williamson, *Eastern Traders*, 86.

32  Williamson, *Eastern Traders*, 86; Parkinson, *War in the Eastern Seas*, 228–30;
    Chatterton, *The Mercantile Marine*, 137.

33  Williamson, *Eastern Traders*, 89.

34  Ibid., 90.

35  Ibid., 116–17. For this information, Williamson cites the Henry Upton
    Papers at the National Maritime Museum and the Journal of Magniac and
    Company at the University Library, Cambridge.

36  Parkinson, *War in the Eastern Seas*, 357–65.

37  Philips, *The East India Company*, 182.

38  Stern, "Company, State and Empire," 149–50.

39  Lawson, *The East India Company*, 139.

40  Ibid., 142.

41  Philips, *The East India Company*, 190.

42  Keay, *The Honourable Company*, 452–3.

43  Williamson, *Eastern Traders*, 114–15; Farrington, *Catalogue of East India
    Company Ships Journals and Logs*, 711.

44  Peyrefitte, *The Immobile Empire*, xxix–xxx; Keay, *The Honourable Company*,
    435–6; Wild, *The East India Company*, 40.

45  Peyrefitte, *The Immobile Empire*, 510.

46  Williamson, *Eastern Traders*, 120–2, 127.

47  Ibid., 127.

48  Jardine's final voyage in the service of the EIC was also the *Windham*'s, for
    Andrews sold her in 1818 to the insurgent navy in Chile, then in revolt
    against Spain.

49  Williamson, *Eastern Traders*, 129.

50  Andrew was the son of William's eldest sister, Jean, who had married David
    Johnstone. Andrew would eventually become a member of the firm and
    his descendants would dominate its leadership in the twentieth century.
    The family genealogy is contained in an appendix in Keswick, ed., *The
    Thistle and the Jade*, 262–3.

51  Farrington, *Catalogue of East India Company Ships Journals and Logs*, 593.
    After seventeen trips, the very durable ship was retired from EIC service in
    1834.

52 The minutes of the Court of Directors for 7 October 1818 contain the following entry: "Ordered: that Mr. William Jardine be permitted to proceed to Bombay under Free Merchant's Indentures upon the nomination of John Thornhill, Esquire, on the usual terms and conditions." Williamson, *Eastern Traders*, 135.

53 Framjee Cowasjee was the most famous member of the Banaji family, who diversified his investments into agriculture and other industries as well as conducting trading and shipping enterprises to China. Palsetia, "The Parsis of India and the Opium Trade in China," 654.

54 The *Bombay Merchant* was a ship consigned to McCullum, Isbister and Hornsley, a firm that appears to have had close relations with Weeding. Williamson speculates that Weeding may have held an interest in the vessel. Williamson, *Eastern Traders*, 136.

55 Reid, "The Steel Frame," 16.

56 Williamson, *Eastern Traders*, 139.

57 Mackenzie, "A History of the Mathesons," 489. The name of the mercantile firm in which he trained is unknown.

58 Reid, "The Steel Frame," 17–18; Blake, *Jardine Matheson*, 38; Williamson, *Eastern Traders*, 138. His nomination was provided by John B. Taylor, a member of the Court of Directors.

59 Lubbock, *The Opium Clippers*, 32. While the account of the undelivered letter remains strong in Jardine, Matheson lore, Alain Le Pichon thinks that it is apocryphal, and considers the possible options as resignation to forestall dismissal or actual dismissal for being too independent. Le Pichon, *China Trade and Empire*, 20n65.

60 Williamson, *Eastern Traders*, 138; Reid, "The Steel Frame," 18; Blake, *Jardine Matheson*, 38.

61 Thomas Stamford Raffles had founded a British settlement on the island of Singapore in February 1819, just three months before Matheson first saw the site.

62 James Matheson (aboard *Marquis of Hastings*, Penang harbour) to M. Larruleta and Company (Calcutta), Penang, 14 May 1819, and Singapore, 24 May 1819, James Matheson – Private Letter Book 1819–1820, Jardine Matheson Archive, University Library, Cambridge (hereafter MS JM), C1/3.

63 James Matheson (aboard *Marquis of Hastings*) to McIntyre and Company (Calcutta), Canton, 11 and 14 August 1819, and to Crattenham Mackillop and Company (Calcutta), Canton, 14 August 1819, Taylor and Matheson – Letter Book, MS JM, C1/3.

64 James Matheson (Canton) to Mrs R. Taylor (Canton), 27 November 1820, James Matheson – Private Letter Book 1820–1821, MS JM, C1/4.

65 James Matheson (Canton) to M. Larruleta and Company (Calcutta), 14 November 1819, James Matheson – Private Letter Book 1819–1820, MS JM, C1/3; Williamson, *Eastern Traders*, 138.

66 Robert Taylor (Canton) to James Matheson (at sea), 4 April 1820, Taylor and Matheson – Letter Book, MS JM, C1/3.

67 James Matheson (Pondicherry) to M. Larruleta and Company (Calcutta), 12 February 1820, James Matheson – Private Letter Book 1820–1821, MS JM, C1/4.

68 James Matheson (Pondicherry) to M. Larruleta and Company (Calcutta), 14 February 1820, James Matheson – Private Letter Book 1820–1821, MS JM, C1/4.

69 James Matheson (Yanam) to M. Larruleta and Compnay (Calcutta), 20 March 1820, James Matheson – Private Letter Book 1820–1821, MS JM, C1/4; Williamson, *Eastern Traders*, 139.

70 James Matheson (Panjim Goa) to M. Larruleta and Company (Calcutta), 1 May 1820, James Matheson – Private Letter Book 1820–1821, MS JM, C1/4; Williamson, *Eastern Traders*, 139.

71 James Matheson (Canton) to Mrs R. Taylor (Canton), 27 November 1820, James Matheson – Private Letter Book 1820–1821, MS JM, C1/4.

72 James Matheson (Canton) to M. De Courson de la Vilettelio, 5 December 1820, James Matheson – Private Letter Book 1820–1821, MS JM, C1/4; James Matheson (Canton) to M. de Arriaga, 13 January 1821, ibid.

73 James Matheson (Canton) to Mrs R. Taylor (Canton). 27 November 1820, James Matheson – Private Letter Book 1820–1821, MS JM, C1/4; James Matheson (Canton) to James Scott and Company (Calcutta), 11 December 1822, Yrissari and Company – Letter Book, MS JM, C2/1. Matheson was not prepared to assume responsibility for his deceased partner's debts.

74 James Matheson (Canton) to Parrisat and Company (Pondicherry), 5 December 1820, James Matheson – Private Letter Book 1820–1821, MS JM, C1/4.

75 James Matheson (Canton) to J. Hoefod (Canton), 5 December 1820, and to D. Brodie (Calcutta), 31 January 1821, James Matheson – Private Letter Book 1820–1821, MS JM, C1/4.

76 James Matheson (Macao) to M. Larruleta and Company (Calcutta), 23 December 1820, and to Thomas Anderson (Batavia), 17 February 1821, James Matheson – Private Letter Book 1820–1821, MS JM, C1/4.

77 Andrew Johnstone (Canton) to William Jardine (Bombay), 27 November 1820, James Matheson – Private Letter Book 1820–1821, MS JM, C1/4;

James Matheson (Canton) to William Jardine and Framjee Cowasjee (Bombay), 12 December 1820, ibid.

## CHAPTER FOUR

1 James Matheson (Macao) to T. Milburn (Bombay), 8 March 1821, James Matheson – Private Letter Book 1820–1821, MS JM, C1 /4; James Matheson (Macao) to D.J. Napier (Singapore), 8 March 1821, ibid.; James Matheson (Canton) to John Morgan (Singapore), 2 June 1821, ibid. We gain an insight into Matheson's business instincts from the letter to Morgan. Apparently for the security of documents at his new house at Macao, he wanted a large iron chest, which he requested that Morgan send him. Having haggled over the price while at Singapore, he now told Morgan: "Had I known you were a Constituent [of Taylor?] I should not have tried to drive *so hard a Bargain*."

2 James Matheson (Macao) to M. Larruleta and Company (Calcutta), 18 June 1821, James Matheson – Private Letter Book 1820–1821, MS JM, C1/4; Williamson, *Eastern Traders*, 140.

3 James Matheson (Canton) to M. Larruleta and Company (Calcutta), 3 June 1821, James Matheson – Private Letter Book 1820–1821, MS JM, C1/4; James Matheson (Canton) to John Morgan (Singapore), 2 June 1821, ibid.

4 Declaration by James Matheson, Canton, 28 May 1822, specifying his partnership in the firm and designating several persons to exercise power of attorney for him. The list included members of the firm of Mackintosh and Company, Calcutta, where Matheson had begun his career as an Eastern trader inauspiciously. We may conclude that his relationship with his uncle's firm had by now been repaired. Yrissari and Company – Letter Book, MS JM, C2/1.

5 In a letter to Jardine, dated 13 April 1822 (Canton), Matheson wrote: "Accompanying is an account of your opium sales and a sketch of your acct. current, which will I trust give you a satisfactory view of your concerns left under our charge." Yrissari and Company – Letter Book, MS JM, C2/1.

6 Williamson, *Eastern Traders*, 140–1; James Matheson (Canton) to William Jardine (Bombay), 13 April 1822, Yrissari and Company – Letter Book, MS JM, C2/1.

7 Greenberg, *British Trade and the Opening of China*, 22–4; Reid, "Sealskins and Singsongs," 50–3; Williamson, *Eastern Traders*, 5; Morse, ed., *The Chronicles of the East India Company Trading to China*, 2: 84–5.

8 Morse, ed., *The Chronicles of the East India Company Trading to China*, 2: 85.

9 John Reid had wound up his affairs at Canton and left China in February 1787 after the Imperial Austrian Company went bankrupt. Williamson, *Eastern Traders*, 12; Greenberg, *British Trade and the Opening of China*, 25; Reid, "Sealskins and Singsongs," 53; Morse, ed., *The Chronicles of the East India Company Trading to China*, 2: 150.

10 Williamson, *Eastern Traders*, 14–16, 22–3; Greenberg, *British Trade and the Opening of China*, 25. The diplomatic status of consul gave him the right of residence, which the EIC could not deny.

11 Greenberg, *British Trade and the Opening of China*, 27.

12 The firm bore the name Hamilton and Reid, in 1799, with the partners being Robert Hamilton, David Reid, Thomas Beale, and Alexander Shank. After Hamilton's death in 1799 and Reid's departure in 1800, the firm employed the name Reid, Beale and Company. By 1804, the name of the firm was Beale and Magniac. Greenberg, *British Trade and the Opening of China*, 27–8, 76.

13 Reid, "Merchant Consuls," 63; Greenberg, *British Trade and the Opening of China*, 27; Williamson, *Eastern Traders*, 48.

14 Spanish dollars long remained overvalued at Canton, to such an extent that there may have been some private minting going on among the foreign merchants, and it seems that James Matheson was engaged in that activity as late as 1840. Downes, *The Golden Ghetto*, 107.

15 Ibid.

16 Ibid., 108–9; Reid, "Sealskins and Singsongs," 52–3.

17 The whole pattern of financing trade within the extended British world is described in detail in Gillett Brothers Discount Company, *The Bill on London*.

18 Downes, *The Golden Ghetto*, 109.

19 Cheong, *Mandarins and Merchants*, 285.

20 Fay, *The Opium War*, 43.

21 Milligan, *Pleasures and Pains*, 25.

22 Ibid., 22.

23 Booth, *Opium*, 51–3; Milligan, *Pleasures and Pains*, 22.

24 Berridge and Edwards, *Opium and the People*, 9–10.

25 Ibid., 21–2.

26 Ibid., 10.

27 Howat, "Godfrey's Cordial or Little Penny Sticks," 24–5.

28 Milligan, *Pleasures and Pains*, 27.

29 Ibid., 24–5.

30  Coleridge, "Kubla Kahn," in Applebaum, ed., *English Romantic Poetry*, 105–6; de Quincey, *Confessions of an Opium Eater*, 36.

31  Trocki, *Opium, Empire and Global Political Economy*, 58.

32  Greenberg, *British Trade and the Opening of China*, 104–5, citing J. Phipps, *A Practical Treatise on the China and Eastern Trade* (1836), introduction.

33  Greenberg, *British Trade and the Opening of China*, 104–5.

34  Trocki, *Opium, Empire and Global Political Economy*, 67.

35  Ibid., 59. Trocki contends that without opium there would have been no British empire, though he concedes that it would be difficult to prove that point. Opium was the largest single item of export from India for the first six decades of the nineteenth century.

36  See ibid., 68–70.

37  Booth, *Opium*, 6–10.

38  Morse, ed., *The Chronicles of the East India Company Trading to China*, 2: 316–17.

39  Fay, *The Opium War*, 44, citing Owen, *British Opium Policy in China and India*, 87.

40  Trocki, *Opium, Empire and Global Political Economy*, 78.

41  Ibid., 87.

42  Fay, *The Opium War*, 14.

43  Booth, *Opium*, 12–13.

44  Trocki, *Opium, Empire and Global Political Economy*, 91. Estimates of drug use for this period are largely guesswork. China's population was nearing 400 million at the start of the nineteenth century. Foreign observers estimated in 1836 that China had 12.5 million opium smokers. Commissioner Lin maintained, in 1838, that 1 per cent of the population was using opium.

45  Trocki, *Opium, Empire and Global Political Economy*, 93.

46  Van Dyke, "Smuggling Networks of the Pearl River Delta before 1842," 49–50.

47  Ibid., 60.

48  Ibid., 61.

49  Van Dyke, *The Canton Trade*, 132.

50  Greenberg, *British Trade and the Opening of China*, 48. Lintin is about eighty miles south of Canton and twenty miles northeast of Macao.

51  Fay, *The Opium War*, 46–8.

52  Van Dyke, "Smuggling Networks of the Pearl River Delta before 1842," 65.

53  Greenberg, *British Trade and the Opening of China*, 49; Lubbock, *The Opium Clippers*, 88–9. Sycee was uncoined silver in ingots or lumps.

54  Booth, *Opium*, 118–19.

55  Van Dyke, *The Canton Trade*, 133.

56  Lubbock, *The Opium Clippers*, 53–5; Fay, *The Opium War*, 48–9; Trocki, *Opium, Empire and Global Political Economy*, 102.

57  See Greenberg, *British Trade and the Opening of China*, chapter 4; and Van Dyke, *The Canton Trade*, 126–41.

58  Williamson, *Eastern Traders*, 140; Greenberg, *British Trade and the Opening of China*, 94–5.

59  Morse, ed., *The Chronicles of the East India Company Trading to China*, 4: 11–19; James Matheson (Canton) to James L. Buckingham, 13 April 1822, Yrissari and Company – Letter Book, MS JM, C2/1.

60  Van Dyke, "Smuggling Networks of the Pearl River Delta before 1842," 68.

61  Ibid., 62.

62  Downes, *The Golden Ghetto*, 122.

63  Trocki, *Opium, Empire and Global Political Economy*, 101.

64  James Matheson (Canton) to William Jardine (Bombay), 13 April 1822, Yrissari and Company – Letter Book, MS JM, C2/1.

65  Williamson, *Eastern Traders*, 141.

66  Morse, ed., *The Chronicles of the East India Company Trading to China*, 4: 64–6. For paintings depicting the fire, its aftermath, and the reconstruction of the factory area, see the Hong Kong Museum of Art and the Peabody Essex Museum, *Views of the Pearl River Delta*, 174–83.

67  Xavier Yrissari (Canton) to Alexander Mackintosh (Bombay), 27 July 1823, Yrissari and Company – Letter Book, MS JM, C2/2.

68  Yrissari and Company (Canton) to M. Uriarte (Calcutta), 26 April 1823, and to Mackintosh and Company, 29 July 1823, Yrissari and Company – Letter Book, MS JM, C2/2.

69  Yrissari and Company (Canton) to Mackintosh and Company (Calcutta), 13 November 1823, Yrissari and Company – Letter Book, MS JM, C2/2; Blake, *Jardine Matheson*, 40.

70  Parliamentary Papers: Opium Trade (1832), cited in Chang, *Commissioner Lin and the Opium War*, 238n7.

71  Williamson, *Eastern Traders*, 141, 145. Not long thereafter both Jardine and Cowasjee sold their shares in the *Sarah*.

72  Ibid., 141; Grace, "Hollingworth Magniac," *ODNB*. Jardine's travels may be traced in letters included in the Yrissari and Company – Letter Book, MS JM, C2/3: James Matheson (Canton) to O. Mortucci (London), 18 December 1824; Yrissari and Company (Canton) to William Jardine (Canton), 26 June 1824, and (Bombay), 11 February 1825; Yrissari and

Company (Canton) reporting Jardine's departure for Bombay to W.H. Hamilton (Van Diemensland), 10 January 1825.

73  Collis, *Foreign Mud*, 66.

74  The quote comes from the entry on Hollingworth Magniac in the (old) *DNB*, by Charles Sebag-Montefiore; documentation for the quote is not listed.

75  Hollingworth Magniac's retirement from commerce was temporary, and he emerged from it in 1833 to support Jardine, Matheson bills of exchange after a financial crisis had caused the collapse of their correspondent firm in Calcutta, Fairlie and Company. In 1835 he entered into a partnership with John Abel Smith and Oswald Smith, creating the firm of Magniac Smith, which later became Magniac Jardine in 1841, and eventually Matheson and Company in 1848, at which time Holllingworth Magniac continued to be a partner. Grace, "Hollingworth Magniac," *ODNB*. Thomas Weeding became sole owner of the *Sarah* by a bill of sale which was registered at London on 26 November 1827. Williamson, *Eastern Traders*, 145.

76  Ibid., 142; Reid, "The Steel Frame," 18.

77  Nye, "The Morning of My Life in China," 28.

78  James Matheson (Canton) to Hood and Son (London), 13 November 1824; to J.H. Gledstanes (London), 12 November 1824; to Gledstanes King and Company (London), 8 February 1827; and to Thomas Dobue and Duboisviolette (Nantes), 30 December 1826, Yrissari and Company – Letter Book, MS JM, C2/3, C2/5, and C2/6.

79  James Matheson (Canton) to Messrs. Smith and Elder (London), 30 April 1824, 22 March 1825, and 11 November 1825, Yrissari and Company – Letter Book, MS JM, C2/3 and C2/4.

80  Most sources give credit for founding the paper to James Matheson, but Downes attributes its origins to Alexander, with James eventually taking control. Downes, *The Golden Ghetto*, 92n117, 399n118; Reid, "The Steel Frame," 18; Blake, *Jardine Matheson*, 39; Greenberg, *British Trade and the Opening of China*, 39.

81  Van Dyke, *The Canton Trade*, 107–8. Notable among the other English-language newspapers were the *Canton Press*, the *Chinese Repository*, and the *Chinese Courier*.

82  He, "Russell and Company and the Imperialism of Anglo-American Free Trade," 85–6. Wood left Canton but returned in 1831 to work for Russell and Company; later he left that firm to establish his second English-language newspaper, the *Chinese Courier and Canton Gazette*.

83 The first issue of the paper was published on 8 November 1827. Thereafter it was published every two weeks. Just a few months after the first issue, the editor presented a fairly complete and frank description of how the opium trade, though illegal, was conducted at Canton. At that point, the "Price Current," listing the market prices for various types of opium, was published by the *Register* on the same schedule as the newspaper. *Canton Register*, 12 April 1828.

84 Yrissari and Company (Canton) to M. Uriarte (Calcutta), 18 June 1825; to Mackintosh and Company (Calcutta), 28 October 1825; to Lyme and Company (Singapore), 14 December 1825; and to John Purvis (Singapore), 25 September 1826, Yrissari and Company – Letter Book, MS JM, C2/4 and C2/5.

85 Yrissari and Company (Canton) to Maclaine and Company (Batavia), 1 March 1827, Yrissari and Company – Letter Book, MS JM, C2/5; Williamson, *Eastern Traders*, 142.

86 Cheong, *Mandarins and Merchants*, 73.

87 Yrissari and Company to Rickards, Mackintosh and Company (London), 13 January 1827; to Mendietta, Uriarte and Company (Calcutta), 12 February 1827; and to Willliam Jardine (Canton), 20 February 1827, Yrissari and Company – Letter Book, MS JM, C2/5.

88 J. Ybar to William Jardine (Canton), 9 March 1827, and James Matheson (Canton) to Mendietta, Uriarte and Company (Calcutta), 3 March 1827, Yrissari and Company – Letter Book, MS JM, C2/5.

89 Cheong, *Mandarins and Merchants*, 85n97.

90 Yrissari and Company (Canton) to Magniac and Company (Canton), 14 February 1827, Yrissari and Company – Letter Book, MS JM, C2/5.

91 Cheong, *Mandarins and Merchants*, 75.

92 James Matheson to Rustomjee Cowasjee (Calcutta), 27 May 1827, and James Matheson (Canton) to Antonio Pereira (Macao), 1 October 1827, Yrissari and Company – Letter Book, MS JM, C2/5; Williamson, *Eastern Traders*, 142–3; Blake, *Jardine Matheson*, 41; Reid, "The Steel Frame," 18.

93 The *Jamesina* was his own ship as far back as 1823 and bore his name. The vessel was a refitted British war vessel. Consigned to Magniac and Company after Matheson became a partner, she was engaged solely in the opium trade. James Matheson to Allport, Ashburner and Company, 25 January 1828, and James Matheson (Canton) to Jose Lopes (Macao), 23 September 1828, Yrissari and Company – Letter Book, MS JM, C2/5; Lubbock, *The Opium Clippers*, 69–70.

94 Cheong, *Mandarins and Merchants*, 114.

95 Williamson, *Eastern Traders*, 143; Reid, "The Steel Frame," 18; Greenberg, *British Trade and the Opening of China*, 148.

96 James Matheson (Canton) to Charles Knowles Robinson (Calcutta), 15 April 1825, Yrissari and Company – Letter Book, MS JM, C2/4.

97 James Matheson (Canton) to Mackintosh and Company (Calcutta), 7 October 1829, Yrissari and Company – Letter Book, MS JM, C2/5.

98 William Jardine (Canton) to Andrew Johnstone (in Britain), 21 March 1830, William Jardine – Private Letter Book, MS JM, C4/1.

99 As late as the 1840s, with the company centred at Hong Kong, it continued to be a convention of the firm that partners remained unmarried. No living accommodations suitable for married couples were provided at the firm's quarters. Reid, "The Steel Frame," 30.

100 Reid, "Love and Marriage," 39.

101 Ibid.

102 Letters from James Matheson (Macao) to John White (Calcutta), 11 March and 16 June 1832, James Matheson – Private Letter Book, MS JM, C5/1.

103 James Matheson (Canton) to Arbuthnot and Company (Madras), 16 June 1832, James Matheson – Private Letter Book, MS JM, C5/1.

104 William Jardine (Canton) to J.H. Gledstanes (London), 22 November 1832, William Jardine – Private Letter Book, MS JM, C4/2.

105 William Jardine (Canton) to Hollingworth Magniac (Colworth), 1 January 1831, William Jardine – Private Letter Book, MS JM, C4/1. The fact that Jardine was in his office at Creek Hong writing letters on Hogmanay, when Scottish custom prescribes a big celebration of the New Year, reveals something of the inner drive that led him to devote so much time to his work.

106 Collis, *Foreign Mud*, 67; Cheong, *Mandarins and Merchants*, 114, 269.

107 In 1993 I asked the firm's honorary archivist, Alan Reid, about the mysterious Mrs Ratcliffe. He replied that he thought she was William Jardine's mistress.

108 William Jardine to Andrew Johnstone, 21 March 1830, and to Thomas Weeding (London), October 1833 and 4 December 1833, William Jardine – Private Letter Book, MS JM, C4/3. Jardine would give his nephew detailed instructions about family matters.

109 William Jardine to Captain John Hine, 27 March 1830, William Jardine – Private Letter Book, MS JM, C4/1.

110 William Jardine to Thomas Weeding (London), 7 November 1834, enclosing a letter for Mrs Ratcliffe, William Jardine – Private Letter Book, MS JM, C4/3.

111 William Jardine (Canton) to Thomas Weeding (London), 3 and 6 December 1838, and to Matilda Jane Ratcliffe, 3 December 1838, William Jardine – Private Letter Book, MS JM, C4/7.

112 Matilda Jane Ratcliffe (London) to Jardine, Matheson and Company (Hong Kong), 19 October 1854, Letters – Great Britain, Private, MS JM, B1/8.

113 There are other possible scenarios for this part of Jardine's life. Mrs Ratcliffe may have been his daughter by a youthful episode during his first years of EIC service, and Tilly thereby his granddaughter; some guardian status for the mother and child may have existed by virtue of a completely hidden commitment preceding his years in China; or perhaps there was a burden of honour to a young widow to whom he had made a promise of marriage which he never fulfilled. While his generosity toward his Scottish relatives is documented, there is nothing to suggest that he was caring for relatives in this situation.

114 Collis, *Foreign Mud*, 68.

115 Morse, ed., *The Chronicles of the East India Company Trading to China*, 4: 244–5.

CHAPTER FIVE

1 William Jardine (Canton) to Andrew Thomson, 11 December 1830, William Jardine – Private Letter Book, MS JM, C4/1.

2 William Jardine (Canton) to Andrew Johnstone (London), 22 October 1832, William Jardine – Private Letter Book, MS JM, C4/2.

3 James Matheson (Canton) to John MacVicar (London), 6 February 1833, James Matheson – Private Letter Book, MS JM, C5/1.

4 Fairbank, *Trade and Diplomacy on the China Coast*, 63, citing Gerald Yorke, "The Princely House: The Story of the Early Years of Jardine Matheson and Company in China 1782–1844" (unpublished manuscript in the collection of Matheson and Company), 111.

5 William Jardine (Canton) to James Matheson (Singapore), 18 March 1830, William Jardine – Private Letter Book, MS JM, C4/1.

6 William Jardine (Canton) to I.H. Gladstone (London), 29 March 1830, William Jardine – Private Letter Book, MS JM, C4/1.

7 Lubbock, *The Opium Clippers*, 33. Lubbock argues that Jardine "was quite ruthless in business and pursued the opium trade with all his might and without any moral scruples."

8 William Jardine (Canton) to R. Rolfe (Bocking, Essex), 6 April 1830, William Jardine – Private Letter Book, MS JM, C4/1.

9 James Matheson (Canton) to Smith Elder and Company (London), 4 May 1831, James Matheson – Private Letter Book, MS JM, C5/1.

10 James Matheson (Canton) to Hugh Matheson (Calcutta), 4 November 1831, and to Thomas Weeding (London), 16 November 1833, James Matheson – Private Letter Book, MS JM, C5/1.

11 Andrew Jardine joined his uncle in China in 1832, but illness necessitated his return home in 1836. He was back in China a year later and became a partner in 1839. Andrew remained in China until 1843, and although he retired from Jardine, Matheson in 1845, he became one of the founding partners of Matheson and Company in 1848.

12 William Jardine (Canton) to Charles Stewart (Hillside near Lockerbie), 23 March 1830, William Jardine – Private Letter Book, MS JM, C4/1. William's second sister, Margaret, and her husband, James (also surnamed Jardine), were known as the Chipknowe family, from their residence. William's youngest sister, Elizabeth, was married to William Dobbie and is referred to in the correspondence as "Mrs. Dobbie."

13 Wiliam Jardine (Canton) to James Stewart (Gillembierigg near Lockerbie), 28 January 1831, William Jardine – Private Letter Book, MS JM, C4/1.

14 William Jardine (Canton) to Andrew Johnstone (Scotland), 26 March 1830, William Jardine – Private Letter Book, MS JM, C4/1. He had already sent certificates worth $1,148 to Andrew Johnstone for the benefit of the Kirkburn family earlier that month. William Jardine (Canton) to Andrew Johnstone (Scotland), 14 March 1830, William Jardine – Private Letter Book, MS JM, C4/1.

15 Very helpful appendices in Keswick's *The Thistle and the Jade*, 262–5, provide a genealogy of the Jardines and their descendants and a listing of partners and directors for Matheson and Company and Jardine, Matheson from their foundings through the early 1980s. Blake, *Jardine Matheson*, 116–19, offers useful information about the family members involved in the operation of the firm and its allied houses in Calcutta and London.

16 Greenberg, *British Trade and the Opening of China*, 146–7.

17 Ibid., 149–50.

18 Ibid., 167n21.

19 James Matheson (Canton) to H.P. Hadow (Bombay), 10 March 1832, James Matheson – Private Letter Book, MS JM, C5/1.

20 Fairbank, *Trade and Diplomacy on the China Coast*, 62.

21 Reid, "Spreading Risks," 181.

22 Fairbank, *Trade and Diplomacy on the China Coast*, 62.

23 Singh, *European Agency Houses in Bengal (1783–1833)*, 276.

24 Ibid., 277–85.

25 James Matheson (Canton) to Hugh Matheson (Calcutta), 4 November 1831, James Matheson – Private Letter Book, MS JM, C5/1; Cheong, *Mandarins and Merchants*, 166.

26 Cheong, *Mandarins and Merchants*, 165–6.

27 James Matheson to unnamed party (addressed "Dear Sir"), 26 May 1834, James Matheson – Private Letter Book, MS JM, C5/1; Cheong, *Mandarins and Merchants*, 167.

28 James Matheson (Canton) to Hugh Matheson (Calcutta), 7 April 1832, James Matheson – Private Letter Book, MS JM, C5/1.

29 Ibid.

30 James Matheson (Canton) to Hugh Matheson (Calcutta), 7 April 1832, James Matheson – Private Letter Book, MS JM, C5/1. Among the firms or individuals whose reliability Jardine and Matheson (still operating as Magniac and Company) trusted when Magniac endorsed bills were: Baring Brothers (London), John Jacob Astor (New York), Gledstanes, Drysdale and Company (London), Thomas Weeding (London), Thomas Wyatt (London), and Spode and Copeland (London).

31 Greenberg, *British Trade and the Opening of China*, 164, citing circular letter from Jardine and Matheson to Bombay merchants regarding remission of funds to England.

32 Ibid., 164–5. The nature and extent of Magniac's financial arrangements are discussed in detail in Cheong, *Mandarins and Merchants*, chapter 3.

33 Fairbank, *Trade and Diplomacy on the China Coast*, 63.

34 Reid, "The Shipping Interest," 132.

35 Van Dyke, "New Sea Routes to Canton in the 18th Century and the Decline of China's Control over Trade," 59.

36 Ibid., 72–7.

37 Ibid., 77.

38 Ibid., 78–82. Van Dyke maintains that the off-season arrivals were one of the early signs that the upper levels of Chinese government were starting to lose control over China's foreign commerce.

39 Fairbank, *Trade and Diplomacy on the China Coast*, 62.

40 Greenberg, *British Trade and the Opening of China*, 173–4.

41 Reid, "The Shipping Interest," 132.

42 Lubbock, *The Opium Clippers*, 66–9; Fay, *The Opium War*, 51; Williamson, *Eastern Traders*, 188.

43 Lubbock, *The Opium Clippers*, 78–9; Reid, "The Shipping Interest," 136.

44 Trocki, *Opium, Empire and the Global Political Economy*, 104–6.

45 Ibid., 106.

46 Fay, *The Opium War*, 51; Lubbock, *The Opium Clippers*, 77–8; Blake, *Jardine Matheson*, 54; Fay, "The Opening of China," 67.

47 James Matheson (Canton) to John MacVicar (London), 26 March 1832, James Matheson – Private Letter Book, MS JM, C5/1.

48 Williamson, *Eastern Traders*, 148.

49 Ibid., 149.

50 James Matheson (Canton) to Charles Thomas (Singapore), April 1831, 23 July 1832, 11 August 1832, 28 January 1833, and 14 October 1833, James Matheson Private Letter Book, MS JM, C5/1; Williamson, *Eastern Traders*, 149; Lubbock, *The Opium Clippers*, 61.

51 Williamson, *Eastern Traders*, 185.

52 Fay, "The Opening of China," 67; Trocki, *Opium, Empire and the Global Political Economy*, 95.

53 It is revealing of Jardine's and Matheson's business propriety that they made an enormous correction in the amount that was to be transferred to Hollingworth Magniac. Their corresponding agency house, Fairlie and Bonham, had determined that Magniac's account was worth £10,000. Jardine and Matheson directed that an additional £20,000 be transferred to Magniac. James Matheson to Hollingworth Magniac (Colworth, England), 22 October 1831, James Matheson – Private Letter Book, MS JM, C5/1.

Magniac's retirement was delayed from its original date of 30 June 1827 to allow him a chance to make up the loss he suffered from the failure of the Hong merchant Manhop. Jardine determined to extend the date of Magniac's retirement to 1830. Like Jardine and Matheson, Hollingworth Magniac was concerned about providing for family members. To some degree, this delay allowed Magniac to be compensated for the financial and personal disappointment attending his brother Daniel's dismissal from the firm (for marrying his Asian mistress). A further extension of two years was the result of the decision by Jardine and Matheson that Francis Hollingworth should retire from the firm. The additional two years that Magniac's capital remained in the firm allowed for earnings on that capital to establish a fund for Francis's retirement home "and other family purposes." James Matheson (Macao) to H.P. Hadow (Bombay), 10 March 1832, James Matheson – Private Letter Book, MS JM, C5/1.

54 William Jardine (Canton) to F.P. Alleyn (London), 27 February 1832; to C. Marjoribanks (London), 27 February 1832; and to Hollingworth Magniac, 2 March 1832, William Jardine – Private Letter Book, MS JM,

c4/1 and c4/2. When Magniac proposed another relative to take Francis Hollingworth's place and become a partner in the firm, Jardine was uncomfortable, since he and his partner had already taken two of their nephews into the firm, and he had to decline a request from Jamsetjee Jejeebhoy to take a Mr Low from Bombay into the firm. William Jardine (Canton) to Jamsetjee Jejeebhoy (Bombay), 27 February 1832, William Jardine – Private Letter Book, MS JM, c4/1.

55 *Canton Register*, 2 July 1832, 1; Morse, ed., *The Chronicles of the East India Company Trading to China*, 4: 327; Reid, "The Steel Frame," 20; Blake, *Jardine Matheson*, 41. A notice of the intended retirement of Hollingworth Magniac had appeared in the *Register* on 15 February.

56 William Jardine (Canton) to C. Marjoribanks (London), 27 February 1832, William Jardine – Private Letter Book, MS JM, c4/1.

57 Grace, "Hollingworth Magniac," *ODNB*.

58 Wakeman, "The Canton Trade and the Opium War," 170–1.

59 *Canton Register*, 2 August 1828.

60 Greenberg, *British Trade and the Opening of China*, 177; William Jardine (Canton) to H. Gledstanes (London), 27 December, 1830, William Jardine – Private Letter Book, MS JM, c4/1.

61 William Jardine (Canton) to F.P. Alleyn (London), 27 February 1832, William Jardine – Private Letter Book, MS JM, c4/1.

62 William Jardine (Canton) to J.R. Reid (London), 28 February 1832, William Jardine – Private Letter Book, MS JM, c4/1.

63 Greenberg, *British Trade and the Opening of China*, 180; Fay, *The Opium War*, 57.

64 Greenberg, *British Trade and the Opening of China*, 183.

65 Ibid., 184.

66 Gardner, *The East India Company*, 202. The Company's profit from China for the fifteen years 1814–29 was £15,414,000, which accounted for three-quarters of its overall profit for that period. For the same period the rest of the Company's total profit was £5,074,000.

67 William Jardine (Canton) to William Baynes (London), 27 February 1828, William Jardine – Private Letter Book, MS JM, c4/1; Fay, *The Opium War*, 57; Morse, ed., *The Chronicles of the East India Company Trading to China*, 4: 332–4.

68 Fay, *The Opium War*, 58.

69 Ibid., 60.

70 Ibid., 61; Morse, ed., *The Chronicles of the East India Company Trading to China*, 4: 334–5.

71 Gardner, *The East India Company*, 203.

72 Wakeman, "The Canton Trade and the Opium War," 173.

73 Extracts from Dispatch of Select Committee to Governor General of India, 25 October 1831, in Morse, ed., *The Chronicles of the East India Company Trading to China*, 4: 313–20.

74 William Jardine (Canton) to Thomas Crawford (Bombay), 16 March 1832, William Jardine – Private Letter Book, MS JM, C4/2.

75 Greenberg, *British Trade and the Opening of China*, 179; William Jardine (Canton) to Thomas Weeding (London), 15 January 1831, William Jardine – Private Letter Book, MS JM, C4/1.

76 Fay, *The Opium War*, 61–2.

77 Ibid., 62.

78 Greenberg, *British Trade and the Opening of China*, 34, citing William Jardine – Private Letter Book, 10 February 1833.

79 William Jardine (Canton) to Thomas Weeding (London), 23 October 1833, William Jardine – Private Letter Book, MS JM, C4/3.

80 William Jardine (Canton) to John MacVicar (Manchester), 10 December 1833, William Jardine – Private Letter Book, MS JM, C4/3.

81 Fay, *The Opium War*, 63; Morse, ed., *The Chronicles of the East India Company Trading to China*, 4: 350, 361–6.

82 Morse, ed., *The Chronicles of the East India Company Trading to China*, 4: 360–6; Fay, *The Opium War*, 63–4.

83 *Canton Register*, 15 November 1833, 98–9. The address, which was unanimously subscribed to by the commanders and officers present, was signed by John Hine, Robert Scott, and W.R. Blakely.

84 Fay, *The Opium War*, 64; Williamson, *Eastern Traders*, 176–7; William Jardine (Canton) to John MacVicar (Manchester), 10 December 1833, and to Rev. Karl Gutzlaff (aboard *Colonel Young*), 14 December 1833, William Jardine – Private Letter Book, MS JM, C4/3.

85 William Jardine (Canton) to Rev. Karl Gutzlaff (aboard *Colonel Young*), 14 December 1833, William Jardine – Private Letter Book, MS JM, C4/3.

## CHAPTER SIX

1 Collis, *Foreign Mud*, 68.

2 Reid, "The Steel Frame," 21.

3 William Jardine (Canton) to John MacVicar (London), 16 June 1833, William Jardine – Private Letter Book, MS JM, C4/3.

4 William Jardine (Canton) to Hollingworth Magniac (Colworth, England), 23 February 1830, 2 February 1831, 3 March 1831, 4 May 1831, and July 21, 1831, William Jardine – Private Letter Book, MS JM, C4/1; William Jardine (Canton) to Hollingworth Magniac, 15 November 1833, ibid., C4/3.

5 William Jardine (Canton) to Thomas Weeding (London), 1 March 1832, William Jardine – Private Letter Book, MS JM, C4/2.

6 William Jardine (Canton) to T.D. Edwards (Sydney), 16 January 1833, William Jardine – Private Letter Book, MS JM, C4/2.

7 William Jardine (Canton) to Hollingworth Magniac (Colworth), 16 November 1830, William Jardine – Private Letter Book, MS JM, C4/1.

8 William Jardine (Canton) to Hollingworth Magniac (Colworth), 9 April, 14 April, and 16 November 1830, William Jardine – Private Letter Book, MS JM, C4/1; James Matheson (Canton) to Sir Andrew Lyningstedt (Macao), 12 May 1831, and to Mr Pearson (no address), 15 March 1832, James Matheson – Private Letter Book, MS JM, C5/1.

9 William Jardine (Canton) to T.D. Edwards (Sydney), 16 January 1833, William Jardine – Private Letter Book, MS JM, C4/2; James Matheson (Canton) to B. Barretto (Macao), 27 January 1834, James Matheson – Private Letter Book, MS JM, C5/1; James Matheson (Canton) to Claudio Adriano DaCosta (Lisbon), 18 March 1832, ibid.

10 William Jardine (Canton) to Jamsetjee Jejeebhoy (Bombay), 29 December 1832 and 27 January 1833, William Jardine – Private Letter Book, MS JM, C4/2.

11 William Jardine (Canton) to Thomas Weeding (London), 20 October 1837, William Jardine – Private Letter Book, MS JM, C4/6.

12 William Jardine (Canton) to F. Halliburton (London), 26 March 1830, William Jardine – Private Letter Book, MS JM, C4/1.

13 Collis, *Foreign Mud*, 67.

14 Their limitations in the Chinese language are suggested by that fact that in 1831 John Morrison, the son of Dr Robert Morrison, was engaged to serve as interpreter for the British merchants of Canton with an annual salary of £1,200 per year. The firm (then still Magniac's) and Dent's agreed to pay two-thirds of the cost, with the rest coming from the other merchants and the ships coming up to Whampoa. James Matheson (Canton) to Jamsetjee Jejeebhoy (Bombay), 31 January 1831, James Matheson – Private Letter Book, MS JM, C5/1.

15 Gutzlaff, *Journal of Three Voyages along the Coast of China*, chapter 1; Reid, "Karl Gutzlaff," 135; Collis, *Foreign Mud*, 69–70; Blake, *Jardine Matheson*, 46.

16  Gutzlaff, *Journal of Three Voyages along the Coast of China*, 181; Fay, *The Opium War*, 57–8.

17  Excerpts from the letter appear in Collis, *Foreign Mud*, 70, and Blake, *Jardine Matheson*, 46–7, both of whom cite the unpublished Yorke manuscript, "The Princely House," as their source.

18  Gutzlaff, *Journal of Three Voyages along the Coast of China*, 425.

19  Ibid., 427.

20  Reid, "Karl Gutzlaff," 135.

21  James Matheson (Canton) to Hugh Matheson (Calcutta), 8 December 1831, James Matheson – Private Letter Book, MS JM, C5/1. Earlier that year James had sent Hugh a bill for 15,000 rupees with instructions to invest it in opium. James Matheson to Hugh Matheson, 26 August 1831, ibid.

22  William Jardine (Canton) to I.R. Latimer (Canton), 10 September 1831, William Jardine – Private Letter Book, MS JM, C4/1.

23  William Jardine (Canton) to J. Colville (Calcutta), 18 March 1832, William Jardine – Private Letter Book, MS JM, C4/2.

24  William Jardine (Canton) to Jamsetjee Jejeebhoy (Bombay), 10 March 1831, William Jardine – Private Letter Book, MS JM, C4/1.

25  William Jardine (Canton) to Thomas Weeding (London), 11 January 1831, William Jardine – Private Letter Book, MS JM, C4/1.

26  Trocki, *Opium, Empire and the Global Political Economy*, 107, and appendix 2, 179–80.

27  James Matheson (Canton) to H.P. Hadow (Bombay), 10 March 1831, James Matheson – Private Letter Book, MS JM, C5/1.

28  William Jardine (Canton) to Jamsetjee Jejeebhoy (Bombay), 9 August and 19 December 1832, William Jardine – Private Letter Book, MS JM, C4/2.

29  William Jardine (Canton) to Jamsetjee Jejeebhoy (Bombay), 5 August 1832, and to M. DeVitre (Bombay), 7 August 1832, William Jardine – Private Letter Book, MS JM, C4/1.

30  Wiliam Jardine (Canton) to Jamsetjee Jejeebhoy (Bombay), 27 November 1831, William Jardine – Private Letter Book, MS JM, C4/1.

31  William Jardine (Canton) to M. DeVitre (Bombay), 26 November 1832, William Jardine – Private Letter Book, MS JM, C4/2. The Malwa prices had actually surged from about $465 per chest in July to as much as $850 per chest in the late fall.

32  James Matheson (Canton) to Charles Thomas (Singapore), 1 November 1833, James Matheson – Private Letter Book, MS JM, C5/1.

33  William Jardine (Canton) to M. DeVitre (Bombay), 9 March 1831, William Jardine – Private Letter Book, MS JM, C4/1.

34 William Jardine (Canton) to Jamsetjee Jejeebhoy (Bombay), 10 March 1831, William Jardine – Private Letter Book, MS JM, C4/1; James Matheson (Canton) to Hormizjee Dorabjee, 10 March 1831, James Matheson – Private Letter Book, MS JM, C5/1.

35 William Jardine (Canton) to M. DeVitre (Bombay), 10 August 1832, William Jardine – Private Letter Book, MS JM, C4/2.

36 William Jardine (Canton) to Captain Serle, 31 March 1830, Wiiliam Jardine – Private Letter Book, MS JM, C4/1 and C4/2.

37 William Jardine (Canton) to John MacVicar (Manchester), 22 October and 14 November 1832, William Jardine – Private Letter Book, MS JM, C4/2.

38 James Matheson (Canton) to Hugh Matheson (Calcutta) 15 December 1832, James Matheson – Private Letter Book, MS JM, C5/1.

39 Ibid.

40 William Jardine (Canton) to W.H. Hamilton (Hobart Town, Australia), 1 April 1831, and to Charles Thomas (Singapore), 16 December 1832, William Jardine – Private Letter Book, MS JM, C4/1 and C4/2.

41 William Jardine (Canton) to J.H. Zobel (Manila), 26 November 1832, William Jardine – Private Letter Book, MS JM, C4/2. The letter books do not reveal whether this deal was actually achieved.

42 William Jardine (Canton) to Charles Marjoribanks (London), 2 January 1833, William Jardine – Private Letter Book, MS JM, C4/2.

43 William Jardine (Canton) to Thomas Weeding (London), 5 May 1831 and 7 May 1832, and to J.W. Graham (London), 24 February 1831 and 6 May 1831, William Jardine – Private Letter Book, MS JM, C4/1 and C4/2.

44 William Jardine (Canton) to Thomas Weeding (London), 27 February 1831, William Jardine – Private Letter Book, MS JM, C4/1.

45 James Matheson (Canton) to Henry Piddington (Calcutta), 6 April 1832, James Matheson – Private Letter Book, MS JM, C5/1.

46 William Jardine (Canton) to C. McLeod (Bombay), 22 December 1832, William Jardine – Private Letter Book, MS JM, C4/2.

47 William Jardine (Canton) to Thomas Weeding (London), 11 December 1832, William Jardine – Private Letter Book, MS JM, C4/2.

48 Reid, "Spreading Risks," 181.

49 "Matheson has been … on a trip to Calcutta. His absence and the press of business must plead my excuse for not addressing you earlier," Jardine wrote to J.F. Davis at the EIC headquarters in London. William Jardine (Canton) to J.F. Davis (London), 3 April 1830, William Jardine – Private Letter Book, MS JM, C4/1.

50 The partners expressed their gratitude to Magniac in a letter that Matheson wrote to him in March 1834, indicating at the same time that he was about to set out for Bombay again. James Matheson (Macao) to Hollingworth Magniac (Colworth), 8 March 1834, James Matheson – Private Letter Book, MS JM, C5/1.

51 William Jardine (Canton) to Jamsetjee Jejeebhoy (Bombay), 21 August 1833, and to M. de Vitre (Bombay), 21 August 1833, William Jardine – Private Letter Book, MS JM, C/2.

52 William Jardine (Canton) to Jamsetjee Jejeebhoy (Bombay), 3 May 1834, William Jardine – Private Letter Book, MS JM, C4/3.

53 William Jardine (Canton) to Captain MacKay (brig *Fairy* off the coast of China), 3 March, 9 May, and n.d. [mid-May] 1834; to James Matheson (en route to India and at Singapore on return journey), 1 April and 10 June 1834; and to Hugh Matheson (Calcutta), 27 May 1834, William Jardine – Private Letter Book, MS JM, C4/3.

54 William Jardine (Canton) to Captain MacKay of the *Fairy* (at Lintin and along the coast of China), 3 March, 9 May, n.d. [mid-May], and 11 June 1834, William Jardine – Private Letter Book, MS JM, C4/3.

55 William Jardine (Canton) to Thomas Weeding (London), 16 November 1833, and to Mr Thomson (location unknown), 30 February 1834, William Jardine – Private Letter Book, MS JM, C4/3.

56 William Jardine (Canton) to Thomas Weeding (London), 16 November 1833, William Jardine – Private Letter Book, MS JM, C4/3.

57 William Jardine (Canton) to Thomas Weeding (London), 18 March 1834, William Jardine – Private Letter Book, MS JM, C4/3.

58 William Jardine (Canton) to James Matheson (en route to India), 22 March 1834, and to Thomas Weeding (London), 20 April 1834, William Jardine – Private Letter Book, MS JM, C4/3.

59 Ibid.

60 Van Dyke, *Merchants of Canton and Macao,* 12–13.

61 William Jardine (Canton) to W.F. Copeland (London), 26 April 1834, William Jardine – Private Letter Book, MS JM, C4/3.

62 William Jardine (Canton) to Henry Templer (London), 31 January 1834, William Jardine – Private Letter Book, MS JM, C4/3.

63 Collis, *Foreign Mud,* 96.

64 Melancon, "Peaceful Intentions," 38.

65 Ibid., 40, citing letter from Grey to Napier, 10 January 1834, Grey Papers.

66 Fay, *The Opium War,* 68–9; Blake, *Jardine Matheson,* 64.

67 Collis, *Foreign Mud*, 113.

68 Melancon, "Peaceful Intentions," 41.

69 Napier, *Barbarian Eye*, 112, 153. She takes a strongly negative view of Jardine.

70 The title "viceroy" was a European form of reference for a Chinese provincial governor.

71 Blake, *Jardine Matheson*, 70.

72 William Jardine (Canton) to Thomas Weeding (London), 23 October 1833, William Jardine – Private Letter Book, MS JM, C4/3.

73 Letter from William Jardine (Canton) to Thomas Weeding (London), 11 June 1834, William Jardine – Private Letter Book, MS JM, C4/3.

74 Lord Napier (Canton) to Mark Napier (Edinburgh), 3 August 1834, Napier Papers, National Library of Scotland, Edinburgh. Collis, who relies on the unpublished Yorke manuscript, asserts in his vivid narrative *Foreign Mud* (114) that Napier accepted Jardine's offer and installed his family in the house which was owned by the firm. Fay, *The Opium War* (68), reports that the house in which they stayed belonged to Captain Alexander Grant of the *Hercules*, one of the Jardine, Matheson floating warehouse ships.

75 Collis, *Foreign Mud*, 114; Fay, *The Opium War*, 68–9.

76 Blake, *Jardine Matheson*, 66.

77 Fay, *The Opium War*, 69, citing *Correspondence Relating to China*, 1840, 36 (223): 5, PP.

78 Collis, *Foreign Mud*, 115; Blake, *Jardine Matheson*, 66; Fay, *The Opium War*, 69–70. Melancon, "Peaceful Intentions" (41), maintains that "while Napier's views coincided with those held by the British merchants, he arrived at them independently and in opposition to his instructions from home." Melancon challenges the interpretations of Greenberg (*British Trade and the Opening of China*), Collis (*Foreign Mud*), and Chang (*Commissioner Lin and the Opium War*) that the free traders had significantly shaped Napier's thinking. However, his argument does not account sufficiently for the regular and continued influence of Jardine as Napier's confidant during these months. Had Jardine been resistant to Napier's strong views, the superintendent would not have maintained their close relationship or he would have been swayed toward a more moderate tone in his approach to the viceroy and the Hong merchants.

79 *Chinese Repository*, August 1834, 3: 189.

80 Ibid., September 1834, 3: 235.

81 Ibid., 3: 236.

82 Lord Napier (Canton) to Mark Napier (Edinburgh), 3 August 1834, Napier Papers; Fay, *The Opium War*, 70–1; Collis, *Foreign Mud*, 116–17; Blake, *Jardine Matheson*, 66–7.

83 Blake, *Jardine Matheson*, 67.

84 Hunter, *The "Fan Kwae" at Canton*, 64.

85 Fay, *The Opium War*, 71.

86 Lord Napier (Canton) to Mark Napier (Edinburgh), 3 August 1834, Napier Papers.

87 William Jardine (Canton) to John MacVicar (Manchester), 20 August 1834, and to Thomas Weeding (London), 21 August 1834, William Jardine – Private Letter Book, MS JM, C4/3.

88 Fay, *The Opium War*, 72.

89 Quoted in Collis, *Foreign Mud*, 130.

90 Ibid., 145

91 Fay, *The Opium War*, 74–5.

92 Lord Napier (Canton) to Mark Napier (Edinburgh), 17 August 1834, Napier Papers.

93 William Jardine (Canton) to Jamsetjee Jejeebhoy (Bombay), 6 September 1834, William Jardine – Private Letter Book, MS JM, C4/3.

94 Lord Napier (Canton) to Mark Napier (Edinburgh), 17 August 1834, Napier Papers.

95 It was Chinese policy that foreign ships proceeding past the Bocca Tigris had to be trading vessels with trade goods aboard. Van Dyke, *The Canton Trade*, 166.

96 Williams, "Recollections of China prior to 1840," 5.

97 Fay, *The Opium War*, 75–7; Collis, *Foreign Mud*, 150–2.

98 James Matheson (Canton) to John Purvis (Singapore) and to H.P. Hadow (Bombay), 25 September 1834, James Matheson – Private Letter Book, MS JM, C5/2.

99 Fay, *The Opium War*, 78.

100 Nye, "The Morning of My Life in China," 40.

101 *Canton Register*, 23 September 1834, 150.

102 Fay, *The Opium War*, 78; Collis, *Foreign Mud*, 160.

103 *Canton Register*, 23 September 1834, 153. In that same issue, the editor was calling for a British blockade of the port of Canton.

104 Ibid., 7 October 1834, 158. The editor commented: "More wanton cruelty to one suffering from fever cannot be imagined."

105 William Jardine (Canton) to H. Hadow (Bombay), 9 October 1834, William Jardine – Private Letter Book, MS JM, C4/3.

106 Fay, *The Opium War*, 79; *Chinese Repository*, October 1834, 3: 283.

107 *Canton Register*, 14 October 1834, 1; Dr Colledge's notes on the painful voyage are excerpted in the same issue. *Chinese Repository*, October 1834, 3: 281; Collis, *Foreign Mud*, 163. The funeral sermon for Napier was preached at Canton on Sunday, 16 October, by Rev. Elijah Bridgman, editor of the *Repository*.

108 Wakeman, "The Canton Trade and the Opium War," 175.

109 Melancon, "Peaceful Intentions," 46.

110 Nye, "The Morning of My Life in China," 15.

111 William Jardine (Canton) to J.H. Gledstanes (London), 27 September 1835, William Jardine – Private Letter Book, MS JM, C4/4. Jardine vigorously denied that Napier had ever received the Hong merchants.

112 William Jardine (Canton) to Thomas Weeding (London), 11 June 1834, Willliam Jardine – Private Letter Book, MS JM, C4/3.

113 Napier, *Barbarian Eye*, 205.

114 William Jardine (Canton) to Thomas Weeding (London), 23 October 1834, William Jardine – Private Letter Book, MS JM, C4/3.

### CHAPTER SEVEN

1 James Matheson (Canton) to Robert Lyall (Calcutta), 4 December 1834, James Matheson – Private Letter Book, MS JM, C5/2.

2 The quote, drawn from J. Phipps, *A Practical Treatise on China and the Eastern Trade* (1836), appears in Greenberg, *British Trade and the Opening of China*, 193.

3 The Chamber would be expanded in 1836 to include non-British foreigners, particularly Parsis and Americans. Although the Chamber had no coercive powers, it did establish the first formal mechanism for the resolution of commercial disputes, usually by means of the appointment of an arbiter. In the last analysis its influence was that of moral suasion, by directing the force of community opinion against offenders. Downes, *The Golden Ghetto*, 103–4.

4 Van Dyke, *The Canton Trade*, 139, 170.

5 William Jardine (Canton) to Jamsetjee Jejeebhoy (Bombay), 8 November and 23 December 1834, William Jardine – Private Letter Book, MS JM, C4/3.

6 William Jardine (Canton) to M. de Vitre (London), 28 February 1834, William Jardine – Private Letter Book, MS JM, C4/4.

7 Van Dyke, *The Canton Trade*, 139–40.

8  Blake, *Jardine Matheson*, 75.

9  "Memorial to the King's Most Excellent Majesty in Council (Petition of the Undermentioned British Subjects at Canton)," 1834, as published with James Matheson's *Present Position and Future Prospects of the British Trade with China*; also published in the *Canton Repository*, December 1834, 3: 354–60.

10  On 3 March 1835 a notice on the front page of the *Register* reported that Wright, Johnstone, and A. Matheson had been admitted as partners in the firm of Jardine, Matheson.

11  Fay, *The Opium War*, 79, citing *Correspondence relating to China*, 1840, 36 (223): 115, PP.

12  The vessels in question were the *Berkshire* and the *Hythe*, whose teas would be able to reach Britain before those under management of Jardine, Matheson and other firms. William Jardine (Canton) to Thomas Weeding (London), 12 December 1834; to Henry Templer (London), 29 December 1834; and to John MacVicar (Manchester), 15 January 1835, William Jardine – Private Letter Book, MS JM, C4/3 and C4/4.

13  William Jardine (Canton) to Henry Templer (London), 29 December 1834 and 15 January 1835, William Jardine – Private Letter Book, MS JM, C4/4.

14  William Jardine (Canton) to Hollingworth Magniac (London), 26 February 1835, William Jardine –Private Letter Book, MS JM, C4/4.

15  James Matheson (Canton) to Robert Lyall (Calcutta), 4 December 1834, James Matheson – Private Letter Book, MS JM, C5/2. His scrivener for the moment was his nephew, Alexander Matheson.

16  William Jardine (Canton) to James Stewart (Gillembie, near Lockerby, Scotland), 1 March 1835, William Jardine – Private Letter Book, MS JM, C4/4.

17  William Jardine (Canton) to Hollingworth Magniac (London), 26 February 1835, William Jardine – Private Letter Book, MS JM, C4/4.

18  William Jardine (Canton) to Andrew Johnstone (Macao), 13 March 1835, William Jardine – Private Letter Book, MS JM, C4/4.

19  William Jardine (Canton) to Thomas Weeding (London), 27 February 1835, William Jardine – Private Letter Book, MS JM, C4/4.

20  William Jardine (Canton) to Lady Napier, 28 February 1835, William Jardine – Private Letter Book, MS JM, C4/4.

21  James Matheson (London) to William Jardine (Canton), 8 July 1835, London Private, MS JM, B1/10.

22  James Matheson (London) to William Jardine (Canton), 11 July 1835, London Private, MS JM, B1/10.

23 James Matheson (London) to William Jardine (Canton), 1 August 1835, London Private, MS JM, B1/10.

24 James Matheson (Canton) to Andrew Johnstone (Halleaths), 9 December 1837, James Matheson – Private Letter Book, MS JM, C5/2. As a friend and patient of Jephson, Matheson was in famous company, for Jephson's other patients included Princess Victoria, King George IV, William E. Gladstone, John Ruskin, and Florence Nightingale.

25 James Matheson (Inverness) to William Jardine (Canton), 24 August 1835, Great Britain – Private, MS JM, B1/8. At some point in his travels he called on Lady Napier, whom he regarded as a "noble lady." He reported that she was feeling deeply hurt that the government had done nothing to address the wrongs inflicted upon her husband.

26 Particularly useful to him were Peter Auber's *China: An Outline of Its Government, Laws and Policy, and of the British and Foreign Embassies to, and Intercourse with, That Empire* (1834), and James Holman's *A Voyage round the World*, volume 4 (1835). In a prefatory note ("advertisement") to the tract, Matheson acknowledges that he has "occasionally adopted the felicitous language of his admirable friend Mr. Holman."

27 Matheson, *Present Position and Future Prospects of the British Trade with China*, 1.

28 Ibid., 3.

29 Ibid., 5–6.

30 Ibid., 33–4. In this portion of the treatise, Matheson relies on the natural-law principles of Emerich de Vattel, the eighteenth-century Swiss philosopher and jurist, whose *Droit de gens* (1758; translated as *The Law of Nations*, 1760) posited that natural law was superior to positive governmental legislation as a source of international law. He cites Vattel as writing that it is a fundamental maxim of the natural law "that it is the duty of nations to fulfill their engagements, whether express or tacit."

31 Ibid., 40. For corroboration he quotes Auber: "Whole fleets detained when on the point of sailing!"

32 Ibid., 44.

33 Ibid., 51.

34 Ibid., 55.

35 Ibid., 61; emphasis in original. Matheson held the emperor responsible for the treatment of Lord Napier, because he had ratified the actions of the local authorities and even awarded them honours for having expelled the "Barbarian Eye" (54, 67).

36  Ibid. He calls attention to the petition of the Canton merchants (on which he was the second signatory), and specifically mentions their advice that the plenipotentiary take up a position on the east cost of China, not far from Peking, aboard a Royal Navy ship of the line with sufficient additional maritime force to impress the Chinese.

37  Memorial of the president, vice-president, and directors of the Chamber of Commerce and Manufactures at Manchester, February 1836, as published with Matheson's *Present Position and Future Prospects of the British Trade with China.*

38  Memorial of the Liverpool East India Association, February 1836, as published with ibid.; and Memorial of the Glasgow East India Association, June 1835, also published with ibid.

39  Ibid.

40  William Jardine (Canton) to James Matheson (in Britain), 3 November 1835, William Jardine – Private Letter Book, MS JM, C4/4.

41  James Matheson to George Armstrong (Liverpool) and J. Garnett (Clithero), 21 January 1836, James Matheson – Private Letter Book, MS JM, C5/2.

42  William Jardine (Canton) to James Matheson (c/o Thomas Weeding, London), 24 and 28 December 1835; Jardine to John MacVicar (Manchester), 30 December 1835, William Jardine – Private Letter Book, MS JM, C4/4.

43  William Jardine (Canton) to Captain McKay (brig *Fairy* at Lintin Island), 30 November 1834, William Jardine – Private Letter Book, MS JM, C4/3.

44  The mandarins were Chinese civil servants ranked hierarchically, with rank indicated by the colour of buttons on their caps.

45  William Jardine (Canton) to Captain John Rees (barque *Colonel Young* on the coast of China), 9 March 1835, William Jardine – Private Letter Book, MS JM, C4/4.

46  Fay, "The Opening of China," 65. Until the end of the EIC's monopoly at Canton, the Americans traded largely in Turkish opium, but they gradually shifted over to Indian opium in the second half of the 1830s. In volume of sales Russell was behind only the two biggest British firms, Jardine, Matheson and Dent, but it announced in 1839 that it would discontinue its opium trade. Downes, *The Golden Ghetto*, 127–8.

47  Downes, *The Golden Ghetto*, 127–8. Malwa came from the princely territories in India, rather than the regions dominated by the EIC. Patna and Benares opium cases were shipped from Calcutta, whereas Malwa initially slipped out of remote coastal regions of western India, to avoid Company control. After EIC commercial operations ended, Malwa was sent out of Bombay.

48 James Matheson (Canton) to M. Uriarte (Calcutta), 17 December 1832, James Matheson – Private Letter Book, MS JM, C5/1.

49 William Jardine (Canton) to P. Niell (Lucknow), 15 July 1834, William Jardine – Private Letter Book, MS JM, C4/3. Jardine reported that the 1832–33 season was extraordinary, bringing in $15,352,429 for 28,003 chests of opium – the largest sum of money ever spent on the drug in one season.

50 William Jardine (Canton) to M. DeVitre (Bombay), 7 April 1833 and 22 May 1833, and to Thomas Weeding (London), 12 July 1833, William Jardine – Private Letter Book, MS JM, C4/2 and C4/3.

51 William Jardine to Captain John Rees (barque *Colonel Young* on the coast of China), 16 February 1835, William Jardine – Private Letter Book, MS JM, C4/4.

52 William Jardine (Canton) to H.K. George (Singapore), 22 July 1835, William Jardine – Private Letter Book, MS JM, C4/4.

53 William Jardine (Canton) to Captain Clifton (aboard *Red Rover* at Macao Roads), 13 March 1835, William Jardine – Private Letter Book, MS JM, C4/4.

54 Ibid. Clifton was the builder and original owner of the *Red Rover*.

55 William Jardine (Canton) to Andrew Johnstone (Macao), 13 March 1835, William Jardine – Private Letter Book, MS JM, C4/4.

56 William Jardine (Canton) to Hugh Matheson (Calcutta), 22 July 1835, William Jardine – Private Letter Book, MS JM, C4/4.

57 William Jardine (Canton) to Captain Rees (aboard *Colonel Young*), 14 August 1835, William Jardine – Private Letter Book, MS JM, C4/4.

58 William Jardine (Canton) to Hugh Matheson (Calcutta), 5 September 1835, William Jardine – Private Letter Book, MS JM, C4/4.

59 William Jardine (Canton) to James Matheson (London), 13 September 1835, William Jardine – Private Letter Book, MS JM, C4/4.

60 Lubbock, *The Opium Clippers*, 116–18. A lac was 100,000 rupees. The *Sylph*, minus her cargo, was refloated, proved durable, and remained in the opium trade for many years.

61 William Jardine (Canton) to James Matheson (c/o Thomas Weeding, London), 23 April 1835, and to Robert Lyall (Calcutta), 4 May 1835, William Jardine – Private Letter Book, MS JM, C4/4; Reid, "The Shipping Interest," 77.

62 William Jardine (Canton) to Captain Ovenstone (aboard barque *Falcon*), 23 April 1835; Jardine (Canton) to Captain Ovenstone, 7 September 1835; Jardine to James Matheson (London), 13 September 1835, William

Jardine – Private Letter Book, MS JM, C4/4. Also, Jardine (Canton) to John Shillaber (Manila), 2 April 1836, William Jardine – Private Letter Book, MS JM, C4/5; and Fay, "The Opening of China," 77.

63  Lubbock, *The China Clippers*, 9–10. Lubbock says that the *Falcon* was the only shiprigged (square-rigged) opium clipper that he is aware of. The barque was 113 feet long and carried 22 guns when it was in military service prior to its years in Jardine's fleet.

64  Ibid., 137–8.

65  Fay, "The Opening of China," 69–70.

66  Greenberg, *British Trade and the Opening of China*, 192.

67  Collis, *Foreign Mud*, 181.

68  Ibid., 182.

69  William Jardine (Canton) to James Matheson (c/o Thomas Weeding, London), 24 December 1835, William Jardine – Private Letter Book, MS JM, C4/4. Robinson had been drawing a salary of £6,000.

70  Fay, *The Opium War*, 80; Collis, *Foreign Mud*, 182–3. Palmerston had decided in June 1836 to dismiss Sir George Robinson from the chief superintendent's post and to appoint Sir Charles Elliot to succeed him. Blake, *Jardine Matheson*, 79.

71  Collis, *Foreign Mud*, 195.

72  Fay, *The Opium War*, 82.

73  Greenberg, *British Trade and the Opening of China*, 200, citing "Correspondence In" (loose letters), Jardine, Matheson Archive, 18 November 1837.

74  Fay, citing *Correspondence Relating to China*, 1840, 36 (223): 190, PP.

75  William Jardine (Canton) to Captain MacKay (aboard *Fairy*), 1 June 1836, William Jardine – Private Letter Book, MS JM, C4/5.

76  William Jardine (Canton) to Captain Rees (aboard *Colonel Young*), 12 April 1835, and Captain Jauncey (aboard *Austin*), 21 July 1835 and 29 August 1835, William Jardine – Private Letter Book, MS JM, C4/4.

77  William Jardine (Canton) to Captain Jauncey (aboard *Austin*), 21 July 1835, William Jardine – Private Letter Book, MS JM, C4/4.

78  Summary of letter from William Jardine (Canton) to Captain McKay (aboard *Fairy*), 29 August, 1835, William Jardine – Private Letter Book, MS JM, C4/4.

79  William Jardine (Canton) to Captain Ovenstone (aboard *Lady Hayes*), 20 March 1836, William Jardine – Private Letter Book, MS JM, C4/5.

80  William Jardine (Canton) to H.P. Hadow (Calcutta), 5 September 1835, William Jardine – Private Letter Book, MS JM, C4/4 .

81 William Jardine (Canton) to James Matheson (c/o Thomas Weeding, London), 3 November 1835, William Jardine – Private Letter Book, MS JM, C4/4.

82 Rumours that Peking might legalize the sale of opium drove drug prices higher; but when the rumours turned out to be inaccurate, the prices fell sharply. Trocki, *Opium, Empire and the Global Political Economy*, 99.

83 Van Dyke, *The Canton Trade*, 138. The outward drain of sycee was very costly to China.

84 William Jardine (Canton) to Jamsetjee Jejeebhoy (Bombay), 7 July 1836; to H.K. George (Singapore), 22 July, 1836; and to Captain Rees (aboard *Austin*), 26 July 1836, William Jardine – Private Letter Book, MS JM, C4/5; Blake, *Jardine Matheson*, 80-1.

85 Van Dyke, *Merchants of Canton and Macao*, 10.

86 Van Dyke, *The Canton Trade*, 162.

87 Trocki, *Opium, Empire and the Global Political Economy*, 97.

88 Collis, *Foreign Mud*, 185.

89 Van Dyke, *The Canton Trade*, 162.

90 Ibid., 138.

91 Ibid., 172.

92 William Jardine (Canton) to T.W. Henderson (Bombay), 5 November 1836, William Jardine – Private Letter Book, MS JM, C4/5; Greenberg, *British Trade and the Opening of China*, 198; Fay, *The Opium War*, 118. When the opium trade was legalized by the Treaty of Tianjin, following the Second Opium War (or Arrow War), in 1860, the effect was, as Jardine and Alexander Matheson had feared, to undercut the advantages that agency houses like Jardine, Matheson had previously enjoyed in the drug trade. Trocki, *Opium, Empire and the Global Political Economy*, 110.

93 William Jardine (Canton) to Captain Rees (aboard *Austin*), 3 November 1836, William Jardine – Private Letter Book, MS JM, C4/5.

94 Edict from the governor, 28 October 1830, published in the *Canton Register*, 1 November 1836, 180; Melancon, *Britain's China Policy and the Opium Crisis*, 70.

95 William Jardine (Canton) to Howqua, senior Hong merchant, and the other members of the Cohong, 4 November 1836, William Jardine – Private Letter Book, MS JM, C4/5.

96 Edict from the governor, December 13, 1836, published in the *Canton Register*, 20 December 1836, 120.

97 Chang, *Commissioner Lin and the Opium War*, 98; William Jardine (Canton) to Howqua and the other Cohong members, 26 November 1836, William Jardine – Private Letter Book, MS JM, C4/5.

98 *Chinese Repository*, November 1836, 5: 336.

99 William Jardine (Canton) to Jamsetjee Jejeebhoy (Bombay), 17 March 1835, William Jardine – Private Letter Book, MS JM, C4/4.

100 William Jardine (Canton) to Captain Jauncey (aboard *Austin*), 9 November 1835, William Jardine – Private Letter Book, MS JM, C4/4.

101 William Jardine (Canton) to Jamsetjee Jejeebhoy (Bombay), 7 March 1836, William Jardine – Private Letter Book, MS JM, C4/5.

102 William Jardine (Canton) to Captain Jauncey (aboard *Austin*), 15 July 1835, and to Captain Mackenzie (aboard *Governor Findlay*), 5 June 1836, William Jardine – Private Letter Book, MS JM, C4/4 and C4/5. Mackenzie was treated to some of Jardine's own grapeshot for being too liberal with his gunpowder and saluting an American warship at Cumsingmoon. "The Commodore would have felt more obliged to you had you not put his civility to the test [by requiring a return of the compliment]. Reserve your powder for more useful purposes."

103 William Jardine (Canton) to T.W. Henderson (Bombay), 17 November 1836, William Jardine – Private Letter Book, MS JM, C4/5; James Matheson (Canton) to E. Bonstead (Singapore), 22 December 1836, and to Captain Larkins, 21 November 1836, James Matheson – Private Letter Book, MS JM, C5/2.

104 William Jardine (Canton) to James Matheson (c/o Thomas Weeding, London), 3 November 1835, William Jardine – Private Letter Book, MS JM, C4/4.

105 William Jardine (Canton) to Andrew Thomson (Bonside, Linlithgow, Scotland), 29 February, 1836, William Jardine – Private Letter Book, MS JM, C4/5.

106 William Jardine (Canton) to Thomas Weeding (London), 11 October 1836, William Jardine – Private Letter Book, MS JM, C4/5.

107 William Jardine (Canton) to Andrew Thomson (Bonside, Linlithgow, Scotland), 29 February, 1836, William Jardine – Private Letter Book, MS JM, C4/5.

108 William Jardine (Canton) to J.H. Gledstanes (London), 16 April 1836, and to James Jardine (Edinburgh), 9 May 1836, William Jardine – Private Letter Book, MS JM, C4/5.

109 William Jardine (Canton) to Howqua et al., 9 and 18 December 1836, William Jardine – Private Letter Book, MS JM, C4/5.

110 William Jardine (Canton) to James Matheson (c/o Thomas Weeding, London), 24 November 1835, William Jardine – Private Letter Book, MS JM, C4/4.

111 William Jardine (Canton) to H.P. Hadow (Bombay), 2 February 1836; to D.L. Burn (Bombay), 10 February 1836; to J.H. Gledstanes (London), 16 February 1836; to Jamsetjee Jejeebhoy (Bombay), 27 February 1836; and to George Moffat (London), 16 April 1836, William Jardine – Private Letter Book, MS JM, C4/5.

112 William Jardine to Thomas Weeding (London), 15 May 1836, William Jardine – Private Letter Book, MS JM, C4/5.

113 William Jardine to John Shillaber (Manila), 27 May 1836; to R.W. Henderson (Bombay), 28 May 1836; and to John Thacker (London), 3 December 1836, William Jardine – Private Letter Book, MS JM, C4/5.

114 Alan Reid, in conversation with this author, indicated that Jardine's stomach troubles began in 1835. Jardine makes passing reference to the problem in letters written in late August 1835. William Jardine – Private Letter Book, MS JM, C4/4.

115 James Matheson (Canton) to Andrew Johnstone (Halleaths, Scotland), 9 December 1837, James Matheson – Private Letter Book, MS JM, C5/2.

116 Gulick, *Peter Parker and the Opening of China*, 151–2.

117 Downes, *The Golden Ghetto*, 25, 98. When families of the partners of Western firms began settling at Macao, they received the best available medical treatment, which was paid for by the firms that secured private physicians on annual retainer.

118 Gulick, *Peter Parker and the Opening of China*, 72. Jardine chaired the initial meeting that prepared the constitution and by-laws. He was elected one of the vice-presidents of the society.

119 Nye, *The Morning of My Life in China*, 54–5.

120 Fay, *The Opium War*, 92–4.

121 Ibid., 96, 136.

## CHAPTER EIGHT

1 Greenberg, *British Trade and the Opening of China*, 201; Fay, *The Opium War*, 119. At the House of Commons Select Committee hearings in May 1840, Jardine testified that the viceroy had four boats flying his flag carrying opium up the river. Great Britain, Parliament, House of Commons, Report of the Select Committee on the China Trade, 1840, 95. Slade offered the same judgment to readers of the *Canton Register* in December

1838: "We consider that the governor, or to speak more generally, the local government, are the most blame worthy parties in this question of river smuggling, which had been practiced in the most open and undisguised manner for the last 18 months at least." *Canton Register*, 13 December 1838, 101.

2 Fay, *The Opium War*, 119.

3 Van Dyke, *The Canton Trade*, 162.

4 William Jardine (Canton) to Jamsetjee Jejeebhoy (Bombay), 10 January 1836, and to J.H. Gledstanes (London), 16 February 1836, William Jardine – Private Letter Book, MS JM, C4/4.

5 William Jardine (Canton) to Capatin MacKay (aboard *Fairy*), 1 June 1836, William Jardine – Private Letter Book, MS JM, C4/5.

6 In July 1837 Dent's ship *Lord Amherst* fired upon and sank one of the Chinese war junks that had been stationed close by the *Lord Amherst* in order to obstruct deliveries of the drug to smugglers. Cheong, *Mandarins and Merchants*, 35.

7 Fairbank, *Trade and Diplomacy on the China Coast*, 71.

8 William Jardine (Canton) to Captain Rees (aboard *Colonel Young*), 1 and 12 April 1836, William Jardine – Private Letter Book, MS JM, C4/5.

9 William Jardine (Canton) to Captain Jauncey (aboard *Austin*), 5 June 1836, and to Captain J. Rees (*Colonel Young*), 30 June 1836, William Jardine – Private Letter Book, MS JM, C4/5.

10 William Jardine (Canton) to Captain J. Rees (aboard *Colonel Young*), 12 April and 4 June 1836, and to Captain MacKay (aboard *Fairy*), 1 June 1836, William Jardine – Private Letter Book, MS JM, C4/5.

11 William Jardine (Canton) to Captain J. Rees (aboard *Colonel Young*), 5 September 1836, William Jardine – Private Letter Book, MS JM, C4/5.

12 William Jardine (Canton) to Captain John Rees (aboard *Colonel Young*), 24 September 1836; to Captain Jauncey (aboard *Austin*), 24 September 1836; and to Captain MacKenzie (aboard *Governor Findlay*), 25 September 1836, William Jardine – Private Letter Book, MS JM, C4/5.

13 William Jardine (Canton) to Captain Rees (aboard *Austin*), 20 November 1836, William Jardine – Private Letter Book, MS JM, C4/5.

14 Lubbock, *The Opium Clippers*, 102.

15 Ibid., 103; William Jardine (Canton) to Captain Rees (aboard *Austin*), 27 January and 17 February 1836, and to John Shillaber (Manila), 27 February 1836, William Jardine – Private Letter Book, MS JM, C4/5; James Matheson (Canton) to Colonel McInnes (Inverness), 30 April 1838, James Matheson – Private Letter Book, MS JM, C5/3.

16 William Jardine (Canton) to John Shillaber (Manila), 31 January 1837, William Jardine – Private Letter Book, MS JM, C4/5; James Matheson (Canton) to Colonel McInnes (Inverness), 30 April 1837, and to J.A. Stewart Mackenzie (Ceylon), 11 April 1837, James Matheson – Private Letter Book, MS JM, C5/3.

17 Wakeman, "The Canton Trade and the Opium War," 178.

18 Cheong, *Mandarins and Merchants*, 133.

19 Respondentia agreements were loans to shipowners with the cargo serving as collateral for the loan.

20 Cheong, *Mandarins and Merchants*, 238–9.

21 Ibid., 240–1; Greenberg, *British Trade and the Opening of China*, 167–8, citing Jardine correspondence, 9 February 1835.

22 Cheong, *Mandarins and Merchants*, 244.

23 William Jardine (Canton) to John Shillaber (Manila), 11 August 1837, William Jardine – Private Letter Book, MS JM, C4/6.

24 James Matheson (Canton) to William Lyall (London), 9 December 1837, James Matheson – Private Letter Book, MS JM, C5/2.

25 James Matheson (Canton) to Captain Alexander Grant (London), 20 October 1837, James Matheson – Private Letter Book, MS JM, C5/2.

26 James Matheson (Canton) to John Abel Smith (London), 9 September 1837, James Matheson – Private Letter Book, MS JM, C5/2.

27 William Jardine (Canton) to Hollingworth Magniac (London), 26 August 1837, William Jardine – Private Letter Book, MS JM, C4/6.

28 Nye, "The Morning of My Life in China," 27.

29 Cheong, *Mandarins and Merchants*, 245.

30 William Jardine (Canton) to Jamsetjee Jejeebhoy (Bombay), 20 August 1837, William Jardine – Private Letter Book, MS JM, C4/6.

31 William Jardine (Canton) to Jamsetjee Jejeebhoy (Bombay), 19 October 1837, William Jardine – Private Letter Book, MS JM, C4/6.

32 William Jardine (Canton) to T.W. Henderson (Bombay), 6 September 1837, William Jardine – Private Letter Book, MS JM, C4/6.

33 James Matheson (Canton) to William Lyall (London), 9 December 1837, James Matheson – Private Letter Book, MS JM, C5/2. Not all the news was bad. Matheson could report that the government of Bengal had granted the partners a "magnificent bonus" to cover their loss stemming from incautious opium purchases made for the firm by Lyall Matheson.

34 James Matheson (Canton) to John Abel Smith (London), 11 December 1837, James Matheson – Private Letter Book, MS JM, C5/2.

35  William Jardine (Canton) to Thomas Weeding (London), 31 May 1837 and 26 August 1837, William Jardine – Private Letter Book, MS JM, C4/6.

36  William Jardine (Canton) to Thomas Weeding (London), 3 December 1838, William Jardine – Private Letter Book, MS JM, C4/7. This is an accurate quotation from the letter as it appears in the Letter Book.

37  Cheong, *Mandarins and Merchants,* 159–60. The Chinese government prohibited shipments of more than 100 piculs of silk in any one vessel. So Jardine, Matheson sometimes stored silk in their opium vessels at Lintin until a favourable opportunity arose for sending them forward to England. James Matheson (Canton) to Robert Garnett (Manchester), 22 November 1836, James Matheson – Private Letter Book, MS JM, C5/2.

38  William Jardine (Canton) to John MacVicar (Manchester), 11 January 1836, William Jardine – Private Letter Book, MS JM, C4/4.

39  Cheong, *Mandarins and Merchants,* 163.

40  James Matheson (Canton) to John MacVicar (Manchester), 24 December 1836, James Matheson – Private Letter Book, MS JM, C5/2.

41  William Jardine (Canton) to John MacVicar (Manchester), 19 January 1837, William Jardine – Private Letter Book, MS JM, C5/3. Cheong (*Mandarins and Merchants,* 166) calls Thom's conduct a "curious lapse into commercial spying." Oddly, while this rift was developing, MacVicar was having an engraved portrait of Matheson printed for distribution, likely a result of the role Matheson had played in rallying English merchants during his trip home. With manifest unease, Matheson wrote to MacVicar in January 1838, saying: "I cannot but feel extremely sorry that under the circumstances you should not have paused before giving effect to the plan … I hope however you will consider me entitled to claim from you the purchase of the plate & copyright which pray put to my debt or rather that of the house."

42  James Matheson (Canton) to Robert Lyall (London), 15 March 1837; to John Abel Smith (London), 3 May 1837; and to Charles Lyall (Calcutta), 18 August 1837, James Matheson – Private Letter Book, MS JM, C5/2 and C5/3; William Jardine (Canton) to Andrew Johnstone (London), 4 April 1837, William Jardine – Private Letter Book, MS JM, C4/6.

43  James Matheson (Canton) to James Walkinshaw (London), 1 August 1838, James Matheson – Private Letter Book, MS JM, C5/3.

44  Law, "Macvicar, John," *ODNB,* http://www.oxforddnb.com.helin.uri.edu:80/view/article/60314 (accessed 7 July 2005). MacVicar and Company was still practising business at Canton as of 1848, and his firm

had taken part in the foundation of the colony of Hong Kong by purchasing lots there when the first land offerings were made available in 1841.

45 Greenberg, *British Trade and the Opening of China*, 189–90; Cheong, *Mandarins and Merchants*, 161.

46 William Jardine (Canton) to John MacVicar (Manchester), 11 January 1836 and 26 April 1836, William Jardine – Private Letter Book, MS JM, C4/5.

47 William Jardine (Canton) to Henry Templer (London), 14 May 1836, William Jardine – Private Letter Book, MS JM, C4/5.

48 William Jardine (Canton) to J.H. Gledstanes (London), 5 April 1836, William Jardine – Private Letter Book, MS JM, C4/5.

49 Greenberg, *British Trade and the Opening of China*, 190; William Jardine (Canton) to Henery Templer (London), 22 November 1836, William Jardine – Private Letter Book, MS JM, C4/5.

50 James Matheson (Canton) to John MacVicar (Manchester), 12 December 1836, James Matheson – Private Letter Book, MS JM, C5/1.

51 Cheong, *Mandarins and Merchants*, 163.

52 William Jardine (Canton) to H.P. Hadow (Bombay), 1 April 1835, William Jardine – Private Letter Book, MS JM, C4/4.

53 William Jardine (Canton) to Hollingworth Magniac (London), 26 August 1836, William Jardine – Private Letter Book, MS JM, C4/6.

54 William Jardine (Canton) to Jamsetjee Jejeebhoy (Bombay), 4 February 1837, William Jardine – Private Letter Book, MS JM, C4/5.

55 William Jardine (Canton) to A. Thomson (Bonside, near Linlithgow, Scotland), 12 February 1837, William Jardine – Private Letter Book, MS JM, C4/5.

56 William Jardine (Canton) to Hollingworth Magniac (London), 16 January 1837, William Jardine – Private Letter Book, MS JM, C4/5.

57 James Matheson (Canton) to Andrew Johnstone (Halleaths, Scotland), 9 December 1837, James Matheson – Private Letter Book, MS JM, C5/2.

58 Ibid.; William Jardine (Canton) to Hollingworth Magniac (London), 15 March 1837, William Jardine – Private Letter Book, MS JM, C4/6.

59 James Matheson (Canton) to B.C. Wilcocks (Philadelphia), 8 March 1837, James Matheson – Private Letter Book, MS JM, C5/2.

60 Greenberg, *British Trade and the Opening of China*, 191, citing Jardine letter of 3 January 1837.

61 William Jardine (Canton) to John Shillaber (Manila), 6 June 1836, William Jardine – Private Letter Book, MS JM, C4/5.

62  William Jardine (Canton) to A.J. Keating (Canton), 5 August and 19 August 1835, William Jardine – Private Letter Book, MS JM, C4/4.

63  William Jardine (Canton) to Jamsetjee Jejeebhoy (Bombay), 9 May 1837, William Jardine – Private Letter Book, MS JM, C5/2.

64  James Matheson (Canton) to Robert Young (Santiago de Chile), 23 October 1837, James Matheson – Private Letter Book, MS JM, C5/2.

65  Cheong, *Mandarins and Merchants*, 252.

66  Ibid., 253.

67  Ibid.

68  Ibid., 268. After examining the firm's correspondence through the 1830s, Cheong concluded that, of the thousands of letters written by the partners, there were only four that were really strongly worded, three of which were products of the years of the financial panic.

69  William Jardine (Canton) to Henry Templer (London), 29 May 1837, William Jardine – Private Letter Book, MS JM, C4/6.

70  William Jardine (Canton) to Jamsetjee Jejeebhoy (Bombay), 3 September 1837, William Jardine – Private Letter Book, MS JM, C4/6.

71  James Matheson (Canton) to C. Thomas (Calcutta), 30 January 1837, and to John Purvis (Singapore or Calcutta), 27 November 1837, James Matheson – Private Letter Book, MS JM, C5/3 and C5/2.

72  James Matheson (Canton) to John Abel Smith (London), 6 January 1838, and to John Purvis (Singapore), 9 January 1838, James Matheson – Private Letter Book, MS JM, C5/2.

73  James Matheson (Canton) to George Moffat (London), 28 February 1838, James Matheson – Private Letter Book, MS JM, C5/3.

74  Cheong, *Mandarins and Merchants*, 255.

75  The pamphlet was forwarded from Calcutta to Bridgman by Archdeacon Dealtry. *Chinese Repository*, November 1836, 5: 297–305.

76  Letter from "A Reader," in *Chinese Repository*, December 1836, 5: 367–70.

77  Two letters to the editor, *Chinese Repository*, January 1837, 5: 407–18.

78  Van Dyke, *The Canton Trade*, 172.

79  Kuo, *A Critical Study of the First Anglo-Chinese War*, 58.

80  Blake (*Jardine Matheson*, 80) describes Elliot as intelligent but over-confident, opinionated, impractical, impetuous, and lacking in judgment. Wakeman ("The Canton Trade and the Opium War," 177), in a softer tone, describes the new superintendent as "one of those fortunate individuals who are usually able to believe that a 'reasonable' solution can be found for even the most difficult problems."

81  Wong, *Deadly Dreams*, 27.

82 Fay, *The Opium War*, 118.

83 Melancon, *Britain's China Policy and the Opium Crisis*, 70.

84 James Matheson (Canton) to Captain Hine (Singapore), 10 July 1837, James Matheson – Private Letter Book, MS JM, C5/2. For an extended examination of the debate about legalization and the closure of that debate, see Chang, *Commissioner Lin and the Opium War*, chapter 4.

85 James Matheson (Canton) to C. Thomas (Calcutta), 27 July 1837, James Matheson – Private Letter Book, MS JM, C5/3.

86 William Jardine (Canton) to Jamsetjee Jejeebhoy (Bombay), 20 February 1837, William Jardine – Private Letter Book, MS JM, C4/5.

87 James Matheson (Canton) to D.S. Burn (Bombay), 21 January 1837, and to R.H. Crawford (Bombay), 19 May 1837, James Matheson – Private Letter Book, MS JM, C5/2.

88 Cheong, *Mandarins and Merchants*, 135.

89 Fay, *The Opium War*, 199; Cheong, *Mandarins and Merchants*, 135.

90 William Jardine (Canton) to T.W. Henderson (Bombay), 6 November 1836 and 3 January 1837, William Jardine – Private Letter Book, MS JM, C4/5.

91 William Jardine (Canton) to Cursetjee Ardaseer (Bombay), 25 March 1837, William Jardine – Private Letter Book, MS JM, C4/6.

92 William Jardine (Canton) to Captain Jauncey (aboard *Governor Findlay* along the coast), 26 April 1837, and to Captain Parry (aboard *Hercules*, along the coast), 30 May 1837, William Jardine – Private Letter Book, MS JM, C4/6. When Jardine received reports of harsh treatment of the Chinese passengers by Jauncey's third mate, he directed Jauncey to "admonish the man gently," because such conduct would give the *Governor Findlay* a bad name among the Chinese and would discourage them "from giving her that preference which they are willing to accord in every other respect." William Jardine to Captain Jauncey, 8 August 1837, William Jardine – Private Letter Book, MS JM, C4/6.

93 William Jardine (Canton) to Captain Rees (aboard *Austin* along the coast), 26 April 1837, and to Jamsetjee Jejeebhoy (Bombay), 10 July 1837, William Jardine – Private Letter Book, MS JM, C4/6.

94 Cheong, *Mandarins and Merchants*, 139; William Jardine (Canton) to T.W. Henderson (Bombay), 13 June 1837, William Jardine – Private Letter Book, MS JM, C4/6. A month later, Jardine indicated that the drug purchasers were willing to adopt any mode of delivery that would relieve them of a portion of the enormously burdensome charge. William Jardine (Canton) to T.W. Henderson (Bombay), 13 July 1837, William Jardine – Private Letter Book, MS JM, C4/6.

95 James Matheson (Canton) to Charles Lyall (Calcutta), 14 June 1837, James Matheson – Private Letter Book, MS JM, C5/3.

96 Fay, *The Opium War*, 120.

97 William Jardine (Canton) to Captain Jauncey (aboard *Governor Findlay* along the coast), 18 July 1837, William Jardine – Private Letter Book, MS JM, C4/6.

98 William Jardine (Canton) to Jamsetjee Jejeebhoy (Bombay), 9 August 1837, William Jardine – Private Letter Book, MS JM, C4/6.

99 William Jardine (Canton) to Captain Rees (aboard *Austin*), 19 August 1837, and to Charles Lyall (Calcutta), 2 September and 4 October 1837, William Jardine – Private Letter Book, MS JM, C4/6. Jardine found it "very disagreeable" that the four lacs of silver sent to Lyall arrived after he had purchased opium on their behalf at higher prices, for it meant that the firm was more heavily committed to Patna than it desired to be. William Jardine to Charles Lyall, 18 October 1837, William Jardine – Private Letter Book, MS JM, C4/6.

100 William Jardine (Canton) to Captain Strachan (aboard schooner *Jardine*), 17 August 1837, and to the commanding officers of the *Findlay*, *Colonel Young*, and *Eleanor*, 2 October 1837, William Jardine – Private Letter Book, MS JM, C4/6.

101 Fay, *The Opium War*, 122. On one occasion Jardine sent directions to Captain Parry to load sixty-three chests of opium aboard the *Hellas*, on the account of the Chinese buyer Affoon. Enclosed with his letter was a piece of Chinese red paper. The counterpart of that piece of red paper was to be handed to Parry by Affoon's friends, in order to identify them before they took delivery of the opium. William Jardine (Canton) to Captain Parry (aboard *Hercules*, at Hong Kong), 12 July 1838, William Jardine – Private Letter Book, MS JM, C4/6.

102 William Jardine (Canton) to Captain Rees (aboard *Austin*), 13 October 1837, William Jardine – Private Letter Book, MS JM, C4/6.

103 William Jardine (Canton) to Captain James Pearson (Calcutta), 27 November 1837, and to T.W. Henderson (Bombay), 6 December 1837, William Jardine – Private Letter Book, MS JM, C4/6.

104 Kuo, *A Critical Study of the First Anglo-Chinese War*, 59–62; Fay, *The Opium War*, 81–2.

105 Melancon, *Britain's China Policy and the Opium Crisis*, 71.

106 Collis, *Foreign Mud*, 196.

107 Kuo, *A Critical Study of the First Anglo-Chinese War*, 64–70. Kuo interprets this action as a commitment on the part of the British government to protection of the opium trade.

108 Melancon, *Britain's China Policy and the Opium Crisis*, 72.

109 Ibid., citing Foreign Office correspondence, Palmerston to Elliot, 15 June 1838, FO 288/8/18–19.

110 Kuo, *A Critical Study of the First Anglo-Chinese War*, 72; Fay, *The Opium War*, 82–3.

111 William Jardine to Captain Strachan (aboard schooner *Jardine*, at Lintin), 2 January 1838, and to Captain Baylis (aboard *Colonel Young*), 11 February 1838, William Jardine – Private Letter Book, MS JM, C4/6.

112 William Jardine (Canton) to Captain Rees (aboard *Austin*), 24 January, 13 February, and 5 June 1838, William Jardine – Private Letter Book, MS JM, C4/6.

113 William Jardine (Canton) to Captain Parry (aboard *Hercules*), 20 February 1838, William Jardine – Private Letter Book, MS JM, C4/6; also, William Jardine (Canton) to Captain Parry (aboard *Hercules*, at Hong Kong), 6 July and 23 July 1838, William Jardine – Private Letter Book, MS JM, C4/7.

114 William Jardine to Captain Jauncey (aboard *Governor Findlay* at Chusan), 27 February 1838; to Jamsetjee Jejeebhoy (Bombay), 13 March 1838; and to T.W. Henderson (Bombay), 28 February, 15 March, and 10 April 1838, William Jardine – Private Letter Book, MS JM, C4/7.

115 William Jardine (Canton) to Captain Alexander Grant (c/o Magniac Smith, London), 1 May 1838; to Captain Rees (aboard *Austin*), 3 May and 3 June 1838; to T.W. Henderson (Bombay), 9 June 1838; and to Captain Baylis (aboard *Colonel Young*), 12 June 1838, William Jardine – Private Letter Book, MS JM, C4/7.

116 Letter from William Jardine (Canton) to J.A. Stewart Mackenzie (Ceylon), 12 June 1838, William Jardine – Private Letter Book, MS JM, C4/7.

117 Fay, *The Opium War*, 125–6; William Jardine (Canton) to J.A. Stewart Mackenzie (Ceylon), 12 June 1838, William Jardine – Private Letter Book, MS JM, C4/7.

118 Fay, *The Opium War*, 126; Blake, *Jardine Matheson*, 86; William Jardine (Canton) to Captain Rees (aboard *Austin*), 14 August 1838, William Jardine – Private Letter Book, MS JM, C4/7.

119 James Matheson (Canton) to Hugh Matheson (Liverpool), 22 June 1838, James Matheson – Private Letter Book, MS JM, C5/3. He contrasted Hugh's reticence with Andrew Johnstone's risk, which was expected to return 20 per cent to 30 per cent on his investment.

120 Kuo, *A Critical Study of the First Anglo-Chinese War*, chapter 7.

121 William Jardine (Canton) to Captain Rees (aboard *Austin*), 14 August 1838; to Captain Parry (aboard *Hercules*), 3 September 1838; and to

Jamsetjee Jejeebhoy (Bombay), 10 September and 22 September 1838, William Jardine – Private Letter Book, MS JM, C4/7.

122 William Jardine (Canton) to Captain Baylis (aboard *Colonel Young*), 1 October 1838, William Jardine – Private Letter Book, MS JM, C4/7.

123 William Jardine (Canton) to Captain Jauncey (aboard *Governor Findlay*), 17 November 1838, William Jardine – Private Letter Book, MS JM, C4/7.

124 James Matheson (Canton) to Cursetjee Ardaseer (Bombay), 6 October 1838, and to John Lyall (Calcutta), 10 and 27 November 1838, James Matheson – Private Letter Book, MS JM, C5/3. William Jardine to Captain Jauncey (aboard *Governor Findlay*), 17 November 1838, and to Captain Rees (aboard *Austin*), 18 November 1838, William Jardine – Private Letter Book, MS JM, C4/7.

125 James Matheson (Canton) to Jamsetjee Jejeebhoy (Bombay), 2 November 1838; to Mrs Alleyn (London), 13 November 1838; and to B. Barretto (Macao), 8 December 1838, James Matheson – Private Letter Book, MS JM, C5/3.

126 William Jardine (Canton) to Jamsetjee Jejeebhoy (Bombay), 29 November 1838, and to Captain Rees (aboard *Austin*), 18 November and 16 December 1838, William Jardine – Private Letter Book, MS JM, C4/7.

127 William Jardine (Canton) to Jamsetjee Jejeebhoy (Bombay), 18 November and 5 December 1838, and to T.W. Henderson (Bombay), 5 December 1838, William Jardine – Private Letter Book, MS JM, C4/7.

128 William Jardine (Canton) to T.W. Henderson (Bombay), 5 December 1838, and to Jamsetjee Jejeebhoy, 5 December 1838, William Jardine – Private Letter Book, MS JM, C4/7.

129 William Jardine (Canton) to Jamsetjee Jejeebhoy (Bombay) and to T.W. Henderson (Bombay), both on 22 December 1838, William Jardine – Private Letter Book, MS JM, C4/7.

130 H.H. Lindsay, Chamber of Commerce, to the Hong merchants, in *Chinese Repository*, 7 December 1838, 7: 441–2; and Fay, *The Opium War*, 131–2.

131 Chang, *Commissioner Lin and the Opium War*, 111–12. Jardine told Jejeebhoy that most of the foreign merchants were disinclined to meet with the Cohong, because of the offensive tone of the Hongs' communications and because the Cohong were not really attempting to be conciliators. William Jardine (Canton) to Jamsetjee Jejeebhoy (Bombay), 6 December 1838, William Jardine – Private Letter Book, MS JM, C4/7.

132 Fay, *The Opium War*, 133–4. In vivid language, Jardine reported to Jeejebhoy that there had been a "grand row" in front of the foreign factories, for which the foreign community was "much to blame for irritating

the rabble." William Jardine (Canton) to Jamsetjee Jejeebhoy, 13 December 1838, William Jardine – Private Letter Book, MS JM, C4/7.

133 *Canton Register,* 18 December 1838, 104.

134 Ibid.

135 Chang, *Commissioner Lin and the Opium War,* 115, citing *Correspondence to China, 1840, Parliamentary Papers,* 326–7.

136 Chang, *Commissioner Lin and the Opium War,* 115; Fay, *The Opium War,* 135.

137 William Jardine (Canton) to Captain Baylis (aboard *Colonel Young*), 13 December 1838; to Jamsetjee Jejeebhoy (Bombay), 13 December 1838; and to T.W. Henderson (Bombay), 1 January 1838, William Jardine – Private Letter Book, MS JM, C4/7.

138 William Jardine (Canton) to Jamsetjee Jejeebhoy (Bombay), 22 December 1838 and 1 January 1839, William Jardine – Private Letter Book, MS JM, C4/7. Jacques Downes disputes Jardine's estimate of Teng and presents him as an honest, rigorous administrator. Downes, *The Golden Ghetto,* 132. Hsin Pao Chang also argues that the accusations concerning Teng's venality were groundless. Chang, *Commissioner Lin and the Opium War,* 101.

139 Wakeman, "The Canton Trade and the Opium War," 171–2.

140 William Jardine (Canton) to John H. Gledstanes (London), 14 March 1837, William Jardine – Private Letter Book, MS JM, C4/6.

141 James Matheson (Canton) to various British residents of Canton (Richard Turner et al.), 6 November 1838, James Matheson – Private Letter Book, MS JM, C5/3.

142 William Jardine (Canton) to T.W. Henderson (Bombay), 26 November 1838, William Jardine – Private Letter Book, MS JM, C4/7. The *Sarah* was once owned jointly by Cowasjee, Jardine, and Weeding. Jardine had appointed H.P. Hadow to act for him in settling such claims, but Hadow died, and Cowasjee lost track of the fact that he had been Jardine's surrogate for resolving these sorts of transactions.

143 William Jardine (Canton) to Captain Jauncey (aboard *Governor Findlay*), 11 January 1838, William Jardine – Private Letter Book, MS JM, C4/7.

144 William Jardine to Captain Hall (aboard the schooner *Harriet*), William Jardine – Private Letter Book, MS JM, C4/7. Matheson showed a similar concern for fairness and decent behaviour when complaints about the conduct of the captain of the *Harriet* were received in 1837, including accusations of serious mistreatment of a Portuguese crewman from Macao. "It is peculiarly painful to us to receive complaints of this description, and we beg you will impress on all the commanders in our employ, how desirous we are they should be guarded against." James Matheson

(Canton) to Captain Parry (aboard *Hercules*), 21 November 1837, James
Matheson – Private Letter Book, MS JM, C5/2.

145  William Jardine (Canton) to Jamsetjee Jejeebhoy (Bombay), 21 January
1839, William Jardine – Private Letter Book, MS JM, C4/7.

146  Fay, *The Opium War*, 128–9; Chang, *Commissioner Lin and the Opium War*,
120–5; Collis, *Foreign Mud*, 192–3; Cheong, *Mandarins and Merchants*,
142. Lin had risen swiftly through the hierarchy of mandarins, had been
a provincial governor since 1832, and had been appointed governor general of Hu-Kuang (Hupeh and Hunan) in 1837.

147  Kuo, *A Critical Study of the First Anglo-Chinese War*, 99–100; Fay, *The Opium
War*, 138–9.


CHAPTER NINE


1  James Matheson (Canton) to Thomas Charles Smith (London), 29 January 1839, James Matheson – Private Letter Book, MS JM, C5/3; *Canton
Register*, 29 January 1839, 22.

2  Kerr, ed., *Letters from China*, 87–90; Fay, *The Opium War*, 138. Some people
thought that Jardine was intending to marry upon his return to England.
"It is said that he has his eye on a widow lady who was out here," reported
Forbes in a bit of flawed gossip.

3  *Canton Register*, 29 January 1839, 23.

4  Kerr, ed., *Letters from China*, 88; Nye, "The Morning of My Life in China,"
57; *Canton Register*, 29 January 1839, 23.

5  Nye, "The Morning of My Life in China," 57.

6  Kerr, ed., *Letters from China*, 90. The occasion is also mentioned by Hunter,
*The "Fan Kwae" at Canton*, 135. Hunter, who was present for the banquet,
admired Jardine for his "sagacity and judgment."

7  Kerr, ed., *Letters from China*, 89; emphasis in original.

8  James Matheson (Canton) to Thomas Charles Smith (London), 29 January 1839, James Matheson – Private Letter Book, MS JM, C5/3.

9  *Canton Register*, 29 January 1839, 1 and 22.

10  William Jardine (Canton) to Captain Rees (aboard *Austin*), 10 December
1838, William Jardine – Private Letter Book, MS JM, C4/7; Blake, *Jardine
Matheson*, 86.

11  Matheson was calculating that mail from Canton to London would arrive
in time to allow Magniac Smith to follow up on the news from Canton by
writing to Jardine at Alexandria. James Matheson (Canton) to Thomas
Charles Smith (London), 29 January 1839, James Matheson – Private

Letter Book, MS JM, C5/3. (Two years earlier, in 1837, two inventors in Britain had developed an electric telegraph, but the telegraph links to India were a couple of generations away.)

12  Blake, *Jardine Matheson*, 86, citing the unpublished manuscript of Gerald Yorke, "The Princely House" (1937), which is in turn citing Jardine's Private Letter Book for 26 January 1839.

13  James Matheson (Canton) to Thomas Charles Smith (London), 17 January 1839, James Matheson – Private Letter Book, MS JM, C5/3.

14  Matheson ordered a morning frock coat and a warm double-breasted waistcoat – both of "the finest black cloth," as well as a "pea jacket" of the thickest cloth, to be worn over a coat. Two coats had recently arrived from the tailor in question, W.I. Cooper, and Matheson was well pleased with the way they fitted him. James Matheson (Canton) to W. I. Cooper (London), 25 and 30 January 1839, James Matheson – Private Letter Book, MS JM, C5/3.

15  William Jardine (Canton) to J. Middleton (Macao), 10 January 1839; to Captain Paterson (of *Lady Hayes*), 10 January 1839; and to Captain Baylis (of *Colonel Young*), 11 January 1839, William Jardine – Private Letter Book, MS JM, C4/7. Even after Lin's confiscation of the opium stocks in the spring of 1839, the firm continued to provide this charter service for a man named Middleton and another named Starkey. James Matheson or the firm (Macao) to Captain Strachan (on *Omega* at Hong Kong), 5 June 1839, and to Captain Hall (on the schooner *Harriet* at Typa), 6 June 1839, William Jardine – Private Letter Book, MS JM, C4/7. (Jardine's letter book continued to be used for some of the firm's correspondence, even though he had been gone from Canton for months.)

16  James Matheson or the firm (Canton) to the commanding officer of the *Lady Hayes*, 18 February 1839, William Jardine – Private Letter Book, MS JM, C4/7; James Matheson (Canton) to Thomas Charles Smith (London), 29 January 1839, James Matheson – Private Letter Book, MS JM, C5/3.

17  James Matheson (Canton) to the Right Honorable J.A. Stewart MacKenzie (Ceylon), 26 January 1839, James Matheson – Private Letter Book, MS JM, C5/3.

18  *Canton Register*, 29 January 1839, supplement.

19  James Matheson (Canton) to John Abel Smith (London), 25 January 1839, James Matheson – Private Letter Book, MS JM, C5/3; and James Matheson (Canton) to Captain Rees (aboard *Lady Hayes*), 29 January 1839, William Jardine – Private Letter Book, MS JM, C4/7.

20  Fay, *The Opium War*, 128.

21  *Chinese Repository*, April 1839, 7: 610.

22  Fay, *The Opium War*, 140.

23  James Matheson (Canton) to Jamsetjee Jejeebhoy (Bombay), 28 February 1839, James Matheson – Private Letter Book, MS JM, C5/3.

24  Kerr, ed., *Letters from China*, 98; Fay, *The Opium War*, 140.

25  James Matheson (Canton) to T.W. Henderson (Bombay), 9 March 1839, James Matheson – Private Letter Book, MS JM, C5/3.

26  James Matheson (Canton) to John Abel Smith (London), 9 March 1839, James Matheson – Private Letter Book, MS JM, C5/3. Two and a half lacs of dollars per annum was his projection.

27  Waley, *The Opium War through Chinese Eyes*, 18; Gelber, *Opium, Soldiers and Evangelicals*, 61.

28  James Matheson (Canton) to Jamsetjee Jejeebhoy (Bombay), 9 March 1839, James Matheson – Private Letter Book, MS JM, C5/3; Kuo, *A Critical Study of the First Anglo-Chinese War*, 100.

29  Fay, *The Opium War*, 142; Hunter, *The "Fan Kwae" at Canton*, 135; Chang, *Commissioner Lin and the Opium War*, 126; Waley, *The Opium War through Chinese Eyes*, 20.

30  Waley, *The Opium War through Chinese Eyes*, 22, quoting Lin's report of 12 March 1839 to the emperor.

31  James Matheson (Canton) to T.W. Henderson (Bombay), 10 March 1839, and to Jamsetjee Jejeebhoy (Bombay), 13 March 1839, James Matheson – Private Letter Book, MS JM, C5/3.

32  James Matheson (Canton) to John Abel Smith (London), 18 March 1839, James Matheson – Private Letter Book, MS JM, C5/4.

33  Waley, *The Opium War through Chinese Eyes*, 28–31. Trying to be diplomatic, and assuming that Victoria was not aware of the opium trade practices of British merchants, Lin stated that "there is a class of evil foreigner that makes opium and brings it for sale, tempting fools to destroy themselves, merely in order to reap profit." Then, in the form of official notification to her, he declared: "What is here forbidden to consume, your dependencies must be forbidden to manufacture, and what has already been manufactured Your Majesty must immediately search out and throw it to the bottom of the sea, and never again allow such poison to exist in Heaven or on earth."

34  James Matheson (Canton) to John Abel Smith (London), 18 March 1839, James Matheson – Private Letter Book, MS JM, C5/4; Waley, *The Opium War through Chinese Eyes*, 32; Fay, *The Opium War*, 144.

35 Waley, *The Opium War through Chinese Eyes*, 33–4; Chang, *Commissioner Lin and the Opium War*, 139.

36 James Matheson (Canton) to John Abel Smith (London), 18 March 1839, James Matheson – Private Letter Book, MS JM, C5/4.

37 James Matheson, "Brief Narrative," manuscript account (draft with corrections in his own hand) of events at Canton, March 1839, MS JM; memorandum by James Matheson, 19 March 1839, James Matheson – Private Letter Book, MS JM, C5/4; Fay, *The Opium War*, 145.

38 James Matheson (Canton) to William Jardine (London), 1 May 1839, James Matheson – Private Letter Book, MS JM, C5/4. This twelve-page letter is the longest piece of correspondence in the private letter books of Jardine and Matheson. Copies of it were sent by way of six different ships in order to be sure that it reached Jardine as soon as possible. When taken together with the "Brief Narrative," it constitutes Matheson's personal history of the dramatic events of March and April 1839 which set in motion the sequence of events leading to the Opium War of 1840–42.

39 Chang, *Commissioner Lin and the Opium War*, 132, 143.

40 Matheson, "Brief Narrative"; Fay, *The Opium War*, 145–6; Chang, *Commissioner Lin and the Opium War*, 145–7; Kuo, *A Critical Study of the First Anglo-Chinese War*, 105.

41 James Matheson (Canton) to William Jardine (London), 1 May 1839, James Matheson – Private Letter Book, MS JM, C5/4.

42 Ibid.; Kerr, ed., *Letters from China*, 109–10; Nye, "The Morning of My Life in China," 61.

43 James Matheson (Canton) to William Jardine (London), 1 May 1839, James Matheson – Private Letter Book, MS JM, C5/4.

44 Kerr, ed., *Letters from China*, 110–11; Collis, *Foreign Mud*, 206–7.

45 Hoe and Roebuck, *The Taking of Hong Kong*, 70–2; Collis, *Foreign Mud*, 210–11; Fay, *The Opium War*, 147–8; Kuo, *A Critical Study of the First Anglo-Chinese War*, 106.

46 Matheson, "Brief Narrative"; Fay, *The Opium War*, 148–9; Collis, *Foreign Mud*, 212–13; Kerr, ed., *Letters from China*, 110–11.

47 Fay, *The Opium War*, 149; Downes, *The Golden Ghetto*, 137.

48 Kerr, ed., *Letters from China*, 111.

49 James Matheson (Canton) to William Jardine (London), 1 May 1839, James Matheson – Private Letter Book, MS JM, C5/4.

50 Gelber, *Opium, Soldiers and Evangelicals*, 66; Chang, *Commissioner Lin and the Opium War*, 153–5. The only serious misfortune among the residents of

No. 1 during the weeks of confinement was that nineteen-year-old David Jardine was injured when he fell down a flight of stairs after dinner one night. Blake, *Jardine Matheson*, 91.

51  Chang includes as appendix D a letter to the *Times*, dated 10 August 1839, written by the surgeon of the Indiaman *George IV*. He reported that, during the detention of the ships at Whampoa, "a round of dinner parties … was given by the principal commanders of the fleet, at which I had the honour of being present, and I am bold to say that the whole of these parties were distinguished by an abundance of joyous hilarity and capital cheer, that would have gratified the most fastidious bon vivant. Who furnished the turkey, mutton, capon, &c., as well as the rich selection of fresh vegetables which graced the tables? The barbaric and inhospitable Chinese Government."

"Thank heaven we are all well and merry as crickets," Forbes wrote after five days of the confinement (Kerr, ed., *Letters from China*, 113). But the tedium and the difficulties of keeping things clean eventually wore down the initial spirit of adventure. The residents could not get enough water to keep their floors clean; moreover, their toilet facilities became repulsive.

52  Fay, *The Opium War*, 151.

53  *Correspondence relating to China, 1840*, cited in Gelber, *Opium, Soldiers and Evangelicals*, 67.

54  Matheson, "Brief Narrative"; Fay, *The Opium War*, 152–4, citing *Correspondence relating to China, 1840*, 36 (223), 374, PP; Kerr, ed., *Letters from China*, 112.

55  Collis, *Foreign Mud*, 215.

56  Hoe and Roebuck, *The Taking of Hong Kong*, 74–5, citing letter from Charles Elliot to Clara Elliot, 4 April 1839.

57  Matheson, "Brief Narrative"; Blake, *Jardine Matheson*, 91 and 261n.4, citing Yorke ms.; Fay, *The Opium War*, 154; Greenberg, *British Trade and the Opening of China*, 203; Kerr, ed., *Letters from China*, 113. Fourteen hundred of the American-held chests came from Russel and Company. One hundred and four chests were turned over by W.S. Wetmore.

58  James Matheson (Canton) to William Jardine (London), 1 May 1839, James Matheson – Private Letter Book, MS JM, C5/4; Fay, *The Opium War*, 154, citing Select Committee on Trade with China 1840 (359), 147, PP.

59  Fay, *The Opium War*, 154; Greenberg, *British Trade and the Opening of China*, 203.

60  Thampi, "Parsees in the China Trade," 21.

61 James Matheson (Canton) to Alexander Matheson (Macao), 29 March
   1839, James Matheson – Private Letter Book, MS JM, C5/4.

62 Blake, *Jardin Matheson*, 91, citing Yorke ms., 240; Collis, *Foreign Mud*, 216.

63 Waley, *The Opium War through Chinese Eyes*, 39, citing Lin's papers, 2: 252;
   Matheson, "Brief Narrative."

64 Fay, *The Opium War*, 155.

65 Jardine, Matheson and Company (Canton, unsigned) to Captain John
   Rees (aboard *Lady Hayes*) "and all the commanders of our vessels on the
   Coast of China," 17 April 1839, William Jardine – Private Letter Book, MS
   JM, C4/7. Matheson wasted no time in telling Captain Parry that, since
   the *Hercules* would no longer be functioning as an opium vessel, "you must
   reduce her expenses, including your own pay." However, he asked that the
   *Hercules* stand off Macao in case it was needed to evacuate English families
   or to serve as a headquarters and residence for the firm if they could not
   reside at Macao.

66 Fay, *The Opium War*, 158–9.

67 James Matheson (Canton) to Jamsetjee Jejeebhoy (Bombay), 3 April 1839,
   James Matheson – Private Letter Book, MS JM, C5/4.

68 James Matheson (Canton) to John Middleton (Macao), 9 April 1839,
   James Matheson – Private Letter Book, MS JM, C5/4.

69 James Matheson (Canton) to John Abel Smith (London), 6 May 1839,
   and to William Jardine (London), 13 May 1839, James Matheson – Private
   Letter Book, MS JM, C5/4.

70 Kuo, *A Critical Study of the First Anglo-Chinese War*, 115.

71 Ibid., 113–14; Fay, *The Opium War*, 163; Hoe and Roebuck, *The Taking of
   Hong Kong*, 79.

72 James Matheson (Canton) to J.C. Green (Canton), 14 May 1839, James
   Matheson – Private Letter Book, MS JM, C5/4; Fay, *The Opium War*, 159.

73 Kerr, ed., *Letters from China*, 127–29; Hoe and Roebuck, *The Taking of Hong
   Kong*, 86–7.

74 Jardine, Matheson and Company (Macao) to Captain John Rees (aboard
   *Lady Hayes*) and Captain Jauncey (aboard *Hellas*), 1 June and 1 July 1839,
   William Jardine – Private Letter Book, MS JM, C4/7; and James Matheson
   (Macao) to Jamsetjee Jejeebhoy (Bombay), 29 May 1839; to T.W.
   Henderson (Bombay), 10 June 1839; and to William Jardine (London),
   13 June 1839, James Matheson – Private Letter Book, MS JM, C5/4.

75 Chang, *Commissioner Lin and the Opium War*, 173–75; Waley, *The Opium War
   through Chinese Eyes*, 47–9, 50–1; Fay, *The Opium War*, 160; Hoe and

Roebuck, *The Taking of Hong Kong*, 82; memorial of Lin Tse-hsu to the emperor, 28 July 1839, doc. 16 in Kuo, *A Critical Study of the First Anglo-Chinese War*, 248–50; James Matheson (Macao) to Jamsetjee Jejeebhoy (Bombay), 25 June 1839, James Matheson – Private Letter Book, MS JM, C5/4. While King was at the site of the destruction, one of the coolies was caught with a small quantity of opium and was immediately decapitated. Collis, *Foreign Mud*, 219.

76 Fay, *The Opium War*, 192–3, citing letter from Elliot to Palmerston, 3 April 1839, Foreign Office files, 17/31.

77 Memorial to Lord Palmerston, in *Chinese Repository*, 8: 32–5.

78 Fay, *The Opium War*, 191; James Matheson (aboard *Hercules*, near Hong Kong) to John Abel Smith (London), 24 September 1839, James Matheson – Private Letter Book, MS JM, C5/4.

79 James Matheson (Macao) to James Ryan (Canton), 10 August 1839, James Matheson – Private Letter Book, MS JM, C5/4.

80 James Matheson (Canton) to Jamsetjee Jejeebhoy (Bombay), 3 May 1839, and to T.W. Henderson (Bombay), 5 May 1839, James Matheson – Private Letter Book, MS JM, C5/4.

81 James Matheson (Macao) to William Jardine (London), 27 June 1839, James Matheson – Private Letter Book, MS JM, C5/4.

82 James Matheson (afloat off Macao, aboard the schooner *Maria*) to Thomas Scott (Singapore), 24 August 1839, James Matheson – Private Letter Book, MS JM, C5/4.

83 James Matheson (Macao) to T.W. Henderson (Bombay), 25 June 1839, James Matheson – Private Letter Book, MS JM, C5/4.

84 James Matheson (first at Canton, then Macao), to William Jardine (no address, since Jardine was travelling), 8 May 1839; to Charles Lyall (Calcutta), 27 June 1839; and to T. Edward (Sydney, New South Wales), 1 June 1839, James Matheson – Private Letter Book, MS JM, C5/4.

85 James Matheson (Macao) to John Abel Smith (London), 7 July 1839, James Matheson – Private Letter Book, MS JM, C5/4.

86 James Matheson (aboard the schooner *Maria*, off Macao) to Jamsetjee Jejeebhoy (Bombay), 19 August 1839, and to Thomas Scott (Singapore), 24 August 1839, James Matheson – Private Letter Book, MS JM, C5/4; Gelber, *Opium, Soldiers and Evangelicals*, 74; Collis, *Foreign Mud*, 236–7.

87 Lovell, *The Opium War*, 74.

88 Hoe and Roebuck, *The Taking of Hong Kong*, 92–3; Fay, *The Opium War*, 172–3; Gelber, *Opium, Soldiers and Evangelicals*, 74; Collis, *Foreign Mud*, 231–4.

89 Fay, *The Opium War*, 175–6; Collis, *Foreign Mud*, 240.

90 Fay, *The Opium War*, 175–6; Collis, *Foreign Mud*, 238–41. Collis states that this episode is generally taken to be the beginning of the first Anglo-Chinese War.

91 Lovell, *The Opium War*, 92–3.

92 James Matheson (aboard *Hercules*, at Hong Kong) to T.W. Henderson (Bombay), 9 September 1839, James Matheson – Private Letter Book, MS JM, C5/4.

93 James Matheson (aboard *Hercules*, at Hong Kong) to John Abel Smith (London), 24 September 1839, James Matheson – Private Letter Book, MS JM, C5/4.

94 Reid, "The Steel Frame," 23; Fay, *The Opium War*, 183.

95 William Jardine (Constantinople) to James Matheson (Canton), 27 May 1839, Incoming Correspondence – Europe/Private, MS JM, B1/8.

96 Reid, "The Steel Frame," 24.

97 Ibid.; Collis, *Foreign Mud*, 255–56.

98 By the terms of the agreement, Turkey was required to close the Dardanelles to the passage of all warships during any war in which Turkey was a neutral party. France eventually backed down and the crisis passed.

99 One of Palmerston's biographers writes: "It is doubtful whether the foreign secretary had any passion or even deep interest to spare to the Chinese issue from the far more vital matters which were on his hands from 1839 to 1841. It occupied surprisingly little space in his private correspondence for those years." Bell, *Lord Palmerston*, 1: 278.

100 William Jardine (London) to James Matheson, 16 September 1839, cited in Collis, *Foreign Mud*, 251. At this time Matheson had no permanent residence, because he had been asked to leave Macao.

101 William Jardine (London) to James Matheson, 25 September 1839, Incoming Correspondence – London, MS JM, B6/10.

102 William Jardine (London) to James Matheson (China), 25–27 September 1839, in Le Pichon, *China Trade and Empire*, 386.

103 Ibid., 387. Melancon (*Britain's China Policy and the Opium Crisis*, 103) argues that Palmerston had already outlined the alternative responses to the China crisis for Lord Melbourne, in a memorandum of 23 September, and that Palmerston had already reached the conclusion that he preferred a naval blockade.

104 William Jardine (London) to James Matheson, 27 September 1839, cited in Blake, *Jardine Matheson*, 93.

105  William Jardine (London) to James Matheson, 27 September 1839, Incoming Correspondence – London, MS JM, B6/10.

106  William Jardine (London) to Jamsetjee Jejeebhoy (Bombay), 5 October 1839, Incoming Correspondence – London Private, MS JM, B1/10.

107  Bourne, *Palmerston*, 587–8.

108  William Jardine (London) to James Matheson, 14 October 1839, Incoming Correspondence – London, MS JM, B6/10.

109  Fay, *The Opium War*, 194.

110  Ibid., 194, 200.

111  Ibid.

112  William Jardine (Scotland) to James Matheson, 14 December 1839, cited in Collis, *Foreign Mud*, 253.

113  Memorandum from William Jardine to Lord Palmerston, 5 December 1839, Palmerston Papers, University of Southampton, MS 62 PP/MM/CH/5. It was headed "A few cursory Remarks on the Present position and future Prospects of British Subjects trading to China."

114  Ibid.

115  Ibid.

116  Ibid.

117  Ibid.

118  "Take a copy & return the original with this note," Palmerston instructed his secretary on 1 May 1840. Palmerston Papers, University of Southampton, MS 62 PP/MM/CH/5.

119  Bourne, *Palmerston*, 587–8.

120  Ibid., 583.

121  Ibid., 586.

122  Collis, *Foreign Mud*, 257; Blake, *Jardine Matheson*, 93–4.

123  The £2 million of 1839 would be equal to £78 million according to Gelber's 2004 conversion scale. Gelber, *Opium, Soldiers and Evangelicals*, 83.

124  Melancon, *Britain's China Policy and the Opium Crisis*, 122; Fay, *The Opium War*, 202.

125  Gelber, *Opium, Soldiers and Evangelicals*, 91; Melancon, *Britain's China Policy and the Opium Crisis*, 123.

126  Great Britain, House of Commons, *Debates*, 7 April 1840, Series 3, vol. 53, 704–20, http://www.hansard.millbanksystems.com/commons/1840/apr/07/war-with-china (accessed 27 June 2013).

127  Ibid., 9 April 1840, vol. 5, 800–20; Gelber, *Opium, Soldiers and Evangelicals*, 93–7; Fay, *The Opium War*, 203; Melancon, *Britain's China Policy and the Opium War*, 125–6.

128 House of Commons, *Debates*, Series 3, vol. 5, 925–48.

129 Fay, *The Opium War*, 202–4; Gelber, *Opium, Soldiers and Evangelicals*, 98–100; Melancon, *Britain's China Policy and the Opium Crisis*, 127–8.

130 Fay, *The Opium War*, 204.

131 Melancon, *Britain's China Policy and the Opium Crisis*, 128.

132 *The Times*, 25 April 1840.

## CHAPTER TEN

1 James Matheson (Toon Koo, China) to John Abel Smith (London), 26 December 1839, James Matheson – Private Letter Book, MS JM, C5/4.

2 A letter concerned with tea being shipped to a client in London contained an additional note that the pursar of the *Kyd*, by which Matheson was transporting the tea, also had a pony to be sent to Matheson's lodge at Achany, just outside Lairg – "an odd whim you will say." Presumably, Matheson intended to catch up with the pony before long. James Matheson (Macao) to Alexander Robertson (London), 4 May 1840, James Matheson – Private Letter Book, MS JM, C5/5.

3 Greenberg, *British Trade and the Opening of China*, 207.

4 James Matheson (Macao) to Charles Lyall (Calcutta), 27 June 1839, James Matheson – Private Letter Book, MS JM, C5/4.

5 Greenberg, *British Trade and the Opening of China*, 207.

6 Ibid., 208; Collis, *Foreign Mud*, 278.

7 Greenberg, *British Trade and the Opening of China*, 208.

8 Collis, *Foreign Mud*, 279.

9 James Matheson (Macao) to William Jardine and Alexander Matheson (London), 26 April 1840, James Matheson – Private Letter Book, MS JM, C5/5.

10 Blake, *Jardine Matheson*, 97; Collis, *Foreign Mud*, 278.

11 James Matheson (Tongku, near Lintin) to William Jardine and Alexander Matheson, 24 November 1839, James Matheson – Private Letter Book, MS JM, C5/4.

12 James Matheson (Hong Kong) to T.W. Henderson (Bombay), 16 October 1839, James Matheson – Private Letter Book, MS JM, C5/4.

13 James Matheson (Hong Kong) to Jamsetjee Jejeebhoy (Bombay), 16 October 1839, James Matheson – Private Letter Book, MS JM, C5/4.

14 James Matheson (Hong Kong) to T.W. Henderson (Bombay), 18 October 1839, James Matheson – Private Letter Book, MS JM, C5/4; James

Matheson (Tytam Bay) to Cursetjee Ardaseer (Bombay), 3 November 1839, ibid.

15 James Matheson (Tongku, near Lintin) to T.W. Henderson (Bombay), 30 November 1839, James Matheson – Private Letter Book, MS JM, C5/4; Gelber, *Opium, Soldiers and Evangelicals*, 76. Chuenpi, which was the site of the naval incident, is at the edge of the Bogue, where the Canton River flows into the Gulf of Canton.

16 Chang, *Commissioner Lin and the Opium War*, 207–8, citing a letter from Joseph Coolidge to Augustine Heard, 13 December 1839.

17 James Matheson (Tongku) to Charles Lyall (Calcutta), 14 December 1839, James Matheson – Private Letter Book, MS JM, C5/4.

18 Fay, *The Opium War*, 201. The ships *Sir Charles Malcolm* and *General Wood* now bore new names as the *Alabama* and *Syden* when they left Canton late in January 1840, carrying teas for Jardine, Matheson clients, for transshipment to the firm's vessels or charters at Tongku.

19 James Matheson (Tongku) to Charles Myall (Calcutta), 1 December 1839, James Matheson Private Letter Book, MS JM, C5/4.

20 James Matheson (Tongku) to John Anderson, 6 January 1840, James Matheson – Private Letter Book, MS JM, C5/5. Anderson was an English merchant who forwarded piece-goods to the China market through Jardine, Matheson.

21 James Matheson (Macao) to William Jardine (London), 29 February 1840, and to John Abel Smith (London), 29 February 1840, James Matheson – Private Letter Books, MS JM, C5/5.

22 James Matheson (Macao) to T.W. Henderson (Bombay), 29 February 1840, James Matheson – Private Letter Book, MS JM, C5/5; and James Matheson (Macao) to T. Scott (Singapore), 14 April 1840, ibid.

23 Matheson even told Henderson in the latter half of April that the firm would be obliged if Henderson would purchase opium for them with any of their funds then in his possession. James Matheson (Macao) to T.W. Henderson (Bombay), 20 April 1840, James Matheson – Private Letter Book, MS JM, C5/5.

24 James Matheson (Macao) to Jamsetjee Jejeebhoy (Bombay), T.W. Henderson (Bombay), William Jardine (London), and John Abel Smith (London), all on or around 19 April 1840, James Matheson – Private Letter Book, MS JM, C5/5.

25 The *Mor* was owned by Jardine, Matheson; Jamsetjee Jejeebhoy; and Remington and Company. Matheson considered it the fastest ship east of the Cape of Good Hope. James Matheson (Macao) to William Jardine

(London), 17 February 1840, James Matheson – Private Letter Book, MS JM, C5/5.

26 The commander of the expedition was to have been Admiral Sir Frederick Maitland of the East Indian Station, but his flagship, the *Wellesley,* was struck by a fever in the fall of 1839 and Maitland was carried off by the disease. George Elliot was named as his replacement. Hence the unusual circumstance of having first cousins directing the British campaign in China.

27 James Matheson (Macao) to Jamsetjee Jejeebhoy (Bombay), 21 March 1840, James Matheson – Private Letter Book, MS JM, C5/5.

28 James Matheson (Macao) to William Jardine and Alexander Matheson (London), 26 April 1840; to Jamsetjee Jejeebhoy (Bombay), 29 May 1840; and to Thomas Scott (Singapore), 29 May 1840, James Matheson – Private Letter Book, MS JM, C5/5; Fay, *The Opium War,* 209.

29 Downes, *The Golden Ghetto,* 205.

30 Jauncey nearly lost the eye, but Parker's surgery helped to save it, and in gratitude Jauncey not only contributed £300 to Parker's mission but persuaded Jardine, Matheson to match that gift. Although the broken jaw was a source of much pain to Jauncey for weeks, he recovered well and, after some time in England, returned to China near the end of the war. Kerr, ed., *Letters from China,* 238–40; Fay, *The Opium War,* 209–10, 237.

31 James Matheson (Macao) to Thomas Scott (Singapore), 29 May 1840, James Matheson – Private Letter Book, MS JM, C5/5.

32 James Matheson (Macao) to William Lyall (London), 6 May 1840, James Matheson – Private Letter Book, MS JM, C5/5.

33 Collis, *Foreign Mud,* 281. The author does not give the date of the letter.

34 Kerr, ed., *Letters from China,* 113n126; Fay, *The Opium War,* 121; Downes, *The Golden Ghetto,* 205–7. Downes acknowledges that, although King railed against the drug trade, his firm could not have survived without it, for Jardine, Matheson opium earnings gave it the silver to discount large quantities of Olyphant's notes. King's younger cousin and partner, William Howard Morss, had a close working relationship with James Matheson.

35 James Matheson (Macao) to William Jardine (London), 17 February 1840, James Matheson – Private Letter Book, MS JM, C5/5. A piece involving King appeared in the *Canton Register* in February 1840, causing Matheson such embarrassment that he felt compelled to write to King expressing his regrets at the piece and disavowing any influence over the paper's editorial policy.

36 James Matheson (Macao) to William Jardine (London), 1 September 1840, James Matheson – Private Letter Book, MS JM, C5/5.

37 James Matheson (Macao) to J.A. Smith (London), 25 June 1840, James Matheson – Private Letter Book, MS JM, C5/5. The actual number was closer to four thousand.

38 Ibid.

39 James Matheson (Macao) to Jamsetjee Jejeebhoy and T.W. Henderson (Bombay), 25 June 1840, James Matheson – Private Letter Book, MS JM, C5/5.

40 James Matheson (Macao) to William Lyall (London), 29 July 1840, James Matheson – Private Letter Book, MS JM, C5/5. A sword stick or sword cane was a hollow walking stick or cane which concealed a narrow sword, with the handle doubling for the cane and the sword.

41 James Matheson (Macao) to John Abel Smith (London), 25 Junes 1840, James Matheson – Private Letter Book, MS JM, C5/5.

42 James Matheson (Macao) to Jamsetjee Jejeebhoy (Bombay), 1 July 1840, James Matheson – Private Letter Book, MS JM, C5/5.

43 James Matheson to T. W. Henderson (Bombay) and Charles Lyall (Calcutta), 4 August 1840, James Matheson – Private Letter Book, MS JM, C5/5.

44 Fay, *The Opium War*, 239.

45 James Matheson (Macao) to John Thacker (London), 2 October 1840, James Matheson – Private Letter Book, MS JM, C5/5.

46 Draft of a document addressed to the House of Lords and entitled "Measures to be Taken with regard to China," 1839, Palmerston Papers, University of Southampton, MS 62 PP/MM/CH/5.

47 Gelber, *Opium, Soldiers and Evangelicals*, 104–5; Fay, *The Opium War*, 217.

48 Gelber, *Opium, Soldiers and Evangelicals*, 103–4; Fay, *The Opium War*, 218.

49 James Matheson (Macao) to William Jardine (London), 1 September 1840, James Matheson – Private Letter Book, MS JM, C5/5.

50 James Matheson (Macao) to John Abel Smith (London), 2 October 1840, James Matheson – Private Letter Book, MS JM, C5/5.

51 James Matheson (Macao) to Jamsetjee Jejeebhoy (Bombay), 12 October 1840, James Matheson – Private Letter Book, MS JM, C5/5.

52 James Matheson (Macao) to Jamsetjee Jejeebhoy (Bombay), 18 September 1840, James Matheson – Private Letter Book, MS JM, C5/5.

53 James Matheson (Macao) to Jamsetjee Jejeebhoy (Bombay), 10 November 1840, James Matheson – Private Letter Book, MS JM, C5/5.

54 Fay, *The Opium War*, 238–9.

55 Wakeman, "The Canton Trade and the Opium War," 196; Kuo, *A Critical Study of the First Anglo-Chinese War*, 139–40; Gelber, *Opium, Soldiers and Evangelicals*, 111; Fay, *The Opium War*, 231–2.

56 Fay, *The Opium War*, 236; Gelber, *Opium, Soldiers and Evangelicals*, 113; James Matheson (Macao) to James Adam Smith (Manila), 2 December 1840, James Matheson – Private Letter Book, MS JM, C5/6. Admiral Elliot feared that he would not live long enough to reach England, but he actually lived for twenty more years.

57 Wakeman, "The Canton Trade and the Opium War," 196.

58 Waley, *The Opium War through Chinese Eyes*, 124; Kuo, *A Critical Study of the First Anglo-Chinese War*, 141; Chang, *Commissioner Lin and the Opium War*, 212. Kuo maintains that Lin was "the first and last Chinese statesman who fought against opium with the zeal of a true patriot." His disgrace was not permanent, for he served as acting governor general of Shensi and Kansu in 1845 and later as governor general of Yunnan and Kweichow. He died in November 1850 at age sixty-seven.

59 *Canton Press*, 5 September 1840, 1.

60 William Jardine (Cheltenham) to Jamsetjee Jejeebhoy, 3 August 1840, Incoming Correspondence – Great Britain/Private, MS JM, B1/8; Reid, "The Steel Frame," 22, 32.

61 William Jardine (Halleaths) to Jamsetjee Jejeebhoy (Bombay), 3 October and 1 November 1840, Incoming Correspondence – Great Britain/Private, MS JM, B1/8.

62 William Jardine (Halleaths) to Jamsetjee Jejeebhoy (Bombay), 3 October 1840, Incoming Correspondence – Great Britain/Private, MS JM, B1/8.

63 William Jardine (London) to Jamsetjee Jejeebhoy (Bombay), 2 November 1840, Incoming Correspondence – London/Private, MS JM, B1/10.

64 James Matheson (Macao) to Charles Lyall (Calcutta), 18 October and 26 October 1840, and to T.W. Henderson (Bombay), 17 October 1840, James Matheson – Private Letter Book, MS JM, C5/6.

65 James Matheson (Macao) to Jamsetjee Jejeebhoy (Bombay), 12 August and 28 November 1840; to T. Scott (Singapore), 15 September 1840; and to T.W. Henderson, 15 September 1840, James Matheson – Private Letter Book, MS JM, C5/5.

66 James Matheson (Macao) to William Jardine (London), 21 and 22 November 1840, James Matheson – Private Letter Book, MS JM, C5/5.

67 James Matheson (Macao) to Charles Lyall (Calcutta), 9 December 1840, and to T.W. Henderson (Bombay), 26 December 1840, James Matheson – Private Letter Book, MS JM, C5/5.

68 James Matheson (Macao) to William Jardine (London), 4 January 1841, James Matheson – Private Letter Book, MS JM, C5/6.

69 James Matheson (Macao) to Jamsetjee Jejeebhoy (Bombay), 9 November 1840 and 16 December 1840, and to William Jardine (London), 29 November 1840, James Matheson – Private Letter Book, MS JM, C5/5.

70 James Matheson (Macao) to William Jardine (London), 29 November 1840, James Matheson – Private Letter Book, MS JM, C5/5.

71 James Matheson (Macao) to T.W. Henderson (Bombay), 26 December 1840, and to C. Ardaseer (Bombay), 27 December 1840, James Matheson – Private Letter Book, MS JM, C5/6.

72 James Matheson (Macao) to Jamsetjee Jejeebhoy (Bombay), 28 December 1849, James Matheson – Private Letter Book, MS JM, C5/6.

73 Gelber, *Opium, Soldiers and Evangelicals*, 114–15.

74 Kuo, *A Critical Study of the First Anglo-Chinese War*, 145, sets the Chinese casualties that day as 500 dead and 300 wounded; and the British casualties as 38 wounded.

75 Fay, *The Opium War*, 272–5; Gelber, *Opium, Soldiers and Evangelicals*, 115–16.

76 James Matheson (Macao) to William Jardine (London), 15 January 1841; emphasis in original. Also to Jamsetjee Jejeebhoy (Bombay), 16 January 1841, James Matheson – Private Letter Book, MS JM, C5/6.

77 Kuo, *A Critical Study of the First Anglo-Chinese War*, 146.

78 James Matheson (Macao) to William Jardine (London), 22 January 1840, James Matheson – Private Letter Book, MS JM, C5/6.

79 James Matheson (Macao) to Wiliam Jardine (London), 23 January 1841, James Matheson – Private Letter Book, MS JM, C5/6.

80 James Matheson (Macao) to William Jardine (London), 22 January 1841, James Matheson – Private Letter Book, MS JM, C5/6.

81 Blake, *Jardine Matheson*, 109–11; Fay, "The Opening of China," 78; Bard, *Traders of Hong Kong*, 41; James Matheson (Macao) to William Jardine (London), 30 January 1841, James Matheson – Private Letter Book, MS JM, C5/6. The superintendent found a shanty town already existing when he arrived.

82 Kuo, *A Critical Study of the First Anglo-Chinese War*, 147–8; Lovell, *The Opium War*, 136–8.

83 James Matheson (Macao) to William Jardine (London), 19 February 1841, James Matheson – Private Letter Book, MS JM, C5/6.

84 James Matheson (Macao) to William Jardine (London), 19 March 1841, James Matheson – Private Letter Book, MS JM, C5/6; emphasis in original.

85 James Matheson (Macao) to William Jardine (London), 19 February 1841; to Jamsetjee Jejeebhoy (Bombay), 26 February 1841; and to John Abel Smith (London), 26 February 1841, James Matheson – Private Letter Book, MS JM, C5/6.

86 *Canton Press* (Macao), 27 March 1841, extra; Fay, *The Opium War*, 278–82.

87 James Matheson (Macao) to T.W. Henderson (Bombay), 20 February 1841; to Jamsetjee Jejeebhoy (Bombay), 24 March 1841; and James Matheson (Canton) to Jamsetjee Jejeebhoy (Bombay), 15 April 1841, James Matheson – Private Letter Book, MS JM, C5/6.

88 James Matheson (Macao) to William Jardine (London) and Jamsetjee Jejeebhoy (Bombay), 21 April 1841, and to T.W. Henderson (Bombay) 2 May 1841, James Matheson – Private Letter Book, MS JM, C5/6.

89 James Matheson (Macao) to T.W. Henderson (Bombay), 2 May 1841, James Matheson – Private Letter Book, MS JM, C5/6.

90 James Matheson (Macao) to T.W. Henderson (Bombay), 2 May 1841; to Jamsetjee Jejeebhoy (Bombay), 2 May 1841; to M.D. Hunter (Sydney, New South Wales), 10 May 1841; and to William Jardine (London), 19 May 1841, James Matheson – Private Letter Book, MS JM, C5/6 and C5/7.

91 *Canton Press*, 29 May 1841.

92 James Matheson (Macao) to William Jardine (London), 19 and 27 May 1841, and to William Haylett (Madras), 20 May 1841, James Matheson – Private Letter Book, MS JM, C5/7; Fay, *The Opium War*, 289.

93 James Matheson (Macao) to William Jardine (London), 27 May 1841, and to Jamsetjee Jejeebhoy (Bombay), 28 May 1841, James Matheson – Private Letter Book, MS JM, C5/7.

94 James Matheson (Macao) to Jamsetjee Jejeebhoy (Bombay), 28 May and 2 June 1841, James Matheson – Private Letter Book, MS JM, C5/7.

95 Fay, *The Opium War*, 297–303.

96 Beeching, *The Chinese Opium Wars*, 154.

97 *Chinese Repository*, vol. 10 (July 1840): 350–1; *Canton Press*, 12 June 1840.

98 Ibid. The terms of sale were detailed in *Chinese Repository* for July. Forty lots with sea frontage of 100 feet were to be auctioned. Successful bidders were expected to build a structure worth at least £1,000 on their sites. The editor of the *Canton Press* was skeptical about the risk of investing in land on Hong Kong: "Many of our neighbors are gone to venture their money, but many are holding back. In this uncertainty many will abstain from purchasing a pig in a poke." *Canton Press*, 12 June 1840.

99 Fay, *The Opium War*, 303; Reid, "East Point," 196–7; Welsh, *A Borrowed Place*, 134–5; Andrew Jardine (Macao) to Jamsetjee Jejeebhoy (Bombay), 8 June 1841, James Matheson – Private Letter Book, MS JM, C5/7. Elliot asked Jardine, Matheson, and Dent to circulate a letter explaining his policies for acquiring property on the island. *Canton Press*, 26 June 1841; *Canton Register*, 22 June 1840, supplement.

100  *Canton Register,* 31 August 1841, 1. Predictably, the editor of the *Press* had reservations about this initiative by Matheson. Regarding the vessels carrying lumber: "We much doubt they will answer as a speculation, labor being here both good and cheap, and all sorts of materials abundant." *Canton Press,* 11 September 1841.

101  James Matheson (Macao) to James Ryan and Joseph Coolidge (Canton), 21, 22, and 24 June 1841, and to John Abel Smith (London), 15 July 1841, James Matheson – Private Letter Book, MS JM, C5/7.

102  James Matheson (Macao) to Jamsetjee Jejeebhoy (Bombay), 15 July 1841, and to T.W. Henderson, 15 July 1841, James Matheson – Private Letter Book, MS JM, C5/7.

103  Fay, *The Opium War,* 305–7; W.S.B. (Boyd) of the Jardine, Matheson Macao office to Joseph Coolidge (Canton), 24 July 1841, James Matheson – Private Letter Book, MS JM, C5/7; James Matheson (Macao) to Charles Lyall (Calcutta), 7 August 1841, James Matheson – Private Letter Book, MS JM, C5/7.

104  On the very day that Elliot received the news, the *Canton Press* reported that Jardine and a number of other merchants, upon learning of the Chuenpi settlement, had called upon Palmerston to declare that Elliot had lost the confidence of the British government by showing himself unequal to the duties entrusted to him. *Canton Press,* 24 July 1841.

105  Fay, *The Opium War,* 311, citing *The Letters of Queen Victoria* (1907) 1: 329; emphasis in original.

106  Gelber, *Opium, Soldiers and Evangelicals,* 124; Fay, *The Opium War,* 309, citing Elliot's letter to Lord Aberdeen, 25 January 1842 (FO 17/61).

107  William Jardine (London) to Jamsetjee Jejeebhoy (Bombay), 3 May 1841, Incoming Correspondence – London/Private, MS JM, B1/10.

108  James Matheson (Macao) to William Jardine (London), 24 August 1841, James Matheson – Private Letter Book, MS JM, C/7.

109  William Jardine (London) to James Matheson (Macao), 31 May 1841, cited by Fairbank, *Trade and Diplomacy on the China Coast,* 82–3, from the Yorke ms., 333.

110  James Matheson (Macao) to William Jardine (London), 24 August 1841, James Matheson – Private Letter Book, MS JM, C5/7.

111  *The Times* (London), 8 November 1841, 4. *The Times* Digital Archive, find.galegroup.com.helin.uri.edu/ttda/newspaperRetrieve.do (accessed 5 July 2013).

112 James Matheson (Macao) to William Jardine (London) and Jamsetjee
Jejeebhoy (Bombay), 24 August 1841, James Matheson – Private Letter
Book, MS JM, C5/7.

113 Gelber, *Opium, Soldiers and Evangelicals*, 125–7.

114 Fairbank, *Trade and Diplomacy on the China Coast*, 82.

115 James Matheson (Macao) to James Adam Smith (Manila), 25 September
1841, James Matheson – Private Letter Book, MS JM, C5/7. He directed
Magniac Smith (London) to place £4,500 at the disposal of Gordon and
Stuart, Edinburgh, and authorized Magniac Smith to deliver to them the
deeds for his estate of Achany, just outside Lairg. In a different communication, he requested that those London agents place £3,000–4,000 at
the disposal of his brother, Major Thomas Matheson. James Matheson to
Magniac Smith (London), 24 August 1841 and 18 March 1841, James
Matheson – Private Letter Book, MS JM, C5/7.

116 James Matheson (Macao) to James Adam Smith (Manila), 25 September
1841 and 29 December 1841, and to Jamsetjee Jejeebhoy (Bombay),
8 October 1841, James Matheson – Private Letter Book, MS JM, C5/7.

117 James Matheson (Macao) to Magniac Smith (London), 12 May and
15 November 1841; to Lyall Brothers and Company, 15 November 1841;
and to John L. Anderson (London), 23 December 1841, James
Matheson – Private Letter Book, MS JM, C5/7.

118 James Matheson (Macao) to Smith, Elder and Company (London),
23 June 1841, and to James Adam Smith (Manila), 29 December 1841,
James Matheson – Private Letter Book, MS JM, C5/7.

119 Greenberg, *British Trade and the Opening of China*, 209; James Matheson
(Macao) to John Abel Smith (London), 8 September 1841; to various
correspondents, November and December 1841; and to Jamsetjee
Jejeebhoy (Bombay) and R.W. Crawford (Bombay), 27 December 1841,
James Matheson – Private Letter Book, MS JM, C5/7.

120 James Matheson (Macao) to John Abel Smith (London), 8 September
1841, James Matheson – Private Letter Book, MS JM, C5/7; Fay, *The
Opium War*, 324.

121 James Matheson (Macao) to James Adam Smith (Manila), 23 November
1840, and to John Abel Smith (London), 28 March 1841, James
Matheson – Private Letter Book, MS JM, C5/6; and to E. de Otadui and
James Adam Smith (Manila), 29 December 1841, MS JM, C5/7.

122 James Matheson (Macao) to E. de Otadui and James Adam Smith
(Manila), 3 November and 29 December 1841, James Matheson

– Private Letter Book, MS JM, C5/7; and James Matheson (Macao) to E. de Otadui, 4 March 1842, Alexander Matheson – Private Letter Book, MS JM, C6/2.

123 James Matheson (Macao) to George James Gordon (Calcutta), 16 August 1841, James Matheson – Private Letter Book, MS JM, C5/7; and Jerome Tannadish, "George Chinnery," 238–9.

124 James Matheson (Macao) to M.D. Hunter and Company (Sydney, New South Wales), April and 27 November 1841, and James Matheson to Mitchell Scobie (Port Philip, Australia), 10 May 1841, James Matheson – Private Letter Book, MS JM, C5/6 and C5/7. He also entertained the alternate possibility of purchasing land in New Zealand.

Matheson's second cousin (whose name was also James Matheson) had joined M.D. Hunter's firm at Sydney in the course of 1841, but he was a young man and not likely to have the sort of influence that could induce Matheson to sink such a great sum of money into a land speculation for emigration purposes.

125 James Matheson (Macao) to R.W. Crawford (Bombay), 3 January and 2 March 1842; to E. de Otadui (Manila), 7 February 1842; and to Jamsetjee Jejeebhoy (Bombay), 4 March 1842, Alexander Matheson – Private Letter Book, MS JM, C6/2.

126 James Matheson (Macao) to R.W. Crawford (Bombay), 3 January 1842; to Jamsetjee Jejeebhoy (Bombay), 19 January 1842; and to Captain Green (aboard *Reliance*), n.d. [early February 1842], Alexander Matheson – Private Letter Book, MS JM, C6/2.

127 James Matheson (Macao) to R.W. Crawford (Bombay), 2 March 1842, Alexander Matheson – Private Letter Book, MS JM, C6/2.

## CHAPTER ELEVEN

1 Jejeebhoy had recently been knighted by Queen Victoria.

2 The address is recorded in Mackenzie, "A History of the Mathesons," 492–3. A slightly different version of the address, taken from the *Bombay Courier*, is reported in *The Scotsman*, 13 August 1842, 4.

3 Mackenzie, "A History of the Mathesons," 494.

4 Thampi maintains that letters written by Jejeebhoy toward the end of his life reveal that he felt a sense of disillusion with Jardine, Matheson and Company, especially after Jardine left Canton. He complained that they had delayed the disposal of cargoes he had shipped to them, that they

had sold goods at low prices, and that they had caused him to incur heavy losses. Thampi, "Parsees in the China Trade," 22.

5  Reid, "The Steel Frame," 24, 136.

6  Blake, *Jardine Matheson*, 114.

7  Ibid.

8  Reid, "The Steel Frame," 24–5.

9  Great Britain, House of Commons, *Debates*, 17 March 1842, Series 3, vol. 61, 786.

10  Ibid., 792–3.

11  Owen, *British Opium Policy in China and India*, 183–4, 190–1.

12  Fay, *The Opium War*, 369.

13  Kuo, *A Critical Study of the First Anglo-Chinese War*, 298, doc. 50.

14  Fay, *The Opium War*, 361.

15  Wakeman, "The Canton Trade and the Opium War," 221.

16  Gelber, *Opium, Soldiers and Evangelicals*, 147.

17  Waley, *The Opium War through Chinese Eyes*, 232.

18  Kuo, *A Critical Study of the First Anglo-Chinese War*, 165–72; Fay, *The Opium War*, 362.

19  Gelber, *Opium, Soldiers and Evangelicals*, 148.

20  Bard, *Traders of Hong Kong*, 38.

21  Deyan, "The Study of Parsee Merchants," 57.

22  Hoe, *The Private Life of Old Hong Kong*, 50.

23  Lord Palmerston to John Abel Smith, 28 November 1842, cited in Greenberg, *British Trade and the Opening of China*, 214–15; Collis, *Foreign Mud*, 254–5; and Blake, *Jardine Matheson*, 106. Privately, Alexander Matheson was unconvinced that peace would be good for the firm.

24  James Matheson (Glasgow) to Jamsetjee Jejeebhoy (Bombay), 2 December 1842, Incoming Correspondence – Great Britain/Private, MS JM, B1/8.

25  John Abel Smith (London) to Jamsetjee Jejeebhoy (Bombay), and from James Matheson (London) to Jejeebhoy, both 6 January 1843, Incoming Correspondence – London/Private, MS JM, B1/10.

26  John Abel Smith (London), 3 March 1843, reporting Jardine's death to an unnamed acquaintance of James Matheson (in Matheson's absence from London), letter 2307, MS JM.

27  His campaign announcement is reprinted in Reid, "The Steel Frame," 25.

28  Owen, *British Opium Policy in China and India*, 230–1.

29  James Matheson to Captain McMinnies, 22 April 1843, cited in Wakeman, "The Canton Trade and the Opium War," 223.

30  Alexander Matheson, 10 September 1843, cited in ibid., 150.

31  Reid, "The Steel Frame, 26; Owen, *British Opium Policy in China and India*, 194.

32  Mary Jane Matheson's parents were both prominent and wealthy persons, with social pedigrees. Ann Mary Fowler was an accomplished linguist (English, French, Italian, Latin) who taught her ten children not only languages but also piano, harp, and drawing. She brought £40,000 into the marriage and subsequently inherited £100,000. Michael Henry Percival was given an imperial appointment as collector of customs at Quebec in 1810, a position that carried an income of £8,000 per year. In 1813 he was made magistrate with authority throughout the province, following which he was named to the Legislative Council of Quebec (1818) and was appointed commissioner of the port of Quebec (1826). In the midst of this flourishing political career, the family had acquired a vast estate at Sillery (just west of Quebec City). He named the property (which would at mid-century become the home of the governor general) "Spencer Wood." The family left Canada in 1828 to spend a year in Florence, Italy (when Mary Jane was nine years old). It had been their intention to return to Spencer Wood. However, her father died at sea in October 1829, and his widow took the family back to Britain rather than returning to Canada.

33  The account of the marriage celebrations appeared in the *Inverness Courier*, 15 November 1843. A notice of the ceremony was published in the *Scotsman*, 15 November 1843.

34  Sutherland Sasines, 1751–1860 (Highland Regional Archive, Inverness Library), 1839: nos. 63 and 64. Ketteringham, *A History of Lairg*, 192. Achany is located south of the town of Lairg.

35  Ketteringham, *A History of Lairg*, 191.

36  Macdonald, *Lewis*, 37–9.

37  Ketteringham, *A History of Lairg*, 189–91.

38  Reid, "Commodities: Tea," 128–9.

39  Fay, "The Opening of China," 78–9; Welsh, *A Borrowed Place*, 44–6.

40  Blake, *Jardine Matheson*, 124.

41  Welsh, *A Borrowed Place*, 184–8, citing the report of the Select Committee of the House of Commons to Enquire into the Present State of the Commercial Relations between Great Britain and China, March 1847.

42  Matheson (aboard *Hercules* at Hong Kong) to John Abel Smith (London), 24 September 1839, James Matheson – Private Letter Book, MS JM, C5/4.

43  Trocki, *Opium, Empire and the Global Political Economy*, 112.

44 Blake, *Jardine Matheson*, 139–40; Fay, "The Opening of China," 79.

45 Blake, *Jardine Matheson*, 117.

46 Ibid.; Reid, "The Steel Frame," 28. In time, Donald inherited the Scottish estates of his uncle James in Sutherland and on the Isle of Lewis after the death of Lady Matheson.

47 John Abel Smith and Hollingworth Magniac were the partners carried over from the old firm. The other partners in the new firm were Alexander Matheson, Hugh Matheson, and Andrew Jardine. Reid, "The Steel Frame," 26–7; Blake, *Jardine Matheson*, 116. The partners are listed in an appendix of Keswick, ed., *The Thistle and the Jade*, 264.

48 Harcourt, *Flagships of Imperialism*, 163–4.

49 The Board of Directors approved his appointment unanimously at their meeting of 5 December 1848, and he wrote to them (from Stornoway) on 26 December expressing his thanks for their confidence in him. He took up his duties as chairman in April 1849. Board of Directors Minutes, 5 December 1848 and 2 January 1849, Records of the Peninsular and Oriental Steam Navigation Company, National Maritime Museum, London.

50 Harcourt, *Flagships of Imperialism*, 155.

51 Trocki, *Opium, Empire and the Global Political Economy*, 112.

52 David and Stephen Howarth, in *The Story of P&O*, acknowledge that opium was carried by the company's ships. However, they maintain that the steamship line did not buy or sell the drug on its own account. They account for the failure of the P&O freight route from Hong Kong to Macao and Canton by saying: "P&O was too law-abiding and the carriers of drugs too ruthless" (78–9). But Freda Harcourt offers abundant evidence to document the steamship company's entrance into the opium-carrying business, and its consideration of head-to-head competition with Jardine's sailing ships between Calcutta and Hong Kong. Harcourt, *Flagships of Imperialism*, chapter 3.

53 Trocki, *Opium, Empire and the Global Political Economy*, 112.

54 Harcourt, *Flagships of Imperialism*, 89–96.

55 Board of Directors minutes, 5 November 1852, P&O Records.

56 Copies of letters between Jardine, Matheson and Company (Hong Kong) and certain Bombay merchants (Jamsetjee Furdoonjee and Cursetjee Furdoonjee), relating to the sale and shipping of opium from Bombay, 9 August 1858 and n.d. but from the same period. The correspondence confirms the use of P&O steamers for opium consigned to Jardine, Matheson. P&O Records.

57  Board of Directors minutes, 22 November 1853, containing letter from James Matheson, Edinburgh, 20 November 1853, P&O Records.

58  Anderson, "Development of the P&O Company."

59  Freda Harcourt clarifies the income statistics by charting the relation of receipts to outlay and then adding the government subsidy for mail delivery. Her table (7.1) makes it clear that the firm's profitability was assured by the mail contracts; otherwise, the P&O operations would have been only marginally profitable in some years and not profitable at all in other years. Harcourt, *Flagships of Imperialism*, 193.

60  Ibid.

61  Reports from the managing directors to the Board, 26 May 1858, P&O Records.

## CHAPTER TWELVE

1  "Election for Ross and Cromarty," *Inverness Courier*, 17 August 1847, 2–3.

2  Index to the *Inverness Courier* for 1852, 258. The vote totals were 288 for Matheson, 218 for Ross.

3  Testimony of James Matheson, MP. Second Report of the Select Committee on Sites for Churches (Scotland), House of Commons (1847), 31–2.

4  Macdonald, *Lewis*, 39; Grant, *A Shilling for Your Scowl*, 37. The last direct male descendant of the Mackenzies of Kintail (the original proprietors by a grant of King James VI) was Francis, Earl of Seaforth, who died in 1815.

5  MacKenzie, "A History of the Mathesons," 496.

6  "History of the Lews Castle," http://www.stornowayhistoricalsociety.org. uk/features/castle/ (accessed 14 June 2007).

7  Macdonald, *Lewis*, 39.

8  Mackenzie, "A History of the Mathesons," 496–7.

9  Gray, "The Highland Potato Famine of the 1840's," 357.

10  Devine, *The Great Highland Famine*, 4–5.

11  Ibid., 15.

12  Gray, "The Highland Potato Famine of the 1840's," 357–66.

13  Ibid., 368.

14  Devine, *The Great Highland Famine*, 43–4.

15  Ibid., 61, 69, 99.

16  Macdonald, *Lewis*, 40.

17  Devine, *The Great Highland Famine*, 89, 159.

18 Ibid., 212, citing the Report to the Board of Supervision by Sir John McNeill on the Western Highlands and Islands (usually called the McNeill Report), Parliamentary Papers, 26 (1851), appendix A.

19 Testimony of James Matheson, Second Report of the Select Committee on Sites for Churches (Scotland), House of Commons, 1847, 32.

20 Ibid., 90.

21 Paterson, "History of Education in the Island of Lewis," 65–7; author's conversation with Duncan Morrison, then resident of the former Seminary building, 13 May 1993.

22 Mackenzie, "A History of the Mathesons," 499.

23 Devine, *The Great Highland Famine*, 102; Macdonald, *Lewis*, 41; Mackenzie, "A History of the Mathesons," 497.

24 Mackenzie, "A History of the Mathesons," 498.

25 Devine, *The Great Highland Famine*, 100–5.

26 Macdonald, *Lewis*, 41.

27 Devine, *The Great Highland Famine*, 103–4.

28 Devine, *The Great Highland Famine*, 213. In spite of the stringent application of the new estate policy, James Shaw Grant allows that Mackenzie was not a cruel man. "If we judge John Munro Mackenzie against his contemporaries on other Highland estates, we must come to the conclusion that, by the standards of his day, he was just, and even, at times, compassionate." Grant, *A Shilling for Your Scowl*, 59. Presumably, James Matheson viewed Mackenzie with favour for precisely the qualities that Grant cites.

29 Devine, *The Great Highland Famine*, 216; Grant, *A Shilling for Your Scowl*, 50–1.

30 Am Baile: Highland History and Culture, http://www.ambaile.org.uk/en/item/item_page.jsp?item_id+9381 (accessed 20 June 2007); "Scotland in the Nineteenth Century," Glasgow Digital Library, http://gdlr.strath.ac.uk/haynin/haynin1403.htm (accessed 20 June 2007).

31 Devine, *The Great Highland Famine*, 212–13, and appendix 10. The figures fluctuate from one author to another. Devine gives a total of 2,337; his statistics seem most reliable because he uses John Munro Mackenzie's estate diary and he accounts for the totals by listing the number of emigrants in a ship-by-ship tabulation.

32 Macdonald, *Lewis*, 42.

33 Devine, *The Great Highland Famine*, 221. In a study of the Scottish and French settlers of Winslow Township in Quebec, J. Irvine Little reveals that Winslow Township was the final destination for 400 of the Lewis emigrants

of 1851, but only 203 were there to be recorded in the census of 1852, which means that they did not immediately settle in that farming community. Little, *Crofters and Habitants,* 45; http://www.books.google.com/books ?id=YOlafx9QE4sC&dq=crofters+and+habitants&printsec=frontcover&sou rce=web&ots=jjEEakWkOi&sig=4GEi2p44uLRpLGQEfNh8lGiTsME#PPA4 6,M1 (accessed 20 June 2007).

34  Devine, *The Great Highland Famine,* 220, citing the *Inverness Advertiser,* 4 November 1851.

35  Devine, *The Great Highland Famine,* 222–3; Little, *Crofters and Habitants,* 26, citing the McNeill Report, 1,045. James Shaw Grant maintains that Mackenzie believed fishing to be the proper remedy for the scarcities of 1851 and tried to persuade James Matheson to develop the necessary harbours and piers, but that Matheson declined to pursue that course of action. Grant, *A Shilling for Your Scowl,* 52.

36  In nineteenth-century usage, the terms "Lewis" and "The Lews" were used more or less interchangeably, with the latter eventually becoming an archaic form of reference to the island.

37  Information from the National Archives (Kew) and the British Library Newspaper Archive (Colindale) provided by John Faid, genealogist and historian of the English branch of the Clan Matheson Society, June 2007.

38  "Rejoicing in Stornoway," *Inverness Courier,* 23 January 1851.

39  "Rejoicings in Sutherland," *Inverness Courier,* 16 January 1851.

40  Ketteringham, *A History of Lairg,* 35.

41  Achany House continued to be a family home for Mathesons until 1948. Sir James had enlarged the house by the addition of wings for dining and drawing rooms, which gave it its current frontal breadth. His nephew Donald developed the house further by adding a third floor and constructing turrets over the bays in the wings. See the drawings of Achany in Ketteringham, *A History of Lairg,* 160.

42  Ibid., 97–8.

43  Macdonald, *Lewis,* 43; Mackenzie, "A History of the Mathesons," 498–9.

44  Mackenzie, "A History of the Mathesons," 500.

45  Ibid.

46  Mackenzie, *The Book of the Lews,* 175. There were eighteen licensed drinking establishments in Stornoway (with a population of just under five thousand) just a decade before James Matheson acquired Lewis.

47  Macdonald, *Lewis,* 42–3.

48  Geddes, *The Isle of Lewis and Harris,* 232.

49  Nicolson, *Lord of the Isles,* 205.

50 Mackenzie, *The Western Isles*, 56–9. Lord Leverhulme had first conceived the challenge of converting Lewis to a new economy at the time of his initial visit in 1884. But he held the estate for only five years, before conceding away that dream. In 1923 he gave the parish of Stornoway to the Stornoway Trust, and over the next two years most of the rest of the estate was sold to individuals or syndicates.

51 Prior to occupying the Lews Castle, James and Mary Jane Matheson had lived in a cottage located at Goathill, to the east of Matheson Road.

52 Extract from the minutes of Lodge Fortrose, for 30 November 1847, provided by George J. Clavey, past secretary of the lodge. Sir James himself was not a Mason.

53 Details of the building are drawn from a site visit and from the following electronic resources: "Buildings at Risk Register for Scotland," http://www.buildingsatrisk.org.uk/view.asp?SCT+Ref+No=1545 (accessed 2 July 2007); Stornoway Historical Society, "History of the Lews Castle," http://www.stornowayhistoricalsociety.org.uk/features/castle (accessed 2 July 2007); "Lews Castle, Stornoway, Scotland," http://www.lews-castle.com/index.asp (accessed 2 July 2007).

54 *The Scotsman*, 23 July 1843, 2. Prince Alfred had been invited to succeed the king of Greece, who abdicated in 1862, but diplomatic considerations precluded his accepting. Being a lieutenant in the navy was not quite the same as being king of Greece, but roaring nights like this at the Lews Castle may have compensated somewhat for the letdown.

55 *The Scotsman*, 19 November 1868, 8.

56 Cunningham, *The Castle Grounds*, 10 and appendixes.

57 Macdonald, *Lewis*, 43.

58 Grant, *A Shilling for Your Scowl*, 9.

59 Ibid., 7–9. This book presents a ringing indictment of Donald Munro, and some of the blameworthiness is assigned to Sir James Matheson.

60 Ibid., 196–7.

61 *The Scotsman*, 20 August 1863, 8.

62 Grant, *A Shilling for Your Scowl*, 120–3.

63 *The Scotsman*, 10 June 1863.

64 Grant, *A Shilling for Your Scowl*, 116. Grant assumes that Matheson's Edinburgh lawyers had advised him to acquire the harbour.

65 Ibid., 127.

66 This traditional Scottish term refers to a summer grazing pasture on which a rough hut may be built.

67 *Report of the Trial of the So-called Bernera Rioters*, 10–12.

68 Macdonald, *Lewis*, 172.

69 Ibid., 4; Grant, *A Shilling for Your Scowl*, 145.

70 Grant, *A Shilling for Your Scowl*, 147; *Report of the Trial of the So-called Bernera Rioters*, 4; MacDonald of Gisla, *Tales and Traditions of the Lews*, 148–52. Accounts differ as to whether Sir James received them in the Castle, or whether he met them outside, or whether they were led into the conservatory where Lady Matheson served them bread and beef, along with milk and coffee.

71 "The Shah" was formally dethroned in May 1875, when Sir James appointed his nephew Hugh Matheson as his baron Baillie, factor, and commissioner. The court document provided a face-saving cover for Munro by recording that he was in the process of resigning. MacDonald of Gisla, *Tales and Traditions of the Lews*, 152; Grant, *A Shilling for Your Scowl*, 186.

72 *Report of the Trial of the So-called Bernera Rioters*, 11.

73 Grant, *A Shilling for Your Scowl*, 156.

74 Macdonald, *Lewis*, 172.

75 Devine, *Clanship to the Crofters' War*, 228.

76 Letter from Hugh M. Matheson to the *Glasgow Weekly Mail*, 2 April 1877, in Geddes, *The Isle of Lewis and Harris*, appendix, 4-6.

77 Additional letters and editorial commentary, from the *Glasgow Daily Mail*, the *Echo* (London), and *The Scotsman* (Edinburgh), are contained in the appendix to *The Island of Lews*.

78 *Inverness Advertiser*, 10 January 1879.

79 Nelson, *Queen Victoria and the Discovery of the Riviera*, 12, citing James Henry Bennet, *Winter and Spring on the Shores of the Mediterranean*, 5th ed. (London: J. and A. Churchill 1875), 8.

80 Extrait des Registres des Actes de L'État-Civil, Ville de Menton, for James Matheson, deceased 31 December 1878; extract issued 18 June 2007.

81 *Inverness Courier*, 2 January 1879, 5.

82 Prior to the funeral, a large public gathering was held at Stornoway on 4 January 1879 to allow residents of Lewis to express their sentiments of loss and to adopt a motion of sympathy and condolence to be sent to Lady Matheson. On 4 February some of them set out to attend the funeral at Lairg, but mechanical problems with the paddle steamer *Ondine*, caught in a gale, imperiled the sixty passengers and forced the steamer to return to Stornoway after nine hours at sea. *Inverness Advertiser*, 10 January 1879 and 7 February 1879.

83 Great Britain, Parliament, Scotland, *Owners of Lands and Heritages*. There were two codicils to the English will and two to the Scottish will; in the latter, the second codicil was attached only two months before his death.

84 In Scottish law, life rent was the entitlement to enjoy the benefits of the property for life, but not the right to dispose of the property.

85 Will of Sir James Matheson, Bart., Scottish Record Office, SC 70/1/194. A tax of £21,000 was paid on the estate on 26 May 1879.

86 *Inverness Courier*, 2 January 1879. The lavish tribute of the *Inverness Courier* must be weighed in keeping with its status as the foremost journal of support for the pro-landlord lobby in northern Scotland.

87 Ibid.

88 Testimonials to Sir James Matheson from local government records held by Tasglann nan Eilean Siar (Hebridean Archives), provided by Comhairle nan Eilean Siar, Stornoway, Lewis.

89 John H. Macleod, "The Late Sir James Matheson of Lewis," *Stornoway Gazette & West Coast Advertiser*, 29 September 1950. An unsigned response on 6 October 1950 described letters from Sir James (now lost) which revealed the "lively and enquiring mind" of a person with naturalist interests. The writer, who was not as effusive as John Macleod, commented that "Lewis was certainly luckier in its landlords, though not in its factors, than most parts of the Highlands and Islands, in the latter half of the 19th century."

90 Ibid.

### POSTLUDE

1 Niebuhr, *Moral Man and Immoral Society*, 4.

2 Brook and Wakabayashi, eds., *Opium Regimes*, 7.

3 Ibid., 2–3. The Introduction to this work offers a good, brief summary of the patterns of historical interpretation of the causes of the Opium War.

4 Palsetia, "The Parsis of India and the Opium Trade in China," 658. In that connection the author immediately raises the name of the much-respected Bombay philanthropist Jamsetjee Jejeebhoy, who was deeply engaged in shipping opium to China: "[His] chief preoccupation was the efficient conduct of his commerce, and in particular the welfare of his goods and the prompt remittance of his payment."

5 Lovell, *The Opium War*, 24

6 William Jardine (Canton) to Thomas Crawford (Bombay), 16 March 1832, William Jardine – Private Letter Book, MS JM, C4/2.

7 Wong, *Deadly Dreams*, 210 and 311.

8 Glenn Melancon argues that Jardine's advice was not as decisive as some scholars, such as Wong, contend. He maintains that Palmerston had

already outlined for Melbourne the alternative responses to China days before he first met with Jardine. Melancon, *Britain's China Policy and the Opium Crisis*, 103.

9  Connell, *A Business in Risk*, 26–37.

10  Cain and Hopkins, *British Imperialism*.

11  Ibid., 119–21.

12  Cain and Hopkins, "Gentlemanly Capitalism and British Expansion Overseas," 518.

13  Ibid., 523, citing C.K. Webster, *The Foreign Policy of Palmerston*, vol. 2 (1951), 750–1.

14  Cain and Hopkins, *British Imperialism*, 48.

15  Ibid., 47.

16  Ibid., 54–6.

17  Cain and Hopkins, "Gentlemanly Capitalism and British Expansion Overseas," 502, citing L.H. Jenks, *The Migration of British Capital to 1875* (1963 repr.), 197.

18  Cain and Hopkins, *British Imperialism*, 308.

# BIBLIOGRAPHY

## MANUSCRIPTS AND ARCHIVES

### *William Jardine and James Matheson*

Jardine Matheson Archive, Cambridge University Library
  William Jardine – Private Letter Books
  James Matheson – Private Letter Books
  Alexander Matheson – Private Letter Book
  Taylor and Matheson – Letter Book
  Yrissari and Company – Letter Book
  Jardine Matheson – Incoming Correspondence, London/Private
  Incoming Correspondence – London
  Incoming Correspondence – Europe/Private, 1839
  Incoming Correspondence – Great Britain/Private
  James Matheson, "Brief Narrative," manuscript account of events at Canton,
    March 1839
Edinburgh University. Extracts from the Matriculation Album for 1810 and
  1811, Manuscripts Division, Edinburgh University Library.
Last Will of William Jardine, 1 September 1843. SC 70/1/64. http://www.
  scotlandspeople.gov.uk/
Royal High School, Edinburgh. Archives of the Royal High School. Extract
  from Class Lists in Library Registers and from Library Ledger of Books
  Borrowed by Pupils, 1809–10.
Sutherland Sasines, 1751–1860. 1839: numbers 63 and 64. Highland
  Regional Archive, Inverness Library.

Ville de Menton, France, Extrait des Registres des Actes de L'État-Civil, for James Matheson, deceased 31 December 1878; extract issued 18 June 2007.

Will of Sir James Matheson, Bart., 5 May 1879. SC 70/1/194. http://www.scotlandspeople.gov.uk/

### Other

Charles N. Talbot Papers, Rhode Island Historical Society, Providence

Napier Papers, William John Napier (9th Lord Napier), National Library of Scotland, Edinburgh

Palmerston Papers, University of Southampton

Peninsular and Oriental Steam Navigation Company. Board of Directors Minutes, 1848–58. Records of the Peninsular and Oriental Steam Navigation Company, National Maritime Museum, London.

### NEWSPAPERS

*Canton Press*, 1839–41

*Canton Register*, 1827–41

*Chinese Repository*, 1834–41

*Inverness Advertiser*, 1879

*Inverness Courier*, 1843, 1847, 1851, 1852, 1879

*The Scotsman*, 1843, 1863, 1868

*The Times* (London), 1840, 1842

### BOOKS, ARTICLES, AND PRINTED SOURCES

Addison, Thomas. *The Journals of Thomas Addison*. Publications of the Navy Records Society, vol. 20: *The Navy Miscellany* (1902). http://books.google.com/books?id=4zQJAAAAIAAJ&pg=PA336&lpg=PA336&dq=The+Journals+of+Thomas+Addison&source=bl&ots=AaxPr9zqZJ&sig=5eu6r_vfWoolfe_JYRbZ–SgfTM&hl=en&sa=X&ei=5-E5U8u2I_XesATtz4LICQ&ved=0CF4Q6AEwCQ#v=onepage&q=The%20Journals%20of%20Thomas%20Addison&f=false (accessed 31 March 2014).

Am Baile: Highland History and Culture. http://www.ambaile.org.uk (accessed 31 March 2014).

Anderson, Sir Donald. "Development of the P&O Company, 1815–1869." In the Company History file, P&O Records, National Maritime Museum, Greenwich.

Antony, Robert J. *Like Froth Floating on the Sea: The World of Pirates and Seafarers in Late Imperial China*. Berkeley, CA: Institute of East Asian Studies 2003.

Applebaum, S., ed. *English Romantic Poetry: An Anthology*. New York: Dover Publications 1996.

Bard, Solomon. *Traders of Hong Kong: Some Foreign Merchant Houses, 1841–1899*. Hong Kong: Urban Council 1993.

Beeching, Jack. *The Chinese Opium Wars*. San Diego, CA: Harcourt Brace Jovanovich 1975.

Bell, Herbert C.F. *Lord Palmerston*. 2 vols. Hamden, CT: Archon Books 1966.

Berridge, Virginia, and Griffith Edwards. *Opium and the People: Opiate Use in Nineteenth Century England*. New Haven, CT: Yale University Press 1981.

Bickers, Robert. *The Scramble for China: Foreign Devils and the Qing Empire, 1832–1914*. London: Penguin Books 2012.

Blake, Robert. *Jardine Matheson, Traders of the Far East*. London: Weidenfeld and Nicolson 1999.

Booth, Martin. *Opium: A History*. New York: St Martin's Press 1996.

Bourne, Kenneth. *Palmerston, The Early Years, 1784–1841*. New York: Macmillan 1982.

Bowen, H.V. *The Business of Empire: The East India Company and Imperial Britain, 1765–1833*. Cambridge: Cambridge University Press 2006.

– "Britain in the Indian Ocean and Beyond." In H.V. Bowen, Elizabeth Mancke, and John G. Reid, eds., *Britain's Oceanic Empire: Atlantic and Indian Ocean Worlds, 1550–1850*. Cambridge: Cambridge University Press 2012. 45–65.

Brook, Timothy, and Bob Tadashi Wakabayashi, eds. *Opium Regimes: China, Britain, and Japan, 1839–1952*. Berkeley, CA: University of California Press 2000.

Buchan, John. *Sir Walter Scott*. Port Washington, NY: Kennikat Press 1967. Repr. of 1932 ed.

"Buildings at Risk Register for Scotland." http://www.buildingsatrisk.org.uk/search/planning_authority/206/p/4/event_id/889149/building_name/lews-castle-tower-lady-lever-park-stornoway (accessed 31 March 2014).

Cable, Boyd. *A Hundred Year History of the P. & O.* London: Ivor Nicholson and Watson 1937.

Cain, P.J., and A.G. Hopkins. "Gentlemanly Capitalism and British Expansion Overseas I: The Old Colonial System, 1688–1850." *Economic History Review*, New Series, 104, no. 4 (1986): 501–25.

– *British Imperialism, 1688–2000*, 2nd ed. Harlow, UK: Pearson Education 2002.

Chang, Hsin-pao. *Commissioner Lin and the Opium War.* New York: Norton 1970.

Chatterton, E. Keble. *The Mercantile Marine.* Boston: Little Brown and Company 1923.

Cheong, W.E. *Mandarins and Merchants: Jardine Matheson & Co.: A China Agency of the Early Nineteenth Century.* London: Curzon Press 1979.

– *The Hong Merchants of Canton: Chinese Merchants in Sino-Western Trade.* Richmond, Surrey, U K: Curzon 1997.

Cockburn, Henry. *Memorials of His Time.* Edited by Karl Miller. Chicago: University of Chicago Press 1974.

Collis, Maurice, *Foreign Mud: The Opium Imbroglio at Canton in the 1830's & the Anglo-Chinese War.* New York: W.W. Norton and Company 1946. Repr. 1968.

Connell, Carol Matheson. *A Business in Risk: Jardine Matheson and the Hong Kong Trading Industry.* Westport, C T: Praeger Publishers 2004.

Cunningham, Peter. *The Castle Grounds.* Stornoway, Lewis, Scotland: Stornoway Trust Estate 1978.

Daiches, David. *Sir Walter Scott and His World.* New York: Viking Press 1971.

Devine, T.M. *The Great Highland Famine.* Edinburgh: John Donald Publishers 1988.

– "Social Responses to Agrarian 'Improvement': The Highland and Lowland Clearances in Scotland." In R.A. Houston and I.D. Whyte, eds., *Scottish Society, 1500–1800.* Cambridge: Cambridge University Press 1989. 152–6.

– *Clanship to the Crofters' War: The Social Transformation of the Scottish Highlands.* Manchester, U K: Manchester University Press 1994.

– *The Scottish Nation.* New York: Viking 1999.

– *To the Ends of the Earth: Scotland's Global Diaspora, 1750–2010.* Washington, D.C.: Smithsonian Books 2011.

Deyan, Guo. "The Study of Parsee Merchants." *Review of Culture,* International edition, 8 (October 2003): 51–60.

Downes, Jacques. *The Golden Ghetto.* Bethlehem, PA: Lehigh University Press 1997.

Downing, C. Toogood. *The Fan-Qui in China.* 3 vols. Shannon, Ireland: Irish University Press 1972. Repr. of 1838 London ed.

Duffy, Christopher. *The '45.* London: Cassell 2003.

"The Faculty of Medicine at Edinburgh." n.d. http://www.med.ed.ac.uk/ history/history3.htm (accessed 13 February 2001).

Fairbank, John K. "Ewo on History." In Maggie Keswick, ed., *The Thistle and the Jade.* London: Octopus Books 1982.

– *Trade and Diplomacy on the China Coast.* Cambridge, M A: Harvard University Press 1964.

Farrington, Anthony. *Catalogue of East India Company Ships Journals and Logs, 1600–1834*. London: British Library 1999.

Fay, Peter Ward. *The Opium War, 1840–1842*. Chapel Hill: University of North Carolina Press 1975.

– "The Opening of China." In Maggie Keswick, ed., *The Thistle and the Jade*. London: Octopus Books 1982. 55–79.

Ferguson, William. *Scotland, 1689 to the Present*. New York: Frederick A. Praeger 1968.

"Flags of the World." http://www.fotw.us/flags/gb-eic.html (accessed 31 March 2014).

Fry, Michael. "Dundas, Henry, First Viscount Melville (1742–1811)." In *The Oxford Dictionary of National Biography* (Oxford: Oxford University Press 2004), http://o-www.oxforddnb.com.helin.uri.edu/view/article/8250?docPos=1 (accessed 5 June 2013).

Gardella, Robert. *Harvesting Mountains: Fujian and the China Tea Trade, 1757–1937*. Berkeley, CA: University of California Press 1994.

Gardner, Brian. *The East India Company: A History*. New York: Barnes and Noble 1971.

Geddes, Arthur. *The Isle of Lewis and Harris: A Study in British Community*. Edinburgh: University Press 1955.

Gelber, Harry. *Opium, Soldiers and Evangelicals*. Basingstoke, UK: Palgrave Macmillan 2004.

Gillett Brothers Discount Co. *The Bill on London*. 2nd rev. ed. London: Chapman and Hall 1959.

Grace, Richard J. Articles in *Oxford Dictionary of National Biography* (Oxford: Oxford University Press 2004): "William Jardine, 1784–1843"; "Hollingworth Magniac, 1786–1867" (revision of earlier DNB entry by Charles Sebag-Montefiore); "Sir James Matheson, Bart., 1796–1878"; "Sir Alexander Matheson, Bart., 1805–1886."

Grant, James Shaw. *A Shilling for Your Scowl*. Stornoway, Lewis: Acair 1992.

Gray, Malcolm. "The Highland Potato Famine of the 1840's." *Economic History Review*, New Series, 7, no. 3 (1955): 357–68.

Great Britain, Parliament. Scotland. *Owners of Lands and Heritages, 1872–73*. Edinburgh: Murray and Gibb 1874.

Great Britain, Parliament, House of Commons. Sessional Papers, 1840, Report of the Select Committee on Trade with China.

– Hansard Parliamentary Debates, Series 3, vol. 53, 7–9 April 1840.

– Hansard Parliamentary Debates, Series 3, vol. 61, 17 March 1842.

– Testimony of James Matheson, Esq., MP, Second Report of the Select
Committee on Sites for Churches (Scotland), House of Commons, 1847.

Greenberg, Michael. *British Trade and the Opening of China, 1840–1842.*
Cambridge: Cambridge University Press 1951. Repr. of Monthly Review
Press ed., n.d.

Gulick, Edward V. *Peter Parker and the Opening of China.* Cambridge, MA:
Harvard University Press 1973.

Gutzlaff, Charles. *Journal of Three Voyages along the Coast of China, in 1831,
1832, & 1833.* Taipei: Ch'eng Wen Publishing Company 1968.

Harcourt, Freda. *Flagships of Imperialism: The P & O Company and the Politics of
Empire from Its Origins to 1867.* Manchester, UK, and New York: Manchester
University Press 2006.

He, Sibing. "Russell and Company and the Imperialism of Anglo-American
Free Trade." In Kendall Johnson, ed., *Narratives of Free Trade.* Hong Kong:
Hong Kong University Press 2012. 83–98.

Hoe, Susanna. *The Private Life of Old Hong Kong.* Hong Kong: Oxford University Press 1991.

Hoe, Susanna, and Derek Roebuck. *The Taking of Hong Kong: Charles and Clara
Elliot in China Waters.* Richmond, UK: Curzon Press 1999.

Hong Kong Museum of Art and the Peabody Essex Museum. Exhibition catalogue. *Views of the Pearl River Delta.* Hong Kong: Urban Council of Hong
Kong 1996.

Horn, D.B. *A Short History of the University of Edinburgh, 1556–1889.* Edinburgh:
University Press 1967.

Howarth, David, and Stephen Howarth. *The Story of P&O.* Rev. ed. London:
Weidenfeld and Nicolson 1994.

Howat, Polly. "Godfrey's Cordial or Little Penny Sticks: Opium Eating in the
Fens." *Cambridgeshire County Life Magazine,* 5 (spring 2008): 24–5.

Hsü, Immanuel H.Y. *The Rise of Modern China.* 6th ed. Oxford: Oxford
University Press 2000.

Hunter, William C. *The "Fan Kwae" at Canton.* Shanghai: Kelly and Walsh 1911.
Repr. of 1882 ed.

Inverness Royal Academy. *The Inverness Academical.* War Memorial Number.
Inverness: December 1921.

*The Island of Lews.* London: Barret, Sons and Company 1878.

Johnson, Edgar. *Sir Walter Scott: The Great Unknown.* 2 vols. New York:
Macmillan 1970.

Keay, John. *The Honourable Company: A History of the English East India Company.*
New York: Macmillan 1994.

Kerr, Phyllis Forbes, ed. *Letters from China: The Canton-Boston Correspondence of Robert Bennet Forbes, 1838–1840.* Mystic, CT: Mystic Seaport Museum 1996.

Keswick, Maggie, ed. *The Thistle and the Jade.* London: Octopus Books 1982.

Ketteringham, Lesley. *A History of Lairg.* Lairg, Scotland: The Byre 1997.

Kuo, Pin-chia. *A Critical Study of the First Anglo-Chinese War, with Documents.* Westport, CT: Hyperion 1973. Repr. of 1935 Shanghai ed.

Kybett, Susan Maclean. *Bonnie Prince Charlie: A Biography of Charles Edward Stuart.* New York: Dodd, Mead and Company 1988.

Law, Philip K. "Macvicar, John (c.1795–1858/9)." *Oxford Dictionary of National Biography.* Oxford: Oxford University Press 2004. http://o-www.oxforddnb. com.helin.uri.edu/view/article/60314?docPos=1 (accessed 31 March 2014).

Lawson, Philip. *The East India Company: A History.* London: Longman 1993.

Lenman, Bruce. *Integration, Enlightenment, and Industrialization: Scotland, 1746–1832.* Toronto: University of Toronto Press 1981.

Le Pichon, Alain. *China Trade and Empire: Jardine, Matheson & Co. and the Origins of British Rule in Hong Kong, 1827–1843.* Records of Social and Economic History, New Series 38. Oxford: Published for the British Academy by Oxford University Press 2006.

Little, J. Irvine. *Crofters and Habitants: Settler Society, Economy, and Culture in a Quebec Township, 1848–1881.* Montreal and Kingston, ON: McGill-Queen's University Press 1991.

Lockhart, John Gibson. *Memoirs of the Life of Sir Walter Scott.* 5 vols. 1837–38. Repr. Boston: Houghton Mifflin Company 1901.

Lovell, Julia. *The Opium War: Drugs, Dreams and the Making of China.* London: Picador 2011.

Lubbock, Basil. *The China Clippers.* 2nd ed. Glasgow: Brown, Son and Ferguson 1946.

– *The Opium Clippers.* Glasgow: Brown, Son and Ferguson 1933. Repr. 1967.

Macdonald, Donald. *Lewis: A History of the Island.* Edinburgh: Gordon Wright Publishing 1978.

MacDonald of Gisla, Dr Donald. *Tales and Traditions of the Lews.* Stornoway, Lewis, Scotland, 1967.

MacGregor, David R., *Merchant Sailing Ships, 1715–1815: Their Design and Construction.* Annapolis, MD: Naval Institute Press 1980.

Mackenzie, Alexander. "A History of the Mathesons." *The Celtic Magazine,* 7, no. 83 (September 1882): 489–503.

– *History of the Mathesons.* Edited and rewritten by Alexander McBain. 2nd ed. Stirling: E. MacKay, and London: Gibbings and Cay 1900.

Mackenzie, William Cook. *The Book of the Lews*. Paisley: Alexander Gardner 1919.

– *The Western Isles: Their History, Tradition, and Place-Names*. Paisley: Alexander Gardner 1932.

Magnusson, Magnus. *Scotland: The Story of a Nation*. New York: Atlantic Monthly Press 2000.

Matheson, James. *Present Position and Future Prospects of the British Trade with China* London: Smith, Elder and Company 1836.

Melancon, Glenn. "Peaceful Intentions: The First British Trade Commission in China, 1833–5." *Historical Research* 73 (February 2000): 33–47.

– *Britain's China Policy and the Opium Crisis*. Aldershot, UK: Ashgate Publishing 2003.

Milligan, Barry. *Pleasures and Pains: Opium and the Orient in Nineteenth-Century British Culture*. Charlottesville: University Press of Virginia 1995.

Mitchison, Rosalind. *A History of Scotland*. 2nd ed. London: Methuen 1982.

Morse, Hosea Ballou, ed., *The Chronicles of the East India Company Trading to China, 1635–1834*. 5 vols. Taipei: Cheng-Wen Publishing Company. Repr. 1966.

Mui, Hoh-cheung and Lorna H. *The Management of Monopoly: A Study of the East India Company's Conduct of Its Tea Trade, 1784–1833*. Vancouver: University of British Columbia Press 1984.

Murray, Dian H. *Pirates of the South China Coast, 1790–1810*. Stanford, CA: Stanford University Press 1987.

Napier, Priscilla. *Barbarian Eye: Lord Napier in China, 1834*. London: Brassey's 1995.

Nelson, Michael. *Queen Victoria and the Discovery of the Riviera*. London: I.B. Tauris Publishers 2001.

Nicolson, Nigel. *Lord of the Isles: Lord Leverhulme in the Hebrides*. London: Weidenfeld and Nicolson 1959.

Niebuhr, Reinhold. *Moral Man and Immoral Society*. New York: Charles Scribner's Sons 1932.

Nye, Jr., Gideon. "The Morning of My Life in China: A Lecture Delivered before the Canton Community on the Evening of January 31st 1873." Canton, 1873.

Owen, David Edward. *British Opium Policy in China and India*. New Haven, CT: Yale University Press 1934. Repr. Archon Books 1968.

Palestia, Jesse S. "The Parsis of India and the Opium Trade in China." *Contemporary Drug Problems*, 35 (winter 2008): 647–78.

Parker, James G. "Scottish Enterprise in India, 1750–1914." In R.A. Cage, ed., *The Scots Abroad: Labour, Capital, Enterprise, 1750–1914*. London: Croom Helm 1985. 191–219.

Parkinson, C. Northcote. *War in the Eastern Seas, 1793–1815*. London: George Allen and Unwin 1954.

– *Trade in the Eastern Seas, 1793–1813*. New York: Augustus M. Kelly 1966. Repr. of 1937 ed.

Paterson, Kenneth R. "History of Education in the Island of Lewis, with Particular Reference to the Nineteenth Century." MEd thesis, University of Glasgow 1970.

Peyrefitte, Alain. *The Immobile Empire*. Translated by Jon Rothschild. New York: Alfred A. Knopf 1992.

Philips, C.H. *The East India Company, 1784–1834*. Manchester, UK: University Press 1940.

Plank, Geoffrey. *Rebellion and Savagery: The Jacobite Rising of 1745 and the British Empire*. Philadelphia: University of Pennsylvania Press 2006.

Porter, Roy, and Mikulas Teich. *Drugs and Narcotics in History*. Cambridge: Cambridge University Press 1997.

Prebble, John. *Culloden*. New York: Atheneum 1962.

– *The Lion in the North*. Harmondsworth, UK: Penguin Books 1973.

Pritchard, Earl H. *Anglo-Chinese Relations during the Seventeenth and Eighteenth Centuries*. New York: Octagon Books 1970. Repr. of 1929 ed.

Quincey, Thomas de. *Confessions of an Opium Eater*. New York: Dover Publications 1995. Repr. of 1821 ed.

Reid, Alan. "East Point." In Maggie Keswick, ed., *The Thistle and the Jade*. London: Octopus Books 1982

– "Karl Gutzlaff." In Maggie Kewswick, ed., *The Thistle and the Jade*. London: Octopus Books 1982.

– "Merchant Consuls." In Maggie Keswick, ed., *The Thistle and the Jade*. London: Octopus Books 1982.

– "Sealskins and Singsongs." In Maggie Keswick, ed., *The Thistle and the Jade*. London: Octopus Books 1982.

– "The Shipping Interest." In Maggie Keswick, ed., *The Thistle and the Jade*. London: Octopus Books 1982.

– "Spreading Risks." In Maggie Keswick, ed., *The Thistle and the Jade*. London: Octopus Books 1982.

– "The Steel Frame." In Maggie Keswick, ed., *The Thistle and the Jade*. London: Octopus Books 1982.

Reid, Margaret. "Commodities: Tea." In Maggie Keswick, ed., *The Thistle and the Jade*. London: Octopus Books 1982.

– "Jamsetjee Jejeebhoy." In Maggie Kewsick, ed., *The Thistle and the Jade*. London, Octopus Books, 1982.

– "Love and Marriage." In Maggie Keswick, ed., *The Thistle and the Jade*. London: Octopus Books 1982.

*Report of the Trial of the So-called Bernera Rioters*. Edinburgh: Donald McCormick 1874.

Risse, Guenter B. *Hospital Life in Enlightenment Scotland*. Cambridge: Cambridge University Press 1986.

Rosner, Lisa. *Medical Education in the Age of Improvement*. Edinburgh: University of Edinburgh Press 1991.

"Scotland in the Nineteenth Century." Glasgow Digital Library, http://gdl. cdlr.strath.ac.uk/haynin/index.html (accessed 31 March 2014).

Shalini, Saksena. "Parsi Contributions to the Growth of Bombay and Hong Kong." *Review of Culture*, International edition, 10 (April 2004): 26–35.

Sinclair, Sir John, ed. *The Statistical Account of Scotland, 1791–1799*, vol. 4: Dumfriesshire. Originally published between 1791 and 1799; reissued at Wakefield, UK: E.P. Publishing 1978.

– *The Statistical Account of Scotland, 1791-1799*, vol. 18: Caithness and Sutherland. Originally published between 1791 and 1799; reissued at Wakefield, UK: E.P. Publishing 1978.

Singh, S.B. *European Agency Houses in Bengal (1783–1833)*. Calcutta: Firma K.L. Mukhopadhyay 1966.

Smith, Philip Chadwick Foster. "Philadelphia Displays 'The Flowery Flag.'" In Jean Gordon Lee, ed., *Philadelphians and the China Trade, 1784–1844*. Philadelphia, PA: Philadelphia Museum of Art 1984. 21–42.

Somerset Fry, Peter and Fiona. *The History of Scotland*. London: Ark Paperbacks 1982.

Stern, Philip J. "Company, State and Empire: Governance and Regulatory Frameworks in Asia." In H.V. Bowen, Elizabeth Mancke, and John G. Reid, eds., *Britain's Overseas Empire: Atlantic and Indian Ocean Worlds, c. 1550–1850*. Cambridge: Cambridge University Press 2012. 130–50.

Stornoway Historical Society. "History of the Lews Castle." http://www. stornowayhistoricalsociety.org.uk/lewis-castle-history.html (accessed 31 March 2014).

Subramanian, Lakshmi. "Seths and Sahibs: Negotiated Relationships between Indigenous Capital and the East India Company." In H.V. Bowen, Elizabeth

Mancke, and John G. Reid, eds., *Britain's Oceanic Empire: Atlantic and Indian Ocean Worlds, c. 1550–1850*. Cambridge: Cambridge University Press 2012. 311–39.

Sutherland, John. *The Life of Walter Scott: A Critical Biography*. Oxford: Blackwell Publishers 1995.

Sutton, Jean. *Lords of the East: The East India Company and Its Ships*. London: Conway Maritime Press 2000.

Sylla, Richard. "Review of Peter Temin's *The Jacksonian Economy*." Economic History Services, 17 August 2001, http://eh.net/book_reviews/the-jacksonian-economy (accessed 31 March 2014).

Tannadish, Jerome. "George Chinnery." In Maggie Keswick, ed. *The Thistle and the Jade*. London: Octopus Books, 1982.

Thampi, Madhavi. "Parsees in the China Trade." *Review of Culture,* International edition, 10 (April 2004): 17–25.

Trevor-Roper, Hugh. "The Invention of Tradition: The Highland Tradition of Scotland." In Eric Hobsbawm and Terence Ranger, eds., *The Invention of Tradition*. Cambridge: Cambridge University Press 1983.

Trocki, Carl A. *Opium, Empire and the Global Political Economy: A Study of the Asian Opium Trade 1750–1950*. London: Routledge 1999.

Van Dyke, Paul A. *The Canton System: Life and Enterprise on the China Coast, 1700–1745*. Hong Kong: Hong Kong University Press 2005.

– *The Canton Trade*. Hong Kong: Hong Kong University Press 2008.

– "New Sea Routes to Canton in the 18th Century and the Decline of China's Control over Trade." *Hai yang shi yan jiu,* 1 (2010): 57–108.

– *Merchants of Canton and Macao*. Hong Kong: Hong Kong University Press 2011.

– "Smuggling Networks of the Pearl River Delta before 1842." In Paul A. Van Dyke, ed., *Americans and Macao: Trade, Smuggling and Diplomacy on the South China Coast*. Hong Kong: Hong Kong University Press 2012. 49–72.

Wakeman, Frederic, Jr. "The Canton Trade and the Opium War." In John K. Fairbank, ed., *The Cambridge History of China*, vol. 10, pt. 1.: *Late Chi'ing 1810–1911*. Cambridge: Cambridge University Press 1978.

Waley, Arthur. *The Opium War through Chinese Eyes*. London: George Allen and Unwin 1958.

Welsh, Frank. *A Borrowed Place: The History of Hong Kong*. New York: Kodansha America 1993.

Wild, Anthony. *The East India Company: Trade and Conquest from 1600*. New York: Lyons Press 1999.

Williams, S. Wells. "Recollections of China prior to 1840." *Journal of the North-China Branch of the Royal Asiatic Society*, New Series 8, no. 8.

Williamson, Captain A.R. *Eastern Traders*. London: Jardine, Matheson and Company. Privately printed, 1975.

Wong, J.Y. *Deadly Dreams: Opium, Imperialism, and the Arrow War (1856–1860) in China*. Cambridge: Cambridge University Press 1998.

# INDEX